The Irony of Democracy

An Uncommon Introduction to American Politics

Thomas R. Dye

•

Harmon Zeigler, Late

WADSWORTH
CENGAGE Learning™

Australia • Brazil • Canada • Mexico • Singapore • Spain • United Kingdom • United States

WADSWORTH
CENGAGE Learning™

The Irony of Democracy:
An Uncommon Introduction to American
Politics, Fourteenth Edition
Thomas R. Dye, Harmon Ziegler, Late

Executive Editor: Carolyn Merrill

Editorial Assistant: Katherine Hayes

Technology Project Manager: Yevgeny Ioffe

Senior Marketing Manager: Trent Whatcott

Marketing Communications Manager:
  Heather Baxley

Sr. Content Project Manager: Josh Allen

Art Director: Linda Helcher

Manufacturing Manager: Barbara Britton

Permissions Editor: Mardell Glinski-Schultz

Production Service: International
  Typesetting and Composition

Cover Designer: Beckmeyer Design

Cover Image: Mike Powell/Stone/© Getty
  Images

Printer: West Group

Compositor: International Typesetting
  and Composition

For product information and technology assistance, contact us at
Cengage Learning Academic Resource Center,
1-800-423-0563

For permission to use material from this text or product, submit all requests online at **www.cengage.com/permissions**
Further permissions questions can be emailed to
permissionrequest@cengage.com

Library of Congress Control Number: 2007934423

Student Edition:

ISBN-13: 978-0-495-50123-7

ISBN-10: 0-495-50123-9

Wadsworth Cengage Learning
25 Thomson Place
Boston, MA 02210-1202
USA

Cengage Learning products are represented in Canada by Nelson Education, Ltd.

For your course and learning solutions, visit **academic.cengage.com**

Purchase any of our products at your local college store or at our preferred online store **www.ichapters.com**

Printed in the United States of America
1 2 3 4 5 11 10 09 08 07

Contents

To the Student

In asking you to read this book, your instructor wants to do more than teach you about "the nuts and bolts" of American government. This book has a theme: only a tiny handful of people make decisions that shape the lives of all of us, and, despite the elaborate rituals of parties, elections, and interest-group activity, we have little direct influence over these decisions. This theme is widely known as *elitism*. Your instructor may not believe completely in this theory but may instead believe that many groups of people share power in the United States, that competition is widespread, that we have checks against the abuse of power, and that the individual citizen can personally affect the course of national events by voting, supporting political parties, and joining interest groups. This theory, widely known as *pluralism*, characterizes virtually every American government textbook now in print—except this one. Your instructor, whether personally agreeing with the elitist or with the pluralist perspective, is challenging you to confront our arguments. He or she wants you to deal thoughtfully with some troubling questions about democracy in the United States.

It is far easier to teach "the nuts and bolts" of American government—the constitutional powers of the president, Congress, and courts; the function of parties and interest groups; the key cases decided by the Supreme Court; and so on—than to tackle the question, How democratic is American society? It is easier to teach the "facts" of American government than to search for their explanations. Although this book does not ignore such facts, its primary purpose is to interpret them—to help you understand why our government works as it does.

The Irony of Democracy is not necessarily "antiestablishment." This book challenges the prevailing pluralistic view of democracy in the United States, but it neither condemns nor endorses American political life. Governance of the United States by a small, homogeneous elite is subject to favorable or unfavorable interpretation, according to one's personal values. Each reader is free to decide whether we as a society should preserve, reform, or restructure the political system described in these pages.

The Irony of Democracy is neither a conservative nor a liberal textbook. It does not apologize for elite rule or seek to defend American institutions or leaders. On the contrary, we are critical of politicians, bureaucrats, corporate chieftains, media moguls, lawyers, lobbyists, and special interests. But we do not advocate fruitless liberal nostrums promising to bring "power to the people" or "citizen movements" that are themselves led by elites with their own self-interests.

The Irony of Democracy is indeed an endorsement of democratic values—individual dignity, limited government, freedom of expression and dissent, equality of opportunity, private property, and due process of law. Our elitist theory of democracy is not an attack on democratic government but rather an effort to understand the realities of politics in a democracy.

TO THE INSTRUCTOR

The fourteenth edition of *The Irony of Democracy* continues its classic theme—elitism in a democratic society. Despite the near-universal acceptance of pluralist ideology in American political science and American government textbooks, we remain unrepentant. *The Irony of Democracy* remains an *elitist* introduction to American government. This is a textbook that will challenge your students to rethink everything they have been taught about American democracy—it is a book of ideas, not just facts.

Elite theory is contrasted to democratic theory and to modern pluralist theory throughout the book, in examining the U.S. Constitution, American political history, power structures, public opinion, mass media, elections, parties, interest groups, the presidency, Congress, the bureaucracy, the courts, federalism, civil rights, and national security policy.

Elite theory is used as an analytic model for understanding and explaining American politics; it is *not* presented as a recommendation or prescription for America.

Is the government "run for the benefit of all the people" or "by a few big interests looking out for themselves"? Years ago, when *The Irony of Democracy* was first written, a majority of Americans believed that their government was being run for the benefit of all; the elitist view was expressed by relatively few people. Today an astounding 80 percent of Americans believe that their government is run "by a few big interests looking out for themselves." The elitist perspective, which we developed as an analytic model of American politics, has now become a part of the popular political culture!

We take no pleasure in observing that the mass public has come to share our view of the American political system. On the contrary, we have become increasingly disenchanted over the years with narrow, self-serving elite behavior. Our elitist theory of democracy has always recognized the potential for danger in mass movements led by extremist and intolerant demagogues. But over the years we have become convinced that the principal threat to democracy in the United States today arises from irresponsible elites seeking power and privilege at the expense of shared social values.

Recent editions of *The Irony of Democracy,* including this fourteenth edition, have been more critical of America's elite, more "antiestablishment" than earlier editions, and for good reason. Chapter 4, "Elites in America," describes the increasingly voracious and predatory nature of global corporations, the growing arrogance of the rich and powerful, and the increasing isolation of the elites from the concerns and troubles of the masses of Americans. We continued to compile evidence of the concentration and globalization of corporate power and its consequences for the masses. In Chapter 5, "Masses in America," we describe the stagnation of real wages of working Americans, the widening gap between rich and poor, and the resulting disaffection of the masses from democratic politics. Yet even if the masses were to shed their ignorance and apathy and turn to political action, we believe the result would be intolerance rather than compassion, racism rather than brotherhood, authoritarianism rather than democracy.

Recent editions have also been more critical of the current functioning of our political institutions. In Chapter 8, "Elections, Money, and the Myths of Democracy," we argue that elections are designed primarily to convince the masses that the government is legitimate; that, in fact, voters have little real impact on the direction of public policy; and that Big Money drives the electoral system. The Campaign Finance Reform Law, passed in 2002, did little to change the role of money in elections. We describe how "fat cat" contributors evade the law by creating independent "527" organizations to throw unlimited millions of dollars into campaigns. We have a section on dirty politics that argues that lies and slurs have long tarnished America's political landscape. Finally, we make sure that students understand that presidential elections are decided by the Electoral College vote, not the popular vote of the masses, and we look back on the Supreme Court's role in determining the outcome of the 2000 presidential election.

We also describe, in this fourteenth edition, the changes in American politics following the terrorist attacks of September 11, 2001. We observe the temporary "rally 'round the flag" effect on the masses, followed by the gradual erosion of national unity and growing conflict over how to conduct the war on terrorism. We describe the Patriot Act as typical of elite repression in times of perceived danger.

A new chapter, "Elites and National Security," has been added to this fourteenth edition. We argue that the elite struggle for power is universal. We describe nuclear threats to American security, nuclear terrorism, and antiballistic missile defenses. We describe the NATO alliance, including the current fighting in Afghanistan. We observe that American elites often differ over when and how to use military force. We contrast the "Powell Doctrine" regarding the use of force with the Bush administration's extended war in Iraq.

Most importantly, we describe the American experience in Iraq, from the initial success in the capture of Baghdad, to the prolonged insurgency, mounting casualties, and changing objectives that ensued. A stated purpose of "Operation Iraqi Freedom," the elimination of weapons of mass destruction, turned out to be illusory; no such weapons were found. The "regime change" was successful; Saddam Hussein was sentenced by an Iraqi tribunal to death by hanging. But the American occupation soon turned disastrous, as civil war broke out among Iraqi factions. The masses in America turned against the war as casualties mounted and no end appeared in sight. A Democratic Congress was elected in 2006; its leadership pledged to end the war in Iraq. But the Bush administration chose to initiate a "surge" in U.S. combat forces in that embattled land.

New sections in the fourteenth edition include "Elite Think Tanks," "Elite Foreign Policymaking: the Council on Foreign Relations," "Elite-Mass Differences over Immigration," "Are You a Liberal or a Conservative?," "Off and Running, 2008," "Why Third Parties Fail," "Super Lobby: the Business Roundtable," "Lawyers, Lobbyists, and Influence Peddlers," "Katrina: Bureaucratic Failure," "The Capital Gains Tax Scam," "The Top Ten Universities in Congress," "Polarization on Capitol Hill," "Women and Minorities Acquiring Elite Status," and "Mass Opposition to the War in Iraq."

Finally, we have endeavored to make *The Irony of Democracy* a better teaching instrument. We do not do so by "dumbing down" our discussions (and we dismissed suggestions to employ an eighth-grade vocabulary). Rather, we have tried to clarify our arguments throughout the text, first by embedding "In Brief" sections within chapters, and second by enhancing chapter summaries with "An Elitist Interpretation." We have also added Internet references throughout our discussions.

Our Epilogue is directed at students. It does not offer platitudinous clichés about citizenship but rather realistic advice about what young people might do to help preserve democratic values in an elitist system.

Thomas R. Dye
Harmon Zeigler

Government is always government by the few, whether in the name of the few, the one, or the many.

Harold Lasswell

THE IRONY OF DEMOCRACY

Elites—not masses—govern the United States. Life in a democracy, as in all societies, is shaped by a handful of people. Major political, economic, and social decisions are made by tiny minorities, not the masses of people.

Elites are the few who have power; the *masses* are the many who do not. Power is deciding who gets what, when, and how; it is participation in the decisions that shape our lives; the masses are the many whose lives are shaped by institutions, events, and leaders over which they have little direct control. Political scientist Harold Lasswell wrote, "The division of society into elite and mass is universal," and even in a democracy "a few exercise a relatively great weight of power, and the many exercise comparatively little."[1]

Democracy is government "by the people," but the survival of democracy rests on the shoulders of elites. This is the irony of democracy: elites must govern wisely if government "by the people" is to survive. The masses do not lead; they follow. They respond to the attitudes, proposals, and behavior of elites.

This book, *The Irony of Democracy,* explains American political life using elite theory. It presents evidence from U.S. political history and contemporary political science describing and explaining how elites function in a modern democratic society. But before we examine American politics, we must understand more about *elitism, democracy,* and *pluralism.*

THE MEANING OF ELITISM

The central idea of elitism is that all societies are divided into two classes: the few who govern and the many who are governed. The Italian political scientist Gaetano Mosca expressed this basic concept as follows:

In all societies—from societies that are very underdeveloped and have largely attained the dawnings of civilization, down to the most advanced and powerful societies—two classes of people appear—a class that rules and a class that is ruled. The first class, always the less numerous, performs all of the political functions, monopolizes power, and enjoys the advantages that power brings, whereas the second, the more numerous class, is directed and controlled by the first, in a manner that is now more or less legal, now more or less arbitrary and violent.[2]

Elites, not masses, govern *all* societies. Elites are not a product of capitalism or socialism or industrialization or technological development. All societies—socialist and capitalist, agricultural and industrial, traditional and advanced—are governed by elites. All societies require leaders, and leaders acquire a stake in preserving the organization and their position in it. This motive gives leaders a perspective different from that of the organization's members. An elite, then, is inevitable in any social organization. As French political scientist Roberto Michels put it nearly a century ago, "He who says organization, says oligarchy."[3] The same is true for societies as a whole. According to the distinguished American political scientist Harold Lasswell, "The discovery that in all large-scale societies the decisions at any given time are typically in the hands of a small number of people" confirms a basic fact: "Government is always government by the few, whether in the name of the few, the one, or the many."[4]

Elitism also asserts that the few who govern are not typical of the masses who are governed. Elites control resources: power, wealth, education, prestige, status, skills of leadership, information, knowledge of political processes, ability to communicate, and organization. Elites in the United States are drawn disproportionately from wealthy, educated, prestigiously employed, socially prominent, white, Anglo-Saxon, and Protestant elements of society.

They come from society's upper classes, those who own or control a disproportionate share of the societal institutions: industry, commerce, finance, education, the military, communications, civic organizations, and law.

Elitism, however, does not necessarily bar individuals of the lower classes from rising to the top. In fact, a certain amount of "circulation of elites" (upward mobility) is essential for the stability of the elite system. Openness in the system siphons off potentially revolutionary leadership from the lower classes; moreover, an elite system is strengthened when talented and ambitious individuals from the masses enter governing circles. However, social stability requires that movement from nonelite to elite positions be a slow, continuous assimilation rather than a rapid or revolutionary change. Only those nonelites who have demonstrated their commitment to the elite system itself and to the system's political and economic values can be admitted to the ruling class.

Elites share a general consensus about the fundamental norms of the social system. They agree on the basic rules of the game and on the importance of preserving the social system. The stability of the system, and even its survival, depends on this consensus. Political scientist David Truman writes, "Being more influential, they [the elites] are privileged; and being privileged, they have, with very few exceptions, a special stake in the continuation of the system in which their privileges rest."[5] However, elite consensus does not prevent elite members from disagreeing or competing with each other for preeminence. But this competition takes place within a narrow range of issues; elites agree on more matters than they disagree on. Disagreement usually occurs over *means* rather than *ends*.

IN BRIEF	ELITE THEORY

- Society is divided into the few who have power and the many who do not.
- The few who govern are not typical of the masses who are governed. Elites are drawn disproportionately from the upper socioeconomic strata of society.
- The movement of nonelites to elite positions must be slow and continuous to maintain stability and avoid revolution. Only nonelites who have accepted the basic elite consensus enter governing circles.
- Elites share a consensus on the basic values of the social system and the preservation of the system. They disagree only on a narrow range of issues.

- Public policy does not reflect the demands of the masses but the prevailing values of the elite. Changes in public policy will be incremental rather than revolutionary.
- Elites may act out of narrow self-serving motives and risk undermining mass support, or they may initiate reforms, curb abuse, and undertake public-regarding programs to preserve the system and their place in it.
- Active elites are subject to relatively little direct influence from the apathetic masses. Elites influence the masses more than the masses influence elites.

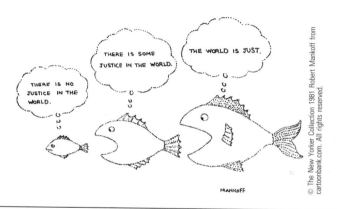

In the United States, the bases of elite consensus are the sanctity of private property, limited government, and individual liberty. Political historian Richard Hofstadter writes about American elite struggles:

> The fierceness of political struggles has often been misleading; for the range of vision embodied by the primary contestants in the major parties has always been bounded by the horizons of property and enterprise. However much at odds on specific issues, the major political traditions have shared a belief in the rights of property, the philosophy of economic individualism, the value of competition; they have accepted the economic virtues of capitalist culture as necessary qualities of man.[6]

Elitism implies that public policy does not reflect demands of "the people" so much as it reflects the interests and values of elites. Changes and innovations in public policy come about when elites redefine their own values. However, the general conservatism of elites—that is, their interest in preserving the system—means that changes in public policy will be *incremental* rather than revolutionary. Public policies are often modified but seldom replaced.

Elites may act out of narrow self-serving interests or enlightened, "public-regarding" motives. Occasionally elites abuse their powers and position and undermine mass confidence in their leadership. At other times, elites initiate reforms designed to preserve the system and restore mass support. Elitism does not necessarily mean that the masses are exploited or repressed, although these abuses are not uncommon. Elitism means only that the responsibility for mass welfare rests with elites, not with masses.

Finally, elitism assumes that the masses are largely passive, apathetic, and ill informed. Mass sentiments are manipulated by elites more often than elite values are influenced by the sentiments of the masses. Most communication between elites and masses flows downward. Masses seldom make decisions about governmental policies through elections or through evaluation of political parties' policy alternatives. For the most part, these "democratic" institutions—elections and parties—have only symbolic value: they help tie the masses to the political system by giving them a role to play on election day. Elitism contends that the masses have at best only an indirect influence over the decision-making behavior of elites.

THE MEANING OF DEMOCRACY

Ideally, *democracy* means individual participation in the decisions that affect one's life. Traditional democratic theory has valued popular participation as an opportunity for individual self-development: responsibility for governing one's own conduct develops one's character, self-reliance, intelligence, and moral judgment—in short, one's dignity. The classic democrat would reject even a benevolent despot who could govern in the interest of the masses. As the English political philosopher John Stuart Mill asked, "What development can either their thinking or active faculties attain under it?" Thus the argument for citizen participation in public affairs depends not on its policy outcomes but on the belief that such involvement is essential to the full development of human capacities. Mill argued that people can know truth only by discovering it for themselves.[7]

Procedurally, in the democratic model, a society achieves popular participation through majority rule and respect for the rights of minorities. Self-development presumes self-government, and self-government comes about only by encouraging each individual to contribute to the development of public policy and by resolving conflicts over public policy through majority rule. Minorities who have had the opportunity to influence policy but whose views have not won majority support accept the decisions of majorities. In return, majorities permit minorities to attempt openly to win majority support for their views. Freedom of speech and press, freedom to dissent, and freedom to form opposition parties and organizations are essential to ensure meaningful individual participation. This freedom of expression is also critical in ascertaining the majority's real views.

The underlying value of democracy is individual dignity. Human beings, by virtue of their existence, are entitled to life, liberty, and property. A "natural law," or moral tenet, guarantees every person liberty and the right to property, and this natural law is morally superior to human law. John Locke, the English political philosopher whose writings most influenced America's founding elites, argued that even in a "state of nature"—that is, a world of no governments—an individual possesses inalienable rights to life, liberty,

U.S. Information Agency
Official U.S. government definitions of democracy and individual rights.
www.usinfo. state.gov

IN BRIEF	DEMOCRATIC THEORY

- Popular participation in the decisions that shape the lives of individuals in a society.
- Government by majority rule, with recognition of the rights of minorities to try to become majorities. These rights include the freedoms of speech, press, assembly, and petition and the freedoms to dissent, to form opposition parties, and to run for public office.
- A commitment to individual dignity and the preservation of the liberal values of life, liberty, and property.
- A commitment to equal opportunity for all individuals to develop their capacities.

and property. Locke meant that these rights are independent of government; governments do not give them to individuals, and no government may legitimately take them away.[8]

Locke believed that a government's purpose is to protect individual liberty. People form a "social contract" with one another to establish a government to help protect their rights; they tacitly agree to accept government authority to protect life, liberty, and property. Implicit in the social contract and the democratic notion of freedom is the belief that governmental authority and social control over the individual must be minimal. This belief calls for removing as many external restrictions, controls, and regulations on the individual as possible without violating the freedom of other citizens.

Another vital aspect of classical democracy is a belief in the equality of all people. The Declaration of Independence states that "all men are created equal." Even the Founding Fathers believed in equality for all persons *before the law,* regardless of their personal circumstances. A democratic society cannot judge a person by social position, economic class, creed, or race. Political equality is expressed in the concept of "one person, one vote."

Over time, the notion of equality has also come to include *equality of opportunity* in all aspects of American life: social, educational, and economic, as well as political. Each person should have an equal opportunity to develop his or her capacities to the fullest potential. There should be no artificial barriers to success in life. All persons should have the opportunity to make of themselves what they can, to develop their talents and abilities to their fullest, and to be rewarded for their skills, knowledge, initiative, and hard work. However, the traditional democratic creed has always stressed *equality of opportunity,* not *absolute equality.* Thomas Jefferson recognized a "natural aristocracy" of talent, ambition, and industry, and liberal democrats since Jefferson have always accepted inequalities that arise from individual merit and hard work. Absolute equality, or "leveling," is not part of liberal democratic theory.

ELITISM IN A DEMOCRACY

Democracy requires popular participation in government. (The Greek root of the word *democracy* means "rule by the many.") But popular participation in government can have different meanings. To our nation's Founders, who were quite ambivalent about the wisdom of democracy, it meant that the people would be given representation in government. The Founders believed that government rests

Freedom House
Dedicated to
expanding freedom
worldwide. Provides
measures of freedom
and classifies 192
nations as "free,"
"partly free," and
"not free."
*www.freedomhouse.
org*

ultimately on the *consent* of the governed. But their notion of *republicanism envisioned decision making by representatives of the people, rather than direct decision making by the people themselves.*

The Founders were profoundly skeptical of direct democracy, in which the people initiate and decide policy questions by popular vote. They had read about direct democracy in the ancient Greek city-state of Athens, and they were fearful of the "follies" of democracy. James Madison wrote,

> *Such democracies have ever been spectacles of turbulence and contention; have ever been found incompatible with personal security of the rights of property and have in general been as short in their lives as they have been violent in their deaths.*[9]

THE FEAR OF DIRECT DEMOCRACY

The Founders were most fearful that unrestrained *majorities* would threaten liberty and property and abuse minorities and individuals, "the weaker party and the obnoxious individual." They recognized the potential contradiction in democratic theory—government by majority rule can threaten the life, liberty, and property of minorities and individuals.

Thus *the U.S. Constitution has no provision for national referenda.* It was not until 100 years after the Constitution was written that political support developed in some states for more direct involvement of citizens in policy making. At the beginning of the twentieth century, populists in the farm states of the Midwest and the mining states of the West introduced the initiative and referendum.

Today only voters in about half the *states* can express their frustrations with elite governance directly. The *initiative* is a device whereby a specific number or percentage of voters, through the use of a petition, may have a proposed state constitutional amendment or a state law placed on the ballot for adoption or rejection by the electorate of a state. This process bypasses the legislature and allows citizens to propose both laws and constitutional amendments. The *referendum* is a device by which the electorate must approve decisions of the legislature before these become law or become part of the state constitution or by which the electorate must approve of proposals placed on the ballot by popular initiative. And voters in eighteen states can *recall* elected officials—petition for an election to decide whether or not an incumbent official should be ousted from office before the end of his or her term.[10]

THE IMPRACTICALITY OF DIRECT DEMOCRACY

Even if it were desirable, mass government is not really feasible in a large society. Abraham Lincoln's rhetorical flourish—"a government of the people, by the people, for the people"—has no real-world meaning. What would "the people" look like if all of the American people were brought together in one place?

> *Standing shoulder to shoulder in military formation, they would occupy an area of about sixty-six square miles. The logistical problem of bringing [300] million bodies together is trivial, however, compared with the task of bringing about a meeting of [300] million minds. Merely to shake hands with that many people would take a*

FOCUS | MASS DISTRUST OF AMERICA'S ELITE

How much trust do the masses have in America's leadership? Public opinion polls show that people are willing to "trust the government in Washington to do what is right" (see the figure). It is no surprise that defeat and humiliation in war undermines mass support for a nation's leadership. Perhaps the most important negative influence on mass confidence in America's elite was the experience of the Vietnam War. This tragic war was followed immediately by the Watergate scandal and the first forced resignation of a president. But Americans traditionally "rally 'round the flag" when confronted with serious national threats. The Gulf War victory in 1991 produced an upward spurt in trust. And following the terrorist attack on America of September 11, 2001, mass trust in government skyrocketed to levels not seen since the 1960s. But victory in the "war on terrorism" proved to be elusive and America found itself in the quagmire of Iraq. Trust in government fell again.

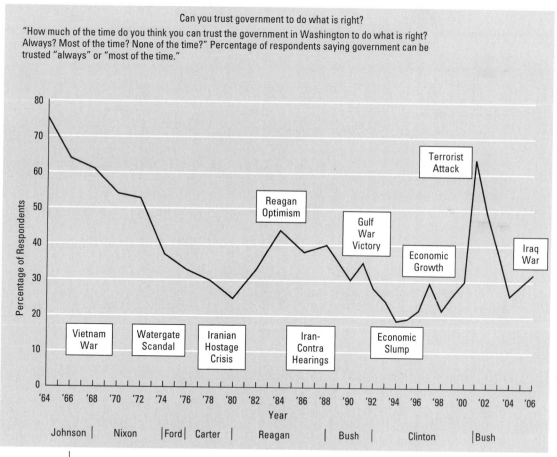

Can you trust government to do what is right?

"How much of the time do you think you can trust the government in Washington to do what is right? Always? Most of the time? None of the time?" Percentage of respondents saying government can be trusted "always" or "most of the time."

MASS SUPPORT FOR AMERICAN GOVERNMENT

Source: Prepared by the authors from National Election Surveys, University of Michigan, data. Data from 1996 onward from various polls reported in The Polling Report, Washington, D.C.

Reprinted with special permission of King Features Syndicate.

century. How much discussion would it take to form a common opinion? A single round of five-minute speeches would require five thousand years. If only one percent of those present spoke, the assembly would be forced to listen to over two million speeches. People could be born, grow old and die while they waited for the assembly to make one decision.

In other words, an all-American town meeting would be the largest, longest, and most boring and frustrating meeting imaginable. What could such a meeting produce? Total paralysis. What could it do? Nothing.[11]

REPRESENTATIVE DEMOCRACY AND THE INEVITABILITY OF ELITES

The solution to the practical problem of popular government is the development of institutions of representation—elections, parties, organized interest groups—as bridges between individuals and their government. *But this solution leads inevitably to elitism, not democracy.*

Individuals in all societies, including democracies, confront the iron law of oligarchy. As organizations and institutions develop in society, power is concentrated in the hands of the leadership. Society becomes "a minority of directors and a majority of directed." Individuals are no match for the power of large institutions.

Power is the ability to influence people and events by granting or withholding valuable resources. To exercise power, one must control valuable resources. Resources are defined broadly to include not only wealth but also position, status, celebrity, comfort, safety, and power itself. Most of the nation's resources are concentrated in large organizations and institutions—in corporations, banks, and financial institutions; in television networks, newspapers, and publishing empires; in organized interest groups, lobbies, and law firms; in foundations and think tanks; in

Documents of American Democracy
Core documents defining American democracy at official site of U.S. Government Printing Office.
www.gpoaccess.gov/coredocs

IN BRIEF | ## WHY ELITISM PREVAILS IN A DEMOCRACY

- The Founders believed in republicanism—decision making by representatives of the people, not the people themselves.
- There is no provision in the U.S. Constitution for national referendum. (Only some states allow referendum voting.)
- Direct individual participation in decision making by 300 million people is not possible.

- Decision making by representatives inevitably leads to elitism—the "iron law of oligarchy."
- Democratic values can be preserved only by multiple competitive elites—the media, parties, interest groups, corporations, unions, and other independent institutions.

---

civic and cultural organizations; and, most important, in government. The government is the most powerful of all these organizations, not only because it has accumulated great economic resources but because it has a monopoly on physical coercion. Only government can legitimately imprison and execute people.

ELITE COMPETITION AS THE BASIS OF DEMOCRACY

In a democratic society, unlike a totalitarian one, multiple elites exist. A defining characteristic of Western democratic nations is the *relative autonomy* of various elites—governmental, economic, media, civic, cultural, and so on.[12] In contrast, a defining characteristic of totalitarian societies is the forced imposition of unity on elites. Fascism asserted the unity of the state in Hitler's words: "Ein Volk, Ein Reich, Ein Fuhrer" (one people, one state, one leader). Socialism asserts the government's control of economic as well as political resources, and communism extols "the dictatorship of the proletariat" and assigns the Communist party the exclusive right to speak for the proletariat.

In Western democracies, elites have *multiple institutional bases* of power. Not all power is lodged in government, nor is all power derived from wealth. Democracies legitimize the existence of opposition parties and of organized interest groups. The power and independence of a media elite is a distinctive feature of U.S. democracy. Even within U.S. government, relatively autonomous multiple elites have emerged—in Congress, in the judiciary, in the executive, and even within the executive, in a variety of bureaucratic domains. But it is really the power and autonomy of nongovernmental elites—media, corporate, financial, union, legal, civic, interest groups, and so on—and their recognized legitimacy that distinguishes the elite structures of democratic nations from those of totalitarian states.

THE MEANING OF PLURALISM

No scholar or commentator, however optimistic about life in the United States, would assert that the U.S. political system has fully realized all the goals of democracy. No one contends that citizens participate in all decisions shaping their lives or that majority preferences always prevail. Nor does anyone argue that the system always protects the rights of minorities, always preserves the values of life, liberty, and property, or provides every American with an equal opportunity to influence public policy.

Pluralism is the belief that democratic values can be preserved in a system where multiple, competing elites determine public policy through bargaining and compromise, voters exercise meaningful choices in elections, and new elites can gain access to power.

Pluralism seeks to affirm that American society is democratic.

HOW ELITISM AND PLURALISM DIFFER

Elite theory differs from the prevailing pluralist vision of democracy in several key respects. Both theories agree that societal decision making occurs through elite interaction, not mass participation; that the key political actors are the leaders of large organizations and institutions, not individual citizens; and that public policy generally reflects the interests of large organizations and institutions, not majority preferences. Yet despite these recognized parallels with pluralist theory, elite theory offers a fundamentally different view of power and society.

First of all, elite theory asserts that the most important division in society is between elites and masses, between the few who govern and the many who do not. Pluralism overlooks this central division of society into elites and masses and emphasizes the fragmentation of society and competition between leadership groups. Elitism emphasizes the importance to leaders of maintaining their positions of power, whereas pluralism emphasizes their devotion to their group interests.

Elite theory asserts that the mass membership of organizations, parties, interest groups, and institutions in society rarely exercises any direct control over the elite leadership. Group membership does *not* ensure effective individual participation in decision making. Rarely do corporations, unions, armies, churches, governmental bureaucracies, or professional associations have any internal democratic mechanisms. They are usually run by a small elite of officers and activists. The pluralists offer no evidence that the giant organizations and institutions in American life really represent the views or interests of their individual members.

Elite theory suggests that accommodation and compromise among leadership groups is the prevailing style of decision making, not competition and conflict. Pluralism contends that competition among leadership groups protects the individual. But why should we assume that leadership groups compete with each other? More likely, each elite group allows other elite groups to govern in their own spheres of influence without interference. According to elite theory, accommodation rather than competition is the prevailing style of elite interaction: "You scratch my back and I'll scratch yours."

Elite theory takes account of *all* power holders in society, private as well as public. Pluralism focuses on governmental leaders and those who interact directly with them. Because governmental leaders are chosen in elections, pluralism asserts that leaders can be held accountable to the people. But even if governmental elites can be held accountable through elections, how can corporation executives, media elites, union leaders, and other persons in positions of private leadership be held accountable?

IN BRIEF	PLURALISM

- Society is divided into numerous groups, all of which make demands on government and none of which dominate decision making.
- Although citizens do not directly participate in decision making, their many leaders make decisions through a process of bargaining, accommodation, and compromise.
- Competition among leadership groups helps protect individuals' interests. Countervailing centers of power—for example, competition among business leaders, labor leaders, and government leaders—can check one another and keep each interest from abusing its power and oppressing the individual.
- Although individuals do not participate directly in decision making, they can exert influence through participating in organized groups, as well as parties and elections.
- Leadership groups are open; new groups can form and gain access to the political system.

- Although political influence in society is unequally distributed, power is widely dispersed. Access to decision making is often determined by how much interest people have in a particular decision. Because leadership is fluid and mobile, power depends on one's interest in public affairs, skills in leadership, information about issues, knowledge of democratic processes, and skill in organization and public relations.
- Multiple leadership groups operate within society. Those who exercise power in one kind of decision do not necessarily exercise power in others. No single elite dominates decision making in all issues.
- Public policy does not necessarily reflect majority preference but is an equilibrium of interest interaction—that is, competing interest group influences are more or less balanced, and the resulting policy is therefore a reasonable approximation of society's preferences.

Elitism emphasizes the shared characteristics of leaders, not only their common interest in preserving the social system and their place in it but also their many shared experiences, values, and goals. Pluralism emphasizes diversity among leaders—differences in backgrounds, ideologies, and viewpoints. Even when elitists show that a disproportionate share of America's leadership is composed of wealthy, educated, prestigiously employed, white, upper- and upper-middle-class males, pluralists respond by asserting that these background characteristics are poor predictors of the decision-making behavior of leaders. Elitism focuses on leadership consensus, asserting that elites differ more over the means than the ends of public policy. Pluralism focuses on elite conflict, asserting that elites differ on a wide variety of issues of vital importance to society.

Pluralism and elitism also differ over the nature and extent of mass influences over societal decision making. Elitism asserts that elites influence the masses more than the masses influence elites. Communication flows primarily downward from the elites to the masses. An enlightened elite may choose to consider the well-being of the masses in decision making, either out of ethical principles or a desire to avoid instability and revolution. But even when elites presume to act in the interests of the masses, the elites act on their *own* view of what is good for the masses, not what the masses decide for themselves. In contrast, pluralists, while acknowledging that elites rather than the masses make society's decisions, nonetheless assert that the masses influence policy through both their membership in organized interest groups and their participation in elections. Interest groups, parties, and elections, according

TABLE I.I | HOW ELITISM AND PLURALISM DIFFER IN THEIR VIEWS OF POWER AND SOCIETY

	Elite Theory	Pluralist Theory
Most important political division(s) in society	*Elites* who have power, and *masses* who do not.	*Multiple competing groups* (economic, racial, religious, ideological, etc.) that make demands on government.
Structure of power	*Hierarchical*, with power concentrated in a relatively small set of institutional leaders who make key social decisions.	*Polyarchal*, with power dispersed among multiple leadership groups who bargain and compromise over key societal decisions.
Interaction among leaders	*Consensus over values and goals* for society, with disagreements largely limited to *means* of achieving common goals.	*Conflict and competition over values and goals* as well as means of achieving them.
Sources of leadership	*Common backgrounds and experiences* in control of institutional resources; wealth, education, upper socioeconomic status; slow continuous absorption of persons who accept prevailing values.	*Diversity in backgrounds and experiences* and activism in organizations; continuous formation of new groups and organizations; skills in organizational activity and gaining access to government.
Principal institutions of power	Corporations, banks, investment firms, media giants, foundations, "think tanks," and other *private organizations, as well as government.*	Interest groups, parties, and the legislative, executive, and judicial branches of *government.*
Principal direction of political influence	*Downward* from elites to masses through mass media, educational, civic, and cultural organizations.	*Upward* from masses to elites through interest groups, parties, elections, opinion polls, etc.
View of public policy	Public policy reflects *elite preferences*, as modified by both altruism and desire to preserve the political system from mass unrest; policy changes occur incrementally when elites redefine their own interests.	Public policy reflects *balance of competing interest groups;* policy changes occur when interest groups gain or lose influence, including mass support.
Principal protection for democratic values	*Elite commitments* to individual liberty, free enterprise, and tolerance of diversity, and their desire to preserve the existing political system.	*Competition among groups:* countervailing centers of power each checking the ambitions of others.

to the pluralists, provide the means by which the masses can hold elites accountable for their decisions.

In short, although elitism and pluralism share some common views on the preeminent role of elites in a democratic society, elitism differs from pluralism in several key respects, as summarized in Table 1.1.

ELITE AND MASS THREATS TO DEMOCRACY

It is the irony of democracy that the survival of democratic values—individual dignity, limited government, equality of opportunity, private property, freedom of speech and press, religious tolerance, and due process of law—depends on enlightened elites. The masses respond to the ideas and actions of elites. When elites abandon democratic principles or the masses lose confidence in elites, democracy is in peril.

ELITE DISTEMPER

Yet democratic elites do not always live up to their responsibilities to preserve the system and its values. Elite behavior is not always enlightened and farsighted but is instead frequently shortsighted and narrowly self-serving. The relative autonomy of separate elites in a democracy—governmental, corporate, financial, media, legal, civic, and cultural—often encourages narrow visions of the common good and a willingness to sacrifice social values for relative advantage.

Examples of narrowly self-serving elite behavior abound. Politicians resort to divisive, racial appeals or to class antagonisms—setting black against white or poor against rich—to win elections, even while knowing that these tactics undermine mass confidence in national leadership. Corporate officials sacrifice long-term economic growth for short-term windfall paper profits, knowing that the nation's competitive position in the world is undermined by shortsighted "bottom-line" policies. Elites move factories and jobs out of the United States in search of low-paid workers and higher profits. Global trade and unchecked immigration lower the real wages of American workers. Inequality in America increases, and elites and masses grow further apart. Members of Congress in pursuit of personal pay and perks as well as lifetime tenure cater to fat-cat political contributors and well-heeled interest groups. They devote more energy to running for office than to running the government. Bureaucrats, seeking to expand their powers and budgets, create a regulatory quagmire, disadvantaging the nation in global competition. Politicians and bureaucrats have burdened future generations with enormous debts. Interest group leaders pursue their quest for special privileges, treatments, and exemptions from law at the expense of the public interest. Network television executives "hype" both news and entertainment shows with violence, scandal, sex, corruption, and scares of various sorts, knowing that these stories undermine mass confidence in the nation's institutions. Lawyers and judges pervert the judicial process for personal advantage, drowning the nation in a sea of litigation, clogging the courts and delaying justice, reinterpreting laws and the Constitution to suit their purposes, and undermining mass respect for the law.

In short, elites do not always act with unity and purpose. They all too frequently put narrow interests ahead of broader, shared values. These behaviors grow out of the relative autonomy of various elites in a democracy. They are encouraged by the absence of any external checks on the power of elites in their various domains. The only effective check on irresponsible elite behavior is their own realization that the system itself will become endangered if such behavior continues unrestrained. So periodically elites undertake reforms, mutually agreeing to curb the most flagrant abuses of the system. The stimulus to reform is the restoration of mass confidence in

| ## MASS VIEWS OF ELITE GOVERNANCE

Elite theory asserts a division between masses and elites. Masses themselves are wary of elite governance. They believe that their political leaders are distant, insensitive to their needs, and inattentive to their views.

Most Americans believe that the government pays little attention to their views on public policy, that people in government have little understanding of popular thinking, and that the nation would be better off if elites followed mass views.

Over the years, how much attention do you feel the government pays to what the people think when it decides what to do: a good deal, some, or not much?

A good deal	7%
Some	36
Not much	54
Don't know	3

In general, do you think people in government understand what people like you think: very well, somewhat well, not that well, or not well at all?

Very well	2%
Somewhat well	27
Not that well	33
Not well at all	35
Don't know	3

If leaders of the nation followed the views of the public more closely, do you think the nation would be better off or worse off than it is today?

Better off	81%
Worse off	10
Don't know	10

Source: Center on Policy Attitudes as reported in *The Polling Report*, February 15, 1999.

elite government and ultimately the preservation of the elite system itself. But reforms often succeed only in creating new opportunities for abuse, changing the rules but failing to restrain self-interested elites.

MASS UNREST

Mass politics can also threaten democratic values. Despite a superficial commitment to the symbols of democracy, the masses have surprisingly weak commitments to the principles of individual liberty, toleration of diversity, and freedom of expression when required to apply these principles to despised or obnoxious groups or individuals. In contrast, elites, and the better-educated groups from which they are recruited, are generally more willing than the masses to apply democratic values to specific situations and to protect the freedoms of unpopular groups.

Masses are dangerously vulnerable to demagogic appeals to intolerance, racial hatred, anti-intellectualism, class antagonisms, anti-Semitism, and violence. Counter-elites, or demagogues, are mass-oriented leaders who express hostility toward the established order and appeal to the mass sentiments. These counterelites, whether they are on the left or the right, are extremist and intolerant, impatient with due process, contemptuous of individual rights, eager to impose their views by sweeping measures, and often willing to use violence and intimidation to do so. Right-wing counterelites talk of "the will of the people," whereas left-wing radicals cry, "All power to the people." Both appeal to mass extremism: the notion that compromise and coalition building and working within the democratic system for change is pointless or even immoral. Democratic politics is viewed with cynicism.

It is the irony of democracy that democratic values can survive only in the absence of mass political activism. Democratic values thrive best when the masses are absorbed in the problems of everyday life and involved in groups and activities that distract their attention from mass political movements. Political stability depends on mass involvement in work, family, neighborhood, trade union, hobby, church, group recreation, and other activities. When the masses become alienated from home, work, and community—when their ties to social organizations and institutions weaken—they become vulnerable to the appeals of demagogues, and democratic values are endangered.

Mass activism inspires elite repression. Mass political movements, when they gain momentum and give rise to hatred, generate fear and insecurity among elites. Elites respond by limiting freedom and strengthening security, banning demonstrations, investigating and harassing opposition, arresting activists, and curtailing speech, writing, and broadcasting—usually under the guise of preserving law and order. Universities, once heralded as society's bastions of free thought and expression, impose "speech codes," "sensitivity training," and other repressive measures on students and faculty in the paradoxical pursuit of tolerance and "diversity." Ironically, elites resort to these repressive actions out of a genuine belief that they are necessary to preserve democratic values (see Focus: Terrorism's Threat to Democracy).

Elite theory, then, recognizes several threats to democracy: *elite misdeeds* (short-sighted and self-interested behavior that undermines popular support for the political system), *mass activism* (extremist and intolerant political movements, led by counter-elites appealing to racial hatred, class antagonism, and personal fears), and *elite repression* (forced indoctrination in "political correctness"; limitations on dissent, speech, and assembly in the name of law and order; and the subversion of democratic values in a paradoxical effort to preserve the system).

AN ELITIST THEORY OF DEMOCRACY

All societies are governed by elites, even democratic societies. The elitist theory of democracy is not an attack on democracy but rather an aid in understanding the realities of democratic politics.

Elite theory is not an apology for elite rule; it is not defense of official misdeeds or repression. Rather, it is a realistic explanation of how democracy works, how democratic values are both preserved and threatened, how elites and masses interact, how public policy is actually determined, and whose interests generally prevail.

Critics of this elitist theory of democracy claim that it is "conservative," that it legitimizes elite rule, that it obstructs social progress of the masses. But elite theory neither endorses nor condemns elite governance; rather, it seeks to expose and analyze the way in which elites function in a democracy.

Elite theory poses the central questions of American politics: Who governs the nation? How do people acquire power? How are economic and political power related? What interests shaped the U.S. Constitution? How have American elites changed over two centuries? How widely is power shared in the United States today? Are leaders in government, business, banking, the media, law, foundations, interest groups, and cultural affairs separate, distinct, and competitive—or are they concentrated, interlocked, and consensual? Do the elites or the masses give greater support to democratic values? Are the elites becoming ever more isolated from the masses? Are the masses losing confidence in the nation's elite, and if so, what does this mean for

FOCUS | TERRORISM'S THREAT TO DEMOCRACY

The terrorist attack on America on September 11, 2001, was the worst act of terrorism in modern history: commercial airliners, loaded and fueled, were hijacked and flown at high speeds directly into the symbols of America's financial and military power—the World Trade Center in New York City and the Pentagon in Washington, D.C. Televised images of the collapse of New York City's largest buildings left a lasting impression on Americans. More lives were lost on American soil than at any time since the Civil War. America found itself in a new war—a war on terrorism—with a hidden enemy whose goal was to kill as many innocent people as possible.

Terrorist Goals

Terrorism is political violence directed against innocent civilians. As barbaric as terrorism appears to civilized peoples, it is not without a rationale. Terrorists are not "crazies." Their first goal is to announce in the most dramatic fashion their own grievances, their commitment to violence, and their disregard for human life, often including their own. In its initial phase, the success of the terrorist act is directly related to the publicity it receives. Terrorist groups jubilantly claim responsibility for their acts. The more horrendous, the more media coverage, the more damage, the more dead—all add to the success of the terrorists in attracting attention to themselves.

A prolonged campaign of terrorism is designed to inspire pervasive fear among the masses, to convince them that their government cannot protect them, and to erode their confidence in their nation's leadership. Democratic elites are particularly vulnerable to terrorism. They must respond quickly and effectively to maintain the confidence of their people. But in doing so, they are almost always forced to sacrifice some of the very liberties they are dedicated to protect—increased surveillance, stopping and searching citizens without cause, searches at airport terminals and public gatherings, detention of persons for long periods without trial, crackdowns on immigrants, and other repressive measures.

Elite Response

The terrorist attack on America on September 11, 2001, motivated elites to enact and enforce more restrictions on individual liberty than the nation had experienced since World War II and the early Cold War period. Congress quickly passed the Aviation Security Act, which federalized security at all U.S. airports, required checked baggage to be inspected, and authorized armed federal marshals on domestic and international flights. Congress also passed a "Patriot" Act that, among other things, allows searches without notice to the suspect, grants "roving" wiretaps that allow any telephones used by suspects to be wiretapped, allows law enforcement authorities to track Internet communications, permits the inspection of business, bank, and library records, authorizes the seizure of properties used to commit or facilitate terrorism, and allows the detention of noncitizens charged with terrorism.

Congress created a new Department of Homeland Security, charged with the responsibility of coordinating more than forty federal agencies that have a role in combating terrorism. President Bush authorized the trial of noncitizens accused of terrorism by military commissions rather than by federal courts. He cited as precedent the actions of President Franklin D. Roosevelt during World War II. The Supreme Court held that only Congress could authorize the creation of special military tribunals,[a] and later at Bush's request, Congress did so. All of these actions enjoyed widespread mass support (see Chapter 5).

---

[a]*Hamdan v. Rumsfield*, June 29, 2006.

democracy? Can democracy long survive when most people are distrustful of government and cynical toward politics?

Are the masses generally informed, sensible, and considerate—or are they largely ill informed, apathetic, and intolerant? Does public opinion shape elite behavior—or do elites shape public opinion through the mass media? How successful are the media elites in molding mass opinion and influencing public debate? Are American political

Power Structure Research
Information on how to conduct research on elites, together with bibliography on power and elites.
www.uoregon.edu/ ~vburris/whorules

parties "responsible" instruments of popular control of government—or are they weakened oligarchies, dominated by ideologically motivated activists? Do elections serve as policy mandates from the people—or are they primarily an exercise in citizenship, choosing personnel, not policy? Are political campaigns designed to inform voters and assess their policy preferences—or are they expensive, commercial adventures in image making? How politically active, informed, knowledgeable, and consistent in their views are the American people? Do organized interest groups fairly represent the views of their members—or do they reflect the views and interests of leaders who are largely out of touch with the members? Does competition among interest groups create a reasonable balance in public policy—or do the special interests dominate policy making at the expense of the mass public?

How much influence do the masses have over the actions of presidents, Congress, and the courts? What role does the president play in America's elite system? What effect does the president's behavior have on the way the masses view their government? Does presidential popularity with the masses affect the power of the president? Is power shifting from elected officials to "faceless bureaucrats"? What are the sources of bureaucratic power, and can bureaucracy be restrained? Whom do members of Congress really represent? Are members of Congress held accountable for their policy decisions by the voters back home—or are they free to pursue their personal interests in Washington, knowing that their constituents are generally unaware of their policy positions? Why are the nation's most important domestic policy questions usually decided by the most elitist branch of the government, the unelected, lifetime-tenured justices of the Supreme Court? Can political decentralization—decision making by subelites in states and communities—increase mass involvement in government? How do elites respond to mass protest movements? Do protest movements themselves become oligarchic over time and increasingly divorced from the views of the masses?

We will address questions such as these from the perspective of *elite* theory. But we will also compare and evaluate the answers suggested by *pluralist* theory and *democratic* theory. The goal is a better understanding not only of American politics but also of elitism, pluralism, and democracy.

SELECTED READINGS

Dahl, Robert A. *Pluralist Democracy in the United States: Conflict and Consensus.* Chicago: Rand McNally, 1967. Most of Dahl's important work on pluralism was conducted at the community level. This book extended pluralism to the national level.

Etzioni-Halevy, Eva. *The Elite Connection.* Cambridge, Mass.: Polity Press, 1993. A scholarly description of "democratic elite theory," with comparisons to classical liberalism, traditional European elite theory, and modern American pluralism. It argues that although Western democracy is not "government by the people," it preserves democratic values through competition among separate and relatively autonomous elites both within and outside the state.

Etzioni-Halevy, Eva, ed. *Classes and Elites in Democracy.* New York: Garland Press, 1997. Advanced students may wish to read key selections from the scholarly literature on classes, elites, and democracy. This well-edited volume contains thirty-eight brief selections from the works of such writers as Karl Marx, Roberto Michels, Gaetano Mosca, Vilfredo Pareto, Joseph A. Schumpeter, C. Wright Mills, Robert A. Dahl, Samuel P. Huntington, and Seymour Martin Lipset.

Henry, William A., III. *In Defense of Elitism.* New York: Doubleday, 1994. A critical debunking of the myths that everyone is alike (or should be), that a just society will produce equal success for everyone, and that the common man is always right.

Katznelson, Ira, Mark Kesselman, and Alan Draper. *The Politics of Power: A Critical Introduction to American Government*, 5th ed. Belmont, Calif.: Wadsworth/Thomson Learning, 2006. An argument that the United States "is characterized by massive disparties in wealth, income, and political resources."

Michels, Roberto. *Political Parties: A Sociological Study of the Oligarchical Tendencies of Modern Democracies*. New York: Free Press, 1962. This classic book first appeared in 1911 in German. Michels was a disciple of Mosca. Like Mosca, he saw elitism as an outcome of social organization. Michels argued that the very fact of organization

in society leads inevitably to an elite. His often quoted thesis is, "Who says organization, says oligarchy." Political scientists have called this the iron law of oligarchy.

Mosca, Gaetano. *The Ruling Class*. Edited by A. Livingston. New York: McGraw-Hill, 1939. This classic book was first published in 1896 in Italy. Mosca added to it in a 1923 edition that reflects the impact of World War I on his ideas. Along with the work of Vilfredo Pareto, Mosca's *Ruling Class* forms the basis of "classical elitism."

Parenti, Michael. *Democracy for the Few*, 7th ed. Boston: Bedford; St. Martin's, 2002. A vitriolic attack on American elite governance, including chapters with titles such as "The Plutocratic Culture," "A Constitution for the Few," "Military Empire and Global Domination," "Unequal before the Law," to name a few.

Notes

1. Harold Lasswell and Abraham Kaplan, *Power and Society* (New Haven, Conn.: Yale University Press, 1950), p. 219.

2. Gaetano Mosca, *The Ruling Class* (New York: McGraw-Hill, 1939), p. 50.

3. Roberto Michels, *Political Parties: A Sociological Study of the Oligarchical Tendencies of Modern Democracies* (1915; reprint, New York: Free Press, 1962), p. 70.

4. Harold Lasswell and Daniel Lerner, *The Comparative Study of Elites* (Stanford, Calif.: Stanford University Press, 1952), p. 7.

5. David Truman, "The American System in Crisis," *Political Science Quarterly* 74 (December 1959): 489.

6. Richard Hofstadter, *The American Political Tradition* (New York: Knopf, 1948), p. viii.

7. John Stuart Mill, *Representative Government* (New York: Dutton, Everyman's Library, 1962), p. 203.

8. For a discussion of John Locke and the political philosophy underlying democracy, see George Sabine, *A History of Political Theory* (New York: Holt, Rinehart & Winston, 1950), pp. 517–541.

9. James Madison, The Federalist, Number 10 (New York: Modern Library, 1937).

10. For a discussion of "Democracy in the States" and a list of states that allow initiative, referenda, and recall voting, see Thomas R. Dye and Susan A. MacManus, *Politics in States in Communities* (Upper Saddle River, N.J.: Prentice-Hall, 2003), Chapter 2.

11. E. E. Schattschneider, *Two Hundred Million Americans in Search of a Government* (New York: Holt, Rinehart & Winston, 1969), p. 63.

12. See Eva Etzioni-Halevy, *The Elite Connection* (Cambridge, Mass.: Polity Press, 1993).

All communities divide themselves into the few and the many. The first are the rich and well-born, the other the masses of people.

Alexander Hamilton

THE FOUNDING FATHERS: THE NATION'S FIRST ELITE

CHAPTER **2**

The Founding Fathers—those fifty-five men who wrote the Constitution of the United States and founded a new nation—were a truly exceptional elite, not only "rich and well-born" but also educated, talented, and resourceful. When Thomas Jefferson, then the nation's minister in Paris, first saw the list of delegates to the Constitutional Convention of 1787, he wrote to John Adams, the minister to London, "It is really an assembly of demigods."[1] The men at the Convention belonged to the nation's intellectual and economic elites; they were owners of landed estates, important merchants and importers, bankers and financiers, real estate and land speculators, and government bond owners. Jefferson and Adams were among the nation's very few notables who were not at the Constitutional Convention.

The Founding Fathers were not typical of the four million Americans in the new nation, most of whom were small farmers, tradespeople, frontier dwellers, servants, or slaves. However, to say that these men were not a representative sample of the American people or that the Constitution was not a very democratic document does not discredit the Founding Fathers or the Constitution. To the aristocratic society of eighteenth-century Europe, the Founding Fathers were dangerous revolutionaries who were establishing a government in which men with the talent of acquiring property could rise to political power even though they were not born into the nobility. And the Constitution has survived the test of time, providing the basic framework for an ever-changing society.

ELITES AND MASSES IN THE NEW NATION

Many visitors from the aristocratic countries of Europe noted the absence of an American nobility and commented on the spirit of equality that prevailed. Yet class lines existed in America. At the top of the social structure, a tiny elite dominated the social, cultural, economic, and political life of the new nation. The French chargé d'affaires reported in 1787 that America had "no nobles" but that certain "gentlemen" enjoyed "preeminence" because of "their wealth, their talents, their education, their families, or the offices they hold."[2] Some of these prominent gentlemen were Tories who fled America after the Revolution, but Charleston still had its Pinckneys and Rutledges; Boston its Adamses, Lowells, and Gerrys; New York its Schuylers, Clintons, and Jays; Philadelphia its Morrises, Mifflins, and Ingersolls; Maryland its Jenifers and Carrolls; and Virginia its Blairs and Randolphs.

Below this thin layer of educated and talented merchants, planters, lawyers, and bankers was a substantial body of successful farmers, shopkeepers, and independent artisans—of the "middling" sort, as they were known in revolutionary America. This early middle class was by no means a majority in the new nation; it stood considerably above the masses of debt-ridden farmers and frontier dwellers who made up most of the population. This small middle class had some political power, even at the time of the Constitutional Convention; it was entitled to vote, and its views were represented in governing circles, even if these views did not prevail at the Convention. The middle class was better represented in state legislatures and was championed by several men of prominence in the revolutionary period—Patrick Henry, Luther Martin, and Thomas Jefferson.

The great mass of white Americans in the revolutionary period were "freeholders," small farmers who worked their own land, scratching out a bare existence for themselves and their families. They had little interest in or knowledge of public affairs. Usually the small farmers who were not barred from voting by property-owning or tax-paying qualifications were too preoccupied with debt and subsistence or too isolated in the wilderness to vote anyway. Nearly eight out of ten Americans made a marginal living in the dirt; one in ten worked in fishing or lumbering; and one in ten worked in commerce in some way, whether as a dockhand, sailor, lawyer, or merchant.

At the bottom of the white social structure in the new republic were indentured servants and tenant farmers; this class, which was perhaps 20 percent of the population, exercised little, if any, political power. Finally, still further below, were the black slaves. Although they made up almost another 20 percent of the population and were an important component of the American economy, they were considered property, even in a country that proclaimed the natural rights and equality of "all men."

ELITE PREFERENCES: INSPIRATION FOR A NEW CONSTITUTION

Our Documents
National Archives website with access to 100 "milestone documents" in American history.
www.ourdocuments. gov

In July 1775, Benjamin Franklin proposed to the Continental Congress a plan for a "perpetual union"; following the Declaration of Independence in 1776, the Congress appointed a committee to consider the Franklin proposal. The committee, headed by John Dickinson, made its report in the form of the Articles of Confederation, which the Congress debated for more than a year before finally adopting them on November 15, 1777. The Articles of Confederation were not to go into effect until every state approved; Delaware withheld its consent until 1779, Maryland until 1781.

GOVERNMENT UNDER THE ARTICLES OF CONFEDERATION

The Articles of Confederation, effective from 1781 to 1789, established a "firm league of friendship" among the states "for their common defense, the security of their liberties, and their mutual and general welfare." The document reassured each state of "its sovereignty, freedom, and independence, and every power, jurisdiction, and right, which is not by this confederation expressly delegated to the United States, in Congress assembled." The Confederation's delegated powers included power to declare war, to send and receive ambassadors, to make treaties, to fix standards of weights and measures, to regulate the value of coins, to manage Indian affairs, to establish post offices, to borrow money, to build and equip an army and navy, and to make requisitions (requests) to the several states for money and people. However, certain key powers remained with the states, including two of the most important ones of government: to regulate commerce and to levy taxes.

REPAYMENT OF LOANS MADE TO CONGRESS

The inability of Congress to levy taxes under the Articles of Confederation was a serious threat to those elites who had given financial backing to the new nation during the Revolutionary War. The Continental Congress and the states had financed the war with money borrowed through the issuance of government bonds. Congress was unable to tax the people to pay off those debts, and the states became less and less inclined, as time passed, to meet their obligations to the central government. The states paid only one-tenth the sums requisitioned by the Congress under the Articles. During the last years of the Articles, the national government was unable even to pay interest on its debt. As a result, the bonds and notes of the national government lost most of their value, sometimes selling on the open market for only one-tenth their original value. Investors who had backed the American war effort were left with nearly worthless bonds.

Without the power to tax, and with the credit of the Confederation ruined, the prospects of the central government for future financial support—and survival— looked dim. Naturally, the rich planters, merchants, and investors who owned government bonds had a direct financial interest in helping the national government acquire the power to tax and to pay off its debts.

ELIMINATION OF BARRIERS TO TRADE AND COMMERCE

The inability of Congress under the Articles to regulate commerce among the states and with foreign nations, and the states' practice of laying tariffs on the goods of other states as well as on those of foreign nations, created havoc among commercial and shipping interests. "In every point of view," Madison wrote in 1785, "the trade of this country is in a deplorable condition."[3] The American Revolution had been fought, in part, to defend American commercial and business interests from oppressive regulation by the British government. Now the states themselves were interfering with the development of a national economy. Merchants and shippers with a view toward a national market and a high level of commerce were vitally concerned that the national government acquire the power to regulate interstate commerce and to prevent the states from imposing crippling tariffs and restrictions on interstate trade.

PROTECTION OF BANKERS AND CREDITORS FROM CHEAP MONEY

State governments under the Articles posed a serious threat to investors and creditors through issuing cheap paper money and passing laws impairing contractual obligations. Paper money issued by the states permitted debtors to pay off their creditors with money worth less than the money originally loaned. States were requiring creditors to accept their money as "legal tender," meaning that the refusal of a creditor to accept it would abolish the debt. Even the most successful farmers were usually heavily in debt, and many of them were gaining strength in state legislatures. They threatened to pass laws delaying the collection of debts and even abolishing the prevailing practice of imprisonment for unpaid debts. Obviously, creditors had a direct financial interest in establishing a strong central government that could prevent the states from issuing public paper or otherwise interfering with debt collection.

PROTECTION OF PROPERTY AGAINST RADICAL MOVEMENTS

A strong central government would help protect creditors against social upheavals by the large debtor class in America. In several states, debtors had already engaged in open rebellion against tax collectors and sheriffs attempting to repossess farms on behalf of creditors. The most serious rebellion broke out in the summer of 1786 in Massachusetts, when bands of insurgents—composed of farmers, artisans, and laborers—captured the courthouses in several western districts and briefly held the city of Springfield. Led by Daniel Shays, a veteran of Bunker Hill, the insurgent army posed a direct military threat to the governing elite of Massachusetts. Shays' Rebellion was put down by a smaller mercenary army, paid for by well-to-do citizens who feared a wholesale attack on property rights. Growing radicalism in the states intimidated the propertied classes, who began to advocate a strong central government to "insure domestic tranquility," guarantee "a republican form of government," and protect property "against domestic violence."

OPENING WESTERN LAND TO SPECULATION

A strong central government with enough military power to oust the British from the Northwest and to protect western settlers against Indian attacks could open the way for the development of the American West. In addition, the protection and settlement of western land would cause land values to skyrocket and make land speculators rich.

Men of property in early America actively speculated in western land. George Washington, Benjamin Franklin, Robert Morris, and even the popular hero Patrick Henry were involved in land speculation. During the Revolutionary War, Congress had often paid the Continental soldiers with land certificates. After the war, most of the ex-soldiers sold the certificates to land speculators at very low prices. The Confederation's military weakness along its frontiers had kept the value of western lands low, for ravaging Indians discouraged immigration to the lands west of the Alleghenies and the British threatened to cut off westward expansion by continuing to occupy (in defiance of the peace treaty) several important fur-trading forts in the Northwest. The British forts were also becoming centers of anti-American influence among the Indians.

PROTECTION OF SHIPPING AND MANUFACTURING

The development of a strong national navy was also important to American commercial interests, because the states seemed ineffective in preventing smuggling, and piracy was a very real danger and a vital concern of American shippers.

*"Religious freedom is my immediate goal, but my
long-range plan is to go into real estate."*

Manufacturing was still in its newborn stages during the revolutionary era in America, but farsighted investors were anxious to protect infant American industries against the import of British goods. Although all thirteen states erected tariff barriers against foreign goods, state tariffs could not provide the same protection for industry as a strong central government with a uniform tariff policy, because the state tariff system allowed low-tariff states to bring in foreign goods and circulate them throughout the country.

Ensuring the Return of Runaway Slaves

Southern planters and slaveholders also sought protection for their ownership of human "property." In 1787, slavery was lawful everywhere except in Massachusetts. Although many leaders in the South as well as the North recognized the moral paradox of asserting in the Declaration of Independence that "all men are created equal," yet at the same time owning slaves (as did the author of the Declaration, Thomas Jefferson), nonetheless the nation's Founders were fully prepared to protect "the peculiar institution" of slavery. (Interestingly, the Founders were too embarrassed to use the word *slave* in the new Constitution, preferring instead the euphemism "persons held to service or labor.") It was especially important to slave owners to guarantee the return of escaped slaves.

- The federal government had no tax powers and therefore could not repay the money lent to it by wealthy bankers, planters, merchants, and investors.
- States were imposing tariffs on goods shipped from state to state, inhibiting trade and commerce.
- States were issuing their own paper money and obliging banks and other creditors to accept it as legal tender.
- Open rebellion against tax collectors and creditors repossessing property (Shays' Rebellion) threatened property classes.
- The absence of a strong U.S. Army allowed Indians to attack Western land setters, and therefore lowered prices that Western land speculators could get for their investments.
- The absence of a strong U.S. Navy allowed pirates to threaten American shipping merchants.
- The absence of federal tariffs and customs duties allow foreign goods to challenge domestic manufacturers.
- Slaves who ran away to free states threatened the "property" of slave owners.
- American elites were hampered in their dealings in the international community by the absence of a strong central U.S. government.

EXERCISING POWER IN WORLD AFFAIRS

Finally, a strong sense of nationalism appeared to motivate America's elites. While the masses focused on local affairs, the educated and cosmopolitan leaders in America were concerned about the weakness of America in the international community. Thirteen separate states failed to manifest a sense of national purpose and identity. The Confederation was held in contempt not only by Britain, as evidenced by the violations of the Treaty of Paris, but even by the lowly Barbary states. Alexander Hamilton expressed the indignation of America's leadership over its inability to swing weight in the world community:

> There is something...diminutive and contemptible in the prospect of a number of petty states, with the appearance only of union, jarring, jealous, and perverse, without any determined direction, fluctuating and unhappy at home, weak and insignificant by their dissentions in the eyes of other nations.[4]

In short, America's elite wanted to assume a respectable role in the international community and exercise power in world affairs.

FORMATION OF A NATIONAL ELITE

In the spring of 1785, delegates from Virginia and Maryland met in Alexandria, Virginia, to resolve certain difficulties that had arisen between the two states over the regulation of commerce and navigation on the Potomac River and Chesapeake Bay. It was fortunate for the new nation that the most prominent man in America, George Washington, took a personal interest in this meeting. As a rich planter and land speculator who owned more than 30,000 acres of western lands upstream on the Potomac, Washington was keenly aware of commercial problems under the Articles. He lent great prestige to the Alexandria meeting by inviting participants to his home at

Mount Vernon. Out of this conference came the idea for a general economic conference for all the states. The Virginia legislature issued a call for such a convention to meet in Annapolis in September 1785.

Judged by its publicly announced purpose—securing interstate agreement on matters of commerce and navigation—the Annapolis Convention was a failure; only twelve delegates appeared, representing five commercial states: New York, New Jersey, Pennsylvania, Delaware, and Virginia. But these twelve men saw the opportunity to use the Annapolis meeting to achieve greater political successes. Hamilton, with masterful political foresight, persuaded the others in attendance to strike out for a full constitutional solution to America's ills. The Annapolis Convention adopted a report, written by Hamilton, that outlined the defects in the Articles of Confederation and called on the states to send delegates to a new convention to suggest remedies for these defects. The new convention was to meet in May 1787 in Philadelphia. Rumors at the time suggested that Hamilton, with the behind-the-scenes support of James Madison in the Virginia legislature, had intended all along that the Annapolis Convention fail in its stated purposes and that it provide a stepping-stone to larger political objectives.

Shays' Rebellion was very timely for men like Hamilton and Madison, who sought to galvanize America's elite into action. Commencing in the fall of 1786, after the Annapolis call for a new convention, the rebellion convinced men of property in Congress and state legislatures that there was cause for alarm.

On February 21, 1787, Congress confirmed the call for a convention to meet in Philadelphia,

> for the sole and express purpose of revising the Articles of Confederation and reporting to Congress and the several legislatures such alterations and provisions therein as shall, when agreed to in Congress and confirmed by the states, render the federal Constitution adequate to the exigencies of government and the preservation of the union.

Delegates to the Convention were appointed by the legislatures of every state except Rhode Island, the only state in which the debtor classes had gained political control of the legislature. The fifty-five men who met in the summer of 1787 to establish a new national government quickly chose George Washington, their most prestigious member—indeed the most prestigious man on the continent—to preside over the assembly. Just as quickly, the Convention decided to hold its sessions behind closed doors and to keep all proceedings a carefully guarded secret. Delegates adhered closely to this decision and informed neither close friends nor relatives of the nature of the discussions. Apparently the Founding Fathers were aware that elites are most effective in negotiation, compromise, and decision making when they operate in secrecy.

The Convention was quick to discard its congressional mandate to "revise the Articles of Confederation"; without much hesitation, it proceeded to write an entirely new constitution. Only men confident of their powers and abilities, men of principle and property, could proceed in this bold fashion. Let us examine the characteristics of the nation's first elite more closely.

GEORGE WASHINGTON'S PRESTIGE

One cannot overestimate the prestige of George Washington at this time in his life. As the commander-in-chief of the successful revolutionary army and founder of the new nation, he had overwhelming charismatic appeal among both elites and masses.

George Washington
Documents, articles, and other resources on the nation's first president.
http://gwpapers. virginia.edu

Preeminent not only as a soldier, statesman, and founder of the nation, he was also one of the richest men in America. Through all the years that he had spent in the revolutionary cause, he had refused any payment for his services. He often paid his soldiers from his own fortune. In addition to his large estate on the Potomac, he possessed many thousands of acres of undeveloped land in western Virginia, Maryland, Pennsylvania, Kentucky, and the Northwest Territory. He owned major shares in the Potomac Company, the James River Company, the Bank of Columbia, and the Bank of Alexandria. And he held large amounts in U.S. bonds and securities. Washington stood at the apex of America's elite structure.

THE FOUNDERS' GOVERNING EXPERIENCE

Biographies of the Founding Fathers
Brief biographies of each of the fifty-five delegates to the Constitutional Convention, as well as bios of the signers of the Declaration of Independence and the Articles of Confederation.
www.colonialhall. com

The Founding Fathers had extensive experience in governing. These same men had made all the key decisions in American history from the Stamp Act Congress to the Declaration of Independence to the Articles of Confederation. They controlled the Congress of the United States and had conducted the Revolutionary War. Eight delegates had signed the Declaration of Independence. Eleven delegates had served as officers in Washington's army. Forty-two of the fifty-five Founding Fathers had already served in the U.S. Congress. Even at the moment of the Convention, more than forty delegates held high offices in state governments; Franklin, Livingston, and Randolph were governors. The Founding Fathers were unsurpassed in political skill and experience.

THE FOUNDERS' EDUCATION

In an age when no more than a handful of men on the North American continent had gone to college, the Founding Fathers were conspicuous for their educational attainment. More than half the delegates had been educated at Harvard (founded in 1636), William and Mary (1693), Yale (1701), the University of Pennsylvania (1740), Columbia College (1754), or Princeton (1756) or in England. The tradition of legal training for political decision makers, which has continued in the United States to the present, was already evident. About a dozen delegates were still active lawyers in 1787, and about three dozen had had legal training.

THE FOUNDERS' WEALTH

The fifty-five men at the Philadelphia Convention formed a major part of the nation's economic elite as well. The personal wealth represented at the meeting was enormous. It is difficult to determine accurately who were the richest men in America at that time because the finances of the period were chaotic and because wealth assumed a variety of forms—land, ships, credit, slaves, business inventories, bonds, and paper money of uncertain worth (even George Washington had difficulty at times converting his land wealth into cash). But at least forty of the fifty-five delegates were known to be holders of government bonds; fourteen were land speculators; twenty-four were moneylenders and investors; eleven were engaged in commerce or manufacturing; and fifteen owned large plantations[5] (see Table 2.1).

TABLE 2.1 | FOUNDERS' MEMBERSHIP IN ELITE GROUPS

Government Bond Holders		Real Estate and Land Speculators	Lenders and Investors	Merchants, Manufacturers, and Shippers	Planters and Slaveholders
Major	Minor				
Baldwin	Bassett	Blount	Bassett	Broom	Butler
Blair	Blount	Dayton	Broom	Clymer	Davie
Clymer	Brearly	Few	Butler	Ellsworth	Jenifer
Dayton	Broom	Fitzsimons	Carroll	Fitzsimons	A. Martin
Ellsworth	Butler	Franklin	Clymer	Gerry	L. Martin
Fitzsimons	Carroll	Gerry	Davie	King	Mason
Gerry	Few	Gilman	Dickinson	Langdon	Mercer
Gilman	Hamilton	Gorham	Ellsworth	McHenry	C. C. Pinckney
Gorham	L. Martin	Hamilton	Few	Mifflin	C. Pinckney
Jenifer	Mason	Mason	Fitzsimons	G. Morris	Randolph
Johnson	Mercer	R. Morris	Franklin	R. Morris	Read
King	Mifflin	Washington	Gilman		Rutledge
Langdon	Read	Williamson	Ingersoll		Spaight
Lansing	Spaight	Wilson	Johnson		Washington
Livingston	Wilson		King		Wythe
McClurg	Wythe		Langdon		
R. Morris			Mason		
C. C. Pinckney			McHenry		
C. Pinckney			C. C. Pinckney		
Randolph			C. Pinckney		
Sherman			Randolph		
Strong			Read		
Washington			Washington		
Williamson			Williamson		

THE FOUNDERS' "CONTINENTAL" VIEW

Perhaps what most distinguished the men in Philadelphia from the masses was their cosmopolitanism. They approached political, economic, and military issues from a "continental" point of view. Unlike the masses, members of the elite extended their loyalties beyond their states; they experienced the sentiment of nationalism half a century before it would begin to seep down to the masses.[6]

ELITE CONSENSUS IN 1787

By focusing on the debates *within* the Convention, many scholars have overemphasized the differences of opinion among the Founding Fathers. True, the Convention was the site of many conflicting views and innumerable compromises; yet the more striking fact is that the delegates were in almost complete accord on essential political questions.

PROTECTING LIBERTY AND PROPERTY

They agreed that the fundamental end of government is the protection of liberty and property. They accepted without debate many of the precedents set by the English constitution and by the constitutions of the new states. Reflecting the advanced ideas of their times, the Founding Fathers were much less religious than most Americans today. Yet they believed in a law of nature with rules of abstract justice to which human laws should conform. They believed that this law of nature endowed each person with certain inalienable rights essential to a meaningful existence—the rights to life, liberty, and property—and that these rights should be recognized and protected by law. They believed that all people were equally entitled to respect of their natural rights regardless of their station in life. Most of the Founding Fathers were even aware that this belief ran contrary to the practice of slavery and were embarrassed by this inconsistency in American life.

But "equality" did *not* mean to the Founding Fathers that people were equal in wealth, intelligence, talent, or virtue. They accepted inequalities in wealth and property as a natural product of human diversity. They did not believe that government had a responsibility to reduce these inequalities; in fact, *they saw "dangerous leveling" as a serious violation of the right to property* and the right to use and dispose of the fruits of one's own industry.

GOVERNMENT AS CONTRACT

The Founding Fathers agreed that the origin of government is an implied contract among people. They believed that people pledge allegiance and obedience to government in return for protection of their persons and property. They felt that the ultimate legitimacy of government—sovereignty—rests with the people themselves and not with gods or kings and that *the basis of government is the consent of the governed.*

REPUBLICANISM

The Founding Fathers believed in republican government. They opposed hereditary monarchies, the prevailing form of government in the world at the time. Although they believed that people of principle and property should govern, they were opposed to an aristocracy or a governing nobility. To them, a "republican government" was a representative, responsible, and nonhereditary government. But they certainly did *not* mean mass democracy, with direct participation by the people in decision making. They expected the masses to consent to government by men of principle and property, out of recognition of their abilities, talents, education, and stake in the preservation of liberty and order. The Founding Fathers believed that the masses should have only a limited role in selecting government leaders. They bickered over how much direct participation was appropriate in selecting decision makers and they bickered over the qualifications necessary for public office, but they generally agreed that the *masses should have only a limited, indirect role in selecting decision makers and that decision makers themselves should be men of wealth, education, and proven leadership ability.*

LIMITED GOVERNMENT

The Founding Fathers believed in limited government that could not threaten liberty or property. Because the Founding Fathers believed that power is a corrupting influence and that the concentration of power is dangerous, *they believed in dividing government power into separate bodies capable of checking, or thwarting, one another should any one branch pose a threat to liberty or property.* Differences of opinion among honest people, particularly differences among elites in separate states, could best be resolved by balancing representation of these several elites in the national government and by creating a decentralized system that permits local elites to govern their states as they see fit, with limited interference from the national government.

NATIONALISM

Finally, and perhaps most important, the Founding Fathers believed that only a strong national government, with power to exercise its will directly on the people, could "establish justice, insure domestic tranquility, provide for the common defense, promote the general welfare, and secure the blessings of liberty."

ELITE CONSENSUS IN A WORLD CONTEXT

National Constitutional Center
Constitutional museum adjoining Independence Hall in Philadelphia. Website includes a virtual tour. *www. constitutioncenter. org*

Elite consensus in 1787 was conservative in that it sought to preserve the status quo in the distribution of power and property in the United States. Yet at the same time, *this elite consensus was radical compared with the beliefs of their elite contemporaries elsewhere in the world.* Nearly every other government adhered to the principles of hereditary monarchy and privileged nobility, whereas American elites were committed to republicanism. Other elites asserted the divine rights of kings, but American elites talked about government by the consent of the governed. While the elites in Europe rationalized and defended a rigid class system, American elites believed in equality and inalienable human rights.

AN ELITE IN OPERATION: CONCILIATION AND COMPROMISE

On May 25, 1787, sessions of the Constitutional Convention opened in Independence Hall, Philadelphia. After the delegates had selected Washington as president of the Convention and decided to keep the proceedings of the Convention secret, Governor Edmund Randolph, speaking for the Virginia delegation, presented a draft of a new constitution.[7]

| IN BRIEF | ELITE CONSENSUS IN 1787 |

- Natural law endows each person with inalienable rights to life, liberty, and property.
- Government originates as a contract among people to protect their liberty and property. Government exists by consent of the governed. A government that violates this contract is illegitimate and may rightfully be overthrown—the right to revolution.
- Republican government—government by representatives of the people—is preferable to

hereditary monarchies and aristocracies. But direct democracy—decision making by the people themselves—is a dangerous idea. The masses should have only a limited role in selecting decision makers.

- Governmental power should be limited, by written constitutional guarantees, and by dividing and separating governmental powers.
- A strong national government is required to protect liberty and property.

REPRESENTATION COMPROMISE

The Virginia plan gave little recognition to the states in its proposed composition of the national government. The plan suggested a two-house legislature: a lower house to be chosen by the people of the states, with representation according to the population, and an upper house to be chosen by the first house. This Congress would have power to "legislate in all cases in which the separate states are incompetent, or in which the harmony of the United States may be interrupted by the exercise of individual legislation." Moreover, Congress would have the authority to nullify state laws that it felt violated the Constitution, thus ensuring national supremacy. The Virginia plan also proposed a parliamentary form of government, with Congress choosing members of the executive and judiciary branches.

The most important line of cleavage at the Convention was between elites of large states and elites of small states over the representation scheme in the Virginia plan. This question was not one of economic interest or ideology, because delegates from large and small states did not divide along economic or ideological lines. After several weeks of debate over the Virginia plan, delegates from the small states presented a counterproposal in a report by William Paterson of New Jersey. The New Jersey plan may have been merely a tactic by the small-state elites to force the Convention to compromise on representation—the plan was set aside after only a week of debate with little negative reaction. The New Jersey plan proposed to retain the representation scheme outlined in the Articles of Confederation, which granted each state a single vote. But the plan went further, proposing separate executive and judiciary branches and expansion of the powers of Congress to include the right to levy taxes and regulate commerce.

The New Jersey plan was not an attempt to retain the Confederation. Indeed, the plan included words that later appeared in the Constitution as the famous national supremacy clause that provides that the U.S. Constitution and federal laws supersede each state's constitution and laws. Thus, even the small states did not envision a confederation. Both the Virginia and New Jersey plans were designed to strengthen the national government; they differed only on how much to strengthen it and on its system of representation.

TABLE 2.2 | REPRESENTATIONAL COMPROMISE, 1787

The Virginia Plan	The New Jersey Plan	The Connecticut Compromise The Constitution of 1787
Two-house legislature, with the lower house directly elected based on state population and the upper house elected by the lower.	One-house legislature, with equal state representation, regardless of population.	Two-house legislature, with the House directly elected based on state population and the Senate selected by the state legislatures; two senators per state, regardless of population.
Legislature with broad power, including veto power over laws passed by the state legislatures.	Legislature with the same power as under the Articles of Confederation, plus the power to levy some taxes and to regulate commerce.	Legislature with broad power, including the power to tax and to regulate commerce.
President and cabinet elected by the legislature.	Separate multiperson executive, elected by the legislature, removable by petition from a majority of the state governors.	President chosen by an Electoral College.
National judiciary elected by the legislature.	National judiciary appointed by the executive.	National judiciary appointed by the president and confirmed by the Senate.
"Council of Revision" with the power to veto laws of the legislature.	National Supremacy Clause similar to that found in Article VI of the 1787 Constitution.	National Supremacy Clause: the Constitution is "the supreme Law of the Land."

On June 29, William Samuel Johnson of Connecticut proposed the obvious compromise: that representation in the lower house of Congress be based on population, whereas representation in the upper house would be equal—two senators from each state. The Connecticut compromise also provided that equal representation of states in the Senate could not be abridged, even by constitutional amendment. (See Table 2.2.)

SLAVERY COMPROMISES

The next question requiring compromise was that of slavery and the role of slaves in the system of representation, an issue closely related to economic differences among America's elite. It was essentially the same question that seventy-four years later divided that elite and provoked the nation's bloodiest war. Planters and slaveholders generally believed that wealth, particularly wealth in slaves, should count in apportioning representation. Non-slaveholders felt that "the people" should include only free inhabitants. The decision to apportion direct taxes among the states in proportion to population opened the way to compromise, because the attitudes of slaveholders and non-slaveholders reversed when counting people in order to apportion taxes. The result was the famous three-fifths compromise: three-fifths of the slaves of each state would be counted for the purpose of both representation and apportioning direct taxes.

A compromise was also necessary on the question of trading in slaves. On this issue, the men of Maryland and Virginia, states already well supplied with slaves, were able to indulge in the luxury of conscience and support proposals for banning the further import of slaves. But the less-developed southern states, particularly South Carolina and Georgia, could not afford this posture because they still wanted additional slave labor. Inasmuch as the southern planters were themselves divided, the ultimate compromise permitted Congress to prohibit the slave trade—but not before the year 1808. The twenty-year delay would allow the undeveloped southern states to acquire all the slaves they needed before the slave trade ended.

EXPORT TAX COMPROMISE

Agreement between southern planters and northern merchants was still relatively easy to achieve at this early date in American history. But latent conflict was evident on issues other than slavery. Although all elite groups agreed that the national government should regulate interstate and foreign commerce, southern planters feared that the unrestricted power of Congress over commerce might lead to the imposition of export taxes. Export taxes would bear most heavily on the southern states, which depended on foreign markets in order to sell the indigo, rice, tobacco, and cotton that they produced. However, planters and merchants were able to compromise again in resolving this issue: articles exported from any state should bear no tax or duty. Only imports could be taxed by the national government.

VOTER QUALIFICATION COMPROMISE

Another important compromise, one that occupied much of the Convention's time (although it has received little recognition from later writers), concerned qualifications for voting and holding office in the new government. Although no property qualifications for voters or officeholders appear in the text of the Constitution, the debates revealed that members of the Convention generally favored property qualifications for holding office. The delegates showed little enthusiasm for mass participation in democracy. Elbridge Gerry of Massachusetts declared that "the evils we experience flow from the excess of democracy." Roger Sherman protested that "the people immediately should have as little to do as may be about the government." Edmund Randolph continually deplored the turbulence and follies of democracy, and George Clymer's notion of republican government was that "a representative of the people is appointed to think for and not with his constituents." John Dickinson considered property qualifications a "necessary defense against the dangerous influence of those multitudes without property and without principle, with which our country like all others, will in time abound." Charles Pinckney later wrote to Madison, "Are you not ... abundantly depressed at the theoretical nonsense of an election of Congress by the people; in the first instance, it's clearly and practically wrong, and it will in the end be the means of bringing our councils into contempt." Many more such elitist statements appear in the records of the Convention.[8]

Given these views, how do we explain the absence of property qualifications in the Constitution? Actually a motion was carried in the Convention instructing a committee to fix property qualifications for holding office, but the committee could not agree on what qualifications to impose. Various propositions to establish property qualifications met defeat on the floor, not because delegates believed they were inherently wrong but, interestingly enough, because the elites at the Convention represented different kinds of property holdings. Madison pointed out that fact in the July debate, noting that a land ownership requirement would exclude from Congress the mercantile and manufacturing classes, who would hardly be willing to turn their money into landed property just to become eligible for a seat in Congress. Madison rightly observed that "landed possessions were no certain evidence of real wealth. Many enjoyed them to a great extent who were more in debt than they were worth." The objections by merchants and investors defeated the "landed" qualifications for congressional representatives.

Thus, the Convention approved the Constitution without property qualifications on officeholders or voters, except those that the states themselves might see fit to impose. Failing to come to a decision on this issue of suffrage, the delegates merely returned the question to state legislatures by providing that "the electors in each state should have the qualifications requisite for electors of the most numerous branch of the state legislatures." At the time, this expedient course of action did not seem likely to produce mass democracy. Only one branch of the new government, the House of Representatives, was to be elected by popular vote. The other three controlling bodies—the president, the Senate, and the Supreme Court—were removed from direct voter participation. The delegates were reassured that nearly all the state constitutions then in force included property qualifications for voters.

Finally, the Constitution did not recognize women as legitimate participants in government. For nearly one hundred years, no state accorded women the right to vote. (The newly formed Wyoming Territory first gave women the right to vote and hold public office in 1869.) Not until 1920 was the U.S. Constitution amended to guarantee women the right to vote.

THE CONSTITUTION AS ELITIST DOCUMENT

The text of the Constitution, together with interpretive materials in *The Federalist Papers,* written by Hamilton, Madison, and John Jay, provides ample evidence that elites in America benefited both politically and economically from the adoption of the Constitution.* Although both elites and nonelites—indeed all Americans—may have benefited from the Constitution, *elites benefited more directly and immediately than*

---

*See the Appendix for the complete text of the Constitution of the United States of America, as well as Numbers 10 and 51 of *The Federalist Papers.*

"You know, the idea of taxation with representation doesn't appeal to me very much, either."

did nonelites. And we can infer that the elites would not have developed and supported the Constitution if they had not stood to gain substantially from it.

Let us examine the text of the Constitution itself and its impact on American elites. Article I, Section 8, grants seventeen types of power to Congress, followed by a general grant of power to make "all laws which shall be necessary and proper for carrying into execution the foregoing powers."

LEVYING TAXES

The first and perhaps most important power is the "power to lay and collect taxes, duties, imposts, and excises." The taxing power is the basis of all other powers, and it enabled the national government to end its dependence on states. This power was essential to the holders of public securities, particularly when combined with the provision in Article VI, "All debts contracted and engagements entered into, before the adoption of this Constitution, shall be as valid against the United States under this Constitution, as under the Confederation." Thus, the national government was

The Constitution
Official U.S.
government website
with annotated
Constitution,
providing caselaw
interpretations of each
Article and Clause.
*www.gpoaccess.
gov/constitution*

committed to paying off all those investors who held bonds of the United States, and the taxing power guaranteed that commitment would be fulfilled.

The text of the Constitution suggests that the Founding Fathers intended Congress to place most of the tax burden on consumers in the form of custom duties and excise taxes rather than direct taxes on individual income or property. Article I, Section 2, states that government can levy direct taxes only on the basis of population; it follows that it could not levy such taxes in proportion to wealth. This provision prevented the national government from levying progressive income taxes; not until the Sixteenth Amendment in 1913 did this protection for wealth disappear from the Constitution.

Southern planters, whose livelihoods depended on the export of indigo, rice, tobacco, and cotton, strenuously opposed giving the national government the power to tax exports. Article I, Section 9, offered protection for their interests: "No tax or duty shall be laid on articles exported from any State." However, Congress was given the power to tax imports so that northern manufacturers could erect a tariff wall to protect American industries against foreign goods.

REGULATING COMMERCE

Congress also had the power to "regulate commerce with foreign nations, and among the several States." The interstate commerce clause, together with the provision in Article I, Section 9, prohibiting the states from taxing either imports or exports, created a free trade area over the thirteen states. This arrangement was very beneficial for American merchants.

PROTECTING MONEY AND PROPERTY

Following the Article I, Section 8, powers to tax and spend, to borrow money, and to regulate commerce is a series of specific powers designed to enable Congress to protect money and property. Congress is given the power to make bankruptcy laws, to coin money and regulate its value, to fix standards of weights and measures, to punish counterfeiting, to establish post offices and post roads, to pass copyright and patent laws to protect authors and inventors, and to punish piracies and felonies committed on the high seas. Each of these powers is a specific asset to bankers, investors, and shippers, respectively. Obviously, the Founding Fathers felt that giving Congress control over currency and credit in the United States would result in better protection for financial interests than would leaving the essential responsibility to the states. Similarly, they believed that control over communication and transportation (by establishing post offices and post roads) was too essential to trade and commerce to be left to the states.

CREATING THE MILITARY

The remaining powers in Article I, Section 8, deal with military affairs: raising and supporting armies; organizing, training, and calling up the state militia; declaring war; suppressing insurrections; and repelling invasions. These powers—together with the provisions in Article II that make the president the commander-in-chief of the army and navy and of the state militia when called into the federal service and that give the president power to make treaties with the advice and consent of the Senate and to send and receive ambassadors—centralized diplomatic and military affairs at the national level. Article I, Section 10, confirms this centralization of diplomatic and military powers by prohibiting the states from entering into treaties with foreign nations, maintaining ships of war, or engaging in war unless actually invaded.

Clearly, the Founding Fathers had little confidence in the state militias, particularly when they were under state control. General Washington's painful experiences with state militias during the Revolutionary War were still fresh in his memory. The militias had proved adequate when defending their own states against invasion, but when employed outside their own states, the militias were often a disaster. Moreover, if western settlers were to be protected from the Indians and if the British were to be persuaded to give up their forts in Ohio and open the way to westward expansion, the national government could not rely on state militias but must have an army of its own. Similarly, a strong navy was essential to the protection of U.S. commerce on the seas (the first significant naval action under the new government was against the piracy of the Barbary states). Thus, a national army and navy were not so much protection against invasion (for many years the national government continued to rely primarily on state militias for this purpose) as they were protection and promotion of the government's commercial and territorial ambitions.

PROTECTING AGAINST REVOLUTION

A national army and navy, as well as an organized and trained militia that could be called into national service, also provided protection against class wars and debtor rebellions. In an obvious reference to Shays' Rebellion, Hamilton warned in *The Federalist*, Number 21:

> *The tempestuous situation from which Massachusetts has scarcely emerged evinces that dangers of this kind are not merely speculative. Who could determine what might have been the issue of her late convulsions if the malcontents had been headed by a Caesar or a Cromwell? A strong military force in the hands of the national government is a protection against revolutionary action.*[9]

Further evidence of the Founding Fathers' intention to protect the government classes from revolution is found in Article IV, Section 4, where the national government guarantees to every state "a republican form of government," as well as protection against "domestic violence." Thus, in addition to protecting western land and commerce on the seas, a strong army and navy would enable the national government to back up its pledge to protect governing elites in the states from violence and revolution.

Protection against domestic insurrection also appealed to the southern slaveholders' deep-seated fear of a slave revolt. Madison drove this point home in *The Federalist*, Number 23:

> *I take no little notice of an unhappy species of population abounding in some of the states who, during the calm of regular government were sunk below the level of men; but who, in the tempestuous seeds of civil violence, may emerge into human character and give a superiority of strength to any party with which they may associate themselves.*[10]

| IN BRIEF | CONSTITUTIONAL PROTECTIONS FOR PROPERTY |

- The debts of the U.S. government, including those incurred prior to the adoption of the Constitution, must be paid.
- The national government is given the power to tax in order to pay off its debts.
- Taxes must be direct, not proportional or based on wealth or income (a provision not changed until the adoption of the Sixteenth Amendment in 1913).
- No taxes can be placed on exports—goods produced in the United States. The national government may tax imports from other countries—a form of protection for domestic industries.
- States cannot interfere with interstate commerce.

- States cannot issue their own paper money or require its acceptance as legal tender.
- The national government will protect creditors in bankruptcy laws and protect authors and inventors in patent and copyright laws. It will punish counterfeiting and piracy.
- A national army will protect Western landholders, and a national navy will protect merchants and shippers.
- The national government will protect property owners against revolution—"domestic violence."
- The Constitution guarantees slave owners the return of escaped slaves (a provision not changed until the adoption of the Thirteenth Amendment in 1865).

PROTECTING SLAVERY

The Constitution permitted Congress to outlaw the import of slaves after 1808. But most southern planters were more interested in protecting their existing property and slaves than they were in extending the slave trade, and the Constitution provided an explicit advantage to slaveholders in Article IV, Section 2:

> No person held to service or labor in one State, under the laws thereof, escaping into another, shall in consequence of any law or regulation therein, be discharged from such service or labor, but shall be delivered up on claim of the party to whom such service or labor may be due.

This provision was an extremely valuable protection for one of the most important forms of property in the United States at the time. Although the U.S. slave trade lapsed after twenty years, slavery itself, as a domestic institution, was better safeguarded under the new Constitution than under the Articles.

LIMITING STATES IN MONETARY AFFAIRS

The restrictions placed on state legislatures by the Constitution also provided protection to economic elites in the new nation. States could not coin money, issue paper money, or pass legal-tender laws that would make any money other than gold or silver coin tender in the payment of debts. This restriction would prevent the states from issuing cheap paper money, which debtors could use to pay off creditors with less valuable currency. Moreover, the states were prohibited from passing legal-tender laws obliging creditors to accept paper money in payment of debts.

LIMITING STATES IN BUSINESS AFFAIRS

The Constitution also prevents states from passing any law "impairing the obligation of contracts." The structure of business relations in a free-enterprise economy depends on governmental enforcement of private contracts, and economic elites seek to prevent government from relieving people of their contractual obligations. If state legislatures could relieve debtors of their contractual obligations, relieve indentured servants of their obligations to their masters, prevent creditors from foreclosing on mortgages, declare moratoriums on debt, or otherwise interfere with business obligations, then the interests of investors, merchants, and creditors would be seriously damaged.

ELITISM AND THE STRUCTURE OF THE NATIONAL GOVERNMENT

The structure of the national government clearly reflects the desire of the Founders to protect liberty and property, especially from *mass majorities*. Those who criticize the U.S. government for its slow, unwieldy processes should realize that the government's founders deliberately built in this characteristic. These cumbersome arrangements—the checks and balances and the fragmentation of authority that make it difficult for government to realize its potential power over private interests—aim to protect private interests from governmental interference and to shield the government from an unjust and self-seeking majority. If the system handcuffs government and makes it easy for established groups to oppose change, then the system is working as intended.

This system of intermingled powers and conflicting loyalties is still alive today. Of course, some aspects have changed; for example, voters now elect senators directly, and the president is more directly responsible to the voters than was originally envisioned. But the basic arrangement of checks and balances endures. Presidents, senators, representatives, and judges are chosen by different constituencies; their terms of office vary, and their responsibilities and loyalties differ. This system makes majority rule virtually impossible.

NATIONAL SUPREMACY

The heart of the Constitution is the supremacy clause of Article VI:

> *This Constitution, and the laws of the United States which shall be made in pursuance thereof; and all treaties made, or which shall be made, under the authority of the United States, shall be the supreme law of the land; and the judges in every State shall be bound thereby, any thing in the Constitution or laws of any State to the contrary notwithstanding.*

This sentence made it abundantly clear that laws of Congress would supersede laws of the states, and it made certain that Congress would control interstate commerce, bankruptcy, monetary affairs, weights and measures, currency and credit, communication, transportation, and foreign and military affairs. Thus, the supremacy clause ensures that the decisions of the national elite will prevail over those of the local elites in all vital areas allocated to the national government.

REPUBLICANISM

The structure of the national government—its republicanism and its system of separated powers and checks and balances—was also designed to protect liberty and property. To the Founding Fathers, a republican government meant the delegation of powers by the people to a small number of citizens "whose wisdom may best discern the true interest of their country, and whose patriotism and love of justice will be least likely to sacrifice it to temporary or partial consideration."[11] Madison explained, in classic elite fashion, "that the public voice, pronounced by representatives of the people, will be more consonant to the public good than if pronounced by the people themselves." The Founding Fathers clearly believed that representatives of the people were more likely to be enlightened persons of principle and property than the voters who chose them and thus would be more trustworthy and dependable.

Voters also had a limited voice in the selection of decision makers. Of the four major decision-making entities established in the Constitution—the House of Representatives, the Senate, the presidency, and the Supreme Court—the people were to elect only one (see Table 2.3). The others were to be at least twice removed from popular control. In the constitution of 1787, the people elected only House members, and for short terms of only two years. In contrast, state legislatures were to elect U.S. senators for six-year terms. Electors, selected as state legislatures saw fit, selected the president. The states could hold elections for presidential electors, or the state legislatures could appoint them. The Founding Fathers hoped that presidential electors would be prominent men of wealth and reputation in their respective states. Finally, federal judges were to be appointed by the president for life, thus removing those decision makers as far as possible from popular control. (See Figure 2.1.)

TABLE 2.3 | DECISION-MAKING BODIES IN THE CONSTITUTION OF 1787

House of Representatives	Senate	President	Supreme Court
Directly elected by "the People of the several States"	Selected by state legislatures (later changed to direct election by 17th Amendment in 1913)	Selected by "electors" in each state "in such Manner as the Legislature may direct"	Appointed by the president "by and with the Advice and Consent of the Senate"
Two-year term	Six-year term	Four-year term	Life term
Members apportioned to each state according to population	Two senators from each state regardless of population	Single executive	No size specified, but by tradition, nine

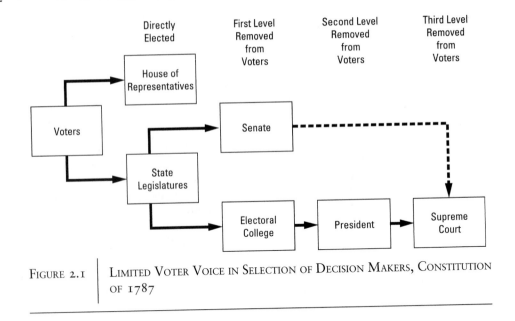

Directly Elected	First Level Removed from Voters	Second Level Removed from Voters	Third Level Removed from Voters

FIGURE 2.1 | LIMITED VOTER VOICE IN SELECTION OF DECISION MAKERS, CONSTITUTION OF 1787

SEPARATION OF POWERS AND CHECKS AND BALANCES

The Founding Fathers also intended the system of separated powers in the national government—separate legislative, executive, and judicial branches—as a bulwark against majoritarianism (government by popular majorities) and an additional safeguard for elite liberty and property. The doctrine derives from the French writer Montesquieu, whose *Spirit of Laws* was a political textbook for these eighteenth-century statesmen. *The Federalist*, Number 51, expressed the logic of the system of checks and balances:

> *Ambition must be made to counteract ambition.... It may be a reflection on human nature, that such devices should be necessary to control the abuses of government. But what is government itself, but the greatest of all reflections on human nature? If men were angels, no government would be necessary. If angels were to govern men, neither external or internal controls on government would be necessary. In framing a government which is to be administered by men over men, the greatest difficulty lies in this: you must first enable the government to control the governed; and in the next place oblige it to control itself.*[12]

The Constitution states the separation-of-powers concept in the opening sentences of the first three articles:

> *[Article I:] All legislative powers herein granted shall be vested in a Congress of the United States, which shall consist of a Senate and House of Representatives.*
> *[Article II:] The executive power shall be vested in a President of the United States....*
> *[Article III:] The judicial power of the United States shall be vested in one Supreme Court, and in such inferior courts as the Congress may from time to time ordain and establish.*

Insofar as this system divides responsibility and makes it difficult for the masses to hold government accountable for public policy, it achieves one of the purposes intended by the Founding Fathers. Each of the four major decision-making bodies of the national government—House, Senate, president, and Supreme Court—is chosen by different constituencies. Because the terms of these decision-making bodies are of varying length, a complete renewal of government at one stroke is impossible. Thus, the people cannot wreak havoc quickly through direct elections. To make their will felt in all the decision-making bodies of the national government, they must wait years.

Moreover, each of these decision-making bodies has an important check on the decisions of the others. No bill can become law without the approval of both the House and the Senate (see Table 2.4). The president shares in the legislative power through the veto and the responsibility to "give to the Congress information of the state of the Union, and recommend to their consideration such measures as he shall judge necessary and expedient." The president can also convene sessions of Congress. But the appointing power of the president is shared by the Senate; so is the power to make treaties. Also, Congress can override executive vetoes. The president must execute the laws but cannot do so without relying on executive departments, which Congress must create. The executive branch can spend only money appropriated by Congress. Indeed, "separation of powers" is a misnomer, for we are really talking

TABLE 2.4 | CHECKS AND BALANCES: "SUPPRESSING FACTIOUS ISSUES"

Congress	President

House and Senate Checks
    Both must agree on bills
	President's Checks on Congress
	    Can veto bills passed by Congress
	    Can call special sessions
	    Can recommend legislation
	    Vice president presides over Senate and
	        can vote to break ties

Congressional Checks on President
    Can override president's veto (with two-
        thirds vote of both House and Senate)
    Can impeach and remove president
    Can reject appointments (Senate)
    Can refuse to ratify treaties (Senate)
    Can reject president's requests for laws
        and funds
    Can investigate president's actions
	President's Checks on Courts
	    Nominates judges (including Supreme
	        Court justices)
	    Can pardon persons convicted by federal
	        courts

Congressional Checks on Courts
    Can reject judicial nominees (including
        those for Supreme Court)
    Can create lower federal courts
    Can amend laws to change court
        interpretations of them
    Can propose constitutional amendments
        to change court interpretations of the
        Constitution
    Can impeach and remove judges
	Courts
	
	Courts Checks on Congress
	    Can interpret laws of Congress
	    Can declare laws unconstitutional
	
	Court Checks on President
	    Can declare actions of president
	        unconstitutional

| IN BRIEF | CONSTITUTIONAL LIMITS ON MASS PARTICIPATION IN GOVERNMENT |

- The Constitution, laws, and treaties of the United States are the "Supreme Law of the Land"; "any thing in the Constitution and or Law of any State to the contrary notwithstanding."

- Of the four decision-making entities established in the Constitution of 1787—the House of Representatives, the Senate, the president, and the Supreme Court—only one, the House of Representatives, was to be elected by the people.

- A guarantee of "republican" government. Voters select only the members of the House of Representatives; the members of the Senate are selected by state legislatures (not changed until the adoption of the Seventeenth Amendment in 1913); the president is selected by "electors" (by custom and usage beginning in 1800 "electors" pledged to presidential candidates came to be elected by voters in the states); justices of the Supreme Court and other federal

- judges are appointed for life by the president and confirmed by the Senate.

- Mass movements are frustrated by separation of powers, including differing terms for each decision-making body—the House of Representatives, two years; Senate, six years; president, four years; courts, lifetime.

- Mass movements are frustrated by checks and balances—both House and Senate must agree to the proposed legislation; the president must sign the legislation, or veto can be overwritten only by a two-thirds vote of both houses; if the legislation is challenged, the courts must decide on its interpretation and whether it is constitutional or not.

- Judicial review can invalidate not only state laws and constitutions, but also any laws of Congress; that nine justices, who are appointed not elected, decide conflict with the Constitution.

Madison's Papers
Biography, correspondence, and papers of James Madison.
www.virginia.edu/pjm

about sharing, not separating, power; each branch participates in the activities of every other branch.

Even the Supreme Court, which was created by the Constitution, must be appointed by the president with the consent of the Senate, and Congress may prescribe the number of justices. Congress must create lower and intermediate courts, establish the number of judges, and fix the jurisdiction of lower federal courts.

JUDICIAL REVIEW

Perhaps the keystone of the system of checks and balances is the idea of judicial review, an original contribution by the Founding Fathers to the science of government. In *Marbury v. Madison* in 1803, Chief Justice John Marshall argued convincingly that the Founding Fathers intended the Supreme Court to have the power to invalidate not only state laws and constitutions but also any laws of Congress that came into conflict with the Constitution. The text of the Constitution nowhere specifically authorizes federal judges to invalidate acts of Congress; at most, the Constitution implies this power. (But Hamilton apparently thought that the Constitution contained this power, since he was careful to explain it in *The Federalist*, Number 78, before the ratification of the Constitution.) Thus, the Supreme Court stands as the final defender of the fundamental principles agreed on by the Founding Fathers against the encroachments of popularly elected legislatures.

Constitutional Law
Cornell University Law School collection of key Supreme Court constitutional decisions.
http://straylight.law.cornell.edu/supct

| FOCUS | JAMES MADISON: SUPPRESSING MAJORITY "FACTIONS" |

Perhaps the most important contributor to the Constitution was James Madison (1751–1836). Not only did he play a key role in writing the Constitution, but his insightful and scholarly defense of it also helped immeasurably in securing its ratification. Indeed, Madison is more highly regarded by political scientists and historians as a *political theorist* than as the fourth president of the United States.

Madison's family owned a large plantation, Montpelier, near present-day Orange, Virginia. Private tutors and prep schools provided him with a thorough background in history, science, philosophy, and law. He graduated from the College of New Jersey (now Princeton University) at age 18 and assumed a number of elected and appointed positions in Virginia's colonial government. In 1776, Madison drafted a new Virginia Constitution. While serving in Virginia's Revolutionary assembly, he met Thomas Jefferson; the two became lifetime political allies and friends. In 1787, Madison represented Virginia at the Constitutional Convention and took a leading role in its debates over the form of a new federal government. Madison's *Notes on the Constitutional Convention of 1787,* published twenty years after the event, is the only account of the secret meeting.

Madison's political philosophy is revealed in *The Federalist Papers,* a series of eighty-five essays published in major newspapers in 1787 and 1788, all signed simply "Publius." Alexander Hamilton and John Jay contributed some of them, but Madison wrote the two most important essays: Number 10, which explains the nature of political conflict (faction) and how it can be "controlled"; and Number 51, which explains the system of separation of powers and checks and balances.

According to Madison, "controlling faction" was the principal task of government. What creates factions? According to Madison, conflict is part of human nature. In all societies, we find "a zeal for different opinions concerning religion, concerning government, and many other points" as well as "an attachment to different leaders ambitiously contending for preeminence and power." Even when there are no serious differences among people, these "frivolous and fanciful distinctions" will inspire "unfriendly passions" and "violent conflicts." However, according to Madison,

the most common and durable source of factions has been the various and unequal distribution of property. Those who hold and those who are without property have ever formed distinct interests in society. Those who are creditors and those who are debtors fall under like discrimination. A landed interest, a manufacturing interest, a mercantile interest, a monied interest, with many lesser interests, grow up of necessity in civilized nations, and divide them into different classes, actuated by different sentiments and views. [The Federalist, Number 10]

In Madison's view, a national government is the most important protection against mass movements that might threaten property. By creating such a government, encompassing a large number of citizens and a great expanse of territory,

you take in a greater variety of parties and interests; you make it less probable that a majority of the whole will have a common motive to invade the rights of other citizens; or if such a common motive exists it will be more difficult for all who feel it to discover their own strength, and to act in unison with each other.

The structure of the new national government should ensure suppression of "factious" issues (those that would generate factions). And Madison did not hedge in naming these factious issues: "A rage for paper money, for an abolition of debts, for an equal division of property, of any other improper or wicked project." Note that Madison's factious issues are all challenges to the dominant economic elites. His defense of the new Constitution was that its republican and federal features would help keep certain threats to property from ever becoming public issues. In short, the Founding Fathers deliberately designed the new U.S. government to make it difficult for any mass political movement to challenge property rights.

RATIFICATION: AN EXERCISE IN ELITE POLITICAL SKILLS

When its work ended on September 17, 1787, the Constitutional Convention sent the Constitution to New York City, where Congress was then in session. The Convention suggested that the Constitution "should afterwards be submitted to a convention of delegates chosen in each state by the people thereof, under the recommendation of its legislature for their assent and ratification." Convention delegates further proposed that ratification by nine states be sufficient to put the new constitution into effect. On September 28, Congress sent the Constitution to the states without further recommendations.

EXTRAORDINARY RATIFICATION PROCEDURE

The ratification procedure suggested by the Founding Fathers was a skillful political maneuver. Because the Convention proceedings had been secret, few people knew that the delegates had gone beyond their instructions to amend the Articles of Confederation and had created a whole new scheme of government. Their ratification procedure was a complete departure from what was then the law of the land, the Articles of Confederation. The Articles provided that Congress make amendments only with the approval of *all* states. But since Rhode Island was firmly in the hands of small farmers, the unanimity required by the Articles was obviously out of the question. The Founding Fathers felt obligated to act outside the existing law.

The Founding Fathers also called for special ratifying conventions in the states rather than risk submitting the Constitution to the state legislatures. This extraordinary procedure gave clear advantage to supporters of the Constitution, because submitting the plan to the state legislatures would weaken its chances for success. Thus, the struggle for ratification began under ground rules designed by the national elite to give them the advantage over any potential opponents.

LIMITED PARTICIPATION IN RATIFICATION

In the most important and controversial study of the Constitution to date, Charles A. Beard compiled a great deal of evidence supporting the hypothesis "that substantially all of the merchants, moneylenders, security holders, manufacturers, shippers, capitalists and financiers, and their professional associates are to be found on one side in support of the Constitution, and that substantially all of the major portion of the opposition came from the non-slaveholding farmers and debtors."[13] Although historians disagree over the solidarity of class divisions in the struggle for ratification, most concede that only about 160,000 people voted in elections for delegates to state ratifying conventions and that not more than 100,000 of these voters favored the adoption of the Constitution. This figure represents about one in six of the adult males in the country, and no more than 5 percent of the general population. Thus, whether or not Beard is correct about class divisions in the struggle for ratification, it is clear that *the number of people who participated in any fashion in ratifying the Constitution was an extremely small minority of the population.*[14]

EMERGENCE OF ANTI-FEDERALIST OPPOSITION

Some men of property and education did oppose the new Constitution. These were men who had greater confidence in their ability to control state governments than to control the new federal government. They called themselves Anti-Federalists, and they vigorously attacked the Constitution as a counterrevolutionary document that could undo much of the progress made since 1776 toward freedom, liberty, and equality. According to the opponents of the Constitution, the new government would be "aristocratic," all powerful, and a threat to the "spirit of republicanism" and the "genius of democracy." They charged that the new Constitution created an aristocratic upper house and an almost monarchical presidency. The powers of the national government could trample the states and deny the people of the states the opportunity to handle their own political and economic affairs. The Anti-Federalists repeatedly asserted that the Constitution removed powers from the people and concentrated them in the hands of a few national officials who were largely immune to popular control; moreover, they attacked the undemocratic features of the Constitution and argued that state governments were much more representative of the people. Also under attack were the secrecy of the Constitutional Convention and the actions of the Founding Fathers, both contrary to the law and the spirit of the Articles of Confederation.

Anti-Federalist Papers
Collection of writings from 1787 to 1788 by opponents of the Constitution.
www.constitution.org/afp

THE BILL OF RIGHTS AS AN AFTERTHOUGHT

Although the Anti-Federalists deplored the undemocratic features of the new Constitution, their most effective criticism centered on the absence of any bill of rights. The omission of a bill of rights was particularly glaring because the idea was very popular at the time, and most new state constitutions contained one. It is an interesting comment on the psychology of the Founding Fathers that the idea of a bill of rights did not come up in the Convention until the final week of deliberations; even then it received little consideration. The Founding Fathers certainly believed in limited government, and they did write a few liberties into the body of the Constitution, such as protection against bills of attainder and ex post facto laws, a guarantee of the writ of habeas corpus, a limited definition of treason, and a guarantee of jury trial. However, they did not include a bill of rights in the Constitution.

When criticism about the absence of a bill of rights began to mount, supporters of the Constitution presented an interesting argument to explain the deficiency: (1) the national government was one of enumerated powers and could not exercise any powers not expressly delegated to it in the Constitution; (2) the power to interfere with free speech or press or otherwise to restrain liberty was not among the enumerated powers in the Constitution; (3) it was therefore unnecessary to deny the new government that power specifically. But this logic was unconvincing; the absence of a bill of rights seemed to confirm the suspicion that the Founding Fathers were more concerned with protecting property than with protecting the personal liberties of the people. Many members of the elite and nonelite alike were uncomfortable with the thought that personal liberty depended on a thin thread of inference from enumerated powers. Supporters of the Constitution thus had to retreat from their demand for unconditional ratification. The New York, Massachusetts, and Virginia conventions agreed to the new Constitution only after receiving the Federalists' solemn promise to add a bill of rights as amendments. Thus, the fundamental guarantees of liberty in the Bill of Rights were political concessions by the nation's elite. Whereas the Founding Fathers deserved great credit for the document that they produced in Philadelphia, the first Congress to meet under that Constitution was nonetheless obliged to submit twelve amendments to the states, ten of which—the Bill of Rights—were ratified by 1791.

THE CONSTITUTION: AN ELITIST INTERPRETATION

Elite theory provides us with an interpretation of the U.S. Constitution and the basic structure of U.S. government. Our analysis of constitutional policies centers on the following propositions:

1. The Constitution of the United States was not "ordained and established" by "the people." Instead it was written by a small, educated, talented, wealthy elite in America, representative of powerful economic interests: bondholders, investors, merchants, real estate owners, and planters.
2. The Constitution and the national government that it established had their origins in elite dissatisfaction with the inability of the central government to pay off its bondholders, the interference of state governments with the development of a national economy, the threat to investors and creditors posed by state issuance of cheap paper money and laws relieving debtors of contractual obligations, the threat to propertied classes arising from post–Revolutionary War radicalism, the inability of the central government to provide an army capable of protecting western development or a navy capable of protecting American commercial interests on the high seas, and the inability of America's elite to exercise power in world affairs.
3. The elite achieved ratification of the Constitution through its astute political skills. The masses of people in the United States did not participate in the writing of the Constitution or in its adoption by the states, and they probably would have opposed the Constitution had they had the information and resources to do so.
4. The Founding Fathers shared a consensus that the fundamental role of government is the protection of liberty and property. They believed in a republican form of government by men of principle and property. They opposed an aristocracy or a governing nobility, but they also opposed mass democracy with direct participation by the people in decision making. They feared mass movements seeking to reduce inequalities of wealth, intelligence, talent, or virtue. "Dangerous leveling" was a serious violation of men's rights to property.
5. The structure of American government was designed to suppress "factious" issues—threats to dominant economic elites. Republicanism, the division of power between state and national governments, and the complex system of checks and balances and divided power were all designed as protections against mass movements that might threaten liberty and property.
6. The text of the Constitution contains many direct and immediate benefits to America's governing elite. Although all Americans, both elites and masses, may have benefited by the adoption of the Constitution, the advantages and benefits for U.S. elites were their compelling motives for supporting the new Constitution.

Selected Readings

Beard, Charles A. *An Economic Interpretation of the Constitution of the United States.* New York: Macmillan, 1913. The Free Press issued a paperback edition in 1965. Much of this chapter reflects data presented by Beard in this classic work. Beard traces the events leading up to the writing of the Constitution and the events surrounding ratification from an economic point of view. He discovers that economic considerations played a major, if not central, role in the shaping of the Constitution.

For several critiques of Beard, see:

1. Beale, Howard K., ed. *Charles A. Beard: An Appraisal.* Lexington: University of Kentucky Press, 1954.
2. Benson, Lee. *Turner and Beard: American Historical Writing Reconsidered.* New York: Free Press, 1960.
3. McDonald, Forrest. *We the People: The Economic Origins of the Constitution.* Chicago: University of Chicago Press, 1958.

Finkelman, Paul. *Slavery and the Founders,* 2nd ed. Armonk, New York: M. E. Sharpe, 2000. A critical account of the Founders' attitudes toward slavery and the resulting three-fifths compromise.

Frohnen, Bruce. *The American Republic: Primary Sources.* Indianapolis, Ind.: Liberty Fund, 2002. Single volume collection of primary sources, including documents, speeches, and essays from the Mayflower Compact to the Civil War.

Madison, James, Alexander Hamilton, and John Jay. *The Federalist,* 2nd rev. ed. Edited by George W. Carey and James MacClellan. New York: Liberty Fund Books, 2001. This collection of the articles published in support of the Constitution offers the most important contemporary comments available on the Constitution. This edition includes cross-references linking provisions of the Constitution to relevant paragraphs of *The Federalist.*

McDonald, Forest. *Novus Ordo Seclorum.* Lawrence: University of Kansas Press, 1985. A now-classic study of the intellectual origins of the Constitution. The Latin title means "New World Order."

Peltason, J. W. *Understanding the Constitution,* 16th ed. New York: Harcourt Brace, 2006. Of the many books that explain parts of the Constitution, this is one of the best. It contains explanations of the Declaration of Independence, the Articles of Confederation, and the Constitution. The book is written clearly and is well suited for undergraduate as well as graduate and faculty use.

Rossiter, Clinton L. *1787, The Grand Convention.* New York: Macmillan, 1966. This readable and entertaining account of the men and events of 1787 contains many insights into the difficulties the Founding Fathers had writing the Constitution.

Notes

1. Lester Cappon, ed., *The Adams-Jefferson Letters* (Chapel Hill: University of North Carolina Press, 1959), vol. 1, p. 106.
2. Max Ferrand, ed., *The Records of the Federal Convention of 1787* (New Haven, Conn.: Yale University Press, 1937), vol. 3, p. 15.
3. Ferrand, *Records,* p. 32.
4. See Clinton Rossiter, *1787, The Grand Convention* (New York: Macmillan, 1966), p. 45.
5. Charles A. Beard, *An Economic Interpretation of the Constitution of the United States* (New York: Macmillan, 1913), pp. 73–151.

6. John P. Roche, "The Founding Fathers: A Reform Caucus in Action," *American Political Science Review* 55 (December 1961): .
7. James Madison kept secret notes on the Convention, which he published many years later. Most of our knowledge about the Convention comes from Madison's notes. See Ferrand, *Records.*
8. See especially Beard, *Economic Interpretation.*
9. James Madison, Alexander Hamilton, and John Jay, *The Federalist* (New York: Modern Library, 1937).
10. Madison et al., *The Federalist,* number 10.

11. Madison et al., *The Federalist,* Number 10.
12. Madison et al., *The Federalist,* Number 51.
13. Beard, *Economic Interpretation,* pp. 16–17.
14. Beard's economic interpretation differs from an elitist interpretation in that Beard believes that the economic elites supported the Constitution and the masses opposed it. Our elitist interpretation asserts only that the masses did not participate in writing or adopting the Constitution and that elites benefited directly from its provisions. Our interpretation does not depend on showing that the masses opposed the Constitution but merely that they did not participate in its establishment. Attacks on Beard appear in Forrest McDonald, *We the People: The Economic Origins of the Constitution* (Chicago: University of Chicago Press, 1958), and Robert E. Brown, *Charles Beard and the Constitution* (Princeton, N.J.: Princeton University Press, 1956). Lee Benson provides a balanced view in *Turner and Beard: American Historical Writing Reconsidered* (New York: Free Press, 1960).

The fierceness of political struggles has often been misleading; for the range of vision embodied by the primary contestants in the major parties has always been bounded by the horizons of property and enterprise.

Richard Hofstadter

THE EVOLUTION OF AMERICAN ELITES

A stable elite system depends on the "circulation of elites"—the movement of talented and ambitious individuals from the lower strata into the elite. An open elite system that provides for "a slow and continuous modification of the ruling classes" is essential for continuing the system and avoiding revolution. Popular elections, party competition, and other democratic institutions in the United States have not enabled the masses to govern, but these institutions have helped keep the elite system an open one. They have assisted in the circulation of elites, even if they have never been a means of challenging the dominant elite consensus.

In this chapter, a historical analysis of the evolution of American elites, we show that American elite membership has evolved slowly, without any serious break in the ideas or values underlying the U.S. political and economic systems. The United States has never experienced a true revolution that forcibly replaced governing elites with nonelites. Instead, American elite membership has been open to those who acquire wealth and property and who accept the national consensus about private enterprise, limited government, and individualism. Industrialization, technological change, and new sources of wealth in the expanding economy have produced new elite members, and the American elite system has permitted the absorption of the new elites without upsetting the system itself (see Focus: Mass Ignorance of American Political History).

Policy changes and innovations in the structure of American government over the decades have been *incremental* (step-by-step) rather than revolutionary. Elites have modified public policies but seldom replaced them. They have made structural adaptations in the constitutional system designed by the Founding Fathers but have kept intact the original framework of U.S. constitutionalism.

Political conflict in the United States has centered on a narrow range of issues. Only once, in the Civil War, have elites been deeply divided over the nature of American society. The Civil War reflected a deep cleavage between southern elites—dependent on

FOCUS	MASS IGNORANCE OF AMERICAN POLITICAL HISTORY		

		Know	Don't Know/Refused (Includes Incorrect Responses)
Who delivered the Gettysburg Address?		67%	33%
Who was the first president of the United States?		92	8
What is the name of the national anthem?		58	42
Two of the three branches of the U.S. government are called the Executive and the Legislative branches. What is the third branch called?		57	43
How many U.S. senators are there from each state?		59	41
In what document are these words found?—"We hold these truths to be self-evident, that all men are created equal."		34	66
Who wrote the "Letter from Birmingham Jail"?		33	67
What are the first 10 amendments to the U.S. Constitution called?		47	53
Who is the current vice president of the United States?		69	31
Who is the current chief justice of the U.S. Supreme Court?		17	83

Source: Gallup poll, October 2003. Available online at www.gallup.com

Thomas Jefferson once wrote, "If a nation expects to be both ignorant and free, it expects what never was and never will be." The brief review of the evolution of American elites in this chapter is no substitute for the study of American political history.

Jefferson would be alarmed today at the widespread ignorance of American history and basic civics among the American people. Most people know that George Washington was the first president of the United States. But beyond such an elementary fact, ignorance of history increases alarmingly. More than half of Americans do not know that the first ten amendments to the Constitution of the United States are the Bill of Rights. Two-thirds of the American people do not recognize the words of the Declaration of Independence or know that Martin Luther King Jr. wrote the "Letter from Birmingham Jail." Sizable minorities cannot name the three branches of the U.S. government or do not know that there are two senators from each state.

a plantation economy, slave labor, and free trade—and northern industrial and commercial elites, who prospered under free labor and protective tariffs.

HAMILTON AND THE NATION'S FIRST PUBLIC POLICIES

The most influential figure in George Washington's administration was Alexander Hamilton, secretary of the treasury. More than anyone else, Hamilton was aware that the new nation had to win the lasting confidence of business and financial elites in order to survive and prosper. Only if the United States were established on a sound financial basis could it attract investors at home and abroad and expand its industry and commerce. Great Britain remained the largest source of investment capital for the new nation, and Hamilton was decidedly pro-British. He also favored a strong central government as a means of protecting property and stimulating the growth of commerce and industry.

Paying the National Debt

Hamilton's first move was to refund the national debt at face value. Most of the original bonds were no longer in the hands of the original owners but had fallen to speculators who had purchased them for only a fraction of their face value. Because these securities were worth only about twenty-five cents on the dollar, the Hamilton refund program meant a 300 percent profit for the speculators. Hamilton's program went beyond refunding the debts owed by the United States; he also undertook to pay the debts incurred by the states themselves during the Revolutionary War. His objective was to place the creditor elite under a deep obligation to the central government.

Establishing a National Bank

Hamilton also acted to establish a Bank of the United States, which would receive government funds, issue a national currency, facilitate the sale of national bonds, and tie the national government even more closely to the banking elites. The Constitution did not specifically grant Congress the power to create a national bank, but Hamilton was willing to interpret the "necessary and proper" clause broadly enough to include the creation of a bank to help carry out the taxing, borrowing, and currency powers enumerated in the Constitution. Hamilton's broad construction of the "necessary and proper" clause looked in the direction of a central government that would exercise powers not specifically enumerated in the Constitution.

Thomas Jefferson, who was secretary of state in the same cabinet with Hamilton, expressed growing concern over Hamilton's tendency toward national centralization. Jefferson argued that Congress could not establish the bank because the bank was not strictly "necessary" to carry out delegated functions. But Hamilton won out, with the support of President Washington; in 1791 Congress voted to charter the Bank of the United States. For twenty years the bank was very successful, especially in stabilizing the currency of the new nation.

Expanding the "Necessary and Proper" Clause

Not until 1819 did the Supreme Court decide the constitutionality of the Bank of the United States. In the famous case of *McCulloch v. Maryland,* the Supreme Court upheld the broad definition of national power suggested by Hamilton under the "necessary and proper" clause. At the same time, the Court established the principle that a state law that interferes with a national activity is unconstitutional.[1] "Let the end be legitimate," Chief Justice John Marshall wrote, "let it be within the scope of the Constitution, and all means which are appropriate, which are plainly adopted to that end, which are not prohibited, but consistent with the letter and spirit of the Constitution, are constitutional." The *McCulloch* case firmly established the principle that Congress has the right to choose any appropriate means for carrying out the delegated powers of the national government. The "necessary and proper" clause is now sometimes called the implied powers clause or the elastic clause because it gives to Congress many powers that the Constitution does not explicitly grant. Congress still traces all its activities to some formal grant of power, but this task is usually not difficult.

RISE OF THE JEFFERSONIANS

The centralizing effect of Hamilton's programs and their favoring of merchants, manufacturers, and shipbuilders aroused some opposition in elite circles. Southern planters and large landowners benefited little from Hamilton's policies, and they were joined in their opposition by local and state elites who feared that a strong central government threatened their own powers. These landed elites were first called Anti-Federalists and later Republicans and Democratic Republicans when those terms became popular after the French Revolution. When Thomas Jefferson resigned from Washington's cabinet in protest of Hamilton's program, Anti-Federalists began to gather around Jefferson.

JEFFERSON AS A WEALTHY PLANTATION OWNER

Historians portray Jefferson as a great democrat and champion of the "common man." And in writing the Declaration of Independence, the Virginia Statute for Religious Freedom, and the famous *Notes on Virginia,* Jefferson indeed expressed concern for the rights of all "the people" and a willingness to trust in their wisdom. But when Jefferson spoke warmly of the merits of "the people," he meant those who owned and managed their own farms and estates. He firmly believed that *only those who owned their own land could make good citizens.* Jefferson disliked aristocracy, but he also held the urban masses in contempt. He wanted to see the United States become a nation of free, educated, landowning farmers. Democracy, he believed, could be founded only on a propertied class in a propertied nation. His belief that landownership is essential to virtuous government explains in part his Louisiana Purchase, which he hoped would provide the American people with land "to the hundredth and thousandth generation."[2]

The dispute between Federalists and Anti-Federalists in the early United States was not between elites and masses. It was a dispute within elite circles between two propertied classes: merchants and bankers on one side and plantation owners and slaveholders on the other.[3]

RISE OF POLITICAL PARTIES

The Anti-Federalists, or Republicans, did not elect their first president, Thomas Jefferson, until 1800. John Adams, a Federalist, succeeded Washington in the election of 1796. Yet the election of 1796 was an important milestone in the development of the American political system. For the first time, two candidates, Adams and Jefferson, campaigned not as individuals but as members of political parties. For the first time, the candidates for the electoral college announced themselves before the election as either "Adams's men" or "Jefferson's men." Most important, for the first time, American political leaders realized the importance of molding mass opinion and organizing the masses for political action. Jefferson's Republican Party first saw the importance of working among the masses to rally popular support. The Federalist leaders made the mistake of assuming that they could maintain the unquestioning support of the less educated and less wealthy without bothering to mold their opinions.

EARLY ATTEMPTS AT ELITE REPRESSION

Rather than trying, as the Republicans did, to manipulate public opinion, the Federalists tried to outlaw public criticism of the government by means of the Alien and Sedition Acts of 1798. Among other things, these acts made it a crime to publish any false or malicious writing directed against the president or Congress or to "stir up hatred" against them. The acts directly challenged the newly adopted First Amendment guarantee of freedom of speech and the press.

In response to the Alien and Sedition Acts, Jefferson and Madison put forward their famous Kentucky and Virginia resolutions. These measures proposed that the states assume the right to decide whether Congress has acted unconstitutionally and, furthermore, that the states properly "interpose" their authority against "palpable and alarming infractions of the Constitution." The Virginia and Kentucky legislatures passed these resolutions and declared the Alien and Sedition Acts "void and of no force" in these states.

REPUBLICANS IN POWER: THE STABILITY OF PUBLIC POLICY

In the election of 1800, the Federalists went down to defeat; Thomas Jefferson and Aaron Burr were elected over John Adams and C. C. Pinckney. Only the New England states, New Jersey, and Delaware, where commercial and manufacturing interests were strongest, voted Federalist. Because the vast majority of American people won their living from the soil, the landed elites were able to mobilize those masses behind their bid for control of the government. The Federalists failed to recognize the importance of agrarianism in the nation's economic and political life. Another half century would pass and America's Industrial Revolution would be in full swing before manufacturing and commercial elites would reestablish their dominance.

The election of 1800 enabled landed interests to gain power in relation to commercial and industrial interests. Yet the fact that an "out" party, the Republicans, peacefully replaced an "in" party, the Federalists, is testimony to the strength of the consensus among the new nation's elite.* The "Virginia dynasty"—Thomas Jefferson,

---

*The original text of the Constitution did not envision an opposing faction. Presidential electors could cast two votes for president, with the understanding that the candidate with the second highest vote total would be vice president. Seventy-three Republican electors pledged to Jefferson and sixty-five Federalists pledged to Adams went to the electoral college. Somewhat thoughtlessly, all the Republicans cast one vote for Jefferson and one vote for Aaron Burr, his running mate, with the result that each man received the same number of votes for the presidency. Because of the tie vote, the decision went to the Federalist-controlled House of Representatives, where a movement was begun to elect Burr, rather than Jefferson, in order to embarrass the Republicans. But Alexander Hamilton used his influence in Congress to swing the election to his old political foe Jefferson, suggesting again that their differences were not so deep that either would deliberately undermine the presidency to strike at the other. Once in power, the Republicans passed the Twelfth Amendment to the Constitution, providing that each presidential elector should thereafter vote separately for president and vice president. Both Federalists and Republicans in the states promptly agreed with this reform, and ratification was completed by the election of 1804.

James Madison, and finally James Monroe—governed the country for six presidential terms, nearly a quarter of a century. It is interesting that once in office the Republicans made few changes in Federalist and Hamiltonian policy. (The only major pieces of legislation repealed by the Republicans were the Alien and Sedition Acts, and it seems clear that in passing these acts the Federalists had violated elite consensus.) The Republicans did not attack commercial or industrial enterprise; in fact, commerce and industry prospered under Republican rule as never before. They did not attempt to recover money paid out by Hamilton in refunding national or state debts. They allowed public land speculation to continue. Instead of crushing the banks, Republicans soon supported the financial interests they had sworn to oppose.

Jefferson was an ardent expansionist; to add to America's wealth in land, he purchased the vast Louisiana Territory. Later, a stronger army and a system of internal roads were necessary to help develop western land. Jefferson's successor, James Madison, built a strong navy and engaged in another war with England, the War of 1812, to protect U.S. commerce on the high seas. The Napoleonic wars and the War of 1812 stimulated American manufacturing by depressing trade with Britain. In 1816, Republicans passed a high tariff in order to protect domestic industry and manufacturing from foreign goods. As for Republican tax policies, Jefferson wrote in 1816:

> To take from one, because it is thought his own industry and that of his fathers has acquired too much, in order to spare to others, who, or whose fathers, have not exercised equal industry and skill, is to violate arbitrarily the first principle of association, "the guarantee to everyone the free exercise of his industry and the fruits acquired by it."[4]

In short, the Republicans had no intention of redistributing wealth in the United States. Indeed, before the end of Madison's second term in 1817, the Republicans had taken over the whole complex of Hamiltonian policies: a national bank, high tariffs, protection for manufacturers, internal improvements, western land development, a strong army and navy, and a broad interpretation of national power. So complete was the elite consensus that by 1820 the Democratic Republican Party (as it had become known by then) had completely driven the Federalist Party out of existence, largely by taking over its programs.

RISE OF THE WESTERN ELITES

According to Frederick Jackson Turner, "The rise of the New West was the most significant fact in American history."[5] Certainly the American West had a profound impact on the political system of the new nation. People went west because of the vast wealth of fertile lands that awaited them there; nowhere else in the world could one acquire wealth so quickly as in the new American West. Because aristocratic families of the eastern seaboard seldom had reason to migrate westward, the western settlers were mainly middle- and lower-class immigrants. With hard work and good fortune, penniless migrants could become wealthy plantation owners or cattle ranchers in a single generation. Thus, the West offered rapid upward social mobility.

New elites arose in the West and had to be assimilated into America's governing circles. No one exemplifies the new entrants into the U.S. elite better than Andrew Jackson. Jackson's victory in the presidential election of 1828 was not a victory of the common people against the propertied classes but rather one of the new western elites against established Republican leadership in the East. Jackson's victory forced established U.S. elites to recognize the growing importance of the West and to open their ranks to the new rich west of the Alleghenies.

THE "NATURAL ARISTOCRACY"

Because Jackson was a favorite of the people, it was easy for him to believe in the wisdom of the common people. But Jacksonian democracy was by no means a philosophy of leveling egalitarianism. The ideal of the frontier society was the self-made man, and people admired wealth and power won by competitive skill. Wealth and power obtained only through special privilege offended the frontiersmen, however. They believed in a *natural aristocracy* rather than an aristocracy by birth, education, or special privilege. Jacksonians demanded not absolute equality but a more open elite system—a greater opportunity for the rising middle class to acquire wealth and influence.

EXPANSION OF THE ELECTORATE

In their struggle to open America's elite system, the Jacksonians appealed to mass sentiment. Jackson's humble beginnings, his image as a self-made man, his military adventures, his frontier experience, and his rough, brawling style endeared him to the masses. As beneficiaries of popular support, the new elites of the West developed a strong faith in the wisdom and justice of popular decisions. The new western states that entered the Union granted universal white male suffrage, and gradually the older states fell into step. Rising elites, themselves often less than a generation away from the masses, saw in a widened electorate a chance for personal advancement that they could never have achieved under the old regime. Therefore the Jacksonians became noisy and effective advocates of the principle that all (white) men should have the right to vote and to hold public office. They also successfully attacked the congressional caucus system of nominating presidential candidates.

After his defeat in Congress in 1824, Jackson wished to sever Congress from the presidential nominating process. In 1832, when the Democratic Party, as it was known by then, held its first national convention, it renominated Andrew Jackson by acclamation. The tradition of nominating presidential candidates by national party convention was viewed as a democratizing reform, but it really originated out of Jackson's frustration at not being nominated by the Democratic Party's congressional caucus in 1824.

ELITE CLEAVAGE: THE CIVIL WAR

During the nation's first sixty years, American elites substantially agreed about the character and direction of the new nation. Conflicts over the national bank, the tariff, internal improvement (such as roads and harbors), and even the controversial war with Mexico in 1846 did not threaten the basic underlying consensus. In the 1850s, however, the status of blacks in American society—the most divisive issue in the history of American politics—drove a wedge into the elites and ultimately led to the nation's bloodiest war. The national political system was unequal to the task of negotiating a peaceful settlement to the slavery problem because America's elites were divided deeply over the question.

SOUTHERN ELITES

In 1787, the southern elites—cotton planters, landowners, exporters, and slave traders—foresaw an end to slavery, but after 1820 the demand for cotton became insatiable, and southern planters could not profitably produce cotton without slave labor. Cotton accounted for more than half the value of all U.S. goods shipped abroad before the Civil War. Although Virginia did not depend on cotton, it sold great numbers of slaves to the cotton states, and "slave raising" itself became immensely profitable.

It was the white *elites* and not the white *masses* of the South who had an interest in the slave and cotton culture. On the eve of the Civil War, probably no more than 400,000 southern families—approximately one in four—held slaves, and many of those families held only one or two slaves each. The number of great planters—men who owned fifty or more slaves and large holdings of land—was probably not more than 7,000, yet their views dominated southern politics.

NORTHERN ELITES

The northern elites were merchants and manufacturers who depended on free labor, yet they had no direct interest in abolishing slavery in the South. But both northern and southern elites realized that control of the West was the key to future dominance of the nation. Northern elites wanted a West composed of small farmers who produced food and raw materials for the industrial and commercial East and provided a market for eastern goods. Southern planters feared the voting power of a West composed of small farmers and wanted western lands for expansion of the cotton and slave culture. Cotton ate up the land and, because it required continuous cultivation and monotonous rounds of simple tasks, was suited to slave labor. Thus, to protect the cotton economy, it was essential to protect slavery in western lands. *This conflict over western land eventually precipitated the Civil War.*

ATTEMPTS AT COMPROMISE

Despite these differences, the underlying consensus of American elites was so great that they devised compromise after compromise to maintain unity. The Missouri Compromise of 1820 divided the land in the Louisiana Purchase exclusive of Missouri between free territory and slave territory at 36° 30' and admitted Maine and Missouri as free and slave states, respectively. After the war with Mexico, the elaborate Compromise of 1850 caused one of the greatest debates in American legislative history, with Senators Henry Clay, Daniel Webster, John C. Calhoun, Salmon P. Chase, Stephen A. Douglas, Jefferson Davis, Alexander H. Stevens, Robert Tombs, William H. Seward, and Thaddeus Stevens all participating. Elite divisiveness was apparent, but it was not yet so destructive as to split the nation. Congress achieved a compromise by admitting California as a free state; creating two new territories, New Mexico and Utah, out of the

Mexican cession; enacting a drastic fugitive slave law to satisfy southern planters; and prohibiting the slave trade in the District of Columbia. Even the Kansas-Nebraska Act of 1854 was to be a compromise; each new territory would decide for itself whether to be slave or free, with the expectation that Nebraska would vote free and Kansas slave. But gradually the spirit of compromise gave way to cleavage and conflict.

CLEAVAGE, VIOLENCE, AND SECESSION

Beginning in 1856, proslavery and antislavery forces fought it out in "bleeding Kansas." Intemperate language in the Senate became commonplace, with frequent threats of secession, violence, and civil war.

In 1857, the Supreme Court decided, in *Dred Scott v. Sandford,* that the Missouri Compromise was unconstitutional because Congress had no authority to forbid slavery in any territory.[6] The Constitution protected slave property, said Chief Justice Roger B. Taney, as much as any other kind of property.

In 1859, John Brown and his followers raided the U.S. arsenal at Harpers Ferry as a first step to freeing the slaves of Virginia by force. Brown was captured by Virginia militia under the command of Colonel Robert E. Lee, tried for treason, found guilty, and executed. Southerners believed that northerners had tried to incite the horror of a slave insurrection, and northerners believed that Brown had died a martyr.

The conflict between North and South led to the complete collapse of the Whig Party and the emergence of a new Republican Party composed exclusively of northerners and westerners. For the first time in the history of American parties, one of the two major parties did not spread across both sides of the Mason-Dixon line; 1860 was the only year in American history when four major parties sought the presidency. The nation was so divided that no party came close to winning the majority of popular votes. Lincoln, the Republican candidate, and Douglas, the Democratic candidate, won most of their votes from the North and West, and John C. Breckinridge (Kentucky), the Southern Democratic candidate, and John Bell (Tennessee), the Constitutional Union candidate, received most of their votes from the South.

More important, the cleavage had become so deep that many prominent southern leaders announced that they would not accept the outcome of the presidential election if Lincoln won. Threats of secession were not new, but this time it was no bluff. For the first and only time in American history, prominent elite members were willing to destroy the American political system rather than compromise their interests and principles. Shortly after the election, on December 20, 1860, the state of South Carolina seceded from the Union. Within six months, ten other southern states followed.

LINCOLN AND SLAVERY

Abraham Lincoln never attacked slavery in the South; his exclusive concern was to halt the spread of slavery in the western territories. He wrote in 1845, "I hold it a paramount duty of us in the free states, due to the union of the states, and perhaps to liberty itself (paradox though it may seem), to let the slavery of the other states alone."[7] Throughout his political career, he consistently held this position. On the other hand, with regard to the western territories he said, "The whole nation is interested that the best use shall be made of these territories. We want them for homes and free white people. This they cannot be, to any considerable extent, if slavery shall be planted within them."[8]

In short, Lincoln wanted to tie the western territories economically and culturally to the northern system. As for Lincoln's racial views, as late as 1858 he said:

> *I will say, then, that I am not, nor ever have been, in favor of bringing about in any way the social and political equality of the white and black races; that I am not, nor ever have been, in favor of making voters or jurors of Negroes, nor qualifying them to hold office, nor to intermarry with white people...and in as much as they cannot so live while they do remain together, there must be a position of superior and inferior; and I as much as any other man am in favor of having the superior position assigned to the white race.*[9]

Lincoln's political posture was essentially conservative. He wished to preserve the long-established order and consensus that had protected American principles and property rights so successfully in the past. He was not an abolitionist, and he did not want to destroy the southern elites or to alter the southern social fabric. His goal was to bring the South back into the Union, to restore orderly government, and to establish the principle that the states cannot resist national authority with force.

EMANCIPATION AS POLITICAL OPPORTUNISM

As the war continued and casualties mounted, northern opinion toward southern slave owners became increasingly bitter. Many Republicans joined the abolitionists in calling for emancipation of the slaves simply to punish the "rebels." They knew that the South's power depended on slave labor. Lincoln also knew that if he proclaimed that the war was being fought to free the slaves, foreign intervention was less likely. Yet even in late summer of 1862, Lincoln wrote:

> *My paramount object in this struggle is to save the Union. If I could save the Union without freeing any slaves, I would do it; if I could save it by freeing some and leaving others alone, I would also do that. I shall do less whenever I shall believe what I am doing hurts the cause, and I shall do more whenever I believe doing more will help the cause. I shall adopt new views as fast as they shall appear to be true views.*[10]

Finally, on September 22, 1862, Lincoln issued his preliminary Emancipation Proclamation. Claiming his right as Commander-in-Chief of the army and navy, he promised that "on the first day of January 1863, all persons held as slaves within any state or designated part of a state, the people whereof shall then be in rebellion against the United States shall be then, thence forward, and forever free." Thus, one of the great steps forward in human freedom in this nation, the Emancipation Proclamation, did not come about as a result of demands by the people and certainly not as a result of demands by the slaves themselves. It was a political and military action by the president for the sake of helping to preserve the Union. It was not a revolutionary action but a conservative one.

RISE OF THE NEW INDUSTRIAL ELITE

The Civil War's importance to the U.S. elite structure lies in the commanding position that the new industrial capitalists won in the course of struggle. Even before 1860, northern industry had been altering the course of American life; the economic transformation of the United States from an agricultural to an industrial nation reached the climax of a revolution in the second half of the nineteenth century. Canals and steam railroads had been opening new markets for the growing industrial cities of the East. The rise of corporations and of stock markets for the accumulation of capital upset old-fashioned ideas of property. The introduction of machinery in factories revolutionized the conditions of American labor and made the masses dependent on industrial capitalists for their livelihood. Civil War profits compounded the capital of the industrialists and placed them in a position to dominate the economic life of the nation. Moreover, when the southern planters were removed from the national scene, the government in Washington became the exclusive domain of the new industrial leaders.

POLITICAL PLUNDER

The protective tariff, long opposed by the southern planters, became the cornerstone of the new business structure of the United States. The industrial capitalists realized that the Northwest Territory was the natural market for their manufactured goods, and the protective tariff restricted the vast and growing American market to American industry alone. The passage of the Homestead Act in 1862 threw the national domain wide open to settlers, and the Transcontinental Railroad Act of 1862 gave the railroads plentiful incentives to link expanding western markets to eastern industry. The northeastern United States was rich in the natural resources of coal, iron, and water power, and the large immigrant population streaming in from Europe furnished a dependable source of cheap labor. The Northeast also had superior means of transportation—both water and rail—to facilitate the assembling of raw materials and the marketing of finished products. With the rise of the new industrial capitalism, power in the United States flowed from the South and West to the Northeast, and Jefferson's dream of a nation of small free farmers faded.

SOCIAL DARWINISM

The new industrial elite found a new philosophy to justify its political and economic dominance. Drawing an analogy from the new Darwinian biology, Herbert Spencer undertook to demonstrate that, just as an elite was selected in nature through evolution, so also society would near perfection as it allowed natural social elites to be selected by free competition. In defense of the new capitalists, Spencer argued: "There cannot be more good done than that of letting social progress go on unhindered; an immensity of mischief may be done in ... the artificial preservation of those least able to care for themselves."[11] Spencer hailed the accumulation of new industrial wealth as a sign of "the survival of the fittest." The "social Darwinists" found in the law of survival of the fittest an admirable defense for the emergence of a ruthless ruling elite, an elite that defined its own self-interest more narrowly, perhaps, than any other in American history.

INDUSTRIAL CAPITALISM

As business became increasingly national in scope, only the strongest or most unscrupulous of the competitors survived. Great producers tended to become the cheapest ones, and little companies tended to disappear. Industrial production rose rapidly, while the number of industrial concerns steadily diminished. Total capital investment and total output of industry vastly increased, while ownership became concentrated. One result was the emergence of monopolies and near monopolies in the major industries of the United States. Another result was the accumulation of great family fortunes.[12] (See Table 3.1, compiled from 1924 tax returns. Admittedly, it fails to record other great personal fortunes, such as Armour and Swift in meat packing, Candler in Coca-Cola, Cannon in textiles, Fleischmann in yeast, Pulitzer in publishing, Golet in real estate, Harriman in railroads, Heinz in foods, Manville in asbestos, Cudahy in food processing, Dorrance in Campbell's Soup, Hartford in A&P, Eastman in film, Firestone in rubber, Sinclair in oil, Chrysler in automobiles, Pabst in beer, and others.)

ELITE POLITICAL DOMINANCE

The only serious challenge to the political dominance of eastern capital came over the issue of "free silver." Leadership of the "free silver" movement came from mine owners in the silver states of the Far West. Their campaigns convinced thousands of western farmers that the unrestricted coinage of silver was the answer to their economic distress. The western mine owners did not care about the welfare of small farmers, but the prospect of inflation, debt relief, and expansion of the supply of money and purchasing power won increasing support among the masses in the West and South.

When William Jennings Bryan delivered his famous Cross of Gold speech at the Democratic convention in 1896, he undid the Cleveland "Gold Democrat" control of the Democratic Party. Bryan was a westerner, a talented orator, an anti-intellectual, and a deeply religious man; he was antagonistic to the eastern industrial interests and totally committed to the cause of free silver. Bryan tried to rally the nation's have-nots to his banner; he tried to convince them that Wall Street was exploiting them. Yet he did not severely criticize the capitalist system, nor did he call for increased federal regulatory powers. In his acceptance speech he declared, "Our campaign has not for its object the reconstruction of society.... Property is and will remain the stimulus to endeavor and the compensation for toil."[13]

The Republican campaign, directed by Marcus Alonzo Hanna of Standard Oil, aimed to persuade the voters that what was good for business was good for the country. Hanna raised an unprecedented $16 million campaign fund from his wealthy fellow industrialists (an amount unmatched in presidential campaigns until the 1960s) and advertised his candidate, William McKinley, as the man who would bring a "full dinner pail" to all.

Bryan's attempt to rally the masses was a dismal failure; McKinley won by a landslide. Bryan ran twice again under the Democratic banner, in 1900 and 1908, but he lost by even greater margins. Although Bryan carried the South and some western states, he failed to rally the masses of the populous eastern states or of the growing cities. Republicans carried working-class, middle-class, and upper-class neighborhoods in the urban industrial states.

LIBERAL ESTABLISHMENT: REFORM AS ELITE SELF-INTEREST

In 1882, William H. Vanderbilt of the New York Central Railroad expressed the ethos of the industrial elite: "The public be damned." This first generation of great American capitalists had little sense of public responsibility. They had built their empires in the

TABLE 3.1 | THE GREAT INDUSTRIAL FORTUNES, 1924

Ranking by 1924 Income Tax	Family	Primary Source of Wealth
1	Rockefeller	Standard Oil Co.
2	Morgan Inner Group (including Morgan partners and families and eight leading Morgan corporation executives)	J. P. Morgan & Co., Inc.
3	Ford	Ford Motor Co.
4	Harkness	Standard Oil Co.
5	Mellon	Aluminum Co.
6	Vanderbilt	New York Central Railroad
7	Whitney	Standard Oil Co.
8	Standard Oil Group (including Archbold, Bedford, Cutler, Flagler, Pratt, Rogers, and Benjamin, but excepting others)	Standard Oil Co.
9	Du Pont	E. I. Du Pont de Nemours
10	McCormick	International Harvester Co. and Chicago Tribune Inc.
11	Baker	First National Bank
12	Fisher	General Motors
13	Guggenheim	American Smelting and Refrigerating Co.
14	Field	Marshall Field & Co.
15	Curtis-Bok	Curtis Publishing Co.
16	Duke	American Tobacco Co.
17	Berwind	Berwind-White Coal Co.
18	Lehman	Lehman Brothers
19	Widener	American Tobacco and Public Utilities
20	Reynolds	R. J. Reynolds Tobacco Co.
21	Astor	Real estate
22	Winthrop	Miscellaneous
23	Stillman	National City Bank
24	Timken	Timken Roller Bearing Co.
25	Pitcairn	Pittsburgh Plate Glass Co.
26	Warburg	Kuhn, Loeb & Co.
27	Metcalf	Rhode Island textile mills

continued

TABLE 3.1 | THE GREAT INDUSTRIAL FORTUNES, 1924 *continued*

Ranking by 1924 Income Tax	Family	Primary Source of Wealth
28	Clark	Singer Sewing Machine Co.
29	Phipps	Carnegie Steel Co.
30	Kuhn	Kuhn, Loeb & Co.
31	Green	Stocks and real estate
32	Patterson	Chicago Tribune, Inc.
33	Taft	Real estate
34	Deering	International Harvester Co.
35	De Forest	Corporate law practice
36	Gould	Railroads
37	Hill	Railroads
38	Drexel	J. P. Morgan & Co.
39	Thomas Fortune Ryan	Stock market
40	H. Foster (Cleveland)	Auto parts
41	Eldridge Johnson	Victor Phonograph
42	Arthur Curtiss James	Copper and railroads
43	C. W. Nash	Automobiles
44	Mortimer Schiff	Kuhn, Loeb & Co.
45	James A. Patten	Wheat market
46	Charles Hayden	Stock market
47	Orlando F. Weber	Allied Chemical & Dye Corp.
48	George Blumenthal	Lazard Freres & Co.
49	Ogden L. Mills	Mining
50	Michael Friedsam	Merchandising
51	Edward B. McLean	Mining
52	Eugene Higgins	New York real estate
53	Alexander S. Cochran	Textiles
54	Mrs. L. N. Kirkwood	
55	Helen Tyson	
56	Archer D. Huntington	Railroads
57	James J. Storrow	Lee Higgins & Co.
58	Julius Rosenwald	Sears, Roebuck and Co.
59	Bernard M. Baruch	Stock market
60	S. S. Kresge	Merchandising

Source: Ferdinand Lundberg, *America's Sixty Families* (Secaucus, N.J.: Citadel Press, 1937). Reprinted by permission.

competitive pursuit of profit. They believed that their success arose from the immutable laws of natural selection, the survival of the fittest; they believed that society was best served by allowing those laws to operate freely.

WILSON'S EARLY WARNING

In 1912, Woodrow Wilson, forerunner of a new elite ethos, criticized America's elite for its lack of public responsibility. Wilson urged America's elite to value the welfare of the masses as an aspect of its own long-run welfare. Wilson did not wish to upset the established order; he merely wished to develop a sense of public responsibility within the establishment. He believed that the national government should see that industrial elites operate in the public interest, and his New Freedom program reflected his high-minded aspirations. The Federal Reserve Act (1914) placed the nation's banking and credit system under government control. The Clayton Antitrust Act (1914) attempted to define specific business abuses, such as charging different prices to different buyers, granting rebates, and making false statements about competitors. Wilson's administration also established the Federal Trade Commission (1914) and authorized it to function in the "public interest" to prevent "unfair methods of competition and unfair and deceptive acts in commerce." Congress established an eight-hour day for railroad workers in interstate commerce (1914) and passed the Child Labor Act (1914) in an attempt to eliminate the worst abuses of children in industry. (The Supreme Court, much less "public regarding," declared this act unconstitutional.) Wilson's program aimed to preserve competition, individualism, enterprise, and opportunity—all considered vital in the American heritage. But he also believed fervently that elites must function in the public interest and that some government regulation might be required to see that they do so.

THE GREAT DEPRESSION

Herbert Hoover was the last great advocate of the laissez-faire capitalism of the old order. The economic collapse of the Great Depression undermined the faith of both elites and nonelites in the ideals of the old order. Following the stock market crash of October 1929, and despite elite assurances that prosperity lay "just around the corner," the American economy virtually stopped. Prices dropped sharply, factories closed, real estate values declined, new construction practically ceased, banks went under, wages dropped drastically, and unemployment figures mounted. By 1932, one out of every four persons in the United States was unemployed, and one out of every five persons was on welfare.

ELITE REFORM

The election of Franklin Delano Roosevelt to the presidency in 1932 ushered in a new era in American elite philosophy. The Great Depression did not bring about a revolution or the emergence of new elites, but it did have an important impact on the thinking of America's governing elites. The victories of fascism in Germany and communism in the Soviet Union and the growing restlessness of the masses in America combined to convince America's elite that reform and regard for the public welfare were essential to the continued maintenance of the American political system and their dominant place in it.

Roosevelt sought a New Deal philosophy that would permit government to devote much more attention to the public welfare than did the philosophy of social Darwinism. The New Deal was not new or revolutionary but rather a necessary reform of the existing capitalist system. It had no consistent unifying plan; it was a series of improvisations, many of them adopted suddenly and some of them even contradictory. Roosevelt believed that government needed to undertake more careful economic planning to adapt "existing economic organizations to the service of the people." And he believed that the government must act humanely and compassionately toward those who were suffering hardship. Relief, recovery, and reform—not revolution—were the objectives of the New Deal.

NOBLESSE OBLIGE

For anyone of Roosevelt's background, it would have been surprising indeed to try to do anything other than preserve the existing social and economic order. Roosevelt was a descendant of two of America's oldest elite families, the Roosevelts and the Delanos, patrician families whose wealth predated the Civil War and the Industrial Revolution. The Roosevelts were not schooled in the scrambling competition of the new industrialists. From the beginning, Roosevelt expressed a more public-regarding philosophy. Soon his personal philosophy of noblesse oblige—elite responsibility for the welfare of the masses—became the prevailing ethos of the new liberal establishment.

VIETNAM: ELITE FAILURE TO LEAD

America's failure in Vietnam—the nation's longest war and only decisive loss—was not the result of military defeat. Rather, it resulted from the failure of the nation's political leadership to set forth clear objectives in Vietnam, to develop a strategy to achieve those objectives, and to rally mass support behind the effort.

INCREMENTAL INVOLVEMENT

Initially, the United States sought to resist communist aggression from North Vietnam and ensure a strong and independent democratic South Vietnamese government. In 1962, President John F. Kennedy sent a large force of military advisers and counterinsurgency forces to assist in every aspect of training and support for the Army of the Republic of Vietnam (ARVN). President Kennedy personally inspired the development and deployment of U.S. counterinsurgency Special Forces ("Green Berets") to deal directly with a guerrilla enemy and help "win the hearts and minds" of the Vietnamese people. President Kennedy's actions were consistent with the long-standing U.S. policy of containing the spread of communism and assisting free people in resisting internal subversion and external aggression.[14]

By 1964, units of the North Vietnamese Army (NVA) had begun to supplement the communist guerrilla forces (Vietcong) in the south. Unconfirmed reports of an attack on U.S. Navy vessels by North Vietnamese torpedo boats led to the "Gulf of Tonkin" resolution by the Congress, authorizing the president to take "all necessary measures" to "repel any armed attack" against any U.S. forces in Southeast Asia. In February 1965, President Lyndon B. Johnson ordered U.S. combat troops into South Vietnam and authorized a gradual increase in air strikes against North Vietnam.

POLITICAL LIMITS

The fateful decision to commit U.S. ground combat forces to Vietnam was made without any significant effort to mobilize American public opinion, the government, or the economy for war. On the contrary, the president minimized the U.S. military effort, placed numerical limits on U.S. troop strength in Vietnam, limited bombing targets, and underestimated North Vietnam's military capabilities as well as expected U.S. casualties. No U.S. ground troops were permitted to cross into North Vietnam, and only once (in Cambodia in 1970) were they permitted to attack NVA forces elsewhere in Indochina. But more important, the U.S. leadership provided no clear-cut military objectives.

MILITARY VICTORY, POLITICAL DEFEAT

The Pentagon Papers,[15] composed of official memos and documents of the war, reveal increasing disenchantment with military results throughout 1967 by Secretary of Defense Robert McNamara and others who had originally initiated U.S. military actions. President Johnson sought to rally support for the war by claiming that the United States was "winning." But on January 30, 1968, Vietcong forces blasted their way into the U.S. embassy compound in Saigon and held the courtyard for six hours. The attack was part of a massive, coordinated Tet offensive against all major cities of South Vietnam. U.S. forces responded and inflicted heavy casualties on the Vietcong. By any *military* measure, the Tet offensive was a "defeat" for the enemy and a "victory" for U.S. forces.[16]

Yet the Tet offensive was Hanoi's greatest political victory. "What the hell is going on?" asked a shocked television anchorman, Walter Cronkite. "I thought we were winning the war."[17] Television pictures of bloody fighting in Saigon and Hue seemed to mock the administration's reports of an early end to the war. The media, believing they had been duped by Johnson and Westmoreland, launched a long and bitter campaign against the war effort. Elite support for the war plummeted.

Deserted by the very elites who had initiated American involvement in the war, hounded by hostile media, and confronting a bitter and divisive presidential election, Lyndon Johnson made a dramatic announcement on national television on March 31, 1968: he halted the bombing of North Vietnam and asked Hanoi for peace talks, and concluded: "I shall not seek, and I will not accept, the nomination of my party for another term as your president." Formal peace talks opened in Paris on May 13.

SHIFTING POLITICAL OBJECTIVES

U.S. objectives in Vietnam shifted again with the arrival in Washington of the new president, Richard M. Nixon, and his national security advisor, Henry A. Kissinger. The Nixon administration immediately began a gradual withdrawal of U.S. forces from Vietnam.

Nixon and Kissinger knew the war must be ended. But they sought to end it "honorably." The South Vietnamese could not be abruptly abandoned without threatening the credibility of U.S. commitments everywhere in the world. They sought a peace settlement that would give South Vietnam a reasonable chance to survive. They hoped that "détente" with the Soviet Union and a new relationship with the People's Republic of China might help to bring about "peace with honor" in Vietnam.

THE END GAME

Meanwhile, National Security Advisor Henry Kissinger and Hanoi's Le Duc Tho had begun meeting secretly in Paris, away from the formal negotiations, to work out "the shape of a deal." U.S. prisoners of war were a major bargaining chip for Hanoi. In the presidential election of 1972, the war became a partisan issue. Democratic candidate George McGovern had earlier stated that he would "crawl on his hands and knees to Hanoi" for peace, whereas Nixon continued his "peace with honor" theme. Nixon's landslide reelection strengthened his position in negotiations.[18] The United States unleashed a devastating air attack directly on Hanoi for the first time in December 1972. When negotiations resumed in Paris in January, the North Vietnamese quickly agreed to peace on the terms that Kissinger and Le Duc Tho had worked out earlier. Both Nixon and Kissinger contend that "the Christmas bombing" secured the final peace.[19]

The Paris Peace Agreement of 1973 called for a cease-fire in place, with NVA troops remaining in its areas of control in the south. The South Vietnamese government and the ARVN also remained in place. All U.S. forces were withdrawn from South Vietnam and U.S. prisoners returned. But the major question of the war—the political status of South Vietnam—was unresolved. The United States promised "full economic and military aid" to the South Vietnamese government and promised to "respond with full force" should North Vietnam violate the cease-fire.

ABANDONING COMMITMENTS

The South Vietnamese government lasted two years after the Paris Peace Agreement. The United States fulfilled none of its pledges. Congress refused to provide significant military aid to the South Vietnamese. Congress passed the War Powers Act in 1973 over Nixon's veto, obligating the president to withdraw U.S. troops from combat within sixty days in the absence of an explicit congressional endorsement. Then the Watergate affair forced Nixon's resignation in August 1974. In early 1975, Hanoi decided that the United States would not "jump back in" and therefore that "the opportune moment" was at hand. NVA forces attacked Hue and Da Nang; the ARVN and thousands of civilians fled southward toward Saigon.

President Gerald Ford never gave serious consideration to the use of U.S. military forces to repel the new invasion, and his requests to Congress for emergency military aid to the South Vietnamese fell on deaf ears.[20] The spectacle of U.S. Marines using rifle butts to keep desperate Vietnamese from boarding helicopters on the roof of the U.S. embassy "provided a tragic epitaph for twenty-five years of American involvement in Vietnam."[21] Unlike past wars, there were no victory parades, and no one could answer the question of the mother whose son was killed in Vietnam: "What did he die for?"

THE GULF WAR: ELITE LEADERSHIP RESTORED

America's leadership performed markedly better in the 1991 Gulf War. Clear strategic objectives were established by President George Bush: to force the immediate and unconditional withdrawal of Iraqi troops from Kuwait. The president relied on his military commanders to devise a plan to achieve this objective, to assemble the necessary forces to carry out the plan without artificial ceilings or limitations, and to execute the plan effectively and with minimum casualties. The president relied on a single direct chain of military command, from Secretary of Defense Richard Cheney to the Chairman of the Joint Chiefs of Staff, General Colin Powell, to a single battlefield commander, General Norman Schwarzkopf, who controlled all Army, Navy, Air Force, and Marine units in the operation, as well as all allied forces.

The U.S. military leadership had learned its lessons from Vietnam: define clear military objectives, use overwhelming and decisive military force, move swiftly and avoid protracted stalemate, minimize casualties, and be sensitive to the image of the war projected back home. The president concentrated his attention on winning political support for the war in world capitals, at the United Nations, and, most important, at home.

OPERATION DESERT SHIELD

Saddam Hussein's invasion of Kuwait on August 2, 1990, was apparently designed to restore his military prestige following eight years of indecisive war against Iran, to secure additional oil revenues to finance the continued buildup of Iraqi military power, and to intimidate and perhaps to invade Saudi Arabia and the Gulf states and thereby secure control over a major share of the world's oil reserves. The Iraqi invasion met with surprisingly swift response from the United Nations in Security Council Resolution 660, condemning the invasion and demanding an immediate withdrawal, and Resolution 661, imposing a trade embargo and economic sanctions. A summit meeting of Arab states reinforced the condemnation and sanctions, with only Libya, Yemen, and the Palestine Liberation Organization (PLO) supporting Iraq. On August 7, the first U.S. forces were sent to Saudi Arabia in Operation Desert Shield to assist in the defense of the kingdom.

MASSIVE MILITARY BUILDUP

Early on, President Bush described the U.S. military deployment as "defensive," but he soon became convinced that neither diplomacy nor an economic blockade would dislodge Saddam from Kuwait. The president ordered the military to prepare an "offensive" option. The top U.S. military commanders, including Generals Powell and Schwarzkopf, had been field officers in Vietnam, and they were resolved not to repeat the mistakes of that war. They wanted to use overwhelming and decisive military force; they wanted to avoid gradual escalation, protracted conflict, target limitations, and political interference in the conduct of the war. They presented the president with an "offensive" plan that called for a very large military buildup: elements of six Army divisions and two Marine divisions; more than a thousand combat aircraft, plus hundreds of tanker and transport aircraft; and six Navy carrier battle groups with nearly five hundred combat aircraft. Coalition forces included British and French heavy armored units and Egyptian, Syrian, Saudi, and other Arab units. Secretary of State James Baker convinced the UN Security Council members, including the Soviet Union (with China abstaining), to support Resolution 678, which authorized states to "use all necessary means" against Iraq unless it withdrew from Kuwait by January 15. Bush had won the support of the world body for offensive action, but the Democratic-controlled Congress balked. The president believed he had constitutional authority as Commander-in-Chief to attack Baghdad, whether or not Congress approved. The Democratic leadership thought otherwise, but after long debate in the Senate, enough Democrats deserted their party to give the president a close 52 to 47 vote in favor of the use of force.

OPERATION DESERT STORM

From Baghdad, CNN reporters Bernard Shaw and Peter Arnett were startled the early morning of January 17 when Operation Desert Storm began with an air attack on key installations in the city. Iraqi forces were also surprised, despite the prompt timing of the attack; Saddam had assured them that the United States lacked the resolve to fight and that, even if war broke out, U.S. public opinion would force a settlement as casualties rose. Air forces quickly won air supremacy and then went on to attack strategic targets and later to degrade Iraqi military forces by cutting off supplies, destroying tanks and artillery, and demoralizing troops with round-the-clock bombardment. U.S. television audiences were treated to videotapes of laser-guided smart bombs entering the doors and air shafts of enemy bunkers. Collateral civilian damage was lower than in any previous air war.

General Schwarzkopf's plan for the ground war emphasized deception and maneuver. While Iraqi forces prepared for attacks from the south and the east coast, Schwarzkopf sent heavy armed columns in a "Hail Mary" play—a wide sweep to the west, outflanking and cutting off Iraqi forces in the battle area. On the night of February 24, the ground attack began, with Marines easily breaching berms, ditches, and minefields and racing directly to the Kuwait City airport; helicopter air assaults lunged deep into Iraq; armored columns raced northward across the desert to outflank Iraqi forces and then attack them from the west; and a surge in air attacks kept Iraqi forces holed up in their bunkers. Iraqi troops surrendered in droves; highways from Kuwait City were turned into massive junkyards of Iraqi vehicles; Iraqi forces that tried to fight were quickly destroyed. After one hundred hours of ground fighting, President George Bush declared a cease-fire.

TRIUMPH WITHOUT VICTORY?

In retrospect, the president's decision to end the war after only one hundred hours of ground operations appears to have been premature. Units of Saddam's elite Republican Guard, which would have been surrounded and destroyed with another day's fighting, escaped back to Baghdad. With these surviving forces, Saddam maintained his cruel grip on the country and proceeded to attack his regime's opponents brutally. Saddam's continuation in power appeared to mock the sacrifices in lives exacted by the war. (For continuation see "The War in Iraq" in Chapter 16.)

AMERICAN POLITICAL HISTORY: AN ELITIST INTERPRETATION

According to elite theory, the movement of nonelites into elite positions must be slow and continuous in order to maintain stability and avoid revolution. Furthermore, potential elite members must demonstrate their commitment to the basic elite consensus before being admitted to elite positions. Elite theory recognizes competition among elites but contends that elites share a broad consensus about preserving the system essentially as it is. It views public-policy changes as a response to elites' redefinition of their own self-interest rather than as a product of direct mass influence. Finally, elite theory views changes in public policy as incremental rather than revolutionary. American political history supports these propositions:

1. America's elite membership evolved slowly, with no serious break in the ideas or values of the American political and economic system. When the leadership of Hamilton and Adams (Federalists) shifted to that of Jefferson, Monroe, and Madison (Republicans), government policies changed little because of the fundamental consensus among elite members.

2. As new sources of wealth opened in an expanding economy, America's elite membership opened to new groups and individuals who had acquired wealth and property and who accepted the national consensus about private enterprise, limited government, and individualism. The West produced new elites, who were assimilated into the governing circle. Public policies changed but were not replaced. The Jacksonians wanted a more open elite system in which the newly wealthy could acquire influence, but they were no more in favor of "dangerous leveling" than were the Founding Fathers.

3. The Civil War reduced southern planters' influence in America's elite structure and paved the way for the rise of the new industrial capitalists. The Industrial Revolution produced a narrowly self-interested elite of industrial capitalists. Mass movements resulted—chiefly one for free silver—but they met with failure.

4. America's elites have divided deeply on the nature of American society only once. This division produced the Civil War, the nation's bloodiest conflict. The Civil War was a conflict between southern elites, dependent on a plantation economy, slave labor, and free trade, and northern industrial commercial elites, who prospered under free labor and protective tariffs. But before, during, and after the Civil War, northern and southern elites continued to strive for compromise in recognition of shared consensus on behalf of liberty and property.

5. The new liberal establishment sought to preserve the existing social and economic order, not to overthrow it. The Great Depression, the victories of fascism in Germany and communism in the Soviet Union, and growing restlessness of the American masses combined to convince America's elites that a more public-regarding philosophy was essential to preserving the American political system and their prominent place in it. Eventually, Franklin D. Roosevelt's philosophy of noblesse oblige—elite responsibility for the welfare of the masses—won widespread acceptance among established American leadership.

6. Policy changes have been incremental. Policy changes, including those launched by the New Deal, occurred when events threatened the system; governing elites—acting on the basis of enlightened self-interest—instituted reforms to preserve the system. Even the reforms and welfare policies of the New Deal were designed to strengthen the existing social and economic fabric of society while minimally dislocating elites.

7. America's defeat and humiliation in Vietnam was a result of the failure of the nation's elite to set forth clear policy objectives, develop a strategy to achieve those objectives, and rally mass support behind the war. Elites, not masses, initially favored the war, and the United States began its withdrawal when elite, not mass, opinion shifted against the war.

8. America's political and military leadership performed much better in the Gulf War in 1991. The decisive use of overwhelming military force to achieve clear objectives with minimum U.S. casualties propelled President George H. W. Bush to all-time highs in approval ratings and established the military as the most trusted institution in American society.

SELECTED READINGS

Burch, Phillip H., Jr. *Elites in American History. Vol. I: The Federalist Years to the Civil War. Vol. II: The Civil War to the New Deal. Vol. III: The New Deal to the Carter Administration.* New York: Holmes and Meier, 1980. The most thorough study available of the class backgrounds of American leaders throughout history. Burch describes the socioeconomic status and financial interests of top government officials from the Washington to the Carter administrations. He links the elite status of these decision makers to their public actions and policy positions.

Commager, Henry Steele, ed. *Documents of American History*, 7th ed. New York: Appleton-Century-Crofts, 1963. Fundamental sources of American history. Six hundred edited documents.

de Tocqueville, Alexis. *Democracy in America.* Chicago: University of Chicago Press, 2000 (1835). The classic early assessment of American political culture by a French traveler.

Elkins, Stanley, and Eric McKitrick. *The Age of Federalism.* New York: Oxford University Press, 1993. An examination of politics in America at the close of the eighteenth century, leading up to the election of 1800.

Hartz, Louis. *The Liberal Tradition in America.* New York: Harcourt, Brace, & World, 1955. The absence of a feudal aristocracy in the United States obstructed the development of social-class consciousness, which in turn prevented the emergence of socialism in this country. The United States as a nation was "born free," and most Americans consider themselves middle class.

Hofstadter, Richard. *The American Political Tradition.* New York: Knopf, Vintage Books, 1948. This book is an important political history from an elite perspective. Hofstadter traces the development of American political elites and their philosophies from Jefferson and the Founding Fathers through Jackson, Bryan, Wilson, and Franklin Roosevelt. He emphasizes that at every stage of U.S. history, elites have been in considerable agreement over major issues (with the possible exception of the Civil War). Finally, Hofstadter discusses the elite practice of incrementalism: that elite leaders have always moved to preserve the established order with as little change in the system as possible.

Morrison, Samuel Eliot. *The Growth of the American Republic.* New York: Oxford University Press, 1958. The classic American history text.

Snow, Donald M., and Dennis M. Drew. *From Lexington to Desert Storm and Beyond: War and Politics and the American Experience.* New York: M. E. Sharpe, 2000. The evolution of U.S. military policy as it was molded by political forces and international challenges.

Notes

1. *McCulloch v. Maryland,* 4 Wheaton 316 (1819).
2. See Richard Hofstadter, *The American Political Tradition* (New York: Knopf, 1948), pp. 18–44.
3. Hofstadter, *American Political Tradition,* pp. 32–33.
4. Hofstadter, *American Political Tradition,* p. 38.
5. Frederick Jackson Turner, "The West and American Ideals," in *The Frontier in American History* (New York: Holt, Rinehart & Winston, 1921).
6. *Dred Scott v. Sandford,* 19 Howard 393 (1857).
7. Hofstadter, *American Political Tradition,* p. 109.
8. Hofstadter, *American Political Tradition,* p. 113.
9. Hofstadter, *American Political Tradition,* p. 116.
10. Hofstadter, *American Political Tradition,* p. 119.
11. Herbert Spencer, *Social Statics* (1851).
12. See Gustavus Myers, *A History of the Great American Fortunes,* 3 vols. (Chicago: Kerr, 1910).
13. V. O. Key Jr., *Politics, Parties, and Pressure Groups* (New York: T. Y. Crowell, 1942), pp. 189–191.
14. See David Halberstam, *The Best and the Brightest* (New York: Random House, 1973).
15. New York Times, *The Pentagon Papers* (New York: Bantam Books, 1971).
16. George C. Herring, *America's Longest War* (New York: Random House, 1979), p. 182.
17. Herring, *America's Longest War,* p. 188.
18. See Henry Kissinger, *The White House Years* (Boston: Little, Brown, 1979), pp. 1301–1446.
19. Kissinger, *The White House Years,* p. 1461; see Richard Nixon, *RN: The Memoirs of Richard Nixon,* vol. 2 (New York: Warner Books, 1978), p. 251.
20. See Frank Snepp, *Decent Interval* (New York: Random House, 1977).
21. Herring, *America's Longest War,* p. 262.

There has always been a privileged class, even in America, but it has never been so dangerously isolated from its surroundings.

Christopher Lasch

ELITES IN AMERICA

Power in the United States is organized into large institutions. Positions at the top of the major institutions in American society are sources of great power. Sociologist C. Wright Mills described the relationship between institutional authority and power in this way:

> *If we took the one hundred most powerful men in America, the one hundred wealthiest, and the one hundred most celebrated away from the institutional positions they now occupy, away from their resources of men and women and money, away from the media of mass communication that are now focused upon them—then they should be powerless and poor and uncelebrated. For power is not of a man. Wealth does not center in the person of the wealthy. Celebrity is not inherent in any personality. To be celebrated, to be wealthy, to have power, requires access to major institutions, for the institutional positions men occupy determine in large part their chances to have and to hold these valued experiences.*[1]

In this chapter we describe the people who occupy high positions in the major private and governmental institutions of American society. We include the major *private* institutions—in industry, finance, media, law, and other "nongovernmental institutions"—because we believe that they allocate values for our society and shape the lives of all Americans. Remember, we defined an elite member as anyone who participates in decisions that allocate values for society, not just those who participate in decision making as part of the government. The decisions of automobile companies to raise prices, of banks to raise or lower interest rates, of computer companies to market new products, of the mass media to determine what is "news," and of schools and colleges to decide what will be taught—all affect the lives of Americans as much as government decisions do.[2]

Governmental elites—the president and top executive officials, congressional leaders, and committee chairs—interact closely with corporate and financial and media elites. Corporate and personal wealth is channeled through foundations to universities and think tanks to undertake policy research and develop policy recommendations.

Research reports and policy recommendations are directed toward both media and governmental elites. The media largely set the agenda for discussion and debate of policy directions. Governmental elites are obliged to respond to media definitions of societal "problems," as well as to policy proposals that the media receive from foundations, universities, and think tanks.

National policy does not reflect demands of "the people" but rather the preferences, interests, and values of the few who participate in the policy-making process. Changes or innovations in public policy come about when elites redefine their own interests or modify their own values. Policies decided by elites need not be oppressive or exploitative of the masses. Elites may be very public regarding, and the welfare of the masses may be an important consideration in elite decision making. Yet it is *elites* who make policy, not the *masses*.

THE CONCENTRATION OF CORPORATE POWER

Economic power in the United States is concentrated in a small number of large corporations and banks. Traditionally, pluralism portrays business as just another interest group, competing with all other interest groups to influence public policy. Corporate power, according to the pluralists, depends on the political skills and resources of particular individuals, groups, and industries within the corporate world, on the performance of the economy, on the climate of public opinion, and on the relative strength of competing groups. In contrast, elitism views economic elites as distinctly powerful, not only in shaping government policy but, more important, in making decisions that directly influence all our lives.

Fortune **Magazine**
Information on corporate and financial institutions, including the largest American ("Fortune 500") and global corporations.
www.fortune.com

Economic elites decide what will be produced, how it will be produced, how much it will cost, how many people will be employed, who will be employed, and what their wages will be. They decide how goods and services will be distributed, how much money will be available for loans, what interest rates will be charged, and what new technologies will be developed.

Of course, these decisions are influenced by governmental regulations, consumer demand, international competition, federal fiscal and monetary policy, and other public and private market forces. But in a free-market economy, corporate elites, not government officials, make most of the key economic decisions.[3]

INDUSTRIAL CONCENTRATION

Formal control of the nation's economic life rests in the hands of a relatively small number of senior officers and directors of the nation's largest corporate institutions. This concentration has occurred chiefly because economic enterprise has increasingly consolidated into a small number of giant corporations. The following statistics only suggest the scale and concentration of modern U.S. corporate enterprise.

About six million corporate tax returns are received by the U.S. Internal Revenue Service each year. But only 25,000 (0.4%) of these returns come from corporations that receive over $50 million in annual revenues. Yet these large corporations account for nearly three-fourths of the total corporate revenues in the nation. America's 500 largest corporations—the "Fortune 500"—collectively take in about $9.1 *trillion* in revenues each year, or more than half of all corporate revenue in the nation. The

TABLE 4.1 | THE NATION'S LARGEST NONFINANCIAL CORPORATIONS

Rank	Corporation	Rank	Corporation
1	Exxon Mobile	26	Sears
2	Wal-Mart	27	Dow Chemical
3	General Motors	28	Wellpoint
4	Chevron	29	AT&T
5	Ford Motors	30	Time Warner
6	ConocoPhillips	31	Lowe's
7	General Electric	32	United Technologies
8	International Business Machine	33	United Parcel Service
9	Hewlett-Packard	34	Walgreen
10	Home Depot	35	Albertson's
11	Valero Energy	36	Microsoft
12	McKesson	37	Intel
13	Verizon	38	Safeway
14	Cardinal Health	39	Medco
15	Altria (Philip Morris)	40	Lockheed Martin
16	Kroger	41	CVS
17	Marathon Oil	42	Motorola
18	Procter and Gamble	43	Caterpillar
19	Dell	44	Archer Daniels Midland
20	Boeing	45	Sprint Nextel
21	AmerisourceBergen	46	Caremark
22	Costco	47	PepsiCo
23	Target	48	Walt Disney
24	Pfizer	49	Plains Pipeline
25	Johnson & Johnson	50	Sonoco

Source: Derived from data provided by *Fortune* at www.fortune.com. Data for 2006.

nation's fifty largest corporations are listed in Table 4.1. The five largest nonfinancial corporations—Exxon Mobil, Wal-Mart, General Motors, Chevron, and Ford Motors—account for about 15 percent of all corporate revenue in the United States.

FINANCIAL CONCENTRATION

The financial elite of America is even more concentrated than the industrial elite and becoming ever more so each year. Table 4.2 lists the ten largest commercial banks in the nation; together they control nearly half of all banking assets.

TABLE 4.2 | THE NATION'S LARGEST COMMERCIAL BANKS

Rank	Commercial Bank	Rank	Commercial Bank
1	Citigroup	6	Wachovia
2	Bank of America	7	Capital One Financial
3	JPMorgan Chase	8	National City Corp
4	Wells Fargo	9	Sun Trust
5	U.S. Bancorp	10	Bank of New York

Source: Derived from data provided by *Fortune* at www.fortune.com. Data for 2006.

Giant banking mergers in the last decade have resulted in greater concentration of banking assets than at any time in recent history. Today, three banking corporations—Citigroup, JPMorgan Chase, and Bank of America—control about one-third of all the nation's banking assets. The merger of JPMorgan and Chase Manhattan and the merger of Bank of America with NationsBank consolidated the nation's financial industry. The financial mega-giant, Citigroup, was created first through the merger of CitiCorp with the Wall Street investment firms of Salomon Brothers and Smith Barney, followed by its acquisition of Travelers Insurance. Robert Rubin, former Secretary of the Treasury, was named the first cochairman of the new giant of the financial world.

Citigroup
Web site of America's largest financial institution.
www.citigroup.com

The nation's largest insurance companies invest nearly half of all insurance investment funds, acting on behalf of the millions of Americans who purchase life, home, and auto insurance (see Table 4.3).

The nation's largest investment firms (see Table 4.4) largely decide how America will invest in its future. They decide whether, when, and under what terms American corporations can borrow money from and sell stocks and bonds to the general public. That is to say, they decide the allocation of capital in our capitalist system.

THE GLOBAL ELITES

International trade—the buying and selling of goods and services between individuals and firms located in different countries—has expanded rapidly in recent decades. Today, almost one-fourth of the world's total output is sold in a country other than the

TABLE 4.3 | THE NATION'S LARGEST INSURANCE COMPANIES

Rank	Insurance Company	Rank	Insurance Company
1	American International Group (AIG)	6	New York Life
2	State Farm	7	Hartford
3	MetLife	8	TIAA-CREF
4	Allstate	9	Travelers
5	Prudential	10	Nationwide

Source: Derived from data provided by *Fortune* at www.fortune.com. Data for 2006.

FOCUS	CORPORATE MERGER MANIA

America's corporate elite is becoming ever more concentrated. Indeed, "merger mania" has largely swept away community banks, smaller stock brokerage firms, and independent newspapers, publishers, and media companies. All but a very few successful independent business entrepreneurs—those who create most of America's new products and services—eventually sell out to the corporate conglomerates.

The U.S. government has relaxed enforcement of its antitrust laws, laws that date back to the Sherman Antitrust Act of 1890. In a mega-merger labeled "Rockefeller's Revenge," Exxon, once the nation's third largest industrial corporation, and Mobil, once the nation's seventh largest, agreed to combine their power in 1998. Actually, their merger is a *recombination* of giant oil companies once owned by John D. Rockefeller's Standard Oil Company monopoly. The U.S. Supreme Court approved President Theodore Roosevelt's trust-busting breakup of Standard Oil in 1911. But today it is argued that global competition in the oil industry requires a reconcentration of economic power in U.S. corporations. The new Exxon Mobil giant claims that it must compete with global oil conglomerates such as Royal Dutch Shell (Netherlands) and British Petroleum (which itself bought up Amoco).

Citicorp (banking) and Travelers Group (insurance) merged their assets in 1998 to become the world's largest financial institution, with nearly $1 trillion in assets. The new Citigroup boasts of over one hundred million customers in more than one hundred countries. And the merger of AOL (America OnLine) with Time Warner in 2000 created the world's largest media conglomerate (see Chapter 6).

Defenders of corporate and financial megamergers argue that these deals are needed to make American firms large enough to compete successfully against giant conglomerates in Japan and Europe. And they argue that in any business—manufacturing, retail sales, or service—larger size grants easier access to capital and supplies and therefore allows the giants to keep prices down. Few locally owned retail stores, for example, can compete in prices with KMart or J. C. Penney, let alone the nation's largest retailer, Wal-Mart.

Nearly every year the nation posts a new record number of mergers and acquisitions. Costs and prices are kept low, and profits are driven up. Perhaps more important, elites further concentrate their power and resources.

But masses face continuing disruption in their lives. Employees face job losses, dislocations, and "downsizing" of their positions and salaries. Even in a strong economy workers must be prepared constantly to move on to new jobs. It is not only factory workers who are regularly displaced but also bank tellers, retail sales persons, stockbrokers, and many other middle-class, "white-collar" employees.

one in which it was produced. Today the United States exports about 11 percent of the value of its gross domestic product (GDP) and imports about 12 percent. Exports and imports were only about 3 percent of GDP in 1970 (see Figure 4.1). Global competition heavily impacts the American economy.

TABLE 4.4	THE NATION'S LARGEST INVESTMENT FIRMS

Rank	Investment Firm	Rank	Investment Firm
1	Morgan Stanley	7	Franklin Resources
2	Merrill Lynch	8	AG Edwards
3	Goldman Sachs	9	ETrade
4	Lehman Brothers	10	Legg Mason
5	Bear Sterns	11	Raymond James
6	Charles Schwab	12	T. Rowe Price

Source: Derived from data provided by *Fortune* at www.fortune.com. Data for 2006.

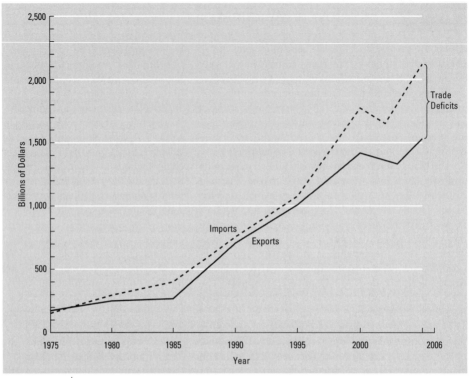

FIGURE 4.1 | U.S. WORLD TRADE

Source: *Statistical Abstract of the United States,* 2006, p. 820. Note that America's economic slowdown in 2001–2002 reduced exports and expanded the trade deficit.

The globalization of economic power has created a global elite—the leaders of the world's largest banks and industrial corporations (see Table 4.5). The economic power of the global elite challenges the notion of national sovereignty. This elite can move, or threaten to move, economic resources—industrial plants, sales and inventory, and capital investment—across national boundaries, and thus shape the economic policies of national governments. And direct international investments and cross-national ownership of economic resources are rising rapidly.

MULTINATIONALISM

America's top exporting corporations (see Table 4.6) have largely dictated U.S. trade policy. Both Democratic and Republican presidential administrations over the past half-century have supported expanded world trade. The U.S. market is the largest in the world and the most open to foreign-made goods. U.S. policy has been to maintain an open market while encouraging other nations to do the same. U.S. tariffs tumbled after World War II, and then continued their downward spiral through to today (see Figure 4.2). Opposition to these policies from American workers and labor unions has been ignored. Indeed, the United States continues to

TABLE 4.5 | THE WORLD'S LARGEST CORPORATIONS

Rank	Corporation	Country
1	Exxon Mobile	USA
2	Wal-Mart	USA
3	Royal Dutch Shell	Netherlands
4	BP	United Kingdom
5	General Motors	USA
6	Chevron	USA
7	Daimler Chrysler	Germany
8	Toyota	Japan
9	Ford Motor	USA
10	Conoco Philips	USA
11	General Electric	USA
12	Total	France
13	ING	Netherlands
14	Citigroup	USA
15	AXA	France
16	Allianz	Germany
17	Volkswagen	Germany
18	Fortis	Belgium
19	Credit Agricole	France
20	American International	USA
21	Assicurazioni Generali	Italy
22	Siemens	Germany
23	Sinopec	China
24	Nippon Tel & Tel	Japan
25	Carrefour	France

U.S. Trade Representative
Information on U.S. trade policy.
www.ustr.gov

lead international efforts to further liberalize world trade, encourage the flow of investment capital around the world, and eliminate foreign market barriers to American exports.

THE WORLD TRADE ORGANIZATION

A multinational General Agreement on Tariffs and Trade organization (GATT) was created following World War II for the purpose of encouraging international trade. Over the years, GATT has been dominated by banking, business, and commercial interests in

TABLE 4.6 | AMERICA'S LARGEST EXPORTERS

Rank	Company Name	Major Export
1	General Motors	Motor vehicles and parts, locomotives
2	Ford Motor	Motor vehicles and parts
3	Boeing	Commercial aircraft
4	Chrysler	Motor vehicles and parts
5	General Electric	Jet engines, turbines, plastics, medical systems, locomotives
6	Motorola	Communications equipment, semiconductors
7	International Business Machines (IBM)	Computers and related equipment
8	Philip Morris	Tobacco, beer, food products
9	Archer Daniels Midland	Protein meals, vegetable oils, flour, alcohol, grain
10	Hewlett-Packard	Measurement, computation, communications products and systems
11	Intel	Microcomputer components, modules, systems
12	Caterpillar	Engines; turbines; construction, mining, and agricultural machinery
13	McDonnell Douglas	Aerospace products, missiles, electronic systems
14	Du Pont	Chemicals, polymers, fibers, specialty products
15	United Technologies	Jet engines, helicopters, cooling equipment
16	Eastman Kodak	Imaging products
17	Lockheed Martin	Aerospace products, missiles, electronic systems
18	Compaq Computer	Computers and related equipment
19	Raytheon	Electronic systems, engineering and construction projects
20	Digital Equipment	Computer, software, related equipment
21	AlliedSignal	Aircraft and automotive parts, chemicals
22	Minnesota Mining & Mfg. (3M)	Industrial, electronics, health care, consumer, and imaging products
23	Westinghouse Electric	Power systems, office furniture, transport refrigeration
24	Dow Chemical	Chemicals, plastics, consumer specialities
25	Merck	Health products

Western nations seeking multilateral tariff reductions and the relaxations of quotas. In 1993, the GATT "Uruguay Round" eliminated quotas on textile products; established more uniform standards for proof of dumping; set rules for the protection of intellectual property rights (patents and copyrights on books, movies, videos, and so on); reduced tariffs on wood, paper, and some other raw materials; and scheduled a gradual reduction of government subsidies for agricultural products.

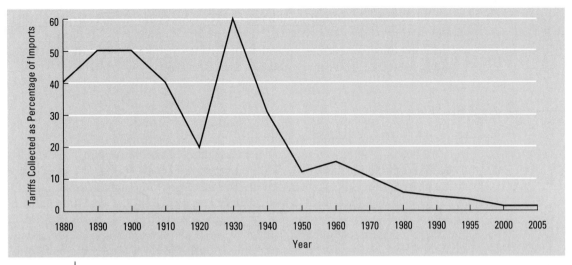

FIGURE 4.2 | DECLINES IN U.S. TARIFFS OVER TIME

Source: Data from *Statistical Abstract of the United States, 2006.*

The World Trade Organization (WTO) was created in 1993 to enforce GATT. Today, the WTO includes 130 nations that agree to a governing set of global trade rules. (China was admitted in 2001.) The WTO is given power to adjudicate trade disputes among countries and to monitor and enforce trade agreements.

THE INTERNATIONAL MONETARY FUND (IMF) AND THE WORLD BANK

The IMF's purpose is to facilitate international trade, allowing nations to borrow to stabilize their balance-of-trade payments. However, when economically weak nations incur chronic balance-of-trade deficits and perhaps face deferral or default on international debts, the IMF may condition its loans on changes in a nation's economic policies. It may require a reduction in a nation's government deficits by reduced public spending and/ or higher taxes, or it may require a devaluation of its currency, making its exports cheaper and imports more expensive. It may also require the adoption of noninflationary monetary policies. Currently, the IMF and the World Bank are actively involved in assisting Russia and other states of the former Soviet Union to convert to free-market economies.

The World Bank makes long-term loans, mostly to developing nations, to assist in economic development. It works closely with the IMF in investigating the economic conditions of nations applying for loans and generally imposes IMF requirements on these nations as conditions for loans.

THE NORTH AMERICAN FREE TRADE AGREEMENT (NAFTA)

In 1993, the United States, Canada, and Mexico signed the North American Free Trade Agreement (NAFTA). Objections by labor unions and environmental groups in the United States were drowned out in a torrent of support by the American corporate community, Democrats and Republicans in Congress, President Bill Clinton, and former president George Bush. NAFTA envisions the removal of tariffs on virtually all products by all three nations over a period of ten to fifteen years. It also allows banking, insurance, and other financial services to cross these borders.

FREE TRADE OF THE AMERICAS

Heading the current agenda for institutionalizing global trade is the "Free Trade of the Americas." The objective is the negotiation of a tariff-free, rules-based, free-trade Western Hemisphere to include thirty-three nations. A meeting of Western Hemisphere nations in Quebec City in 2001 set a goal for such an agreement for 2005. Recent U.S. presidents, both Democrats and Republicans, have pressed Congress for "fast-track authority" for trade agreements, essentially requesting that Congress pass presidentially negotiated trade agreements without amendments. In 2002, Congress granted President Bush's request for "trade promotion authority."

GLOBALIZATION AND DEMOCRACY

The globalization of corporate power is moving economic elites in America even further away from the people. International elites in industry, banking, finance, and the media are increasingly removed from the values, beliefs, and concerns of the masses of people in their countries. Indeed, global elites are becoming increasingly free from the restraints of national governments. America's global elite is becoming ever more isolated from the masses. Social historian Christopher Lasch observes:

> It is a question whether they think of themselves as Americans at all. Patriotism, certainly, does not rank very high in their hierarchy of virtues. "Multiculturalism," on the other hand, suits them to perfection, conjuring up the agreeable images of a global bazaar. . . . The new elites are at home only in transit, en route to a high-level conference, to the grand opening of a new franchise, to an international film festival, or to an undiscovered resort. Theirs is essentially a tourist's view of the world—not a perspective likely to encourage a passionate devotion to democracy.[3]

CORPORATE ELITES

Following the Industrial Revolution in America in the late nineteenth century and well into the twentieth century, the nation's largest corporations were controlled by the tycoons who created them—Andrew Carnegie (Carnegie Steel, later United States Steel), Andrew Mellon (Alcoa and Mellon banks), Henry Ford (Ford Motor Co.), J. P. Morgan (J. P. Morgan), and, of course, John D. Rockefeller (Standard Oil Company, later broken into Exxon, Mobil, Chevron, Atlantic Richfield, and other large oil companies). However, by the 1930s control of most large corporations had passed to professional managers. As early as 1932, Adolf Berle and Gardiner Means, in their classic book, *The Modern Corporation and Private Property*, described the separation

- The world's twenty-five largest corporations include nine American firms. European nations and Japan complete the global elite, which in the future may also include China.
- U.S. exporting companies support a domestic open market—the elimination of tariffs and trade barriers—in order to encourage other nations to open their doors to their products.
- The World Trade Organization (WTO) is the principal instrument for formulating global trade policy.

- American elites have created a common market with Mexico, Canada, and the United States through NAFTA, despite objections by unions and environmental groups. NAFTA is a blueprint for expanding trade throughout Central America (CAFTA) and throughout North and South America (FTA).
- Globalization of corporate power moves economic elites even further away from people, and increasingly removes the restraints of national governments from worldwide corporate activities.

of ownership from control. The theory of "managerialism" became the conventional wisdom about corporate governance.[4]

Corporate power does not rest in the hands of the masses of corporate employees or even in the hands of the millions of middle- and upper-class Americans who own corporate stock.

MANAGEMENT POWER

Corporate power is generally wielded by the top managers of the nation's large industrial corporations and financial institutions. Theoretically, stockholders have ultimate power over management, but in fact individual stockholders seldom have any control over the activities of the corporations they own. When confronted with mismanagement, individual stockholders simply sell their stock rather than try to challenge the powers of the managers. Indeed, most stockholders sign over "proxies" to top management so that top management can cast these proxy votes at the annual meetings of stockholders. Management itself usually selects its own slate for the board of directors and easily elects them with the help of proxies.

Large control blocks of stock in corporations are usually held by banks and financial institutions or pension trusts or mutual funds. Occasionally, the managers of these institutions will demand the replacement of corporate managers who have performed poorly. But more often than not, banks and trust funds vote their stock for the management slate. Institutional investors usually allow the management of corporations essentially to appoint themselves and their friends to the board of directors and thus to become increasingly unchallengeable.

The number of board members in major U.S. banks and corporations averages between twelve and fifteen. Board members are divided among "inside" directors (top executive officers of the corporation itself), "outside" directors (usually top executive officers of other banks or corporations), and "public interest" directors (persons selected to give symbolic representation to consumers, minorities, or civic groups). (See Table 4.7.)

TABLE 4.7 | INSIDE THE BOARDROOM AT EXXON MOBIL

Insiders

Rex W. Tillerson
President
Director: The Business Council, The Business
    Roundtable

J. Stephen Simon
Senior VP, Exxon Mobile

Public Interest

Marilyn Carlson Nelson
Chairman and CEO: Carlson Companies
Chair: National Women's Business Council

Reatha Clark King
Chairman: General Mills Foundation
Director: Wells Fargo; Lenox Group
Trustee: Atlanta-Clark University, University
    of Chicago

Michael J. Boskin
Friedman Professor of Economics, Hoover
    Institute, Stanford University
Director: National Bureau of Economic
    Research; Oracle Corp., Shinse,
    Vodafone

Outside Corporate

Henry A. McKinnel
Chairman and CEO: Pfizer Inc.
Director: Moody's Corporation, John Wiley
    Inc., The Business Council, The Business
    Roundtable, New York Public Library

James R. Houghton
Chairman and CEO: Corning (Glass)
    International
Director: MetLife, Metropolitan Museum of
    Art, Pierpont Morgan Library, The
    Business Council, The Council on
    Foreign Relations, Harvard Corporation

William W. George
Professor of Management, Harvard
    University
Former Chairman and CEO: Medronic
Former Asst. Secretary of the Navy
Director: Goldman Sachs, Medtronic, Novitis
    AG, Dayton Hudson, Global Center for
    Leadership and Business Ethics, Union
    Theological Seminary, Macalaster
    College, Minnesota Symphony Orchestra

Phillip E. Lippincott
Chairman and CEO: Scott Paper
Retired Chairman: Campbell Soup
Director: Campbell Soup, Penn Mutual Life
Member: The Business Council

Samuel J. Palmisano
Chairman and CEO: IBM

Walter V. Shipley
Retired Chairman of the Board: Chase
    Manhattan Corp.
Director: Verizon Communications, Wyeth,
    Goodwill Industries, American Museum
    of Natural History
Member: The Business Council

William R. Howell
Chairman Emeritus: J. C. Penney Co.
Director: Duetsche Bank, American Electric
    Power, Halliburton, Pfizer

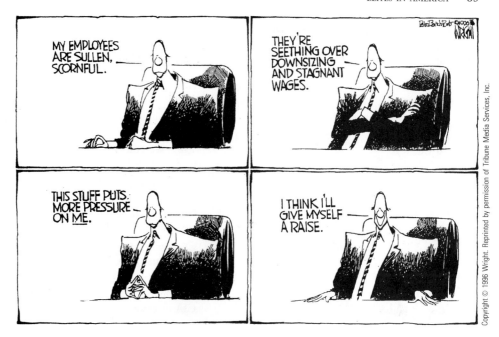

INTERLOCKING DIRECTORATES

ExxonMobil
Web site of the world's largest corporation, including information on officers and directors.
www.exxonmobil.com

Corporate power is further concentrated by a system of interlocking directorates. Interlocking directorates, in which a director of one corporation also sits on the boards of other corporations, enable key corporate elites to wield influence over a large number of corporations. It is not uncommon for top members of the corporate elite to hold several directorships.

GOVERNMENT ELITES

Politicians specialize in office seeking. They know how to run for office, but they may not know how to run the government. After victory at the polls, wise politicians turn to experienced executive elites to run the government. Both Democratic and Republican presidents select essentially the same type of executive elite to staff the key positions in their administrations. Frequently, these top government executives—cabinet members, presidential advisers, special ambassadors—have occupied key posts in private industry, finance, or law or influential positions in education, the arts and sciences, or social, civic, and charitable associations. The executive elites move easily in and out of government posts from their positions in the corporate, financial, legal, and education worlds. They often assume government jobs at a financial sacrifice, and many do so out of a sense of public service.

REVOLVING DOORS

The elitist model of power envisions a single group of people exercising power in many sectors of American life. Elitists do not necessarily expect to see individuals *simultaneously* occupying high positions in both business and government, but they do

TABLE 4.8 | THE BUSH CABINET, 2007

Position	Occupation	Career Highlights	Corporate Connections
President George W. Bush	Oil company executive; manager/director, Texas Rangers	Governor, Texas, 1994–2000	Harkin Energy,* Enron, Philip Morris, AT&T, Microsoft
Vice President Richard Cheney	Oil company executive	U.S. Rep. Wyo., 1979–1989; secretary of defense, 1989–1993	Halliburton Oil,* Enron, Philip Morris, AT&T, Microsoft
Secretary of State Condoleezza Rice	Educator	Hoover Institute (think tank); provost, Stanford University; national security advisor, 2001–2004	Chevron,* Charles Schwab,* TransAmerica
Secretary of Treasury Henry M. Paulson	Investment banker	Chairman and CEO, Goldman Sachs	Goldman Sachs
Secretary of Defense Robert Gates	Intelligence officer	President, Texas A&M; CIA director	Fidelity Investments, NACCO Investments, Brinker, Parker Drilling
Attorney General Alberto Gonzales	Attorney	Texas Supreme Court	Vinson & Elkins (corporate law firm)
Secretary of Commerce Carlos Gutierrez	Cereal company executive	President, Kellogg Co.	Kellogg Co.*
Secretary of HUD Alphonso Jackson	Attorney	Dallas Housing Authority; deputy secretary of HUD; president, American Electric Power	JPMorgan,* American Electric Power*
Secretary of Labor Elaine Chao	Banker, president of civic organization	Director, Peace Corps, 1991–1992; president, United Way, 1992–1996	Northwest Airlines,* Clorox,* HCA,* Bank of America,* Dole Food*
Secretary of Transportation Mary E. Peters	Transportation administrator	Administrator, Federal Highway Administration, 2003–2005	HDR Inc. (Arizona engineering firm)
Secretary of Interior Dirk Kempthorne		Mayor of Boise, 1985–1986; Governor, Idaho, 1998–2006; U.S. Senator, 1992–1998	Idaho Homebuilders Association, FMC corp.*
Secretary of Health and Human Services Michael Leavitt	Business executive	Governor, Utah; administrator, EPA	Pacificorp,* Utah Power and Light,* Great Western*
Secretary of Education Margaret Spellings	Educator	Assistant to governor of Texas; assistant to president	None

TABLE 4.8 | THE BUSH CABINET, 2007 *continued*

Position	Occupation	Career Highlights	Corporate Connections
Secretary of Agriculture Mike Johanns	Attorney	Mayor, Lincoln, Nebraska	Kraft, Tyson, ConAgra
Secretary of Energy Samuel L. Bodman	Investments	Chairman and CEO, Cabot Corp.	Cabot Corp., Fidelity Investments,* John Hancock,* Thermo Electron,* Security Capital*
Secretary of Veterans Administration John Nicholson	Army officer; attorney; real estate developer	U.S. ambassador to Vatican; chairman, Republican National Committee	None
Secretary of Homeland Security Michael Chertoff	Attorney	U.S. attorney for New Jersey; Judge, U.S. Court of Appeals	None

*Corporate connections provided by the Center for Responsive Politics. Connections include services as officer or director (shown with asterisk), together with major stock holdings and/or heavy campaign contributions.

expect to see a "revolving door" by which elites move from power positions in banking, industry, the media, law, the foundations, and education to power positions in government, then frequently returning to prestigious private posts after a term of "public service." The previous elite positions held by cabinet members in the Bush administration, together with their corporate connections, are shown in Table 4.8.

ELITE POLICY-MAKING INSTITUTIONS

America's elite is not only found in the higher echelons of business, banking and investments, insurance, and government itself but, equally important, in the nation's leading foundations, think tanks, mass media, and universities. These institutions can be thought of as a "third force" in American society (the other two being business and government) that funds, plans, formulates, and directs the policy-making process.

The most influential institutions have been labeled the American Establishment. They include the top policy-oriented foundations—the Ford Foundation, the Rockefeller Foundation, the Carnegie Corporation. They include the nation's leading policy-planning organizations or "think tanks"—the Brookings Institution, the RAND Corporation, the American Enterprise Institute, the Council on Foreign Relations, the Trilateral Commission. Top business and financial leaders look to the Business Roundtable and the Committee for Economic Development for policy advice. Elites communicate with the masses and with each other through the *Washington Post*, the *New York Times*, and the *Wall Street Journal* (see Chapter 6). They sit on the boards of trustees, provide financial support, and rely on policy recommendations generated by Harvard University, Yale University, Princeton University, the University of Chicago, and Stanford University. They support the Metropolitan Museum of Art, the Museum of Modern Art, and the Metropolitan Opera.

FOCUS | ELITE ATTITUDES TOWARD MASS GOVERNANCE

Since the early days of the Republic, American elites have adopted a democratic rhetoric that obscures their disdain for the masses. Alexander Hamilton may have been the last national leader to publicly acknowledge elitist views:

> All societies divide themselves into the few and the many. The first are the rich and the well-born; the other the masses of people. And however often it is said that the voice of the people is the voice of God, it is not true in fact. The people are forever turbulent and changing; they seldom judge right.[a]

Today, as well as two centuries ago, elites have little confidence in the judgment of the masses.

It is difficult to query elites about their true opinion of the masses. Elites are difficult to survey by standard polling methods, and even when questioned, they know enough to give socially acceptable responses. The rhetoric of democracy is so ingrained that elites instinctively recite democratic phrases. But consider the following responses obtained in a special survey of congressional, executive, and bureaucratic elites in Washington conducted by the Princeton Survey Research Associates:

QUESTION: "How much trust and confidence do you have in the wisdom of the American people when it comes to making choices on election day: a great deal, a fair amount, not very much, or none at all?"

	Congress Members	Presidential Staff	Senior Bureaucrats
Great deal	64	34	34
Fair amount	31	51	44
Not very much	1	12	20
None at all	0	1	1
Don't know/ No answer	4	2	1

QUESTION: "Do you think the American public knows enough about the issues you face to form wise opinions about what should be done about these issues, or not?"

	Congress Members	Presidential Staff	Senior Bureaucrats
Yes	31	13	14
No	47	77	81
Maybe/ Depends (vol.)	17	7	3
Don't know/ No answer	5	3	2

[a]Quoted in Richard Hofstadter, *The American Political Tradition*, (New York: Knopf, 1948), p. 6.

Source: Pew Research Center/*National Journal* survey conducted under the direction of Princeton Survey Research Associates, October 1997—February 1998. *N* = 81 members of Congress, 98 presidential appointees, and 151 members of the Senior Executive Service of the federal government. As reported in *Polling Report*, May 4, 1998.

The Establishment is influential whether the Republicans or the Democrats control the White House or Capitol Hill. "A change of the guard in Washington pulls to the new president those prominent establishmentarians most friendly to his aims, while pushing their counterparts from the previous administration back to the staffs and boards of the Establishment's private institutions."[5]

PUBLIC POLICY AS ELITE PREFERENCE

The major directions of public policy in America are determined by a relatively small group of like-minded individuals interacting among themselves and reflecting their own values and preferences in policy making. (By contrast, the pluralist model of the policy process portrays public policy as the product of competition, bargaining, and compromise among many diverse groups in society. Interest groups are viewed as the

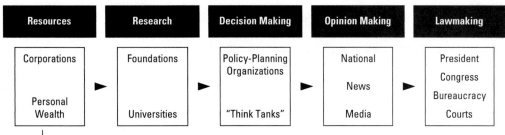

FIGURE 4.3 | AN ELITIST MODEL OF THE PUBLIC POLICY-MAKING PROCESS*

*For a more detailed model, see Thomas R. Dye, *Who's Running America? The Bush Restoration* (Upper Saddle River, N.J.: Prentice Hall, 2002), p. 173

principal actors in the policy-making process—the essential bridges between individuals and government. Public policy, according to the pluralists, reflects an equilibrium of the relative influence of interest groups.)

Brookings Institution
Washington's most influential think tank, responsible for many significant policy initiatives.
www.brookings.org

The elite model of the public policy-making process is presented in Figure 4.3. The model suggests that the initial resources for research, study, planning, and formulation of national policy are derived from corporate and personal wealth. This wealth is channeled into foundations, universities, and policy-planning groups in the form of endowments, grants, and contracts. Moreover, corporate presidents, directors, and top wealthholders also sit on the governing boards of the foundations, universities, and policy-planning groups to oversee the spending of their funds. In short, corporate and personal wealth provide both the financial resources and the overall direction of policy research, planning, and development.

THE FOUNDATIONS

The foundations provide a link between wealth and the intellectual community. They provide the initial "seed money" to identify social problems, to determine national priorities, and to investigate new policy directions. Universities must respond to the policy interests of foundations, and of course they also try to convince foundations of new and promising policy directions. But research proposals originating from universities that do not fit the "emphasis" of foundations are usually lost in the shuffle of papers. Although university intellectuals working independently occasionally have an impact on the policy-making process, on the whole, intellectuals respond to policy directions set by the foundations, corporations, and government agencies that underwrite the costs of research.

THE THINK TANKS

Heritage Foundation
Conservative think tank influential in Republican policy initiatives.
www.heritage.org

The *policy-planning groups,* or think tanks, are the central coordinating points in the policy-making process. They review the relevant university and foundation-supported research on topics of interest, with the goal of developing *policy recommendations*—explicit programs designed to resolve or ameliorate national

FOCUS | GREEN IN THE BOARDROOM

There is abundant evidence that the corporate managers put *personal motives*—especially their own pay, benefits, and perquisites—above the interests of the corporation and its stockholders. The pay of chief executive officers (CEOs) of the largest corporations has mushroomed in recent years, as has the pay of corporate directors. The average CEO in the largest corporations in 2005 took home nearly $12 million in pay and benefits.[a] According to business professor Edward E. Lawler, "It just seems to get more absurd each year. What is outrageous one year becomes a standard for the next. And no one is in a position to say no."[b]

Boards of directors are supposed to oversee top executive pay and protect stockholders, but CEOs generally win approval for their own salaries from compliant directors.

The pay gap in the United States between corporate chieftains and average factory workers has increased dramatically over the last few decades.

In the early 1980s, the median pay package (pay, benefits, and perquisites) of a corporate CEO was approximately fifty times greater than the pay of the average factory worker. By 2000 that gap had become a chasm, with the median CEO earning 525 times the pay of the average factory worker. This gap declined slightly in 2005 to 411 times the pay of the average worker. (In Japan, by contrast, the average CEO receives only seventeen times the pay of an ordinary worker.) It is difficult to explain to workers, whose average real hourly earnings have stagnated steadily since 1970, why the pay packages of top corporate (and governmental) leaders have sky-rocketed.

---

[a]AFL-CIO *Executive Paywatch*. Available online at www.aflcio.org.

[b]Quoted by Thomas A. Stewart, "The King Is Dead," *Fortune* (January 11, 1993), p. 34.

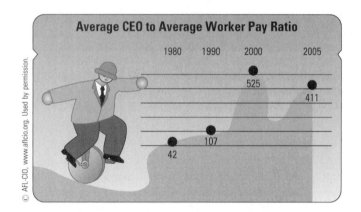

Average CEO to Average Worker Pay Ratio

© AFL-CIO, www.aflcio.org. Used by permission.

	1980	1990	2000	2005
	42	107	525	411

Council on Foreign Relations
Most influential elite foreign policy organization, developing, discussing, and publishing in *Foreign Affairs* policy prescriptions.
www.cfr.org

problems. At the same time, they endeavor to build consensus among corporate, financial, media, civic, intellectual, and government leaders around major policy directions. Certain policy-planning groups—notably the Council on Foreign Relations, the American Enterprise Institute, the Heritage Foundation, and the Brookings Institution—are influential in a wide range of key policy areas (see Focus: The Elite Think Tanks).

| ## HOW ELITES MAKE POLICY

- Public policy in America primarily reflects the values and preferences of the elite.
- The initial resources for research, planning, and formulation of national policy come from corporate and personal wealth. This wealth is channeled into universities and policy planning organizations; corporate directors and wealth holders serve on the boards of directors of these organizations.
- The foundations provide the initial seed money to identify social problems, determine national priorities, and investigate policy directions. Universities respond to the availability of grants from foundations.
- The policy-planning organizations, or "think tanks," are central coordinating points in the policy-making process. They undertake their own research, as well as review relevant university- and foundation-supported research, with the goal of developing policy recommendations. They also endeavor to build consensus among corporate, financial, media, civic, intellectual, and government elites around major policy directions.
- Media elites set the agenda for policy making by allocating valuable network broadcast time to what they define as societal "problems." The media frequently base their broadcasts on university and think tank research and recommendations.
- The White House, congressional committees, and top executives maintain contact with think tanks, and must respond to the issues presented them by the media. Thus, the groundwork is laid for making policy into law.

THE MEDIA

American Enterprise Institute
Think tank influential in moderate Republican and Democratic circles.
www.aei.org

Policy recommendations of the leading policy-planning groups are distributed to the mass media, federal executive agencies, and Congress. The mass media play a vital role in preparing public opinion for policy change. The media define the "problem" as a problem and thus set the agenda for policy making. They also encourage politicians to assume new policy stances by allocating valuable network broadcast time to those who will speak out in favor of new policy directions.

THE WASHINGTON INSIDERS

The White House staff, congressional committee staffs, and top executive administrators usually maintain close contact with policy-planning groups. Often these groups help prepare legislation for Congress to implement policy decisions. Particular versions of bills will pass between executive agencies, the White House, policy-planning groups, and the professional staffs of the congressional committees that eventually will consider the bills. Thus groundwork is laid for making policy into law.

POWER IN AMERICA: AN ELITIST INTERPRETATION

Power in the United States is organized into large institutions, private as well as public: corporations, banks and financial institutions, universities, law firms, religious institutions, professional associations, and military and government bureaucracies.

FOCUS	THE ELITE THINK TANKS

The nation's private policy-planning organizations, popularly referred to as think tanks, compose the center of our elitist model of national policy making. There are a host of think tanks in Washington, but among the generally recognized elite organizations are the Brookings Institution, the American Enterprise Institute, and the Heritage Foundation. The leading think tank in the fields of foreign affairs, national security, and international trade is the Council on Foreign Relations, together with its multinational arm, the Trilateral Commission.[a]

The Brookings Institution

This organization has long been the dominant policy-planning group for American domestic policy, despite the growth of other think tanks over the years. Brookings has been described as the central locus of the Washington "policy network."[b] The Brookings Institution was started early in the twentieth century with grants from Robert Brookings, a wealthy St. Louis merchant; Andrew Carnegie, head of U.S. Steel (now USX); John D. Rockefeller, founder of the Standard Oil Company (now Exxon); and Robert Eastman, founder of Kodak Corporation. Its early recommendations for economy and efficiency in government led to the Budget and Accounting Act of 1921, which established the annual unified federal budget. (Before 1921, each department submitted separate budget requests to Congress.) In the 1960s, the Brookings Institution, with grants from the Ford Foundation, helped design the war on poverty. Brookings staffers were influential in developing Clinton's comprehensive, but unsuccessful, health care package, and Brookings economists long pushed for the North American Free Trade Agreement.

The American Enterprise Institute

For many years, Republicans dreamed of a "Brookings Institution for Republicans" that would help offset the liberal bias of Brookings. In the late 1970s, that role was assumed by the American Enterprise Institute (AEI). The AEI attracted many distinguished "neoconservative" scholars who were beginning to have doubts about big government. Their work was influential in shaping Reagan administration efforts in deregulation, tax reduction, and anti-inflationary monetary policy. Today the AEI harbors both moderate Republicans and progrowth "new" Democrats.

Policy work by AEI scholars laid the groundwork for the Welfare Reform Act of 1996. This work convinced many Democrats as well as Republicans in Congress that federal welfare entitlement programs, notably Aid to Families with Dependent Children, were contributing to family breakdown and welfare dependency. Welfare reform generally followed AEI-sponsored recommendations to eliminate the federal entitlement to cash aid, return welfare policy making to the states, set limits on the length of time that people could be on welfare, and require teenage mothers to stay with their parents and in school as a condition of receiving cash aid.

The Heritage Foundation

Conservatives gradually came to understand that without an institutional base in the capital city they could never establish a strong and continuing influence in the policy network. The result of their efforts to build a "solid institutional base" and establish "a reputation for reliable scholarship and creative problem solving" is the Heritage Foundation. The initial funding came from Colorado businessman—brewer Joseph Coors, who was later joined by two drugstore magnates, Jack Eckerd of Florida and Lewis I. Lehrman of New York. Heritage boasts that it accepts no government grants or contracts and that it has a larger number of individual contributors than any other think tank. Heritage is "unabashedly conservative," but there are no specific policy initiatives that can be traced to Heritage. President Ronald Reagan once hailed the foundation as changing "the intellectual history of the West" and testified to its "enormous influence on Capitol Hill—and believe me, I know—at the White House."[c]

The Heritage Foundation "is committed to rolling back the liberal welfare state and building an America where freedom, opportunity, and civil society flourish."[d]

Heritage has addressed many of the "hot-button" conservative issues: abortion, racial preferences in affirmative action programs, public vouchers for pupils to attend private religious schools, and religion and morality in public life.

---

[a]The Council on Foreign Relations is described in Chapter 16.

[b]Leonard Silk and Mark Silk, *The American Establishment* (New York: Basic Books, 1980), p. 160.

[c]Heritage Foundation, *Annual Report* (1985), p. 1.

[d]Heritage Foundation, *Mission Statement*, 2000.

This chapter develops several propositions in analyzing power and the institutional structure of the United States:

1. The corporate structure of American society concentrates great authority in a relatively small number of positions. 500 of the largest industrial corporations receive over 50 percent of the nation's industrial revenues, and the ten largest banks control nearly half of the nation's banking assets.

2. Top corporate management wields corporate power rather than the mass of employees or individual stockholders. Only occasionally do large institutional investors, such as pension funds, investment firms, banks, and insurance companies, challenge top management.

3. There is ample evidence of excessive greed in corporate boardrooms, especially in the pay, benefits, and perquisites of top managers. The average CEO of a large corporation earns over 400 times the pay of an average factory worker.

4. Despite democratic rhetoric, American elites doubt that the masses of people have the knowledge or judgment to make wise decisions about public affairs.

5. Public policy reflects the preferences and values of the elites. Elites may consider the welfare of the masses in policy making, but it is the elites, not the masses, who make policy.

6. The initial resources for policy planning are derived from corporations and personal wealth. These resources are channeled through foundations and universities in the form of grants, contracts, and endowments. The elite policy-planning organizations, such as the Brookings Institution, the American Enterprise Institute, and the Council on Foreign Relations, play a central role in preparing policy recommendations and developing policy consensus among corporate, governmental, and media elites.

SELECTED READINGS

Domhoff, G. William. *Who Rules America?* Englewood Cliffs, N.J.: Prentice-Hall, Spectrum Books, 1967; *The Higher Circles.* New York: Random House, Vintage Books edition, 1970; *Who Rules America Now?* Englewood Cliffs, N.J.: Prentice-Hall, 1983. In these books, Domhoff argues that there is a governing class in the United States. By the term *governing class,* he means the part of the national upper class that holds positions of power in the federal government and industry and their upper-middle-class hired executives. He spends a great deal of time in these books developing the notion of class indicators. In *Who Rules America?* he examines elite control of the federal government; in *Higher Circles* he develops in detail the role of private planning organizations in the formation of foreign and domestic policy; and in *Who Rules America Now?* he revises and updates his theory of upper-class American life.

Dye, Thomas R. *Top Down Policymaking.* New York: Chatham House Publishers, 2001. An elitist view of national policy making, arguing that public policy is made from the top down, not from the bottom up. It describes how policy agenda flows downward from elites to government through a network of foundations, "think tanks," policy-planning organizations, interest groups, campaign finance contributors, and the media.

Dye, Thomas R. *Who's Running America?* 7th ed. Upper Saddle River, N.J.: Prentice-Hall, 2002. This book studies 5,000 top institutional leaders in industry, banking, utilities, government, the media, foundations, universities, and civic and cultural organizations. The book names names, studies concentration of power and interlocking

at the top, examines recruitment and social backgrounds, discusses elite values, examines cohesion
and competition among leaders, and outlines the
elite policy-making process.

Halberstam, David. *The Best and the Brightest.* New
York: Random House, 1973. This book assesses
the men who advised presidents Kennedy and
Johnson on conduct of the war in Vietnam. Based
on interviews conducted by the author, a former
New York Times Vietnam correspondent, the
book reveals an excellent view of the men and
processes responsible for decision making at the
highest levels of the federal executive branch.

Lasch, Christopher. *The Revolt of the Elites.* New
York: W. W. Norton, 1998. Lasch believes that
the decline of public-regarding elites is a greater

threat to democracy than a mass revolt led by
demagogues (counterelites; see Chapter 5). He is
therefore in accord with our premise that elites
have squandered their positions of trust.

Mills, C. Wright. *The Power Elite.* New York:
Oxford University Press, 1956. This book is a
classic of elite literature. Mills takes an institutional approach to roles within an "institutional
landscape." Three institutions—the big corporations, the political executive, and the military—
are of great importance. The individuals who fill
the positions within these institutions form a
power elite. These higher circles share social
attributes (such as similar lifestyles, preparatory
schools, and clubs) as well as positions of power.
Thus Mills's power elite is relatively unified.

NOTES

1. C. Wright Mills, *The Power Elite* (New York:
Oxford University Press, 1956), pp. 10–11.

2. Even the leading pluralist scholars have revised
their views about corporate power in the United
States. For many years pluralist political scientists,
notably Yale University's Robert A. Dahl and
Charles E. Lindblom, argued that no single interest group, including "business," dominated American politics. But later Dahl and Lindblom
publicly confessed their "error": *In our discussion
of pluralism we made another error—and it is a
continuing error in social science—in regarding
business and business groups as playing the same
interest group role as the other groups in polyarchal systems, though more powerful. Businessmen*

*play a distinctive role in polyarchal politics that is
qualitatively different from that of any interest
group. It is also much more powerful than an
interest group role.*
Robert A. Dahl and Charles E. Lindblom, *Politics
and Economic Welfare,* 2nd ed. (Chicago: University of Chicago Press, 1976). See preface.

3. Christopher Lasch, *The Revolt of the Elites* (New
York: W. W. Norton, 1995), p. 6.

4. John Kenneth Galbraith, *The New Industrial
State* (Boston: Houghton Mifflin, 1967), p. 323.

5. Leonard Silk and Mark Silk, *The American Establishment* (New York: Basic Books, 1980),
p. 20.

Let us transport ourselves into a hypothetical country that, in a democratic way, practices the persecution of Christians, the burning of witches, and the slaughtering of Jews. We should certainly not approve of these practices on the ground that they have been decided on according to the rules of democratic procedure.

Joseph Schumpeter

MASSES IN AMERICA

Democratic government envisions an active, informed, participating citizenry. It also envisions a citizenry committed to democratic values—liberty and equality, freedom of speech and the press, tolerance of diversity, and due process of law. And perhaps most important, democracy envisions a people who believe in equality of opportunity—that is, people who believe that they or their children have a reasonable opportunity to improve their lives if they study and work hard, save and invest wisely, and display initiative and enterprise. The United States describes itself as the "land of opportunity." The promise of upward mobility and the absence of an extreme difference between rich and poor diminish class consciousness—that is, an awareness of one's class position and a motive for class conflict.

But despite a robust economy, the masses in America—especially unskilled and semiskilled workers—have seen their average hourly wages stagnate over time. The nation's labor force has been *de*unionized. Despite mass opposition, immigration, both legal and illegal, has skyrocketed. More important, inequality in America is increasing. Differences between rich and poor in both income and wealth are growing. These disturbing trends are largely a product of elite support for the globalization of trade. Elites in America benefit directly from the expansion of international trade, the globalization of capital markets, and worldwide competition among workers for jobs.

Most Americans are ignorant of public affairs and apathetic about politics. Although they may voice superficial agreement with abstract statements of democratic values, they do not translate these values into specific attitudes or behaviors, especially toward people and ideas that they despise. The real question is how democracy and individual freedom can survive in a society where the masses give only limited support to these values.

ELITE GAINS, MASS LOSSES

The U.S. economy performs very well, but the benefits from that performance are unevenly distributed. The global economy produces growth and profit for America's largest corporations and amply rewards the nation's highest-skilled workers. Indeed, global trade *raises aggregate income* for the nation. But at the same time, it contributes to a *decline in average hourly earnings* of American workers and *worsened inequality* in America. Elite gains are accompanied by mass losses.

STAGNATING WORKER EARNINGS

Average hourly and weekly earnings of American workers have stagnated over the past three decades (see Figure 5.1). In real 1982 dollars (controlling for the effects of inflation), average hourly earnings declined from $8.40 in 1970 to $7.50 in 1995. The prosperous 1990s brought a modest recovery in worker earnings. But real worker wages are still below what they were thirty-five years ago.

Stagnating real wages in the United States have been obscured by the fact that median family income has been rising. In 1970, median family income was $38,123 (in constant 2005 dollars); by 2005, this figure had risen to $46,326.[1] But *family income rose because more family members entered the workforce*, not because workers were paid more. Workforce participation among married women rose from 40 percent in

Bureau of Labor Statistics
Official source of information on income, wages, employment, and other economic data.
www.bls.gov

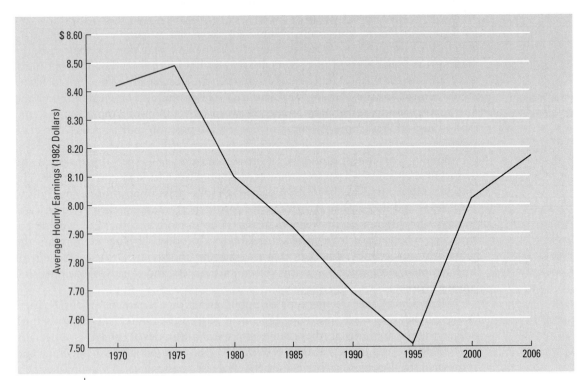

FIGURE 5.1 | WORKER'S AVERAGE HOURLY EARNINGS

Source: U.S. Bureau of Labour Statistics (www.bls.gov).

1970 to 70 percent in 2005.[2] In short, American families raised their incomes despite lower hourly wages simply by having more family members go to work.

This stagnation in the earnings of American workers, especially the less skilled, has occurred simultaneously with the growth of international trade. Although this coincidence does not prove that trade is causing earnings to stagnate or decline, it raises a question: In a global economy, is the huge supply of unskilled labor pushing down the wages of American workers? Increased trade, especially with less developed economies such as Mexico, China, and India, with their huge numbers of low-wage workers, creates competition for American workers. It is difficult to maintain the wage levels of American jobs, especially in labor intensive industries, in the face of such competition. Moreover, it is not uncommon for U.S. corporations to move their manufacturing plants to low-wage countries, especially to northern Mexico, where the transportation costs of moving finished products back to the U.S. market are minimal.

CAPITAL MOBILITY

The global economy encourages the unrestricted movement of investment capital across borders. Large investors—banks, investment firms, corporations, mutual funds—regularly transfer assets from New York to London to Tokyo to Hong Kong to Singapore and to other financial centers around the world. Communications technology has greatly accelerated multinational capital flows in recent years. This allows companies to buy products and build factories ("outsourcing") where they can take advantage of cheaper unskilled and semiskilled labor.

"Human Resources."

DEUNIONIZATION

Fifty years ago, American unions were a significant force in determining workers' wages, especially in manufacturing. Industrial unions, such as the United Steel Workers, United Automobile Workers, and United Mine Workers, set wage rates that influenced the entire national wage structure. Nearly 40 percent of the nation's labor force was unionized.

Today about 13 percent of the nation's labor force is unionized (see Figure 5.2). The major industrial unions have shrunk in membership; only unions of government employees (American Federation of State, County, and Municipal employees), teachers (National Education Association), and some transportation and service workers (International Brotherhood of Teamsters) have gained members in recent years.

AFL-CIO
Information from union federation on workers' wages and executives' salaries.
www.aflcio.org

The AFL-CIO (American Federation of Labor–Congress of Industrial Organizations) is a federation of national unions. Today the AFL-CIO and its members appear to devote more attention to Washington lobbying than to negotiating wage contracts with employers. Indeed, union wage demands have been modest in recent years and nationwide strikes rare.

Deunionization is largely a product of the globalization of the economy. Employers can move, or threaten to move, their factories outside the country in response to union demands. Or they can replace striking union members with nonunion workers.

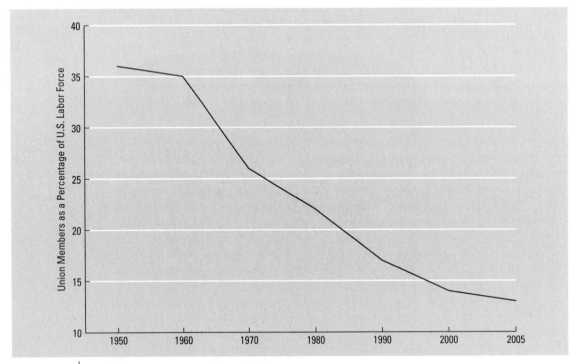

FIGURE 5.2 | DEUNIONIZATION

Source: Data derived from www.aflcio.org.

Heavy immigration into the United States maintains a large pool of available low-wage workers.

ELITE–MASS DIFFERENCES OVER IMMIGRATION

The United States accepts more immigrants than all other nations of the world combined (see Figure 5.3). The vast majority of immigrants in recent years have come from the less-developed nations of Asia (43 percent) and Latin America (47 percent). Most immigrants come to the United States for economic opportunity. Most personify the traits we typically think of as American: opportunism, ambition, perseverance, initiative, and a willingness to work hard. As immigrants have always done, they frequently take dirty, low-paying, thankless jobs that other Americans shun.

Elites, notably the nation's business and corporate leaders, tend to support immigration, in order to increase the supply of low-wage workers in the United States. But mass support for immigration is lacking, especially after the terrorist attack of September 11, 2001.

Center for Immigration Studies
Information on legal and illegal immigration and its effects.
www.cis.org

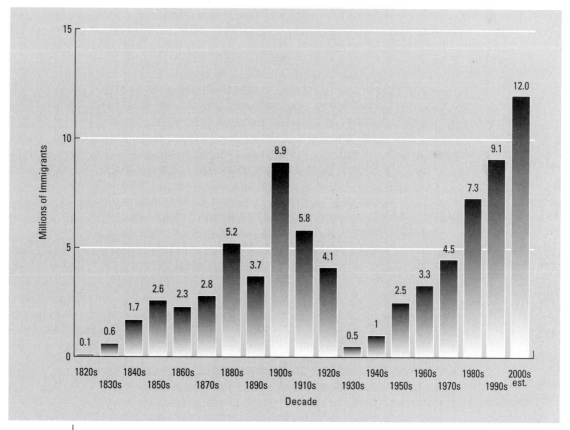

FIGURE 5.3   IMMIGRATION TO THE UNITED STATES

Source: *Statistical Abstract of the United States,* 2006, p. 9. Estimate for 2000s based on 4 million immigrants in 2001–2004.

QUESTION: *In your view, should immigration be kept at its present level, increased, or decreased?*

Present level	42	30	36	37	33	31	32
Increased	14	8	12	14	14	15	17
Decreased	41	58	49	47	49	51	49
	June 2001	Oct 2001	June 2002	June 2003	June 2004	June 2005	June 2006

And when asked what should be done about current levels of immigration into the United States, nearly half of Americans say that they should be decreased, whereas only about one-third want them kept at current levels. Very few say they should be increased.[3]

Most Americans agree that immigrants make valuable contributions—that they "are productive citizens once they get their feet on the ground" (63 percent), "are hard-working" (58 percent), and "are basically good honest people" (55 percent). However, majorities also believe that immigrants "are a burden on taxpayers" (66 percent), "take jobs from Americans" (58 percent), and "add to the crime problem" (56 percent).[4]

ILLEGAL IMMIGRATION

Estimates of illegal immigration vary widely, from the official U.S. Immigration and Customs Enforcement (ICE) estimate of 400,000 per year (about 40 percent of the legal immigration) to unofficial estimates ranging up to three million per year. The ICE estimates that about four million illegal immigrants currently reside in the United States; unofficial estimates range up to twelve million or more. Many illegal immigrants slip across U.S. borders or enter ports with false documentation, and many more overstay tourist or student visas (and are not counted by the ICE as illegal immigrants).

As a free society, the United States is not prepared to undertake massive roundups and summary deportations of millions of illegal residents. The Fifth and Fourteenth Amendments to the U.S. Constitution require that every *person* (not just citizens) be afforded "due process of law." ICE may turn back people at the border or even hold them in detention camps. The Coast Guard may intercept boats at sea and return the occupants to their country of origin.[5] Aliens have no constitutional right to come to the United States. However, *once in the United States, whether legally or illegally, every person is entitled to due process of law and equal protection of the laws*. People are entitled to a fair hearing before any government attempt to deport them. Aliens are entitled to apply for asylum and to present evidence at a hearing of their "well-founded fear of prosecution" if returned to their country.

ELITE SUPPORT FOR IMMIGRATION

Powerful industry groups that benefit from the availability of legal and illegal immigrants have led the fight in Washington to keep America's doors open. They have fought not only to expand legal immigration but also to weaken enforcement of laws against illegal immigration.

Current U.S. immigration policy—the admission of more than one million *legal* immigrants per year and weak enforcement of laws against *illegal* immigration—is largely driven by industry groups seeking to lower their labor costs. Agriculture, restaurants, the clothing industry, manufacturers, and hospitals, for example, all lobby heavily in Washington to weaken immigration laws and their enforcement. Large agribusinesses benefit from a heavy flow of unskilled immigrants who harvest their crops at very low wages. Meat and poultry processing plants depend heavily on illegal alien labor. Clothing, textile, and shoe companies that have not already moved their manufacturing overseas are eager to hire low-paid immigrants for their assembly lines. Even high-tech companies have found that they can recruit skilled computer analysts and data processors from English-speaking developing nations (India, for example) for wages well below those paid to American citizens with similar skills. These business interests frequently operate behind the scenes in Washington, allowing pro-immigration ethnic and religious groups to capture media attention. And indeed, large numbers of Americans identify with the aspirations of people striving to come to the United States, whether legally or illegally. Many Americans still have family and relatives living abroad who may wish to immigrate. Hispanic groups have been especially concerned about immigration enforcement efforts that may lead to discrimination against all Hispanic Americans.

Conflict over Immigration Policy

Political elites are caught in a dilemma. The masses strongly oppose increased immigration, legal or illegal. Business interests support increased immigration, and as the Hispanic population increases in the United States (currently more than 14 percent of the population), a political base arises in support of immigration. So far, elites have followed an uncomfortable policy of doing nothing to control immigration and overlooking the millions of illegal immigrants who pour into the United States each year.

Conflict in Washington over immigration policy is intense. To date, this conflict has prevented any effective action to halt illegal immigration, or to determine the status of millions of illegal immigrants currently living in the United States, or to decide how many aliens should be admitted each year and what the criteria for their admission should be. Congress and President George W. Bush wrestled with these questions in a comprehensive 789-page bill in 2007. The bill tried to compromise diverse interests—employers seeking to keep immigration as open as possible, millions of illegal immigrants seeking a legal path to citizenship, citizens seeking border security and opposed any form of amnesty for illegal aliens. The bill's major provisions included: strengthening border enforcement, including funding of 700 miles of fencing along the 2,000-mile Mexican border; granting legal status to millions of undocumented immigrants currently living in the country; providing a path to citizenship that included criminal background checks, paying fines and fees, and acquiring English proficiency; establishing a temporary (two-year) guest worker program; and shifting the criteria for legal immigration from family-based preferences to a greater emphasis on skills and education. Opponents of one or another of these various provisions, both Democrats and Republicans, united to defeat the bill in the U.S. Senate.

INEQUALITY IN AMERICA

Income inequality is and has always been a significant component of the American social structure. The top one-fifth (20 percent) of income recipients in the United States receives nearly 48 percent of all income in the nation, and the bottom fifth receives only about 4 percent (see Table 5.1). Historically, the income share of the top fifth declined since the pre–World War II years. But inequality has risen dramatically since 1970.

Various theories have been put forward to explain why inequality has worsened: the decline of the manufacturing sector of the economy with its relatively high-paying blue-collar jobs; a rise in the number of two-wage families, making single-wage households relatively less affluent; and demographic trends, which include larger proportions of older Americans and larger proportions of female heads of households.

But the globalization of trade is emerging as the principal cause of increasing inequality in America. Americans are now competing economically with peoples around the world. Our unskilled and semiskilled workers are obliged to compete with very-low-wage workers in developing nations, from China, Taiwan, South Korea, Mexico, and the Caribbean. In contrast, our highly skilled workers, entrepreneurs, executives, and investors are well positioned to gain from trade. The result is that inequality worsens even though the aggregate income of the nation rises.

INEQUALITY OF WEALTH

Wealth is even more unequally distributed than income. (Wealth is the total value of a person's assets—bank accounts, stocks, bonds, mutual funds, business equity, houses, properties, etc.—minus debts, mortgages, and unpaid bills.) Millionaires in America

TABLE 5.1 | DISTRIBUTION OF FAMILY INCOME IN THE UNITED STATES

Quintiles*	Percentage of Total Income Received								
	1929	1936	1950	1962	1972	1980	1990	1995	2005
Lowest	3.5	4.1	4.8	4.6	5.5	5.2	4.6	4.4	4.1
Second	9.0	9.2	10.9	10.9	12.0	11.6	10.8	10.1	9.6
Third	13.8	14.1	16.1	16.3	17.4	17.5	16.6	15.8	15.5
Fourth	19.3	20.9	22.1	22.7	23.5	24.2	23.8	23.2	23.2
Highest	54.4	51.7	46.1	45.5	41.6	41.5	44.3	46.5	47.6
Total	100.0	100.0	100.0	100.0	100.0	100.0	100.0	100.0	100.0
Top 5 percent	30.0	24.0	21.4	19.6	14.4	15.7	17.4	20.0	20.5

*Each quintile is 20 percent of the population.

Source: *Statistical Abstract of the United States,* 2006, p. 464.

TABLE 5.2 | TOP TEN WEALTHHOLDERS, 2006

William H. Gates Jr.	Microsoft
Warren E. Buffet	Berkshire Hathaway
Sheldon Adelson	Casinos, hotels
Lawrence T. Ellison	Oracle
Paul G. Allen	Microsoft
Christy Walton	Wal-Mart Inheritance
S. Robson Walton	Wal-Mart inheritance
Michael Dell	Dell
Alice L. Walton	Wal-Mart Inheritance

are no longer considered rich. To be truly rich today, one must be worth $1 *billion*. Most of the nation's wealthy are reluctant to reveal their net worth; thus any listing is only an estimate. *Forbes* magazine lists 400 *billionaires* in the United States.[6] (See Table 5.2.)

The top 1 percent of families in the United States currently owns about 40 percent of all family wealth.[7] Moreover, inequality of wealth has worsened in recent years. Harvard economist Richard B. Freeman summarizes these distressing views:

> *An economic disaster has befallen low-skilled Americans, especially young men. Researchers using several data sources—including household survey data from the Current Population Survey, other household surveys, and establishment surveys—have documented that wage inequality and skill differentials in earnings and employment increased sharply in the United States from the mid-1970s through the 1980s and into the 1990s. The drop in the relative position of the less skilled shows up in a number of ways: greater earnings differentials between those with more and less education; greater earnings differentials between older and younger workers; greater differentials between high-skilled and low-skilled occupations; in a wider earnings distribution overall and within demographic and skill groups; and in less time worked by low-skill and low-paid workers.*[8]

MASS DISAFFECTION FROM POLITICS

Distrust and cynicism characterize mass attitudes toward government and politics. Surveys of American public opinion since the 1960s have shown dramatic increases in public disdain of politics and politicians: "Public officials don't care what people like me think!" "Government is run by a few big interests looking out for themselves!" "Quite a few government officials are crooked!" (See Figure 5.4.)

The rise in mass cynicism and the decline in mass trust of government deeply concerns American elites. Their concerns are that if the trust of the masses in government is weakened, "citizens may become less likely to comply with the laws, to support government programs through taxes, and to enter government service. Without those critical resources, government will be unable to perform well, and

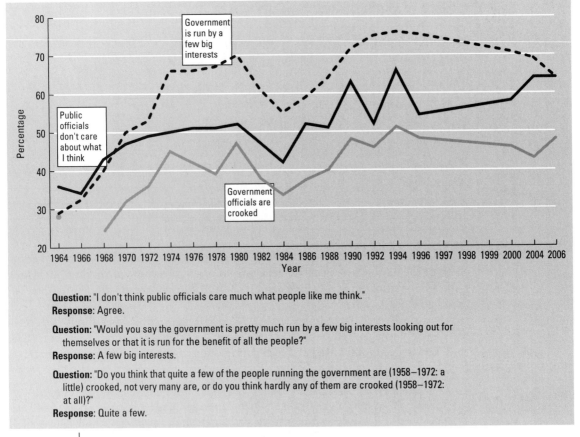

Question: "I don't think public officials care much what people like me think."
Response: Agree.

Question: "Would you say the government is pretty much run by a few big interests looking out for themselves or that it is run for the benefit of all the people?"
Response: A few big interests.

Question: "Do you think that quite a few of the people running the government are (1958–1972: a little) crooked, not very many are, or do you think hardly any of them are crooked (1958–1972: at all)?"
Response: Quite a few.

FIGURE 5.4 │ MASS DISAFFECTION FROM POLITICS

Source: National Election Studies to 2000; The Polling Report for 2004, 2006.

Polling Report
Source for trends in mass opinion, including data from a variety of current polls.
www.pollingreport.com

people will become even more disaffected—a dangerous downward spiral that can weaken democratic institutions."[9]

Studies frequently argue that the underlying causes of declining confidence are complex. While acknowledging that elite actions themselves—notably the Vietnam War and the Watergate scandal—were influential in causing mass disaffection, these studies point to several other underlying factors. First, they bemoan a long-term trend toward disrespect of authority (as elites throughout the ages have done). Second, they acknowledge that globalization of the economy involves some "creative destruction"—disruption of the lives of many people and a resulting insecurity that is blamed on government. Third, they contend that changes in the political process—the decline in allegiance to political parties, the increased role of television in political campaigns, the professionalization of politics—make average citizens feel that they have less control over their elected representatives. Finally, some elite studies have also acknowledged the effect of negative media reporting on popular attitudes toward government and politics.[10]

IN BRIEF

CONDITIONS AFFECTING THE MASSES

- Average worker earnings have stagnated over time. Family income has risen only because more family members have gone to work.
- Legal and illegal immigration has reached an all-time high. Elites support immigration as a source of low-cost labor.
- Inequality of income has increased over time, with the lowest 20 percent receiving only

about 4 percent of the nation's total income, and the highest 20 percent receiving nearly 50 percent.

- Mass distrust and cynicism toward government has grown over the years. Only in crisis periods do the masses "rally 'round the flag."

Although the masses continue to distrust elites, there are signs that hostility toward government has begun to diminish. Several factors combine to counter mass dissatisfaction with government. First of all, a strong economy reduces mass distrust and cynicism. The prosperity of recent years appears to have moderated mass dissatisfaction with elites. Second, it is clear that the masses continue to want government to play a significant role in many different areas of life:

QUESTION: *It should be the responsibility of the federal government to:*

Guarantee national security	91%
Ensure health standards	70%
Ensure fair treatment of women and minorities	67%
Protect the natural environment	65%
Finance health care	63%
Ensure that the poorest Americans have enough to eat	58%

Source: Pew Center for the People and the Press, *Deconstructing Distrust: How Americans View Government* (Philadelphia, PA: Pew Center, 2000).

Finally, Americans are very patriotic, more so than the citizens of most other nations. Mass opinion remains very positive toward the constitutional framework of American government, even though it is critical of the people who run it. The attack on the United States on September 11, 2001, united the masses behind the elites as no other event in American history, except, perhaps, the attack on Pearl Harbor in 1941. Americans are quick to "rally 'round the flag."

The American people are quick to unite behind their leadership when attacked from foreign soil. This was as true following the Japanese attack on Pearl Harbor as it was sixty years later with the terrorist attack in 2001. Not only does mass support for the nation's leadership skyrocket, but also the masses are quite willing to grant new powers to the elites to achieve security. Indeed, mass support for civil liberties almost disappears in times of national crisis.

ANTIDEMOCRATIC ATTITUDES AMONG THE MASSES

The masses give only superficial support to fundamental democratic values—freedom of speech and the press and due process of law. People *say* they believe in those values when they are expressed as abstract principles; for example, they answer yes to the question "Do you believe in freedom of speech for everyone?" However, the public is unable or unwilling to apply the principles to specific situations, especially situations involving despised or obnoxious groups or individuals. In contrast, elites and the well-educated groups from which they are recruited are much more willing than the masses to apply democratic values in specific situations and to protect the freedoms of unpopular groups.

After years of studying the differences between the elites and masses in their attitudes toward freedom, political scientists Herbert McClosky and Alida Brill reached the following conclusions regarding the *masses* in the United States:

> *If one judges by the responses of the mass public to survey questions, one has little reason to expect that the population as a whole will display a sensitive understanding of the constitutional norms that govern the free exercise of speech and publication. Only a minority of the mass public fully appreciate why freedom of speech and press should be granted to dissenters and to others who challenge conventional opinion.*[11]

In contrast, these scholars are much more optimistic regarding freedom and tolerance among *elites:*

> *Insofar as these matters are better understood and more firmly believed by those who, in one role or another, help to govern the society, one is tempted to conclude that, owing to the vagaries of the social process, the protection of First Amendment rights rests principally upon the very groups the Amendment was mainly designed to control—the courts, the legislature, political leaders, and the opinion elites of the society.*[12]

Differences between elites and masses in support of democratic values are illustrated in Table 5.3. These questions were asked of a national sample of community leaders (the press, clergy, teachers, men and women in business, lawyers and judges, union officials, and leaders of voluntary organizations), as well as a national sample of the public.

SOCIAL CLASS AND DEMOCRATIC ATTITUDES

Clearly, the masses do not fully understand or support the ideas and principles on which the U.S. political system rests. We are left asking how the system survives.

The distribution of antidemocratic attitudes among various social classes may provide part of an answer. The upper social classes (from which members of the elites are largely recruited) give greater, more consistent support to democratic values than do the lower social classes. Political sociologist Seymour Martin Lipset has observed that "extremist and intolerant movements in modern society are more likely to be based on the lower classes than on the middle and upper classes."[13] Analyzing the ideologies of the lower class, Lipset notes:

> *The poorer strata everywhere are more liberal or leftist on economic issues; they favor more welfare state measures, higher wages, graduated income taxes, support of trade unions, and so forth. But when liberalism is defined in noneconomic terms—as*

TABLE 5.3 | ELITE VERSUS MASS SUPPORT OF DEMOCRATIC VALUES

	% Mass Public	% Community Leaders
Academic Freedom		
When inviting guest speakers to a college campus:		
____ students should be free to invite the ones they want to hear.	41	60
____ speakers should be screened beforehand to be sure they don't advocate dangerous or extreme ideas.	45	26
Freedom of Speech		
Should foreigners who dislike our government or criticize it be allowed to visit or stay here?		
____ yes	41	69
____ no	47	24
If a group asks to use a public building to hold a meeting denouncing the government, their request should be:		
____ granted	23	51
____ denied	57	26
Religious Freedom		
The freedom of atheists to make fun of God and religion:		
____ should be legally protected no matter who might be offended.	26	53
____ should not be allowed in a public place where religious groups gather.	53	30
Due Process of Law		
A person suspected of serious crimes:		
____ should have the right to be let out on bail.	16	31
____ should be kept safely in prison until the trial.	68	36
Homosexuality		
Should a community allow its auditorium to be used by gay liberation movements to organize for homosexual rights?		
____ yes	26	46
____ no	58	40
Complete equality for homosexuals in teaching and other public service jobs:		
____ should be protected by law.	29	49
____ may sound fair but is not really a good idea.	51	33

Note: Percentages exclude "neither," "undecided," and no response.

Source: Herberty McClosky and Alida Brill, *Dimensions of Tolerance: What Americans Believe About Civil Liberties.* Copyright © 1983 Russell Sage Foundation, 112 East 64th Street, New York, NY 10021. Reprinted with permission.

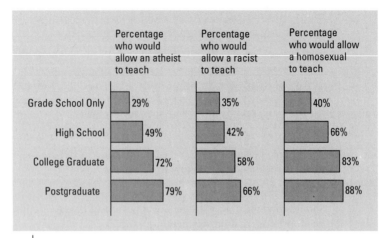

FIGURE 5.5 | EDUCATIONAL LEVELS AND TOLERANCE

Source: General Social Survey, Cumulative Index, 2000.

support of civil liberties, internationalism, and so forth—the correlation is reversed. The more well-to-do are more liberal; the poorer are more intolerant.[14]

EDUCATION AND DEMOCRATIC ATTITUDES

Public Agenda Online

Mass opinion on a variety of issues. *www. publicagenda.org*

Education is a very important factor in developing tolerance and respect for civil liberty. Clearly, Americans' level of education is related to their degree of tolerance, as is illustrated by Figure 5.5. Each increment of education adds to the respondents' willingness to allow atheists, racists, or homosexuals to teach.

Indeed, a lack of education may be more important than any other characteristic in shaping antidemocratic attitudes. Within occupational levels, higher educational status makes for greater tolerance. Increases in tolerance associated with educational level are greater than those related to occupation. No matter what the occupation, tolerance and education are strongly related.

Education also affects tolerance by influencing an individual's ability to apply an abstract principle to a concrete situation. It is one thing to agree that peaceful demonstrations are legitimate; it is quite another to allow an *unpopular* demonstration. For example, even when less-educated people agree with the general statement "People should be allowed to hold a protest demonstration to ask the government to act on some issue," only about one-third of them would allow a demonstration in favor of legalizing marijuana. But well-educated people are able to apply their abstract principles to specific situations: Among the well-educated who agree with this general statement, more than 80 percent would allow a pro-marijuana demonstration.[15]

ELITE EXPERIENCE AND DEMOCRATIC ATTITUDES

Finally, leadership experience itself may also contribute to tolerance. Although education is the most influential factor in promoting tolerance, leadership and activity in public affairs also develop tolerance. Political scientists Herbert McClosky and

Alida Brill compared mass attitudes with those of community leaders—local government officials, judges and lawyers, journalists, clergy, school administrators, and leaders of unions and civic organizations. McClosky and Brill asked a variety of questions designed to ascertain support for civil liberty. For example, they asked, "Should demonstrators be allowed to hold a mass protest march for some unpopular cause?" with possible answers being "Yes, even if most people in the community do not want it" and "No, not if the majority is against it." Among community leaders, 71 percent said yes, but among the mass public only 41 percent would allow a mass demonstration protest for an unpopular cause.[16]

Perhaps leadership activity socializes people to democratic norms; they may become more familiar with democratic values because they are active in the democratic process. Or, perhaps, their public activity exposes them to a wider variety of attitudes, opinions, and lifestyles, broadens their perspective, and generates empathy for people different from themselves.

ARE THE MASSES BECOMING MORE DEMOCRATIC?

There is some evidence suggesting that over time Americans are becoming more tolerant of different social groups. This is particularly true of groups that elites themselves have come to accept and have undertaken to instruct the masses on what should be their proper attitudes.

Consider, for example, the historic change in white mass attitudes toward school integration that occurred in the years following the historic Supreme Court decision of *Brown v. Board of Education of Topeka, Kansas*, holding that racial segregation violated the equal protection clause of the U.S. Constitution.

From 1942 to 1982, a national sample of white Americans was asked the question "Do you think white and black students should go to the same schools or separate schools?" In 1942, not one white American in three (30 percent) approved of integrated schools. In 1956, two years after the historic *Brown v. Board of Education* court decision, white attitudes had shifted markedly (49 percent approved). By 1963, two out of every three whites (67 percent) supported integrated schools, and there was a continuation of the upward trend until more than 90 percent of white Americans favored school integration by the 1980s. (Note, however, that despite increasing tolerance of integration *in principle*, white parents do not want their children to become a minority in their schools.) Additional survey information suggests that whites are becoming increasingly accommodating toward equal rights for blacks over time in other areas as well. But it should be noted that white opinion generally *follows* public policy, rather than leads it.

It is also argued that Americans are becoming more tolerant over time. For example, over time Americans have become more willing to allow "communists," "atheists," and "homosexuals" to hold meetings, make speeches, and place their books in public libraries. An optimistic interpretation is that increased education as well as increased exposure of the masses to media messages of tolerance are having a positive effect.

A more cynical interpretation is that there has been little change in "real" tolerance for unpopular groups but rather a change in *which* groups are considered particularly obnoxious. Over time, communists and atheists have become less

TABLE 5.4 | CONTINUING INTOLERANCE TOWARD DESPISED GROUPS

Statement	Percentage Agreeing
Members of the (least-liked group) should be allowed to teach in public schools.	19
The (least-liked group) should be outlawed.	29
Members of the (least-liked group) should be allowed to make a speech in this city.	50
The (least-liked group) should have their phones tapped by our government.	59
The (least-liked group) should be allowed to hold public rallies in our city.	34

Source: Data from John L. Sullivan, James Pierson, and George Marcus, *Political Tolerance and American Democracy* (Chicago: University of Chicago Press, 1982), p. 67.

threatening. But people are still willing to restrict the liberties of those they dislike, for example, racists, prochoice or anti-abortion groups, and neo-Nazis. In other words, some people who would defend the liberties of communists and atheists may be willing to deny the same liberties to racists or Nazis. "Liberty" may depend on who says what.

Indeed, "content-controlled" questions, in which respondents were first given a list of groups and asked which they liked least and then asked whether they would restrict the liberties of their "least-liked" group, revealed surprising levels of intolerance (see Table 5.4).

PUTTING CIVIL RIGHTS TO POPULAR VOTE

In states with the initiative and referendum, civil rights issues often come up for popular vote. And when they do, the restrictive, anti-civil-rights side regularly wins! Indeed, one study of seventy-four referenda votes in the states on civil rights issues—housing and public accommodation laws protecting minorities, school desegregation, protection for homosexuals, English-only laws, and protection for AIDS victims—reports anti-minority victories on more than three-fourths of the votes.[17] James Madison's concerns about "the tyranny of the majority" appear to be as well founded today as they were over 200 years ago.

MASS POLITICAL IGNORANCE

If elections are to be a means of popular control over public policy, voters must be reasonably well informed about policy issues and must hold opinions about them. Yet large numbers of the electorate are politically uninformed, have no real opinions on policy issues, and therefore respond inconsistently to policy questions.

MASS CONFIDENCE IN AMERICAN INSTITUTIONS

Mass confidence in American institutions is generally higher than mass confidence in the people who run the same institutions. Indeed, American support for the institutional structure of society is often cited as a barrier to mass attacks on institutions themselves, and even revolution.

However, mass confidence in institutions is limited. The strongest mass support among institutions is for the military. It may seem ironic that in a democratic society the military is the most popular institution. Only the military, the church, and the police garner a "great deal" or "quite a lot" of mass confidence. The following figure details responses to the statement/question:

I am going to read you a list of institutions in American society. Please tell me how much confidence you, yourself, have in each one—a great deal, quite a lot, some, or very little?

Among the branches of the national government, the Supreme Court (the only unelected branch) wins more confidence than the president or Congress. Indeed, mass confidence in the Congress is no greater than mass confidence in labor unions, big business, or electric power utilities. And only a little more than one-third of the general public expresses confidence in newspapers or television news (see Chapter 6).

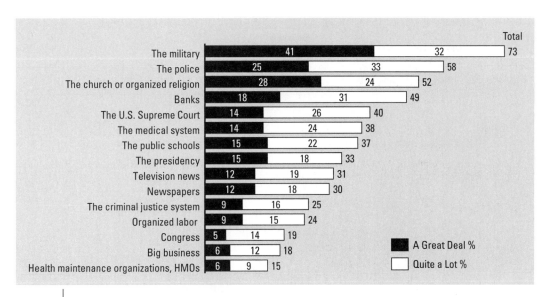

MASS CONFIDENCE IN AMERICAN INSTITUTIONS

Source: Gallup Poll, June 2006.

IGNORANCE

Public opinion surveys regularly report what is now the typical finding of a low level of political information among adult Americans (see Figure 5.6). Only about half of the public knows the elementary fact that each state has two U.S. senators; fewer still know the terms of members of Congress or the number of Supreme Court justices.

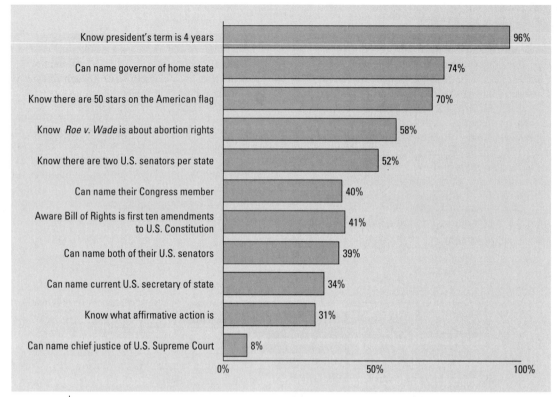

Know president's term is 4 years — 96%
Can name governor of home state — 74%
Know there are 50 stars on the American flag — 70%
Know *Roe v. Wade* is about abortion rights — 58%
Know there are two U.S. senators per state — 52%
Can name their Congress member — 40%
Aware Bill of Rights is first ten amendments to U.S. Constitution — 41%
Can name both of their U.S. senators — 39%
Can name current U.S. secretary of state — 34%
Know what affirmative action is — 31%
Can name chief justice of U.S. Supreme Court — 8%

FIGURE 5.6 | MASS POLITICAL IGNORANCE

Source: Data from Robert S. Erikson and Kent L. Tedin, *American Public Opinion,* 6th ed. (New York: Longman, 2001), p. 55, citing various polls by Gallup, Harris, National Opinion Research Center (NORC), and CBS/*New York Times.*

Although most Americans can name the president, fewer than half can name their congressional representative, and fewer still can name both of their U.S. senators. Knowledge of state and local officeholders is even worse. Elites view such political ignorance as irrational. For active and influential elites, the stakes of competition in politics are high and the cost of information is cheap; their careers, self-esteem, and prestige are directly and often daily affected by political decisions. For such elites, ignorance would be irrational.

Among the masses, however, political ignorance may be a rational stance—that is, the cost of informing oneself about politics may outweigh the benefits. Most people do not have friends in public office and do not benefit directly from the victory of one candidate or another. Moreover, because one vote among millions is only infinitesimally influential, to most people it must seem quite reasonable to remain ignorant about politics. Thus, the average citizen generally tunes out political information.

PHANTOM OPINIONS

Contradictions in mass opinion are frequently revealed in public opinion polls. Because opinion polls ask questions that are meaningless to many people, the answers are often meaningless as well. Many people have never thought about the question before it is asked and will never think about it again. Their spontaneous responses do not reflect preexisting opinion. Many respondents do not wish to appear uninformed, and therefore they offer an "opinion," even though they had never thought about the issue before the interview. Few people acknowledge they have no opinion, even when that option is provided on a survey question. Many respondents simply react to question wording, responding positively to positive phrases ("helping poor people," "improving education," "cleaning up the environment," and the like) and negatively to negative phrases (such as "raising taxes," "expanding governmental power," "restricting choice"). Many respondents succumb to a "halo effect"—giving socially approved responses to questions, regardless of their true feelings.

INCONSISTENT OPINIONS

Because so many people hold no real opinion on political issues, question wording frequently produces inconsistent responses. A study of attitudes toward pornography provides an example of inconsistent response. When respondents were asked whether they agreed that "people should have the right to purchase a sexually explicit book, magazine, or movie if that's what they want to do," an overwhelming 80 percent endorsed the statement. However, when the same respondents were also asked whether they agreed with the opposite statement that "community authorities should be able to prohibit the selling of magazines or movies they consider to be pornographic," 65 percent approved of this view as well.[18]

MASS POLITICAL APATHY

Political apathy also characterizes mass politics (see Figure 5.7). Nearly half of eligible voters in the United States stay away from the polls, even in presidential elections.* Voter turnout is lower yet in off-year congressional elections, when it falls to 35 percent of the voting-age population. City or county elections, when they are held separately from state or national elections, usually produce turnouts of 20 to 35 percent of eligible voters. Less than 1 percent of the American adult population ever run for public office. Only about 5 percent ever actively participate in parties and campaigns, and about 10 percent ever make financial contributions. About 15 percent wear political buttons or display bumper stickers. Less than 20 percent ever write their congressmember or contact any other public official. About one-third of the population belongs to organizations that could be classified as interest groups, and only a few more ever try to convince their friends to vote for a certain candidate.

---

* The 2004 presidential election produced a voter turnout of about 58 percent, the heaviest since the 1960s. Various explanations have been offered for this surge in voter participation: the expected closeness of the election, the experience of 2000 when only a few hundred votes in Florida decided the outcome, the war in Iraq, and an apparent increase in voters concerned with "moral values."

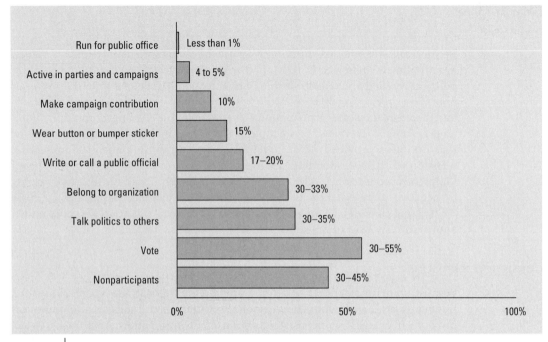

FIGURE 5.7 | MASS POLITICAL APATHY

Sustained political participation—voting consistently in election after election for state and local offices as well as Congress and the president—is rare. One study of voter participation over ten elections (including presidential, congressional, gubernatorial, and state and local legislative elections) showed that only 4 percent of the voting-age population voted in nine or all ten of the elections; only 26 percent voted in half of the ten elections; and 38 percent did not vote in any election.[19] Age is the best predictor of sustained political activity; older citizens are more likely than young people to be regular voters.

THE DANGERS OF MASS ACTIVISM

It is the irony of democracy that democratic ideals survive because the masses are generally apathetic and inactive. Thus, the capacity of the American masses for intolerance, authoritarianism, scapegoating, racism, and violence seldom translates into organized, sustained political movements.

The survival of democracy does *not* depend on mass support for democratic ideals. It is apparently not necessary that most people commit themselves to democracy; all that is necessary is that they fail to commit themselves actively to antidemocratic movements. The masses' tendency to avoid political activity makes their antidemocratic attitudes less destructive. Those with the attitudes most dangerous for democracy are the least involved in politics.

| IN BRIEF | MASS POLITICAL ATTITUDES |

- The masses give rhetorical support to democratic values, including freedom of speech, press, assembly, and religion. But when confronted with the application of these values to despised groups, the masses are willing to restrict their liberties.
- The elites are more supportive of basic liberties than the masses. In part this is a product of greater educational levels of the elites, but it is also attributable in part to the experience of leadership.
- Polls suggest that the masses have become more tolerant of minorities over time. But referenda voting in the states indicates continuing strong mass support for restrictive measures.
- Political ignorance is widespread among the masses. This may be a rational response to the belief among the masses that their opinions matter very little to elites.
- Mass political apathy results in "halo" responses to positively worded questions and negative responses to negatively worded questions in mass polling. Mass opinion is nonexistent on many issues, resulting in contradictory and inconsistent responses in mass polling.

Occasionally, however, mass apathy gives way to mass activism. Reflecting the masses' antidemocratic, extremist, hateful, and violence-prone sentiments, this activism occasionally threatens democratic values.

SOURCES OF MASS ACTIVISM

Mass activism tends to occur in crises—defeat or humiliation in war, and economic depression and unemployment. Political sociologist William Kornhauser correctly observes:

> There appears to be a close relation between the severity of crises and the extent of mass movements in Western societies. The more severe the depression in industrial societies, the greater the social atomization, and the more widespread are mass movements. . . . The stronger a country's sense of national humiliation and defeat in war, the greater the social atomization, and the greater the mass action (for example, there is a close association between military defeat and the rise of strong mass movements).[20]

Defeat in war, or even failure to achieve any notable victories in a protracted military effort, reduces mass confidence in established leadership and makes the masses vulnerable to the appeals of counterelites. Both fascism in Germany and communism in Russia followed on the heels of national humiliation and defeat in war. The antiestablishment culture of the late 1960s and early 1970s owed a great deal to the mistakes and failures of the nation's leadership in Vietnam.

Mass anxiety and vulnerability to counterelites also increase in periods of economic dislocation—depression, unemployment, or technological change—that threaten financial security. Poverty alone causes less anxiety than does change or the threat of change in people's level of affluence. Another source of anxiety among the masses is their perceived level of personal safety. Crime, street violence, and terrorism can produce disproportionately strong anxieties about personal safety. Historically, masses that believe their personal safety is threatened have turned to vigilantes, the Ku Klux Klan, and "law and order" movements.

Extremism
Jewish Anti-
Defamation League:
information on anti-
Semitic and ex-
tremist movements
in America.
www.adl.org

The masses are most vulnerable to extremism when they are alienated from group and community life and when they feel their own lives are without direction or purpose. Mass participation in the established organizations of the community—church groups, PTAs, Little League, fraternal orders—provides a sense of participation, involvement, and self-esteem. Involvement shields the masses from the despairing appeals of demagogues who play on latent mass fears and hatreds. People who are socially isolated are most likely to become mobilized by totalitarian movements. Thus, a thriving group and community life very much serves the interest of the elites; it helps protect them from the threat of demagogues who wish to challenge the established system of values.

COUNTERELITES

Mass activism presents potentially serious threats to democratic values. Demagogues (or counterelites) seek to exploit the worst attributes of mass politics—intolerance, racial hatred, class antagonism, anti-Semitism, impatience with democratic processes, and the tendency to resort to violence to achieve "the will of the people."

Counterelites have arisen in American politics from both the extreme left and the extreme right. But all appeal to similar mass sentiments.

Although left counterelites in the United States are just as antidemocratic, extremist, and intolerant as are right counterelites, their appeal is not as broadly based as is the appeal to the right. Left counterelites have no mass following among workers, farmers, or middle-class Americans. In contrast, right counterelites in the United States historically have been more successful in appealing to broad mass followings.

RIGHT-WING EXTREMISM

Nazi Movement
The official site of
the National Social-
ist Movement (Nazi
Party) reveals the
nature and activities
of the most extrem-
ist groups in
America.
www.nsm88.com

Many changes in American society over the years have contributed to the popular appeal of right counterelites: shifts in power and prestige from the farms to the cities, from agriculture to industry; shifts away from racial segregation toward special emphasis on opportunities for blacks; shifts from religion to secularism; shifts in scale from small to large, from personal to impersonal, from individual to bureaucratic; increases in crime, racial disorder, and threats to personal safety. Any genuine "people's" revolution in the United States would undoubtedly take the form of a right-wing, nationalist, patriotic, religious-fundamentalist, racist, anti-intellectual, "law and order" movement.[21]

CITIZEN MILITIAS

In recent years self-styled citizen "militias" have cropped up across the nation—armed groups that more or less regularly get together dressed in camouflage to engage in military tactics and training. Their politics are generally superpatriotic, occasionally racist, and often conspiracy minded. They frequently view federal government agencies as the enemy and the United Nations as a threat to American independence. They view themselves as modern-day descendants of the American patriot militias who fought the Revolutionary War. They believe the Constitution's Second Amendment "right to bear arms" guarantees individual Americans the right to arm themselves against tyrannical government. This often places them in conflict with

| IN BRIEF | DANGERS OF MASS ACTIVISM |

- It is the irony of democracy that democratic values survive because of support from the elites, not the masses.
- The survival of democracy depends on mass apathy. Mass political activism threatens democratic values.
- Mass activism can be inspired by economic depressions, defeat in war, and perceived threats to personal safety.

- Mass movements, led by counterelites (demagogues), are frequently intolerant, racist, hateful, anti-Semitic, superpatriotic, and violence prone.
- Elites become repressive during periods of crisis when they perceive threats from domestic or foreign sources. Both antidemocratic mass activism and elite repression endanger democratic values.

regulatory efforts of the Bureau of Alcohol, Tobacco, and Firearms (ATF). It was the ATF's violent efforts to enforce federal gun-control laws that led to the deaths of more than seventy people near Waco, Texas, in 1993. This incident reportedly inspired the bombing of the Oklahoma City federal building and the deaths of 168 people there in 1995.

ELITE REPRESSION

Elites are more committed to democratic values than the masses are, but they frequently abandon these values in periods of crisis and become repressive. Antidemocratic mass activism has its counterpart in elite repression. Both endanger democratic values.

REPRESSION AND THE WAR ON TERRORISM

The current "war on terrorism" was inspired by foreign terrorists rather than by domestic mass activism. Yet elites have adopted various repressive measures in the wake of that attack. They did so with the early enthusiastic support of the masses of Americans. All the polls taken shortly after the attack indicated that Americans were prepared to accept many new restrictions on their freedom—more surveillance of their papers and communications, more searches of their belongings, roundups of suspected immigrants, and even prolonged detention without recourse to the courts. Indeed, in the months immediately following September 11, 2001, almost half of all Americans said that the government should take "all steps necessary" to prevent additional acts of terrorism "even if it means your basic civil liberties would be violated." As the initial surprise and fear of terrorist attacks in the United States subsided, however, Americans became more concerned with civil liberties and less willing to give their government the authority to violate these liberties to fight terrorism.

QUESTION: *Which comes closer to your view—the government should take all steps necessary to prevent additional acts of terrorism in the United States even if it means your basic civil liberties would be violated, or the government should take steps to prevent additional acts of terrorism but not if those steps would violate your basic civil liberties?*

Jan. 2002	Jun. 2002	Sep. 2002	Apr. 2003	Aug. 2003	May 2004
Take steps, even if civil liberties violated					
49%	40%	33%	33%	29%	31%
Take steps, but not violate civil liberties					
47%	56%	62%	64%	67%	64%

A Brief History of Elite Repression

Repressive behavior is typical of elites who feel threatened in crises. The Alien and Sedition Acts (1798), passed in the administration of John Adams, closed down Jeffersonian newspapers and jailed their editors. Abraham Lincoln suspended the writ of habeas corpus (the requirement that authorities bring defendants before a judge and show cause for their detention) during the Civil War. In the wake of World War I, Congress passed the Espionage Act, which outlawed "any disloyal, profane, scurrilous, or abusive language intended to cause contempt, scorn, contumely, or disrepute" to the government. Socialist presidential candidate Eugene V. Debs was imprisoned for speaking against the war and the draft; his conviction was upheld by the U.S. Supreme Court, as were convictions of other antiwar protesters of that period.

Shortly after the Japanese attack on Pearl Harbor, President Franklin D. Roosevelt authorized removal and internment of Japanese Americans living on the West Coast. The U.S. Supreme Court upheld this flagrant violation of the Constitution. Not until 1988 did the U.S. Congress vote to make reparations and public apologies to the surviving victims.

During the Cold War, the U.S. government prosecuted top leaders of the Communist Party for violating the Smith Act, which made it unlawful "to knowingly and willfully advocate, abet, advise, or teach the duty, necessity, or propriety of overthrowing any government in United States by force or violence." Again, the U.S. Supreme Court upheld their convictions. Not until the 1960s did the Court begin to reassert freedom of expression, including the advocacy of revolution.

The Patriot Act

Following the terrorist attack of September 11, 2001, Congress moved swiftly to enact the "Patriot Act," officially the Uniting and Strengthening America Act by Providing Appropriate Tools Required to Intercept and Obstruct Terrorism of 2001. President Bush and Attorney General John Ashcroft successfully lobbied Congress to increase the federal government's powers of searches, seizures, surveillance, and detention of suspects. The concerns of civil libertarians were largely swept aside. The act was passed nearly unanimously in the Senate (98–1) and overwhelmingly in the House (357–66) with the support of both Democrats and Republicans. (For details of the act, see "Homeland Security" in Chapter 16.)

Patriot Act
Official government
arguments in support
of the Patriot Act.
*www.lifeandliberty.
gov*

What factors affect Americans' willingness to trade off restrictions on civil liberties in order to provide for safety and security from terrorism? Political science research suggests that the greater people's sense of threat, the greater their support for restrictions on civil liberties.[22] The lower people's trust in government, the less willing they are to trade off civil liberties for security. Liberals are less willing to trade off civil liberties than moderates or conservatives. Overall it seems clear that Americans' commitment to civil liberties is highly contingent on their concerns about threats to national or personal security.

MASS CONDITIONS: AN ELITIST INTERPRETATION

Democratic theory envisions an active, informed citizenry who believe in equality of opportunity. Democracy is said to thrive in the absence of extreme differences between rich and poor, in the promise of upward social mobility. Democracy is said to depend on popular support for individual liberty, freedom of expression, and due process of law. But our analysis of mass conditions and attitudes in America today suggests the following propositions:

1. The earnings of American workers have stagnated over the past three decades. Earnings decline, especially among unskilled and semiskilled workers, has occurred simultaneously with the growth of international trade.
2. Inequality in America has worsened since 1970. The gap between rich and poor has widened as elites have moved investment capital across national borders, lowered tariffs for foreign goods coming to America, and encouraged legal and illegal immigration.
3. Distrust and cynicism characterized mass attitudes toward government and politics. However, elites have benefited politically from a strong economy that has dampened mass enthusiasm for political activism.
4. Despite mass disaffection from government and politics, the masses expect their government to provide for their economic security.
5. Mass support for democratic values is at best superficial. Elites are more consistent than the masses in applying general principles of democracy to specific individuals and groups.
6. Although the targets of mass hatred and intolerance change over time, giving the appearance of increasing respect for democratic values, the willingness of the masses to deny fundamental liberties to despised groups remains unchanged.
7. The survival of democracy depends on elite rather than mass commitment to democratic ideals. Political apathy and nonparticipation among the masses contribute to the survival of democracy. Fortunately for democracy, the antidemocratic masses are generally more apathetic than elites are. Only an unusual demagogue or counterelite can arouse the masses from their apathy and create a threat to the elite consensus.
8. Occasionally, mass apathy turns into mass activism, which is generally extremist, intolerant, antidemocratic, and violence prone. Conditions that encourage mass activism include defeat or humiliation in war, economic dislocation, and perceived threats to personal safety.

9. Although left counterelites are as antidemocratic as right counterelites, their appeal is not as broadly based as the appeal of the right. Right counterelites have mobilized mass support among large numbers of farmers, workers, and middle-class Americans.

10. Although more committed to democratic values than the masses are, elites may abandon these values in crises. When war or revolution threatens the existing order, elites may deviate from democratic values to maintain the system. They may then cease tolerating dissent, censor mass media, curtail free speech, jail counterelites, and strengthen police and security forces.

SELECTED READINGS

Erikson Robert S., and Kent L. Tedin. *American Public Opinion,* 7th ed. New York: Longman, 2007. Authoritative text describing the forces influencing mass opinion and an assessment of the influence of mass opinion in American politics.

Hibbing, John R., and Elizabeth Theiss-Morse. *Stealth Democracy.* New York: Cambridge University Press, 2003. Argues that Americans are not really democratic and that the government they want, and the politics they approve of, are a considerable distance from the classic vision of democracy.

Jacobs, Lawrence R., and Theda Skocpal, eds. *Inequality and American Democracy.* New York: Russell Sage Foundation, 2005. A series of essays on the political consequences of growing income inequality in America.

Keister, Lisa A. *Wealth in America: Trends in Wealth Inequality.* New York: Cambridge University Press, 2000. A description and analysis of inequality in wealth (as opposed to income) distribution, including data on increasing inequality of wealth over time in the United States.

Kornhauser, William. *The Politics of Mass Society.* Glencoe, Ill.: Free Press, 1959. A classic work in political sociology arguing that "atomization" of individuals in the masses makes them vulnerable to the appeals of demagogues and leads to mass movements of intolerance, hatred, and violence. The survival of democracy, Kornhauser argues, depends on "insulating" elites from mass movements by involving the masses in community, family, church, and recreational activities.

Lipset, Seymour Martin, and Earl Raab. *The Politics of Unreason.* New York: Harper & Row, 1970.

A historical recounting of right-wing extremism in America from colonial times through the 1960s.

McClosky, Herbert, and Alida Brill. *Dimensions of Tolerance.* New York: Russell Sage Foundation, 1983. A report of survey results of support for civil liberties among the mass public and a selected sample of civic leaders. The results reveal consistent differences in levels of tolerance between the mass public and elites in speech and press, due process, fair trial, equal opportunity, privacy, and women's and homosexuals' rights.

McClosky, Herbert, and John Zaller. *The American Ethos.* Cambridge, Mass.: Harvard University Press, 1984. A report of public attitudes toward capitalism and democracy showing that "influentials" (in other words, elites) both understand and support these components of the American ethos more than the general public.

Stouffer, Samuel A. *Communism, Conformity, and Civil Liberties.* New York: Wiley, 1955. The earliest study, now a classic, of intolerance and authoritarianism among the American people. Based on surveys during the McCarthy period, Stouffer shows that the willingness to curtail the liberties of atheists, socialists, and communists is greatest among the least-educated segments of the population.

Sullivan, John L., James Pierson, and Gregory Marcus. *Political Tolerance and American Democracy.* Chicago: University of Chicago Press, 1982. The authors demonstrate that tolerance has *not* increased over time but rather that the objects of intolerance change. Americans, both liberal and conservative, are willing to curtail the freedoms of groups that they most despise.

NOTES

1. *Statistical Abstract of the United States,* 2006, p. 463.

2. U.S. Bureau of the Census, *Income, Poverty and Health Insurance Coverage, 2005* (Washington, D.C.: Government Printing Office, 2006).

3. Public Agenda On-Line. Available at www. publicagenda.com (December 2006).

4. National polls reported in *The Polling Report.* www.pollingreport.com/immigration (December 2006).

5. *Sale v. Haitian Centers Council,* 125 L. Ed. 2d 128 (1993).

6. "The *Forbes* Four Hundred," *Forbes,* published annually in the October issue.

7. Edward N. Wolff, *Top Heavy* (New York: Twentieth Century Fund, 1995), p. 104.

8. Richard B. Freeman, "Are Your Wages Set in Beijing?" *Journal of Economic Perspectives,* 9 (Summer 1995): 15.

9. Quotations attributed to elites are taken from Harvard professor Joseph S. Nye Jr., "Finding Ways to Improve the Public's Trust in Government," *Chronicle of Higher Education* (January 16, 1998): B6–7. See also Joseph S. Nye Jr., *Why People Don't Trust Government* (Cambridge, Mass.: Harvard University Press, 1997).

10. See Robert S. Erikson and Kent L. Tedin, *American Public Opinion,* New York: Pearson Longman, 2007, chapter 6.

11. Herbert McClosky and Alida Brill, *Dimensions of Tolerance* (New York: Russell Sage Foundation, 1983), p. 249.

12. McClosky and Brill, *Dimensions of Tolerance,* p. 249.

13. Seymour Martin Lipset, *Political Man* (Garden City, N.Y.: Doubleday, 1963), p. 87.

14. Lipset, *Political Man,* p. 92.

15. William Kornhauser, *The Politics of Mass Society* (Glencoe, Ill.: Free Press, 1959), p. 174.

16. McClosky and Brill, *Dimensions of Tolerance,* p. 249.

17. See Barbara S. Gamble, "Putting Civil Rights to a Popular Vote," *American Journal of Political Science,* 41 (January 1997): 245–269.

18. *Public Opinion* (September/October 1986): 32; also cited in Robert S. Erikson, Norman R. Luttbeg, and Kent L. Tedin, *American Public Opinion,* 3rd ed. (New York: Macmillan, 1988), p. 55.

19. Lee Sigelman et al., "Voting and Nonvoting: A Multi-Election Perspective," *American Journal of Political Science,* 29 (November 1985): 749–765.

20. Kornhauser, *Politics of Mass Society,* p. 174.

21. Seymour Martin Lipset and Earl Raab, *The Politics of Unreason* (New York: Harper & Row, 1970), p. 348.

22. Darren W. Davis and Brian D. Silver, "Civil Liberties vs. Security: Public Opinion in the Context of the Terrorist Attacks on America," *American Journal of Political Science,* 48 (January 2004): 28–46.

For most people most of the time politics is a series of pictures in the mind, placed there by television news, newspapers, magazines, and discussions.... Politics for most of us is a passing parade of symbols.

Murray Edelman

ELITE–MASS COMMUNICATION

Communication in the American political system flows downward from elites to masses. Television and the press are the means by which elites communicate to the masses not only information but also values, attitudes, and emotions. Professional pollsters in turn try to measure mass response to these elite communications. But elite–mass communication often fails. Masses frequently misinterpret elite messages to them, and elites cannot always shape mass opinion as they intend.

THE NEWS MAKERS

Elites instruct the masses about politics and social values chiefly through television, the major source of information for the vast majority of Americans. Those who control this flow of information are among the most powerful people in the nation.

Television is the principal form of *mass* communication. Fully 98 percent of all households have TV sets, and about 70 percent of all households receive cable television. Local TV broadcasts, with community news, sports, and weather mixed with national news, are most popular among the masses. In recent years cable news (Fox and CNN especially) has surpassed the combined nightly network news broadcasts of ABC, CBS, and NBC, which once had a near monopoly on the news. The elderly (people older than 65) still read newspapers (60 percent), but young people (18–29) rarely do so on a regular basis (23 percent). The Internet is a source of news for only relatively few, mostly younger people.[1] (See Figure 6.1.)

The power of television arises not only from its mass viewership but also from its ability to communicate emotions as well as information. Television's true power is in its visuals—angry faces in a rioting mob, police beating an African American motorist, wounded soldiers being unloaded from a helicopter—all scenes that convey an emotional message. The dramatic televised collapse of the World Trade Center buildings on September 11, 2001, united the country in grief and anger. It is doubtful

Pew Research Center for People and the Press
Information, including opinion polls, on the media.
http://www.people-press.org

123

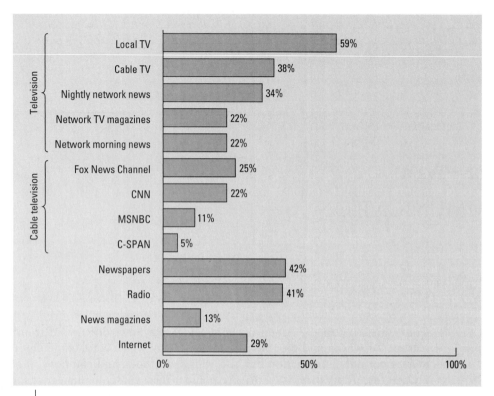

FIGURE 6.1 | WHERE THE MASSES GET THEIR NEWS

Source: Data from Pew Research Center for the People and the Press, June 2, 2005. http://people-press.org.

that the nation would have responded with such unity and purpose if the tragedy had not been televised.

The media elite—television and newspaper executives, reporters, editors, anchors, and producers—do not see themselves as neutral "observers" of American politics but rather as active "participants." They not only report events but also discover events to report, assign them political meaning, and interpret their importance for their mass viewers. They seek to challenge government officials, debate political candidates, and define the problems of society. "TV is the great Legitimator. TV confirms reality. Nothing happens in America, practically everyone seems to agree, until it happens on television."[2]

THE MYTH OF THE MIRROR

The media elite frequently make contradictory remarks about their own power. They sometimes claim that they do no more than "mirror" reality. The "mirror" myth is nonsense. A mirror makes no choices about what images it reflects, but television executives have the power to create some national issues and ignore others, to elevate obscure people to national prominence, to reward politicians they favor and punish those they disfavor. Indeed, at times the news makers proudly credit themselves with the success of the civil rights movement, ending the Vietnam

War, and forcing two presidents—Lyndon Johnson and Richard Nixon—out of office. These claims contradict the mirror image theory, but they more accurately reflect the power of the mass media.

THE CONCENTRATION OF MEDIA POWER

Media mega-mergers in recent years have created corporate empires that spread across multiple media—television, film, print, music, and the Internet. Conglomerate media corporations combine television broadcasting and cable programming, movie production and distribution, magazine and book publication, music recording, sports and recreation, and Internet access and e-commerce. The six multinational corporations listed in Table 6.1 dominate media and cultural markets.

INTERELITE COMMUNICATION

The nation's leading television networks (ABC, CBS, NBC, Fox, and CNN), the nation's influential national newspapers (*Washington Post, New York Times, Wall Street Journal, USA Today*), and leading news magazines (*Newsweek, Time, U.S. News & World Report*) also function as channels of interelite communication. These media are read and viewed by corporate, financial, and government leaders each day. These media provide the agenda for interelite discussion on a fairly regular basis. It is especially important for top government officials to be familiar with both the news stories and opinion columns that appear each day in the *Washington Post, New York Times, Wall Street Journal,* and *USA Today.*

THE MEDIA'S POLITICAL FUNCTIONS

The political power of the mass media arises from several of its vital functions: news making, interpretation, socialization, persuasion, and agenda setting.

NEWS MAKING

Newspaper Web Sites
Virtually all major daily newspapers have Web sites that summarize each day's stories. For national news the most frequently consulted sites are *USA Today, Wall Street Journal, New York Times,* and *Washington Post.*
www.usatoday.com
www.nytimes.com
www.washingtonpost.com
www.wallstreetjournal.com

News making is deciding what and who are "newsworthy" and allocating precious television time and newspaper space accordingly. Television producers and newspaper and magazine editors focus attention on certain people, issues, and events, and that attention in turn generates public concern and political action. Without media coverage, the mass public would not know about these personalities, issues, or events. And without public interest, government officials would not consider the topics important.

The media must select from a tremendous oversupply of information and decide what is "news," and the selection process is the root of their power. Television cannot be "a picture of the world" (as some television executives pretend) because the whole world cannot squeeze into the picture (or into the twenty-four noncommercial minutes of the network evening news). Media attention creates events, issues, and personalities; media inattention means obscurity, even nonexistence. Of course, politicians, public relations people, interest group leaders, and aspiring "celebrities" know that the decisions of news executives are vital to their success and even to their existence. So they try, sometimes desperately, to attract the media's attention—to get

TABLE 6.1 | THE MEDIA EMPIRES

1. *Time Warner*
   Television: Turner Network television (TNT), Turner Broadcasting System (TBS), Cable News Network (CNN), Home Box Office (HBO), Cinemax, Time Warner Cable, Cartoon Network (CN).
   Motion Pictures: Warner Brothers, New Line Cinema, Castle Rock, Looney Tunes, Warner Independent Pictures.
   Magazines: Time, People, Sports Illustrated, Fortune, MAD Magazine, DC Comics, plus many other speciality magazines.
   Books: Warner Books; Little, Brown Publishing; Book-of-the-Month Club.
   Music: Warner Brothers Records, Atlantic Records, Elektra.
   Sports and Entertainment: Atlanta Braves, Atlanta Hawks, World Championship Wrestling.
   Internet: AOL, Netscape, Mapquest, Moviefone, AOL Latino.

2. *Walt Disney*
   Television: ABC-TV, plus ten stations; ESPN, ESPN-2, Disney Channel, A&E, E!, Lifetime.
   Motion Pictures: Walt Disney Pictures, Miramax, Touchstone, Buena Vista.
   Music: Walt Disney Records, Mammoth.
   Sports and Recreation: Disney theme parks in Florida, California, France, Japan, and Hong Kong; Disney Cruise Line; Anaheim Angels, Mighty Ducks.

3. *Viacom*
   Television: CBS, plus forty TV stations; MTV, BET, CMT, Nickelodeon, Showtime, VH1, Comedy Central, Nick-At-Nite, Spike TV.
   Motion Pictures: Paramount Pictures, Dreamworks, Viacom.
   Books: Simon & Schuster.
   Music: Famous Music Publishing.

4. *NewsCorp (Fox)*
   Television: Fox Network plus thirty-five TV stations; Fox News, Fox Sports, Fox Family Channel, Direct TV.
   Motion Pictures: 20th Century Fox, Searchlight, Blue Sky Studios.
   Magazines: TV Guide.
   Books: HarperCollins.
   Music: Mushroom Records.
   Sports and Recreation: Los Angeles Lakers.
   Internet: MySpace, BroadSystems.
   Newspapers: Wall Street Journal, London Times, New York Post, and others.
   Financial: Dow Jones

5. *Sony* (U.S. subsidiary of Sony, Japan)
   Television: Sony Pictures Television (Jeopardy, Wheel of Fortune, etc.).
   Motion Pictures: Columbia Pictures, Sony Pictures, TriStar, Screen Gems.
   Music: Columbia Records, Epic Records, Nashville Records, Sony Classical.
   Sports and Recreation: Sony Theaters, PlayStation.
   Manufacturing: Sony TVs, computers, electronics.

6. *General Electric*
   Television: NBC Network, NBC Universal, plus thirteen TV stations; CNBC, MSNBC, Telemundo.
   Motion Pictures: Universal Pictures.
   Manufacturing: GE appliances.

Source: Thomas R. Dye, *Who's Running America?* 7th ed. (Upper Saddle River, N.J.: Prentice-Hall, 2002). Updated by the author.

just ten seconds on the network news. The result is the "media event"—an activity arranged primarily to stimulate media coverage and attract public attention to an issue or personality. The more bizarre, dramatic, and sensational the event, the more likely it is to attract media attention.

INTERPRETATION

Interpretation of events, issues, and personalities begins when news makers search for an "angle" on the story—a way to put it into context and speculate about its meaning and consequences. Through interpretation, news makers provide the masses with explanations and meanings for events and personalities.

Most network news broadcasts now include a "special segment" or "news special"—two or three minutes of "in-depth" coverage of a particular topic, such as gun control, nuclear plant safety, or international terrorism. News staffs prepare the specials well in advance of their showing and use film or videotape and a script with a "lead-in," "voice-over," and "recapitulation." The interpretive function is clearest in these stories, but interpretation takes place in every news story.

SOCIALIZATION

The media's socialization function is to teach mass audiences the elite's preferred political norms and values. Both news and entertainment programming contribute to socialization. Election night coverage shows "how democracy works" and reinforces the values of political participation. Entertainment programs socialize the mass public by introducing social themes and ways of life—for example, racial tolerance, new sexual mores, feminism, and homosexuality. Television executives and producers frequently congratulate themselves on socially progressive themes.

PERSUASION

Center for Media and Public Affairs Studies of news and entertainment media, including election coverage. *www.cmpa.com*

Persuasion occurs when governments, corporations, unions, political parties, and candidates make deliberate attempts, usually but not always through paid advertising, to affect people's beliefs, attitudes, or behavior. Corporate advertisers ask Americans not only to buy products but also to believe that the corporations are concerned with the environment or with health or with the economic welfare of the nation.

The most obvious efforts at political persuasion take place during political campaigns. Candidates no longer rely on Democratic and Republican party organizations to run their campaigns but instead seek out advertising and public relations specialists to direct sophisticated media campaigns. Television has made candidate image a major factor in voters' choices.

AGENDA SETTING

The real power of the mass media lies in deciding what will be decided. Defining the issues, identifying alternative policies, focusing on political, economic, or social "crises"—these are critical aspects of national policy making. We can refer to these activities as *agenda setting*. Conditions in society that are not defined as "crises" or

| IN BRIEF | Political Functions of the Media |

- Agenda setting—deciding what will be decided, defining issues, and identifying "problems" and "crises".
- News making—deciding what and who are "newsworthy" and deserving of limited media time and space.
- Interpretation—placing reports into context and providing mass audiences with explanations and meanings.

- Socialization—teaching mass audiences the elite's preferred norms and values in both news and entertainment programming.
- Persuasion—direct attempts, usually through paid advertising, to affect mass beliefs, attitudes, and behaviors.

even as "problems" by the mass media never become policy issues. Such conditions do not get on political leaders' agendas. Political leaders, eager to get coverage on the evening news programs, speak out on the issues the mass media have defined as important. These issues are placed on the agenda of decision makers. Governments must then decide what to do about them.

Policy issues do not just happen. Creating an issue, dramatizing it, calling attention to it, turning it into a "crisis," and pressuring government to do something about it are important political tactics. Influential individuals, organized interest groups, political candidates and officeholders, and, perhaps most important, the mass media all employ these tactics.

The power of television is not in persuading viewers to take one side of an issue or another or to vote for one candidate or another. Instead, the power of television is in setting the agenda for decision making: deciding which issues and candidates will be given attention and which will be ignored. Systematic research has shown that issues that receive the greatest attention in the mass media are most likely to be viewed by voters as "important."

BASHING AMERICA FOR FUN AND PROFIT

American television and the news media in general have a bad-news bias. They cover bad news very well. They do not cover good news very well or very often. Bad news is big news: it is dramatic and sensational. Scandals, rip-offs, violent crimes, threatening budget cuts, sexual deviance, environmental scares, and similar fascinations all capture audience attention. But the good news—improved health statistics, longer life spans, better safety records, higher educational levels, and so on—does not stir audience interest so easily. *The result is an overwhelming bias toward negative news stories in the media,* especially on television. Bad-news stories outnumber good-news stories ten to one.

The networks select news for its emotional impact. Stories that inspire mass fears (bombing and terrorism, mass killings, nuclear power plant accidents, AIDS, global warming, and so on) are especially favored. Violence, sex, and government corruption are favorite topics because they attract popular interest. When faced with more complex problems—inflation, government deficits, foreign policy—the news makers feel they must simplify, dramatize, or else ignore them altogether.

Entertainment programs reinforce the negative picture of American life. Consider the popularity of crime programs. In the real world, about three out of one hundred Americans will be victims of a crime *in a year*. In prime-time television entertainment, approximately ten crimes are committed *each night*. Murder is the least common crime in the real world, but it is by far the most common crime on television, which averages one killing every two and a half programs! It is little wonder that Americans who watch a great deal of television tend to overestimate the real amount of crime in society greatly.[3]

SEX SELLS

Historically, reputable newspapers and magazines declined to carry stories about the sex lives of political figures. This unwritten rule of journalism protected Presidents Franklin D. Roosevelt, Dwight D. Eisenhower, and especially John F. Kennedy during their political careers. But today, journalistic ethics (if there are any at all) do not limit reporting of sexual charges, rumors, or innuendoes or public questioning of candidates and appointees about whether they ever "cheated on their spouse," "smoked marijuana," or "watched pornographic movies."

The media's rationale is that these stories reflect on the *character* of a candidate and hence deserve reporting to the general public as information relevant to their choice for national leadership. Yet it seems clear that scandalous stories are pursued by the media primarily for their commercial value. Sex sells; it attracts viewers and readers. But the media's focus on sexual scandal and other misconduct obscures other issues. Politicians defending themselves from personal attack cannot get their political themes and messages across to voters. Moreover, otherwise qualified people may stay out of politics to avoid the embarrassment to themselves and their families that results from invasion of personal privacy.

Television entertainment has become increasingly sex obsessed and profanity ridden. Recordings are released with lyrics that glamorize cop killing, rape, and suicide. Critic Michael Medved writes:

> *Our fellow citizens cherish the institution of marriage and consider religion an important priority in life; but the entertainment industry promotes every form of sexual adventurism and regularly ridicules religious believers as crooks or crazies.*[4]

Hollywood claims that its movies simply reflect the sex, vulgarity, and violence already present in our culture, that restraints on movie makers would inhibit "creative oratory," and that censorship would violate "freedom of expression." And they contend that the popularity of their movies, television shows, and records (judged in terms of money received from millions of moviegoers, viewers, and listeners) prove that Americans are entertained by the current Hollywood output, regardless of what socially approved responses they give to pollsters. "Movies drenched in gore, gangster rap, even outright pornography are not some sort of alien interstellar dust malevolently drifting down to us, but products actively sought out and beloved by millions."[5]

MASS REACTION

However, fun and profit for the media come with high costs for American society. People heavily exposed to political scandal and corruption by the media lose trust and confidence in government and its institutions. Increased mass cynicism and declining voter participation can be attributed to "television malaise"—feelings of distrust, powerlessness, and disaffection from government stemming from television's emphasis on the negative in politics.[6]

LIBERAL BIAS IN TELEVISION NEWS

Overall, network television—through entertainment, newscasts, and news specials—communicates established liberal elite values to the masses. These are the values of the media elite: liberal reform and social welfare, a concern for the problems of minorities and the poor, skepticism toward organized religion and the "traditional" family, suspicion of business, hostility toward the military, and an urge to use government power to "do good" (see Focus: The Hollywood Liberals). Only recently has the Fox television network brought conservative news reports and commentators to cable TV viewers. And conservatism prevails on *talk radio,* both among mass callers and the hosts. Rush Limbaugh garners the highest ratings on talk radio.

LIBERALISM IN THE NEWSROOM

The liberal bias of the news originates in the values of the news makers. The owners (stockholders) of the major corporations that own the television networks, magazines, and newspaper chains usually share the moderate conservatism and Republicanism of the business community, but the producers, directors, and reporters are clearly left leaning and Democratic in their political views.

People for the American Way Web site founded by Hollywood "liberals" to combat "right-wing" influence. *www.pfaw.org*

Elite national newsrooms are populated by liberals more so than local newsrooms. Among national media people, self-described liberals outnumber conservatives five to one. Although many describe themselves as moderates, even these "moderates" are decidedly more liberal in their views than "moderates" in the general public. Moreover, there are sharp differences between media elites and the general public regarding religion and morality (see Table 6.2).

In summarizing the social and political bias of the mass media in America, political scientist Doris A. Graber wrote, "Economic and social liberalism prevails, as does a preference for an internationalist foreign policy, caution about military intervention, and some suspicion about the ethics of established large institutions, particularly government."[7]

DIVISIONS AMONG MASS AUDIENCES

Only a few years ago, four major networks, ABC, CBS, NBC, and CNN, supplied virtually all television news. But the Fox News Channel broke this near monopoly and provided an alternative viewpoint on the news. The result has been a "politicization" of news audiences.

Accuracy in Media A self-described watchdog organization critical of liberal bias in the media. *www.aim.org*

Increasingly, Democrats and Republicans are choosing different television and radio news sources. A national poll of "regular viewers" indicates that Republicans prefer Fox News, whereas Democrats favor CNN as well as the nightly network news broadcasts of ABC, CBS, and NBC.

Ideology also splits viewers. Fox viewers, especially regular viewers of the *O'Reilly Factor,* Fox's leading show, are decidedly conservative. In contrast, self-described

FOCUS	THE HOLLYWOOD LIBERALS

The motion picture and television industry centered in Hollywood has a profound effect on the nation's political culture. Much of the commercial products of Hollywood—both television entertainment programming and motion pictures—are directed toward young people. They are the heaviest watchers of television and the largest buyers of movie tickets. Thus Hollywood plays an important role in socializing young Americans to their political world.

With a few exceptions, Hollywood producers, directors, writers, studio executives, and actors are decidedly liberal in their political views, especially compared with the general public. Of the Hollywood elite, more than 60 percent describe themselves as liberal and only 14 percent as conservative, whereas in the general public, self-described conservatives outnumber liberals by a significant margin. Hollywood leaders are five times more likely to be Democrats than Republicans, although many claim to be independents. And on both economic and social issues, the Hollywood elite is significantly more liberal than the nation's general public or college-educated public.

	Hollywood Leaders	American Public
When it comes to politics do you usually think of yourself as:		
Liberal	60%	30%
Conservative	14	43
Other	23	3
Neither/Don't Know	3	24
In politics of today, do you consider yourself:		
Republican	9	28
Democrat	49	33
Independent	40	28
Other/None/ Don't Know	2	11
Favor a constitutional amendment to permit prayer in public schools	16	74
Describe themselves as		
A religious person	24	62
An anticommunist	37	69
Support gay rights	68	12
Support women's movement (men only)	75	46

Source: David Prindle, "Hollywood Liberalism," *Social Science Quarterly*, 74 (March 1993): 121.

moderates and liberals prefer CNN, including the show *Larry King Live*. Radio is another news source that has been politicized. Republicans and conservatives are far more likely than Democrats and liberals to listen to news on the radio and radio talk shows, especially Rush Limbaugh (see Table 6.3).

BIAS AND SLANDER: FREEDOMS OF THE PRESS

Media elites claim that the First Amendment's guarantee of freedom of the press gives them a constitutional right to be biased. Certainly the drafters of the Bill of Rights agreed with Thomas Jefferson that a free and critical press was essential to the proper functioning of democracy. The media argue that they must be free to say

TABLE 6.2 | IDEOLOGY IN THE NEWSROOM

	General Public	National Media	Local Media
Ideological Self-Identification			
Liberal	20%	34%	23%
Moderate	41	54	61
Conservative	33	7	12
No opinion	6	5	4
Religion and Values			
Belief in God...			
Is necessary to be moral	58	6	18
Is not necessary to be moral	40	91	78
Homosexuality should be...			
Accepted by society	51	88	74
Discouraged by society	42	5	14
No opinion	6	7	12

Source: Pew Research Center for the People and the Press, "Values and Press," June 7, 2004.

and print whatever they wish, whether or not it is biased, unfair, negative, sensational, unfounded, dangerous, or offensive. Generally, the U.S. Supreme Court has agreed.

NO PRIOR RESTRAINT

The Court has interpreted freedom of the press to mean that government may place "no prior restraint" on speech or publication (that is, *before* it is said or published). Originally this doctrine was designed to prevent the government from closing down or seizing newspapers. Today the doctrine prevents the government from censoring any news items. For example, the Supreme Court ruled against the federal government and in favor of the *New York Times* in the famous case of the Pentagon Papers. The *New York Times* and the *Washington Post* undertook to publish secret information stolen from the files of the State Department and Department of Defense regarding U.S. policy in Vietnam while the war was still in progress. No one disputed the fact that stealing the secret material was illegal. What was at issue was the ability of the government to prevent publication of the stolen materials in order to protect national security. But the Supreme Court rejected the national security argument and reaffirmed that the government may place no prior restraint on publication.[8] If the government wishes to keep military secrets, it must not let them fall into the hands of the U.S. press.

TABLE 6.3 | POLITICAL DIVISIONS OF AUDIENCES

Partisanship	General Public	Nightly Network News	CNN	Fox News
Republican	29%	27%	25%	41%
Democrat	35	39	44	29
Independent	26	26	25	22
Other/Don't know	10	8	6	8

Ideology	Conservative	Moderate	Liberal	Don't Know
General public	36	38	18	8
CNN	36	39	20	5
Fox	52	30	13	5
O'Reilly Factor	72	23	4	1
Larry King Live	35	41	17	5
Newspapers	58	41	17	5
Call-in radio	45	33	18	4
Rush Limbaugh	77	16	7	0

Source: Pew Research Center for the People and the Press, "Where Americans Go for News," June 25, 2004.

ABSENCE OF "FAIRNESS"

National Association of Broadcasters
News and views of the media industry from their trade association.
www.nab.org

In the early days of radio, broadcast channels were limited and anyone with a radio could broadcast on any frequency. Interference was a common frustration of early broadcasters. The industry petitioned the federal government to regulate and license the assignment and use of broadcast frequencies.

The Federal Communications Commission (FCC) was established in 1934 to allocate broadcast frequencies and license stations for the "public interest, convenience, and necessity." The enabling act clearly instructed the FCC: "Nothing in this Act shall be understood or construed to give the Commission the power of censorship." For many years a "fairness doctrine" required radio and television stations that provided air time to a political candidate to offer competing candidates the same amount of air time at the same price. In addition, stations that broadcast editorials had to provide an opportunity for responsible individuals to present conflicting views. But there was always a huge hole in the fairness doctrine: news programs were exempt. Newscasts, news specials, and even long documentaries were exempt from the fairness doctrine. A biased news presentation did *not* require the network or station to grant equal time to opponents of its views. Moreover, the FCC did little to enforce the fairness doctrine. No station ever lost its license because of the doctrine.

This modest check on media bias was eliminated by the FCC itself in 1987. As part of an effort to deregulate the broadcasting industry, the FCC scrapped the fairness

| **MEDIA BIASES**

- Negativism—an emphasis on bad news that captures audiences' attention, including crime, scandal, environmental scares, terrorism, and other dramatic topics that attract popular interest.
- Sensationalism—an emphasis on violence, sex, government corruption, and other themes that lend themselves to dramatic presentations.
- Liberalism—a bias toward liberal reform and social welfare, problems of minorities and the poor, skepticism toward organized religion and the traditional family, suspicion of big business, and a propensity to call upon government to use its power to "do good." Only recently has the Fox News and talk radio broken the liberal monopoly and begun to divide liberal and conservative audiences.

doctrine despite strong opposition from Congress and watchdog groups. (The decision did not affect the equal-time provision for political candidates.) The FCC defended its decision by arguing (1) that the doctrine chilled debate by leading broadcasters to avoid controversy and (2) that the rapid rise in the number of broadcast outlets (for example, through cable television) showed that market competition rather than government regulation best served the public interest in receiving a variety of perspectives on public affairs. Congress tried to overrule the FCC by passing legislation designed to make the fairness doctrine legally binding, but President Ronald Reagan successfully vetoed it. Thus, broadcasters have no legal obligation to be "fair" in their presentation of public issues.

"ABSENCE OF MALICE"

Communications that wrongly damage an individual are known in law as libel (written) and slander (spoken). The injured party must prove in court that the communication caused actual damage and that it was either false or defamatory. A damaging falsehood, or words or phrases that are inherently defamatory ("Joe Jones is a rotten son of a bitch"), are libelous and not protected by the First Amendment from lawsuits seeking compensation.

However, media elites have successfully sought over the years to narrow the individual's protection against libel and slander. They were successful in *New York Times v. Sullivan*[9] in depriving public officials of the right to recover damages for false statements unless they are made with "malicious intent." The "Sullivan rule" requires public officials not only to show that the media published or broadcast false and damaging statements but also to prove that they did so *knowing at the time* that their statements were false and damaging or that they did so with "reckless disregard" for the truth or falsehood of their statements. The effect of the Sullivan rule is to free the media to say virtually anything about public officials. Indeed, the media have even sought to expand the definition of "public officials" to "public figures"—that is, virtually anyone the media choose as the subject of a story.

| FOCUS | CRACKS IN THE MEDIA ELITE? |

For many years the media elite was united in its liberal views. The major television networks (ABC, CBS, NBC, CNN), the leading influential newspapers (*New York Times, Washington Post*), and the national news magazines (*Newsweek, Time, U.S. News & World Report*) all reflected the prevailing liberal bias. Conservatives often complained but largely failed to crack the liberal media monopoly.

It was an Australian billionaire, Rupert Murdoch, who eventually came to the rescue of American conservatives. Murdoch himself is not particularly conservative in his politics, and his formula for success in his global media empire of newspapers and television networks is to inject as much glitz and vulgarity into his media outlets as possible. But he also recognized an unfilled market for conservative views on American television. In 1996, he founded the Fox News Channel and hired Roger Ailes (former TV ad producer for Richard Nixon, Ronald Reagan,

and George Bush) to head up the new network. Ailes quickly signed Bill O'Reilly for an hour-long nightly conservative talk show, which soon became the leading talk show on all of cable TV, even surpassing the previous leader, CNN's *Larry King Live*.

The Fox network proclaims "fair and balanced" news—"We report, you decide." The implication is that Fox is rectifying the liberal bias of the mainstream media; if its reporting appears conservative, it is only because the country has become so accustomed to left-leaning media that a truly balanced network just seems conservative.

This apparent split in the media elite may not be very deep. Regular news reporting on Fox is not much different from that of other networks. It is the talk and commentary shows that outrage liberals and warm the hearts of conservatives. But whatever its flaws, Fox News has added a diversity of views to American television.

MEDIA POWER

In summary, no effective governmental checks on media power really exist. The constitutional guarantee of freedom of the press is more broadly interpreted in the United States than in any other democracy. The First Amendment guarantees a powerful, independent, and critical media elite.

POLITICS AND THE INTERNET

The Internet provides a channel for mass participation in politics. It is unruly and chaotic by design. It offers a promise of abundant and diverse information and the opportunity for increased political participation. It empowers anyone who can design a Web site to spread his or her views, whether those views are profound and public-spirited or hateful and pornographic.

CHAOTIC BY DESIGN

During the Cold War, the RAND Corporation, a technological research think tank, proposed the Internet as a communications network that could survive a nuclear attack. It was deliberately designed to operate without any central authority or organization. Should any part of the system be destroyed, messages would still find their way to their destinations. The later development of the World Wide Web language allowed any connected computer in the world to communicate with any other connected computer. The introduction of the World Wide Web in 1992 also meant

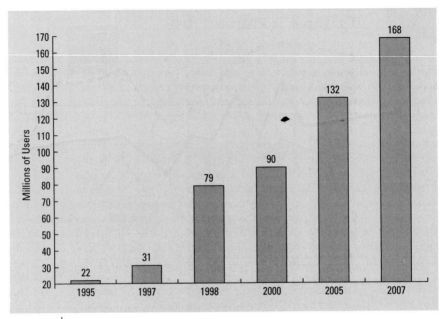

FIGURE 6.2 | THE GROWTH OF INTERNET USERS

Source: *Statistical Abstract of the United States,* 2007, p. 751.

that users no longer needed computer expertise to communicate. By 1995 Americans were buying more computers than television sets and sending more e-mail than "snail mail." Since then, Internet usage has continued to mushroom (see Figure 6.2).

POLITICAL WEB SITES

The Internet is awash in political Web sites. Almost all federal agencies, including the White House, Congress, the federal judiciary, and executive departments and agencies, maintain Web sites. Individual elected officeholders, including all members of Congress, maintain sites that include personal biographies, committee assignments, legislative accomplishments, issue statements, and press releases. The home pages of the Democratic and Republican parties offer political news, issue positions, opportunities to become active in party affairs, and invitations to send money. No serious candidate for major public office lacks a Web site; these campaign sites usually include flattering biographies, press releases, and invitations to contribute financially to the candidates' campaigns. All major interest groups maintain Web sites—business, trade, and professional groups; labor unions; ideological and issue groups; women's, religious, environmental, and civil rights groups. Indeed, this tidal wave of politics on the Internet may offer so much information in such a fragmented fashion that it simply adds to the apathy and indifference of the masses.[10]

Popular Government Web sites

www.whitehouse.gov
www.house.gov
www.senate.gov
www.fbi.gov
www.cia.gov

" INTERESTING.....IT'S LIKE A PORTABLE 500K FILE and YOU DON'T HAVE TO WAIT FOR IT TO DOWNLOAD.... AND YOU SAY IT'S CALLED A NEWSPAPER ? "

THE INTERNET UNCENSORED

The Internet allows unrestricted freedom of expression, from scientific discourses on particle physics and information on the latest developments in medical science, to invitations to join in paramilitary "militias" and offers to exchange pornographic photos and messages. Commercial sex sites outnumber any other category on the Web.

Drudge Report
Controversial blog that links to stories not always carried by mainstream media. Links to all major media outlets. *www.drudgereport. com*

Congress unsuccessfully attempted to outlaw "indecent" and "patently offensive" material on the Internet in its Communications Decency Act of 1996. But the U.S. Supreme Court struck down that act in 1997 and granted the Internet First Amendment protection. Congress had sought to make it a federal crime to send or display indecent material on the Internet to persons under 18 years of age. But the Supreme Court reiterated its view that government may not limit the adult population to "only what is fit for children."[11]

THE BLOGGERS

The Internet has spawned a myriad of individual Web sites, commonly known as "blogs," that frequently criticize the mainstream media. The more reputable blog sites fact-check stories in the mainstream media, or publish stories overlooked by them, as well as toss in their own opinions. They have been labeled the media's "backseat" drivers. Although many bloggers offer little more than their own sometimes heated opinions, they frequently succeed in forcing professional journalists to cover stories they would otherwise have ignored.

MEDIA CAMPAIGNS

Television has contributed to the decline of political parties, it has replaced party leaders as "king makers," it has encouraged voting on the basis of candidate image, it has fostered the development of media campaigns with professional advertising techniques, and it has significantly increased the costs of running for public office. All these changes reduce the influence of the masses in politics and contribute to the power of the elites.

THE DECLINE OF PARTIES

The media have replaced the party organizations as the principal link between the candidates and the voters. Candidates can take their campaigns directly to the voters. They can capture party nominations in primary elections dominated by television advertising. Party organizations have little to say about who wins the party's nomination and next to nothing to say about who wins in the general election. Aspiring candidates no longer begin their quest for public office by calling on party leaders but start instead by hiring professional media advertising firms. Both primary and general elections are now fought largely in the media.

THE MEDIA AS KING MAKERS

Heavy media coverage creates candidates. The media provide name recognition, the first requirement for a successful candidate. Indeed, heavy media attention can transform unknown figures into instant candidates; candidates no longer need to spend years in political apprenticeship in minor offices to run for Congress or a governorship. The media can also condemn an aspiring candidate to obscurity and defeat simply by failing to report his or her activities. News makers select the "serious" candidates for coverage at the beginning of a race. In primary elections, the media even select the "real winner": if the favorite does not win by as large a margin as the media predicted, the media may declare the runner-up the "real winner" even when his or her vote total is less than that of the favorite. People who cannot perform well in front of a camera are no longer feasible candidates for major public office.

IMAGE ELECTIONS

In covering elections, television largely ignores policy questions and focuses on candidate image—the personal traits of the candidates. Candidates are presented on television not in terms of their voting records or policy positions but instead on their ability to project a personal image of charm, warmth, "compassion," youth and vigor, honesty and integrity, and so forth. Elections are presented on television as struggles between competing personalities.

The media cover elections as a political game, consisting of speeches, rallies, press conferences, travels, and perhaps debates. The media report on who is winning or losing, what their strategies are, how much money they are spending, how they look in

their public appearances, the response of their audiences, and so on. It is not surprising that policy issues do not play a large role in voters' decisions, because the media do not pay much attention to policy issues.

THE MEDIA CAMPAIGN

Professional media campaigns, usually directed by commercial advertising firms, have replaced traditional party-organized or amateur grassroots campaigns. Today, professional media people may plan an entire campaign; develop computerized mailing lists for fund-raising; select a (simple) campaign theme and desirable candidate image; monitor the progress of the campaign with continuous voter polls; produce television tapes for commercials, as well as signs, bumper stickers, and radio spots; select the candidate's clothing and hairstyle; write speeches and schedule appearances that will attract new coverage; and even plan the victory party.

Professional campaign management begins with assessing the candidate's public strengths and weaknesses, evaluating those of the opponent, and determining the concerns uppermost in voters' minds. Early polls can test for name recognition, favorable or unfavorable images, and voter concerns; these polls then feed into the campaign strategy. Polls during the campaign chart the candidate's progress, assess the theme's effectiveness, and even identify undecided groups as targets for last-minute campaign efforts. "Negative" campaigns can stress the opponent's weaknesses. Most professional campaigning takes the form of paid television commercials, produced by experienced advertising agencies and shown in specific voter "markets." But a good media campaign manager also knows how to get the candidate "free" time on the evening news. Candidates must attract the media and convey a favorable image: they may visit a retirement home, a coal mine, a ghetto, or a pig farm to appeal to specific groups of voters. A candidate may work a day digging ditches (particularly if perceived as a playboy millionaire), walk from

IN BRIEF	POLITICAL EFFECTS OF THE MEDIA

- The media has replaced parties as the principal link between candidates and voters.
- The media have assumed the "king making" function in their decisions to cover some candidates and ignore others, and to tell audiences who are the "real winners" in primary elections.
- The media, especially television, emphasizes candidates' "image"—personal traits of the candidates—over their policy positions.

- Media campaigning has dramatically increased the costs of running for office.
- Increased media expenses have candidates more dependent on corporations, wealthholders, and interest groups for campaign contributions.

city to city (particularly if the opponent flies in a chartered airplane), or participate in a hog-calling contest (particularly if viewed as too intellectual). Such activities are more likely to win a spot on the evening news than is a thoughtful speech on nuclear terrorism.

EMPOWERING ELITES

All these media effects on elections contribute to the relative power of elites. Local party organizations have been replaced by national media campaigns. Policy questions are largely ignored in elections in favor of easily manipulated candidate images. (More about campaigning and voter choice appears in Chapter 8.) Grassroots campaigning has been displaced by expensive, professional media campaigns, usually directed by commercial advertising agencies. The costs of campaigning have risen dramatically because of the high cost of television advertising. The first question any aspiring candidate faces today—from city hall to county courthouse to state capital to Washington—is how much money can be raised for the campaign. The high costs of a media campaign require that (1) the candidate be personally wealthy or have wealthy friends or (2) the candidate receive financial support from organized interests, usually the political action committees (or PACs) established by corporations, banks, professional associations, industry groups, unions, and other special interests. (The power of interest groups is discussed in Chapter 9.)

MEDIA COVERAGE OF PRESIDENTIAL ELECTIONS

Most Americans are exposed to presidential election campaigns through television. But how well does television cover presidential elections?

HORSE RACE REPORTING

The media treat election campaigns as horse races—reporting on who is ahead or behind, how much money is being spent by the candidates, and their current standing in the polls. These stories account for about half of all the television news coverage of a presidential election. Additional stories are centered on campaign issues—controversies arising on the campaign trail itself, including verbal blunders by the candidates,

TABLE 6.4 | PRESIDENTIAL ELECTION NEWS COVERAGE ON TELEVISION

	2004 (Bush–Kerry)	2000 (Bush–Gore)	1996 (Clinton–Dole)	1992 (Clinton–Bush)
Amount of Coverage				
Number of stories	504	462	483	478
Minutes per day	27	13	12	25
Average sound bite (in seconds)	7.8	7.8	8.2	8.4
Focus of Coverage				
Horse race	48%	71%	48%	58%
Policy issues	49%	40%	37%	32%
Topic of Coverage (percentage of good press)				
Democratic nominee	59%	40%	50%	52%
Republican nominee	37%	37%	33%	29%

Note: Percentages do not add to 100%; some stories were classified in more than one category, and some stories did not fit categories shown.

Source: Derived from *Media Monitor,* Center for Media and Public Affairs.

as well as character issues, such as candidates' sex lives. In contrast, policy issues typically account for only about one-third of television news stories on a presidential election campaign (see Table 6.4). However, in 2004, policy issues, notably terrorism and the war in Iraq, received substantial news coverage.

NEGATIVE COVERAGE

Typically, news stories about presidential candidates are negative. This usually applies to both Republican and Democratic candidates, although Republicans regularly suffer more negative coverage than Democrats. The national news networks—ABC, CBS, NBC—were especially biased against Bush in 2004. On-air evaluations of Kerry were positive by a two to one margin, whereas evaluations of Bush were negative by a two to one margin.[12] Only Fox News's evaluations favored Bush over Kerry. CNN commentators Paul Begala and James Carville accepted advisory roles with the Kerry campaign while still retaining their jobs as news commentators for CNN.

SHRINKING SOUND BITES

Perhaps the most distorting of all television news practices is the reluctance of anchors and reporters to allow the candidates to speak for themselves during the campaign. Instead, most campaign airtime is used by anchors and reporters discussing the campaigns. Only 13 percent of television news story time features direct comments by the candidates themselves.[13] In other words, viewers hear almost six times more campaign talk from journalists than from candidates. And the average "sound bite" for presidential candidates—words actually spoken by the candidates themselves—has shrunk to less than eight seconds.[14]

LATE-NIGHT LAUGHS

The late-night talk shows—*The Tonight Show* (Jay Leno), *The Late Show with David Letterman,* and *Late Night with Conan O'Brien*—are playing an increasing role in television campaigning. Indeed, young people are more likely to get their campaign news from late-night shows than from early evening news shows. In 2004, Bush was the target of twice as many jokes as Kerry. Questioning Bush's intellect, Leno said that the president, when told of the rising Democratic star and Illinois Senate candidate, Barak Obama, replied, "Isn't that the guy we can't find?"

ASSESSING MEDIA IMPACT

What impact do media elites have on mass opinion and behavior? For many years, political scientists advanced the curious notion that the mass media had only "minimal effects" on political behavior. Of course, wiser business elites never believed the minimal-effects theory, as the growth of the multibillion-dollar advertising industry attests. Nor did the politicians believe it, as they turned increasingly to expensive television advertising. Presumably, political scientists were basing their theory on the fact that newspaper editorial endorsements seldom changed people's votes. Systematic research on the political effects of the mass media, particularly television, is fairly recent. This research tells a far different story.

Media effects can be categorized as influencing (1) cognition and comprehension, (2) attitudes and values, (3) public opinion, and (4) behavior. These categories of effects are ranked by the degree of influence the media are likely to have over us. That is to say, the strongest effects of the media are in cognition and comprehension—in generating awareness and increasing information levels. The media also influence attitudes and values, but the strength of media effects is diluted by many other sources of attitudes and values. Public opinion, especially on prominent issues, is seldom changed by the media. However, opinion change, when it does occur, is likely to swing in the direction favored by media reporting. Finally, it is most difficult to establish the independent effect of the media on behavior.

COGNITION AND COMPREHENSION

Media elites strongly influence what we know about our world and how we think and talk about it. Years ago, foreign policy expert Bernard Cohen, in the first book to assess the effects of media on foreign policy, put it this way: "The mass media may not be successful in telling people what to think, but the media are stunningly successful in telling their audience what to think about."[15]

However, the masses generally suffer from *information overload;* so many communications are directed at them that they cannot possibly process them all in their minds. A person's ability to recall a media report is dependent on repeated exposure to it and reinforcement through personal experience. For example, an individual who has a brother in a trouble spot in the Middle East is more likely to be aware of reports from that area of the world. But most viewers become narcotized by information overload; too many voices with too many messages cause them to block out nearly all information. Information overload may be especially heavy in political news. Television tells most viewers more about politics than they really want to know. Political scientist Austin Ranney writes: "The fact is that for most Americans politics is still far from being the most interesting and important thing in life. To them, politics is usually confusing, boring, repetitive, and above all irrelevant to the things that really matter in their lives."[16]

ATTITUDES AND VALUES

Media elites can create new opinions more easily than they can change existing ones. The media often tell the masses how they should feel about news events or issues—those about which the masses have no prior feelings or experiences. And the media can reinforce values and attitudes that the masses already hold. But there is little evidence that the media can change existing mass values.

The masses defend against bias in news and entertainment programming by *selective perception*—mentally screening out information or images with which one disagrees. Selective perception causes people to tend to see and hear only what they want to see and hear. Selective perception reduces the impact of media elites on mass attitudes and behavior.

The networks' concentration on scandal, abuse, and corruption in government, for example, has not always produced the desired liberal, reformist notions in the minds of the masses of viewers. Contrary to the expectations of network executives, their focus on governmental scandals has produced feelings of general political distrust and cynicism toward government and the political system.

PUBLIC OPINION

Can media elites change public opinion? This question was confronted directly by political scientists Benjamin I. Page, Robert Y. Shapiro, and Glenn R. Dempsey in an extensive study of eighty policy issues over fifteen years. They examined public opinion polls on various policy issues at a first point in time, then media content over a following interval of time, and finally public opinion on these same issues at the end of the interval. The purpose was to learn whether media content—messages scored by their relevance to the issue, their salience in the broadcast, their pro or con direction, the credibility of the news source, and quality of the reporting—changed public opinion. Although most people's opinions remained constant over time (opinion in the first time period is the best predictor of opinion in the second time period), opinion changes were heavily influenced by media messages. Page, Shapiro, and Dempsey concluded that "news variables alone account for nearly half the variance in opinion change." They also learned that:

- *Anchors, reporters, and commentators* had the greatest impact on opinion change. Television newscasters have high credibility and trust with the general public. Their opinions are crucial in shaping mass opinion.

- *Independent experts* interviewed by the media have a substantial impact on opinion but not as great as newscasters themselves.
- *A popular president* can also shift public opinion somewhat. On the other hand, unpopular presidents do not have much success as opinion movers.
- *Interest groups* on the whole have a slightly negative effect on public opinion. "In many instances they seem to actually have antagonized the public and created a genuine adverse effect"; such cases include Vietnam War protesters, nuclear freeze advocates, and other demonstrators and protesters, even peaceful ones.[17]

BEHAVIOR

Media elites have a difficult task in changing behavior. But television can motivate people who are already predisposed to act in a certain way.

Many studies have been conducted concerning the effect of the media on behavior—the effect of TV violence, the effect of television on children, and the effects of obscenity and pornography. It is difficult to generalize from these studies. However, it appears that television is more likely to reinforce behavioral tendencies than to change them. For example, televised violence may trigger violent behavior in children who are already predisposed to such behavior, but televised violence has little behavioral effect on the average child. Likewise, there is little evidence that pornography itself causes rape or other deviant sexual behavior among viewers.

Nonetheless, we know that television advertising sells products. And we know that political candidates spend millions to persuade audiences to go out and vote for them on election day. Both manufacturers and politicians create name recognition, employ product differentiation, try to associate with audiences, and use repetition to communicate their messages. These tactics are designed to affect our behavior both in the marketplace and in the election booth.

Political ads are more successful in motivating a candidate's supporters to go to the polls than they are in changing opponents into supporters. It is unlikely that a voter who dislikes a candidate or is committed to a candidate and who has a lot of information about both candidates will be persuaded by political advertising to change his or her vote. But many potential voters are undecided, and the support of many others is "soft." Going to the polls on election day requires effort—people have errands to do, it may be raining, they may be tired. Television advertising is more effective with these marginal voters.

THE MEDIA: AN ELITIST INTERPRETATION

Communications in the American political system flow downward from elites to masses. Elites influence mass opinion more than masses influence elite opinion.

1. Television is the principal means by which elites communicate to masses. Control of the flow of information to the masses is highly concentrated. A handful of prestigious news organizations decide what will be the "news."
2. The political functions of the mass media include news making (deciding what to report), interpretation (providing the masses with explanations of

events), socialization (teaching about preferred norms, values, and lifestyles), persuasion (making direct efforts to affect behavior), and agenda setting.

3. The most important power of the mass media is agenda setting—deciding what will be decided. The media decide what conditions in society to label "crises" or "problems" or "issues" and thereby place these topics on the agenda of national decision makers.

4. Bias in the news arises from the news makers' own liberal-establishment views plus the need to dramatize and sensationalize the news. However, the news makers' concentration on scandal and corruption in government often produces "television malaise"—social distrust, political cynicism, and feelings of powerlessness—instead of reform.

5. At one time, just four networks—ABC, CBS, NBC, and CNN—monopolized television news and presented a common liberal interpretation of the news. Today, however, Fox News provides a conservative viewpoint, and audiences are increasingly divided by ideology in their viewing habits.

6. The First Amendment's guarantee of freedom of the press has been expanded by the Supreme Court to remove virtually all checks on media power. The Sullivan rule renders public officials especially vulnerable to media attacks.

7. The Internet allows the masses to communicate. Although virtually all government agencies, corporate trade and professional groups, political parties, and interest groups maintain elaborate Web sites, any individual with the knowledge to create a Web site can express his or her views.

8. The media have largely replaced political parties as the principal link between the candidates and the voters. The media focus on the personal image of candidates rather than on issues. The high cost of media campaigning adds to the influence of wealthy contributors.

9. The media are most effective at influencing mass cognition and comprehension—what people know, think, and talk about. The media are somewhat less effective in shaping attitudes and values; "selective perception" enables the masses to screen out media messages with which they disagree. The media seldom change public opinion, but when change occurs, it is generally in the direction favored by the media. The media are least effective at directly influencing behavior; for example, political ads are more successful in motivating a candidate's supporters to go to the polls than they are in changing opponents into supporters.

SELECTED READINGS

Ansolabehere, Stephen, Roy Behr, and Shanto Iyengar. *The Media Game.* New York: Macmillan, 1993. A comprehensive text assessing the changes in the political system brought about by television since the 1950s.

Fallows, James. *Breaking the News: How the Media Undermine American Democracy.* New York: Pantheon Books, 1996. A well-known reporter describes how the media distort democracy and lose the trust of the American people.

Goldberg, Bernard. *Bias: A CBS Insider Exposes How the Media Distort the News.* New York: Perennial, 2003. The title says it all.

Graber, Doris A. *Mass Media and American Politics,* 7th ed. Washington, D.C.: CQ Press, 2005. A wide-ranging description of media effects on campaigns and elections, as well as on social values and public policy.

Lichter, S. Robert, Stanley Rothman, and Linda S. Lichter. *The Media Elite*. Bethesda, Md.: Adler & Adler, 1986. A comprehensive study of the social, psychological, and political orientations of the leadership of the mass media, based on extensive interviews in the most influential media outlets.

Medved, Michael. *Hollywood vs. America*. New York: HarperCollins, 1992. An informative and amusing description of the ongoing cultural war between Hollywood and its audiences.

Patterson, Thomas E. *Out of Order*. New York: Random House, 1993. A devastating attack on television news coverage of political campaigns, its negativism, and the resulting cynicism it inspires among citizens.

Prindle, David F. *Risky Business: The Political Economy of Hollywood*. Boulder, Colo.: Western Press, 1993. The politics and economics that drive Hollywood's political liberalism and activism.

Sabato, Larry. *Feeding Frenzy*. New York: Free Press, 1992. An assessment of "how attack journalism has transformed American politics," produced "titillation rather than scrutiny," and resulted in "trivialization rather than enlightenment."

West, Darrel M. *Air Wars*, 4th ed. Washington, D.C.: CQ Press, 2005. In-depth examination of political advertising in election campaigns, from 1952 through the 2004 elections.

NOTES

1. Pew Research Center for the People and the Press, *Where Americans Go for News* (Philadelphia: Pew Center, 2004).
2. William A. Henry, "News as Entertainment," in *What's News: The Media in American Society*, Elie Abel, ed. (San Francisco: Institute for Contemporary Studies, 1981), p. 134.
3. *Media Monitor*, January 1998.
4. Michael Medved, *Hollywood vs. America* (New York: Harper, 1992), p. 70.
5. Quoting Katha Pollit, *Time*, June 12, 1995, pp. 33–36.
6. See Michael J. Robinson, "Public Affairs Television and the Growth of Political Malaise," *American Political Science Review*, 70 (June 1976): 409–432.
7. Doris A. Graber, *Mass Media and American Politics* (Washington, D.C.: Congressional Quarterly, 1980), p. 41.
8. *New York Times v. United States*, 403 U.S. 713 (1973).
9. *New York Times v. Sullivan*, 376 U.S. 254 (1964).
10. See Arthur Lupia and Tashia S. Philpot, "Views from Inside the Net," *Journal of Politics*, 67 (November, 2005): 1122–1142.
11. *Reno v. American Civil Liberties Union*, 521 U.S. 844 (1997).
12. *Media Monitor*, November/December 2004.
13. See Thomas Patterson, *Out of Order* (New York: Random House, 1993).
14. See Larry Sabato, Mark Stencil, and S. Robert Lichter, *Peepshow: Media and Politics in an Age of Scandal* (New York: Rowland and Littlefield, 2001).
15. Bernard Cohen, *The Press and Foreign Policy* (Princeton, N.J.: Princeton University Press, 1963), p. 10.
16. Austin Ranney, *Channels of Power* (New York: Basic Books, 1983), p. 11.
17. Benjamin I. Page, Robert Y. Shapiro, and Glenn R. Dempsey, "What Moves Public Opinion," *American Political Science Review*, 81 (March 1987): 23–24, 37.

Organization implies the tendency to oligarchy. Every party ... becomes divided into a minority of directors and a majority of directed.

Roberto Michels

POLITICAL PARTIES AND IDEOLOGIES

Traditional political science asserted that parties were necessary instruments of popular control of government. But the two major political parties in the United States have little incentive to offer clear policy alternatives. Democratic and Republican voters do not divide clearly along liberal and conservative lines. Party organizations are oligarchic and dominated by activists who are largely out of touch with the voters. Candidates are selected in primary elections in which personal organization and financial assets, not party organizational support, are crucial to victory. Television has replaced party organizations as a means of linking candidates to voters. In short, the American party system fails to provide the masses with an effective means to direct public policy.

THE RESPONSIBLE PARTY MODEL IN DISARRAY

Pluralist political theory developed a "responsible party" model of the American system that viewed the parties as principal instruments of popular control of government. Responsible parties were supposed to:

- Develop and clarify alternative liberal and conservative policy positions for the voters
- Educate the people about the issues and simplify choices for them
- Recruit candidates for public office who agreed with party policy positions
- Organize and direct their candidates' campaigns to win office
- Hold their elected officials responsible for enacting party policy positions after they were elected
- Organize legislatures to ensure party control of policy making

In carrying out these functions, responsible parties were supposed to modify the demands of special interests, build a consensus that could win majority support, and provide simple and identifiable, yet meaningful, choices for the voters on election day.

In this way, disciplined, issue-oriented, liberal and conservative competitive parties would be the principal means by which the people would direct public policy.

But this responsible party model fell into disarray over the years, if indeed it ever accurately described the American political system. There are some fundamental problems with this "responsible" model of the parties:

First of all, in the American two-party system, the parties have no real incentive to offer strong liberal or conservative policy positions. Instead, each tries to capture the broad center of most policy dimensions, where it believes most Americans can be found. Standing on the far right or on the far left, when most Americans are found in the center, is a recipe for defeat. So the parties mostly echo each other. And indeed, voter decisions are seldom based on the policy stands of candidates or parties anyway.

Second, the Democratic and Republican parties are organized as oligarchies, dominated by active, ideologically motivated elites. These party activists, including delegates to the national conventions, hold policy views that do not reflect the opinions of rank-and-file voters in either party. Democratic Party activists are far more liberal than Democratic voters, and Republican Party activists are more conservative than Republican voters.

Third, party loyalties among voters have been declining over time. Most people remain registered as Democrats or Republicans in order to vote in primary elections. But increasing numbers of people identify themselves as Independents. Split-ticket voting (where a single voter casts his or her vote for a Democrat in one race and a Republican in another) is also increasing.

The parties are no longer the principal intermediary between candidates and voters. It is the mass media, particularly television, that has replaced the party as a means of political communication. Candidates can come directly into the voters' living rooms via television. Campaigning is now largely a media activity. Candidates no longer need party workers to carry their message from block to block.

The parties have no direct way to hold their elected officials responsible for enacting party positions, to carry out party platforms, or to ensure that legislators vote the party line. Party leaders within legislative bodies may use committee assignments, preferences in bill consideration, and occasional perks of office to round up votes for the parties' positions. But there are no significant disciplinary measures that party leaders can employ against wayward legislators. Party leaders cannot deny renomination to rebellious officeholders.

Finally, and perhaps most important, primary elections undermine the power of party organizations. Primary elections determine nominees, not party organizations. The progressive reformers who introduced primary elections at the beginning of the twentieth century wanted to undercut the power of party machines in determining who runs for office, and they succeeded in doing so. Nominees now establish personal organizations for campaigning in primary elections; they are not really obliged to negotiate with party leaders.

Despite these problems, the American political parties survive. They are important in the selection of *personnel* for public office, if not for the selection of public policy. Few Independents are ever elected to high political office. Serious candidates for the presidency, the U.S. Senate, the House of Representatives, state governorships, and state legislatures (in every state except nonpartisan Nebraska) must first win Democratic or Republican party nomination.

IN BRIEF	PROBLEMS WITH THE RESPONSIBLE PARTY MODEL

- The parties do not offer the voters clear liberal or conservative policy alternatives.
- The parties themselves are oligarchies, dominated by active, ideologically motivated delegates.
- Party loyalties among the masses have been declining over the years.
- The mass media, particularly television, has replaced the party as the principal means of

- communication between candidates and the electorate.
- The parties cannot hold their elected officials responsible for following party positions.
- Primary elections determine nominees, not party organizations.

DEMOCRATIC AND REPUBLICAN PARTIES: WHAT'S THE DIFFERENCE?

The Democratic and Republican parties reflect prevailing elite consensus on basic democratic values: the sanctity of private property, a free-enterprise economy, individual liberty, limited government, majority rule, and due process of law. Moreover, since the 1930s both parties have supported the public-oriented, mass-welfare domestic programs of the "liberal establishment": social security, fair labor standards, unemployment compensation, a national highway program, a federally aided welfare system, countercyclical fiscal and monetary policies, and government regulation of banking, transportation, food and drugs, labor relations, and the environment. Finally, both parties have supported the basic outlines of U.S. foreign and military policy since World War II: international involvement, containing Soviet expansion during the Cold War, the North Atlantic Treaty Organization, military preparedness, and the Korean, Vietnam, and Persian Gulf wars. Currently, both parties support the war on terrorism. Both parties voted overwhelmingly to authorize President Bush to use military force in Iraq. Rather than promoting competition over national goals, the parties reinforce social consensus and limit the area of legitimate political conflict.

CORE CONSTITUENCIES OF THE PARTIES

The major parties are not, of course, identical. Although both parties draw their support from all social groups in the United States, the social bases of the parties are somewhat different. Democratic voters are drawn disproportionately from labor union members and their families, big-city dwellers, Jews, Catholics, and African Americans. The core activists in the Democratic Party are often drawn from labor and teachers' unions, government employees, and feminist, civil rights, and environmental organizations. Republican voters are drawn disproportionately from rural, small-town, and suburban Protestants and business and professional people. The core Republican activists are often drawn from small businesses and business organizations, religious and church groups, and civic and service organizations. To the extent that the aspirations of these groups differ, the thrust of party ideology also differs.

Democratic Party elites (as represented by delegates to the national Democratic Party convention) are more likely to identify themselves as liberals (41 percent) than

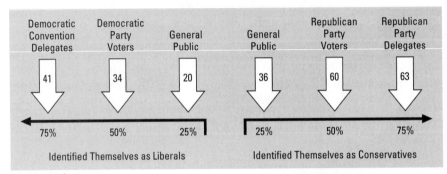

FIGURE 7.1 | LIBERALS AND CONSERVATIVES: PARTY ELITES VERSUS PARTY VOTERS AND THE GENERAL PUBLIC

Source: From data reported in the *New York Times*, August 29, 2004, 13.

Democratic voters (34 percent) or the general public (20 percent). Republican Party elites are more likely to identify themselves as conservatives (63 percent) than Republican voters (60 percent) or the general public (38 percent). (See Figure 7.1.)

THE ATTRACTION TO THE CENTER

Both parties' nominees, if they are to succeed, must appeal to the center. With only two parties and an overwhelmingly nonideological electorate, "consumer demand" requires that party ideologies be ambiguous and moderate. Therefore we cannot expect the parties, which seek to attract the maximum number of voters, to take up liberal and conservative positions supported by only minorities in the population.

Why can't we have a strongly principled party system, with a liberal party and a conservative party, each offering the voters a clear ideological choice? We can diagram the centrist tendencies of the American party system as in Figure 7.2. Let us assume that the parties seek to win public office by appealing to a majority of voters, and let us assume that voters choose the party that is *closest* to their own ideological position. If the voters distribute themselves along a normal curve on these liberal–conservative dimensions, with most voters occupying the moderate center and only small numbers of voters occupying the far left and far right positions, then both parties would have a strong incentive to move to the center. If the liberal party (L) took a strong ideological position to the left of most voters, the conservative party (C) would move toward the center, winning more moderate votes even while retaining its conservative supporters, who would still prefer it to the more liberal opposition party. Likewise, if the conservative party took a strong ideological position to the right of most voters, the liberal party would move to the center and win. Thus, both parties must abandon strong ideological positions and move to the center, becoming moderate in the fight for support of the majority of voters—the moderates.

In short, because the first goal of a party is to win elections, strong ideological and policy positions are counterproductive. Firmer, more precise statements of ideology by the political parties would probably create new lines of cleavage and eventually

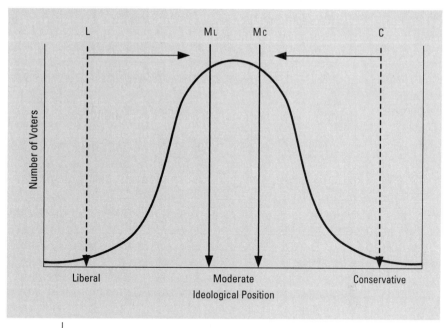

FIGURE 7.2 | WHY THE PARTIES STRIVE FOR MODERATION

fragment the parties. The development of a clear liberal or conservative ideology by either party would only cost it votes.

LIBERAL AND CONSERVATIVE LABELS

Even though politicians often avoid ideological labeling, "liberal" and "conservative" references are common in political debate and commentary. In fact, political *elites*—elected and appointed officeholders; journalists, writers, and commentators; party officials and interest group leaders; and others active in politics—are generally more stable and consistently liberal or conservative in their political views than the masses. Elites are also more likely to use ideological terms in describing politics.

References to conservatism generally mean a belief in the value of free markets, limited government, and individual self-reliance in economic affairs combined with a belief in the value of tradition, law, and morality in social affairs. It is important to note that conservatism in America incorporates different views of the role of government in economic versus social affairs. Conservatives generally prefer limited non-interventionist government in *economic* affairs—that is, minimal government regulatory activity, social welfare programs limited to the "truly needy," and low taxes. On the other hand, conservatives would strengthen government's power to regulate *social* conduct—fighting crime, encouraging religion, restricting abortion, opposing drugs and pornography, and discouraging homosexuality. It is possible, of course, for some to label themselves as economic conservatives and social liberals or vice versa.

American Conservative Union
Conservative news and views and rankings of Congress members on conservative index.
www.conservative.org

References to liberalism generally mean a belief in a strong government to provide economic security and protection for civil rights combined with a belief in freedom from government intervention in social conduct. Today's liberals believe that a large powerful government can change people's lives by working to end racial and sexual discrimination, abolish poverty, create jobs, provide medical care for all, educate the masses, and protect the environment. The prevailing impulse is to "do good"—to use the power of the national government to find solutions to society's troubles. Note that liberals also have different views about the role of government in *economic* affairs versus *social* affairs. Liberals prefer an active powerful government in economic affairs—a government that provides a broad range of public services, regulates business, protects consumers and the environment, and provides generous unemployment, welfare, and old-age benefits. But liberals oppose government restrictions on abortion, oppose school prayer, oppose the death penalty, and oppose government intrusions into personal privacy.

Americans for Democratic Action
The ADA is the nation's oldest liberal political action organization.
www.adaction.org

IDEOLOGY AND THE MASSES

The masses are less likely to understand the meaning of liberalism or conservatism and are less likely to use ideology as a guide to their positions on specific issues. We can ask a question such as "How would you describe your own political philosophy—conservative, moderate, or liberal?" The results of surveys over recent years are shown in Figure 7.3. Self-described conservatives outnumber liberals, but many people prefer to think of themselves as "moderate" or "middle-of-the-road."

What do Americans mean when they label themselves liberal, moderate, or conservative? This question has no clear answer. People who label themselves conservative do not consistently oppose social-welfare programs or government regulation of the economy. People who label themselves liberals do not consistently support tax

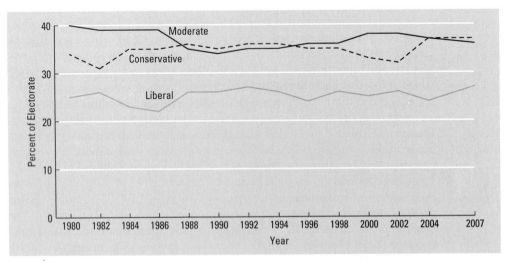

FIGURE 7.3 | LIBERALS, MODERATES, AND CONSERVATIVES IN THE ELECTORATE

increases or expansion of government services. For many years "conservative" has been a more popular label than "liberal" among the masses, yet government services have continued to expand, civil rights have been strengthened, and the regulation of social conduct has become less restrictive—all presumably liberal policy directions.

Recall, however, that Democratic and Republican *elites* are ideologically separated from each other and from their voters. (See Figure 7.1.) Although exact percentages and specific questions vary from one election to the next, the general pattern is clear: Democratic Party activists are far more liberal than Democratic voters or the general electorate. Republican leaders are more conservative than either Republican voters or the general electorate.

Indeed, in recent years Democratic and Republican Party activists have become more ideologically separate. This "party polarization" is even becoming apparent to the masses.[1]

Bill O'Reilly
Popular Web site for conservative views as well as promotion of O'Reilly programs, books, editorials, etc.
www.billoreilly.com

PARTY AND IDEOLOGY

Despite incentives for the parties to move to the center of the political spectrum, the electorate tends to perceive the Republican Party as conservative and the Democratic Party as liberal.

Indeed, polls suggest that voters who described themselves as conservatives voted overwhelmingly for Bush in 2004. And voters who identified themselves as liberals voted overwhelmingly for Kerry (see Table 7.1).

This relationship between ideological self-identification and party self-identification is relatively stable over time. It suggests that the parties are not altogether empty jars.

DECLINING MASS ATTACHMENTS TO PARTIES

For many years, party identification among voters remained remarkably stable. (Party identification is determined by survey responses to the question, "Generally speaking, do you usually think of yourself as a Republican, a Democrat, an Independent, or what?") However, indications of a weakening of the American party system are found in the steady rise of self-described "Independents" over the years and the relatively few voters who describe themselves as "strong" Democrats and Republicans (see Figure 7.4).

The Democratic Party has long held a decided edge among American voters in both registration and self-identification. Nationwide, Democratic registration exceeds Republican registration. But this Democratic Party loyalty has gradually eroded over the years.

TABLE 7.1 | PARTY AND IDEOLOGY AMONG VOTERS

	Total	Voted Democratic	Voted Republican
Liberal	21%	85%	13%
Moderate	45	54	45
Conservative	34	15	84

Source: As reported in *USA Today*, November 17, 2004.

| FOCUS | ARE YOU A LIBERAL OR A CONSERVATIVE? |

	You Are *Liberal* if You Agree That	You Are *Conservative* if You Agree That
Economic policy	Government should regulate business to protect the public interest. The rich should pay higher taxes to support public services for all. Government spending for social welfare is a good investment in people.	Free-market competition is better at protecting the public than government regulation. Taxes should be kept as low as possible. Government welfare programs destroy incentives to work.
Crime	Government should place primary emphasis on alleviating the social conditions such as poverty and joblessness that cause crime.	Government should place primary emphasis on providing more police and prisons and stop courts from coddling criminals.
Social policy	Government should protect the right of women to choose abortion and fund abortions for poor women. Government should pursue affirmative action programs on behalf of minorities and women in employment, education, and so on. Government should keep religious prayers and ceremonies out of schools and public places.	Government should restrict abortion and not use taxpayer money for abortions. Government should not grant preferences to anyone based on race or sex. Government should allow prayers and religious observances in schools and public places.
National security policy	Government should support "human rights" throughout the world. Military spending should be reduced now that the Cold War is over.	Government should pursue the "national interest" of the United States. Military spending must reflect a variety of new dangers in this post-Cold War period.

Party identification is closely associated with voter choice at the polls. Most voters cast their ballots for the candidates of their party. This is true in presidential elections (see Table 8.2 in Chapter 8) and even more true in congressional and state elections.

REALIGNMENT OR DEALIGNMENT?

In recent decades, two clear trends have appeared in party identification among the public. First, the percentage of voters preferring neither party has increased substantially, and, second, the Democratic Party has lost adherents (see Figure 7.4). The rise of Independents and the decline of Democratic partisans are two major developments that tend to complement one another.

FOCUS | IDEOLOGICAL BATTLEFIELDS

Elites are more consistent in their ideological position and more likely to employ ideology in assessing issues and describing politics. But neither the elites nor the masses always align themselves along a single liberal-conservative dimension. We have already defined liberals as supporting government intervention in economic affairs and civil rights, but opposing government intervention in social affairs. And we have described conservatives as wanting to limit government intervention in economic affairs and civil rights, but favoring government regulation of social conduct. Thus, neither liberals nor conservatives are really consistent in their view of the role of government in society, each differentiating between economic and social affairs.

Yet it is possible to support a strong government to regulate business and provide economic security, and also a strong government to closely regulate social conduct. Although few people to use the term *populist* to describe themselves, populists may actually make up a fairly large proportion of the electorate. Liberal politicians can appeal to populists by stressing government intervention to provide economic security, while conservative politicians can appeal to them by stressing the maintenance of traditional social values.

It is also possible to oppose government interference in both economic affairs and the private lives of citizens. The term *libertarian* is only occasionally employed to describe people who consistently call for limited government. Libertarians are against most environmental regulations, consumer protection laws, antidrug laws, defense spending, foreign aid, and government restrictions on abortion. In other words, they favor minimal government intervention in all sectors of society.

The result may be a two-dimensional ideological battlefield—identifying more or less government intervention and separating economic from social affairs. This produces four separate possible ideological stances—liberals, conservatives, populists, and libertarians (see figure).

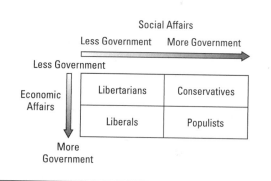

DEALIGNMENT

Dealignment refers to the decline in the attractiveness of both parties. Dealignment is suggested by the growing number of people who have negative or neutral images of the parties and the growth in the belief that neither party can provide solutions for important problems.

There are several other indicators of party dealignment. Almost two-thirds of Americans say they split their votes between Democratic and Republican candidates for separate offices on election day. A majority say that they have voted for different parties in past presidential elections, and more than one-third say they have voted for an Independent or a third-party candidate. However, relatively few voters register as Independents. This is because many states have "closed" primaries that allow only registered Democratic and Republican party members to vote in their party's primary elections. In these states voters *must* register as either Republicans or Democrats in order to vote in a primary election.

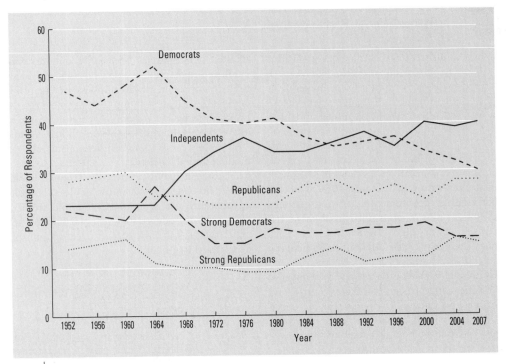

FIGURE 7.4 | PARTY IDENTIFICATION, 1952–2004

Source: Calculated from National Election Surveys data (Ann Arbor: Center for Political Studies, University of Michigan).

REALIGNMENT

Realignment is a more long-term change. Scholars are not in agreement as to whether a single election can be said to realign party identification or whether it takes several elections. But scholars do share a basic understanding of what realignment looks like; it occurs when

> *social groups change their party alignment; the party system realigns when the parti- san bias of groups changes in ways that alter the social group profile of the parties. The changes may result from a previously Democratic group becoming Republican, [they] may reflect the development of a partisan cleavage among a group of voters who had not displayed any distinctive partisan bias, [and they] might also come about as a highly aligned group begins to lose its partisan distinctiveness.*[2]

The major party realignment in recent decades has been the erosion of the Democratic Party loyalty of white southern voters. White southerners, conserva- tives in disposition, have been drifting away from their traditional Democratic ties. Republican candidates swept the southern states in four presidential elections (Nixon in 1972, Reagan in 1980 and 1984, and Bush in 1988). In 1992 and

| FOCUS | MASS PERCEPTIONS OF THE PARTIES |

Over the years, the Democratic Party has usually managed to maintain an image among the masses of being "the party of the common people." The Republican Party (also called the Grand Old Party, or GOP) has been saddled with an image of being "the party of the rich." The Democratic Party is also seen as the party "more concerned with people like yourself." The Republican Party is trusted to do a better job in handling foreign affairs and maintaining a strong national defense. It is also seen as better at fighting crime and illegal drugs and holding down taxes.

In contrast, the Democratic Party is perceived to hold an advantage in many key domestic concerns of Americans. The Democrats are seen as better at protecting the environment and helping the middle class. The strongest Democratic advantage appears in protecting social security and helping the poor and elderly (see the figure).

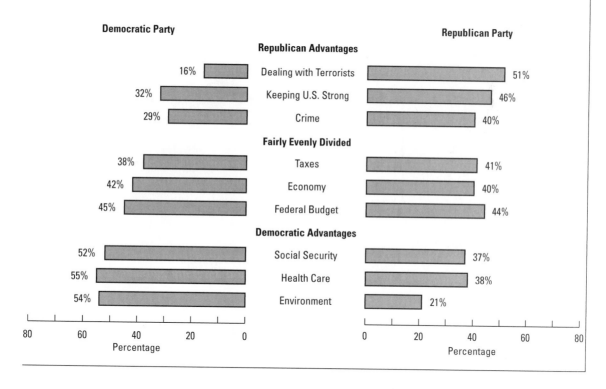

1996, Arkansan Bill Clinton moved several southern states back into the Democratic column. But in 2000, George W. Bush again swept the southern states (even Gore's home state of Tennessee). The result appears to be a Republican "L" on the map, with the Republican Party the strongest in the South and the Rocky Mountain states, and the Democratic Party dominating the Northeast and West Coast (see Figure 7.5).

Yet many of the characteristics of great historical party realignments (such as the creation of the New Deal coalition that elected Franklin Roosevelt in the 1930s) are absent. Realignments in the past resulted in increased turnout, because massive shifts in preference generally were accompanied by increased interest in politics. But this

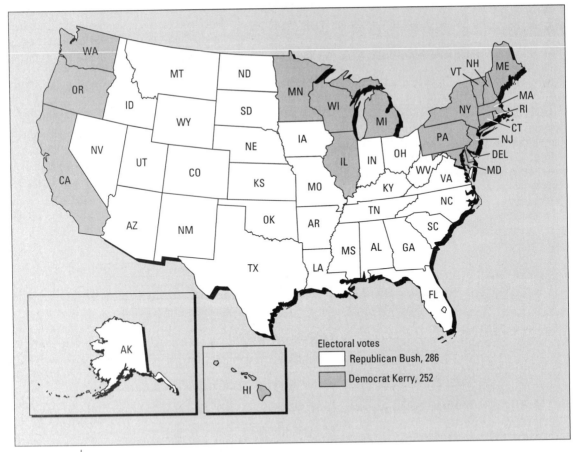

FIGURE 7.5   STATE PARTY ALIGNMENTS IN THE 2004 PRESIDENTIAL ELECTION

effect has been notably absent in recent elections. Turnout has declined, not risen (see Figure 8.4 in Chapter 8).

PRESIDENTIAL PRIMARIES AND THE DETERIORATION OF PARTIES

The growth of presidential primaries over the last several decades contributed a great deal to the decline in importance of party organizations. In their efforts to make the parties' presidential nominations more "democratic," reformers forced more and more states over the years to use primary elections for selecting delegates to their national nominating conventions. It was not until 1972 that a majority of party convention delegates were selected in presidential primary elections. The increased use of primaries was written into state laws and now generally applies to both parties.

Given the expanded role of primaries, do "the voters" now select the presidential nominees? Actual participation in presidential primaries is far less than in general elections. Whereas voting for president in *general elections* varies between 50 percent and 60 percent, participation in presidential *primaries* usually does not exceed 20 percent to 30 percent of eligible voters. Clearly, with an average turnout of this size, primaries do not represent the "voice of the people."

In low-turnout elections, the higher social classes are the principal participants. Such is the case in primary elections. Participants come disproportionately from the college-educated, professionally employed upper-middle classes. Conspicuously underrepresented in the primary electorate are working-class voters and ethnic minorities.

MoveOn
Website of the liberal wing of the Democratic Party.
www.moveon.org

Democratic Leadership Council/New Democrats Online
Moderate Democrats in the House and Senate set forth their views.
www.ndol.org

Primary elections strengthen the influence of the ideological activists in each party. Liberals are overrepresented among Democratic primary voters, and conservatives are overrepresented among Republican primary voters. These ideological voters generally give an advantage in Democratic presidential primaries to candidates with a liberal record, and in Republican presidential primaries to candidates with a conservative record. However, image often triumphs over ideology: primary voters are attracted to charismatic candidates regardless of their ideological leanings. And some primary voters knowingly abandon their ideological preference in order to select a more moderate candidate who appears to have a better chance of winning in November.

The nomination process begins with the Iowa caucuses in February, followed by the first primary election: New Hampshire, a tiny state that jealously guards its position as the first state to hold a primary in every presidential year. The tradition certainly has nothing to do with the strategic importance of New Hampshire in terms of delegate strength. New Hampshire's voters account for less than 1 percent of all votes cast in Democratic primaries, and they choose less than 1 percent of the delegates to the Democratic convention. Were it not for the fact that New Hampshire kicks off the season, its primary election would be ignored. However, the extensive media coverage in the state might lead one to conclude that New Hampshire is a crucial state in the general election. New Hampshire *is* crucial—but as a media event.

Other states long envied New Hampshire's media prominence in presidential primaries. In order to increase their own clout, many states moved up the date of their own presidential primaries to earlier in the year.

Primaries provide an opportunity for the media to separate the serious candidates from the aspirants (see Chapter 6). Although the primary electorate is more ideological than the electorate in general elections, the candidates rarely develop the issues well. Not only are early primaries frequently crowded with candidates, but the fact that the candidates are from the same party reduces the opportunity for exploring issues.

Thus a candidate's media image becomes crucial. Before the primary season, candidates seek to establish credibility as serious contenders of presidential caliber. They attempt to generate name familiarity (as revealed in public opinion surveys) and thus recognition first as serious candidates, not necessarily as front-runners. The proliferation of primaries and attendant media attention make it possible for a candidate to become well known quickly. A reputation can be created by a large campaign chest, an appealing campaign style, and a good image on television.

The consequence of the primary system is that political party leaders—governors, senators, representatives, mayors, the heads of state party organizations, and the

| FOCUS | THE DEMOCRATIC PRESIDENTIAL PRIMARIES, 2004 |

The "preprimary" season began in earnest in August 2003—well over a year before the presidential election. President George W. Bush had no opposition in the Republican primaries, but a small army of Democratic candidates announced their intention to run. However, the two most popular Democratic candidates—former vice president Al Gore and New York's Senator Hillary Clinton—both announced that they would not seek their party's nomination.

Based on initial "name recognition," Connecticut Senator Joe Lieberman started in the lead but soon fell to fourth or fifth place as the battle progressed.

Missouri Congressman Dick Gephardt and Massachusetts Senator John Kerry began to rise in the polls toward the end of 2003. Former NATO commander General Wesley Clark also appeared to be a serious contender; he was rumored to be the choice of Bill and Hillary Clinton.

The Dean Attack
In early November the media began to focus on a little-known Vermont governor, Howard Dean. Dean separated himself from the other candidates with his heated opposition to the war in Iraq and his vitriolic attacks on President Bush. The media were entranced with his "Hate Bush" rhetoric and his fanatical supporters. He was also successful in exploiting the Internet to amass $50 million in campaign funds from his zealous fans. For a while it was the largest war chest of any of the Democratic candidates.

Iowa and New Hampshire
Grassroots Democrats in the Iowa caucuses and the New Hampshire primary appeared unfazed by Dean's intensity and the media attention given to him. Many admired his "raw meat" attacks on Bush, but more seemed committed to finding an "electable" Democrat. John Kerry's relatively lowkey yet well-organized work in Iowa and New Hampshire paid off. He surprised the media commentators with come-from-behind victories in both states. Dean was stunned. He reacted with a high-volume shouting speech that appeared to confirm the voters' notion that he was perhaps too emotional and too unstable for the presidency.

Front-Loaded Victories
Kerry's Iowa and New Hampshire victories gave him the momentum for a series of Democratic primaries that had been moved up into February. By March 2, Kerry had effectively won the Democratic nomination. (He lost only to Clark in Oklahoma and to Edwards in South Carolina.) His Democratic poll numbers skyrocketed, and one by one his competitors dropped out of the race. Although Kerry's liberal voting record matched that of his mentor, Ted Kennedy, he appeared moderate in contrast to Dean.

A Long Campaign
The front-loading of the primary season in 2004 produced a Democratic challenger to President Bush eight months before the general election in November. Kerry's victories, and the media attention they attracted, catapulted the Massachusetts senator to a competitive standing with President Bush in the polls. The stage was set for a long and brutal general election campaign.

---

like—cannot control the selection of presidential candidates. And among voters within the same party, public opinion becomes more volatile, more susceptible to media manipulation, and even more issueless than in the general election. The primary system has been a major factor in the demise of parties and the creation of the new media elite: "Because the competing candidates often share most ideological orientations, personal attributes such as appearance, style, and wit attain new importance (presidents today must be fit and not fat, amusing not dull, with cool not hot personalities)."[3]

POLITICAL PARTIES AS OLIGARCHIES

It is something of an irony that the parties, as the agents of democratic decision making, are not themselves democratic in their structures. American political parties are skeletal organizations, "manned generally by small numbers of activists and involving the great masses of their supporters scarcely at all."[4] In essence, power in the parties rests in the hands of those who have the time and the money to make it a full-time, or nearly full-time, occupation. Party activists—people who occupy party offices and committee posts, who attend local, county, state, or national party meetings and conventions, and people who regularly solicit and/or contribute campaign funds to their party and its candidates—are no more than 3 or 4 percent of the adult population.

Who are the party activists? We know, from research cited earlier, that the activists are strongly ideological. And it is not surprising that party activists are of relatively high socioeconomic status and come from families with a history of party activity. The highest socioeconomic levels are found in the highest echelons of the party organization. More than 70 percent of delegates to the Democratic and Republican national conventions are college graduates, and almost half have graduate degrees. All but a handful are professionals or managers, and most enjoy incomes well above that of the average American.

Most Republican and Democratic primary voters pay little or no attention to candidates for *party* offices. Indeed, there is seldom much competition for these offices at the local level, with only a single name appearing on the ballot for each party post.

Voters in party primary elections decide who will be their party's nominee for public office. Party primary elections decide state legislative candidates (in every state except nonpartisan Nebraska), gubernatorial candidates, congressional candidates, and in presidential party primaries, delegates pledged to support one or another of the candidates for the party's presidential nomination.

Mass participation in party affairs resembles a pyramid, with *all eligible voters* in the United States (about 200 million) at the bottom (see Figure 7.6). About half of all eligible voters go to the polls in a November general presidential election (90 million to 100 million). Between 30 percent and 40 percent of eligible voters cast ballots in off-year congressional elections. But party primary elections, even in presidential years, draw only about 25 percent of eligible voters. Yet these elections in effect choose the Democratic and Republican presidential candidates. Finally, as mentioned earlier, party activists are no more than 3 percent or 4 percent of the electorate.

The Democratic and Republican party organizations formally resemble the American federal system, with national committees, officers and staffs, and national conventions, fifty state committees, and more than 3,000 county committees with city, ward, and precinct levels under their supervision. Members of local and county party committees are usually elected in their party's primary election, although many of these posts across the country are vacant and/or filled with appointees. Both the Democratic and Republican parties have national committees with full-time staffs, and both parties have various policy commissions and caucuses that attract the attention of the energetic few.

Financial support for both the Democratic and Republican national committees comes primarily from corporate, banking, and investment interests; labor unions; real estate interests; and lawyers, lobbyists, and law firms (see Focus: Where the Parties Get Their Money). Both committees combined spent more than $1 *billion* in the 2004 elections.

Democratic Party
Web site of the Democratic National Committee (DNC). With news, press releases, policy positions, etc.
www.democrat.org

Republican Party
Web site of the Republican National Committee (RNC). With GOP news, press releases, policy positions, etc.
www.rnc.org

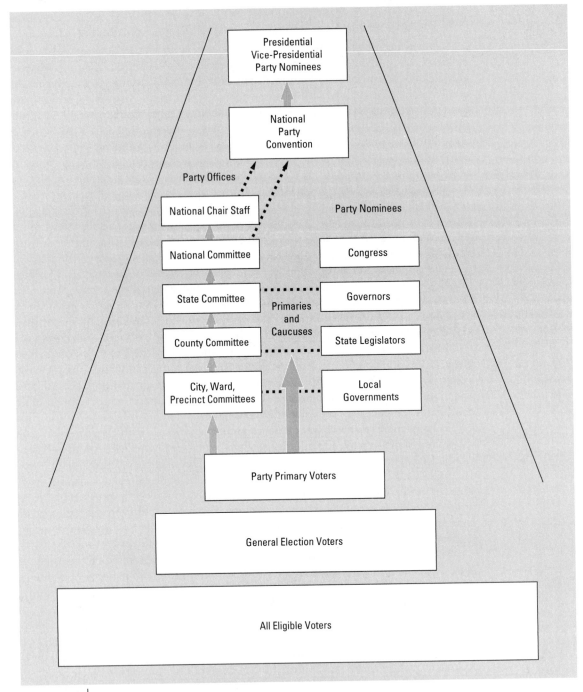

FIGURE 7.6 | PARTIES AS OLIGARCHIES

| FOCUS | WHERE THE PARTIES GET THEIR MONEY |

Both the Democratic and Republican parties rely principally on large corporations, banks, and insurance companies, investment firms, real estate interests, and lawyers and lobbyists for their money. But their sources of money differ in significant ways. First of all, labor unions, especially public employee and teacher unions, are a major source of funding for the Democratic Party. Labor unions give very little to the Republican Party. The Democratic Party relies more heavily on lawyers, lobbyists, and law firms, receiving about four times as much money from this source as the Republican Party. And Hollywood gives more than twice as much money to the Democrats as to the Republicans. Banks divide their money fairly evenly between the parties. The Republican Party relies more heavily on real estate and home-building industries, the oil and gas industry, the pharmaceutical (drug) companies, and manufacturing firms.

TOP CONTRIBUTORS TO THE NATIONAL DEMOCRATIC AND REPUBLICAN CAMPAIGNS IN 2004

Republican Party		Democratic Party	
Top Industries	Top Contributors	Top Industries	Top Contributors
Real estate	National Assn. of Realtors	Lawyers	Goldman Sachs
Drug, health care	National Auto Dealers Assn.	Education	Microsoft
Commercial banks	National Beer Wholesalers	TV/movies	JPMorgan
General contractors	United Parcel Service	Computers	Laborers Union
Manufacturers	SBC Communications	Government employees	Time Warner
Oil and gas	Wal-Mart	Publishing/newspapers	Assn. of Trial Lawyers
Automotive	Deloitte Touche (accounting)	Investment firms	Electrical Workers Union
Insurance	American Medical Assn.		United Auto Workers
	Natl. Assn. of Home Builders		Machinists Union
			Carpenters Union

Source: Data from Center for Responsive Politics.

INDEPENDENT AND THIRD-PARTY POLITICS

Dealignment from the parties would seem to create a favorable environment for Independent candidates and third parties. However, the American tradition of the two-party system, combined with winner-take-all elections for district (for the House) and state (for the Senate) offices and for each state's presidential electors, works against the development of third parties. In addition, the laws of the fifty states governing access to the November general election ballot erect high barriers to Independent candidates who would challenge the Democratic and Republican nominees. The major parties' candidates are automatically included on general election ballots, but Independents and third parties must meet varied requirements in the fifty states to get their names printed on the ballot. These requirements often include filing petitions signed by 5 or 10 percent of the registered voters; this means securing tens of thousands of signatures in smaller states, and hundreds of thousands in larger states.

TABLE 7.2 | HISTORY OF MODERN THIRD-PARTY PRESIDENTIAL CANDIDATES

Third-Party Presidential Candidate	Popular Vote (Percentage)	Electoral Votes (Number)
Theodore Roosevelt (1912), Progressive (Bull Moose) Party	27.4	88
Robert M. La Follette (1924), Progressive Party	16.6	13
George C. Wallace (1968), American Independent party	13.5	46
John Anderson (1980), Independent	6.6	0
Ross Perot (1992), Independent	18.9	0
Ross Perot (1996), Reform Party	8.5	0
Ralph Nader (2000), Green Party	2.7	0
Ralph Nader (2004), Independent	0.1	0

THE RISE AND FALL OF THE REFORM PARTY

Although no Independent candidate has ever made it to the White House, Independent presidential candidates have affected the outcome of the race between the major-party candidates. For example, Teddy Roosevelt's 1912 "Bull Moose" effort split off enough votes from Republican William Howard Taft to allow Democrat Woodrow Wilson to win. But, historically, the American two-party system has discounted Independent candidates (see Table 7.2).

In 1992, Ross Perot initially defied the conventional wisdom about Independent candidates. He motivated tens of thousands of supporters in a grassroots effort, "United We Stand, America," that succeeded in placing Perot's Reform Party with his name as its presidential candidate on the ballot in all fifty states. Perot promised to resolve the financial obstacle by spending "whatever it takes" from his own huge fortune to mount a "world-class campaign." (He ended up spending about $70 million.)

With his own personal fortune, Perot launched the first real electronic campaign—shunning the traditional cross-country airport speeches, rallies, photo ops, and press conferences in favor of TV talk-show appearances, spot commercials, and paid half-hour "infomercials." In all three televised presidential debates, Clinton and Bush treated Perot with kid gloves, not wanting to alienate his middle-class supporters. In the end, Perot garnered 19 percent of the popular vote, the highest percentage won by a third candidate since Teddy Roosevelt in 1912. Moreover, the Perot campaign played a major part in increasing overall voter turnout for the first time in over thirty years. Perot's candidacy prevented Bill Clinton from claiming majority support, holding the winner to 43 percent of the total votes cast. But Perot's voters were spread across the nation. He failed to win in a single state and thus came up with *no* electoral votes.

In his second national campaign, in 1996, Perot was no longer a media novelty. Indeed, in many TV appearances he often appeared brusque, prickly, irritating, and

Reform Party
The Reform Party Web site provides information about founder Ross Perot and the principles of and news about the party.
www.reformparty.org

autocratic. With only 5 to 6 percent support in the early polls and no real chance of winning any electoral votes, Perot was excluded from the presidential debates. On election day he won fewer than half the votes he had garnered four years earlier and again failed to win any state's electoral votes.

The Reform Party imploded at a raucous summer 2000 convention with rival factions almost coming to blows over control of the microphone. Firebrand conservative commentator Pat Buchanan appeared to control a majority of the delegates. But Perot followers viewed Buchanan's candidacy as a hostile takeover of the Reform Party. However, the Federal Elections Commission recognized Buchanan as the official nominee and awarded him the $12.6 million due to the Reform Party based on Perot's vote total in 1996. But Buchanan's right-wing rhetoric attracted less than 1 percent of the voters. Ralph Nader outpolled the combative commentator, and the Reform Party was left in a shambles, its future in doubt.

WHY THIRD PARTIES FAIL

Mass distrust of parties, politicians, and politics in general would seem to create an environment for the success of a third party, perhaps an "antiparty party." And indeed, Ross Perot's Reform Party was partially successful in mobilizing dissatisfied voters. Yet the Reform Party eventually collapsed, as have all other third parties in modern times. Why do these parties fail?

IDEOLOGICAL AND PROTEST PARTIES

Libertarian Party
This Web site reflects the Libertarian Party's strong ideological commitments to individual liberty, free markets, and nonintervention in world affairs.
www.lp.org

Some "third parties," more accurately called minor parties, are not formed to win elections so much as to promote an ideology or express protest. They use the electoral process to express their views and recruit activists to their cause. They measure success not by victory at the polls but rather by their ability to bring their views to the attention of the American public. For example, socialist parties have run candidates in virtually every presidential election in this century. At the opposite end of the ideological spectrum, the Libertarian Party promotes limited government intervention in all aspects of American life. The Libertarian Party regularly nominates presidential candidates to carry the message of less government regulation of the economy, less government control of social life, removal of laws making drug use a crime, opposition to defense spending, and opposition to U.S. involvement in international affairs.

SINGLE-ISSUE PARTIES

Green Party
Although centered on the issue of "ecological wisdom," the Green Web site also promotes "grassroots democracy," "social justice," "peace," "feminism," and "diversity."
www.gro.org

Occasionally issue activists will promote a separate party as a means to call attention to their concerns. Perhaps the most persistent of these parties over the years has been the Prohibition Party. It achieved temporary success with the passage of the Eighteenth Amendment to the U.S. Constitution in 1919—an amendment that prohibited the manufacture, sale, or transportation of "intoxicating liquors." Yet the Eighteenth Amendment did little more than inspire the growth of organized crime in America. What the Prohibitionists referred to as a "noble experiment" failed and was repealed by the Twenty-first Amendment in 1933. Today the Green Party provides an example of a single-issue party, with its primary emphasis on environmental protection. However, the Green Party itself contends that it is "part of the worldwide movement that promotes ecological wisdom, social justice, grass-roots democracy and nonviolence."

CULTURAL CONSENSUS

One explanation of the strength of the two-party system focuses on the broad consensus supporting the American political culture. Both the elites and the masses express commitment to the values of democracy, capitalism, free enterprise, religious freedom, and equality of opportunity. No party directly challenging these values has ever won much of a following. There is little support in the American political culture for avowedly fascist, communist, authoritarian, or other blatantly antidemocratic parties. Political parties with religious affiliations, common in European democracies, are absent from U.S. politics. Socialist parties opposed to the free enterprise system have frequently appeared on the scene under various labels—the Socialist Party, the Socialist Labor Party, and the Socialist Workers Party. But the largest popular vote ever won by a socialist candidate in a presidential election was the 6 percent won by Eugene V. Debs in 1912. In contrast, socialist parties have frequently won control of European governments.

CUSTOM

The cultural explanation blends with the influence of historical precedent. The American two-party system has gained acceptance through custom. The nation's first party system developed from two coalitions, Federalists and Anti-Federalists, and this dual pattern has been reinforced over two centuries.

A WINNER-TAKE-ALL ELECTORAL SYSTEM

Yet another explanation of the continuing domination of the Republican and Democratic parties focuses on the electoral system itself. Winners in presidential and congressional elections, as well as in state gubernatorial and legislative elections, are determined by a plurality, winner-take-all vote. Even in elections that require a majority (more than 50 percent) to win—which may involve a runoff election—only one party's candidate wins in the end. Because of this winner-take-all system, parties have an overriding incentive to broaden their appeal to a plurality or majority of voters. Losers come away empty-handed. There's not much incentive in such a system for a party to form to represent the views of 5 or 10 percent of the electorate. In contrast, many European countries employ proportional representation in elections to their legislative bodies. All voters cast a single ballot for the party of their choice and legislative seats are then apportioned to the parties in proportion to their total vote in the electorate. Minority parties can win legislative seats, perhaps with as little as 5 or 10 percent of the vote. The U.S. system is *not* designed for proportional representation. It's "winner take all."

LEGAL ACCESS TO THE BALLOT

Yet another factor in the preservation of the two-party system is the difficulty third parties have in gaining access to the ballot. The Democratic and Republican nominees are automatically included on all general election ballots, but third-party and independent candidates face serious obstacles in getting their names listed. In presidential elections, a third-party candidate must meet the varied requirements of fifty separate states to appear on their ballots along with the Democratic and Republican nominees. These requirements often include filing petitions signed by 5 or 10 percent of registered voters; accomplishing this requires considerable expenditure of effort and money that the major parties did not incur.

PARTIES AND IDEOLOGIES: AN ELITIST INTERPRETATION

Elitism asserts that the elites share a consensus about the fundamental values of the political system. The elite consensus does not mean that elite members never disagree or never compete with one another for preeminence. But elitism implies that competition centers on a narrow range of issues and that the elites agree on more matters than they disagree on. Our elite model suggests that parties agree about the general direction of public policy and limit their disagreement to relatively minor matters. Our analysis of the party system in the United States suggests the following propositions:

1. U.S. political parties do not present clear ideological alternatives to the American voter. Both major parties are overwhelmingly middle class in organization, values, and goals. Deviation from the shared consensus by either party is more likely to lose than attract voters.
2. Both parties draw support from all social groups in the United States, although the Democrats draw disproportionately from labor union members and their families, big-city dwellers, Jews, Catholics, and African Americans. The Republicans draw disproportionate support from rural, small-town, and suburban Protestants and business and professional people.
3. Democratic and Republican party leaders differ over public policy more than Democratic and Republican mass followers do. However, all observed party differences fall well within the range of elite consensus on the values of individualism and capitalism.
4. The parties are dominated by small groups of activists who formulate party objectives and select candidates for public office. The masses play a passive role in party affairs. They are not really members of the party; they are more like consumers. Party activists differ from the masses because they have the time and financial resources to be able to "afford" politics, the information and knowledge to understand it, and the organization and public relations skills to be successful in it.
5. Individual political party identification is reasonably stable. However, recent years have seen dealignment from both parties—a growth of independent voters, a decline in "strong" party identifiers, and more split-ticket voting.
6. Despite mass disenchantment with the Democratic and Republican parties, Independent third-party candidates face formidable barriers in the American electoral system, including winner-take-all district and state elections and state laws limiting access to the ballot.

Selected Readings

Beck, Paul Allen, and Marjorie Hershey. *Party Politics in America*, 11th ed. New York: Longman, 2005. An authoritative text on the American party system—party organizations, the parties in government, and the parties in the electorate.

Downs, Anthony. *An Economic Theory of Democracy*. New York: Harper & Row, 1959. Downs develops his now classic abstract model of party politics based on rational theory. He discusses the relationships among voters, parties, and governmental policy according to this theory and deduces empirical propositions.

Lowi, Theodore E., and Joseph Romange. *Debating the Two-Party System*. Boulder, Colo.: Rowman & Littlefield, 1997. Lowi argues that the two-party system is no longer adequate to represent the people of a diverse nation; Romange counters that two parties help unify the country and instruct Americans about the value of compromise.

Wattenberg, Martin P. *The Decline of American Political Parties*. Cambridge, Mass.: Harvard University Press, 1990. An illuminating discussion of growing negative views of the parties and the increasing dealignment of the electorate from the party system.

White, John Kenneth, and Daniel M. Shen. *New Party Politics*, 2nd ed. Belmont, Calif.: Wadsworth, 2004. A historical approach to the evolution of the American party system.

Notes

1. Geofrey C. Layman and Thomas M. Carsey, "Party Polarization and Conflict Extension in the American Electorate," *American Journal of Political Science*, 46 (October 2002): 786–802.

2. John Petrocik, "The Post New Deal Party Coalitions and the Election of 1984," paper presented at the meeting of the New Orleans, Political Science Association, American 1985, p. 7.

3. Jeane Kirkpatrick, *Dismantling the Parties* (Washington, D.C.: American Enterprise Institute, 1978), p. 7.

4. Frank J. Sorauf, *Party Politics in America* (Boston: Little, Brown, 1968), pp. 79–80.

As long as people are people, democracy, in the full sense of the word, will always be no more than an ideal. One may approach it as one would the horizon in ways that may be better or worse, but it can never be fully attained. In this sense, you, too, are merely approaching democracy.

Vaclav Havel

ELECTIONS, MONEY, AND THE MYTHS OF DEMOCRACY

CHAPTER **8**

Are elections a means by which the masses can hold the elites responsible for their policy decisions? Do elections enable the masses to direct public policy by voting for one candidate or party or another on election day?

We argue that elections *do not* serve as policy mandates; instead, they function as symbolic reassurance to the masses. By allowing the masses to participate in a political activity, elections contribute to the legitimacy of government. Elected officeholders can claim that their selection by the voters legitimizes what they do in office; that the voters' collective decision to install them in office morally binds citizens to obey the laws; that the masses' only recourse to unjust laws is to wait until the next election to "throw the bums out." Yet even if the "bums" could be thrown out of office (and more than 90 percent of them are regularly reelected), there is no guarantee that public policy would change.

Finally, we argue that money drives political campaigns in America, not policy positions or voting records or even party or ideology. The influence of money in elections and the influence of those who make campaign contributions have grown dramatically in recent decades.

THE MYTH OF THE POLICY MANDATE

For elections to serve as *policy mandates*—that is, for voters to exercise influence over public policy through elections—four conditions would be necessary: (1) competing parties and candidates would offer clear policy alternatives; (2) voters would be concerned with policy questions; (3) election results would clarify majority preferences on these questions; and (4) elected officials would be bound by their campaign positions.

IN BRIEF | ## WHY ELECTIONS ARE NOT POLICY MANDATES

- The parties do not offer clear policy alternatives.
- Policy considerations are not the primary motivators of voter decisions.

- Majority preferences on policy questions cannot be determined from election results.
- Elected officials frequently ignore their campaign policy pledges.

However, politics in the United States fulfills none of these conditions. Voters consequently cannot directly control public policy, for several reasons:

1. Because both parties agree on the major direction of public policy (see Chapter 7), the voters cannot influence it by choosing between the parties. Indeed, inasmuch as more voters describe themselves as "moderate" or "middle-of-the-road" than "liberal" or "conservative," it would be irrational for the Democratic and Republican parties to clearly differentiate their policy positions.
2. For a mandate to be valid, the electorate must make informed policy-oriented choices. But most voters are poorly informed on policy questions and have no strong, consistent policy positions. Traditional party ties and candidate personalities influence voters more than policy questions do. These factors dilute the voters' influence over policy.
3. Victory for a candidate's party need not mean that the voters support all of its programs. Among the voters for a candidate are opponents as well as advocates of the candidate's position on a given issue. A popular majority may be composed of many policy minorities. How is a candidate to know which (if any) of his or her policy positions brought electoral victory?
4. Finally, for voters to exercise control over public officials, elected officials would have to be bound by their campaign pledges. However, elected officials frequently ignore their campaign pledges.

THE MYTH OF THE POLICY-ORIENTED VOTER

For the masses to influence policy through elections, not only would the parties have to offer clear and divergent policy alternatives to the voters, but the voters would also have to make their electoral choices on the basis of their policy preferences. But as we have already noted (see Chapter 5), most voters have no information or opinion about many specific policy issues and therefore cannot be expected to base their electoral choices on these issues. However, it is sometimes argued that, in lieu of specific policy stances, voters have broad liberal or conservative policy dispositions they use as a basis for voting. Moreover, party identification correlates closely with voter choice, with self-identified Democrats choosing the Democratic candidates as the "best person" and self-identified Republicans choosing the Republican candidate.

DETERMINANTS OF VOTER CHOICE

To assess the determinants of voters' choice, the University of Michigan Survey Research Center regularly examines the responses of samples of voters in presidential and congressional elections.[1] Researchers have derived the following categories as a

TABLE 8.1 | DETERMINANTS OF VOTER CHOICE

Voter Category	Percentage
Issues/ideology	19.4
Group benefits	30.0
Nature of the times (economy)	28.1
Candidate image/other	21.5

Source: Calculated by the authors as averages over elections from 1986 through 2000 from data supplied by the University of Michigan Survey Research Center.

American National Election Studies (ANES)
Data on voting, public opinion, and political participation in presidential and congressional elections.
www.electionstudies. org

result. *Ideologues* are respondents who are either "liberal" or "conservative" and are likely to rely on these principles in evaluating candidates and issues. *Near ideologues* are those who mention liberalism or conservatism but do not rely on these dimensions as much as the ideologues do and may not clearly understand the meaning of these political terms. At the next level, the *group benefits* class contains those who do not exhibit any ideological thinking but are able to evaluate parties and candidates by expected favorable or unfavorable treatment for social groups. Subjects favor candidates they consider sympathetic to a group with which they identify. A fourth group is respondents who base their judgment on their perception of the nature of the times— that is, the "goodness" or "badness" of the times. They blame or praise parties and candidates because of their association with conditions of war or peace, prosperity or depression. Finally, as party and ideological affiliations have moderated, increasing numbers of voters are casting their ballots based on the personal characteristics of candidates. Television, including the presidential debates, allows voters to assess the personal qualities of the candidates—their warmth, compassion, strength, confidence, sincerity, and good humor. Of course, voters see only the images the candidates project through the media, that is, *candidate image.*

Issue and ideological voting appeared to be significant determinants of voter choice for less than 20 percent of the voters (see Table 8.1). Clearly, the vast majority of voters do *not* base their choice primarily on issues or ideology. (However, it is interesting to note that issue and ideological voting is most likely to occur among college-educated voters.) Issue and ideological debates between the candidates have relatively little meaning for the masses of Americans.

PARTY VOTING

Party identification remains a powerful influence on voter choice. Party ties among voters have weakened over time, with increasing proportions of voters labeling themselves as independents or only weak Democrats or Republicans, and more voters opting to split their tickets or cross party lines than they did a generation ago (see Chapter 7). Nevertheless, party identification correlates closely with voter choice. Party identification is more important in congressional than in presidential elections, but even in presidential elections the tendency to see the candidate of one's own party as "the best person" is very strong. Consider, for example, three presidential elections

TABLE 8.2 | PARTY AND VOTER CHOICE

2004	Kerry (Democrat)	Bush (Republican)
Democrats	90%	9%
Republicans	7	92
Independents	45	48
2000	Gore (Democrat)	Bush (Republican)
Democrats	86%	11%
Republicans	8	91
Independents	45	47
1996	Clinton (Democrat)	Dole (Republican)
Democrats	84%	10%
Republicans	13	80
Independents	43	35

Source: Election exit polls, reported by Voter News Service.

(see Table 8.2): self-identified Republicans voted overwhelmingly for Dole in 1996 and for George W. Bush in 2000 and 2004. Self-identified Democrats voted overwhelmingly for Clinton in 1996, for Gore in 2000, and for Kerry in 2004. Because self-identified Democrats outnumber self-identified Republicans in the electorate, Republican candidates must broaden their appeal to independent and Democratic crossover voters to win elections.

THE GROUP BASIS OF VOTING

The social group basis of voting is easily observed in presidential elections. Different social groups give disproportionate support to Republican and Democratic candidates. No group is *wholly* within one party or the other, and group differences are modest, with the exception of the strong Democratic loyalty shown by African American voters over the years. If no group influences were involved in voter choices, we would expect that the percentage of each group's vote for Democratic and Republican candidates would be the same as the national percentages. But it is clear that Democratic presidential candidates have drawn disproportionate support from blacks, union members, less-educated manual workers, Catholics, and Jews. Republican presidential candidates, meanwhile, have drawn disproportionate support from whites, the college educated, professional and business people, and Protestants. And recently a significant "gender gap" has developed between the parties, with Democratic candidates doing better among women than men (see Table 8.3).

Pluralists argue that these social group differences in voting are evidence of a "responsible" electorate. Pluralists may acknowledge that most voters have no knowledge of specific policy issues, and some pluralists will even acknowledge that

TABLE 8.3 | GROUP VOTING IN PRESIDENTIAL ELECTIONS

Demographic Factors	1984		1988		1992			1996			2000		2004	
	Mondale (D)	Reagan (R)	Dukakis (D)	Bush (R)	Clinton (D)	Bush (R)	Perot (I)	Clinton (D)	Dole (R)	Perot (I)	Gore (D)	Bush (R)	Kerry (D)	Bush (R)
National (%)	41	59	46	54	43	38	19	49	41	8	48	48	48	51
Sex														
Male	37	62	41	54	41	38	21	43	44	10	42	53	45	54
Female	44	56	49	50	45	37	17	54	38	7	54	43	52	47
Race/ethnicity														
White	35	64	40	59	39	40	20	43	46	9	42	54	42	57
Black	89	9	86	12	83	10	7	84	12	4	90	8	89	11
Hispanic	61	37	69	30	61	25	14	72	21	6	62	35	55	42
Religion														
Protestant	27	72	33	66	33	47	21	36	53	10	42	56	41	58
Catholic	45	54	47	52	44	35	20	53	37	9	50	47	48	51
Jewish	67	31	64	35	80	11	9	78	16	3	79	19	76	24
Education														
Not high school graduate	50	49	56	43	54	28	18	59	28	11	59	38	50	49
High school graduate	39	60	49	50	43	36	21	51	35	13	48	49	48	51
Some college	37	61	42	57	41	37	21	48	40	10	45	51	46	53
College graduate	41	58	43	56	44	39	17	47	44	7	45	51	47	51
Union														
Labor union family	53	46	57	42	55	24	21	59	30	9	67	30	62	36

most voters do not consistently or accurately apply liberal or conservative policy dimensions to their electoral choice. However, pluralists argue that many voters use a *group benefits* standard in making their electoral choice. For example, many black voters may not follow specific arguments on civil rights legislation or study the candidates' records on the issue. But they have a general idea that the Democratic Party, beginning with President Franklin D. Roosevelt and continuing

through the administration of President Lyndon Johnson, took the lead in supporting civil rights legislation. Thus, it is not irrational for black voters to give
disproportionate support to Democratic candidates, even when particular Republican and Democratic candidates have similar records in support of civil rights.
Likewise, voters in other social groups may use a group benefits standard in
evaluating parties and candidates. In short, group identification becomes the
essential mediating device between the individual voter and electoral choice.

For many years the group basis of voter choice directed political campaign
strategy. Candidates conscientiously solicited the support of identifiable social
groups—union members, teachers, farmers, small-business owners, Jews, the
aged, ethnic groups, and so on—by appearing at rallies, securing the endorsement
of group leaders, pledging to look after a group's interests, or citing their personal
(sometimes manufactured) identification with the group they were addressing.
And, indeed, all candidates continue to be sensitive to group identifications among
voters.

Group identifications in the electorate constitute the strongest arguments in
support of pluralist political theory (see Chapter 1). However, there is evidence that
these group identifications may be declining in importance in electoral politics.

THE ECONOMIC BASIS OF VOTING

Ever since the once-popular Republican incumbent Herbert Hoover was trounced by
Franklin D. Roosevelt as the Great Depression of the 1930s deepened, politicians have
understood that *voters tend to hold the incumbent party responsible for hard
economic times.* Perhaps no other lesson has been as well learned by politicians:
hard economic times hurt incumbents and favor challengers. The economy may not be
the only important factor in presidential voting, but it is certainly a factor of great
importance.

Economic conditions at election time—recent growth or decline in personal
income, the unemployment rate, consumer confidence, and so on—are usually closely
related to the vote given the incumbent versus the challenger. Economic recessions
played a major role in the defeat of Presidents Herbert Hoover (1932), Jimmy Carter
(1980), and George H. W. Bush (1992).

Campaigns and Elections
The Web site for "Campaigns and Elections," a magazine directed toward candidates, campaign managers, political TV advertisers, political con-
sultants, and lobbyists.
www.campaignline. com

There is some evidence that it is not the voter's *own* personal economic well-being
that affects his or her vote but rather the voter's perception of *general* economic
conditions. People who perceive the economy as getting worse are likely to vote
against the incumbent party, whereas people who think the economy is getting better
support the incumbent.

However, Democrat Al Gore was unable to ride the strong economy to victory in
2000. By traditional expectations, Gore's election should have been a "slam dunk."
The nation was enjoying economic prosperity, low unemployment, low inflation,
budget surpluses, and relative peace. Most political science "models" of election
outcomes projected Gore as an easy victor. But, contrary to expectations under these
conditions, not enough Americans supported the incumbent party's presidential
candidate. Al Gore won the popular vote but failed to offer the voters the *image*
that they sought in a president.

CANDIDATE IMAGE VOTING

Today's media-oriented campaigning, emphasizing direct television communication with individual voters, reduces the mediating function of parties and groups. Media campaigning emphasizes *candidate image*—personal qualities such as leadership, compassion, character, humor, and charm. As independent and middle-of-the-road identifications among voters have grown, the personal characteristics of candidates have become central to many voters. Indeed, the personal qualities of candidates are most important in the decision of less partisan, less ideological voters. Candidate image is more important in presidential than congressional contests, inasmuch as presidential candidates are personally more visible to the voter than candidates for lesser offices.

It is difficult to identify exactly what personal qualities appeal most to voters. Warmth, compassion, strength, confidence, honesty, sincerity, good humor, appearance, and "character" all seem important. "Character" has become a central feature of media coverage of candidates (see Chapter 6). Reports of extramarital affairs, experimentation with drugs, draft dodging, cheating in college, shady financial dealings, conflicts of interest, or lying or misrepresenting facts receive heavy media coverage because they attract large audiences. But it is difficult to estimate how many voters are swayed by "character" issues.

Attractive personal qualities can win support from opposition-party identifiers and people who disagree on the issues. John F. Kennedy's handsome and youthful appearance, charm, self-confidence, and disarming good humor defeated the heavy-jowled, shifty-eyed, defensive, and ill-humored Richard Nixon. Ronald Reagan's folksy mannerisms, warm humor, and comfortable rapport with television audiences

"We're not saying that nobody likes you. We're just saying you need to work on your likability."

| FOCUS | IMAGES OF BUSH AND KERRY, 2004 |

President George Bush projected an image as "a strong and decisive leader" to most Americans. The nation was in a war on terrorism and George Bush was believed to be a capable Commander-in-Chief. Bush held the advantage on most personal qualities— "takes a stand," "strong leader," "good in a crisis," "down to earth," and "personally likable."

John Kerry was respected for his service in Vietnam, and early in the campaign he attempted to contrast his combat experience in that war to Bush's service at home in the Texas Air National Guard. But events of thirty-five years ago did not seem to motivate many voters.

Kerry's strength rested on his image as better at handling the economy, providing jobs, and ensuring health care for all. He was also seen as "understanding the needs of people like yourself." But the Bush team was able to convince many Americans that Kerry flip-flopped on the issues. For example, paid Republican TV ads stressed his changing positions on Iraq, at first voting to support military action and later voting against appropriations to support that action.

CHARACTER TRAITS THAT BETTER DESCRIBE . . .

	Bush	**Kerry**
Takes a stand	62%	29%
Strong leader	57	34
Good in a crisis	50	38
Down to earth	48	39
Personally likable	43	41
Honest and truthful	42	38
Cares about people	39	45
Changes his mind	28	47

Source: Pew Center for the People and the Press, September 23, 2004.

justly earned him the title "the Great Communicator." Reagan disarmed his critics by laughing at his own flubs—falling asleep at meetings, forgetting names—and by telling his own age jokes. His personal appeal won more Democratic voters than any other Republican candidate had won in modern history, and he won the votes of many people who disagreed with him on the issues.

MONEY DRIVES ELECTIONS

The high costs of media campaigning add to the political influence of wealthy contributors and thus add further to elitism in electoral politics. Campaign spending by *all* presidential and congressional candidates, the Democratic and Republican parties, and independent political organizations now approaches $3 *billion* per election! The most important hurdle for any candidate for public office is raising the funds to meet campaign costs.

**Center for Respon-
sive Politics**
The Web site of an organization devoted to the study of campaign finance laws, the role of money in elections, PACs, "soft money," and special-interest groups.
www.opensecrets.org

The presidential elections of 2000 and 2004 set new records for spending (see Figure 8.1). George W. Bush spent about one-third more than Al Gore and John Kerry, but both Democratic and Republican candidates broke spending records of all previous presidential candidates.

Expenditures for congressional campaigns have also reached new highs. The typical winning campaign for a U.S. Senate seat cost $10 to $12 million. But Senate campaign costs vary a great deal from state to state. The U.S. Senate race in New York in 2000, featuring former first lady Hillary Clinton, set a new spending record for a congressional election at more than $85 million. Senator Clinton spend $57 million in her 2006 reelection campaign. A new individual congressional spending record of $65

IN BRIEF	## DETERMINANTS OF VOTER CHOICE

- Elections are not policy mandates. The vast majority of voters do not base their electoral choices on candidates' stands on issues.
- Party identification remains a strong influence over voter choice.
- Different social groups give disproportionate support to Democratic and Republican

candidates. This is the strongest argument for a pluralist interpretation of politics.
- Voters tend to hold the incumbent party responsible for hard economic times.
- Media campaigning emphasizes candidate "image" in voter choice.

million was set by multibillionaire investment banker (Goldman Sachs) Democrat Jon Corzine, who dug into his own fortune to win the U.S. Senate seat from New Jersey.

The typical winning campaign for a seat in the House of Representatives now costs more than $1.2 million.[2] House members seeking to retain their seats must raise this amount *every two years!* Even losers typically spend over $200,000.

FINDING AND FEEDING THE "FAT CATS"

Most campaign funds are raised from individual contributions. Only about one-third of 1 percent (0.33 percent) of the adult population of the nation contributes $200 or more to presidential or congressional campaigns.[3] (In national surveys, about 7 percent to 10 percent of the population *claims* to have contributed to candidates running for public office.) Contributors are disproportionately high-income, well-educated professional

FOCUS | ## DIRTY POLITICS

Political campaigning frequently turns ugly with negative advertising that is vicious and personal. It is widely believed that television's focus on personal character and private life—rather than on policy positions and governmental experience—encourages negative campaigning. But vicious personal attacks in political campaigns began long before television. They are nearly as old as the nation itself.

"If Jefferson is elected," proclaimed Yale's president in 1800, "the Bible will be burned and we will see our wives and daughters the victims of legal prostitution." In 1864, *Harper's Weekly* decried the "mudslinging" of the day, lamenting that President Abraham Lincoln was regularly referred to by his opponent as a "filthy storyteller, despot, liar, thief, braggart, buffoon, monster, ignoramus Abe, robber, swindler, tyrant, fiend, butcher, and pirate."

Television's first memorable attack advertisement was the "Daisy Girl" commercial broadcast by Lyndon Johnson's presidential campaign in 1964 against his Republican opponent, Barry Goldwater. Although never mentioning Goldwater by name, the purpose of the ad was to "define" him as a warmonger who would plunge the world into a nuclear holocaust. The ad opens with a small, innocent girl standing in an open field plucking petals from a daisy and counting, "1, 2, 3...." When she reaches 9, an ominous adult male voice begins a countdown: "10, 9, 8..." as the camera closes in on the child's face. At "0," a mushroom cloud appears, reflected in her eyes, and envelops the screen. Lyndon Johnson's voice is heard: "These are the stakes."

"Attack ads" have multiplied at all levels of government in recent elections. Following Kerry's own references to his Vietnam combat record, an independent group, Swift Boat Veterans for Truth, challenged the legitimacy of Kerry's story about his Bronze Star and asserted that at least one of his Purple Hearts was awarded for self-inflicted wounds

and not as a result of enemy action. The Swift Boat TV ads were widely condemned; John Kerry had volunteered for Vietnam and had served honorably. Later, the Swift Boat group redirected their ads toward Kerry's post-Vietnam behavior as a leader in the Vietnam Veterans Against the War. These ads showed a young Kerry at a congressional hearing accusing his fellow veterans of terrible atrocities, "murdering civilians, cutting off heads, and burning villages." These ads corresponded to a slight drop in Kerry's poll numbers.

But Bush's service in the Texas Air National Guard during the Vietnam War was also a target of attack. Bush joined the Guard with the possible help of family friends, but he won his wings as a fighter pilot. The Texas Guard was never called to active duty, and Bush never saw combat. But a CBS News report by Dan Rather based on forged documents asserted that Bush failed to meet his Guard responsibilities. Later CBS News recanted the charge. The affair may have helped Bush somewhat, by convincing viewers that Dan Rather and others at CBS were biased against him.

What are the effects of negative advertising? First of all, it works more often than not. Controlled experiments indicate that targets of attack ads are rated less positively by people who have watched these ads. But another effect of negative advertising is to make voters more cynical about politics and government in general. There is conflicting evidence about whether or not negative campaigning by opposing candidates reduces voter turnout.

Sources: Kathleen Hall Jamieson, *Dirty Politics: Deception, Distraction, and Democracy* (New York: Oxford University Press, 1992); also Stephen Ansolabehere et al., "Does Attack Advertising Demobilize the Electorate?" *American Political Science Review*, 88 (December 1994): 829–838; Kim Fridkin Kahn and Patrick J. Kenney, "Do Negative Campaigns Mobilize or Suppress Turnout?" *American Political Science Review*, 93 (December 1999): 877–889.

people with strong partisan views (see Figure 8.2). There are networks of contributors in every state, and campaign staffs use sophisticated computerized mailing lists and telephone directories of regular Democratic and Republican and liberal and conservative contributors to solicit funds.

Small donors (people who give less than $200 in a single contribution) account for the largest category of contributors. But fat cats (people who write checks to the candidates or parties for $2,000, $5,000, or more) are the most valued contributors.

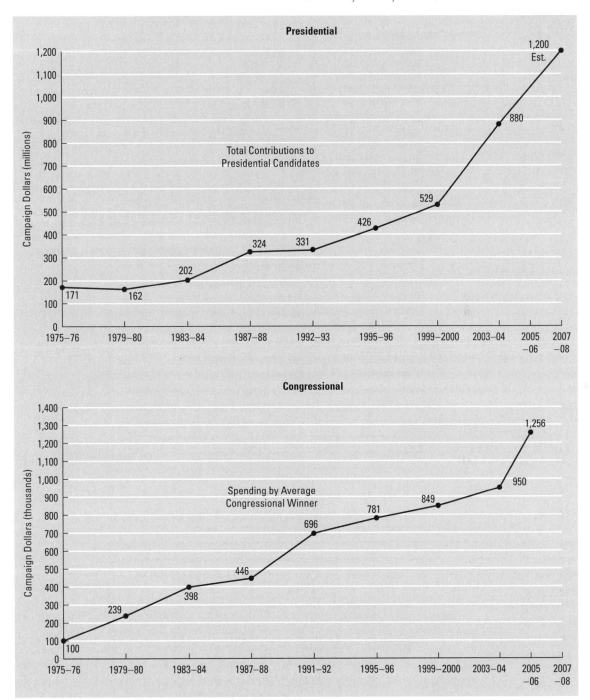

FIGURE 8.1 | THE GROWING COSTS OF CAMPAIGNS

Note: Figures include campaign and party expenditures but exclude expenditures by independent groups. Estimate for 2007–08 by Center for Responsive Politics.

Source: Center for Responsive Politics.

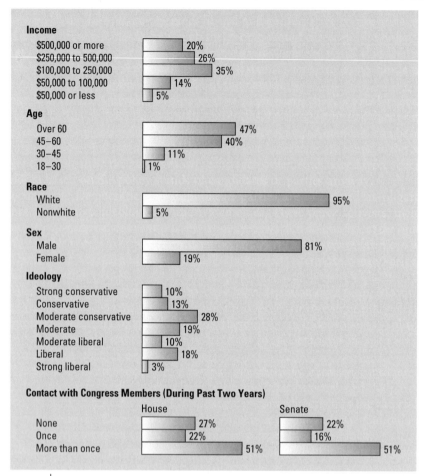

FIGURE 8.2 | CHARACTERISTICS OF INDIVIDUAL POLITICAL CAMPAIGN DONORS

Source: Data from John Green, Paul Herrnson, Lynda Powell, and Clyde Wilcox, "Individual Congressional Campaign Contributions," June 9, 1998, Center for Responsive Politics.

Despite their financial importance, these donors make up less than one-fifth of 1 percent (0.07 percent) of the nation's adult population. A $2,300 check is only the entry fee for fat-cat status; a contribution of $100,000 is preferred. These are the donors whose names are on the candidates' Rolodexes. These are the ones in attendance when the president, the speaker of the house, or other top political dignitaries travel around the country for fund-raisers. They are also the ones who are wined, dined, prodded, and cajoled in a seemingly ceaseless effort by the parties and the candidates to raise funds for the next election.

Fund-raising occupies more of a candidate's time than any other campaign activity. Fund-raising dinners ($2,300 or more per plate), cocktail parties, barbecues, fish fries, and so on are scheduled nearly every day of a campaign. The candidates are expected to appear personally to "press the flesh" of big contributors, the "fat cats."

Movie and rock stars and other assorted celebrities may also be asked to appear at fund-raising affairs to generate attendance. Tickets may be "bundled" to well-heeled individual contributors or sold in blocks to organizations.

THE FAT CATS: TOP CAMPAIGN CONTRIBUTORS

The Center for Responsive Politics, a Washington-based reform organization, studies Federal Elections Commission campaign records for all presidential and congressional contributions. Contributions from 1989 to 2004 have been combined in a list of the top donors (see Table 8.4). This donors list reflects the total contributions to candidates or political parties of the top fifty givers, their political action committees (PACs), employees, and members of their immediate families, according to a study by the Center for Responsive Politics. Not included are independent expenditures, money for issue advertisements, or other indirect expenses.

MILKING THE PACs

Interest groups generally channel their campaign contributions through political action committees. Corporations and unions are not allowed to contribute directly from corporate or union funds, but they may form PACs to seek contributions from managers and stockholders and their families or from union workers and their families. PACs are organized not only by corporations and unions but also by trade and professional associations, environmental groups, and liberal and conservative ideological groups. PAC contributions account for nearly 50 percent of all House campaign financing and about 25 percent of all Senate campaign financing. (For a list of the top PACs, see Table 9.2.)

PAC money goes overwhelmingly (80 percent or more) to incumbent officeholders. When Democrats control Congress, business PACs split their dollars nearly evenly between Democrats and Republicans; when Republicans control Congress, they shift their dollars heavily to the GOP. Labor PACs, however, do not back down from their traditional support of Democrats, even when Republicans control Congress.

WEALTHY CANDIDATES

Candidates for federal office also pump millions of dollars into their own campaigns. (Jon Corzine [D.-New Jersey] won his U.S. Senate seat in 2000 with $65 million of his *own* money.) Candidates can put their own money into their campaigns either through outright gifts or personal loans. (If a candidate lends himself or herself the money to run, he or she is able to pay the loan back later from outside contributions.)

The Supreme Court opened this loophole by declaring that, as an exercise of one's First Amendment right of free speech, individuals can spend as much of their personal wealth on their own campaigns as they wish. Specifically, in *Buckley v. Valeo* in 1976, the U.S. Supreme Court held that the government could not limit individuals' rights to spend money to publish or broadcast their own views on issues or elections. This means not only that candidates can spend unlimited amounts of their own money on their own campaigns but also that private individuals can spend unlimited amounts to circulate their own views on an election (although their contributions to candidates and parties can still be limited).[4]

TABLE 8.4 | ALL-TIME FAT-CAT CAMPAIGN CONTRIBUTORS, 1989–2004

Rank	Organization Name	Total ($ Millions)	Democrats (%)	Republicans (%)
1	American Fedn. of State, County and Municipal Employees	$35.0	98	1
2	National Assn. of Realtors	$24.5	50	49
3	National Education Assn.	$23.6	88	11
4	Assn. of Trial Lawyers of America	$23.4	89	9
5	Communications Workers of America	$22.1	98	0
6	Service Employees International Union	$21.9	87	11
7	Intl. Brotherhood of Electrical Workers	$21.6	96	3
8	Carpenters and Joiners Union	$21.0	69	30
9	Teamsters Union	$20.9	85	13
10	American Medical Assn.	$20.7	27	72
11	Altria Group	$20.6	42	57
12	FedEx Corp	$20.6	34	65
13	Laborers Union	$20.6	86	13
14	United Auto Workers	$20.1	98	0
15	AT&T	$19.5	46	53
16	American Federation of Teachers	$19.4	98	1
17	Goldman Sachs	$18.9	50	49
18	Machinists and Aerospace Workers Union	$18.7	99	0
19	United Food and Commercial Workers Union	$18.4	97	2
20	Citigroup Inc.	$17.2	50	49
21	United Parcel Service	$16.9	29	70
22	National Auto Dealers Assn.	$16.6	28	71
23	National Assn. of Home Builders	$15.1	37	62
24	National Assn. of Letter Carriers	$14.8	75	24
25	National Rifle Assn.	$14.4	13	86
26	AFL-CIO	$14.1	89	10
27	American Bankers Assn.	$13.8	38	61
28	Time Warner	$13.5	72	27
29	SBC Communications	$13.1	34	65
30	Verizon Communications	$12.7	37	62
31	BellSouth Corp.	$12.5	41	58

TABLE 8.4 | ALL-TIME FAT-CAT CAMPAIGN CONTRIBUTORS, 1989–2004 *continued*

Rank	Organization Name	Total ($ Millions)	Democrats (%)	Republicans (%)
32	Microsoft Corp.	$12.5	60	39
33	National Beer Wholesalers Assn.	$12.4	29	70
34	EMILY's List	$11.9	100	0
35	Sheet Metal Workers Union	$11.8	97	2
36	Ernst and Young	$11.7	32	67
37	JPMorgan Chase and Co.	$11.5	50	49
38	Lockheed Martin	$11.5	39	60
39	American Dental Assn.	$11.0	43	56
40	RJR Nabisco/RJ Reynolds Tobacco	$11.0	11	88
41	Morgan Stanley	$11.0	34	65
42	American Hospital Assn.	$10.9	44	55
43	Blue Cross/Blue Shield	$10.8	42	57
44	General Electric	$10.7	44	55
45	National Assn. of Insurance and Financial Advisors	$10.7	37	62
46	American Institute of CPAs	$10.4	38	61
47	Credit Union National Assn.	$10.2	42	57
48	Union Pacific Corp.	$10.2	21	78
49	Bank of America	$10.2	45	54
50	United Steelworkers of America	$10.1	98	1

Source: Center for Responsive Politics.

"FOOD STAMPS FOR POLITICIANS"

Federal funding is available to presidential candidates in both primary and general elections. Candidates seeking the nomination in presidential primary elections can qualify for federal funds by raising $5,000 from private contributions no greater than $250 each in each of twenty states. In the general election, the Democratic and Republican nominees are funded equally at levels determined by the Federal Election Commission.

Federal funding is financed by a $3 "check-off" box on individual income tax returns. All taxpayers are asked whether they wish $3 of their tax payments to go into the federal presidential election campaign fund. But taxpayers have grown increasingly reluctant to have their tax dollars spent for political campaigning, even though the $3 contribution does not increase their taxes. Today only about 13 percent of taxpayers check off the box for presidential campaign funding.

SOFT MONEY   Before 2002, "soft money"—political contributions given directly to the Democratic and Republican parties—was unlimited as to amount. Nearly all soft money was raised in large contributions—indeed, the reason soft money was so popular with parties was that it allowed big donors to give without having to abide by the limits imposed on direct campaign contributions. Direct contributions to the candidates were referred to as "hard money," and the amount any individual could contribute was limited. Technically, soft money was supposed to be used for party building, get-out-the-vote drives, or general party advertising ("Vote Democratic" or "Vote Republican"). But in reality, both parties used their soft money in direct support of their candidates rather than for building the party.

BIPARTISAN CAMPAIGN REFORM ACT (BCRA)   Campaign finance reform, notably the elimination of soft money contributions, became a national issue when Senator John McCain challenged George W. Bush in the Republican primary elections in 2000. McCain failed to win the GOP presidential nomination, but he forced Bush and many Republican Congress members to voice their support for campaign reform. Following the election, McCain and other reformers in Congress pressed the issue, resulting in a major rewrite of campaign finance laws. Among the more important reforms of the BCRA:

- *Hard money:* Contributions from individuals to federal candidates are limited (initially to $2,000) and indexed to grow with inflation (to $2,300 in 2008). Individual contributions to political parties are limited to $25,000 per year.
- *Soft money:* Contributions to national party committees are limited to $5,000. Parties may no longer accept or spend unregulated soft money. State and local party committees can solicit contributions of up to $10,000 for get-out-the-vote activities and registration efforts in federal elections.
- *Broadcast advertising:* Ads by corporations, unions, and interest groups, in support of a federal candidate, cannot be run 60 days before a general election or 30 days before a primary.

THE SUPREME COURT AND CAMPAIGN FINANCE   The U.S. Supreme Court has recognized that limitations on campaign *contributions* help further a compelling government interest—"preventing corruption and the appearance of corruption" in election campaigns. But the Court has been reluctant to allow governments to limit campaign *expenditures,* because paying to express political views is necessary in the exercise of free speech. In an important early case, *Buckley v. Valeo* (1976), the Court held that limiting a candidate's campaign *expenditures* violated the First Amendment's guarantee of free speech.[5]

Later, when called upon to consider the constitutionality of the BCRA, the Court upheld limitations on contributions directly to candidates and to national parties.[6] It also upheld limits on "soft money" contribution to state and local parties, recognizing that these provisions were designed to prevent circumventions of valid prohibitions on campaign contributions. In addition, the Court also upheld a prohibition on spending for "electioneering communications" by individuals and interest groups that are controlled or coordinated with parties or candidates.

Later, the Supreme Court reconsidered the BCRA's provisions limiting individual and organization electioneering communications. The Court distinguished between "express advocacy" on behalf of a candidate or party and "issue ads" that are *not* the functional equivalent of express advocacy. (In other words, ads that do not urge viewers or listeners to vote for or against a particular candidate or party.) "When it comes to defining what speech qualifies as the functional equivalent of express

| FOCUS | How Fat Cats Evade Campaign Finance Reform |

Campaign cash is like the Pillsbury Doughboy: push in one place and it pops out in another. The Bipartisan Campaign Finance Reform Act does not prohibit individuals or nonprofit independent groups from accepting large contributions and spending as much as they want to broadcast their views. Early in the 2004 election, campaign fat-cat contributors and politically savvy consultants, especially in the Democratic Party, began to build a network of independent organizations—organizations into which they could funnel millions of dollars to use in the presidential campaign.

George Soros, one of the world's richest men, is giving away billions to promote democracy in former Soviet bloc nations, including his birthplace, Hungary. In addition, Soros funds a wide variety of liberal causes through his Open Society Institute. In 2003, he declared financial war on George Bush. He gave millions to a series of often newly created liberal organizations, including:

- *MoveOn:* an organization originally formed to defend President Bill Clinton against impeachment. MoveOn is now the leading ultra-liberal group in the Democratic Party.
- *America Votes:* originally created by former Texas governor Ann Richards to get out the anti–George Bush vote. It is now a "progressive voter mobilization" group.
- *The Media Fund:* organized to raise big money to buy TV and radio ads attacking George Bush.
- *Grassroots Democrats:* organized by the Communications Workers of America and the Association of Trial Lawyers to elect Democrats.

These organizations and others like them accept millions of dollars from fat-cat contributors for political TV ads, so long as these do not mention a candidate by name.

MoveOn
Leading liberal organization Web site.
www.moveon.org

advocacy, the Court should give the benefit of doubt to speech, not censorship."[7] The effect of the decision is to permit political contributors to support organizations unaffiliated with a candidate or party, including nonprofit "527" organizations, that air television ads not expressly endorsing a candidate right up to the election day.

INDEPENDENT GROUP EXPENDITURES, "527s" Expenditures by independent groups (sometimes referred to as "527s" based on the authorizing provision in the U.S. Tax Code) are unregulated so long as they are not coordinated with a candidate's campaign. Contributions to these organizations are also unregulated. Big money contributors who can no longer provide large amounts of cash to candidates or to parties can establish these 527 independent groups to produce and broadcast campaign advertisements (see Focus: How Fat Cats Evade Campaign Finance Reform).

DEMOCRACY VERSUS THE ELECTORAL COLLEGE

Elections are designed to confer legitimacy on governmental elites. Elections are supposed to reassure the masses that elites who exercise governmental power do so with popular consent. Because citizens are offered a role in the selection of governmental officials, elections are supposed to morally bind citizens to respect governmental authority and to obey the laws that elected officials enact. But the irony of the 2000 presidential election was that the Supreme Court of the United States, rather than the voters, conferred legitimacy on the president.

George W. Bush was chosen president by the Supreme Court of the United States, not by the masses of voters on election day. Al Gore received 500,000 more popular votes nationwide than Bush. But the Founders—those fifty-five men who wrote the Constitution of the United States in 1787—never intended the president to be chosen by popular vote. Rather, they declared that the president was to be chosen by a majority of "electors": "Each state shall appoint, in such Manner as the Legislature thereof may direct, a Number of Electors equal to the whole number of Senators and Representatives to which the State shall be entitled in the Congress" (Article II). As Madison explained, "The public voice, pronounced by representatives of people, will be more consonant to the public good than if pronounced by the people themselves" (see "Elitism and the Structure of the National Government" in Chapter 2).

Yet, as political parties emerged in the early 1800s, the states chose to hold popular elections for slates of "electors" pledged to one or the other of the presidential candidates. In other words, popular voting for presidential electors in the states came about later by custom, not because the Founders wanted a popularly elected president (see "Rise of the Western Elites," in Chapter 3).

The Center for Voting and Democracy
A Web site with material on possible changes in the Electoral College.
www.fairvote.org

The Electoral College worked reasonably well over time. In 1876, rival slates of electors were forwarded to Congress from the southern states. The Republican-controlled Congress picked the slates pledged to Republican Rutherford B. Hayes rather than the winner of the popular vote, Democrat Samuel J. Tilden (and in the process agreed to end efforts at "Reconstruction" in the southern states; see "The History of Black Subjugation" in Chapter 15). In 1888, the Electoral College failed to reflect popular vote; Republican Benjamin Harrison received 235 electoral votes to incumbent President Grover Cleveland's 168, even though Cleveland won more popular votes nationwide. Not until 112 years later—in the 2000 presidential election—did the Electoral College again fail to reflect the nationwide popular vote.

The Supreme Court Chooses a President, 2000

It is an irony, indeed, that the most elitist branch of the U.S. government, the Supreme Court, actually chose the president in 2000. Yet only the High Court seemed to possess sufficient legitimacy to resolve the first contested presidential election in over a century. (A Gallup poll, conducted before the Supreme Court's decision, indicated that 73 percent of Americans said they would accept the Court's decision as a "legitimate outcome no matter which candidate it favors.")

The Electoral College outcome in 2000 depended on Florida's twenty-five electoral votes. After several machine recounts and counts of absentee ballots, Florida's secretary of state (separately elected Republican Katherine Harris) declared Bush the winner by 537 votes.

Armies of lawyers descended on Florida. The Gore campaign demanded hand recounts of the votes in the state's three most populous and democratic counties—Miami-Dade, Broward, and Palm Beach. Bush's lawyers argued that the hand recounts in these counties were late, unreliable, subjective, and open to partisan bias. Gore's lawyers argued that each punch card ballot should be inspected to ascertain the "intent" of the voter. Partially detached "chads" (small perforated squares in the punch cards that should fall out when the voter punches the ballot) as well as "dimpled chads" where voters may have intended to punch cards but failed to break through them, should be counted. The Democratic-controlled Florida Supreme Court ordered these recounts and set back the Florida legislature's enacted deadline for the certification of the vote.

Meanwhile Bush appealed to the Supreme Court of the United States. In *Bush v. Gore,* finally decided a month after the election, the U.S. Supreme Court held that "the use of standardless manual recounts violates the Equal Protection and Due Process clause of the Constitution" and that setting back the Florida legislature's enacted deadline violated Article II of the U.S. Constitution granting state legislatures the authority to determine the "manner" of choosing presidential electors.

The Court divided 5 to 4 along ideological lines. The five justices in the majority included acknowledged conservatives Rehnquist, Scalia, and Thomas together with moderates O'Connor and Kennedy. The minority included ideological liberals Stevens, Breyer, and Ginsburg together with Souter. Yet despite the prolonged contest, the bitter feelings of many of the participants, and the apparent partisan split, George W. Bush was recognized as the president of the United States immediately after the Supreme Court's historic decision.

Most Americans were willing to acknowledge that the nationwide popular vote for Al Gore was secondary in importance to the Constitution of the United States and its provision for choosing the president by state electoral votes. (Electoral votes of the states are shown in Figure 8.3.)

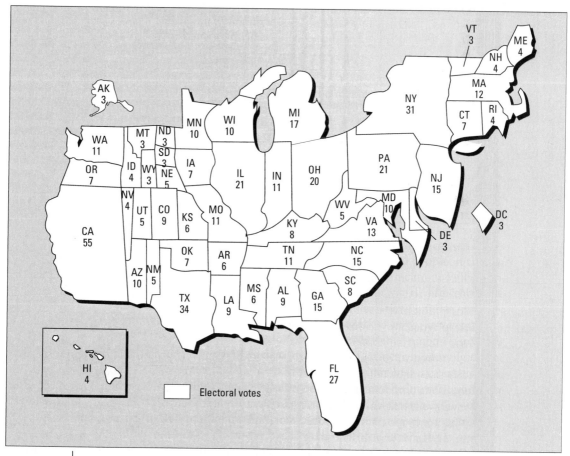

FIGURE 8.3 | ELECTORAL VOTE, 2008

Note: States drawn in proportion to number of electoral votes. Total electoral votes: 538. Needed to win: 270.

| FOCUS | OFF AND RUNNING, 2008 |

Campaigning for the next election begins the day after the polls close from the last election. In presidential politics, candidates have about three years of "pre-campaigning" before officially announcing their candidacy. During this time, they must seek "media mentions" as possible presidential contenders, get their names in presidential polls, begin recruiting a campaign staff, give speeches to organizations influential in their party, meet with party officials across the country, travel to Iowa and New Hampshire, and, most of all, make contacts with wealthy, potential campaign contributors. Knowing that they must first win their party's nomination, most of these activities take place *within* party circles.

Early front runners in the polls do not always win their party's nomination. Three or four years is a long time in politics. Relative unknowns have won their party's nomination in the final year, for example Jimmy Carter in 1976, and Bill Clinton in 1992. But prominence in the polls helps to raise campaign funds and often deters potential competitors.

EARLY VOTER PREFERENCES FOR PRESIDENT 2008

Democratic Candidates		Republican Candidates	
Respondents: Registered Democrats		Respondents: Registered Republicans	
Hillary Clinton	48%	Rudy Giuliani	32%
Barack Obama	25	Fred Thompson	19
John Edwards	13	Mitt Romney	14
Dennis Kuchinich	2	John McCain	11
Bill Richardson	1	Mike Huckabee	4
Christopher Dodd	1	Ron Paul	3
Joseph Biden	1	Duncan Hunter	2
		Sam Brownbeck	2
		Tom Tancredo	1

Note: Candidates with less than 1 percent not shown.

Source: Data from Gallup poll, August 2007.

STAYING HOME ON ELECTION DAY

Another problem with the pluralist theory of popular control over public policy through elections is the fact that almost *half the adult population fails to vote*, even in presidential elections. Off-year (nonpresidential) elections bring out fewer than 40 percent of the eligible voters (see Figure 8.4), yet in these off-year contests the nation chooses all its U.S. representatives, one-third of its senators, and about half of its governors.

The 2004 election produced a surprisingly high turnout. Perhaps the closeness of the 2000 election between Bush and Gore, decided by only 537 votes in Florida, inspired voters to go to the polls. The race between Bush and Kerry appeared to be close. The war in Iraq also may have contributed to the high turnout. Turnout in 2004 reached 55 percent, and more voters went to the polls than at any other time in history.

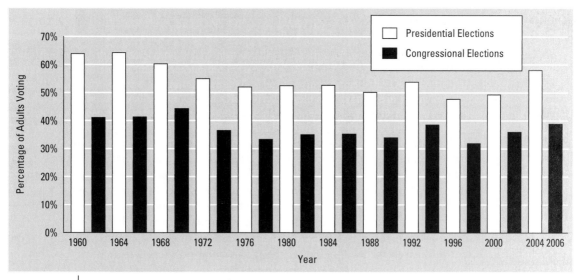

FIGURE 8.4 | PARTICIPATION IN PRESIDENTIAL AND CONGRESSIONAL ELECTIONS

Participation is not uniform throughout all segments of the population (see Table 8.5). Voter turnout relates to such factors as age, race, education, and occupation. Although these figures pertain to voting, other forms of participation—running for

TABLE 8.5 | VOTER TURNOUT IN PRESIDENTIAL ELECTIONS BY SELECTED GROUPS

Age	Percentage	Race	Percentage
18–20	31	White, non-Hispanic	56
21–24	24	Blacks	51
25–34	43	Hispanics	27
35–44	55		
45–64	68		
65+	70		

Education	Percentage	Employment	Percentage
Eighth grade or less	28	Employed	55
Some high school	34	Unemployed	37
High school graduate	49		
Some college	61		
College graduate	73		

Source: *Statistical Abstract of the United States*, 2004.

office, becoming active in campaigns, contributing money, and so on—follow substantially the same pattern. Older, white, middle-class, college-educated Americans participate more in all forms of political activity than do younger, nonwhite, grade-school-educated Americans.

ELECTIONS AS SYMBOLIC REASSURANCE

If elections do not enable voters to direct public policy, if they are largely money driven, if most eligible voters stay home on election day, then what are the purposes of elections? Elite theory views the principal function of elections to be the legitimization of government. Elections are a symbolic exercise to help tie the masses to the established order, to obligate the masses to recognize the legitimacy of government authority, and to obey the law. Political scientist Murray Edelman contends that elections are primarily "symbolic reassurance." According to Edelman, elections serve to "quiet resentments and doubts about particular political acts, reaffirm belief in the fundamental rationality and democratic character of the system, and thus fix conforming habits of future behavior."[8]

ELECTIONS GIVE LEGITIMACY TO GOVERNMENT

Virtually all modern political systems—authoritarian and democratic, capitalist and communist—hold elections. Indeed, communist dictatorships took elections very seriously and strove to achieve 90 to 100 percent voter turnout rates, despite the fact that the Communist Party offered only one candidate for each office. Why did these nations bother to hold elections when the outcome had already been determined? All political regimes seek to tie the masses to the system by holding symbolic exercises in political participation to give the ruling regime an aura of legitimacy. This is the first function of elections. Of course, democratic governments gain even greater legitimacy from elections; democratically elected officeholders can claim that the voters' participation legitimizes their activities and their laws.

ELECTIONS CHOOSE PERSONNEL, NOT POLICY

In democratic nations, elections serve a second function: choosing personnel to hold public office. In 2004, the American voters decided that George Bush and not John Kerry would occupy "the nation's highest office" for the next four years. (The vast majority of people in the world today have never had the opportunity to participate in such a choice.) However, this choice is one of personnel, not policy. Parties do not offer clear policy alternatives in election campaigns; voters do not choose the candidates' policy positions; and candidates are not bound by their campaign pledges anyway. Political scientist Gerald M. Pomper explains:

> To choose a government is not to choose governmental policies. Whereas the voters largely do determine the players in the game of American politics, they have far less control over the signals the players will call, the strategies they will employ, or the final score. The popular will, as represented by a majority of voters, does not determine public policy.[9]

DO ELECTIONS ALLOW FOR RETROSPECTIVE JUDGMENTS?

A third function of elections is to give the masses an opportunity to express themselves about the conduct of the public officials who have been in power. Elections do not permit the masses to direct *future* events, but they may permit the masses to render retrospective judgment about *past* political conduct.[10]

Elections give voters the opportunity to express their displeasure by ousting incumbents from office. But it is not always easy to decipher what the incumbents did wrong that aroused the voters' displeasure.

VIETNAM   Consider, for example, the crucial 1968 presidential election at the height of the Vietnam War. Democrat Lyndon Johnson, who had first committed U.S. ground combat troops to battle in 1965, announced that he would not be a candidate for reelection, and he halted bombing raids and opened peace talks with the North Vietnamese. In the general election that year, voters could choose between Republican Richard Nixon, Democrat Hubert Humphrey, and Independent George Wallace. All three promised to end the war, but none provided a specific program for doing so—whether surrender, all-out bombing, or anything in between. But the voters were able to express their discontent with Johnson's handling of the war by voting against a continuation of the Democratic administration.

CONSERVATISM   Was Ronald Reagan's landslide reelection victory in 1984 over Democrat Walter Mondale a policy mandate for cutting taxes, reducing domestic spending, and a military buildup—the key policy directions in Reagan's first term? Or was it simply an expression of approval of Reagan's presidential style—his warmth, patriotism, good humor, and optimism about America? Throughout the eight years of Reagan's presidency, liberal academics and journalists argued strongly that Reagan's victories reflected his personal popularity, not support for his conservative message. In contrast, conservative commentators urged Reagan to use his voter "mandate" to advance a conservative policy agenda.

RECESSIONS   Perhaps the strongest support for the retrospective voting argument is found in the relationship between economic downturns and the vote for the incumbent party. In presidential elections, the candidate of the incumbent party (whether a president seeking reelection or the president's party nominee) tends to lose votes if the economy is experiencing a downturn during the election year. However, this message from the voters—keep the U.S. economy strong and growing—is hardly a policy directive.

In 1992, during a national recession, voters opted for *change!* Fully 62 percent of the voters cast their votes against incumbent President George H. W. Bush—43 percent for Clinton and 19 percent for Perot. Voters cited the economy as the primary issue on their minds in polls taken as they exited the voting booth. But few voters knew what plans Clinton and Perot had offered to remedy the nation's economic ills. Clinton's stump speech offered everything to everybody: "We can be progrowth and proenvironment, we can be probusiness and prolabor, we can make government work again by making it more aggressive and leaner and more effective at the same time, and we can be pro-family and pro-choice." What kind of policy mandate could Clinton claim from such promises?

It is possible to challenge the retrospective judgment thesis. Bill Clinton presided over a booming economy during most of the 1990s. He was overwhelmingly reelected in 1996. But what was the voters' "retrospective judgment" in the presidential election of 2000? Vice President Al Gore represented an incumbent administration that had presided over economic prosperity, budget surpluses, and relative peace. Democratic President Bill Clinton's approval ratings remained high. So it is unlikely that Republican George W. Bush's victory meant that voters were unhappy with the performance of the Clinton administration.

IRAQ   In 2004, voters were almost equally divided over whether the war in Iraq was "worth it" or not. Initially, the invasions of both Afghanistan and Iraq seemed to go well, with quick advances of American troops, early capitulation by the regimes, and relatively few American casualties. Following the initial invasions, however, the emerging guerrilla war in Iraq and continuing American casualties slowly eroded public support for the war, as well as Bush's approval ratings. The experience in Vietnam remained a haunting reminder for presidents to avoid the "quagmire" of a protracted guerrilla war. Americans want and expect quick victories.

Despite the voters' concerns about continuing American casualties in Iraq, Bush was still seen as a "strong leader" and better at "fighting terrorism" than Kerry. Kerry attacked Bush for having wrongly asserted that there were WMDs (weapons of mass destruction) in Iraq before the invasion. But he failed to offer any significant alternative to continuing the commitment of U.S. troops to Iraq. Neither Kerry nor Bush offered an early "exit" strategy. Voters had no way to directly influence the war in Iraq.

Voters in the 2006 congressional elections appear to have voted against Bush's Iraq policy of "stay the course." Americans had lost confidence in Bush's handling of the war in Iraq: in response to the query "Do you approve or disapprove of the way George W. Bush is handling the situation in Iraq?" 25 percent approved and 70 percent disapproved (November 2006).[11] Yet while it was clear that voters were opposed to Bush's policies in Iraq, there was no way to determine what course of action the voters preferred. Democrats in general offered no real alternative policies. At best, retrospective voting can only indicate what policies voters object to; retrospective voting says very little about the voters' preferences for new policy directions.

ELECTIONS PROVIDE PROTECTION AGAINST OFFICIAL ABUSE

Elections also serve to protect individuals and groups from official abuse. John Stuart Mill wrote, "Men, as well as women, do not need political rights in order that they might govern, but in order that they not be misgoverned."[12] He went on:

> Rulers in ruling classes are under a necessity of considering the interests of those who have the suffrage; but of those who are excluded, it is in their option whether they will do so or not, and however honestly disposed, they are in general too fully occupied with things they must attend to, to have much room in their thoughts for anything which they can with impunity disregard.[13]

Certainly, the long history of efforts to ensure black voting rights in the South suggests that many concerned Americans believed that if blacks could secure access to the polls, they could better protect themselves from discrimination. The vote is a symbol of full citizenship and equal rights that can contribute to black self-respect, but questions remain about how much blacks can gain through the exercise of their vote. It has proven much more difficult to resolve social and economic inequities through the electoral process than to eliminate discriminatory laws and regulations (see Chapter 15).

ELECTIONS: AN ELITIST INTERPRETATION

Elite theory contends that the masses do not participate in policy making and that the elites who do are subject to little direct influence from the apathetic masses. But many scholars who acknowledge that all societies are governed by elites seek to reaffirm democratic values by contending that voters can influence elite behavior in elections. In other words, modern pluralists sometimes challenge elitism on the ground that elections give the masses a voice in policy making by holding governing elites accountable to the people.

Our analysis suggests that elections are imperfect instruments of accountability. Even if the people can hold *government* elites accountable through elections, how can they hold accountable corporate elites, financial elites, union leaders, and other private leadership? The accountability argument usually ignores the realm of *private* decision making to focus exclusively on public decision making by elected elites. But certainly our lives are vitally affected by the decisions of private institutions and organizations. So the first problem with the accountability thesis is that, at best, it applies only to elected government elites. However, our analysis of elections also suggests that it is difficult for the voters to hold even government elites accountable.

1. Competing candidates in elections do not usually offer clear policy alternatives; hence voters seldom can affect policy by selecting a particular candidate for public office.
2. Voters are not well informed about the policy stands of candidates, and relatively few voters are concerned with policy questions. The masses cast their votes in elections based on traditional party ties, candidates' personalities, group affiliations, and a host of other factors with little relation to public policy.
3. The only reasonably stable aspect of mass politics is party identification. But party identification in the mass electorate is not an indication of policy preferences.
4. Money, in the form of campaign contributions, drives elections. Elitism is strengthened by the ever-increasing role of "fat cat" corporate, PAC, and wealthy individual contributions.
5. Campaign finance laws have proven ineffective. The Supreme Court has held that campaign *expenditures* are protected as free speech. Expenditures for issue advocacy by independent "527" organizations are also protected speech.

6. The Constitution places the choice of president in the hands of the Electoral College, not the masses of people. Electoral votes are allocated to the states based on their number of members of Congress (plus three for the District of Columbia). In 2000, Gore won the popular vote, but Bush won a majority of the electoral votes following the Supreme Court's decision regarding Florida's disputed election.

7. Elections are primarily symbolic exercises that help tie the masses to the established order. Elections offer the masses an opportunity to participate in the political system, but electoral participation does not enable them to determine public policy.

8. Elections are a means of selecting personnel, not policy. Voters choose on the basis of a candidate's personal image, filtered through partisan commitment. A candidate's election does not imply a policy choice by the electorate.

9. At best, elections provide the masses with an opportunity to express themselves about the conduct of past administrations, but they do not help them direct the course of future events. A vote against the party or candidate in power does not identify the policy being censured. Moreover, voters have no guarantee that a newly elected official will pursue any specific policy alternatives.

10. Few individuals participate in any political activity other than voting. Almost half the adult population fails to vote even in presidential elections.

Selected Readings

Abramson, Paul R., John H. Aldrich, and David W. Rohde. *Change and Continuity in the 2004 Elections*. Washington, D.C.: CQ Press, 2005. An analysis of the 2004 presidential and congressional elections assessing the impact of party loyalties, presidential performance, group memberships, and policy preferences on voter choice.

Campbell, Angus, Phillip Converse, Warren Miller, and Donald Stokes. *The American Voter: An Abridgement*. New York: Wiley, 1964. An abridged version of the classic study of voting behavior in the United States conducted by the Survey Research Center at the University of Michigan.

Conway, M. Margaret. *Political Participation in the U.S.*, 3rd ed. Washington, D.C.: CQ Press, 2000. The standard text on political participation in American politics, summarizing the research literature on who participates, how, and with what effects.

Fiorna, Morris P. *Retrospective Voting in American Elections*. Princeton, N.J.: Princeton University Press, 1988. A classic description and argument in support of retrospective voting.

Flannagan, William H., and Nancy H. Zingale. *Political Behavior of the American Electorate*, 11th ed. Washington, D.C.: CQ Press, 2002. A text summary of the extensive research literature on the effects of party identification, opinion, ideology, the media, and candidate image on voter choice and election outcomes.

Niemi, Richard G., and Herbert F. Weisberg. *Controversies in Voting Behavior*, 4th ed. Washington, D.C.: CQ Press, 2001. A comprehensive review and critique of political science research on voter choice and electoral decisions.

Sabato, Larry J., and Glenn R. Simpson. *Dirty Little Secrets: The Persistence of Corruption in American Politics*. New York: Random House Times Books, 1996. A political scientist and a journalist combine to produce a lurid report on unethical and corrupt practices in campaigns and elections.

Notes

1. For an introduction to and discussion of the extensive political science literature on determinants of voter choice, see Richard G. Niemi and Herbert F. Weisberg, *Controversies in Voting Behavior*, 4th ed. (Washington, D.C.: CQ Press, 2001). Among the most important works: Angus Campbell et al., *The American Voter* (New York: Wiley, 1960); Norman H. Nie, Sidney Verba, and John R. Petrocik, *The Changing American Voter* (Cambridge, Mass.: Harvard University Press, 1976); Eric Smith, *The Unchanging American Voter* (Berkeley: University of California Press, 1989). See also Robert S. Erikson and Kent L. Tedin, *American Public Opinion*, 7th ed. (New York: Longman, 2007); William H. Flannagan and Nancy H. Zingale, *Political Behavior of the American Electorate*, 10th ed. (Washington, D.C.: CQ Press, 2002).

2. Center for Responsive Politics, www.opensecrets.org (2007).

3. Center for Responsive Politics.

4. *Buckley v. Valeo*, 424 U.S. 1 (1976).

5. *Buckley v. Valeo*, 424 U.S. 1 (1976).

6. *McConnell, Senator, et. al. v. Federal Elections Commission*, 540 U.S. 93 (2003).

7. *Federal Elections Commission v. Wisconsin Right to Life*, June 25, 2007.

8. Murray Edelman, *The Symbolic Uses of Power* (Urbana: University of Illinois Press, 1964), p. 17.

9. Gerald M. Pomper, *Elections in America: Control and Influence in Democratic Politics* (New York: Dodd, Mead, 1980), p. 51.

10. See Morris P. Fiorina, *Retrospective Voting in American National Elections* (Princeton, N.J.: Princeton University Press, 1988).

11. As reported in the *Washington Post* (December 12, 2006).

12. John Stuart Mill, *Considerations on Representative Government* (Chicago: Henry Regnery, Gateway, 1962), p. 144.

13. Mill, *Considerations*, pp. 130–131.

There is overwhelming evidence that participation in voluntary organizations is related to upper social and economic status. . . . The flaw in the pluralist heaven is that the heavenly chorus sings with a strong upper class accent.

E. E. Schattschneider

ORGANIZED INTERESTS: NOT "THE PEOPLE"

CHAPTER 9

Organized interest groups, not "the people," have the most direct day-to-day influence over government. The public interest is a fiction, but the organized interests are potent political realities in Washington, state capitals, and city halls. Interest-group activity, including lobbying, is generally protected by the First Amendment to the U.S. Constitution—"the right of the people peaceably to assemble and to petition the government for redress of grievances." But how democratic is the interest-group system? Do interest groups represent "the people" fairly? Or is the interest-group system another source of elite influence over government?

INTEREST GROUPS: DEMOCRATIC OR ELITIST?

Pluralists contend that interest groups perform several important functions for their members and for a democratic society. First, the organized group links the individual and the government. Political scientists Gabriel Almond and Sidney Verba wrote:

> *Voluntary associations are the prime means by which the function of mediating between the individual and the state is performed. Through them the individual is able to relate himself effectively and meaningfully to the political system.*[1]

But is mediation by organized groups better than direct citizen–government interaction? Why do we need middlemen?

Pluralists also argue that interest groups enhance individual well-being. In a complex society, with primary associations (small groups, such as the family) diminishing in importance, secondary associations (less intimate but more goal oriented) may help people overcome the sense of powerlessness characteristic of mass societies. Groups help integrate the individual with society.

Finally, the pluralists feel that interest groups help reduce potentially divisive conflicts. According to the theory of overlapping group memberships, all citizens are members of groups (some organized, some not).[2] Each person is a product of group affiliations. A person may be, for example, a lawyer, a southerner, a military veteran, and a Protestant, with each affiliation imposing its own values. No single group affiliation could claim the individual's total, undivided loyalty. Hence multiple group affiliations help modify the demands of any one group and reduce social conflict.

In short, pluralists consider interest groups "good" because (1) they provide a more effective voice for citizens who are competing for resources, (2) they reduce the anxiety produced by feelings of powerlessness, and (3) they provide an element of stability.

However, the pluralist theory rests on several assumptions about interest groups that may or may not be correct:

- Membership in organizations is widespread and thus broadly represents all individual interests.
- Organized groups efficiently translate members' expectations into political demands; nothing is lost in the translation, and members gain a great deal by presenting demands through a representative association.
- Although interest groups are not always and uniformly successful (some win and some lose), each group, whatever its demands, has equal access to the political resources necessary for success.
- Organizations help bring about social change.

We refute all these assumptions. We argue that interest groups, rather than articulating the demands of the masses, protect the values of the established elites. Rather than advance social changes, they help maintain the status quo. Indeed, they contribute to political "gridlock"—the inability of the nation to deal effectively with its problems.

THE BUSINESS, PROFESSIONAL, AND CLASS BIAS OF INTEREST GROUPS

It is widely believed that Americans are joiners, and most of the population does in fact belong to at least one formal organization. Yet membership in organized interest groups is clearly linked to socioeconomic status. Membership is greatest among the professional and managerial, college-educated, and high-income people. The upper-middle and upper classes are the primary joiners of organized groups.

THE DOMINANCE OF BUSINESS AND PROFESSIONAL ORGANIZATIONS

Economic organizations dominate interest-group politics in Washington (see Table 9.1). Certainly in terms of the sheer number of organizations with offices and representatives in Washington, business and professional groups and occupational and trade associations predominate.

Business interests are represented, first of all, by large inclusive organizations, such as the U.S. Chamber of Commerce, representing thousands of local chambers of commerce across the nation; the National Association of Manufacturers; the Business Roundtable, representing the nation's largest corporations; and the National Federation of Independent Businesses, representing small business. Specific business interests are

TABLE 9.1 | MAJOR ORGANIZED INTEREST GROUPS BY TYPE

Business
Business Roundtable
National Association of
  Manufacturers
National Federation of Independent
  Businesses
National Small Business
  Association
U.S. Chamber of Commerce

Trade
American Bankers Association
American Gas Association
American Iron and Steel Institute
American Petroleum Institute
American Tobacco Institue
American Truckers Association
Automobile Dealers Association
Home Builders Association
Motion Picture Association
  of America
National Association of
  Broadcasters
National Association of Real
  Estate Boards

Professional
American Bar Association
American Medical Association
Association of Trial Lawyers

Union
AFL-CIO
American Federation of State,
  County, and Municipal Employees
American Federation of Teachers
International Brotherhood of
  Teamsters
International Ladies' Garment
  Workers Union
National Association of Letter
  Carriers
National Education Association
United Auto Workers
United Postal Workers
United Steel Workers

Agricultural
American Farm Bureau Federation
National Cattlemen's Association
National Farmers Union
National Grange
National Milk Producers Federation

Women
EMILY's List
League of Women Voters
National Organization for Women

Public Interest
Common Cause
Consumer Federation of America
Public Citizen
Public Interest Research Groups

Ideological
American Conservative Union
Americans for Constitutional
  Action (conservative)
Americans for Democratic Action
  (liberal)
People for the American Way
  (liberal)
MoveOn (liberal)
National Conservative Political
  Action Committee

Single Issue
Mothers Against Drunk Driving
National Abortion Rights Action
  League, Pro-Choice America
National Rifle Association
National Right-to-Life Committee
Planned Parenthood Federation of
  America
National Taxpayers Union

Environmental
Environmental Defense Fund
Greenpeace
National Wildlife Federation
Natural Resources Defense Council
Nature Conservancy
Sierra Club
Wilderness Society

Religious
American Israel Public Affairs
  Committee
Anti-Defamation League
  of B'nai B'rith
Christian Coalition
National Council of Churches
U.S. Catholic Conference

Civil Rights
American Civil Liberties Union
American Indian Movement
Mexican-American Legal Defense
  and Education Fund
National Association for the
  Advancement of Colored People
National Council of LaRaza
National Urban League
Rainbow Coalition
Southern Christian Leadership
  Conference

Age Related
American Association of Retired
  Persons
Children's Defense Fund

Veterans
American Legion
Veterans of Foreign Wars
Vietnam Veterans of America

Defense
Air Force Association
American Security Council
Army Association
Navy Association

Government
National Association of Counties
National Conference of State
  Legislators
National Governors Association
National League of Cities
U.S. Conference of Mayors

Note: All major organized interest groups maintain informative Web sites, usually accessed on the World Wide Web by the initials of the organization followed by .org.

| FOCUS | SUPER LOBBY: THE BUSINESS ROUNDTABLE |

Arguably the most powerful lobby in Washington is the Business Roundtable. It was established in 1972 "in the belief that business executives should take an increased roll in the continuing debates about public policy." The Roundtable is composed of the chief executives of the largest corporations in America and is financed through corporate membership fees.

The power of the Business Roundtable arises in part from its "firm rule" that a corporate chief executive officer (CEO) cannot send a substitute to its meetings. Moreover, corporate CEOs lobby the Congress in person rather than sending paid lobbyists. Members of Congress are impressed when the CEO of IBM appears at a congressional hearing on business regulation, or when the chair of Prudential Insurance talks to Congress about Social Security.

One congressional staff member explained, "If the Corporation sends his Washington representative to our office, he is probably going to be shunted over to a legislative assistant. But the chairman of the board is going to get to see the senator." Another aide echoed: "Very few members of Congress would not meet with the president of a Business Roundtable corporation."

Among the current issues of concern to the Roundtable are support for free trade agreements and the World Trade Organization; driving down health insurance costs for employers; lowering the corporate income tax; support for federal efforts to improve the workforce with education and performance standards in schools; and reform of tort laws that allow businesses to be sued for product liability.

Business Roundtable
Organization representing the largest U.S. corporations.
www.broundtable.org

also represented by thousands of trade associations. These associations can closely monitor the interests of their specialized memberships. Among the most powerful of these associations are the American Bankers Association, the American Gas Association, the American Iron and Steel Institute, the National Association of Real Estate Boards, the American Petroleum Institute, and the National Association of Broadcasters.

Professional associations rival business and trade organizations in lobbying influence. The American Bar Association and the American Medical Association are two of the most influential groups in Washington. For example, the American Bar Association, which includes virtually all of the nation's practicing attorneys, and its more specialized offspring, the American Association of Trial Lawyers, have successfully resisted efforts to reform the nation's tort laws.

THE INFLUENCE OF ORGANIZED LABOR

Labor unions have declined in membership over the last several decades (see Chapter 5). Nevertheless, labor unions remain a major political influence in Congress and the Democratic Party. The American Federation of Labor–Congress of Industrial Organizations (AFL-CIO) is a federation of more than 100 separate unions with more than 14 million members. The AFL-CIO has long maintained a large and capable lobbying staff in Washington, and it provides both financial contributions and campaign services (registration, get-out-the-vote, information, endorsements) for members of Congress it favors. Many of the larger industrial unions (e.g., the International Brotherhood of Teamsters, United Auto Workers, and United Steel Workers) maintain effective lobbying staffs in Washington.

AFL-CIO
Union federation Web site with information on wages as well as executive salaries.
www.aflcio.org

However, power within the labor movement has shifted dramatically in recent years to government employee unions, notably the American Federation of State, County, and Municipal Employees, the National Education Association, and the American Federation of Teachers.

PIGs, Ideological, and Single-Interest Groups

Public-interest groups (PIGs) claim to represent broad classes of people—consumers, voters, reformers, or the public as a whole. Groups with lofty-sounding names—such as Common Cause, Public Citizen, and the Consumer Federation of America—perceive themselves as balancing the narrow, "selfish" interests of business organizations, trade associations, unions, and other "special" interests. PIGs generally lobby for greater government regulation of consumer products, public safety, campaign finance, and so on. Many PIGs were initially formed in the 1970s by "entrepreneurs" who saw an untapped "market" for the representation of these interests. Among the most influential public-interest groups are Common Cause, a self-styled "citizens' lobby," and the sprawling network of organizations created by consumer advocate Ralph Nader. The Nader network of groups also includes Public Interest Research Groups, which he established on college campuses throughout the nation, frequently by convincing idealistic students to vote to hand over student fees to his organizations.

Like PIGs, single-issue groups appeal to principle and belief. But as their name implies, these groups concentrate their attention on a single cause. They attract the support of individuals with a strong commitment to that cause. Among the most vocal single-issue groups in recent years have been the organizations on both sides of the abortion issue. The National Abortion Rights Action League describes itself as prochoice and opposes any restrictions on a woman's right to obtain an abortion. The National Right-to-Life Committee describes itself as prolife and opposes abortion for any reason other than to preserve the life of the mother. Other prominent single-issue groups include the National Rifle Association (opposed to gun control) and Mothers Against Drunk Driving.

Ideological organizations pursue liberal, conservative, environmental, or feminist agendas, often with great passion and considerable financial resources derived from true-believing contributors. These groups rely heavily on computerized mailings to solicit funds from persons identified as sympathetic to their views. The oldest of the established ideological groups is the liberal Americans for Democratic Action, well known for its annual liberalism ratings of members of the Congress according to their support for or rejection of liberal policies. Yet another prominent ideological group, People for the American Way, was formed by television producer Norman Lear to coordinate the efforts of liberals in the entertainment industry as well as the general public.

Environmental Groups

Environmental organizations have proliferated in recent decades. Among the largest and most prominent are the Environmental Defense Fund, Greenpeace, the National Wildlife Federation, the Natural Resources Defense Council, the Nature Conservancy, the Sierra Club, and the Wilderness Society.

Civil Rights Organizations

NAACP
Civil rights issues and advocacy.
www.naacp.org

Most civil rights organizations grew out of early protest movements (see Chapter 15). The National Association for the Advancement of Colored People (NAACP) is the oldest civil rights organization in the United States. It was founded in 1909 with W. E. B.

LaRaza
Civil rights and
economic concerns
of Hispanic
Americans.
www.nclr.org

DuBois as the editor of its magazine *Crisis*. Its Legal Defense Fund, headed by Thurgood Marshall, later to become the nation's first African American Supreme Court Justice, won the historic case of *Brown v. Board of Education, Topeka, Kansas*, in 1954, declaring school segregation unconstitutional. The Southern Christian Leadership Conference (SCLC) was organized around the nonviolent protest efforts of Martin Luther King Jr. in the 1960s and led to the landmark Civil Rights Act of 1964. The National Council of LaRaza began in the 1970s as a strike by Hispanic migrant laborers against California grape growers.

WOMEN'S GROUPS

NOW
National Organiza-
tion for Women
advocates feminist
issues and supports
women candidates
for public office.
www.now.org

Women's organizations date back to the antislavery societies in pre–Civil War America (see Chapter 15). Today the largest women's group is the League of Women Voters, an organization that provides information to voters, backs registration and get-out-the-vote drives, and generally supports measures seeking to ensure honesty and integrity in government. But the most active feminist organization is the National Organization for Women, founded in 1966.

CLASS BIAS

The class bias of organized groups varies according to the organization. Unions (which frequently are not voluntary) recruit from the working class. But most other organizations have a strong middle- and upper-class bias. Upper-middle-class blacks lead civil rights organizations. Liberal causes, such as the women's movement and Common Cause, draw disproportionately from the university-educated and academically connected liberal establishment and rarely appeal to the lower classes. The social bias in association membership is complemented by the high social origins of lobbyists and the predominance of business and professional organizations in effective lobbying.

The business, professional, and class biases of interest groups challenge pluralist theories about representation in government. Whether or not interest groups are an effective link between the citizen and government, it is clear that many citizens do not avail themselves of this benefit. Even if the formal organization reduces anxiety or increases feelings of power, it does not serve the poor and the uneducated, whose alienation from society is the greatest and whose need for such services is most extreme.

Among members of organizations, active participation—and holding formal office—relates directly to social status. Whereas the majority of Americans are *members* of organizations, only a minority of members are *active* in them. Control typically rests with a small elite. The "iron law of oligarchy" states that even the most democratically inclined organizations gradually evolve into oligarchies.[3] The oligarchs, who help shape the goals of the organizations, come disproportionately from the upper social classes.

HOW WELL DO GROUPS REPRESENT MEMBERS?

The next test of pluralist group theory is how well interest groups translate members' demands into political action—or whether they do so at all.

LARGE VERSUS SMALL ORGANIZATIONS

The size of the group is an important variable in its leadership's political effectiveness. Because elected officials are sensitive to numbers, a large membership enhances a group's access to legislators. However, large groups find it difficult to commit themselves to an explicit position because their membership is so heterogeneous. The policy positions of mass membership organizations are often vague and broad, devoid of specific content—and thus harmless. The U.S. Chamber of Commerce, for example, seeks to represent "businesspeople" without regard for the nature of the business. Because intrabusiness disputes are often as bitter as labor–management disputes, the chamber cannot take a position on many of the legislative and administrative details that affect the economic health of various segments of the business community. Narrowly focused organizations, such as the American Petroleum Institute, which represents only the oil industry, are far more effective than the broad-based U.S. Chamber of Commerce.

In contrast to large groups, small and highly organized groups have attained tangible benefits. Small groups with narrow interests can achieve cohesion more readily and can concentrate their resources on a limited, tangible objective. They can act decisively and persistently based on precise information. Such organizations are most frequently business, professional, or industrial; they are also the major employers of lobbyists at the state and national levels. Many businesspeople organize into trade associations representing many industrial and commercial activities. Because their membership represents a specific form of business activity—for example, the American Bankers Association—many trade associations are quite small; some have as few as twenty-five members. Their power to advocate specific issues is disproportionate to the business community as a whole, which is less focused.

LEADERS VERSUS FOLLOWERS

Leaders and followers differ. *All* groups are afflicted with the curse of oligarchy. For example, civil rights organization leaders do not necessarily represent the views of black masses. Black leaders think black people are going backward, whereas followers think they are making progress. Leaders support racial preferences, but followers do not. Black followers are *social* conservatives, but for leaders the opposite is true.[4]

SINGLE-INTEREST VERSUS TRADITIONAL INTEREST GROUPS

The leadership of single-interest groups may reflect the views of their members better than larger, traditional, better-financed organizations. Because single-issue groups focus on one narrow concern (abortion or gun control, for example), their leaders do not have much flexibility for bargaining or compromise. Their strength is almost solely the intensity of their beliefs. They offer no benefits to members other than political commitment that ranges from "merely strong" to "fanatical."

AARP
Discounts, services, and issues for the elderly.
www.aarp.org

The intense commitment of members to a particular issue has at least two important consequences. First, leaders have far less freedom of action than they would have with a membership recruited for nonissue reasons. The second consequence is that the clearer link between leaders and followers and the dedication of both

LEADERS AND FOLLOWERS—THE AMERICAN ASSOCIATION OF RETIRED PERSONS

There is little evidence to suggest that members know or care very much about what their leaders are doing in their name.[a] The larger the organization becomes, the more difficult is the task of speaking accurately for its members. Consider the largest interest group currently extant, the American Association of Retired Persons (AARP), which has nearly 40 million members. Because the membership is open to anyone over age fifty who pays the modest dues, it is easy to imagine the cross-cutting cleavages that characterize its membership. Other than age, what do they have in common, and how can an organization speak for them on issues of such complexity as increased funding for home health care, coverage of prescription drugs, expansion of state Medicaid criteria, more extensive coverage of nursing home care, increased professional training for caregivers, supplements to food stamps, housing supplements for the aged, energy assistance, and—simultaneously—opposition to budget cuts designed to reduce national deficits? The AARP led the successful fight in Congress against the Balanced Budget Amendment to the Constitution. It is doubtful that all 40 million agree on even a portion of this expansive agenda.

Yet even though common sense tells them that such large groups cannot deliver a vote, Congress members are frequently intimidated by these groups. After each election, myriad organizations lay claim to having been the decisive bloc. More than the politicians of most democracies, American legislators feel that they are vulnerable, that they have no reliable defense against an organization's demands. During testimony at committee hearings, an annoyed legislator might ask for some evidence that an organization does indeed reflect the views of its members, but these outbursts are rare.

The most widely followed example of a legislator calling an organization to task was Republican senator Alan Simpson of Wyoming, who investigated the complex web of the AARP's varied and lucrative business enterprises. The organization earns more than $180 million annually from insurance, travel clubs, discount drugs, credit cards, and annuities.

Simpson, troubled by the AARP's tax-exempt status, cut to the heart of big organization politics: "They're a huge cash flow operation, 38 million people paying $8 dues, bound together by a *common love of airline discounts and automobile discounts and pharmacy discounts,* and they haven't the slightest idea what the organization is asking for."[b] Simpson also alleged that AARP field representatives are subject to immediate dismissal if they disagree with its national board and that those board members are chosen by the association's cadre of lobbyists.

He described the interests of the AARP members as "selective" economic advantages and "collective" advantages. The selective advantages are available only to those who join the organization. If the organization did not offer such benefits, a person would decline to join, because whatever policy advantages that the organization secures apply to all, not just to the members. If the AARP and its allies persuade Congress to expand Medicare, all people over 65 benefit. These benefits are "collective." The incentives are the "selective" benefits, and there is probably no organization that can match the AARP in providing them. For $8 a year, members have access to a mouth-watering list of economic opportunities: health and life insurance discounts; savings on mail-order drugs; low-interest-rate bank cards (the "geezer Visas"); discounted hotels, motels, and rental cars; a newsletter, the *AARP Bulletin;* and a semimonthly magazine, *Modern Maturity.* Some members may, of course, develop a keen interest in the political aspirations of the organization, but most do not; they are there because it makes good economic sense.[c]

---

[a]Terry Moe, *The Organization of Interests* (Chicago: University of Chicago Press, 1980).

[b]These were Simpson's remarks of 1995, when he chaired a two-day hearing on the AARP. See Charles R. Morris, *The AARP: America's Most Powerful Lobby and the Clash of Generations* (New York: Times Books, 1996).

[c]Mancur Olson, *The Logic of Collective Action* (Cambridge, Mass.: Harvard University Press, 1965).

to the cause hampers leaders from fully using the traditional processes of political compromise. Clearly, a person who sees abortion as a form of murder cannot compromise by saying, "I would agree to 30,000 federally funded abortions and no more."

Why have single-issue groups proliferated in recent years? Much of the explanation lies in the decline of political parties (see Chapter 7). As political parties were reformed to increase their responsiveness, the strength of party organizations faded. More and more states turned to open primaries. Candidates came to rely more on personal organization and media exposure than on party organization support (see Chapter 6). Candidates turned to single-interest organizations, whose electoral influence grew in contrast to the decline of parties. Such groups, of course, represent minorities, but so do all other interest groups. The essential difference is that they are *more* representative of the views of their members—because they cannot compromise—than are the established groups. They are not the functional equivalent of political parties, because their causes are limited. They are, however, more responsive to issues than parties and traditional interest groups are.

LOBBYING: HOW ORGANIZED INTERESTS INFLUENCE GOVERNMENT

Lobbying is any communication directed at a government decision maker with the hope of influencing decisions. For organized interests, lobbying is a continuous activity—in congressional committees, in congressional staff offices, at the White House, at executive agencies, at Washington cocktail parties. If a group loses a round in Congress, it continues the fight in the agency in charge of executing the policy, or it challenges the policy in the courts. The following year it resumes the struggle in Congress: it fights for repeal of the offending legislation, for weakening amendments, or for budget reductions that would cripple enforcement efforts. The process can continue indefinitely.

One technique that most experienced lobbyists shun is the *threat*. Amateur lobbyists may threaten legislators by vowing to defeat them at the next election, a tactic guaranteed to produce a defensive reaction among members of Congress. Out of self-respect, legislators are likely to respond to crude pressures by demonstrating their independence and voting against the threatening lobbyist. Moreover, experienced members of Congress know that such threats are empty; lobbyists can seldom deliver enough votes to influence the outcome of an election.

ACCESS

To communicate with decision makers, an organized interest first needs access to them. As a prominent Washington lobbyist explained: "Number 1 is the access—to get them in the door and get a hearing for your case...knowing the individuals personally, knowing their staffs and how they operate and the kind of information they want...that kind of personal knowledge can help you maximize the client's hearing."[5]

"Trust me Mort—no electronic-communications superhighway, no matter how vast and sophisticated, will ever replace the art of the schmooze."

"Opening doors" is a major business in Washington. Individuals who have personal contacts with decision makers (or who say they do) sell their services at high prices. Washington law firms, public relations agencies, and consultants all offer their insider connections and their advice to potential clients. Many professional lobbyists are former members of Congress, former White House aides, or former congressional staff personnel who "know their way around." The personal prestige of the lobbyist, together with the group's perceived political influence, helps open doors in Washington.

INFORMATION

Once lobbyists gain access, their knowledge and information become their most valuable resources. A lobbyist may contribute such information as (1) knowledge of the legislative process, (2) expertise on the issue under debate, and (3) information about the group's position on the issue. Because legislators and their aides value all three types of knowledge, lobbyists can often trade their knowledge for congressional support.

Lobbyists must spend considerable time and effort tracking information about bills affecting their interests. They must be thoroughly familiar with the ins and outs of the legislative process—the relevant committees and subcommittees, their schedules of meetings and hearings, their key staff members, the best moments to act, the precise language for proposed bills and amendments, the witnesses for hearings, and the political strengths and weaknesses of the legislators themselves.

FOCUS	LAWYERS, LOBBYISTS, AND INFLUENCE PEDDLERS

Washington is a awash in lawyers, lobbyists, and influence peddlers. Their offices are concentrated on "K Street" near the Capitol, and they are often collectively referred to as simply "K Street." But as in other sectors of American life, an elite few dominate the influence peddling business.

Direct lobbying expenditures, in addition to PAC contributions to candidates, provide a reasonably good indicator of who is influential in Washington. The nearly $3 billion dollars spent each year on direct lobbying expenditures amount to nearly $5 million dollars for each member of Congress! At the industry group level, pharmaceutical and health products manufacturers spend the most on lobbying. The insurance industry ranks second in direct lobbying expenditures, followed by telephone industries, the oil and gas industry and the electric utilities. Of the top groups spending money on lobbying, only three might be considered noneconomic groups; these include public employee unions, the National Education Association, the American Association of Retired People, and the National Rifle Association. Many individual corporations also spend millions of dollars each year in direct lobbying activities. Lobbying spending by industry tends to reflect the legislative agenda of Congress: when health insurance is being considered, the insurance companies, health maintenance organizations, hospitals, and medical associations appear at near the top of the lobbying spending lists; when tobacco legislation is considered, the American Tobacco Institute, Philip Morris, and other tobacco companies spend heavily; and when tort reform is on the agenda, the American Trial Lawyers Association and the nation's top law firms lobby heavily.

Most large corporations, as well as industry, professional, and trade groups, have their own "in-house" lobbyists. But when particularly important legislation is considered by the Congress, these organizations turn to the top Washington lobbying firms. In his classic book, *The Power Elite*, sociologist C. Wright Mills describes these firms as "professional go-betweens...who act to unify the power elite".[6] They are active at all institutional levels—communicating, negotiating, and mediating among corporations, banks, and wealthholders; foundations and think tanks; and the president, Congress, administrative agencies, and the courts. They are the "insiders" and "fixers" "inside the Beltway" in Washington.

The nation's top lawyers, lobbyists and influence peddlers are listed in Table 9.2. These are firms that are reported to have spent the most in direct lobbying. The firms at the top—Cassidy & Associates, Patton Boggs, Akin Gump—regularly compete each year for the coveted reputation as "the most powerful firm in Washington." All three of these firms have more than 100 clients and spend more than $150 million each year in lobbying (not including their PAC expenditures).

Many influential law firms do not register as lobbyists and do not submit financial statements that would allow us to estimate their activities on Capitol Hill or in the executive bureaucracy. But Table 9.3 lists what is reported to be the nation's most prestigious law firms. The senior partners of these firms do not admit to being lobbyists, but they are key advisers and "go-betweens" in Washington.

The lobbyist's policy information must be accurate as well as timely. A successful lobbyist never supplies faulty or inaccurate information; his or her success depends on maintaining the trust and confidence of the decision makers. A reputation for honesty is as important as a reputation for influence. Lobbyists provide the information and argumentation that members of Congress use in legislative debate and in speeches back home. In this role, the lobbyist complements the functions of congressional staff. Testimony at legislative hearings is a common form of information exchange between lobbyists and legislators. Lobbyists also provide the technical reports and analyses used by congressional staffs in their legislative research.

TABLE 9.2 | TOP LOBBYING FIRMS BY TOTAL OFFICIALLY SPENT FOR LOBBYING 1998–2005

Firm	Total ($ millions)
Cassidy & Associates	210
Patton Boggs LLP	197
Akin, Gump et al.	149
Van Scoyoc Associates	127
Williams & Jensen	102
Barbour, Griffith & Rogers	93
Verner, Liipfert et al.	89
Greenberg Traurig LLP	87
Hogan & Hartson	78
Washington Council Ernst & Young	76
PodestaMattoon	72
Preston, Gates et al.	69
Quinn, Gillespie & Associates	69
Dutko Group	66
PMA Group	61
Timmons & Co.	58
Clark & Weinstock	58
Holland & Knight	55
Alcalde & Fay	55
Swidler, Berlin et al.	52

Source: Center for Responsive Politics. www.opensecrets.org.

GRASSROOTS MOBILIZATION

Many organized interests also lobby Congress by mobilizing constituents to apply pressure on their behalf. Many lobbyists believe that legislators, especially insecure ones, pay close attention to letters, e-mails, and calls from "folks back home." The larger organized interests often have local chapters throughout the nation and can mobilize these local affiliates to apply pressure when necessary. Lobbyists encourage influential local elites to visit a Congress member's office personally or to make a personal phone call on behalf of the group's positions.

Of course, experienced lawmakers recognize attempts by lobby groups to orchestrate "spontaneous" grassroots outpourings of cards and letters. Pressure mail is often identical in wording and content. Nevertheless, members of Congress dare not ignore a flood of letters and e-mails from home, because the mail shows that constituents are aware of the issue and care enough to sign their names.

TABLE 9.3 | AMERICA'S MOST PRESTIGIOUS LAW FIRMS

Arnold & Porter

Covington & Burling

Dewey, Ballantine, Vinson & Elkins

Wilmer, Cutler & Pickering

Arent, Fox et al.

Davis, Polk & Wardwell

Milbank, Tweed et al.

Sullivan & Cromwell

Cadwalader, Wickersham & Taft

Wilkie, Farr & Gallager

Mudge, Rose et al.

Source: Thomas R. Dye, *Top Down Policymaking* (Washington, D.C.: CQ Press, 2001).

Another grassroots tactic is to mobilize the press in a Congress member's home district. Lobbyists may provide news, analyses, and editorials to local newspapers and then clip favorable articles to send to lawmakers. Lobby groups may also buy advertisements in hometown newspapers. And nearly every issue of the *Washington Post* carries full- or half-page ads placed by lobby groups.

DIRECT CONTACTS

Lobbying is expensive. Influential lobbyists make more money than the Congress members they are lobbying. Indeed, many former Congress members, as well as former White House staff and cabinet members, pursue lucrative careers in Washington as lobbyists after leaving office.

Big money is spent on congressional lobbying activity—between $2 and $3 *billion* each year. (This money spent for direct lobbying is *in addition* to political campaign contributions, discussed later.) These expenditures may seem high, but they pale in comparison to the many billions of dollars that hinge on congressional decisions. Among broad economic sectors, banking, finance, insurance, and real estate interests spend the most for lobbying, closely followed by oil and gas, communications and electronics, and the pharmaceutical and health care industry.

CAMPAIGN SUPPORT

However, *the real key to success in lobbying is the campaign contribution.* Interest-group contributions not only help lobbyists gain access and a favorable hearing but also help elect people friendly to the group's goals. As the costs of campaigning increase, legislators must depend more heavily on the contributions of organized interests.

It is illegal for a lobbyist to extract a specific vote pledge from a legislator in exchange for a campaign contribution. Crude "vote buying" is usually (but not always) avoided. Instead, organized interests contribute to the campaign fund of a member of

---

IN BRIEF

Lobbying is any communication directed at government policy makers with the hope of influencing their decisions. Among the techniques of lobbying are:

- Gaining access to policy makers in Congress, the White House, and the bureaucracy.
- Providing information to policy makers and their staffs, directly and by testifying at committee and administrative hearings.

- Mobilizing the grassroots constituents of elected policy makers, inspiring letters, e-mails, and calls from "the folks back home."
- Direct contacts with policy makers, or "schmoozing," at social occasions, dinners, trips, outings, and the like.
- Campaign contributions, direct to candidates (especially incumbents) or through PACs.

Congress over a long period of time and leave it to the lawmaker to figure out how to retain their support. When a legislator consistently votes against an organized interest, that interest may then contribute to the opposition candidate in the next election.

REGULATION OF LOBBIES

Although the First Amendment protects lobbying, government can regulate lobbying activities. The principal method is disclosure: the law requires lobbyists to register as lobbyists and to report how much they spend. But definitions of lobbying are unclear and enforcement is weak. Many of the larger lobby groups—for example, the National Association of Manufacturers, the National Bankers Association, and Americans for Constitutional Action—have never registered as lobbyists. These organizations claim that because lobbying is not their "principal" activity, they need not register under the law. Financial reports of lobbyists grossly underestimate the extent of lobbying in Congress because the law requires reports only on money spent on direct lobbying before Congress, not on money spent for public relations or for campaign contributions. Another weakness in the law is that it applies only to attempts to influence Congress and does not regulate lobbying activities in administrative agencies or the executive branch. However, restrictive legislation might violate the First Amendment freedom to "petition the government for a redress of grievances."

Lobbying
Information on lobbying spending.
www.opensecrets.org/lobbyists

PAC POWER

Political parties are large, disorganized, and largely devoid of ideology. A contributor wishing to support a specific political cause gets more for his or her money by contributing to a PAC. A PAC, or political action committee, is a nonparty organization that solicits voluntary contributions to disburse to political candidates. PACs have been organized by labor unions, trade associations, and liberal and conservative groups. However, the largest number of PACs is in the corporate sector. Contributions to PACs must be voluntary; corporations and labor unions cannot legally use corporate or union treasuries for political campaigns.

PACs have become a major force in Washington politics in recent years. An estimated one-third of all campaign contributions now originates with them. The increasing cost of television campaigning makes many legislators dependent on PAC contributions to run their campaigns.

"A very special interest to see you, Senator."

PACs Prefer Incumbents

PACs
Information on PAC contributions.
www.opensecrets. org/pacs

The PACs give most of their money to incumbent members of Congress. Not only does this practice strengthen incumbents against their opponents, but it also makes incumbents less likely to change the law governing PAC contributions. The object is *access*.

PACs even give money to officeholders not up for election in a particular year, in order to help them retire debts or prepare for a future election. In addition, PACs spend money in "indirect" expenditures. Indirect expenditures include ads and endorsements that are not paid for directly by the candidates' campaign organizations.

The Big-Money PACs

PAC contributions come in larger lumps than most individual contributions. PACs are easier for Congress members to contact for contributions; only about 4,000 PACs regularly contribute to congressional campaigns. Table 9.4 lists the top twenty PAC contributors in the 2004 election.

CONSERVATIVE INFLUENCE OF ORGANIZATIONS

EMILY's List
Political network for prochoice Democratic women that raises early money for women candidates.
www.emilyslist.org

Organizations perform a conservative, stabilizing function for society. Formal organizations seldom cause social change. Of course, the goals of associations vary, but in general, organizations gradually become more moderate as the goal of perpetuating themselves takes priority over their original goals.

In other words, as organizations grow older, they shift from trying to implement their original values to maintaining their structure, even if they thereby sacrifice the organization's central mission. The people who have the greatest stake in the existing social system thus come to dominate the organization. Of course, organizations do not

| FOCUS | EMILY's List |

The greatest obstacle to challenging an incumbent is fund raising. And the most difficult problem facing challengers is raising money *early* in the campaign, when they have little name recognition and little or no standing in the polls.

EMILY's List is a politically adroit and effective effort to support liberal Democratic women candidates who support abortion rights by infusing *early* money into their campaigns. EMILY stands for Early Money Is Like Yeast, because it "makes the dough rise." Not too many years ago, most women candidates confronted incumbent men. These women challengers needed early contributions to provide the initial credibility to their candidacy. EMILY's List is a fundraising network of thousands of contributors,

each of whom pays at least $100 to join and pledges to give at least another $100 to two women from a list of candidates prepared by EMILY's leaders. Most of the contributors are professional women who appreciate EMILY's screening of prochoice, liberal women candidates around the country.

EMILY's List was begun in 1985 by Ellen Malcolm, wealthy heir to a founder of IBM. It claims to have helped drive the dramatic increase in women members of Congress over the last twenty years. Today, the largest number of women in history are serving in the Congress—sixteen senators, and seventy House members, including the Democratic Speaker of the House, Nancy Pelosi.

stop seeking change or increased benefits, but the extent of change they seek is minimal. Once they achieve even a few of their goals, they then have a stake in the ongoing system and a rational basis for pursuing more moderate politics. Social stability is a product of this organizational system.

Bias against Change

Because groups serve society by cementing their members to the established social system, those who seek to radically alter this system find organizations an unsatisfactory mechanism. True, some groups develop with radical change in mind, but the process of bureaucratization of leadership from "have-nots" to "haves" gradually reduces any organization's commitment to substantial change. Impoverished people and blacks have gained little from groups because the group structure is dominated by people with a favored position in society. For segments of society effectively barred from other forms of participation, violent protest may be the only method of entry into the political process. Ironically, if deprived people succeed in organizing themselves, violence will probably decline, to be replaced by organizational activity. But in time, the new organizations will develop their own commitment to the status quo, thus again leaving the truly deprived with little to show for their sacrifices.

"Organization breeds counter-organization," wrote political scientist David Truman.[7] This continuing proliferation of organizations has been said to create "demosclerosis":

More groups demand more benefits, more benefits spawn more groups. As the group formation process picks up speed, an invisible threshold may be crossed. At some point, there might be so many groups and so many more groups forming every year, that they would begin to choke the system that breeds them, to undermine confidence in politics, even to erode political stability.[8]

TABLE 9.4	BIG MONEY PACS: LARGEST PAC CONTRIBUTORS TO THE 2006 CONGRESSIONAL ELECTIONS

PAC	Total (Millions)	Democrat %	Republican %
National Association of Realtors	$3.7	48	51
National Beer Wholesalers Association	$2.9	30	70
National Association of Home Builders	$2.8	26	74
National Auto Dealers Association	$2.7	29	71
Operating Engineers Union	$2.7	78	21
International Brotherhood of Electrical Workers	$2.6	97	3
Laborers Union	$2.6	85	14
American Bankers Association	$2.5	32	67
Association of Trial Lawyers of America	$2.5	96	4
Credit Unions National Association	$2.3	44	55
AT&T Inc.	$2.3	33	66
United Parcel Service	$2.2	31	68
Carpenters and Joiners Union	$2.1	73	26
United Auto Workers	$2.1	99	1
American Federation of Teachers	$2.0	99	1
American Federation of State, County, and Municipal Employees	$1.9	98	1
Plumbers/Pipefitters Union	$1.9	91	9
American Medical Association	$1.9	30	70
Teamsters Union	$1.8	89	9
International Association of Fire Fighters	$1.8	72	27

Source: Center for Responsive Politics.

THE CASE AGAINST INTEREST GROUPS

Pluralist theory rejects the notion of a "public interest." Regarding such an idea as naive, pluralist writers prefer to regard the public interest as the sum of the competing demands; a Darwinian notion that the strongest coalition will—and should—win.

But in the absence of a recognized public interest, governments become so ensnared in interest-group squabbles that they cannot address broader, more distant goals. Political scientist Thomas Mann grieves that "when effective action on the country's most pressing problems requires the imposition of losses on organized interests, with benefits to all on the distant horizon, the odds of success in the U.S. political system are not very high."[9] Only a government strong enough to impose costs on interest groups

---

FOCUS | ### Payback: Money and Prescription Drugs

Congress struggled for many years to pass a prescription drug benefit for Medicare recipients. The bill was one of the most heavily lobbied pieces of legislation in Congress. In 2003, the House and Senate passed very different measures, and the conference committee required large amounts of behind-the-scenes negotiations before sending the bill to both chambers for final passage.

The principal beneficiaries of the bill were supposed to be the nation's senior citizens. And indeed the AARP was heavily involved in every stage of the bill's progress. But the biggest campaign contributors, and arguably the biggest beneficiaries of the final bill, were the drug manufacturers, the health maintenance organizations (HMOs), and the insurance industry.

Republicans sought a bill that allowed insurance companies to play a major role in providing prescription drug insurance and that did not place any price limits on drug manufacturers. Democrats sought a bill that would simply add prescription drug benefits to the current Medicare program. The Republican-controlled House passed the bill by a close vote of 220–215. An analysis of congressional voting on the bill shows that the lawmakers who voted to approve the Republican version of the legislation received on average roughly twice as much in campaign contributions from drug companies, HMOs, and insurance companies as those who voted against the bill (see table).

PAC Contributions and the Prescription Drug Vote in the House

	Average Contributions (1990–2003) to:	
	Supporters	**Opponents**
Drug manufacturers	$27,618	$11,308
HMOs	11,582	6,630
Health insurers	19,510	10,128

Source: Center for Responsive Politics, 2003.

---

can truly serve the public interest. But the United States does not have that government. Mann therefore settles on a realistic if bleak prediction about the future of American politics: "a continuation of the escapism and deadlock of recent years."

INTEREST GROUPS: AN ELITIST INTERPRETATION

Pluralism asserts that organized interest groups provide the individual with an effective way to participate in the political system. It contends that individuals can make their voices heard through membership in the organized groups that reflect their views on public affairs. Pluralists further believe that competition among organized interests provides a balance of power that protects the individual's interests. Interest groups divide power among themselves and hence protect the individual from rule by a single oppressive elite.

Earlier, we pointed out that pluralism diverges from classical democratic theory. Even if the plural elite model accurately portrays the reality of American politics, it does not guarantee the implementation of democratic values. Our analysis of interest groups produces the following propositions:

1. Interest groups draw disproportionately from middle- and upper-class segments of the population. The pressure group system is not representative of the entire community.

2. Leadership of interest groups is recruited from the middle- and upper-class population.

3. Business and professional organizations predominate among organized interest groups.

4. In general, mass membership groups achieve only symbolic success, and smaller, more cohesive groups are able to achieve more tangible results.

5. Considerable inequality exists among organized interest groups. Business and producer groups with narrow membership but cohesive organization achieve their tangible goals at the expense of broad, unorganized groups seeking less tangible goals.

6. Organized interest groups are governed by small elites whose values do not necessarily reflect the values of most members.

7. Business groups and associations are the most highly organized and active lobbyists in Washington and in the state capitals. Their influence is especially evident in the growth of political action committees.

8. Organizations tend to become conservative as they acquire a stake in the existing social order. Therefore pressures for substantial social change must generally come from forces outside the structure of organized interest groups.

Selected Readings

Berry, Jeffrey M. *The New Liberals: The Rising Power of Citizen Groups.* Washington, D.C.: CQ Press, 1999. A description of the increasing number and activities of liberal interest groups in Washington and their success in defeating business and conservative groups.

Ciglar, Allan J., and Burdett A. Louis. *Interest Group Politics,* 6th ed. Washington, D.C.: CQ Press, 2002. An authoritative text on the formation, operations, and effectiveness of organized interests in politics, including a discussion of how interest-group politics has changed over time.

Goldstein, Kenneth M. *Interest Groups, Lobbying and Participation in America.* New York: Cambridge University Press, 2003. Discusses when and why people join interest groups, how members are recruited, and how groups try to influence policy.

Lowi, Theodore J. *The End of Liberalism.* New York: Norton, 1969. The classic critique of "interest group liberalism," describing how special interests contribute to the growth of government and the development of "clientism."

Olson, Mancur. *The Logic of Collective Action.* Cambridge, Mass.: Harvard University Press, 1965. The classic theoretical inquiry into the benefits and costs to individuals of joining groups and the obstacles (including the free-rider problem) to forming organized interest groups.

Olson, Mancur. *The Rise and Decline of Nations.* New Haven, Conn.: Yale University Press, 1982. Argues that, over time, the development of powerful special-interest lobbies has led to institutional sclerosis, inefficiency, and slowed economic growth.

Rozell, Mark J., Clyde Wilcox, and David Madland. *Interest Groups in American Campaigns.* Washington, D.C.: CQ Press, 2005. Describes the activities of interest groups in political campaigns, including their circumvention of the Campaign Reform Act of 2002 through the creation of "527" organizations.

Truman, David B. *The Governmental Process.* New York: Alfred A. Knopf, 1951. The classic description and defense of interest-group pluralism.

NOTES

1. Gabriel A. Almond and Sidney Verba, *The Civic Culture: Political Attitudes and Democracy in Five Nations* (Boston: Little, Brown, 1965), p. 245.
2. David B. Truman, *The Governmental Process* (New York: Alfred A. Knopf, 1951).
3. Roberto Michels, *Political Parties: A Sociological Study of the Oligarchical Tendencies of Modern Democracy* (1915; reprint, New York: Dover, 1959), esp. p. 248.
4. Linda S. Lichter, "Who Speaks for Black America?" *Public Opinion* (August/September 1985): 44.
5. Congressional Quarterly, *The Washington Lobby,* 4th ed. (Washington, D.C.: CQ Press, 1982), p. 5.
6. C. Wright Mills, *The Power Elite* (New York: Oxford University Press, 1956), p. 391.
7. Truman, *The Governmental Process,* p. 65.
8. Jonathan Rauch, *Demosclerosis: The Silent Killer of American Government* (New York: Times Books, 1994), p. 61.
9. Thomas E. Mann, "Breaking the Political Impasse," in Henry J. Aaron, ed., *Setting National Priorities: Policy for the Nineties* (Washington, D.C.: Brookings Institution, 1990), pp. 303, 313.

The Presidency is the focus for the most intense and persistent emotions....The President is...the one figure who draws together the people's hopes and fears for the political future.

James David Barber

THE PRESIDENCY

Governmental elites in the United States do not command; they seek consensus with other elites. Decision making by governmental elites is a process of bargaining, accommodation, and compromise among the dominant interests in American society. Governmental elites act essentially as go-betweens and mediators, seeking policies that are mutually beneficial to the major interests—industrial, financial, bureaucratic, and so on.

The presidency stands at the center of elite interaction in the American political system. For the elite, the president proposes policy initiatives, mobilizes influence within the political system, and supervises the management of government and the economy. For the masses, the president is a symbol of national unity, an outlet to express their emotions toward government, and a vicarious means of taking political action. For *both* elites and masses, the presidency provides a means of handling national crises—taking whatever actions are necessary in an emergency to stabilize the nation, protect its security, and calm its citizens.

THE PRESIDENT AS SYMBOLIC LEADER

More than any other political figure, the president attracts the attention and emotion of the American masses. The people look to the presidency for leadership and reassurance. They want a president who will personalize government, simplify political issues, and symbolize the "compassionate" and protective role of the state. They want someone who seems to be concerned about their welfare.

The people also look for toughness, competence, and decisiveness in the presidency. They are prepared to support a president who is willing to *do something*, whether "something" is a good idea or not. National surveys regularly gauge presidential popularity by asking, "Do you approve or disapprove of the way (____) is handling his job as president?" (see Figure 10.1). Presidential popularity

217

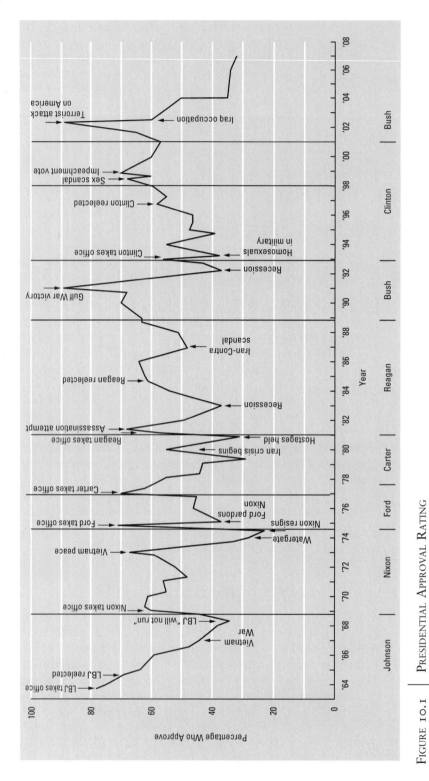

FIGURE 10.1　PRESIDENTIAL APPROVAL RATING

Source: Data based on *Gallup* Reports, 1962–2004.

goes up when the president takes dramatic action or when the nation faces an external crisis or threat.

The people *want* to support the president. All presidents begin their terms with broad public support. Over time, however, support wanes as troubles pile up and the president is unable to cope with them. Indeed, the popular expectations of a president far exceed the president's powers to meet them. The result is an inevitable decline in public support until a new crisis occurs or dramatic action is necessary.

Variations in Presidential Approval Ratings

A brief overview of presidential popularity ratings over time confirms these notions: that a president takes office with broad public support, that support tends to decline over time, and that renewal of support can occur with dramatic action or crisis. Figure 10.1 compares approval ratings of eight presidents. Each took office, whether through election or assassination or resignation, with broad popular support. Over time this support declined. But dramatic action—peace in Vietnam for Nixon, the assassination attempt on Reagan, victory in the Persian Gulf War for the elder Bush, and the terrorist attack of September 11 early in George W. Bush's presidency—produced dramatic increases in presidential support.

Nothing inspires elite support among the masses more than *decisive* military victory. President George Bush achieved nearly 90 percent public approval ratings following victory in the Persian Gulf War. This unprecedented peak was followed by a rapid, disastrous slide, as the nation turned its attention to the economic recession at home. And George W. Bush matched his father's historic peak in approval ratings following the terrorist attack on the United States of September 11, 2001, and the successful ousting of the terrorist-supporting Taliban regime in Afghanistan.

Presidential Approval
Public approval ratings for the president, Congress, and Supreme Court, as well as other public opinion information.
www. pollingreport.com

But prolonged stalemated war, with continuing casualties, gradually erodes presidential support. (Only during World War II, 1941–1945, did the president's approval—Franklin D. Roosevelt—remain high for the duration of the conflict.) The seven-year Vietnam War with no victory in sight brought down President Lyndon B. Johnson and led to his decision not to run for reelection in 1968. The year-long hostage holding of the American embassy personnel by Iran hurt Jimmy Carter's popularity. Following initial victory in Iraq and strong presidential approval, President George W. Bush's ratings gradually slumped with continuing insurgent attacks, almost daily casualties, and no real end to the conflict in sight.

Recessions also erode presidential popularity. Arguably, presidents can do little about economic cycles, but the American people hold them responsible anyhow. Early in President Reagan's term, a recession undercut the otherwise well-liked president's approval ratings. And the steepest decline in presidential approval ever recorded came after the elder President Bush's victory in the Persian Gulf War and the onset of a recession.

Scandals in a presidential administration usually undermine presidential popularity. Indeed, the Watergate affair (see Focus: Watergate and the Limits of Presidential Power later in this chapter) brought Richard Nixon to a new low in presidential polls just before his resignation. President Ford suffered from pardoning

PRESIDENTIAL APPROVAL

- Presidential approval among the masses is high:

  - At the beginning of the president's term in office
  - During crisis periods
  - When decisive military action is undertaken

- Presidential approval erodes:

  - Over time in office
  - Over prolonged stalemated wars
  - During economic recessions
  - Usually during administrative scandals

Nixon. President Reagan was hurt by the Iran-Contra scandal in his second term. But paradoxically, President Bill Clinton's popularity was unaffected by the sex scandal that engulfed him in his second term. On the contrary, his approval ratings went *up* when the scandal broke and when the House of Representatives voted for impeachment (see Focus: Sex, Lies, and Impeachment later in this chapter).

THE PRESIDENCY AND THE MASSES

The president is the nation's leading celebrity. When the president chooses to address the entire nation, the television networks cancel their regular programming and provide free television time.

The presidency possesses enormous symbolic significance. The president affects popular images of authority, legitimacy, and confidence in the American political system. The president can arouse feelings of patriotism or cynicism, hope or despair, honor or dishonor. Political scientist James David Barber wrote:

> The Presidency is the focus for the most intense and persistent emotions.... The President is ... the one figure who draws together the people's hopes and fears for the political future. On top of all of his routine duties, he has to carry that off—or fail.[1]

THE PRESIDENT AND MASS PSYCHOLOGY

We might classify the "psychological functions of the presidency." The president:

- "Simplifies perception of government and politics" by serving as "the main cognitive 'handle' for providing busy citizens with some sense of what their government is doing."

The White House
Official presidency site with news and information, presidential policy views, speeches, pronouncements appointments, etc. plus links to all executive agencies.
www.whitehouse.gov

- Provides "an outlet for emotional expression" through public interest in his and his family's private and public life.

- Is a "symbol of unity" and of nationhood (as the national shock and grief over the death of a president clearly reveal).

- Provides the masses with a "vicarious means of taking political action" in that the president can act decisively and effectively while they cannot do so.

- Is a "symbol of social stability" in providing the masses with a feeling of security and guidance. Thus, for the masses, the president is the most visible member of the elite.[2]

PRESIDENTIAL CHARACTER

Traditionally, Americans expected their presidents to be exemplary in their personal lives. Presidential scholar James David Barber, in his widely read book *Presidential Character,* observed:

> *The President is expected to personify our virtuousness in an inspiring way, to express in what he does and is (not just what he says) a moral idealism which, in the public mind, is the very opposite of politics.*[3]

Traditionally the news media protected the president by not reporting on his private moral conduct. President John F. Kennedy's encounters with a number of women, including movie star Marilyn Monroe and mobster girlfriend Judith Exner, were widely known during his term in office but not revealed until after his death.[4]

But the masses appear to distinguish between private morality and public trust in the president. Even before President Clinton's admission of "inappropriate behavior" with Monica Lewinsky, the overwhelming majority of Americans believed he had engaged in a sexual affair with the 21-year-old White House intern. Yet most Americans continued to approve of the way that Clinton was performing his job as president. Although the public held a negative opinion about Clinton "as a person" (58 percent), they continued to give him strong support in his handling of his job as president (68 percent).[5]

PRESIDENTIAL POWERS OF PERSUASION

The presidency's real power depends not on formal authority but on the president's abilities at persuasion. The president does not command American elites but stands in a central position in the elite structure. *Responsibility for initiating public policy falls principally on the president* and the presidential staff and executive departments.

Through the power to initiate policy alone, the president's influence on the nation is considerable. The president sets the agenda for public decision making. The president presents programs to Congress in various presidential messages, including the annual State of the Union message, and in the annual budget of the U.S. government. The president thereby largely determines the business of Congress in any session. Few major undertakings ever get off the ground without presidential initiation; the president frames the issues, determines their context, and decides their timing.

THE PRESIDENT'S FORMAL POWERS

American Presidents
Biographical facts
and key events in the
lives of all U.S.
presidents.
*www.
americanpresidents.org*

The president has many sources of formal power as chief administrator, chief legislator, party leader, chief diplomat, commander-in-chief, and chief of state and crisis manager. But despite the great powers of the office, no president can monopolize policy making. The president functions within an established elite system and can exercise power only within the framework of that system. The choices available to the president are only those alternatives for which elite support can be mobilized. The president cannot act outside existing elite consensus—outside the "rules of the game"—and must be sensitive to the interests of major elites—business, agriculture, military, education, bureaucracy, and so on.

FOCUS | RATING PRESIDENTS

Historians tend to rank activist presidents who led the nation through war or economic crisis higher than passivist presidents who guided the nation in peace and prosperity. Abraham Lincoln, George Washington, and Franklin Roosevelt are regularly ranked as the nation's greatest presidents. It is more difficult for historians to rate recent presidents; the views of historians are influenced by their own (generally liberal and reformist) political views.

Schlesinger (1962)	Murray (1982)	Schlesinger (1996)	W. J. Ridings and S. B. McIver (1997)
Great	1. Lincoln	**Great**	**Overall Ranking**
1. Lincoln	2. F. Roosevelt	1. Lincoln	1. Lincoln
2. Washington	3. Washington	2. Washington	2. F. Roosevelt
3. F. Roosevelt	4. Jefferson	3. F. Roosevelt	3. Washington
4. Wilson	5. T. Roosevelt		4. Jefferson
5. Jefferson	6. Wilson	**Near Great**	5. T. Roosevelt
	7. Jackson	4. Jefferson	6. Wilson
Near Great	8. Truman	5. Jackson	7. Truman
6. Jackson	9. J. Adams	6. T. Roosevelt	8. Jackson
7. T. Roosevelt	10. L. Johnson	7. Wilson	9. Eisenhower
8. Polk/Truman (tie)	11. Eisenhower	8. Truman	10. Madison
9. J. Adams	12. Polk	9. Polk	11. Polk
10. Cleveland	13. Kennedy		12. L. Johnson
	14. Madison	**High Average**	13. Monroe
Average	15. Monroe	10. Eisenhower	14. J. Adams
11. Madison	16. J. Q. Adams	11. J. Adams	15. Kennedy
12. J. Q. Adams	17. Cleveland	12. Kennedy	16. Cleveland
13. Hayes	18. McKinley	13. Cleveland	17. McKinley
14. McKinley	19. Taft	14. L. Johnson	18. J. Q. Adams
15. Taft	20. Van Buren	15. Monroe	19. Carter
16. Van Buren	21. Hoover	16. McKinley	20. Taft
17. Monroe	22. Hayes		21. Van Buren
18. Hoover	23. Arthur	**Average**	22. Bush
19. B. Harrison	24. Ford	17. Madison	23. Clinton
20. Arthur/Eisenhower (tie)	25. Carter	18. J. Q. Adams	24. Hoover
21. A. Johnson	26. B. Harrison	19. B. Harrison	25. Hayes
	27. Taylor	20. Clinton	26. Reagan
Below Average	28. Tyler	21. Van Buren	27. Ford
22. Taylor	29. Fillmore	22. Taft	28. Arthur
23. Tyler	30. Coolidge	23. Hayes	29. Taylor
24. Fillmore	31. Pierce	24. Bush	30. Garfield
25. Coolidge	32. A. Johnson	25. Reagan	31. B. Harrison
26. Pierce	33. Buchanan	26. Arthur	32. Nixon
27. Buchanan	34. Nixon	27. Carter	33. Coolidge
	35. Grant	28. Ford	34. Tyler
Failure	36. Harding		35. W. Harrison
28. Grant		**Below Average**	36. Fillmore
29. Harding		29. Taylor	37. Pierce
		30. Coolidge	38. Grant
		31. Fillmore	39. A. Johnson
		32. Tyler	40. Buchanan
			41. Harding
		Failure	
		33. Pierce	
		34. Grant	
		35. Hoover	
		36. Nixon	
		37. A. Johnson	
		38. Buchanan	
		39. Harding	

Sources: Arthur Murphy, "Evaluating the Presidents of the United States," *Presidential Studies Quarterly*, 14 (1984): 117–126; Arthur M. Schlesinger Jr., "Rating the Presidents: Washington to Clinton," *Political Science Quarterly*, 112 (1997): 179–190; William J. Ridings and Stuart B. McIver, *Rating the Presidents* (Secaucus, N.J.: Citadel Press, 1997).

CHIEF EXECUTIVE

The president is the chief executive of the nation's largest bureaucracy: fifteen departments, sixty independent agencies, 2.8 million civilian employees, and a large executive office of the president. An organizational chart of the federal government (see Figure 11.1 in Chapter 11) places the president at the head of this giant bureaucracy. But the president cannot really govern this bureaucracy in the fashion of a military officer or corporate president. The Constitution gives the president authority to appoint principal officers of the government, but only "by and with the Advice and Consent of the Senate." And as we will see (in Chapter 12), the Senate can and does constrain the president in his appointment powers. Moreover, Congress can establish or abolish executive departments and regulate their operations by law. And Congress's "power of the purse" allows it to determine the budget of each department each year and thereby to limit or broaden or even "micromanage" the activities of these departments. (The Constitution mandates that "No Money shall be drawn from the Treasury, but in Consequence of Appropriations made by Law" [Article I, Section 9].) The president is responsible for developing "The Budget of the United States Government" each year and sending it to Congress for its consideration (see "The Budget Maze" in Chapter 11). But clearly Congress has the last word on spending.

The president can issue executive orders directing specific federal agencies to carry out the president's policies or directing all federal agencies to pursue the president's preferred course of action. Presidents regularly issue fifty to one hundred executive orders each year. (In 1948, President Harry Truman issued Executive Order 9981 to desegregate the U.S. armed forces. In 1965, President Lyndon Johnson issued Executive Order 11246 instituting affirmative action programs in the federal government.) Executive orders have legal force. They can be overturned only by an act of Congress or, of course, by the federal courts if found to be unconstitutional.

Center for the Study of the Presidency Studies of the office of the president and publication of the journal *Presidential Studies Quarterly.* *www.thepresidency. org*

Presidents rely heavily on their White House staff to exercise their powers. The senior staff normally includes a chief of staff, the national security adviser, the press secretary, a counsel to the president (an attorney), a director of personnel (in charge of appointments), and assistants for political affairs, legislative liaison, and domestic policy. Staff organization depends on each president's personal taste. Some presidents organize their status hierarchically, concentrating power in the chief of staff. Others maintain direct contact with several staff members.

CHIEF LEGISLATOR

The president has principal responsibility for the initiation of national policy. About 80 percent of the bills considered by Congress originate in the executive branch. The Founders understood that the president would be involved in policy initiation. The Constitution requires the president to "recommend to their Consideration such Measures as he shall judge necessary and expedient" (Article II, Section 3). Each year the principal policy statement of the president comes in the State of the Union message to Congress. It is followed by the president's Budget of the United States Government, which sets forth the president's programs with price tags attached. Many other policy proposals are developed by executive departments and agencies, transmitted to the White House for the president's approval, and then sent to Congress.

Presidents are expected to be the chief lobbyist on behalf of the administration's bills as they make their way through Congress. Presidents may exchange many favors, large and small, in exchange for the support of individual members; they may help direct "pork" to a member's district or promise White House support for a member's pet project. Presidents may also issue or withhold invitations to the White House for prestigious ceremonies, dinners with visiting heads of state, and other glittering social occasions—an effective resource because most members of Congress value the prestige.

The veto gives the president great power in legislative affairs. Confronted with the threat of a veto, congressional leaders must decide whether they can get a two-thirds vote in both houses to override the veto. In other words, the president needs only to hold the loyalty of more than one-third of either the House or the Senate in order to sustain a veto. Presidents have had a long history of success in preventing Congress from overriding their vetoes.

PARTY LEADERSHIP

Presidents are the recognized leaders of their party. They usually control the national committee and its Washington staff and largely direct the national party convention. More important, perhaps, presidents enjoy much stronger support in Congress from members of their own party than from members of the opposition party (see "Presidential Support" in Chapter 12).

CHIEF DIPLOMAT

The president of the United States is the leader of the world's largest and most powerful democracy. As the nation's chief diplomat the president has principal responsibility for formulating U.S. foreign policy. The constitutional authority to do so appears relatively modest. Presidents have the power to make treaties with foreign nations "with the Advice and Consent of the Senate." They may "appoint Ambassadors and other public Ministers, and Consuls" and "receive Ambassadors." This power of diplomatic recognition permits a president to grant legitimacy or to withhold it from regimes around the world. For example, to date, all presidents have withheld diplomatic recognition of Fidel Castro's regime in Cuba.

But presidents have expanded on these modest constitutional powers to dominate American foreign policy making. Although nations may also watch the words and actions of the U.S. Congress, the president's statements are generally taken to represent the official position of the U.S. government. But most important, presidents have come to dominate U.S. foreign policy as a product of their role as Commander-in-Chief of the armed forces. Military force is the ultimate diplomatic language.

MANAGING CRISES: 9/11

On the evening of September 11, 2001, President George W. Bush spoke to the American people from the Oval Office in a nationally televised address:

> *The pictures of airplanes flying into buildings, fires burning, huge structures collaps-ing, have filled us with disbelief, terrible sadness, and a quiet, unyielding anger. These mass murders were intended to frighten our citizens into chaos and retreat. But they*

failed, our country's strong. . . . These deliberate and deadly attacks were more than acts of terror. They were acts of war.

Later the president spoke standing side by side with firefighters and rescue workers at the site of the World Trade Center. Both words and pictures were designed to reassure the American people that the president and the U.S. government were committed to dealing effectively with this new crisis.

The president outlined a broad "response to terrorism" to be fought both at home and abroad through diplomatic, military, financial, investigative, homeland security, and humanitarian means. He warned that the new war on terrorism would require a long-term sustained effort (see "Homeland Security" in Chapter 16).

COMMANDER-IN-CHIEF

Defense link
Official Web site of the Department of Defense, with news, data, and links to all service branches.
www.defenselink.mil

In 1775, George Washington was commissioned as Commander-in-Chief by the Continental Congress and given command of all regular (Continental) troops as well as all militia called to duty in the Revolutionary War. Washington later chaired the Constitutional Convention of 1787, and his prestige convinced the Convention to add the title Commander-in-Chief to the presidency. "The President shall be the Commander in Chief of the Army and Navy of the United States" (Article II, Section 2). However, Congress retained for itself the power to "declare war" (Article I, Section 8).

Historically, presidents have exercised the nation's war-making powers. Since 1789, U.S. forces have participated in military actions overseas on more than 150 occasions, but Congress has declared war only five times: the War of 1812, the Mexican War, the Spanish-American War, World War I, and World War II. The Supreme Court has generally refused to take jurisdiction in cases involving the war powers of the president and Congress.

Thus, whereas Congress retains the formal power to "declare war," in modern times wars are not "declared." Instead, they begin with direct military actions, and the president, as Commander-in-Chief of the armed forces, determines what those actions will be. Over the years, Congress has generally recognized the supremacy of the president in military affairs. John Adams fought a war against the French without a congressional declaration; Thomas Jefferson fought the Barbary pirates; presidents throughout most of the nineteenth century fought the Indians; Abraham Lincoln carried presidential war-making powers further than any president before or since; Woodrow Wilson sent troops to Mexico and a dozen Latin American nations; Franklin D. Roosevelt sent U.S. destroyers to protect British convoys in the North Atlantic before Pearl Harbor; and Harry Truman committed U.S. forces to a major war in Korea. President Lyndon Johnson ordered bombing attacks on North Vietnam in 1965 and eventually committed more than half a million men to the Vietnam War. U.S. troops were withdrawn from Vietnam by President Richard Nixon following the Paris Peace Agreement in 1973. But the controversy over the war led Congress to pass the War Powers Act.

THE WAR POWERS ACT

In the early days of the Vietnam War, the liberal leadership of the nation strongly supported the effort, and no one questioned the president's power to commit the nation to war. However, by 1969 most liberal Democratic congressional leaders who had supported the war in its early stages had rushed to become doves. Moreover, with a new Republican president, Richard Nixon, and a Democratic Congress, congressional attacks on presidential policy became much more partisan. As public opposition to the Vietnam War grew and with the presidency and Congress now controlled by different parties, Congress sought to reassert its role in war-making decisions.

In 1973, Congress passed the War Powers Act, designed to restrict presidential war-making powers. President Nixon vetoed the bill, but the Watergate affair appeared to undermine his support in this struggle with Congress, and Congress overrode his veto. The act is an interesting example of the continuing struggle over checks and balances in the U.S. government.

The act includes these provisions:

1. In the absence of a congressional declaration of war, the president can commit armed forces to hostilities or to "situations where imminent involvement in hostilities is clearly indicated by the circumstances" only:

   a. To repel an armed attack on the United States or to forestall the "direct and imminent threat of such an attack."
   b. To repel an armed attack against U.S. armed forces outside the United States or to forestall the threat of such attack.
   c. To protect and evacuate U.S. citizens and nationals in another country if their lives are threatened.
   d. With specific statutory authorization by Congress, not to be inferred from any existing or future law or treaty unless Congress so specifies.

2. The president must report promptly to Congress the commitment of forces for such purposes.
3. Involvement of U.S. forces must be no longer than sixty days unless Congress authorizes their continued use by specific legislation.
4. Congress can end a presidential commitment by a concurrent resolution, an action that does not require the president's signature.

PRESIDENTIAL NONCOMPLIANCE

The War Powers Act raises serious constitutional questions. Clearly, the Commander-in-Chief can order military forces to go anywhere. Congress cannot constitutionally command troops, yet that is what the act attempts to do by specifying that troops must come home if Congress orders them to do so or if Congress simply fails to endorse the president's decision to commit them. No president—Democrat or Republican—can allow Congress to usurp this presidential authority.

President Ford ignored the act in sending U.S. forces to rescue the U.S. ship *Mayaguez* from the Cambodians in 1976. President Carter did not notify Congress before ordering U.S. military forces to attempt rescuing American embassy personnel held hostage in Iran, an effort that ended in disaster in the desert. President Reagan committed troops to Lebanon in 1983. U.S. troops invaded the tiny Caribbean island of Grenada in 1983. President Reagan informed Congress *after* the action (see Table 10.1).

President George H. W. Bush ignored the War Powers Act in ordering the invasion of Panama in 1989 and in sending U.S. forces to Saudi Arabia in August 1990

TABLE 10.1	MAJOR DEPLOYMENTS OF U.S. MILITARY FORCES SINCE WORLD WAR II

Year	Area	President
1950–53	Korea	Truman
1958	Lebanon	Eisenhower
1961–64	Vietnam	Kennedy
1962	Cuban waters	Kennedy
1965–73	Vietnam	Johnson, Nixon
1965	Dominican Republic	Johnson
1970	Laos	Nixon
1970	Cambodia	Nixon
1975	Cambodia	Ford
1980	Iran	Carter
1982–83	Lebanon	Reagan
1983	Grenada	Reagan
1989	Panama	Bush
1990–91	Persian Gulf	Bush
1992–93	Somalia	Bush, Clinton
1994–95	Haiti	Clinton
1995–2000	Bosnia	Clinton
1999–2000	Kosovo	Clinton
2001–	Afghanistan	Bush
2002–	Philippines	Bush
2003–	Iraq	Bush
2004	Haiti	Bush

following Saddam Hussein's invasion of Kuwait. Bush claimed he had the constitutional power to order U.S. military forces to liberate Kuwait from Iraqi occupation, whether or not Congress authorized the action. Bush ordered military preparations to begin, and despite its misgivings, Congress voted to authorize the use of force a few days before U.S. air attacks began. Rapid military victory in the ensuing Persian Gulf War silenced congressional critics.

President Clinton ordered U.S. troops into Bosnia as part of a peace-keeping operation in 1995; later, he ordered extensive bombing of Serbia to force the Serbian president to withdraw his troops from Bosnia. No mention was made of the War Powers Act.

President George W. Bush asked Congress for resolutions authorizing the use of military force, first in Afghanistan in 2001 and later in Iraq in 2003. Congress voted overwhelmingly to approve the use of force in both countries. But neither the president nor Congress cited the War Powers Act in these resolutions.

FORMAL PRESIDENTIAL POWERS

The formal powers of the president include:

- Chief administrator—supervise the executive branch of government; appoint and remove policy officials; prepare executive budget
- Chief legislator—initiate policy; veto legislation passed by Congress; convene special session of Congress "on extraordinary occasions" (Art. II, Sec. 3)
- Party leader—control national party organization; control federal patronage
- Chief diplomat—make treaties ("with the advice and consent of the Senate"); make executive agreements; exercise power of diplomatic recognition—"receive ambassadors and other public ministers"
- Crisis manager and chief of state—oversee formal national action—"The executive Power shall be vested in a President"; represent the nation as chief of state
- Commander-in-chief—command U.S. armed forces; appoint military officials; initiate military actions; exercise broad war powers

INTELLIGENCE AND THE PRESIDENCY

The president is responsible for the intelligence activities of the United States. Nothing in the Constitution refers to intelligence. But presidents have undertaken intelligence activities since the founding of our nation. During the Revolutionary War, General George Washington nurtured small groups of patriots behind British lines who supplied him with information on Redcoat troop movements. (One of these patriots, Nathan Hale, was captured by the British and hanged. His last words: "I only regret that I have but one life to lose for my country." His statue stands at the entrance of CIA headquarters.)

THE INTELLIGENCE COMMUNITY

The intelligence community consists of a group of organizations (see Figure 10.2). Some elements of the intelligence community—the Central Intelligence Agency (CIA), the Defense Intelligence Agency, the National Security Agency (NSA), the National Reconnaissance Office (NRO), and the National Geospatial Intelligence Agency (NGA)—deal exclusively with intelligence collection, analysis, and distribution. Other elements of the intelligence community are located in the Department of Defense, the Department of Homeland Security, the Federal Bureau of Investigation, the Department of State, the Department of Energy, and the Department of Treasury.

ORGANIZING INTELLIGENCE

Congress and the president created a National Commission on Terrorist Attacks, the "9/11 Commission," in 2002 with a sweeping mandate to investigate the facts and circumstances surrounding the September 11 attack and to design a long-term strategy for the war on terrorism. Much of the commission report is a highly readable description of the events leading up to the attack and the actions taken before, during, and after it by all relevant government agencies. The report concludes with a series of recommendations, including a complete reorganization of the intelligence community.

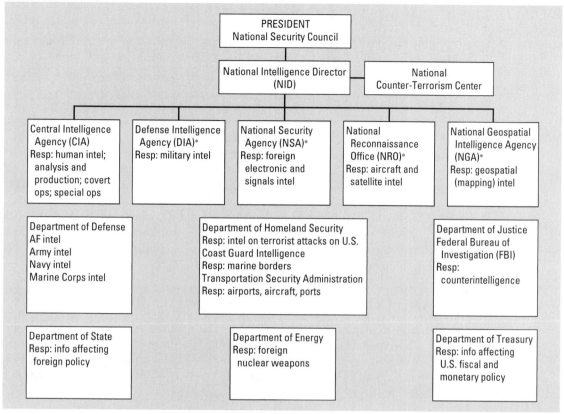

*DIA, NSA, NBO, and NGA are located in the Department of Defense.

FIGURE 10.2 | THE INTELLIGENCE COMMUNITY

The 9/11 Commission recommended the creation of a national intelligence director (NID) to replace the director of central intelligence (DCI) as the head of the intelligence community and principal adviser to the president. (The responsibility of the DCI would be limited to directing the CIA.) The new national intelligence director would have budgetary authority over all elements of the intelligence community and would manage the intelligence effort. The CIA, NSA, NGA, NRO, and the intelligence divisions of the FBI and the Department of Homeland Security would report to the new national intelligence director. A new National Counterterrorist Center would be created under the direction of the NID.

CIA
Information on the CIA together with lists of publications, including the *World Fact Book.*
http://cia.gov

THE CENTRAL INTELLIGENCE AGENCY

The Central Intelligence Agency (CIA) is the leading intelligence agency. It prepares the President's Daily Briefing (PDB) with current intelligence information each day. It also prepares national intelligence estimates (NIE), which provide in-depth analysis of intelligence questions. These documents provide background information for the National Security Council. The CIA is responsible for (1) assembly, analysis, and dissemination of intelligence information from all agencies in the intelligence community; (2) the collection of human intelligence from abroad; and (3) with a specific "presidential finding," the conduct of covert actions, including paramilitary special operations.

Covert actions refer to activities in support of the national interest of the United States that would be less effective if their sponsorship were made public. For example, one of the largest covert actions ever undertaken by the United States was the support for nearly ten years of the Afghan rebels fighting Soviet occupation of their country during the Soviet-Afghanistan War (1978–1988). Public acknowledgment of U.S. aid would have assisted the Soviets in claiming that the rebels were not true Afghans but rather "puppets" of the United States. The rebels themselves did not wish to acknowledge U.S. aid publicly. Hence Presidents Carter and Reagan aided the Afghan rebels through covert action. The "presidential finding" authorizing the covert action is shared with the chairs of the Senate and House committees on intelligence, but congressional approval is *not* required.

THE PRESIDENT AND CONGRESS

The American people expect their president to take the lead in initiating national policy. The masses hold the president responsible for anything that happens in the nation during his term of office, whether or not he has the authority or the capacity to do anything about it. Presidents have every incentive not only to propose policy initiatives but also to get them enacted by the Congress.

WHITE HOUSE LOBBYING

Presidents cannot simply send their bills to Congress and then await the outcome. The White House staff includes "legislative liaison" people—lobbyists for the president's programs. They organize the president's legislative proposals, track them through committee and floor proceedings, arrange committee appearances by executive department and agency representatives, count votes, and advise the president on when and how to "cut deals" and "twist arms." The president may choose to undertake congressional contacts individually—by telephoning and meeting with wavering members of Congress. But direct arm-twisting is generally reserved for the president's most important legislative battles. There is seldom time for a president to contact individual members of Congress personally about many bills in various stages of legislative process—in subcommittee, full committee, floor consideration, conference committee, and final passage—in both the House and Senate.

PRESIDENTIAL "BOX SCORES"

How successful are presidents in getting their legislation through Congress? Presidential success in Congress is generally measured by "box scores"—percentages of presidential victories on congressional votes on which the president took a position. This measure does not distinguish between bills that were important to the president and bills that may

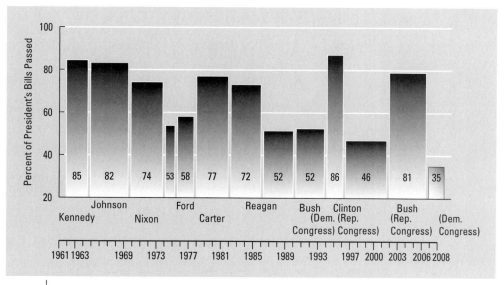

| PRESIDENTIAL SUCCESS IN CONGRESS

have been less significant. But viewed over time (see Figure 10.3), presidential box scores provide insights into the factors that affect the presidents' legislative success.

The most important determinant of presidential success in Congress is party control. Presidents are far more successful when the Congress is controlled by their own party (see Figure 10.3). For example, Democratic presidents John F. Kennedy and Lyndon Johnson enjoyed the support of Democratic-controlled Congresses and enjoyed average success scores of over 80 percent. Jimmy Carter was hardly a popular president, but he enjoyed the support of a Democratic Congress and recorded high box scores. But Republican presidents Richard Nixon and Gerald Ford fared poorly with Democratic-controlled Congresses. Republican president Ronald Reagan was very successful in his first term when he faced a Democratic House and a Republican Senate, but after Democrats took over both houses of Congress, Reagan's success rate plummeted. In President Bill Clinton's first two years in office he enjoyed the support of a Democratic Congress and he succeeded in getting 86 percent of his legislative proposals enacted. But when the Republicans took control of Congress in 1994, Clinton's box scores declined dramatically. George W. Bush enjoyed the support of a Republican-controlled Congress for the first six years of his two terms; but with the election of a Democratic Congress in 2006, Bush's success in Congress ended abruptly.

THE VETO POWER

The veto is the president's most powerful weapon in dealing with Congress. It is especially important to a president facing a Congress controlled by the opposition party. Even the *threat* of the veto enhances the president's bargaining power with Congress. Confronted with such a threat, congressional leaders must calculate

TABLE 10.2 | PRESIDENTIAL VETOES

President	Total Vetoes*	Vetoes Overridden	Percentage of Vetoes Sustained
F. Roosevelt	633	9	99%
Truman	250	12	95
Eisenhower	181	2	99
Kennedy	21	0	100
L. Johnson	30	0	100
Nixon	43	5	90
Ford	66	12	85
Carter	31	2	94
Reagan	78	8	91
Bush	46	1	98
Clinton	37	2	95
Bush (Republican Congress)	1	0	100
Bush (Democratic Congress)	5	0	100

*Regular vetoes plus pocket vetoes.

Source: Harold W. Stanley and Richard G. Niemi, *Vital Statistics on American Politics*, 2005–2006 (Washington, D.C.: CQ Press, 2006) p. 256. Updated by author.

whether they can muster a two-thirds vote of both houses to override the veto. The president needs only one-third plus one of either the House or the Senate in order to sustain the veto. This usually forces congressional leaders of the opposition party to bargain with the president: "What will the president accept?" The president's bargaining power with Congress has been enhanced over the years by a history of success in sustaining presidential vetoes. From George Washington to George Bush more than 96 percent of all presidential vetoes have been sustained (see Table 10.2).

For many years, both Democratic and Republican presidents petitioned Congress to give them a "line-item veto"—the ability to veto some provisions of a bill while accepting other provisions. This power would have been especially important in dealing with appropriations bills because presidents would be able to veto specific pork-barrel items from major spending bills without losing the entire appropriation. But when Congress finally granted the president a form of the line-item veto in 1996, the Supreme Court held it to be unconstitutional, because it "authorizes the president himself to elect to repeal laws, for his own policy reasons" and therefore violates the law-making provisions set forth in Article I of the Constitution.

IMPEACHMENT

The Constitution grants Congress the power of impeachment over the president, vice president, and "all civil Officers of the United States" (Article II, Section 4). Technically, impeachment is a charge similar to a criminal indictment brought against an

FOCUS | SEX, LIES, AND IMPEACHMENT

Bill Clinton is the second president in the nation's history (following Andrew Johnson in 1867) to be impeached by the U.S. House of Representatives. (President Richard Nixon resigned just before an impeachment vote in 1974.) The 1998 House impeachment vote split along partisan lines (228 to 106, with all but five Republicans voting yes and all but five Democrats voting no). It followed a report to the House by Independent Counsel Kenneth Starr that recommended impeachment for perjury, obstruction of justice, witness tampering, and "abuse of power."

The Starr Report describes in graphic and lurid detail Clinton's sexual relationship with young White House intern Monica Lewinsky. It cites as impeachable offenses Clinton's lying about their relationship to his staff, friends, and the nation; his misleading testimony in a sworn statement in the Paula Jones case; his conversations with close friend Vernon Jordan about finding Lewinsky a job; his attempts to impede Starr's investigation; and his evasive testimony before Starr's grand jury:

QUESTION: *"I have a question regarding your definition [of sexual relations] then. And my question is, is oral sex performed on you within that definition . . . ?"*
ANSWER: *"As I understood it, it was not, no."*
QUESTION: *"Well, the grand jury would like to know, Mr. President, why it is you think that oral sex performed on you does not fall within the definition of sexual relations?"*
ANSWER: *"Because that is—if the deponent is the person who has oral sex performed on him, then the contact is with—not with anything on that list, but with the lips of another person."* [a]

Does engaging in extramarital sex and lying about it meet the Constitution's standard for impeachment—"treason, bribery, or other high crimes and misdemeanors"? Perjury—knowingly giving false testimony in a sworn legal proceeding—is a criminal offense. But does the Constitution envision more serious misconduct—crimes that undermine the Constitution or abuse presidential power? Is sex and lying about it

serious enough to warrant Congress's impeachment and removal of a president elected by the people? In *The Federalist,* Number 65, Alexander Hamilton wrote that impeachment should deal with "the abuse or violation of some public trust." Is Clinton's acknowledged "inappropriate behavior" a private affair or a violation of the public trust?

The American people apparently did *not* believe that Clinton's misconduct should have resulted in his impeachment and removal from office:

QUESTION: *"Do you approve or disapprove of the House decision to vote in favor of impeaching Clinton and sending the case to the Senate for trial?"* Yes–35%, No–63%
QUESTION: *"Do you think Bill Clinton should resign now and turn the presidency over to Al Gore?"* Yes–30%, No–69%
QUESTION: *"Should the Senate vote in favor of convicting Clinton and removing him from office or vote against convicting?"* Vote to convict–29%, Vote against convicting–68% [b]

But the decision about what is impeachable is entirely in the hands of the House of Representatives, and the decision about whether or not to remove the president from office is entirely in the hands of the Senate. There is no appeal from the decisions of these chambers. The judgment of the House and the Senate is political as well as judicial, partisan as well as legal, and personal as well as driven by public opinion.

Clinton's Senate impeachment trial ended in acquittal. Indeed, the strongest charge—that President Clinton tried to obstruct justice—failed to win even a majority of Senate votes, far less than the required two-thirds. All forty-five Democrats were joined by five Republicans to create a 50–50 tie vote that left Clinton tarnished but still in office.

---

[a]*Congressional Quarterly Weekly Report,* September 26, 1998, pp. 2607–2613.
[b]Gallup poll reported in *USA Today,* December 21, 1998.

official. The power to bring charges of impeachment is given to the House of Representatives. The power to try all impeachment is given to the Senate, which must convict by a two-thirds vote. Impeachment by the House and conviction by the Senate only removes an official from office; a subsequent criminal trial is required to inflict any other punishment.

The Constitution specifies that impeachment and conviction can only be for "Treason, Bribery, or other High Crimes and Misdemeanors." These words indicate that Congress is not to impeach presidents, federal judges, or any other officials simply because Congress disagrees with their decisions or policies. Indeed the phrase implies that only serious criminal offenses, not political conflicts, can result in impeachment. Nevertheless, politics was at the root of the impeachment of President Andrew Johnson in 1867. (Johnson was a Southern Democratic and remained loyal to the Union. Lincoln had chosen him as vice president in 1864 as a gesture of national unity. A Republican House impeached him on a party-line vote, but after a month-long trial in the Senate, the "guilty" vote fell one vote short of the two-thirds needed for removal.) Partisan politics also played a key role in the House impeachment of Bill Clinton (see Focus: Sex, Lies and Impeachment).

PRESIDENTIAL EXECUTIVE POWER

The Constitution declares that the "executive Power" shall be vested in the president, but it is unclear whether this statement grants presidents any powers that are not specified elsewhere in the Constitution or given to the president by acts of Congress. In other words, does the grant of "executive Power" give presidents constitutional authority to act as they deem necessary *beyond* the powers granted them in the Constitution or granted by laws of Congress?

Historically, U.S. presidents have indeed acted beyond specified constitutional powers or laws of Congress. Among the most notable:

- George Washington issued a Proclamation of Neutrality during the war between France and Britain following the French Revolution, thereby helping to establish the president's power to make foreign policy.
- Thomas Jefferson, who prior to becoming president argued for a narrow interpretation of presidential powers, purchased the Louisiana Territory despite the fact that the Constitution contains no provision for the acquisition of territory, let alone authorizing presidential action to do so.
- Andrew Jackson ordered the removal of federal funds from the national bank and removed his secretary of the treasury from office, establishing the president's power to *remove* executive officials, a power not specifically mentioned in the Constitution.
- Abraham Lincoln, asking, "Was it possible to lose the nation yet to preserve the Constitution?," established the precedent of vigorous presidential action in national emergencies. He blockaded Southern ports, declared martial law in parts of the country, and issued the Emancipation Proclamation, all without constitutional or congressional authority.
- Franklin D. Roosevelt, battling the Great Depression during the 1930s, ordered the nation's banks to close temporarily. Following the Japanese

attack on Pearl Harbor in 1941, he ordered the incarceration without trial of many thousands of Americans of Japanese ancestry living on the West Coast.

CHECKING PRESIDENTIAL POWER

President Harry Truman believed that the president had broad authority "to keep the country from going to hell," and he was willing to use means beyond those specified in the Constitution or authorized by Congress. In 1952, while U.S. troops were fighting in Korea, steel workers at home were threatening to strike. Rather than offend organized labor by forbidding the strike under the terms of the Taft-Hartley Act of 1947 (which he and the unions had opposed), Truman chose to seize the steel mills by executive order and continue their operation under U.S. government control. But the U.S. Supreme Court ordered the steel mills returned to their owners. The Court acknowledged that the president may have inherent powers to act in a national emergency, but argued that Congress had provided a legal remedy in the Taft-Hartley Act. The Court established that the president can act to keep the country from "going to hell," but if Congress has already acted to do so, the president must abide by the law.[6] Nonetheless, presidents have interpreted both the Constitution and the laws of Congress in ways that give them great power (see Focus: Presidential Power over Domestic Intelligence).

EXECUTIVE PRIVILEGE

Yet another argument over implied presidential powers centers on the question of "executive privilege"—the right of the president to keep confidential communications from other branches of government. Traditionally presidents have argued that the Constitution's establishment of separate branches of government entitles the president to conduct the affairs of the executive branch without interference by Congress or the courts. Public exposure of internal executive communications would inhibit the president's ability to obtain candid advice from subordinates, would obstruct the president's ability to conduct negotiations with foreign governments, and would interfere with his command of military operations.

But Congress has never recognized executive privilege. It frequently tries to compel the testimony of executive officials at congressional hearings. Presidents have regularly refused to appear themselves at congressional hearings and have often refused to allow other executive officials to appear or divulge information, citing executive privilege. The federal courts have generally refrained from interfering in this dispute between the executive and legislative branches.

PRESIDENTIAL RESPONSIBILITY TO THE COURTS

The president is not "above the law"; that is, his conduct is not immune from judicial scrutiny. The president's official conduct must be lawful; federal courts may reverse presidential actions found to be unconstitutional or in violation of the laws of Congress. Presidents are not immune from criminal prosecution; they cannot ignore demands to provide information in criminal cases. The Supreme Court ruled that

FOCUS | PRESIDENTIAL POWER OVER DOMESTIC INTELLIGENCE

In the Foreign Intelligence Surveillance Act of 1978 (FISA), Congress created a special FISA court to oversee the collection of electronic intelligence within the United States. It required all intelligence agencies, including the National Security Agency (NSA), which is responsible for the collection of electronic intelligence, to obtain warrants upon a showing that the surveillance is required for investigation of possible attacks upon the nation. The FISA court is secret and the persons under surveillance are not notified.

Nevertheless, President Bush authorized the National Security Agency to intercept international calls to and from Americans—calls involving known or suspected terrorists—without a FISA warrant. The president claimed that he has inherent constitutional powers as Commander-in-Chief to gather intelligence during war or armed conflict, and that the United States is currently at war with international terrorists.

Opponents of warrantless surveillance argued that the president was bound by the FISA Act, which specifically requires court warrants for surveillance within the United States, including international calls. Congress authorized surveillance of U.S. citizens in terrorist investigations *but only* with a warrant issued by the FISA court. Congress was direct and specific on the subject of domestic surveillance in the FISA Act even during wartime. The president, opponents claim, was acting unconstitutionally and unlawfully in authorizing warrantless surveillance of U.S. citizens.

President Bush, with the support of the intelligence community, pressed Congress to revise the FISA Act to allow warrantless surveillance of incoming foreign-to-domestic calls routed through the United States. The administration argued that FISA warrants were too slow to process and that new satellite and fiber obtic cable communications systems made the old FISA law antiquated. Congress obliged in 2007 and authorized warrantless surveillance of foreign-to-domestic and foreign-to-foreign calls.

President Nixon was not immune from court orders when illegal acts were under investigation. Although the Court acknowledged that the president might legitimately claim executive privilege where military or diplomatic matters are involved, such a privilege cannot be invoked in a criminal investigation.[7]

The Court ordered Nixon to surrender tape recordings of White House conversations between the president and his advisers during the Watergate scandal. (See Focus: Watergate and the Limits of Presidential Power.)

The Supreme Court has held that the president has "absolute immunity" from civil suits "arising out of the execution of official duties." The president cannot be sued for damages caused by actions or decisions that are within his constitutional or legal authority. But the president can be sued for private conduct beyond the scope of his official duties. The Supreme Court rejected the notion of presidential immunity from civil claims in a sexual harassment suit by a former Arkansas employee against President Bill Clinton when he was governor of that state.[8]

GEORGE W., IN HIS FATHER'S FOOTSTEPS

George W. Bush was born into his family's tradition of wealth, privilege, and public service. (Bush's grandfather, investment banker Prescott Bush, was a U.S. senator from Connecticut and chairman of the Yale Corporation, the university's governing board.) He grew up in Midland, Texas, where his father had established himself in the oil business before going into politics—first as a Houston Congressman, then Republican national chairman, director of the CIA, ambassador to China, and finally vice president and president of the United States. George W. followed in his father's

| FOCUS | WATERGATE AND THE LIMITS OF PRESIDENTIAL POWER |

Richard Nixon was the only president ever to resign the office. He did so to escape certain impeachment by the House of Representatives and a certain guilty verdict in trial by the Senate. Yet Nixon's first term as president included a number of historic successes. He negotiated the first ever strategic nuclear arms limitation treaty, SALT I, with the Soviet Union. He changed the global balance of power in favor of the Western democracies by opening relations with the People's Republic of China and dividing the communist world. In his second term, he withdrew U.S. troops from Vietnam, negotiated a peace agreement, and ended one of America's longest and bloodiest wars. But his remarkable record is forever tarnished by his failure to understand the limits of presidential power.

On the night of June 17, 1972, five men with burglary tools and wiretapping devices were arrested in the offices of the Democratic National Committee in the Watergate Building in Washington. Also arrested were E. Howard Hunt Jr., G. Gordon Liddy, and James W. McCord Jr., all employed by the Committee to Reelect the President (CREEP). All pleaded guilty and were convicted, but U.S. District Court Judge John J. Sirica believed that the defendants were shielding whoever had ordered and paid for the operation.

Although there is no evidence that Nixon himself ordered or had prior knowledge of the break-in, he discussed with his chief of staff, H. R. Haldeman, and White House advisers John Ehrlichman and John Dean the advisability of payoffs to buy the defendants' silence. Nixon hoped his landslide electoral victory in November 1972 would put the matter to rest.

But a series of sensational revelations in the *Washington Post* kept the story alive. Using an inside source known only as Deep Throat, Bob Woodward and Carl Bernstein, investigative reporters for the *Post*, alleged that key members of Nixon's reelection committee, including its chairman, former attorney general John Mitchell, and White House staff were actively involved in the break-in and, more important, in the subsequent attempts at a cover-up.

In February 1973 the U.S. Senate formed a Special Select Committee on Campaign Activities—the "Watergate Committee"—to delve into Watergate and related activities. The committee's nationally televised hearings enthralled millions of viewers with lurid stories of "the White House horrors." John Dean broke with the White House and testified before the committee that he had earlier warned Nixon the cover-up was "a cancer growing on the presidency." Then, in a dramatic revelation, the committee—and the nation—learned that President Nixon maintained a secret tape-recording system in the Oval Office. Hoping that the tapes would prove or disprove charges of Nixon's involvement in the cover-up, the committee issued a subpoena to the White House. Nixon refused to comply, arguing that the constitutional separation of powers gave the president an "executive privilege" to withhold his private conversations from Congress. However, the U.S. Supreme Court, voting 8 to 0 in *United States v. Nixon*, ordered Nixon to turn over the tapes.[a]

Despite the rambling nature of the tapes, committee members interpreted them as confirming Nixon's involvement in the payoffs and cover-up. Informed by congressional leaders of his own party that impeachment by a majority of the House and removal from office by two-thirds of the Senate were assured, on August 9, 1974, Richard Nixon resigned his office.

On September 8, 1974, new president Gerald R. Ford pardoned former President Nixon "for all offenses against the United States which he, Richard Nixon, has committed or may have committed or taken part in" during his presidency. Upon his death in 1994, Nixon was eulogized for his foreign policy successes.

---

[a]*United States v. Nixon* 418 U.S. 683 (1974).

footsteps to Yale University, but he was not the scholar–athlete that his father had been. Rather, he was a friendly, likeable, heavy-drinking president of his fraternity. Upon graduation in 1968, he joined the Texas Air National Guard and completed flight school, but he never faced combat in Vietnam. He earned an M.B.A. degree from the Harvard Business School and returned to Midland to enter the oil business himself.

Later in his career he would acknowledge his "youthful indiscretions," including a drunk driving arrest in 1976.

Although his famous name attracted investors in a series of oil companies he managed, virtually all of them lost money (including the Harvard Management Company, which invests that university's endowment funds). Even a deal with the government of oil-rich Bahrain, negotiated while his father was president, failed to bail out Bush's Harken Energy Company. But Bush was able to sell off his oil interests and reinvest the money in the Texas Rangers baseball team; he eventually sold his interest in the Rangers in a deal that netted him over $15 million.

STARTING NEAR THE TOP

George W. Bush had never held public office before running for governor of Texas in 1994. But he had gained valuable political experience serving as an unofficial adviser to his father during his presidential campaigns. He went up against the sharp-tongued Democratic governor Ann Richards, who ridiculed him as the "shrub" (little Bush). Bush heavily outspent Richards and won 54 percent of the vote to become Texas's second Republican governor in modern times.

George W.'s political style fitted comfortably with the Texas "good-old boys" in both parties. Although the Texas legislature was controlled by Democrats, Bush won most of his early legislative battles. He supported legislation that gave law-abiding adult Texans the right to carry concealed handguns. A strong economy allowed him to improve public services yet keep Texas among the few states without an income tax. He supported educational reform by opposing the practice of "social promotion" and requiring third-, fifth-, and eighth-grade pupils to pass statewide tests before advancing to the next grade.

Bush's style was to meet frequently and privately with his Democratic opponents and remain on friendly terms with them. He was willing to accept legislative compromises and to try to avoid controversies wherever possible. He helped to lead the gradual realignment of Texas away from its traditional Democratic roots and toward its current Republican coloration. Bush was overwhelmingly reelected governor of Texas in 1998.

RUNNING FOR PRESIDENT

Reportedly, Bush was at first ambivalent about running for president, but a "pilgrimage" of senior Republican stalwarts came to Austin to urge him to run and to prep him on the issues. Bush denies that his father ever tried to influence his decision, but many of his father's friends and political associates did, believing that only he could reclaim the White House for the GOP. They compared "Dubya" to Ronald Reagan—amiable, charming, and good-humored, even if a little vague on the details of public policy. His mother's 10,000-name Christmas card list of closest friends and family helped in building a bankroll of more than $100 million *before* the campaign ever began. And the GOP establishment stuck with him when he was challenged in the early primary elections by maverick Arizona Republican senator and Vietnam War hero John McCain. Bush's father avoided public appearances with his son, not wishing to diminish the younger man's presidential stature. But George senior was an effective fund-raiser in the most expensive presidential campaign in the nation's history.

His Father's Friends

While "Dubya's" father remained in the background, the president's White House and cabinet appointments indicated his reliance on experienced people to run the government. People who served in the Reagan and earlier Bush administrations surrounded George W. Bush. Bush chose Richard Cheney as his vice president, even though Cheney, as a former small-state (Wyoming) congressman, brought no significant electoral votes to the ticket. But Cheney had won the confidence of the Bushes as secretary of defense during the Gulf War. Bush also brought former chairman of the Joint Chiefs of Staff, Colin Powell, into his administration as secretary of state. President Gerald Ford's secretary of defense, Donald Rumsfeld, was reappointed to his old job. National Security Adviser Condoleezza Rice brought a reputation for brilliance and independence to her position. It was clear that "Dubya" was not afraid of being overshadowed by "heavyweights" in his administration.

A Uniter, Not a Divider

George W. Bush always claimed to be a "uniter, not a divider." Early in his administration his claim was tested. He had come to the White House having lost the popular vote; Republicans held a narrow margin of control in the House of Representatives; and when Vermont's U.S. Senator James Jeffords broke a 50–50 tie in the Senate by switching parties, Bush faced a Democrat-controlled Senate.

Politically the nation was split down the middle. It did not appear that any major domestic policy issues—projected deficits in Social Security, prescription drug coverage under Medicare, campaign finance reform, and others—would be resolved. Bush's "good ole boy" style of leadership seemed less effective in Washington than in Austin, Texas.

September 11

The terrorist attack on the United States on September 11, 2001, dramatically changed the political landscape in Washington and the nation. It was time to "rally 'round the president," to suspend partisan bickering, and to unite the masses and elites against a common enemy. The attack became the defining moment in the presidency of George W. Bush. He grew in presidential stature, respect, and decisiveness. His public appearances and statements reassured the American people. He promptly declared a "war on terrorism" against both the terrorist organizations themselves and the nations that harbor and support them. Congress rushed to approve money for home defense and reconstruction and to support the president's use of force. Domestic issues, including a developing recession, were temporarily placed on the policy-making back burner.

Bush clearly explained to an anxious nation that the new war on terrorism had many fronts: prevention through heightened security, the redirection of domestic law enforcement, a strengthening of intelligence-gathering capabilities, the creation of an international coalition to hunt down terrorists and to seize their assets, and initiating direct military attacks on terrorist networks and the governments that harbor them (see Focus: Terrorism's Threat to Democracy, in Chapter 1). Military action in Afghanistan followed quickly. Bush showed no hesitation, no indecision, no willingness to negotiate with terrorists. His public approval ratings skyrocketed: fully 90 percent of Americans approved of the way he was handling his job. The rapid collapse of the hated Taliban government in Afghanistan seemed to confirm Bush's actions. It would be Bush's "finest hour."

GOOD VERSUS EVIL

George Bush convinced the American people that the war on terrorism is "a monumental struggle of good versus evil." In his 2002 State of the Union message he specifically identified an "axis of evil"—Iraq, Iran, and North Korea. Although many in the media scoffed at Bush's portrayal of the war on terrorism as a struggle between good and evil, most Americans heralded what they saw as Bush's "moral clarity" and the firmness of his convictions. He tried to define the enemy as the terrorists and not Islam itself. "The face of terror is not the true faith of Islam." Bush failed to win the support of the United Nations to oust Saddam Hussein from power in Iraq, but he succeeded in getting Congress to pass the joint resolution granting him authority to launch a preemptive military strike against Iraq. The early military phase of the war in Iraq went well; U.S. forces captured Baghdad in a mere 21 days, with precious few casualties. But remnants of Saddam's forces together with terrorists and other hardline organizations began an insurgency against American and other coalition forces. Confronted with a prolonged struggle, costly in lives and money, critics at home and abroad questioned American purposes in Iraq. Bush's high approval ratings began a slow decline.

BUSH REBOUNDS

Throughout most of 2004, Bush's prospects for reelection were cloudy. His approval ratings sank to 50 percent—a danger sign for an incumbent president. After the Democratic convention in July, Bush and Massachusetts Democratic Senator John Kerry ran neck and neck in the polls. The economy was improving, but there were still fewer jobs than when Bush took office. Bush clearly fumbled away the debates, losing to a more articulate, strong-voiced, authoritative, erect, and presidential-looking Kerry. Every day brought reports of more American casualties in Iraq, and Americans divided almost evenly on whether going to war was "worth it."

Yet to the surprise of pollsters, pundits, and commentators, Bush won a convincing victory in November. A huge voter turnout not only gave Bush over 51 percent of the vote but also increased Republican margins in both the Senate and the House. Voters perceived Bush as a "strong leader" with a "strong religious faith" who took "a clear stand on the issues." Kerry was seen as more "intelligent" and capable of "bringing needed change," but Bush was more "trusted" as Commander-in-Chief (see Focus: Images of Bush and Kerry, 2004). Bush interpreted his victory as approval for his "agenda." He gave no indication of any significant changes for his second term.

SECOND TERM FAILURE

George W. Bush began his second term by violating long-standing advice describing Social Security, "the third rail of politics—touch it and you die." Bush campaigned nationwide for a reform plan that would allow workers to invest some of their Social Security payments into private accounts. But the campaign failed badly and Bush began a long decline in mass approval.

The war in Iraq became a national ordeal as casualties mounted and no end appeared to be in sight. Bush offered no realistic strategy for America's exit from the deepening quagmire (see "The War in Iraq" in Chapter 16). Voters responded by electing a Democratic-controlled Congress in 2006, the clearest possible negative retrospective judgment on Bush's performance. His presidential approval ratings fell to 35 percent (see Focus: Mass Opposition to the War in Iraq in Chapter 16). Bush fired his controversial Secretary of Defense Donald Rumsfeld, replacing him with the respected former CIA director Robert Gates. But Bush ignored the report of the Iraq Study Group and began to isolate himself from elites outside of his own administration. He ordered a "surge" in American ground troops in Iraq, a course of action that directly conflicted with recommendations from the Congress and was strongly opposed by the American people.

THE PRESIDENCY: AN ELITIST INTERPRETATION

The president is the popular symbol of governmental authority. However, presidents are substantially less able to control decisions than they would like.

1. Governmental elites in the United States do not command; they seek consensus. Governmental decision making involves bargaining, accommodation, and compromise among government and nongovernment elites. Our examination of the presidency provides clear evidence of the consensual nature of elite interaction and the heavy price a president must pay for failure to accommodate other elites.

2. Presidential power depends not on formal authority but on his or her personal abilities of persuasion.

3. For the masses, the president is the symbol of the government and the nation itself. Presidential popularity with the masses depends on their perception of dynamic leadership in the face of crises. Prolonged stalemated wars erode presidential popularity, as do economic recessions.

4. Good economic times raise presidential popularity. Clinton's continued high ratings, despite widely publicized charges of sexual misconduct, suggest that the masses believe that private morality is unrelated to the evaluation of presidential performance in office.

5. The president can use his popularity with the masses to strengthen his position in dealings with other elites, notably Congress. Clinton's high ratings in the polls were his best defense against removal from office.

6. Controversies over presidential power are always linked to their political context. Although liberal writers generally praise strong presidents in history, during the Vietnam War they turned against the presidency under

Johnson and Nixon. Congress passed the War Powers Act in an unsuccessful effort to gain control over military interventions.

7. The forced resignation of President Nixon was a dramatic illustration of the president's dependence on elite support. A president must govern within the boundaries of elite consensus or face removal from office. The Constitution states that the president can be removed only for "treason, bribery, or other high crimes and misdemeanors." But in fact the president can also be removed for *political* offenses—violating elite consensus.

8. The president is expected to be Commander-in-Chief and global leader, as well as leader in domestic policy. George H. W. Bush performed well as Commander-in-Chief during the Gulf War. But he was widely perceived as ineffective in dealing with the domestic economy.

9. George W. Bush is the second president to follow his father to the White House. (John Quincy Adams, the nation's sixth president, followed his father, John Adams, the nation's second president.) Like his father, George W. Bush's popularity skyrocketed following a crisis, the terrorist attack on the United States on September 11.

10. George W. Bush was successful with a Republican-controlled Congress in his first term. He won reelection in 2004 prior to mass disaffection from the war in Iraq. Voters appeared to express retrospective judgment against the conduct of the war by electing a Democratic-controlled Congress in 2006. Bush's approval ratings plummeted; he ignored the advice of elites outside of his administration regarding his conduct of the war; and he faced a bitter partisan battle with Congress in his last two years in office.

SELECTED READINGS

Barber, James David. *The Presidential Character: Predicting Performance in the White House*, 4th ed. Englewood Cliffs, N.J.: Prentice-Hall, 1992. A controversial classification of presidents along two continua: an "active–passive" baseline, according to the amount of energy and enthusiasm displayed in the exercise of presidential duties, and a "positive–negative" baseline, dealing with the degree of happiness or "fun" each president displays in manipulating presidential power. Using these two baselines, Barber classifies the modern presidents into four types: active–positive (FDR, Truman, Kennedy), active–negative (Wilson, Hoover, Johnson), passive–positive (Taft, Harding), and passive–negative (Coolidge, Eisenhower).

Brody, Richard A. *Assessing Presidents: The Media, Elite Opinion, and Public Support*. Stanford, Calif.: Stanford University Press, 1991. Develops the thesis that media and elite interpretations of presidential actions shape public evaluations of the president; includes analysis of the president's "honeymoon," "rally around the president" events, and the rise and fall of public approval ratings.

Edwards, George C., and Stephen J. Wayne. *Presidential Leadership*, 6th ed. Belmont, Calif.: Wordsworth, 2003. Comprehensive text covering the nomination and election of presidents and their relationships with the public, the media, the bureaucracy, Congress, and the courts.

Kessel, John H. *Presidents, the Presidency, and the Political Environment*. Washington, D.C.: CQ Press, 2001. Emphasizes the role of presidential office staff in accomplishing presidential tasks and in representing outside interests in the White House.

Lowi, Theodore. *The Personal President*. Ithaca, N.Y.: Cornell University Press, 1985. Lowi traces the process by which "the president" and "the government" become synonymous terms.

Milkus, Stanley, and Michael Nelson. *The American Presidency: Origin and Development, 1776–1990*. Washington, D.C.: CQ Press, 1990.

A comprehensive history of the presidency that argues that the institution is best understood by examining its development over time; describes the significant presidential actions in the early days of the Republic that shaped the office, as well as the modern era in which the president has replaced Congress and the political parties as the leading instrument of popular rule.

Nelson, Michael. *The Presidency and the Political System,* 8th ed. Washington, D.C.: CQ Press, 2005. Essays on various aspects of the presidency by leading scholars.

Pika, Joseph A., John Maltese, and Norman C. Thomas. *The Politics of the Presidency,* 6th ed. Washington, D.C.: CQ Press, 2003. A standard text presentation of presidential roles: chief executive, head of state, commander-in-chief, legislative manager, party leader.

Notes

1. James David Barber, *The Presidential Character,* 3rd ed. (Englewood Cliffs, N.J.: Prentice-Hall, 1985), p. 2.
2. Fred I. Greenstein, "The Psychological Functions of the Presidency for Citizens," in Elmer E. Cornwell, ed., *The American Presidency: Vital Center* (Chicago: Scott, Foresman, 1966), pp. 30–36.
3. Barber, *The Presidential Character,* p. 25.
4. Thomas Reeves, *John F. Kennedy* (New York: Kreiger, 1990), p. 190.
5. Gallup poll, as reported in *USA Today,* September 14, 1998.
6. *Youngstown Sheet and Tube Co. v. Sawyer* 393 U.S. 579 (1952).
7. *United States v. Nixon* 418 U.S. 683 (1974).
8. *Clinton v. Jones* 520 U.S. 681 (1997).

The problem is not conspiracy or corruption, but unchecked rule. And being unchecked, the rule reflects not the national need but the bureaucratic need.

John K. Galbraith

THE BUREAUCRATIC ELITE

Power in the United States is gradually shifting from those who control economic and political resources to those who control technology, information, and expertise. The Washington bureaucracy has become a major base of power in American society—independent of Congress, the president, the courts, and the people. Government bureaucracies invade every aspect of modern life: the home, communications, transportation, the environment, the workplace, schools, the streets.

In theory, a *bureaucracy* is a form of social organization that the German sociologist Max Weber described as having (1) a chain of command (hierarchy); (2) a division of labor among subunits (specialization); (3) specification of authority for positions and units by rules and regulation (span of control); (4) impersonality in executing tasks (neutrality); (5) adaptation of structure, authority, and rules to the organization's goals (goal orientation); and (6) predictability of behavior based on maintenance of records and assurance of rules (standardization).[1] If we use Weber's definition, then both corporations and governments, and many other organizations in society, are bureaucracies.

In practice, *bureaucracy* has become a negative term. People have come to view bureaucracy as bringing with it red tape, paper shuffling, duplication of effort, waste and inefficiency, impersonality, insensitivity, and overregulation. More important, people have come to view governmental bureaucracy as unresponsive to the needs of the nation or the people.

Certainly, "the people" have no direct means of altering bureaucratic decisions. Even the president, the White House staff, and cabinet officials have great difficulty establishing control over the bureaucracy. Congress and the courts can place only the broadest restrictions on bureaucratic power. The bureaucrats control information and technology, and they almost invariably outlast their political superiors in office. Often, in fact, the bureaucrats feel a certain contempt for their superiors because political leaders do not have the information, technical expertise, and experience of the bureaucrats.

SOURCES OF BUREAUCRATIC POWER

The power of bureaucracies grows with advances in technology, increases in information, and growth in the size and complexity of society. Large, complex, technological societies cannot be governed by a single president and 535 members of Congress who lack the expertise, time, and energy to look after the myriad details involved in nuclear power or environmental protection or occupational safety or communications or aviation or fair employment or hundreds of other aspects of American life. So the president and Congress create bureaucracies, appropriate money for them, and authorize them to draw up detailed rules and regulations to govern us. The bureaucracies receive only vague and general directions from the president and Congress. Actual governance is in the hands of the Nuclear Regulatory Commission, the Environmental Protection Agency, the Occupational Safety and Health Administration, the Federal Communications Commission, the Federal Aviation Administration, the Equal Employment Opportunity Commission, and hundreds of similar bureaucratic agencies. (There are approximately 2,000 federal government agencies with rule-making powers.) One estimate suggests that the bureaucracies announce *twenty* rules or regulations for every *one* law of Congress. In this way, the power to make policy has passed from the president and Congress to the bureaucratic elite.

ORGANIZED EXPERTISE

Why is policy making shifted to the bureaucracy? The standard explanation is that Congress and the president do not have the time, energy, or expertise to handle the details of policy making. A related explanation is that the increasing complexity and sophistication of technology require technical experts ("technocrats") to actually carry out the intent of Congress and the president. No single bureaucrat can master the complex activities of even a single large governmental agency—from budgeting, purchasing, personnel, accounting, planning, communication, and organization to the complexities of nuclear plants, energy transmission, the internal revenue (tax) code, or the computerized social security files. Each bureaucrat has relatively little knowledge of overall policy. But that person's narrow expertise, when combined with the narrow expertise of thousands of other bureaucrats, creates an organized base of power that political leaders find difficult to control.

SHIFTS IN RESPONSIBILITY

A second reason policy making is shifted to the bureaucracy is that Congress and the president deliberately pass vague and ambiguous laws, largely for symbolic reasons—to ensure nuclear safety, protect the environment, ensure occupational safety, allocate broadcasting channels, guarantee flight safety, prevent unfair interstate charges, guarantee "equal employment opportunity," and so on. The bureaucrats' role is to use the "authority" of these symbolic laws to decide what actually will be done. Thus, bureaucrats must give meaning to symbolic measures. Frequently, Congress and the president do not want to take public responsibility for unpopular policies. They find it easier to blame the bureaucrats and pretend that unpopular policies are a product of an ungovernable Washington bureaucracy. This explanation allows an elected president and an elected Congress to impose regulations without accepting responsibility for them.

| IN BRIEF | SOURCES OF BUREAUCRATIC POWER |

Bureaucratic power arises from the following sources:

- Political elites do not have time or expertise to handle the details of policy.
- The increasing complexity and sophistication of the economy and society.

- Deliberate shifting of responsibility by the political elites to bureaucrats.
- Bureaucratic elites seek to expand their own power and budgets.

BUREAUCRATIC EXPANSIONISM

Finally, the bureaucracy itself is now sufficiently powerful to have its own laws passed—laws that allow agencies to expand in size, acquire more authority, and obtain more money. Bureaucracy has become its own source of power. Political scientist James Q. Wilson comments on "the great, almost overpowering, importance of the existing government and professional groups in shaping policy":

> *I am impressed by the extent to which policy making is dominated by the representatives of those bureaucracies and professions having a material stake in the management and funding of the intended policy and by those political staffs who see in a new program a chance for publicity, advancement, and a good reputation for their superiors.*[2]

ORGANIZATION OF THE WASHINGTON BUREAUCRACY

How big is the government? All governments in the United States—the federal government together with fifty state governments and over 80,000 local governments, including cities, counties, and school and special districts—collectively spend an amount equivalent to about 30 percent of the gross domestic product (GDP), the sum of all the goods and services produced in the nation. The federal government alone accounts for about 20 percent of the GDP and all state and local governments combined account for 10 percent.

The executive branch of the U.S. government includes fifteen departments, more than sixty independent executive agencies operating outside these departments, and the large Executive Office of the President (see Figure 11.1).

Internal Revenue Service
The tax-collecting IRS is potentially the most powerful of all government agencies, with financial records on every tax-paying American.
www.irs.gov

CABINET   The cabinet rarely functions as a group. It consists of the secretaries of the fifteen executive departments and the vice president, with the president as its head. From time to time presidents grant "cabinet level status" to other officials, for example, the U.N. ambassador, CIA director, national security adviser, U.S. trade representative, and administrator of the EPA. Cabinet officers in the United States are powerful because they head giant administrative organizations. The secretary of state, the secretary of defense, the secretary of the treasury, the attorney general, and to a lesser extent the other departmental secretaries are all people of power and prestige in America. But the cabinet, as a council, does not make policy.[3] Presidents do not hold cabinet meetings to decide important policy questions. More frequently, the president knows what he wants and holds cabinet meetings only to help him sell his views.

FOCUS | MASS ATTITUDES TOWARD WASHINGTON BUREAUCRACIES

Opinion polls regularly report that Americans believe "the federal government in Washington" has "too much power." However, Americans rate individual agencies fairly highly. Although the poll results in the table do not ask about all government agencies, the poll does give a sense of how the public views some of the more prominent ones. Among those missing from the poll, however, is "the military," which regularly receives the highest job rating by Americans (80 percent) of any federal organization.

QUESTION: *How would you rate the job being done by _____? Would you say it is doing an excellent job, good, only fair, or poor job?*

"REMEMBER, HAGEDORN, YOU NO LONGER WORK FOR THE PRIVATE SECTOR. IN THE PUBLIC SECTOR, THE CUSTOMER IS NEVER RIGHT."

Harley Schwadron from NATIONAL REVIEW, May 6, 1996. Reprinted by permission. www.CartoonStock.com

	Percentage Saying "Excellent" or "Good"
Centers for Disease Control and Prevention (CDC)	66
Federal Bureau of Investigation (FBI)	53
Federal Reserve Board	53
NASA—The U.S. Space Agency	50
Department of Homeland Security	48
Central Intelligence Agency (CIA)	45
Internal Revenue Service (IRS)	44
Environmental Protection Agency (EPA)	39

Source: Gallup poll, September 30, 2003.

National Security Council
Official NSC Web site includes news, meetings, and current updates on national defense, immigration control, the war on terrorism, etc.
www.whitehouse.gov/nsc

NATIONAL SECURITY COUNCIL   The National Security Council (NSC) resembles an inner cabinet; the president is chairman, and the vice president, secretary of state, secretary of defense, and secretary of the treasury are participating members. The chairman of the joint chiefs of staff and the director of central intelligence are advisers to the NSC. A special assistant to the president for national security affairs heads the NSC staff. The purposes of the council are to advise the president on security policy and to coordinate the foreign, military, and domestic policies.

OFFICE OF MANAGEMENT AND BUDGET   The Office of Management and Budget (OMB) is the largest agency in the Executive Office of the President. Its function is to prepare the budget of the United States for the president to submit to Congress. The federal government cannot spend money without appropriations by Congress, and all requests for congressional appropriations must clear the OMB first, a

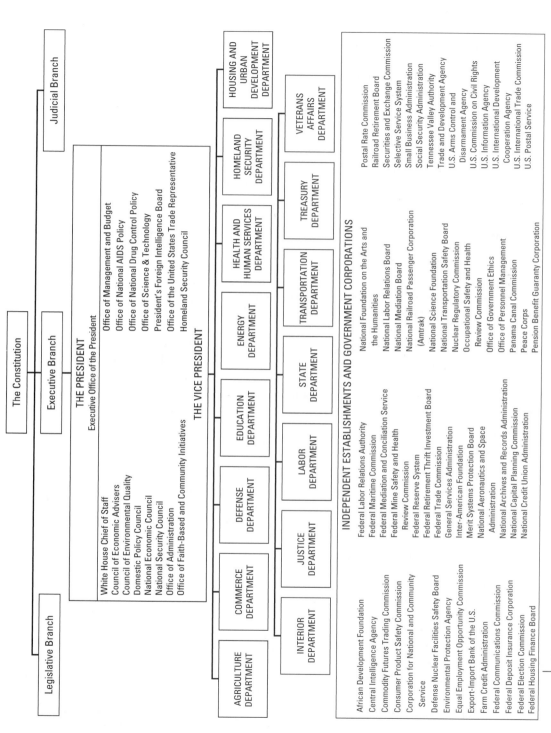

FIGURE 11.1 | THE FEDERAL BUREAUCRACY

Source: U.S. Government Organizational Manual (Washington, D.C.: Government Printing Office, 2005), updated from www.whitehouse.gov.

Federal Departments and Agencies
Many federal departments can be accessed directly by using their initials followed by .gov, for example the Department of Justice—*www.doj.gov,* Federal Bureau of Investigation—*www.fbi.gov.* Where other forms of address are employed, for example, Department of Defense—*www.defenselink. mil,* this book identifies these Web sites in the margins of appropriate chapters.

requirement that gives the OMB great power over the executive branch. Because all agencies request more money than they can receive, the OMB has primary responsibility for reviewing, reducing, and approving estimates submitted by departments and agencies (subject, of course, to appeal to the president). It also continuously scrutinizes the organization and operations of executive agencies in order to recommend changes promoting efficiency and economy. Like members of the White House staff, the top officials of the OMB are responsible solely to the president; thus they must reflect the president's goals and priorities in their decision making.

The most dramatic change in federal tax laws in recent decades occurred during the Reagan years when the top marginal tax rate fell in two steps from 70 percent to 28 percent (see Figure 11.6). At the Republican national convention in 1988, presidential nominee George H. W. Bush made a firm pledge to American voters that he would veto any tax increases passed by the Democratic-controlled Congress: "Read my lips! No new taxes!" Yet in a 1990 budget summit with Democratic congressional leaders, President Bush agreed to raise the top marginal rate to 31 percent, breaking his solemn pledge and contributing to his defeat in the 1992 presidential election. President Clinton pushed the Congress to raise the top marginal rate to 39.6 percent. President George W. Bush came into office vowing not to make the same mistake as his father, raising tax rates in an effort to compromise with the Democrats. On the contrary, Bush was committed to lowering taxes, arguing that an "economic stimulus" package of additional tax cuts would aid the economy. He inspired the Republican-controlled Congress to lower the top marginal rate to 35 percent. But Bush's tax cuts were accompanied by a provision that they would expire in 2010 unless reauthorized by Congress. Republicans argue that a failure to reauthorize these cuts amounts to a "tax increase." Democrats claim that the cuts favor the rich.

PRESIDENTIAL CONTROL OF THE BUREAUCRACY

Constitutionally, the president has authority over the federal bureaucracy. The president has formal power to appoint all secretaries (subject to Senate confirmation), undersecretaries, and deputy secretaries and most bureau chiefs in the federal government. The president also has the power to reorganize the federal bureaucracy, subject to congressional veto. And, of course, the president exercises formal control over the budget. The OMB works directly under presidential supervision.

The president's formal powers over the bureaucracy center on appointments, reorganization, and the budget. We should, however, consider the *real* limitations on these three powers.

APPOINTMENTS

Although the federal bureaucracy consists of 2.8 million civilian employees, the president actually appoints only about 2,500 people. Approximately 600 of those appointments are policy-making positions; the rest are subordinate positions often used for patronage. Many patronage positions go to professional bureaucrats by default because a president cannot find qualified political appointees. Many political appointees are baffled by the career bureaucrats in the agencies. The bureaucrats have the knowledge, skills, and experience to continue existing programs with little or no supervision from their nominal political chiefs. Many political heads "go native"; they yield to the pressures of the career bureaucrats. The president's appointee whose charge is to control a bureau ends up the bureau's captive instead.

Inasmuch as a majority of career bureaucrats are Democrats, exercising policy control over the bureaucracy is particularly difficult for a Republican president. Richard Nixon attempted to deal with this problem by increasing the power of his immediate White House staff; he placed control of major programs in the hands of White House staff, at the expense of the cabinet departments. Ronald Reagan's approach was to appoint conservatives and Republicans to head many key agencies. But the bureaucracy fought back by isolating and undermining Reagan's appointees within the agencies.

George H. W. Bush experienced less conflict with the bureaucracy because he did not pursue any clear domestic policy goals. Bush himself held a variety of bureaucratic posts during his career—UN ambassador, CIA director, and ambassador to the People's Republic of China. The Washington bureaucracy was generally supportive of Bill Clinton's policy activism, with its promise of expanded governmental services and budgets. The only serious bureaucratic opposition Clinton encountered was the 1996 battle with the Department of Health and Human Services over welfare reform.

George W. Bush's cabinet appointees were more experienced in government affairs than those of previous administrations (see Table 4.8 in Chapter 4). Vice President Richard Cheney, Secretary of Defense Robert Gates, former Secretary of State Colin Powell, and former Secretary of Defense Donald Rumsfeld, among others, all served in high positions in previous Republican administrations. Their experience gave them greater knowledge and power over the Washington bureaucracy than top political elites in previous administrations.

REORGANIZATION

Presidents can choose to reorganize the bureaucracy to reflect their priorities. However, most presidents limit this practice to one or two key presidential programs (presidential reorganizations are subject to legislative veto). For example, in the 1960s, President Kennedy created the National Aeronautics and Space Administration as an independent agency to carry out his commitment to a national space program. President Carter created the Department of Education to fulfill his campaign pledge to emphasize educational matters, even though the department's parent organization, the Department of Health, Education, and Welfare, bitterly opposed it. President Reagan promised in his 1980 campaign to eliminate the Department of Education as well as the Department of Energy. But reorganization is a difficult task. Nothing arouses the fighting instincts of bureaucrats as much as the rumor of reorganization. President Reagan was eventually forced to drop his plans to eliminate these two departments. Instead, Reagan ended his administration by creating a new cabinet-level department—the Department of Veterans Affairs—in response to demands for greater status and prestige by veterans' interests.

To reassure the public of the government's efforts to prevent further terrorist attacks after September 11, President George W. Bush first created an Office of Homeland Security inside the Executive Office of the President, with high-profile

FOCUS	KATRINA: BUREAUCRATIC FAILURE

Hurricane Katrina was one of the nation's largest natural disasters. Perhaps it was inevitable that government bureaucracies—federal, state, and local—would be unable to respond to such a crisis. But the lack of competence among bureaucrats at all levels of government, the inertia and stupidity, the disorganized relief that led directly to the deaths of many, all combined to make Katrina "the worst man-made relief disaster ever."[a]

Katrina was a powerful Category Four hurricane when it hit east of New Orleans, practically leveling the city of Biloxi, Mississippi. The first day New Orleans seemed to be spared, but the next day the levees began to crumble—levees that had protected the below-sea-level "Big Easy" for over a century. Soon water submerged 80 percent of the city and 100,000 were stranded with little or no food or water or electricity. For three days emergency efforts floundered badly. Survivors gathered on rooftops and highway flyovers. Reporters got themselves to the scenes of tragedies, but government agents failed to do so. Soon armed looters appeared on the streets. Hospitals functioned in the dark and in the heat; doctors and nurses cried out for the rescue of their patients.

The first rescuers, including private citizens with small boats, dropped people off on highway overpasses, with 100-degree heat and no water or food. Other makeshift rescue efforts took over 25,000 survivors to the leaking Superdome, where there was no light, no water, and no working toilets.

No one was in charge. Local, state, and federal bureaucrats failed to lead, but instead battled over turf. The mayor urged residents to evacuate, but tens of thousands had no cars or other means of transportation. When the mayor finally ordered mandatory evacuation, hundreds of city buses were already underwater. Some nursing homes were overlooked in evacuation efforts and some elderly died unnecessarily. Meanwhile, the mayor, the governor, and Federal Emergency Management Agency (FEMA) officials, and even the president, were giving press conferences boasting of all the aid that was on its way. But the governor refused to request federal troops or to place the Louisiana National Guard under federal authority. President Bush could have done so on his own, but he hesitated, waiting for the governor's request. Only the U.S. Coast Guard and military helicopters seem to perform well—indeed heroically, in many cases rescuing survivors from rooftops.

But FEMA's performance was a disaster. For three days FEMA sat and waited to be called by the governor. When asked by a TV reporter what he intended to do about the horrid conditions in the Superdome, conditions that had been shown on TV for days, the FEMA director responded that he did not know that anyone was in the Superdome. Hundreds of FEMA house trailers sat outside the city unused, as did truckloads of food and water. As flames consumed buildings in New Orleans, FEMA held back 600 firefighters in order to lecture them on equal opportunity, sexual harassment, and customer service.[b] At the airport, frustrated medics waited in empty helicopters to evacuate patients while FEMA delayed over paperwork. When outside doctors and nurses tried to help, FEMA rejected their assistance because they "weren't certified members of a National Disaster Medical Team." "FEMA kept stone-walling us with paperwork. Meanwhile, every 30 or 40 minutes someone was dying."[c] About 150 trucks full of ice purchased for hurricane victims sat uselessly in a parking lot in Maine.[d] The FEMA emergency number was out of service.

[a]*U.S. News and World Report*, September 19, 2005, p. 30.
[b]*Time*, September 19, 2005, p. 18.
[c]*New York Times*, September 18, 2005.
[d]*Ft. Lauderdale Sun-Sentinel*, October 7, 2005, p. 1.

FEMA
Web site of FEMA: disaster information.
www.fema.gov

Pennsylvania governor Tom Ridge as its first director. But continued criticism of security arrangements forced President Bush to propose a more thorough-going reorganization of the executive branch. He proposed and Congress created a new Department of Homeland Security, which would not only coordinate domestic and international antiterrorist efforts but also exercise direct responsibility over the Transportation Security Administration, Immigration and Customs Enforcement,

| FOCUS | BUREAUCRATIC MANEUVERS |

How can bureaucrats outmaneuver the president? One illustration of bureaucratic leeway and discretion in implementing presidential decisions has been widely quoted:

Half of a President's suggestions, which theoretically carry the weight of orders, can be safely forgotten by a cabinet member. And if the President asks about a suggestion the second time, he can be told that it is being investigated. If he asks a third time, the wise cabinet officer will give him at least part of what he suggests. But only occasionally do Presidents ever get around to asking three times.[a]

Bureaucratic maneuvers can become even more complex. Morton Halperin, former staff member of the National Security Council under Henry Kissinger (Halperin later charged Kissinger and others with bugging his telephone), describes "ten commandments" of bureaucratic infighting.[b] These suggest the power of the bureaucracy and the frequently bitter nature of bureaucratic warfare:

1. Never play "politics" with security. But use your own notions of politics to screen out information from the president that conflicts with your own objectives.
2. Tell the president only what is necessary to persuade him of the correctness of your own position. Avoid giving him "confusing" information. Isolate the opposition by excluding them from deliberations.
3. Present your own policy option in the middle of two other obviously unworkable alternatives to give the president the illusion of choice.
4. If the president selects the "wrong" policy anyhow, demand "full authority" to deal with the undesirable consequences, which you say are sure to arise.
5. Always predict the consequences of not adopting your policy in terms of worst cases, making predictions of dire consequences that will follow.
6. If the president chooses your own policy, urge immediate action; if he selects another policy, you may agree in principle but argue that "now is not the time."
7. If the opposition view looks very strong, "leak" damaging information to your supporters in the press or Congress and count on "public opposition" to build.
8. Fully implement orders that result from the selection of your own policy recommendation; circumvent or delay those that do not.
9. Limit the issues that go to the president. Bring up only those favorable to your position or that he is likely to favor.
10. Never oppose the president's policy in such extreme terms that you lose his trust. Temper your disagreements so that you can live to argue another day.

Bureaucrats do not really consider these "commandments" cynical. Indeed, they may not realize when they are following them. They often sincerely believe that their own policies and projects are in the nation's best interest.

---

[a]Graham T. Allison, *Essence of Decision* (Boston: Little, Brown, 1971), p. 172.

[b]Leslie H. Gelb and Morton H. Halperin, "The Ten Commandments of the Foreign Policy Bureaucracy," *Harper's* (June 1972): 28–36.

Border Patrol, the U.S. Coast Guard, the Secret Service, and the Federal Emergency Management Agency (see "Homeland Security" in Chapter 16).

THE BUDGET

The president exercises budgetary power over the bureaucracy through the Office of Management and Budget (OMB). Thus, the OMB director must be a trusted ally of the president, and the OMB must support the president's programs and priorities if

Presidential control over the bureaucracy derives primarily from:

- Presidential power over appointments to the White House, Cabinet, and other high offices, most, however, requiring congressional approval.

- Presidential power over reorganization and the creation of new bureaucracies, subject to congressional approval.
- Presidential power over budget recommendations to Congress.

presidential control over the bureaucracy is to be effective. But even the OMB must accept the budgetary base of each department (the previous year's budget, adjusted for inflation) and engage in "incremental" budgeting. Despite its own expertise, the OMB rarely challenges the budgetary base of agencies but instead concentrates its attention on requested increases.

Any agency that feels shortchanged in the president's budget can leak the fact to its supporting interest groups and congressional subcommittee. Any resulting "public outcry" may force the president to restore the agency's funds. Or Congress can appropriate money not requested by the president. The president may go along with the increased expenditures simply to avoid another confrontation with Congress.

THE BUDGET MAZE

The budget is the most important policy statement of any government. The expenditure side of the budget shows "who gets what" from government, and the revenue side shows "who pays the costs." The budget lies at the heart of the policy-making process.

THE PRESIDENTIAL BUDGET

Office of Management and Budget
Official OMB Web site, includes latest presidential budget.
www.whitehouse. gov/omb

The president is responsible for submitting the annual federal budget, with estimates of revenue and recommendations for expenditures, to Congress. Congress controls the purse strings; no federal monies may be spent without congressional appropriation. The president relies on the OMB to prepare a budget for Congress. The president's budget is usually submitted in late January of each year. The federal fiscal year (FY) begins October 1; this gives Congress about eight months to consider the president's budget and pass the appropriations acts for the coming fiscal year.

Preparation of the budget by the OMB starts more than a year before the beginning of the fiscal year for which it is intended. (Fiscal years are named for the year in which they *end*, so, for example, the OMB prepares FY 2009 in 2007 for presentation to Congress in January 2008 and passage before October 1, 2008; FY 2009 ends September 30, 2009.) The OMB considers budget requests by all executive departments and agencies, adjusting them to fit the president's overall policy goals. It prepares the Budget of the United States Government for the president to submit to Congress. Table 11.1 summarizes the steps in the overall schedule for budgetary preparation.

TABLE 11.1 | THE BUDGET PROCESS

Approximate Schedule	Actors	Tasks
Presidential Budget Making		
January–March	President and OMB	The Office of Management and Budget presents long-range forecasts for revenues and expenditures to the president. The president and the OMB develop general guidelines for all federal agencies. Agencies are sent guidelines and forms for their budget requests.
April–July	Executive agencies	Agencies prepare and submit budget requests to the OMB.
August–October	OMB and agencies	The OMB reviews agency requests and holds hearings with agency officials. The OMB usually tries to reduce agency requests.
November–December	OMB and president	The OMB presents revised budget to the president. Occasionally, agencies may appeal OMB decisions directly to the president. The president and the OMB write budget messages for Congress.
January	President	The president presents budget for the next fiscal year to Congress.
Congressional Budget Process		
February–May	Congressional Budget Office (CBO) and congressional committees	Standing committees review taxing and spending proposals for reports to House and Senate budget committees. The CBO also reviews the entire presidential budget and reports to budget committees.
May–June	Congress; House and Senate budget committees	House and Senate budget committees present first concurrent resolution, which sets overall total for budget outlays in major categories. Full House and Senate vote on resolution. Committees are instructed to stay within budget committee's resolution.
July–September	Congress; House and Senate appropriations committees and budget committees	House and Senate appropriations committees and subcommittees draw up detailed appropriations bills. Bills are submitted to House and Senate budget committees for second concurrent resolution. Budget committees may force reductions through "reconciliation" provisions to limit spending. The full House and Senate vote on "reconciliations" and second (firm) concurrent resolution.

continued

TABLE 11.1 | THE BUDGET PROCESS *continued*

Approximate Schedule	Actors	Tasks
Congressional Budget Process		
September–October	Congress and president	The House and Senate pass various appropriations bills (nine to sixteen bills, by major functional category, such as "defense"). Each is sent to the president for signature. (If vetoed by the president, the appropriations bills go back to the House and Senate, which must override veto with two-thirds vote in each body or revise bills to gain president's approval.)
Executive Budget Implementation		
After October 1	Congress and president	Fiscal year for all federal agencies begins October 1. If no appropriations bill has been passed by Congress and signed by the president for an agency, Congress must pass and the president must sign a continuing resolution to allow the agency to spend at last year's level until a new appropriations act is passed. If no continuing resolution is passed, the agency must officially cease spending government funds and must officially shut down.

CONGRESSIONAL CONSIDERATION

The Constitution gives Congress the authority to decide how the government should spend its money: "No money shall be drawn from the Treasury but in consequence of appropriations made by law" (Article I, Section 9). The president's budget is sent initially to the House and Senate budget committees, whose job it is to draft a *budget resolution* for Congress, setting future target goals for appropriations in various areas. The House and Senate budget committees rely on their own bureaucracy, the Congressional Budget Office, to review the recommendations made by the president and the OMB. Congress is supposed to pass a budget resolution by late spring. The resolution should guide the House and Senate appropriations committees and their subcommittees in writing the appropriations acts.

There are usually thirteen separate *appropriations acts* each year. Each one covers a broad area of government—for example, defense, labor, human services and education, commerce, justice, state, and judiciary. These appropriations bills must pass both the House and the Senate in identical form, just as any other legislation must. All the acts are supposed to be passed before the start of the fiscal year, October 1. These procedures were mandated in the Congressional Budget and Impoundment Control Act of 1974. However, Congress rarely follows its own timetable or procedures.

The common goal of the congressional budget procedures, the House and Senate budget committees, and the Congressional Budget Office is to allow Congress to consider the budget in its entirety rather than in separate segments. But after the budget resolution is passed, the thirteen separate appropriations bills begin their tortuous journeys through specialized appropriations subcommittees. Agency and department leaders from the administration are frequently called to testify before these subcommittees to defend the president's request. Lobbying activity is heavy in these subcommittees.

If the appropriations committees report bills that exceed the ceilings established by the budget resolution, Congress must prepare a *reconciliation bill* to reconcile the amounts set by the budget resolution and the amounts set by the appropriations committees. This procedure tends to match the power of the House and Senate budget committees against the House and Senate appropriations committees. When passed, the reconciliation bill binds the appropriations committees and Congress to ceilings in each area. However, all this congressional infighting generally runs beyond the October 1 deadline for the start of the fiscal year.

Continuing Resolutions and Government Shutdowns

All appropriations acts *should* be passed by both houses and signed by the president into law before October 1, but Congress rarely meets this deadline. Government agencies frequently find themselves beginning a new fiscal year without a budget. Constitutionally, any U.S. government agency for which Congress does not pass an appropriations act may not draw money from the Treasury and thus is obliged to shut down. To get around this problem, Congress usually adopts a *continuing resolution* that authorizes government agencies to keep spending money for a specified period at the same level as in the previous fiscal year.

A continuing resolution is supposed to grant additional time for Congress to pass, and the president to sign, appropriations acts. But occasionally this process has broken down in the heat of political combat over the budget: the time period specified in a continuing resolution has expired without agreement on appropriations acts or even on a new continuing resolution. Shutdowns occurred during the bitter battle between President Bill Clinton and the Republican-controlled Congress over the FY 1996 budget. In theory, the absence of either an appropriations act or a continuing resolution should cause a federal agency to shut down, that is, to cease all operations and expenditures for lack of funds. But in practice, such shutdowns have been only partial, affecting only "nonessential" government employees and causing relatively little disruption.

Presidential Vetoes of Appropriations Bills

Presidents can veto an appropriations bill, but they cannot veto specific provisions in the bill. (Presidents, both Democratic and Republican, have long struggled to obtain the line-item veto—the ability to veto some spending items in a bill while accepting others. In 1996, Congress finally agreed to allow presidents to do so, but the U.S. Supreme Court held the line-item veto unconstitutional, arguing that it gave the president the power to amend bills, a legislative power reserved for Congress in Article I of the Constitution.) As a result, presidents rarely veto appropriations bills, even those with spending provisions they dislike. However, presidents can send Congress a list of "rescissions," and Congress by resolution (which cannot be vetoed by the president) must approve a rescission; otherwise, the government must spend the money.

ELITE FISCAL RESPONSIBILITY?

Over the years, total federal spending has grown dramatically. In 1962, federal spending amounted to only $92 billion; in 2008, this figure was $2.9 trillion (see Figure 11.2). The growth of federal spending is being driven primarily by "entitlement" programs, notably Social Security, which is now the single largest item in the budget, and Medicare and Medicaid, the fastest-growing items in the budget. National defense, which in 1960 constituted 56 percent of all federal spending, declined to 15 percent in the late 1990s and then grew to 19 percent with the war on terrorism.

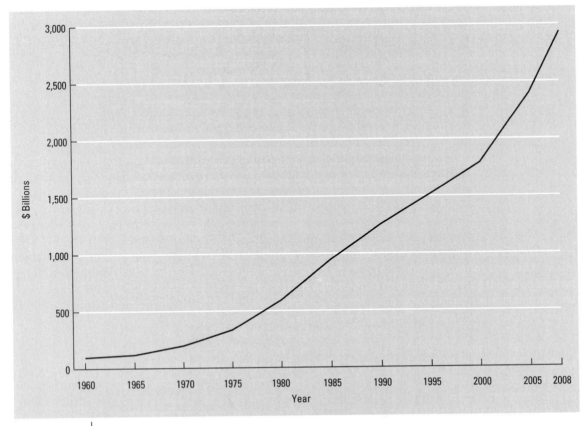

FIGURE 11.2 | FEDERAL SPENDING

Source: Data from *Budget of the United States Government*, 2008.

Overall Federal Spending

The enormous growth of federal spending in billions of dollars, however, is offset in part by America's dynamic economy. Expressed as a percentage of the gross domestic product (GDP)—the sum of all the goods and services produced in the United States in a year—federal spending rose only modestly from 18.8 percent in 1962 to a high of 23.1 percent in 1998. Since then, federal spending as a percentage of GDP has actually declined to about 19 percent. In other words, although total dollar spending by Washington has grown enormously, this spending has remained relatively stable in relation to the nation's overall economy.

Entitlement Spending

Entitlement spending accounts for about 60 percent of all federal spending. Entitlements are items determined by past decisions of Congress and represent commitments in future budgets. They provide classes of people with legally enforceable rights to benefits. Social Security and Medicare benefits for seniors make up the largest entitlement spending. Neither of these programs is directed at the poor. Welfare payments, food stamps, and Medicaid are "means tested"—that is, benefits are limited to lower-income families. In addition to entitlements, other "mandatory" spending (including interest payments on the national debt, federal employees' retirement, unemployment compensation, veterans' benefits, and so on) together with spending for national defense leaves only about 12 percent of the budget for "nondefense discretionary" spending (see Figure 11.3).

"Capping entitlements" is widely recognized by economists as the only way to rein in future federal spending. But no one in Washington—president, Congress

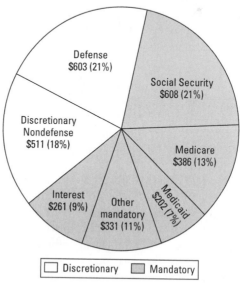

FIGURE 11.3 | MANDATORY SPENDING IN THE FEDERAL BUDGET

Source: *Budget of the United States Government*, 2008.

members, bureaucrats, Republicans or Democrats—is willing to challenge the powerful senior citizen lobby (see Focus: Leaders and Followers—The American Association of Retired Persons in Chapter 9).

Balancing the Budget

Washington regularly spends more than it receives in revenue. Annual deficits put the U.S. government over *$9 trillion in debt*, a figure equal to $30,000 for every man, woman, and child in the nation. The debt is about 65 percent of the size of GDP. The debt is owed to banks, insurance companies, investment firms, and anyone else who buys U.S. government bonds. International investors own about 20 percent of the national debt. Government interest payments to holders of the debt amounts to about 8 percent of governmental expenditures. The debt need not ever be paid off, but future generations of American taxpayers must continue to pay the annual interest on it as long as it is not paid. The booming economy of the 1990s enabled the federal government to finally end its more than thirty years of annual deficits in 1998. (Deficits refer to the *annual* excess of expenditures over revenues; debt refers to the accumulated deficits of the national government over the years.) For four years the government actually incurred surpluses, and congressional debate centered on how to spend the surpluses (see Figure 11.4).

But the terrorist attack of September 11, 2001, ended all hopes of continuing federal surpluses—hopes that had already been eroded by a recession that began in early 2001. The recession resulted in lower than expected federal revenues, and the terrorist attack inspired additional spending for homeland security and military operations. President Bush's fiscal response to the recession was to push the Republican-controlled Congress to enact major tax reductions in 2001 and again in 2003. Democrats argued that these reductions contributed to the return of deficit spending. Republicans argued that tax reductions would stimulate the economy and that economic growth would eventually increase revenues and reduce deficits.

TAX POLITICS

The federal government finances itself primarily from individual income taxes (47 percent) and Social Security payroll taxes (35 percent). Corporations currently pay only about 12 percent of total federal revenues (see Figure 11.5).

Social Security and Medicare taxes (also known as FICA) are paid by wage earners (15.3 percent of total payrolls, paid half by employers and half by employees). Social Security taxes (12.4 percent combined employer-employee rate) are considered "regressive"—that is, they capture a larger share of the income of lower-income Americans than of higher-income Americans. This is because, first of all, Social Security taxes are imposed on only the first $97,500 (in 2007, rising slightly every year) of *wage* income; wages above that amount are not subject to these taxes. (Medicare taxes, 2.9 percent combined rate, are levied against all wage income.) Second, Social Security taxes are not levied against *nonwage* income (interest, dividends, rents, profits from the sale of stocks and bonds, and so on)—sources of income concentrated among high-income taxpayers.

In contrast, the federal individual income tax is highly "progressive"—that is, it captures a larger share of the income of higher-income Americans than lower-income

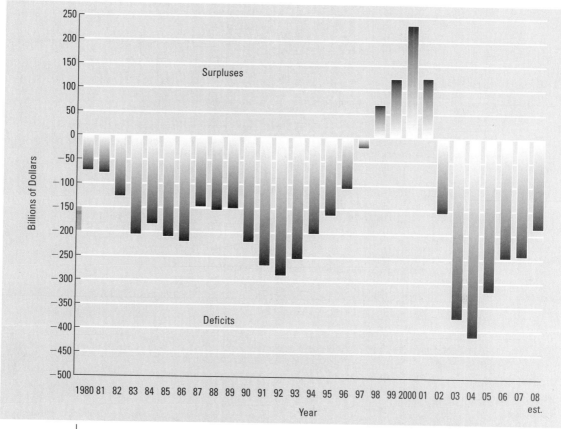

FIGURE 11.4 | ANNUAL FEDERAL DEFICITS AND SURPLUSES

Source: *Statistical Abstract of the United States,* 2006; *Budget of the United States Government,* 2008.

Internal Revenue Service

The IRS Web site provides tax tables and forms for individuals and corporations. *www.irs.gov*

Social Security

The Social Security Administration Web site provides information as well as access to individual accounts. *www.ssa.gov*

Americans (see Figure 11.6). Personal income is taxed at six separate rates—10, 15, 25, 28, 33, and 35 percent. These rates are applied progressively to levels of income, or "brackets," indexed annually to reflect inflation.

The progressivity of the federal individual income tax and the personal and standard exemptions for families and earned income tax credits for low-income earners combine to remove most of the tax burden from middle- and low-income Americans. Indeed, the lower 50 percent of income earners in America pay only about 4 percent of all federal income taxes (see Figure 11.7).

The progressive nature of the federal individual income tax is frequently cited by pluralists as evidence of the political influence of low- and middle-income Americans. However, as noted earlier, Social Security taxes provide almost as much revenue to the federal government as the individual income tax, and Social Security taxes are decidedly regressive. Moreover, the corporate income tax, supposedly set at 35 percent of net profits, produces relatively little revenue owing to a host of exemptions, deductions, and special treatments written into the lengthy and complex U.S. Tax Code.

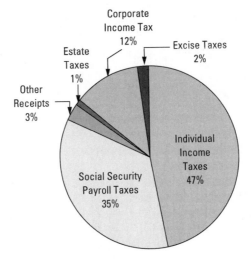

FIGURE 11.5 | SOURCES OF FEDERAL REVENUE

Source: *Budget of the United States Government*, 2008.

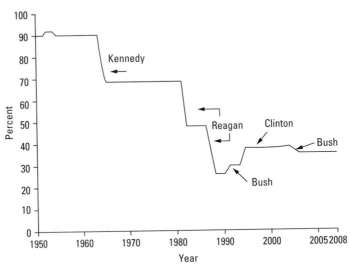

FIGURE 11.6 | MAXIMUM INCOME TAX RATES: PRESIDENT KENNEDY REDUCED THE TOP INCOME TAX RATE TO 70 PERCENT; PRESIDENT RONALD REAGAN REDUCED IT IN TWO STEPS TO 28 PERCENT; PRESIDENT BUSH (THE ELDER) AND CLINTON RAISED IT TO 39.6 PERCENT; AND PRESIDENT GEORGE W. BUSH REDUCED IT TO 35 PERCENT.

FOCUS | ## THE CAPITAL GAINS TAX SCAM

Why should some types of income be given preferential treatment in the tax laws? In Reagan's Tax Reform Act of 1986 all types of income—wage, salary, profits, and capital gains—were to be taxed at the same low rates. (A capital gain is a profit made from buying and selling any asset—real estate, bonds, stocks, etc.) But preferential treatment for capital gains appeals to a wide variety of elites—especially Wall Street investment firms and the real estate industry. Reducing taxes on capital gains increases the turnover (buying and selling) of stocks, bonds, and real estate, and hence the income of investment and real estate firms. And, of course, it significantly reduces the tax burden on high-income taxpayers—those most likely to have income from the sale of these assets (see figure).

Preferential treatment for capital gains has been supported by both Democratic and Republican presidents. When President George H. W. Bush and the Democratic Congress raised the top income tax rate to 31 percent in 1990 they quietly made this rate applicable only to *earned* income. Income from capital gains continued to be taxed at the 28 percent rate. This ploy succeeded in restoring preferential treatment for capital gains. The same tactic was employed again in 1993 when President Clinton won congressional approval for an additional increase in the top marginal rate to 39.6 percent; the capital gains tax rate remained at 28 percent. Republicans continued to urge further reductions in capital gains taxation. Following their congressional victory in the 1994 midterm elections, Republicans pushed through a 20 percent tax rate on capital gains, about one-half of the then existing tax rate on earned income. And President

George W. Bush and a Republican Congress further reduced the capital gains tax to 15 percent in 2003.

Preferential treatment for capital gains means that income from capital investment is taxed at a much lower rate than income from wages and salaries. The elites argue that high tax rates for capital gains discourages economic growth. But if it is true that high tax rates discourage investment, high tax rates must also discourage labor, which is also essential to economic growth. The only real explanation for preferential treatment for capital gains is the power of the elite interests that benefit from the disparity between the treatment of income from investments and income from work.

WHO BENEFITS FROM CAPITAL GAINS

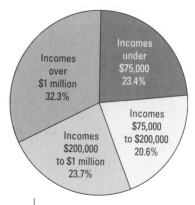

WHO BENEFITS FROM CAPITAL GAINS?

Finally, capital gains—profits from the sale of stocks, bonds, real estate, and so on—are currently taxed at only 15 percent, a rate less than half the top marginal rate on earned income of 35 percent.

BUREAUCRATIC POWER, IRON TRIANGLES, AND REVOLVING DOORS

Traditionally, it was assumed that when Congress passed a law and then created a bureaucracy and appropriated money to carry out the intent of the law, that was the end of the political process. It was assumed that the intent of Congress would be

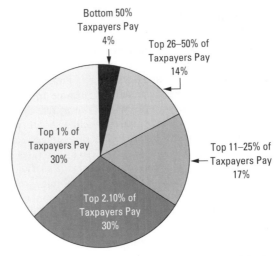

FIGURE 11.7 | WHO PAYS THE FEDERAL INDIVIDUAL INCOME TAX?

carried out—the political battle having been resolved—and that government would get on with the job of "administering" the law.

It turns out, however, that political battles do not end with victory or defeat in Congress. Organized interests do not abandon the fight and return home simply because the site of the battle shifts from the political arena to an administrative one. We tend to think that "political" questions are the province of the president and Congress and that "administrative" questions are the province of the bureaucracy. Actually, "political" and "administrative" questions do not differ in content; they differ only in who decides them.

IMPLEMENTATION, REGULATION, ADJUDICATION

Bureaucracies are not *constitutionally* empowered to decide policy questions. But they do so, nevertheless, as they perform their tasks of implementation, regulation, and adjudication.

Implementation is the development of procedures and activities to carry out policies legislated by Congress. It requires bureaucracies to translate laws into operational rules and regulations and to allocate resources—money, personnel, offices, supplies—to functions. All these tasks involve decisions by bureaucrats—decisions that drive how the law will actually affect society. In some cases, bureaucrats delay the development of regulations based on a new law, assign enforcement responsibility to existing offices with other higher-priority tasks, and allocate few people with limited resources to the task. In other cases, bureaucrats act forcefully in making new regulations, insist on strict enforcement, assign responsibilities to newly created aggressive offices with no other assignments, and allocate a great deal of staff time and agency resources to the task. Interested groups have a strong stake in these decisions, and they actively seek to influence the bureaucracy.

Regulation involves the development of formal rules for implementing legislation. The federal bureaucracy publishes about 60,000 pages of rules in the *Federal Register* each year. Regulatory battles are important because regulations that appear in the *Federal Register* have the effect of law. Congress can amend or repeal a regulation only by passing new legislation and obtaining the president's signature. Controversial bureaucratic regulations often remain in place because Congress is slow to act, because key committee members block corrective legislation, or because the president refuses to sign bills overturning the regulation.

Adjudication involves bureaucratic decisions about individual cases. In adjudication, bureaucrats decide whether a person or firm is failing to comply with laws or regulations and, if so, what penalties or corrective actions are to be applied. Regulatory agencies and commissions—for example, the National Labor Relations Board, the Federal Communications Commission, the Equal Employment Opportunity Commission, the Federal Trade Commission, and the Securities and Exchange Commission—are heavily engaged in adjudication. Their elaborate procedures and body of previous decisions closely resemble the court system. Some agencies authorize specific hearing officers, administrative judges, or appellate divisions to accept evidence, hear arguments, and decide cases. Individuals and firms involved in these proceedings usually hire lawyers specializing in the field of regulation. Administrative hearings are somewhat less formal than a court trial, and the "judges" are employees of the agency itself. Losers may appeal to the federal courts, but the record of agency success in the federal courts discourages many appeals.

BUREAUCRATIC GOALS

Bureaucrats generally believe strongly in the value of their programs and the importance of their tasks. Senior military officers and civilian officials of the Department of Defense believe in the importance of a strong national defense, and top officials in the Social Security Administration are committed to maintaining the integrity of the retirement system and serving the nation's senior citizens. Beyond these public-spirited motives, bureaucrats, like everyone else, seek higher pay, greater job security, and added power and prestige for themselves.

These public and private motives converge to inspire bureaucrats to seek to expand the powers, functions, and budgets of their departments and agencies. Rarely do bureaucrats request a reduction in authority, the elimination of a program, or a decrease in their agency's budget. Rather, bureaucracies strive to add new functions, acquire more authority and responsibility, and increase their budgets and personnel.

"IRON TRIANGLES"

Once an issue is shifted to the bureaucracy, three major power bases—the "iron triangles"—come together to decide its outcome: the executive agency administering the program; the congressional subcommittee charged with overseeing it; and the most interested groups, generally those directly affected by the agency. The interest groups develop close relationships with the bureaucratic policy makers. And both the interest groups and the bureaucrats develop close relationships with the congressional subcommittees that oversee their activities. Agency–subcommittee–interest group relationships become established; even the individuals involved remain the same over fairly long periods of time, as senior members of Congress retain their subcommittee memberships.

Note that the parts of this triumvirate do *not* compete (as pluralist ideology suggests). Instead, bureaucratic agency, congressional subcommittee, and organized interest come together to "scratch each other's back" in bureaucratic policy making. Bureaucrats get political support from interest groups in their requests for expanded power and authority and increased budgetary allocations. Interest groups get favorable treatment of their members by the bureaucracy. Congressional committee members get political and financial support from interest groups as well as favorable treatment for their constituents and contributors who are served or regulated by the bureaucracy.

REVOLVING DOORS

Center for Public Integrity
Reform organization committed to "exposing" corruption, mismanagement, and waste in government.
www.publicintegrity.org

Washington "insiders"—bureaucrats, lobbyists, former members of Congress, White House and congressional staffers—frequently change jobs. They may move from a government post (where they acquired experience, knowledge, and personal contacts) to a job in the private sector as a consultant, lobbyist, or salesperson. Defense contractors may recruit high-ranking military officers or Defense Department officials to help sell weapons to their former employers. Trade associations may recruit congressional staffers, White House staffers, or high-ranking agency heads as lobbyists, or these people may leave government service to start their own lobbying firms. Attorneys from the Justice Department, the Internal Revenue Service, and federal regulatory agencies may be recruited by Washington law firms to represent clients in dealings with their former employees. Following retirement, many members of Congress turn to lobbying their former colleagues.

Concern about *revolving doors* centers not only on individuals cashing in on their knowledge, experience, and contacts obtained through government employment but also on the possibility that some government officials will be tempted to tilt their decisions in favor of corporations, law firms, or interest groups that promise these officials well-paid jobs after they leave government employment. (The Ethics in Government Act limits post-government employment: former members of Congress are not permitted to lobby Congress for one year after leaving that body; former employees of executive agencies are not permitted to lobby their agency for one year after leaving government service, and they are not permitted to lobby their agency for two years on any matter over which they had any responsibility while employed by the government.)

THE REGULATORY QUAGMIRE

The Washington bureaucracy has become the regulator of the national economy, the protector of business against its rivals, and the guardian of the American people against everything from tainted foods to rickety stepladders. Federal regulatory bureaucracies began in 1887 with the creation of the Interstate Commerce Commission to regulate

IN BRIEF	BUREAUCRATIC POWER

- Bureaucracies make policy when they perform their tasks of implementation, regulation, and adjudication.
- Implementation is the development of procedures and activities to carry out laws passed by Congress.
- Regulation is the development of formal rules for implementing congressional legislation.
- Adjudication involves decision making about individual cases, whether or not individuals or firms are complying with laws and regulations, and what penalties or corrective actions are to be applied.
- Bureaucratic policy making generally aspires to the expansion of the powers,

functions, and budgets of departments and agencies.

- "Iron triangles"—executive bureaucracies administering a program, the congressional subcommittee charged with overseeing it, and the interest groups most directly affected by the program—contribute to the power of bureaucrats.
- "Revolving doors" allow bureaucrats, as well as lobbyists, former members of Congress, and White House and congressional staffers, to move from one post to another, often cashing in on their knowledge, experience, and contacts to obtain government employment.

railroad rates. Since then, thousands of laws, amendments, court rulings, and executive orders have expanded the powers of the regulatory commissions over every aspect of our lives (see Figure 11.1 for a list of independent commissions and agencies).

Federal regulatory bureaucracies are legislatures, investigators, prosecutors, judges, and juries—all wrapped into one. They issue thousands of pages of rules and regulations each year; they investigate thousands of complaints and conduct thousands of inspections; they require businesses to submit hundreds of thousands of forms each year; they hold hearings, determine "compliance" and "noncompliance," issue corrective orders, and levy fines and penalties. Most economists agree that overregulation adds greatly to the cost of living, that it is an obstacle to innovation and productivity, and that it hinders economic competition. Most regulatory commissions are *independent*; they are not under an executive department, and their members are appointed for long terms by a president who has little control over their activities. The most independent of all federal regulatory agencies is the Federal Reserve System (see Focus: The Fed: Money Is Too Important to Be Left to Elected Officials).

Code of Federal Regulations
All fifty titles of federal regulations can be found at the Cornell Law School Web site.
www.cfr. law.cornell.edu

THE CAPTURED REGULATORS

Over the years, the reform movements that led to the establishment of many of the older regulatory agencies have diminished in influence. Some regulatory agencies have become closely identified with regulated industry. The capture theory of regulation describes how regulated industries come to benefit from government regulation and how regulatory commissions come to represent the industries they are supposed to regulate rather than "the people." From time to time, various regulatory commissions have behaved as if "captured" by their industry. These have included the (now extinct) Interstate Commerce Commission with railroads and trucking, the Federal Reserve

| FOCUS | THE FED: MONEY IS TOO IMPORTANT TO BE LEFT TO ELECTED OFFICIALS |

Money is too important to be left to democratically elected officials. It became apparent at the beginning of the twentieth century that the control of money would have to be removed from government and placed in the hands of bankers themselves. Moreover, it was generally agreed that bankers' power over money would have to be unrestricted by Congress or the president.

The Federal Reserve Act of 1913 created the Federal Reserve System, popularly known as "the Fed." Its purpose is to decide the nation's monetary policy and credit conditions, to supervise and regulate all banking activity, and to provide various services to banks. Federal Reserve banks are banks' banks; only banks can open accounts at Federal Reserve banks.

The Federal Reserve System is fully independent—its decisions need not be ratified by the president, Congress, the courts, or any other governmental institution. It does not depend on annual federal appropriations but instead finances itself. Theoretically, Congress could amend or repeal the Federal Reserve Act of 1913, but to do so would be economically unthinkable. The only changes to the Act throughout the century have been to *add* to the powers of the Fed.

Controlling the Money Supply

The Federal Reserve System was created by bankers primarily to stabilize the banking system and control the supply of money. The Fed requires all banks to maintain a reserve in currency or in deposits with a Federal Reserve bank. If the "reserve ratio" is set at 20 percent, for example, a bank may create demand deposits only up to five times the amount of its reserve. (If it has $100 million in reserve, its total demand deposits cannot exceed $500 million.)

If the Fed decides that there is too much money in the economy (inflation), it can raise the reserve requirement, for example, from 20 to 25 percent, reducing what a bank can create in demand deposits

to only four times its reserve. (If a bank has $100 million in reserve, its total demand deposits would be limited to $400 million.) In this way the Fed can expand or contract money supply as it sees fit.

The Fed can also alter the money supply by changing the interest it charges member banks to borrow reserve. A bank can expand its deposits by borrowing reserve from the Fed, but it must pay the Fed an interest rate, called the "discount rate," in order to do so. The Fed regularly raises and lowers the discount rate, thereby making it easier or harder for banks to borrow reserve. Raising the discount rate tends to contract money supply; lowering it expands the money supply.

The Fed is also authorized to buy and sell U.S. Treasury bonds and notes in what is called open-market operations. Indeed, the assets of the Fed consist of U.S. bonds and notes. Each day the Open Market Desk of the Fed buys and sells billions of dollars worth of government bonds. If it sells more than it buys, it reduces its own reserve and hence its ability to lend reserve to banks; this contracts the money supply. If it buys more than it sells, it adds to its own reserve, enabling it to lend reserve to member banks and expand the money supply.

Fed Governance

The governance of the Fed ensures its isolation from democratic politics. Its board of governors is made up of seven members appointed by the president and confirmed by the Senate. The full term of a member is *fourteen* years, however, and appointments are staggered so that one expires in each even-numbered year. The chairman of the board is appointed for a four-year term, starting midway through each presidential term. This ensures that the new president cannot immediately install a new chairman. Each Federal Reserve bank has its own board of nine directors chosen by member banks. All meetings of the Fed are held in secret.

Board with banking, the Federal Communications Commission (FCC) with television and radio, the Securities and Exchange Commission (SEC) with the stock market, and the Federal Power Commission with the natural gas industry.

Historically, regulatory commissions have acted against only the most wayward members of an industry. By attacking the businesses giving the industry bad publicity, the commissions actually help improve the public's opinion of the industry as a whole.

Regulatory commissions provide symbolic reassurance to the public that the behavior of the industry was proper.

By limiting entry into an industry by smaller firms (either directly, by denying them routes or broadcast channels, for example, or indirectly, by making the requirements for entry costly), the regulatory commissions reduce competition. This function is an important asset to larger, established businesses; they no longer fear new cut-rate competitors.

THE ACTIVIST REGULATORS

Federal Reserve System
This Federal Reserve System Web site covers general information about "Fed" operations, including monetary policy, reserve bank services, international banking, and supervisory and regulatory functions.
www.federalreserve. gov

Congress has created several regulatory agencies to cover areas in which members of Congress have little or no expertise. To make matters worse, their jurisdiction extends to *all* industries rather than specific ones. Prime examples are the Equal Employment Opportunity Commission (EEOC), the Occupational Safety and Health Administration (OSHA), and the Environmental Protection Agency (EPA). The business community widely resents regulations by these agencies. Rules developed by the EEOC to prevent discrimination in employment and promotion (affirmative action guidelines) have been awkward, and the EEOC enforcement of these rules has been nearly chaotic. Many businesses do not believe that the EEOC has the expertise to understand their industry or their labor market. The same is true of the much-despised OSHA, which has issued thousands of safety regulations that appear costly and ridiculous to those in the industry. The complaint about the EPA is that it seldom considers the costs of its rulings to business or the consumer. Industry representatives contend that the EPA should weigh the costs of its regulations against the benefits to the environment.

The EEOC, EPA, and OSHA have general responsibilities across all business and industry. Thus, these agencies are unlikely to develop expertise in the fashion of the FCC, SEC, or other single-industry regulators. They are unlikely to be captured by industry. Rather, they are bureaucratic extensions of civil rights (EEOC), consumer (OSHA), and environmental (EPA) lobbies to whom they owe their existence.

THE HIDDEN COSTS OF REGULATION

Occupational Safety and Health Administration
This Web site covers news and information directly related to OSHA's mission "to ensure safe and healthful workplaces in America."
www.osha.gov

The costs of government regulation do not appear in the federal budget. Rather, they are paid for by businesses, employees, and consumers. Indeed, politicians prefer a regulatory approach to the environment, health, and safety precisely because it forces costs on the private sector—costs that are largely invisible to voters and taxpayers.

How large is the regulatory bill? Proponents of a regulatory activity usually object to estimating its cost. Politicians who wish to develop an image as protectors of the environment, of consumers, of the disabled, and so on do not want to call attention to the costs of their legislation. Only recently has the Office of Management and Budget even attempted to estimate the costs of federal regulatory activity. Overall, regulatory activity costs Americans between $300 billion and $500 billion a year, an amount equal to about one-quarter of the total federal budget. This means that each of America's 100 million households pays about $4,000 per year in the hidden costs of regulation. Paperwork requirements consume more than 5 billion hours of people's time, mostly to comply with the administration by the Internal Revenue Service of the tax laws. However, the costs of environmental controls, including the Environmental Protection Agency's enforcement of clean air and water and hazardous waste disposal regulations, are the fastest growing regulatory costs.

DEREGULATION

The demand for deregulation has echoed in Washington for many years. Complaints about excessive regulation include the following:

1. The increased costs to businesses and consumers of complying with many separate regulations, issued by separate regulatory agencies, are excessive. Environmental regulation alone may be costing Americans $100 to $200 billion a year, but the costs never appear in a federal budget because businesses and consumers absorb them.
2. Overregulation hampers innovation and productivity. For example, the United States lags behind all other advanced nations in the introduction of new drugs because of lengthy testing by the Food and Drug Administration (FDA). Most observers feel that the FDA would not approve aspirin if it were proposed for marketing today. The costs and delays in winning permission for a new product tend to discourage invention.
3. Regulatory bureaucracies' involvement in licensing and business start-up reduces competition. The red tape involved—the cost of complying with federal reporting requirements—is in itself an obstacle to small businesses.
4. Regulatory agencies do not weigh the costs of complying with their regulations against the benefits to society. Regulators generally introduce controls with little regard for the cost–benefit trade-offs.

In 1978, Congress acted for the first time to significantly reduce the burden of regulation. Acting against the objections of the airline industry, which wanted continued regulation, Congress stripped the Civil Aeronautics Board (CAB) of its power to allocate airline routes to various companies and to set rates. The CAB went out of existence in 1985. The airlines were "set free" (against their will) to choose where to fly and what to charge and to compete openly with one another.

Airline deregulation brought about a huge increase in airline travel. The airlines doubled their seating capacity and made more efficient use of their aircraft through the development of hub-and-spoke networks. Air safety continued to improve. Fatalities per millions of miles flown declined, and, because travelers were diverted from far more dangerous highway travel, overall transportation safety was improved. But these favorable outcomes were overshadowed by complaints about congestion at major airports and increased flight delays, especially at peak hours. (The major airports are publicly owned, and governments have been slow in responding to increased air traffic.) Congestion, delays, and accidents are widely reported in the media, usually accompanied by demands for reregulation.

REREGULATION

Deregulation threatens to diminish politicians' power and eliminate bureaucrats' jobs. It forces industries to become competitive and diminishes the role of interest-group lobbyists. Thus, in the absence of strong popular support for continued deregulation, pressures for reregulation remain strong in Washington.

Public scandals in any sector of the economy frequently result in Congress's acting to impose new regulations. The collapse of Enron, once the nation's seventh largest corporation, with evidence that top executives lived lavishly and hid assets in private accounts, led to new SEC regulatory oversight. Evidence that Enron's accounting firm was involved in the scandal led to new legislation regulating the accounting industry.

CONTROLLING THE BUREAUCRACY: CONGRESS AND THE COURTS

Congress or the courts can overturn the decisions of bureaucracies if sufficient opposition develops to bureaucratic policies. But such opposition is unlikely if bureaucracies work closely with their congressional subcommittees and their interest groups.

CONGRESSIONAL CONSTRAINTS

Congress can restrain the bureaucracy by:

1. Passing direct legislation that changes rules or regulations or limits bureaucratic activity.
2. Altering or threatening to alter the bureau's budget.
3. Retaining specific veto powers over certain bureaucratic actions. (Agencies must submit some proposed rules to Congress; if Congress does not act within a specified time, the rules take effect.)
4. Conducting investigations, usually during legislative or appropriations hearings, that publicize unpopular decisions, rules, or expenditures by bureaus.
5. Making direct complaints to the bureaucracy through formal contacts.

Yet it is difficult for Congress to use these powers as a truly effective check on the bureaucracy.

JUDICIAL CONSTRAINTS

The federal courts exercise more direct control over the bureaucracy than Congress does. Decisions by executive agencies usually can be appealed to federal courts. Moreover, federal courts can issue injunctions (orders) to executive agencies before they institute their rules, regulations, projects, or programs.

Judicial control of the bureaucracy has its limitations, however:

1. Judicial oversight usually emphasizes *procedural* fairness rather than policy content.
2. Bureaucracies have set up elaborate administrative processes to protect their decisions from challenge on procedural grounds.
3. Lawsuits against bureaucracies are expensive; the bureaucracies have armies of attorneys paid for out of tax monies to oppose anyone who attempts to challenge them in court.

4. Excessive delays in federal courts add to the time and expense of challenging bureaucratic decisions.

In fact, citizens have not had much success in court cases against bureaucracies. The courts rarely reverse the decisions of federal regulatory commissions. For example, the Federal Power Commission and the Federal Trade Commission win 91 percent of the cases they argue before the Supreme Court; the National Labor Relations Board wins 75 percent; and the Internal Revenue Service wins 73 percent.[4]

THE BUREAUCRACY: AN ELITIST INTERPRETATION

The federal bureaucracy is a major base of power in the United States, largely independent of the other branches of government and not very responsive to the American people. Governmental bureaucracies invade every aspect of modern life, and their power is growing each year. A bureaucratic elite that both formulates and implements public policy is emerging. Elitism in bureaucracy takes several forms:

1. Bureaucratic power increases with the size and technological complexity of modern society. Official lawmaking bodies—Congress and the president—set forth only general policy statements. Bureaucracies write tens of thousands of rules and regulations and actually undertake the tasks of government.
2. Bureaucratic power increases because (1) Congress and the president do not have the time or expertise to master policy details; (2) Congress and the president deliberately pass vague laws for symbolic reasons, then turn over actual governance to bureaucracies; and (3) the bureaucracy has now amassed sufficient power to influence the president and Congress.
3. Although the president is officially in charge of the executive branch of government, presidential control is limited by (1) the relatively small number of policy-making patronage positions appointed by the president versus the large numbers of professional civil service bureaucrats, (2) the difficulty of achieving meaningful reorganization, and (3) the large number of "uncontrollable" items in the budget.
4. The budget is the most important policy statement of a government. The president, through the Office of Management and Budget, is responsible for the preparation of the Budget of the U.S. Government each year for submission to Congress. But only Congress can authorize the expenditure of federal funds; it does so through annual appropriations acts for major areas of government spending.
5. Federal spending has grown dramatically over the years, driven largely by "entitlement" spending, notably Social Security and Medicare. A booming economy in the 1990s produced four years of balanced budgets, but deficits resumed with recession, the war on terrorism, and tax reductions. Future generations will be burdened with an accumulated national debt of more than $7 trillion.
6. Once a political question shifts to the bureaucracy, an "iron triangle" of power bases comes together to decide its outcome: the executive bureaucracy, the congressional subcommittee, and the organized interest groups.

7. The federal regulatory commissions are investigators, prosecutors, judges, and juries—all wrapped into one. Members of these commissions serve long, overlapping terms, and they do not report to executive departments. They are relatively free from mass influence.

8. The "Fed" (the Federal Reserve Board that governs the Federal Reserve System) is the most independent of all federal agencies. It controls the nation's supply of money and directly influences interest rates.

9. Regulations hide the true costs of government by shifting them from the government itself to businesses, employees, and consumers. Bureaucrats seldom weigh the costs of their actions against whatever benefits are produced.

10. In theory, Congress restrains the bureaucracy directly by ordering changes in rules, altering the budget, retaining veto powers over bureaucratic action, conducting investigations, and registering complaints. In practice, however, Congress rarely reverses bureaucratic decisions and seldom tampers with "uncontrollable" budget items. In theory, the courts can also restrain the bureaucracy, but rarely do they actually reverse administrative decisions.

SELECTED READINGS

Bozeman, Barry. *Bureaucracy and Red Tape.* Upper Saddle River, N.J.: Prentice-Hall, 2000. Distinguishes between bureaucratic "normalities" and democratic "pathologies." Argues that some red tape is required for reasonable accountability.

Henry, Nicholas. *Public Administration and Public Affairs*, 9th ed. Upper Saddle River, N.J.: Prentice-Hall, 2004. Authoritative introductory textbook on public organizations (bureaucracies), public management, and policy implementation.

Howard, Philip K. *The Death of Common Sense: How Law Is Suffocating America.* New York: Random House, 1995. Outrageous stories of bureaucratic senselessness coupled with a plea to allow bureaucrats flexibility in achieving the purposes of laws and holding them accountable for outcomes.

Kerwin, Cornelius M. *Rulemaking: How Government Agencies Write Law and Make Policy*, 3rd ed. Washington, D.C.: CQ Press, 2003. A thorough examination of the regulatory process and the power of rule-making agencies.

Osbourne, David, and Ted Gaebler. *Reinventing Government.* New York: Addison-Wesley, 1992. The respected manual of the "reinventing government" movement with recommendations to overcome the routine tendencies of bureaucracies and inject "the entrepreneurial spirit" in them.

Radin, Beryl. *The Accountable Juggler: The Art of Leadership in a Federal Agency.* Washington, D.C.: CQ Press, 2002. A close-up look at managers in the Department of Health and Human Services and how they juggle competing accountability demands.

Smith, Robert W., and Thomas D. Lynch. *Public Budgeting in America*, 5th ed. Upper Saddle River, N.J.: Prentice-Hall, 2004. Authoritative text describing public budgetary processes, behaviors, and administration.

Wildavsky, Aaron. *The New Politics of the Budgetary Process.* Boston: Scott Foresman, 1988. The revised version of the classic work on politics and incrementalism in budgeting, including strategies by bureaucrats, the OMB, the president, and Congress, with emphasis on the collapse of political consensus, the entitlements problem, and the failure of budget-balancing efforts.

Wilson, James W. *Bureaucracy: What Bureaucrats Do and Why They Do It.* New York: Basic Books, 1989. In the author's words, "an effort to depict the essential features of bureaucratic life in the government agencies of the United States." An examination of what really motivates middle-level public servants. Wilson argues that congressional attempts to "micromanage" government activities hamper the ability of bureaucrats to do their jobs.

NOTES

1. Max Weber, *The Theory of Social and Economic Organization*, A. M. Henderson and Talcott Parsons, trans. (New York: Oxford University Press, 1947). Summary by Robert C. Fried, *Performance in American Bureaucracy* (Boston: Little, Brown, 1976).

2. James Q. Wilson, "Social Science: The Public Disenchantment, a Symposium," *American Scholar* (Summer 1976): 358; also cited by Aaron Wildavsky, *Speaking Truth to Power* (Boston: Little, Brown, 1979), p. 69.

3. *Clinton v. City of New York,* 524 U.S. 417 (1998).

4. Bradley Cannon and Michael Giles, "Recurring Litigants: Federal Agencies before the Supreme Court," *Western Political Quarterly*, 15 (September 1972): 183–191.

Your representative owes you, not his industry only, but his judgement; and he betrays instead of serving you, if he sacrifices it to your opinion.

Edmund Burke

CONGRESS: THE LEGISLATIVE ELITE

The Founders intended that Congress be the first and most powerful branch of government. Article I of the Constitution describes the national government's powers, for example, "to lay and collect Taxes Duties Imposts and Excises and provide for the common Defense and general Welfare of the United States," *as powers given to Congress.* The Founders also intended that the House of Representatives represent "the people" in government. Among the governmental bodies created by the Constitution of 1787, *only the House of Representatives was to be directly elected by the people.* The Senate was to be elected by state legislatures (until the Seventeenth Amendment in 1913 provided for their direct election); the president was to be chosen by the Electoral College; and the Supreme Court was to be appointed for life. House members were to be elected every two years to ensure their responsiveness to the people. Indeed, even today House members fondly refer to their chamber as "the people's House."

But who are "the people" that Congress really represents? It is our argument that Congress members principally represent themselves. We contend that they are recruited from local elite structures; that the masses are largely inattentive to congressional affairs and elections; that the overriding interest of Congress members is their own reelection; that in pursuit of that goal they depend heavily on large campaign contributors; that Congress has structured itself as "an incumbent protection society," that is, to assist its members to remain in office; that even *within* Congress a leadership "establishment" controls legislation; and finally that Congress has largely ceded policy initiation to the president, the bureaucracy, the courts, and organized interest groups.

THE ELITE BIAS OF CONGRESSIONAL RECRUITMENT

The elite bias of Congress begins with the recruitment of its members. Senators and House members are seldom recruited from the masses; they are drawn from the well-educated, prestigiously employed, affluent, upper and upper-middle classes of their home constituencies. They are drawn from the most ambitious, politically motivated, skilled communicators in their communities. Their social ties are mainly to state and community elite structures; they retain their local contacts, club memberships, business ties, and contributor networks. Members who sacrifice local ties and succumb to the attractions of Washington's "inside the beltway" social life do so at some risk.

POLITICAL ENTREPRENEURSHIP

U.S. House of Representatives
Official Web site of the House, with schedule of floor and committee actions, legislative information, and links to every Representative's Web site and every committee Web site.
www.house.gov

U.S. Senate
Official Senate Web site, with floor and committee schedules, Senate news, and links to each Senator's Web site.
www.senate.gov

"Who sent these people to Washington? They sent themselves."[1] The most important qualification for Congress is political entrepreneurship—the ability and desire to sell oneself to others as a candidate, to raise money from political contributors, to organize and motivate others to work on one's campaign, and to communicate to others personally, in small groups and large audiences, and, most important, through the media.

For most members of Congress politics has become their career. They are professional public officeholders. "Citizen officeholders"—people with business or professional or commercial careers who get into politics part-time—have largely been driven out of political life in America by people who enter politics early in life and become career professionals in it. Both holding office and campaigning for it demand the full-time attention of politicians.

Increasingly, political careers are begun early in life. Politically ambitious young people, fresh out of college or law school, seek out internships or staff positions with members of Congress or with congressional committees or in state capitols or city halls. Others volunteer to work in political campaigns. They find political mentors to guide them in learning to organize campaigns, contact financial contributors, and deal with the media. They prudently wait for open seats in their state legislatures, city councils, or perhaps Congress itself, to launch their own initial campaigns for elective office.

Political parties seldom recruit candidates any more; candidates recruit themselves. Nor do interest groups recruit candidates; rather, candidates seek out interest groups in the hope of winning their support. Once elected to office, most successful members of Congress devote full time to staying there.

PROFESSIONALISM

Professional backgrounds dominate the halls of Congress. Congress members are almost always of higher social standing than their average constituent. Candidates for Congress have a better chance at election if their occupations are socially "respectable" and provide opportunities for extensive public contacts. Lawyers, bankers, insurance brokers, and real estate brokers establish in their businesses the wide circle of friends necessary for political success.

The overrepresentation of lawyers in Congress and other public offices is particularly marked. Lawyers have always played a prominent role in the American political system. Twenty-five of the fifty-two signers of the Declaration of Independence and thirty-one of the fifty-five members of the Continental Congress were lawyers. The legal profession has also provided 70 percent of the presidents,

FOCUS	TOP TEN UNIVERSITIES IN CONGRESS			
Harvard University	39	University of Michigan	12
Georgetown University	20	George Washington University	11
Yale University	16	University of Florida	10
University of Virginia	14	University of Pittsburgh	10
Stanford University	13	University of Texas	9

Note: It might not always seem so, especially when Congress is in gridlock or unable to address important national problems, but in fact Congress members on the whole are very well educated. Indeed, the largest number of university graduates obtained their degree at prestigious Harvard University, followed by Georgetown University and Yale University.

Source: *Congressional Quarterly Weekly Report*, January 31, 2005.

vice presidents, and cabinet officers of the United States and about 40 percent of the U.S. senators and House members. Lawyers are in a reasonably high-prestige occupation, but so are physicians, business executives, and scientists. Why, then, do lawyers dominate Congress?

It is sometimes argued that lawyers bring a special kind of skill to Congress. They represent clients in their work; therefore they can use the same skill to represent constituents in Congress. Also, lawyers deal with public policy as it is reflected in the statute books, so they may be reasonably familiar with public policy before entering Congress. But professional skills alone cannot explain the dominance of lawyers in public office. Of all the high-prestige occupations, only lawyers can really enhance their careers through political activities. Physicians, corporate managers, and scientists pay a high cost if they neglect their vocations for politics. But political activity can help boost lawyers' careers; free public advertising and contacts with potential clients are two important benefits. Moreover, lawyers have a monopoly on public offices in law enforcement and the court system, and the offices of judge or prosecuting attorney often provide lawyers with stepping-stones to higher public office, including Congress.

EDUCATION

Congressional members are among the most highly educated occupational groups in the United States. Their educational level is considerably higher than that of the populations they represent. Their education reflects their occupational background and their middle- and upper-class origins (see Focus: Top Ten Universities in Congress).

RACE AND GENDER

African Americans make up over 12 percent of the nation's population. Beginning in 1993, their membership in the House of Representatives reached 9 percent. The leap in black membership was a product of judicial interpretations of the Voting Rights Act, which requires that minorities be given maximum opportunity to elect minorities to Congress through redistricting.

| FOCUS | NANCY PELOSI, SPEAKER OF THE HOUSE |

Nancy Pelosi is the first woman in the history of the U.S. Congress to serve as Speaker of the House of Representatives. In 2001, her Democratic colleagues elected her Minority Leader, the highest ranking leadership position among Democratic members. Pelosi has represented her San Francisco district since her first election to Congress in 1986.

Congresswoman Pelosi comes from a highly political family. Her father, Thomas D'Alesandro, served five terms in Congress and later twelve years as mayor of Baltimore. Pelosi's brother also served as mayor of Baltimore. Young Nancy grew up in Washington and graduated from that city's Trinity College in 1962. She served as a congressional intern to her Maryland senator. She married Paul Pelosi, moved to his hometown of San Francisco, and raised five children. Before her election to Congress, she served on the Democratic National Committee.

In her years in Congress, Pelosi built a solid liberal reputation, serving on the powerful Appropriations Committee. She won the post as Democratic whip in 2001 in a close election against a more moderate Democrat. She automatically ascended to the post of Democratic Leader with the resignation of Tom Daschle.

But Pelosi's real strength within the Democratic Party has long been her fund-raising ability. Her San Francisco district is the home of some of the party's wealthiest individual donors, and Democrats across the nation rely heavily on money from California. Pelosi created her own leadership PAC and regularly hands out millions to her Democratic colleagues. She spends relatively little on her own reelection races in her heavily Democratic district.

When the Democrats won control of the House in the 2006 congressional elections, Pelosi was elevated to Speaker of the House, the first woman ever to achieve that post. She announced her intentions to drive a Democratic agenda through the House and immediately began by tightening House ethics rules. She is described as hard-driving, yet willing to recognize that her strong liberal views are not necessarily shared by all other Democrats. She has been quoted as saying: "Tell them what you're going to do. Do it. And then tell them what you did."[a]

_____

[a]*Congressional Quarterly Weekly Report*, January 8, 2007, p. 123.

It was not until 1966 that the first African American, Republican Edward Brooke of Massachusetts, was popularly elected to the Senate; he served until 1979. Carol Moseley Braun was the first black woman to be elected to the Senate in 1992; she was defeated for reelection in 1998. Barak Obama won election to the Senate from Illinois in 2004.

Hispanics make up more than 14 percent of the nation's population, somewhat more than African Americans. However, to date, Hispanics have not achieved the political power of African Americans. Only twenty-three currently serve in the House, less than 6 percent of that body.

Women also have made great strides in congressional representation. In 2007, seventy-one women took their seats in the House. And sixteen women took their seats in the Senate. More important, perhaps, women are moving up the party hierarchy in each house in achieving leadership positions (see Focus: "Nancy Pelosi, Speaker of the House"). For an overview of the ethnic and gender make-up of Congress, see Table 12.1.

PARTY

For forty years (1954–1994) Democrats controlled the House of Representatives, and for most of these years they also held a majority in the Senate (see Table 12.2). The Republican victory in the congressional election of 1994 was described as

TABLE 12.1 | GENDER AND RACE IN CONGRESS

	Women	African Americans	Hispanics
House Members (435)			
1985–1987	22	19	11
1987–1989	23	22	11
1989–1991	25	23	11
1991–1993	29	25	10
1993–1995	48	38	17
1995–1997	49	39	18
1997–1999	51	37	18
1999–2001	58	39	19
2001–2003	59	36	19
2003–2005	59	37	23
2005–2007	65	40	23
2007–2009	71	40	23
Senators (100)			
1985–1987	2	0	0
1987–1989	2	0	0
1989–1991	2	0	0
1991–1993	2	0	0
1993–1995	6	1	0
1995–1997	8	1	0
1997–1999	9	1	0
1999–2001	9	0	0
2001–2003	13	0	0
2003–2005	14	0	0
2005–2007	14	1	3
2007–2009	16	1	3

an "earthquake" in Washington. The GOP "revolution" was widely attributed to Republican leader Newt Gingrich, who recruited most Republican candidates to support a "Contract with America," which incorporated many popular provisions (for example, a constitutional amendment to balance the budget, term limits, tax reductions, reduced federal spending, and welfare reform). But the "revolution" soon fizzled when Republicans failed to deliver on most of their promises and President Bill Clinton vetoed their budget cuts. Clinton went on to easily win reelection in 1996. Yet Republicans held on to control both the House and the Senate until the Democratic victory in 2006.

TABLE 12.2 | PARTY CONTROL OF CONGRESS

Year	Session	House		Senate	
		D	R	D	R
1959	86th	**282**	153	35	**65**
1961	87th	**262**	173	35	**65**
1963	88th	**258**	177	33	**67**
1965	89th	**295**	140	32	**68**
1967	90th	**248**	187	36	**64**
1969	91st	**243**	192	42	**58**
1971	92nd	**255**	180	45	**55**
1973	93rd	**243**	192	43	**57**
1975	94th	**291**	144	38	**61**
1977	95th	**292**	143	38	**62**
1979	96th	**277**	158	41	**59**
1981	97th	**243**	192	**53**	47
1983	98th	**269**	166	**55**	45
1985	99th	**253**	182	**53**	47
1987	100th	**258**	177	45	**55**
1989	101st	**260**	175	43	**57**
1991	102nd	**269**	166	43	**57**
1993	103rd	**259**	176	44	**56**
1995	104th	205	**230**	**53**	47
1997	105th	208	**227**	**55**	45
1999	106th	212	**223**	**55**	5
2001	107th	213	**222**	50	50
2003	108th	206	**229**	**51**	49
2005	109th	203	**232**	45	**55**
2007	110th	**234**	201	**51**	49

Note: Majority party in bold. Figures include self-described "independents" who align themselves with one or the other party.

Partisanship rose in both the House and the Senate following the disputed presidential election of 2000. Democrats were convinced that Bush had "stolen" the presidency. The rhetoric at the Capitol became more and more inflammatory.

President George W. Bush became "campaigner in chief" in the congressional elections of 2002, and he appeared to have "coattails" in the 2004 elections, as Republicans solidified their control of both Houses. But the war in Iraq seriously eroded Bush's popularity (see Chapter 16) and led to the election of a Democratic-controlled House and Senate in the 2006 midterm congressional elections. Republican congressional control had lasted twelve years, and Democrats were anxious to bring their agenda to the Capitol.

Divided government, with a Republican in the White House and Democrats controlling the House and Senate, does not *necessarily* mean policy gridlock, yet that is often the result. The bitter partisanship that has infected Washington in recent years is a prohibitive barrier to cooperation between the president and Congress. Democratic majorities in both houses are major obstacles to any policy initiatives by President Bush. And the president can threaten vetoes to any major new Democratic programs passed in the Congress.

The president is the Commander-in-Chief, and there is little that Congress can do by itself to compel changes in strategy in Iraq. In theory, Congress can cut off funds for the war, but it is politically risky for Congress to vote to deny funds for American troops in the field. The policy agenda of the Democratic congressional leadership includes strengthening congressional ethics rules, increasing the minimum wage, and reducing interest rates on student loans. Bush's "comprehensive" immigration reform proposal—a guest worker program with a promise of citizenship for immigrants who are here now, as well as increased border enforcement—failed despite Democratic cooperation. Perhaps the most contentious issue between Democrats in Congress and the Republican president is taxation. Bush's first-term tax cuts are set to expire in 2010 unless Congress makes them permanent. Republicans characterize a failure to do so as a "tax increase." Democrats call Bush's cuts "tax cuts for the rich" and oppose making them permanent.

"Bipartisanship" is a popular term in political rhetoric, but it seldom describes what actually occurs in Washington, especially with divided party government.

ACCESS TO MONEY

The cost of a winning campaign for a seat in the U.S. House of Representatives continues to spiral upward (see Figure 12.1). In 2006, the average House winner spent about $1.1 million; winning senators averaged nearly $10 million. (For House members this means raising over $10,000 *each week* during their two-year tenure in office.) These amounts require access to, and support of, fat-cat contributors (see "Money Drives Elections" in Chapter 8). Of course, some wealthy candidates fund their own campaigns. In 2000, four winning U.S. Senators (John Corzine of New Jersey, Mark Dayton of Minnesota, Maria Cantwell of Washington, and Herb Kohl of Wisconsin—all Democrats) spent over $5 million of their own money in their campaigns. Corzine holds the self-funding record, having spent more than $62 million out his own pocket to win his Senate seat; later Corzine would spend heavily to win the governorship of New Jersey.

PERSONAL WEALTH

The personal wealth of members of Congress is well above that of the average American. Members are required to submit annual financial statements that list their assets and liabilities as well as income, guests, and more. But it is difficult to gauge

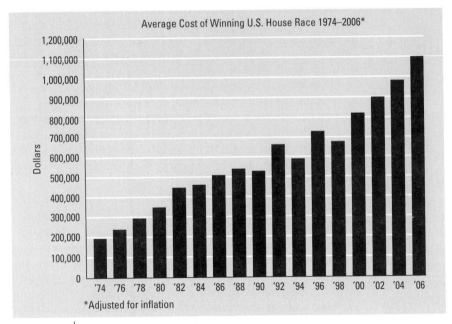

FIGURE 12.1 | AVERAGE COST OF WINNING A U.S. HOUSE RACE

Source: Center for Responsive Politics.

what lawmakers are worth based on what they file, inasmuch as disclosure forms do not require exact values but rather ranges of worth. The Center for Responsive Politics tries to estimate the personal wealth of members based on these filings. The wealthiest members—members with an estimated $55 million or more—are listed in Table 12.3.

WHOM DOES CONGRESS REALLY REPRESENT?

The relevant political constituencies of members of Congress are the elites of their districts rather than their districts' mass populations. In reality, their constituencies are small groups of political activists with the time, interest, and skill to communicate about political events.

MASS INATTENTION

For the great mass of people, Congress is an institution with low visibility and low esteem. Opinion polls consistently report grim facts about the public's lack of awareness of Congress. Only 59 percent of Americans can identify one U.S. senator from their state; only 25 percent can name both of their state's senators. Members of the House of Representatives fare even worse. Only 29 percent of the general public can identify their representative.[2]

Even when constituents know a congressional member's name, few know the member's specific policy positions or, for that matter, the member's overall political position. One study found that among those who offered a reason for candidate

TABLE 12.3	ESTIMATED* PERSONAL WEALTH OF CONGRESS MEMBERS

Rank	Name	$ Millions
1	Darrell Issa (R-Calif)	$677
2	Jane Harman (D-Calif)	$289
3	John Kerry (D-Mass)	$235
4	Herb Kohl (D-Wis)	$234
5	Jay Rockefeller (D-WVa)	$101
6	Dianne Feinstein (D-Calif)	$ 99
7	Edward M. Kennedy (D-Mass)	$ 93
8	Frank R. Lautenberg (D-NJ)	$ 91
9	John Campbell (R-Calif)	$ 78
10	Rodney Frelinghuysen (R-NJ)	$ 67
11	Nita M. Lowey (D-NY)	$ 61
12	Robin Hayes (R-NC)	$ 60
13	Michael McCaul (R-Texas)	$ 58
14	Kenny Ewell Marchant (R-Texas)	$ 55
15	Nancy Pelosi (D-Calif)	$ 55

*Estimates by Center for Responsive Politics based on official filings of Congress members. Figures represent estimated maximum net wealth (assets minus debts). www.opensecrets.org.

choice, only 7 percent indicated that their choice had any "discernible issue content." If one asks for detailed information about policy stands, only a "chemical trace" of the population qualifies as attentive to their congressional candidate's policy positions.[3]

ELITES AS THE RELEVANT CONSTITUENTS

A legislator's relevant constituents, then, are the home district's active, interested, and resourceful elites. In an agricultural district, they are the leaders of the American Farm Bureau Federation and the major agricultural producers—cotton producers, wheat growers, and so on; in the Southwest, oil producers or ranchers; in the mountain states, the copper, lead, and silver mining interests; in northern New England, the lumber, granite, and fishing interests; in central Pennsylvania and West Virginia, the coal interests and leaders of the United Mine Workers. More heterogeneous urban constituencies may contain a variety of influential constituents—bankers and financial leaders, real estate owners and developers, owners and managers of large industrial and commercial enterprises, top labor leaders, and the owners and editors of newspapers and radio and television facilities. In certain big-city districts with strong, disciplined party organizations, the key congressional constituents may be the city's political and governmental elites—the city or county party chairpersons or the mayor. And, of course, anyone who makes major financial contributions to a congressional candidate's campaign becomes a *very* important constituent.

HOME STYLE

Congress members spend as much time cultivating their home districts and states as they do legislating in Washington. "Home style" refers to the activities of senators and representatives in promoting their images among their constituents. These activities include members' allocations of their personnel and staff resources to constituent services; members' personal appearances in their home district or state; and members' efforts to bring federally funded projects, grants, and contracts to their home district or state.

Casework is a form of "retail" politics. Members of Congress win votes and campaign contributors one at a time by helping people on a personal level. Over time grateful voters and contributors accumulate, giving incumbents an advantage at election time. "Pork" describes the efforts of senators and representatives to "bring home the bacon"—to bring federally funded roads, parks, post offices, and redevelopment projects to cities, research grants to universities, weapons contracts to local plants, "demonstration" projects of all kinds, and other "goodies" inside each year's annual appropriations bills. On Capitol Hill much of this pork comes in the form of "earmarks"—special provisions for expenditures tucked inside larger appropriations bills. (Only recently has Congress ruled that members must reveal their sponsorship of earmarks.)

Roll Call
This online magazine covers a variety of current topics about Congress but is especially strong on stories dealing with running for Congress and campaign financing.
www.rollcall.com

Members of Congress spend as much time in their home districts as they do in Washington "moving between two contexts, Washington and home, and between two activities, governing and campaigning."[4] It is important to be seen at home "pressing the flesh," giving speeches and attending dinners, hosting fundraising events, attending civic meetings, and so on. Congress usually follows a Tuesday to Thursday schedule of legislative business, allowing members to spend long weekends at home. Congress also enjoys long recesses during the late summer and over holidays.

CONGRESS IN DISREPUTE

Congress is the least popular branch of government. Polls reveal that a large majority of Americans believe (perhaps accurately) that members of Congress "spend more time thinking about their own political futures than they do in passing legislation."[5] Rarely has the Congress achieved a 50 percent approval rating among the general public (see Figure 12.2). And the Congress's approval rating is almost always well below that of the president.

THROW THE RASCALS OUT?

If Congress is so unpopular, we should reasonably expect voters to "throw the rascals out." The theory of representative democracy implies that dissatisfied voters will defeat incumbents running for reelection. But just the opposite occurs in congressional elections. Well over 90 percent of House members and usually over 75 percent of senators seeking reelection succeed in doing so (see Figure 12.3). Even when the Republican and Democratic parties switch control of Congress, incumbents prevail. In 1994, when Republicans gained control of both the House and the Senate, 90 percent of House incumbents running for reelection won, as well as 92 percent of Senate incumbents.

"Listen, pal! I didn't spend seven million bucks to get here so I could yield the floor to you."

Congressional Quarterly (CQ)
The *Congressional Quarterly Weekly Report* provides the most comprehensive coverage of events in Congress, including key issues, House and Senate roll call votes, backgrounds of members, and political and election information. The CQ Press is a major publisher of books on politics and government. *www.cq.com*

In 2006, when Democrats won control of both houses, 97 percent of House incumbents won reelection and 85 percent of Senate incumbents won. The failure of voters to throw the rascals out, despite mass disapproval of the performance of Congress, is more consistent with elite theory than with democratic theory.

Popular Members, Unpopular Congress

In an apparent paradox, most voters approve of their own representative yet disapprove of the Congress as a whole. Individual members of Congress are generally popular in their districts, even though Congress itself is an object of distrust and even ridicule. Obviously, if most incumbents are popular in their home districts, incumbents will continue to be reelected. The real question is, how do they maintain their popularity?

Incumbent Advantages

Why do incumbents win? First of all, name familiarity—in the absence of any knowledge of issues—can be a powerful advantage. The average voter, even if only vaguely aware of the incumbents, is likely to recognize their names on the ballot and vote for them. Even during a political campaign, an incumbent enjoys much higher name recognition than a challenger.

More important, incumbents use the resources of their office—staff time, travel funds, perks, and privileges—to tend to the needs of their constituents. Over time,

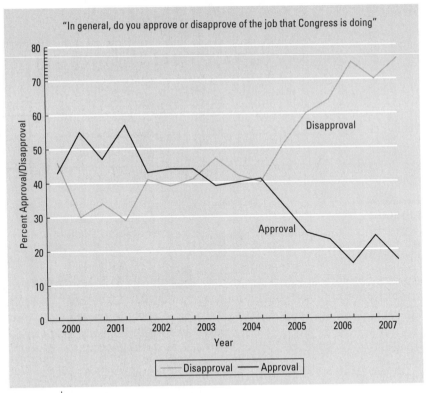

"In general, do you approve or disapprove of the job that Congress is doing"

FIGURE 12.2 | CONGRESSIONAL APPROVAL RATINGS

Source: Various Gallup polls.

incumbents are likely to have developed an effective political organization and a stable network of communication with local elites. They use their franking privilege for mailing newsletters, polls, and other information; they appear at various public events, call news conferences, address organizational meetings, and, in general, make themselves as visible as possible, largely at taxpayers' expense.

Finally, incumbents attract heavy campaign contributions. Because the "smart money" backs a winner, incumbents have more to spend in their campaigns. Indeed, incumbents enjoy an enormous financial advantage over their challengers (see Table 12.4).

MASS REACTION: TERM LIMITS

Mass distrust of politicians fueled a national grassroots movement to limit the terms of public officials—notably members of Congress and state legislators. Term limits are popular with voters; national surveys regularly show overwhelming support for limiting the terms of senators and representatives.

Proponents of term limits rely on antielitist arguments: citizen legislators have largely been replaced by career professional politicians. Over time, professional

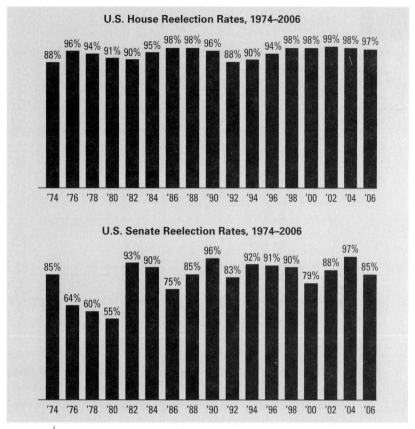

FIGURE 12.3 | INCUMBENT REELECTION RATES

Source: Center for Responsive Politics, 2007.

U.S. Term Limits
Web site of national organization advocating term limits for all public officials.
www.ustl.org

officeholders become isolated from the lives and concerns of average citizens; they acquire an "inside the beltway" mentality (a reference to the circle of interstate highways that surrounds Washington, D.C.). They respond to the media, to polls, to interest groups, but have no direct feeling for how their constituents live. Term limits would force politicians to return home and live under the laws that they make. Term limits would increase competition in the electoral system. Creating "open-seat" races on a regular basis would encourage more people to seek public office.

TABLE 12.4 | CONGRESSIONAL CAMPAIGN SPENDING: INCUMBENTS VERSUS CHALLENGERS

	House	Senate
Average incumbent	$1,265,462	$11,293,45
Average challenger	$ 279,544	$ 1,802,64

Source: Center for Responsive Politics, 2006.

| IN BRIEF | INCUMBENT ADVANTAGES |

Incumbent advantages include:

- Name recognition
- "Home style" service to constituents and contributors

- "Pork" for the home district or state
- Overwhelming advantage in campaign contributions

ELITE OPPOSITION TO TERM LIMITS

However, the enthusiasm of the mass public for term limits is more than matched by the intense opposition the proposal meets on Capitol Hill. It is not likely that members of Congress will ever vote to limit their own terms of office, especially since a constitutional amendment to do so would require two-thirds of the members of both houses to vote to limit their own legislative careers.

Elites argue that term limits infringe on the voters' freedom of choice. If voters are upset with the performance of Congress or their state legislature, they can always "throw the rascals out." If they want to limit the terms of their own members of Congress, they can do so by not reelecting them.

DECIDING ON TERM LIMITS

If the question were left to voters in the states, Congress would certainly confront term limits. Congressional term limits have won by landslide margins almost every time they have appeared on statewide referenda ballots. However, the U.S. Supreme Court held in 1995 that the voters in state referenda cannot limit terms of members of *Congress*. In a controversial 5 to 4 decision, the Court argued that the founders intended that age, citizenship, and residency be the *only* qualifications for membership in Congress, inasmuch as these are the only qualifications mentioned in Article I of the Constitution.[6] The effect of this decision, together with Congress's steadfast opposition to term limits, was to largely destroy the hopes of the congressional term-limit movement.

THE ELABORATE PROCEDURES OF LEGISLATIVE ELITES

Library of Congress
The Thomas system allows the tracing of bills from their introduction, through the committee system, floor schedule vote, and so on. *http:// thomas.loc.gov*

The rules and procedures of Congress are elaborate but important to the functioning of legislative elites. Legislative procedures and rules make the legislative process fair and orderly. Without established customs, rules, and procedures, 535 men and women could not arrive at collective decisions about the thousands of items submitted to them during a congressional session. Yet the same rules also delay or obstruct proposed changes in the status quo; they strengthen Congress's conservative role in policy making. In congressional procedures, legislation faces many opportunities for defeat and many obstacles to passage.

The elaborate procedures of Congress ensure that few of the bills introduced are ever passed. In a two-year congressional session, more than 10,000 bills will be introduced, but fewer than 800 bills will be enacted. In other words, fewer than 10 percent of the measures introduced will ever find their way through the lawmaking process.

THE LAWMAKING PROCESS

Congress follows a fairly standard pattern in the formal process of making laws; Figure 12.4 describes briefly some of the most important procedural steps. Bills generally originate in the president's office, in executive departments, or in the offices of interested elites, but a member of the House or Senate must formally introduce them into Congress. Except for bills raising revenue, which must begin in the House of Representatives according to the Constitution, bills can be introduced in either house. Upon introduction, a bill moves to one of the standing committees of the House or Senate. Most bills are shuffled down to subcommittees, but it is the full committee that eventually decides a bill's fate. The committee may (1) recommend it for adoption with only minor changes, (2) virtually rewrite it into a new policy proposal, (3) ignore it and prevent its passage through inaction, or (4) kill it by majority vote. The full House or Senate *may* overrule a committee decision, but they do so rarely. Most members of Congress are reluctant to upset the prerogatives of the committees and the desires of recognized leaders. Therefore committees have virtual power of life or death over every legislative measure.

STANDING CONGRESSIONAL COMMITTEES

Committee work is essential to the legislative process; Congress as a body could never hope to review all the measures put before it. As early as 1885, Woodrow Wilson described the American political process as "government by the standing committees of Congress."[7] Although it reduces legislative work to manageable proportions, the committee system allows a minority of the legislators, sometimes a single committee chairman, to delay and obstruct the legislative process.

In the Senate, the most prestigious committees are Foreign Relations, Appropriations, and Finance; in the House, the most powerful are the Rules Committee, Appropriations, and Ways and Means. (Table 12.5 lists the twenty-one standing committees in the House and twenty in the Senate.) To expedite business, most standing committees create subcommittees to handle particular matters falling within their jurisdiction. This practice further concentrates power over a particular subject matter in the hands of a few congressional members. Considerable power lies in the hands of subcommittee members, especially the chairpersons; interested elites cultivate the favor of powerful subcommittee and committee chairpersons.

PUBLIC HEARINGS   In examining legislation, a committee or subcommittee often holds public hearings on bills deemed worthy by the chairperson or, in some cases, by the majority of the committee. Influenced by the legal profession, the committees tend to look upon public hearings as trials in which contestants present their sides of the argument to the committee members, who act as judges. Presumably, during this trial the skillful judges (legislators) will sift facts on which to base their decisions. In practice, however, committees use public hearings primarily to influence public opinion or executive action or, occasionally, to discover the position of major elite groups on the measure under consideration. Major decisions take place in secret executive sessions.

COMMITTEE MEMBERSHIP   The membership of the standing committees on agriculture, labor, interior and insular affairs, and the judiciary generally reflects the interest of

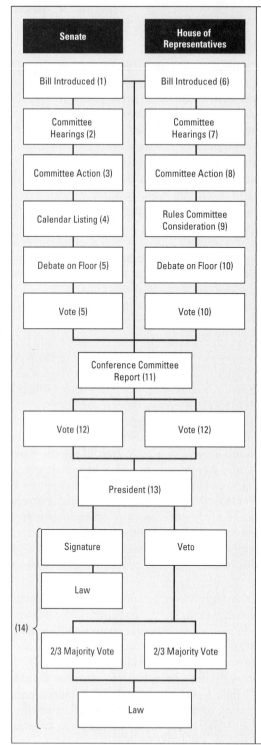

Senate	House of Representatives
Bill Introduced (1)	Bill Introduced (6)
Committee Hearings (2)	Committee Hearings (7)
Committee Action (3)	Committee Action (8)
Calendar Listing (4)	Rules Committee Consideration (9)
Debate on Floor (5)	Debate on Floor (10)
Vote (5)	Vote (10)

Conference Committee Report (11)

Vote (12)	Vote (12)

President (13)

Signature	Veto
Law	

(14)

2/3 Majority Vote	2/3 Majority Vote

Law

1. **Introduction.** Bills can be introduced in either house; often "Companion" bills are introduced in both houses. (In this example, a bill is first introduced in the Senate.) It is given a number and referred to the proper committee.

2. **Hearings.** The subcommittees and/or full standing committees may hold public hearings on the bill.

3. **Committee action.** The full committee meets in executive (closed) session. It may kill the bill, approve it with or without amendments, or draft a new bill. It is here that most bills "die."

4. **Calendar.** If the committee recommends the bill for passage, it is listed on the calendar.

5. **Debate, amendment, vote.** In the Senate, the majority and minority leader decide when the bill goes to the floor for debate. Amendments may be added. The bill is voted on. (A "filibuster" may prevent a vote; 60 votes are needed to halt a filibuster.)

6. **Introduction to the second house.** If the bill passes, it goes to the House of Representatives, where it is referred to the proper committee.

7. **Hearings.** Hearings may be held again, by subcommittees and/or full standing committees.

8. **Committee action.** The committee rejects the bill, prepares a new one, or accepts the bill with or without amendments. Most bills "die" in committee.

9. **Rules Committee consideration.** If the committee recommends the bill, it is listed on the calendar and sent to the Rules Committee. The Rules Committee can block a bill or clear it for debate before the entire House. Bills are given "rules" that determine length of debate, whether amendments will be considered. etc.

10. **Debate, amendment, vote.** The bill goes before the entire body and is debated and voted on.

11. **Conference Committee.** If the bill as passed by the second house contains major changes, either house may request a conference committee. The conference—persons from each house, representing both parties—meets and tries to reconcile its differences.

12. **Vote on conference report.** When committee members reach an agreement, they report back to their respective houses. Their report is either accepted or rejected.

13. **Submission to the president.** If the report is accepted by both houses, the bill is signed by the speaker of the House and the president of the Senate and is sent to the president of the United States.

14. **Presidential action.** The president may sign or veto the bill within ten days. If the president does not sign and Congress is still in session, the bill automatically becomes law. If Congress adjourns before the ten days have elapsed, it does not become law. (This is called the pocket veto.) If the president returns the bill with a veto message, it may still become a law if passed by a two-thirds majority in each house.

FIGURE 12.4 | HOW A BILL BECOMES A LAW

TABLE 12.5 | THE COMMITTEES OF CONGRESS

Senate

Agriculture, Nutrition, and Forestry	Health, Education, Labor, and Pensions
Appropriations	Homeland Security and Environmental Affairs
Armed Services	Judiciary
Banking, Housing, and Urban Affairs	Rules and Administration
Budget	Small Business and Entrepreneurship
Commerce, Science, and Transportation	Select Aging
Energy and Natural Resources	Select Ethics
Environment and Public Works	Select Indian
Finance House	Select Intelligence
Foreign Relations	Veterans Affairs

House

Agriculture	Judiciary
Appropriations	Resources
Armed Forces	Rules
Budget	Science
Energy and Commerce	Small Business
Education and the Workforce	Standards of Official Conduct
Financial Services	Transportation and Infrastructure
Government Reform	Veterans Affairs
Homeland Security	Ways and Means
House Administration	Select Intelligence
International Relations	Veterans Affairs

Joint Committees

Joint Economic Committee	Joint Committee on Printing
Joint Taxation	Joint Committee on the Library

particular elite groups in the nation. Legislators representing farm interests sit on the agricultural committees; representatives of land, water, and natural resource interests serve on interior and insular affairs committees; members of Congress with labor ties and urban industrial constituencies gravitate toward the labor committee; and lawyers dominate the judicial committees of both houses.

Given the power of congressional committees, the assignment of members to committees is one of the most significant activities of Congress. In the House of

Representatives, the Republicans assign their members to committees through the Committee on Committees, which consists of one representative from each state that sends a Republican to Congress. But the real business of this committee is conducted by a subcommittee appointed by the Republican party leader. The subcommittee fills committee vacancies with freshman members and those who request transfer from other committees. The Committee on Committees considers the career backgrounds of members, their seniority, and their reputation for soundness, which usually means support for the party leadership. Often the chairperson of a standing committee tells the Committee on Committees his or her preferences for committee members. Democrats in the House make committee assignments through the Steering and Policy Committee. This committee is composed of the party leadership.

In the Senate, the Committee on Committees fills Republican committee positions, and a steering committee appointed by the Democratic leader selects Democratic committee members. Usually only senators with seniority are eligible for positions on the major Senate committees, such as the foreign relations, armed services, and appropriations committees.

THE POWER OF THE CHAIR   Committee and subcommittee chairpersons are powerful. They usually determine the bills the committee will consider, select issues for public hearings, and establish the agenda of the committee. Governmental and nongovernmental interests officially must consult the chairperson on all questions relating to his or her committee; this procedure confers status on the chairperson with the executive branch and with interested nongovernmental elites. Only occasionally does a majority within the committee-subcommittee "baronage" overrule a chairperson's decision on a committee matter.

THE SENIORITY SYSTEM

The practice of appointing chairpersons according to seniority guarantees conservatism in the legislative process. The member of the majority party with the longest continuous service on the committee becomes chairperson; the member of the minority party with the longest continuous service on the committee is the ranking minority member. Therefore, chairpersons are not chosen by their own committees, by their own party, or by the House and Senate as a whole. They are chosen by the voters of noncompetitive congressional districts whose representatives are likely to stay in office the longest. The major decisions in Congress rest with those members from areas where party competition and voter participation are low. In both houses, the seniority system works against the politically competitive districts.

As their influence within Congress grows, high-seniority legislators tend to identify with Congress as an institution, to the detriment of possible influence of their constituencies. Two factors are at work here. Legislators get to know each other well (they see one another more regularly than they see constituents), and older legislators probably have learned from experience that a perceived unpopular vote will not bring the vigorous constituency response they once thought was inevitable. Thus, the experienced legislator tends to develop a more realistic view of the electorate, expressed well in one senator's remarks: "After several terms, I don't give a damn anymore. I'm pretty safe now and I don't have to worry about reaction in the district."[8] Legislators also specialize in certain kinds of legislation, thus developing expertise that draws their colleagues to them as credible sources of information. As one put it, "That's the beauty of the seniority system—there are informed, experienced people on each Committee you can consult."[9]

DECENTRALIZATION: SUBCOMMITTEES AND "IRON TRIANGLES"

Over time, the specialized subcommittees of Congress have gained power. At present, the House has about 150 subcommittees and the Senate about 90 subcommittees. Each subcommittee develops its own specialized policy network. These policy networks are the "iron triangles" of interest groups, executive bureaucracies, and subcommittee members and staff. These "sub-governments" develop to the benefit of all participants: legislators benefit from campaign contributions by interest groups; lobbyists benefit from personal working relationships with committees and their staffs; administrative agencies benefit from interest groups' and congressional committees' support of their budget requests. Gradually, legislators, lobbyists, and bureaucrats develop a common bond whose strength frequently exceeds that of loyalty to the party.

THE HOUSE RULES COMMITTEE

After a standing committee reports a bill in the House (step 8 in Figure 12.4), the Rules Committee must issue a special rule or order before the bill can go before the House membership for consideration. Consequently, each bill must go through two committees. (The only exceptions are bills reported by the House Appropriations and the Ways and Means committees; the House may consider their bills at any time as privileged motions.) The Rules Committee can kill a bill by shelving it indefinitely. It can insist that the bill be amended as the price of permitting it on the floor and can even substitute a new bill for the one framed by another committee. The Rules Committee determines how much debate will be permitted on any bill and the number and kind of amendments that may be offered from the floor. The only formal limits on Rules Committee authority are the *discharge petition* (which is rarely used and hardly ever successful) and *calendar Wednesday*, a cumbersome procedure that permits standing committees to call up bills the Rules Committee has blocked. The Rules Committee, clearly the most powerful committee in Congress, is dominated by senior members elected from noncompetitive districts.

SENATE FILIBUSTERS

In the Senate, control of floor debate rests with the majority leader. But the majority leader does not have the power to limit debate; a senator who has the floor may talk without limit and may choose to whom he or she yields the floor. If enough senators wish to talk a bill to death, they may do so in what is known as a *filibuster*. This device permits a minority to tie up the business of the Senate and prevent it from voting on a bill. Debate can be limited only by a process called *cloture*. Sixteen members' signatures on a petition will bring cloture to a vote; a three-fifths vote of the full Senate is required to end debate. *This means that forty-one senators can, if they choose, block legislation by voting against cloture.* The filibuster is a means by which a minority can defend itself against majority preferences.

- Committee chairperson support
- Subcommittee and committee hearings, mark-ups, and approval
- Seniority rules
- Decentralization and "iron triangles"

- House Rules Committee
- Senate filibuster rules
- Leadership scheduling floor vote
- Conference committee agreement

THE FLOOR VOTE

Of the 10,000 bills introduced into Congress every year, fewer than a thousand, fewer than one in ten, become law. After approval of a bill by the standing committee in the Senate or by the standing committee and the Rules Committee in the House, the bill moves to the floor for a vote. Usually the most crucial votes come on the amendments to the bill that are offered to the floor (however, the Rules Committee may prevent amendments in the House). Once the membership defeats major amendments or incorporates them into the bill, the bill usually picks up broad support, and the final vote is usually heavily in favor of it.

CONFERENCE COMMITTEES

One of the most conservative features of American government is its *bicameralism;* after following a complicated path in one house, a bill must repeat the process in the other. A bill must pass both branches of Congress in *identical form* before it goes to the president for signature. However, the Senate often amends a House bill, and the House usually amends Senate bills. And every time one house amends a bill, it must resubmit the bill to the originating house for concurrence with the changes. If either house declines to accept changes in the bill, an ad hoc joint committee, called a *conference committee,* must iron out specific differences. Disagreements between the houses are so frequent that from one-third to one-half of all public bills, including virtually all important ones, must go to conference committees after passage by both houses.

Conference committee members, appointed by the presiding officers of each house, usually come from the two standing committees that handled the bills in each house. Because the final bill produced by the conference committee is generally accepted by both houses, these committees have tremendous power in determining the final form of legislation. Both houses must accept or reject conference committee reports as a whole; they cannot further amend them. Most conference committee meetings are closed and unrecorded; the committees hold no hearings and listen to no outside testimony.

The bill that emerges from their deliberations may not represent the view of either house and may even contain items never considered by either one. Some people have dubbed conference committees a "third house" of Congress, whose members are not elected by the people, keep no record of their work, and usually operate behind closed doors—with no debate about their products allowed.

ELITES WITHIN ELITES:
THE CONGRESSIONAL ESTABLISHMENT

A power hierarchy exists among federal government elites that is supported by protocol, by the distribution of formal constitutional powers, by the powers associated with party office, by the committee and seniority systems of Congress, and by the "informal folkways" of Washington. According to the protocol of Washington society, the president holds the highest social rank, followed by former presidents and their widows, the vice president, the speaker of the House, members of the Supreme Court, foreign ambassadors and ministers, cabinet members, U.S. senators, governors of states, former vice presidents, and, finally, House members.

SENATORIAL POWER

The Constitution grants greater formal powers to senators than to House members. With only 100 senators, individual senators are more visible than House members in the social and political life of Washington, as well as in their home states. Senators also have special authority in foreign affairs not accorded to House members, because the Senate must advise and consent by a two-thirds vote to all treaties entered into by the United States. The threat of Senate repudiation of a treaty makes it desirable for the president to solicit Senate views on foreign affairs; in general, the secretary of state works closely with the Senate Foreign Relations Committee on such matters. Influential senators undertake personal missions abroad and serve on delegations to international bodies. Another constitutional power afforded senators is to advise and consent on executive appointments, including Supreme Court justices, cabinet members, federal judges, ambassadors, and other high executive officials. Although the Senate generally approves the presidential nominations, the added potential for power contributes to the difference between the influence of senators and of House members. Finally, senators serve six-year terms and represent broader and more heterogeneous constituencies. Thus, they have a longer guaranteed tenure in Washington, more prestige, and greater freedom from minor shifts in opinion among nongovernmental elites in their home states.

Senators can enhance their power through their political roles; they often wield great power in state parties and can usually control federal patronage dispensed in their state. The power of the Senate to confirm nominations has given rise to the important political custom of "senatorial courtesy": senators of the same party as the president have virtual veto power over major appointments—federal judges, postmasters, customs collectors, and so on—in their states. Presidential nominations that go to the Senate are referred to the senator or senators from the state involved. If the senator declares the nominee personally obnoxious to him or her, the Senate usually respects this declaration and rejects the appointment. Thus, before the president submits a nomination to the Senate, he usually makes sure that the nominee will be acceptable to his party's senator or senators from the state involved.

THE SPEAKER OF THE HOUSE

Party leadership roles in the House and the Senate are major sources of power in Washington. (See Table 12.6 for a list of Senate and House leaders for the

TABLE 12.6 | LEADERSHIP IN THE 110TH CONGRESS, 2007–2009

Speaker of the House — Nancy Pelosi, D-Calif.

Democrats

Majority leader — Steny H. Hoyer, Md.

Majority whip — James E. Clyburn, S.C.

Caucus chairman — Rahm Emanual, Ill.

Caucus vice chairman — John B. Larson, Conn.

Republicans

Minority leader — John A. Boehner, Ohio

Minority whip — Roy Blunt, Mo.

Conference chairman — Adam H. Putnam, Fla.

Conference vice chairman — Kay Granger, Texas

Conference secretary — John Carter, Texas

Policy Committee chairman — Thaddeus
McCotter, Mich.

Chairman, National Republican Congressional
Committee — Tom Cole, Okla.

Chief deputy minority whip — Eric Cantor, Va.

President pro tempore — Robert C. Byrd, D-W.Va.

Democrats

Majority leader — Harry Reid, Nev.

Majority whip — Richard J. Durbin, Ill.

Conference vice chairman, Democratic Senatorial
Campaign Committee chairman — Charles E.
Schumer, N.Y.

Policy Committee chairman — Byron L. Dorgan, N.D.

Conference secretary — Patty Murray, Wash.

Steering & Outreach Committee chairwoman —
Debbie Stabenow, Mich.

Chief deputy majority whip — Barbara Boxer,
Calif.

Republicans

Minority leader — Mitch McConnell, Ky.

Minority whip — Trent Lott, Miss.

Conference chairman — Jon Kyl, Ariz.

Conference vice chairman —John Cornyn, Texas

Policy Committee chairwoman — Kay Bailey
Hutchison, Texas

National Republican Senatorial Committee
chairman — John Ensign, Nev.

110th Congress, 2007–2009.) The speaker of the House of Representatives, elected by the majority party of the House, exercises more power over public policy than any other member of either house. Before 1910, the speaker appointed all standing committees and their chairs, possessed unlimited discretion to recognize members on the floor, and served as chair of the Rules Committee. But in 1910, progressives severely curtailed the speaker's authority. Today the speaker shares power over committee appointments with the Committee on Committees; committee chairs are selected by seniority, not by the speaker; and the speaker no longer serves as chair of the Rules Committee. However, the speaker retains considerable authority: referring bills to committees, appointing all conference committees, ruling on all matters of House procedure, recognizing those who wish to speak, and generally directing the business of the floor. More important, the speaker is the principal figure in House policy formulation, leadership, and responsibility. Although sharing these tasks with standing committee chairs, the speaker is generally "first among equals" in relation to them.

FLOOR LEADERS AND WHIPS

Next to the speaker, the most influential party leaders in the House are the majority and minority floor leaders and the party whips. These party leaders are chosen by their respective party caucuses at the beginning of each congressional session. The party caucus, composed of all the party's members in the House, usually does little more than elect these officers; it makes no major policy decisions. The floor leaders and whips have little formal authority; their role is to influence legislation through persuasion. Party floor leaders must combine parliamentary skill with persuasion, maintain good personal relationships with party members, and cultivate close ties with the president and administration. They cannot deny party renomination to members who are disloyal to the party, but because they can control committee assignments and many small favors in Washington, they can prevent a maverick from becoming an effective legislator.

The whips, or assistant floor leaders, keep members informed about legislative business, see that members are present for important floor votes, and communicate party strategy and position on particular issues. They also serve as the eyes and ears of the leadership, counting noses before important votes. Party whips should know how many votes a particular measure has, and they should be able to get the votes to the floor when the roll is called.

THE VICE PRESIDENT

The vice president of the United States, who serves as president of the Senate, has less control over Senate affairs than the speaker has over House affairs. The vice president votes only in case of a tie and must recognize senators in the order in which they rise. The majority party in the Senate also elects from its membership a president pro tempore, who presides in the absence of the vice president. (Actually, presiding over the Senate is such a tedious task that it often falls to junior senators.)

MAJORITY AND MINORITY LEADERS

The key power figures in the Senate are the majority and minority leaders, who are chosen by their respective parties. The majority leader usually has great personal influence within the Senate and is a power figure in national affairs. The majority leader, when of the same party as the president, is in charge of getting the president's legislative program through the Senate. Although having somewhat less formal authority than the speaker of the House, the majority leader has the right to be the first senator to be heard on the floor and, with the minority floor leader, determines the Senate's agenda. But on the whole, the majority leader's influence rests on powers of persuasion.

COMMITTEE CHAIRS

The committee system and the seniority rule also create powerful congressional figures: the chairs of the most powerful standing committees, particularly the Senate Foreign Relations, Appropriations, and Finance Committees and the House Rules, Appropriations, and Ways and Means Committees. The chairs of the standing committees in both houses have become powerful through members' respect for the authority of their committees. The standing committee system is self-sustaining because an attack on the authority of one committee or committee chairperson is much like a threat to all; members know that if they allow one committee or committee chairperson to be bypassed on a particular measure, they open the door to other similar infringements of power. Hence, committee chairs and ranking committee members tend to stand by one another and support one another's authority over legislation assigned to their respective committees.

Committee chairs and ranking committee members also earn respect because of their seniority and experience in the legislative process. They are often experts in parliamentary process as well as in the substantive area covered by their committees. Finally, and perhaps most important, committee chairs and ranking committee members acquire power through their close relationships with the bureaucratic and interest-group elites within their committee's jurisdiction.

LEADERSHIP PACs

Money is another source of power for congressional leaders. Congressional leaders of both parties, as well as some individual members of Congress, maintain their own political action committees (PACs). Contributors to these PACs increase their influence with the leadership, and the leadership increases its influence with members by distributing PAC money to their supporters in Congress. Leadership PACs are separate from the leaders' personal campaign funds (see Table 12.7).

POLARIZATION ON CAPITOL HILL

Politics on Capitol Hill has become highly polarized in recent years. The Democratic and Republican parties in Congress are further apart ideologically than ever before. The Republicans are more uniformly conservative, and the Democrats more liberal,

TABLE 12.7 | TOP CONGRESSIONAL LEADERSHIP PACs, 2006

PAC for the Future	Nancy Pelosi (D-Calif.)	Speaker of the House
AmeriPAC	Steny H. Hoyer (D-Md.)	House majority leader
Keep Our Majority	Dennis Hastert (R-Ill.)	Former speaker of the House
Freedom Project	John A. Boehner (R-Ohio)	House minority leader
Searchlight Leadership	Harry Reid (D-Nev.)	Senate majority leader
Bluegrass Committee	Mitch McConnell (R-Ky.)	Senate majority leader
New Republican Majority	Trent Lott (R-Miss.)	Senate minority whip
Rely on Your Beliefs	Roy Blunt (R-Mo.)	House minority whip
HILLPAC	Hillary Clinton (D-N.Y.)	U.S. Senator
Hope Fund	Barack Obama (D-Ill.)	U.S. Senator
Center for Democratic Majority	Edward M. Kennedy (D-Mass.)	U.S. Senator
Straight Talk America	John McCain (R-Ariz.)	U.S. Senator

Source: Center for Responsive Politics. www.crp.org.

than in previous years. The proportion of political moderates—conservative Democrats or liberal Republicans—hovered at about 30 percent in the 1960s and 1970s. Fewer than one in ten of today's lawmakers fall into this centrist category.[10] The result is more conflict, less bipartisan cooperation, and more acrimony in the halls of Congress.

The most common explanation for this increased polarization is the realignment of Southern voters from the Democratic to the Republican party. Southern conservatives moved almost en bloc into the Republican Party in the 1980s. As conservatives gained strength in the Republican Party, liberal Republicans, mostly from the Northeast, lost ground. Geographically, the Republican Party became centered in the Mountain States and the South, while the Democratic Party held the Northeast and West Coast.

PARTY VOTING

Party votes, those roll-call votes in which a majority of voting Democrats oppose a majority of voting Republicans, occur on more than half the roll-call votes in Congress. Indeed, roll-call voting follows party lines more often than it follows sectional, urban–rural, or any other divisions that have been studied.

How much cohesion exists within the parties? Table 12.8 shows the percentage of party votes in Congress in recent years, and the average support Democratic and Republican members of Congress have given to their parties. Members of both parties vote with their party majority more than 80 percent of the time.

However, party-line votes are the result more of members' personal predispositions than of explicitly formulated party policy. We can make the distinction between party "regularity," which is strong, and party organization and discipline, of which there is very little.

CONFLICT

Conflict between parties occurs most frequently over taxation, social-welfare programs, health care, antipoverty programs, and the regulation of business and labor. Party conflict is particularly apparent on spending and taxing proposals in the budget. The budget is the president's product and carries the label of the president's party. On some issues, voting generally follows party lines during roll calls on preliminary motions and amendments, but swings to a bipartisan vote on the final legislation. In such situations the parties disagree on certain aspects of the bill but compromise on its final passage.

PRESIDENTIAL SUPPORT

The president generally receives greater support from his own party than from the opposition party in Congress. Thus, the presidents who have run up the highest legislative "box scores"—victories for bills that they supported—are those whose party has controlled one or both houses of Congress (see "The President and Congress" in Chapter 10).

TABLE 12.8 | PARTY VOTING IN CONGRESS

Year	Party Votes as Percentage of Total Votes	Percentage of Party Support: Democrats*	Percentage of Party Support: Republicans*
1990			
Senate	54	82	77
House	49	86	78
1992			
Senate	64	82	83
House	53	86	84
1994			
Senate	52	84	79
House	62	83	84
1996			
Senate	62	84	89
House	56	80	87
1998			
Senate	56	89	88
House	56	83	86
2000			
Senate	49	89	88
House	43	88	82
2002			
Senate	43	83	84
House	46	86	90
2004			
Senate	52	83	90
House	47	86	88
2006			
Senate	57	86	88
House	55	86	86

*Average percentage of times a member voted with the majority of his or her own party in disagreement with the other party's majority.

Source: *Congressional Quarterly Weekly Report*, various years.

CONGRESS AND THE PRESIDENT: AN UNSTABLE BALANCE OF POWER

THE PRESIDENT INITIATES, CONGRESS DELIBERATES

How do the roles of Congress and the other governmental elites differ? Policy proposals are usually initiated outside Congress. The role of Congress primarily is to respond to proposals from the president, bureaucratic elites, and interested non-governmental elites. Congress does not merely ratify or rubber-stamp decisions; it plays an independent role in the policy-making process. But the role is essentially deliberative; Congress accepts, modifies, or rejects the policies initiated by others. For example, the annual federal budget, perhaps the most important policy document of the national government, is written by executive elites and modified by the president before Congress receives it. Of course, Congress is the critical conduit through which appropriations and revenue measures must pass. But sophisticated lawmakers are aware that they function largely as arbiters rather than initiators of public policy.

However, the relationship between Congress and other policy-making elites is not necessarily stable. Whether Congress merely ratifies the decisions of others or asserts its voice independently depends on many factors, such as the aggressiveness and political skills of the president, the strength of congressional leadership, and whether there is divided party control of the White House and Capitol Hill. A politically weakened president, combined with opposition party control of the Congress, provides the environment for congressional assertions of power.

MASS PREFERENCE FOR DIVIDED GOVERNMENT

The masses of voters actually prefer a split between the parties in control of Congress and the presidency. They do not appear to want "responsible party government"—where the party winning an election is fully responsible for public policy. Rather, they appear to prefer that the parties check each other in government.

QUESTION: *"Do you think it is better when one party controls both the presidency and the Congress, better when control is split between the Democrats and Republicans, or doesn't it matter?"*

Better one party	23.8%
Better control split	52.4%
Doesn't matter	23.8%

Source: *National Election Study*, 2000.

THE POWER OF THE PURSE

Theoretically, Congress can control the president through its power over government spending. The Constitution (Article I, Section 9) states that "no money shall be drawn from the Treasury, but in consequence of appropriations made by law." Congress can

| FOCUS | SENATOR HILLARY RODHAM CLINTON |

Hillary Rodham Clinton is the first First Lady ever elected to the Congress and the first woman senator from New York. Her celebrity attracts the media wherever she goes, sometimes causing resentment among her ninety-nine other Senate colleagues, all of whom think of themselves as stars in their own right. Her initial efforts in the Senate have been directed toward establishing herself as a serious, knowledgeable, and effective legislator. And she tries particularly hard to identify herself with the interests of her adopted state, New York.

Hillary Rodham grew up in suburban Chicago, the daughter of wealthy parents who sent her to the private, prestigious Wellesley College. A 1969 honors graduate with a counterculture image—horn-rimmed glasses, long, straggling hair, no makeup—she was chosen by her classmates to give a commencement speech, a rambling statement about "more immediate, ecstatic, and penetrating modes of living."

At Yale Law School Hillary met a long-haired, bearded Rhodes scholar from Arkansas, Bill Clinton, who was just as politically ambitious as she was. Both Hillary and Bill received their law degrees in 1973. Bill returned to Arkansas to build a career in state politics, and Hillary went to Washington as an attorney—first for a liberal lobbying group, the Children's Defense Fund, and later on the staff of the House Judiciary Committee seeking to impeach President Richard Nixon. But Rodham and other Yale grads traveled to Arkansas to help Clinton run, unsuccessfully, for Congress in 1974. Hillary decided to stay with Bill in Little Rock; they married before his next campaign, a successful run for state attorney general in 1976. Hillary remained Hillary Rodham, even as her husband went on to the governorship in 1978.

Her husband's 1980 defeat for reelection as governor was blamed on his liberal leanings; therefore, in his 1982 comeback Bill repackaged himself as a moderate and centrist. Hillary cooperated by becoming Mrs. Bill Clinton, shedding her horn-rims for contacts, blonding her hair, and echoing her husband's more moderate line. These tactics helped propel them back into the governor's mansion. Hillary soon became a full partner in Little Rock's Rose law firm, regularly earning more than $200,000 a year (while Bill earned only $35,000 as Arkansas governor). She won national recognition as one of the "100 most influential lawyers in the United States," according to the *American National Law Journal*. She chaired the American Bar Association's Commission on Women and the Profession.

Hillary's steadfast support of Bill during the White House sex scandals and subsequent impeachment by the House of Representatives in all likelihood saved his presidency. Her approval ratings in public opinion polls skyrocketed during the affair. Whatever she thought in private, she never chastised her husband in public and blamed much of the scandal on "a vast right-wing conspiracy."

Her Senate race attracted national media attention as well as campaign contributions from supporters throughout the nation. When New York City's Mayor Rudolph Giuliani announced that he would *not* run for the Senate, Hillary was relieved to confront a little-known opponent, Congressman Rick Lazio. New York voters were unimpressed with charges that Hillary was not a true New Yorker. She studied New York problems diligently, and overwhelmed Lazio in the campaign. Over $85 million were spent by the candidates, making the campaign the most expensive congressional campaign in history.

She crushed her Republican opponent in her 2006 reelection to the Senate, spending a mere $57 million. Shortly thereafter she announced her intention to run for president in 2008: "I'm in, to win!"

withhold funds or place elaborate restrictions on the use of funds in order to work its will over the president. But even through the use of budgetary power, its most effective tool, Congress has *not* been able to dominate the presidency. More often than not, the president's budget recommendations are accepted by Congress with relatively minor changes (see Chapter 11).

Occasionally, Congress and the president have engaged in highly publicized budgetary battles. President Clinton twice vetoed budget resolutions passed by the

| FOCUS | CONGRESSIONAL ETHICS: AN OXYMORON? |

Congressional ethics has long simmered as an issue on Capitol Hill, occasionally boiling over into well-publicized scandals.

Bribery is a criminal act: it is illegal to solicit or receive anything of value in return for the performance of a governmental duty. But Congress members are expected to perform services for their political contributors. A direct quid pro quo—receiving a financial contribution specifically for the performance of a particular service—is illegal. Few Congress members would be so foolish as to openly state a price to a potential contributor for a specific service, and most contributors know not to state a dollar amount that would be forthcoming if the member performed a particular service for them. But what if the contribution and the service occur close together? A Senate Ethics Committee once found a close relationship between a service and a contribution to be an "impermissible pattern of conduct [that] violated established norms of behavior in the Senate . . . [and] was improper and repugnant."

Yet scandals have tarnished the image of Congress. During its notorious Abscam investigation in 1980, the FBI set up a sting operation in which agents posing as wealthy Arabs offered bribe money to members of Congress while secretly videotaping the transactions. Six representatives and one senator were convicted; only one member of Congress approached by the FBI turned down the bribe. In 1994 the powerful chair of the House Ways and Means Committee, Dan Rostenkowski, was indicted by a federal grand jury for misuse of congressional office funds. He refused to resign from Congress, but his Chicago constituents voted him out of office. Other representatives and senators have resigned following charges of sexual misconduct, including Republican Senator Robert Packwood, who faced official expulsion following a Senate Ethics Committee report in 1995 charging him with numerous counts of sexual harassment of female staff. In 2002 Representative James A. Traficant was expelled following his conviction on ten federal corruption charges. And Representative Randy Cunningham resigned in 2005 after pleading guilty to charges of accepting $2.4 million in bribes from lobbyists. In 2006, former lobbyist Jack Abramoff pleading guilty to bribery charges; Representative Tom DeLay was

forced to step down as Republican majority leader and later resigned from Congress; Representative Bob Ney was convicted of conspiracy to commit fraud. Representative Tom Foley resigned in disgrace in 2006 rather than face an investigation into sexually inappropriate e-mail messages to congressional pages. Representative William Jefferson was forced to resign his committee posts after an FBI raid found $90,000 in alleged bribe money in his home freezer.

Congress has an interest in maintaining the integrity of the institution itself. Congress has established its own rules of ethics, including the following: All members must file personal financial statements each year; members cannot accept fees for speeches or personal appearances; surplus campaign funds cannot be put to personal use; members may not except gifts worth more than $50; former members may not lobby Congress for at least one year after retirement. In 2007, the House strengthened the rules: Members and staff are not be able to accept *any* gifts or meals from lobbyists; lobbyists cannot pay for travel; and requests for "earmarks" (pet projects of members added to appropriations bills) require the disclosure of their sponsors as well as justifications and certification that the earmarks will not benefit lawmakers or their spouses.

The Constitution gives Congress the power to discipline its own members. "Each House may . . . punish its Members for disorderly Behavior, and, with the Concurrence of two thirds, expel a Member." A lesser punishment then expulsion is

continued

| **CONGRESSIONAL ETHICS: AN OXYMORON?** *continued*

official "censure." Censured members are obliged to "stand in the well" and listen to charges read against them. It is supposed to be a humiliating experience and fatal to one's political career. Representative Barney Frank was censured for sexual misconduct with teenage congressional pages in 1983, but he has been regularly reelected by his Massachusetts constituents. Lesser forms of punishment include a public reprimand by the Ethics Committee and orders to a member to repay funds improperly received.

Republican-controlled Congress in late 1995. The federal government temporarily shut down because appropriations acts had not been passed. But when opinion polls showed that more Americans blamed Congress rather than the president for the gridlock, Congress relented and sent the president a budget that more closely reflected his preferences.

CONGRESSIONAL INVESTIGATIONS

Congress retains the power to embarrass a presidential administration and occasionally even to force it to change course through congressional investigations. Such investigations, with the cooperation of the television media, can compel presidents to abandon unpopular actions. In the Iran-Contra hearings in 1987, a Democratic-controlled Congress exposed President Reagan's arms-for-hostages dealings with Iran.

Most congressional investigations are conducted by standing committees of Congress. Occasionally, however, investigations are deemed so important as to merit the appointment of independent commissions. This was the case in the investigation of the assassination of President John F. Kennedy in 1963. President Lyndon B. Johnson appointed a President's Commission on the Assassination of President John F. Kennedy, chaired by the Chief Justice of the Supreme Court, Earl Warren; its findings were distributed as the "Warren Report." And in 2002 the president and Congress created the National Commission on Terrorist Attacks upon the United States; this Commission issued its widely read *9/11 Commission Report* in 2004.

IMPEACHMENT

The ultimate congressional power over the president is impeachment. Despite the Constitution's admonition that impeachment can only be voted for "Treason, Bribery, and other high Crimes and Misdemeanors" (Article II, Section 4), all impeachment movements in U.S. history have developed on political grounds (see Chapter 10).

Despite pious rhetoric in Congress about the "search for truth," "impartial investigation," and "unbiased constitutional judgment," the impeachment process, whatever the merits of the charges against a president, is political, not judicial.

The House vote to impeach President Clinton (228 to 106) followed partisan lines with all but five Republicans voting yes and all but five Democrats voting no.[*]

The subsequent Senate "trial" of President Clinton was perfunctory. Although Republicans held a slim majority in the Senate, they lacked the necessary two-thirds vote to remove Clinton from office. Indeed, Republicans even failed to obtain a majority vote for conviction.

Why is the impeachment of a president so rare, even during periods of divided government? Opinion polls clearly indicated that most Americans did not believe that Clinton's misconduct should result in his removal from office. (See Focus: Sex, Lies, and Impeachment, in Chapter 10.) A public backlash appeared to develop against the House impeachment. Clinton's approval ratings actually *rose* after the House action, and his high popular approval ratings appeared to be the key to his acquittal by the Senate.

CONGRESS: AN ELITIST INTERPRETATION

The Founders intended that Congress be the first and most powerful branch of government and that the House of Representatives represent "the people." But the Founders' intentions are not an accurate description of Congress today. Rather, elite theory suggests several contrary propositions regarding Congress.

1. Congress tends to represent locally organized elites, who inject a strong parochial influence into national decision making. Members of Congress are responsible to national interests that have a strong base of support in their home constituencies.

2. A member's relevant political constituency is not the general population of the home district but its elite. Less than half the general population of a district knows its legislator's name; fewer still have any idea of how their representative voted on any major issue. Only a tiny fraction ever express their views to their legislators.

---

[*]The only precedent for a presidential impeachment—the impeachment and trial of Andrew Johnson in 1868—was also political. No evidence proved President Johnson's personal involvement in a crime for which he could be indicted and found guilty in a court of law. Johnson was a southern Democrat, a U.S. senator from a seceding state (Tennessee) who had remained loyal to the Union. Lincoln chose him as vice president in 1864 as a gesture of national unity. When Johnson acceded to the presidency after Lincoln's assassination, he resisted attempts by "radical" Republicans in Congress to restructure southern society by force. When Johnson dismissed some federal officials who opposed his conciliatory policies, Congress passed the Tenure of Office Act over Johnson's veto, forbidding executive removals without Senate consent. Johnson contended that the act was an unconstitutional infringement of his powers as chief executive. (Years later the Supreme Court agreed, holding that the power of removal is an executive power and specifically declaring that the Tenure of Office Act had been unconstitutional.) When Johnson dismissed his "radical" Republican secretary of war, Edwin M. Stanton, Congress was enraged. The House impeached Johnson on a party-line vote, charging that Johnson had violated the Tenure of Office Act. The Civil War had left a legacy of bitterness against Johnson as a southerner and a Democrat. But following a month-long trial in the Senate, the result was thirty-five "guilty" votes and nineteen "not guilty" votes—one vote short of the necessary two-thirds vote for removal. Seven Republicans joined the twelve Democrats in supporting the president. John F. Kennedy, in his book *Profiles in Courage,* praised the strength and courage of those senators who resisted popular emotions and prevented the president's removal. See Michael Les Benedict, *The Impeachment and Trial of Andrew Johnson* (New York: Norton, 1973).

3. Congress seldom initiates changes in public policy. Instead, it responds to policy proposals initiated by the president and by executive, military, and interested nongovernmental elites. The congressional role in national decision making is usually deliberative: Congress responds to policies initiated by others.

4. Congressional committees are important to communication between governmental and nongovernmental elites. "Iron triangles" (or "policy clusters") consisting of alliances of leaders from executive agencies, congressional committees, and private business and industry tend to develop in Washington. Committee chairs are key members of the policy clusters because of their control over legislation in Congress.

5. The elaborate rules and procedures of Congress delay and obstruct proposed changes in the status quo, thus strengthening Congress's conservative role in policy making. Transforming a bill into law is a difficult process; congressional procedures offer many opportunities for defeat and many obstacles to passage.

6. An elite system within Congress places effective control over legislation in the hands of relatively few members. Most of these congressional "establishment" members are conservatives from both parties who have acquired seniority and therefore control key committee chairs.

7. Most bills that do not die before the floor vote pass unanimously. The greatest portion of the national budget passes without debate. The conflict that exists in Congress tends to follow party lines more often than any other factional division. Conflict centers on the details of domestic and foreign policy but seldom on its major directions.

SELECTED READINGS

Davidson, Roger H., and Walter T. Oleszek. *Congress and Its Members*, 9th ed. Washington, D.C.: CQ Press, 2004. An authoritative textbook on Congress and congressional affairs.

Fenno, Richard F. *Home Style*. Boston: Little Brown, 1978. The classic description of how attention to constituency by members of Congress enhances their reelection prospects. Home-style activities, including casework, pork-barreling, travel and appearances back home, newsletters, and surveys, are described in detail.

Fiorina, Morris P. *Congress: Keystone to the Washington Establishment*, 2nd ed. New Haven, Conn.: Yale University Press, 1989. A lively description of members of Congress as independent political entrepreneurs serving themselves by serving local constituencies and ensuring their own reelection, often at the expense of the national interest.

Herrnson, Paul S. *Congressional Elections: Campaigning at Home and in Washington*, 4th ed. Washington, D.C.: CQ Press, 2004. A well-documented argument that Congress members conduct two campaigns each election, one at home to win votes and the other in Washington to win campaign contributions.

Oleszek, Walter J. *Congressional Procedures and the Policy Process*, 6th ed. Washington, D.C.: CQ Press, 2003. An explanation of the interaction between congressional rules and policy making that includes a description of committee and floor procedures and an explanation of the role of the leadership.

Ornstein, Norman J., Thomas E. Mann, and Michael J. Malbin. *Vital Statistics on Congress*. Washington, D.C.: CQ Press, published biennially. Excellent source of data on members of Congress, congressional elections, committees, and voting alignments.

Sinclair, Barbara. *Unorthodox Lawmaking*, 2nd ed. Washington, D.C.: CQ Press, 2000. A description of the various detours and shortcuts a major bill is likely to take in Congress, including five recent case studies.

NOTES

1. See Alan Ehrenhalt, *The United States of Ambition* (New York: Random House, 1991).

2. Michael X. DelliCarpini and Scott Keeter, "The U.S. Public's Knowledge of Politics," *Public Opinion Quarterly*, 55 (May 1991): 583–612.

3. Warren Miller and Donald Stokes, "Constituency Influence in Congress," *American Political Science Review*, 57 (March 1963).

4. Richard Fenno, *The Making of a Senator* (Washington, D.C.: CQ Press, 1989), p. 119.

5. Survey by Louis Harris, reported in *American Enterprise* (May/June 1992): 103.

6. *U.S. Term Limits v. Thornton*, 514 U.S. 779 (1994).

7. Woodrow Wilson, *Congressional Government* (1885; reprint, New York: Meridian Books, 1956), p. 178.

8. John W. Kingdon, *Congressmen's Voting Decisions* (New York: Harper & Row, 1973), p. 62.

9. Kingdon, *Voting Decisions*, p. 88.

10. See Juliet Eilperin, *Fight Club Politics* (Lanham, Md.: Rowen & Littlefield, 2006).

Scarcely any political question arises in the United States that is not resolved, sooner or later, into a judicial question.

Alexis de Tocqueville

Courts: Elites in Black Robes

The Supreme Court of the United States and the federal court system compose the most elitist institution in American government. Nine justices—none of whom is elected and all of whom serve for life—possess ultimate authority over all the other institutions of American government. These people have the power to declare void the acts of popularly elected presidents, Congresses, governors, state legislators, school boards, and city councils. No appeal is possible from their determination of what is the "supreme law of the land," short of undertaking the difficult task of amending the Constitution itself.

The Supreme Court, rather than the president or Congress, has made many of the nation's most important domestic policy decisions. The Supreme Court took the lead in eliminating segregation from public life, ensuring separation of church and state, defining rights of criminal defendants and the powers of law enforcement officials, ensuring voter equality in representation, defining the limits of free speech and a free press, and declaring abortion a fundamental right of women. Sooner or later in American politics, most important policy questions come before these justices—who are not elected to office and cannot be removed for anything other than "treason, bribery, or high crimes and misdemeanors." As de Tocqueville observed as early as 1835, "Scarcely any political question arises in the United States that is not resolved, sooner or later, into a judicial question."[1] In a paradox for democratic theory, the masses express greatest confidence in the most elitist, nonelected branch of the government. Polls regularly report that the masses have more trust and confidence in the Supreme Court than the presidency or Congress. Among government institutions, only the U.S. military (even more hierarchical and more removed from popular control) inspires more mass confidence than the Supreme Court.

JUDICIAL REVIEW AS AN ELITIST PRINCIPLE

Recognition of the undemocratic character of judicial power in the United States is not new. The Founders viewed the federal courts as the final bulwark against mass threats to principle and property:

> *Limited government ... can be preserved in practice no other way than through the medium of courts of justice, whose duty it is to declare all acts contrary to the manifest tenor of the Constitution void.*[2]

In *Marbury v. Madison* (1803), the historic decision establishing the power of judicial review, John Marshall argued persuasively that (1) the Constitution is "the supreme law of the land" and U.S. and state laws must be congruent with it; (2) Article III of the Constitution gives the Supreme Court the judicial power, which includes the power to interpret the meaning of laws and, in case of conflict between laws, to decide which law shall prevail; and (3) the courts are sworn to uphold the Constitution, so they must declare void a law that conflicts with the Constitution.

Since 1803, the federal courts have struck down more than 100 laws of Congress and uncounted state laws that they believed conflicted with the Constitution. Judicial review and the power to interpret the meaning and decide the application of law are judges' major sources of power.

The Founders' decision to grant federal courts the power of judicial review over *state* court decisions and *state* laws is easy to understand. Article VI states that the Constitution and national laws and treaties are the supreme law of the land, "anything in the Constitution or laws of any state to the contrary notwithstanding." Federal court power over state decisions is probably essential in maintaining national unity, because fifty different state interpretations of the meaning of the Constitution or of the laws and treaties of Congress would create unimaginable confusion. Thus, the power of federal judicial review over state constitutions, laws, and court decisions is seldom questioned.

However, at the *national* level, why should an appointed court's interpretation of the Constitution prevail over the views of an elected Congress and an elected president? Members of Congress and presidents swear to uphold the Constitution, and we can assume that they do not pass laws they believe to be unconstitutional. Because both houses of Congress and the president must approve laws before they become effective, why should federal courts be allowed to set aside these decisions?

Supreme Court Cases
This Cornell Law School's Legal Information Institute Web site contains up-to-date information about important legal decisions rendered by federal and state courts, along with an exhaustive online law library available to researchers.
www.law.cornell.edu

The answer is that the Founders distrusted popular majorities and the elected officials subject to their influence. They believed government should be prevented from attacking principle and property, whether to do so was the will of the majority or not. So the Founders deliberately insulated the courts from popular majorities; by appointing judges for life terms, they sought to ensure their independence. The Founders originally intended that the president (who was not to be directly elected) would appoint judges and that the Senate (also originally not to be directly elected) would confirm the president's appointments. Only in this way, the writers of the Constitution believed, would judges be sufficiently protected from the masses to permit them to judge courageously and responsibly.

THE MAKING OF A SUPREME COURT JUSTICE

All federal judges are appointed by the president and confirmed by a majority vote of the Senate. The recruitment process is highly political. The attorney general's office assists the president in screening candidates for all federal judgeships. For positions on the Supreme Court, presidents usually nominate judges who share their political philosophy. One might assume that this practice is a democratizing influence on the Court, assuming that the people elect a president because they agree with his or her political philosophy. But Supreme Court justices frequently become independent once they reach the Court. Former chief justice Earl Warren, as Republican governor of California, had swung critical delegate votes to Eisenhower in the 1952 Republican convention. When the grateful president rewarded him with the chief justiceship, little in Warren's background suggested that he would lead the most liberal era in the Court's history. Later, Eisenhower complained that the Warren appointment was "the biggest damn mistake I ever made."[3]

Social Background

Justices' social backgrounds generally reflect close ties with the upper social strata. More than 90 percent of the Supreme Court justices have been from socially prominent, politically influential, upper-class families. More than two-thirds of the justices ever serving on the Court attended Ivy League or other prestigious law schools (see Table 13.1).

Of course, social background does not necessarily determine judicial philosophy. However, "if . . . the Supreme Court is the keeper of the American conscience, it is essentially the conscience of the American upper-middle class, sharpened by the imperative of individual social responsibility and political activism, and conditioned

TABLE 13.1 | BACKGROUNDS OF U.S. SUPREME COURT JUSTICES

Justice	Year of Birth	Law School	Position at Time of Appointment	Appointed by (Year)
John G. Roberts, chief justice	1955	Harvard	Judge, U.S. Court of Appeals	Bush (2005)
John Paul Stevens	1920	Northwestern	Judge, U.S. Court of Appeals	Ford (1975)
Antonin Scalia	1936	Harvard	Judge, U.S. Court of Appeals	Reagan (1986)
Anthony M. Kennedy	1936	Harvard	Judge, U.S. Court of Appeals	Reagan (1987)
David Souter	1939	Harvard	Judge, New Hampshire	Bush (1990)
Clarence Thomas	1948	Yale	Judge, U.S. Court of Appeals	Bush (1991)
Ruth Bader Ginsburg	1933	Columbia	Judge, U.S. Court of Appeals	Clinton (1993)
Stephen G. Breyer	1938	Yale	Judge, U.S. Court of Appeals	Clinton (1994)
Samuel A. Alito Jr.	1950	Princeton	Judge, U.S. Court of Appeals	Bush (2006)

by the conservative impact of legal training and professional legal attitudes and associations."[4]

POLITICIZING THE CONFIRMATION PROCESS

Historically, the Senate Judiciary Committee, which holds hearings and recommends confirmation to the full Senate, has consented to nominations by the president with a minimum of dissent; the Senate has rejected only 29 of the 132 Supreme Court nominations ever sent to it. The prevailing ethos had been that a popularly elected president deserves the opportunity to appoint judges; that the opposition party will have its own opportunity to appoint judges when it captures the presidency; and that partisan bickering over judicial appointments is undesirable. But the U.S. Senate's rejection of President Reagan's nomination of Judge Robert H. Bork in 1987 ended the traditional confirmation ethos. Securing the Senate's confirmation of a Supreme Court nominee is now a highly partisan political campaign. (See Focus: Senate Confirmation as Sleazy Spectacle.)

REJECTION BY FILIBUSTER

The Constitution requires only a majority consent of the Senate for presidential nominees to federal courts. However, in recent years Democrats in the Senate have used the filibuster and cloture rules to hold up Republican President Bush's nominees, notably nominees to federal Appeals Court seats. Senators can filibuster the nomination, and the filibuster cannot be ended without a successful cloture motion, which itself requires a three-fifths vote of the Senate. This means that Democrats can defeat cloture with only forty-one votes (see Chapter 12) and leave the president's judicial nominee unconfirmed. Republican leaders have complained bitterly that the filibuster and cloture rules undermine the Constitution's requirement of only majority consent of the Senate.

BUSH'S SUPREME COURT NOMINATIONS

President George W. Bush was successful in his first Supreme Court nomination. John G. Roberts Jr. was eminently qualified to replace William Rehnquist as chief justice: B.A., Harvard; J.D. Harvard Law School; editor of the *Harvard Law Review*; assistant to the attorney general; and since 2003 judge on the D.C. Circuit Court of Appeals. At the Senate Judiciary Committee hearings he was pleasant, courteous, and extraordinarily knowledgeable about the law. He testified for days without any notes. He promised judicial restraint—to interpret the law not to make it—but appeared more moderate than conservative in judicial philosophy. His nomination was confirmed by 72 to 22, with all Republicans and half of the Democrats supporting him.

Upon the resignation of Sandra Day O'Connor, President Bush nominated Harriet Miers, a longtime personal friend serving as counselor to the president. Miers received her B.A. and law degrees from Southern Methodist University and served two years on the Dallas City Commission, and was appointed Texas Lottery Commissioner. She had

The battle over the nomination of Clarence Thomas to the U.S. Supreme Court marked the Senate's collapse into disgraceful spectacle. Indeed, the Senate Judiciary Committee's sleazy performance in the Thomas confirmation established a new low in public ethics.

Clarence Thomas, as President George H. W. Bush's nominee to replace Thurgood Marshall, the first African American Supreme Court justice, reflected the generally conservative judicial philosophy of earlier Reagan appointees. Born to a teenage mother who earned $10 a week as a maid, Clarence Thomas and his brother lived in a dirt-floor shack in Pin Point, Georgia, where they were raised by strict, hard-working grandparents. They taught young Clarence the value of education and sacrificed to send him to a Catholic school. He excelled academically and went on to mostly white Immaculate Conception Seminary College in Missouri to study for the Catholic priesthood. But when he overheard a fellow seminarian express satisfaction at the assassination of Dr. Martin Luther King Jr., Thomas left the seminary in anger and enrolled at Holy Cross College in Washington, D.C., where he helped found the college's Black Student Union. He graduated with honors and went on to Yale Law School.

Thomas began his legal career as an assistant Missouri attorney general under John C. Danforth, before Danforth became a popular Republican U.S. senator. Thomas came to Washington with Danforth and was appointed assistant secretary for civil rights in the U.S. Department of Education and later chairman of the U.S. Equal Employment Opportunity Commission. In the latter role, Thomas spoke out against racial quotas in favor of individual rights and against welfare programs that create permanent dependency.

The Bush White House strategists believed that Thomas provided them with an opportunity to push a strong conservative past the liberal, Democratic-controlled Senate Judiciary Committee and win confirmation by the full Senate. They reasoned that liberal groups who had blocked the earlier nomination of conservative Robert Bork would be reluctant to launch personal attacks on an African American.

But behind the scenes, liberal interest groups, including the National Abortion Rights Action League, People for the American Way, and the National Organization for Women, were searching for evidence to discredit Thomas. On the third day of the hearings,

a University of Oklahoma law professor, Anita Hill, a former legal assistant to Thomas both at the Department of Education and later at the Equal Employment Opportunity Commission, contacted the staff of the Judiciary Committee with charges that Thomas had sexually harassed her in both jobs. Initially, Hill declined to make her charges public, but when Chairman Biden refused to circulate anonymous charges, she agreed to be interviewed by the FBI and went on to give a nationally televised press conference, elaborating on her charges against Thomas. Her bombshell became a media extravaganza and sent the Senate into an uproar.

Thomas's Senate supporters were outraged at what they believed to be a sleazy last-minute ploy to destroy Thomas. But Anita Hill was a convincing witness on her own behalf in front of the Senate Judiciary Committee. She began by saying that only three months after coming to the civil rights office in the Department of Education, Thomas, who was then single, asked her to go out with him. She testified that he initiated sexual conversations with her. Chairman Joseph Biden and other Democrats on the committee treated Hill with great deference, asking her to talk about her feelings and provide explicit details of Thomas's alleged misconduct.

In contrast, Senator Arlen Specter, a Republican moderate with a history of strong support for abortion rights, was not convinced that Hill was telling the truth. Why, he asked, with her legal education and knowledge of civil rights, had she failed to report this harassment? Why did she accept another job at the EEOC from Thomas if she had been harassed by him earlier at the Department of Education? Why had she made many calls to Thomas over the years, leaving friendly messages with his secretary? Senator Orrin Hatch, a conservative Republican, was more hostile, suggesting that Hill was either fantasizing her charges or making them up for political reasons.

The televised hearings captured the nation's attention, touching directly on emotional issues of race and sex. Feminist groups cast the issue as one of sexual harassment and male insensitivity to women's concerns. But Clarence Thomas fought back hard, denying all charges and accusing the committee of conducting a "high-tech lynching" of an "uppity" black man who dares to have conservative opinions.

continued

The mass public may not know or care much about judicial philosophy. Yet race and sex elicit strong opinions. And the "truth" in Washington is all too often determined by opinion polls. An astonishing 86 percent of the general public said they had watched the televised hearings. A majority of blacks as well as whites and a majority of women as well as men sided with the nominee. (In response to the question "Who do you believe more—Anita Hill or Clarence Thomas?" 54 percent said Thomas and 27 percent said Hill. Black opinion was even more heavily weighted in

Thomas's direction, 61 to 19.[a]) In a fitting close to the most bitter and sleazy conflict over a Supreme Court nominee in congressional history, the final Senate confirmation vote was 52 to 48, the closest vote in the history of Supreme Court confirmations.

---

[a]*Gallup Opinion Reports* (October 15, 1991), p. 209. A year later these percentages would shift in Hill's favor, following widespread attention in the media to the issue of sexual harassment.

---

never served in a judicial capacity. Neither Republicans nor Democrats in the Senate were impressed with these meager credentials. After weeks of personal visits with senators, Miers was obliged to withdraw her nomination.

U.S. Courts
The goal of this Web site is "to function as a clearinghouse for information from and about the Judicial Branch of the U.S. government." The site covers the U.S. Supreme Court, U.S. Courts of Appeals, U.S. District Courts, and U.S. Bankruptcy Courts.
www.uscourts.gov

President Bush promptly nominated Samuel A. Alito Jr., a judge with fifteen years of experience on the Circuit Court of Appeals. Alito received his B.A. from Princeton and his law degree from Yale. Following graduation, he became a Reagan Justice Department official and wrote many memos in support of Reagan policies. Liberals would accuse him of personally endorsing these policies, but Alito responded that he was only serving his client as any lawyer would do. At the Senate Judiciary Committee hearings he was respectful of questioning senators but stopped short of providing any views on pending cases that might later come before the court (as had all preceding nominees). He declined to say whether or not he "supported" *Roe v. Wade*, but acknowledged that it was established precedent. Overall he gave the impression that he would be a moderate on the Court, rather than a regular member of the conservative block. His nomination was confirmed by the Senate on a 58 to 42 vote.

SENATE QUESTIONING OF COURT NOMINEES

Senators on the Judiciary Committee, questioning presidents' nominees, have traditionally been frustrated by the refusal of nominees to comment on issues that are likely to come before the court in future cases. The nominees have argued that giving specific opinions may impinge upon their judicial impartiality when faced with specific cases. A true judicial approach requires that they examine specific facts in each case, listen to the arguments on both sides, and confer with their colleagues on the Court before rendering an opinion. Thus, when asked if he supported *Roe v. Wade*, John Roberts said "I should stay away from issues that may come before the Court again." But Democratic Senator Joseph Biden insisted that Roberts should at least discuss his views about abortion and the right of privacy as well as other general legal views: "Without any knowledge of your understanding of the law, because you will not share it with us, we are rolling the dice with you, judge."

THE STRUCTURE OF THE FEDERAL COURT SYSTEM

The federal court system consists of three levels of courts with general jurisdiction, together with various special courts (the Court of Claims, Customs Court, Patent Court, and Court of Military Appeals). The Constitution establishes only the Supreme Court, although Congress determines the number of Supreme Court justices—traditionally nine. Article III authorizes Congress to establish "such inferior courts" as it deems appropriate. Congress has designed a hierarchical court system consisting of nearly 100 U.S. federal district courts and eleven U.S. circuit courts of appeals, in addition to the Supreme Court of the United States (see Figure 13.1).

FEDERAL DISTRICT COURTS

Federal district courts are the trial courts of the federal system. Each state has at least one district court, and larger states have more. (New York, for example, has four.) More than 600 judges, appointed for life by the president and confirmed by the Senate, preside in these courts. The president also appoints U.S. marshals for each district court to carry out orders of the court and maintain order in the courtroom. Federal district courts hear criminal cases prosecuted by the U.S. Department of Justice, as well as civil cases. As trial courts, the district courts use both grand juries (juries composed to hear evidence and, if warranted, to indict a defendant by bringing formal criminal charges against that person) and petit, or regular, juries (juries that determine guilt or innocence). District courts may hear as many as 300,000 cases in a year.

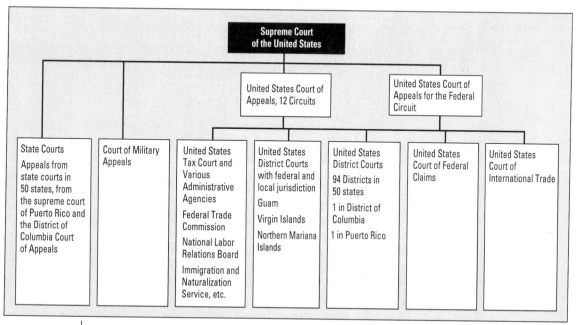

FIGURE 13.1 | THE U.S. COURT SYSTEM

CIRCUIT COURTS OF APPEALS

Circuit courts of appeals are *appellate courts*. They do not hold trials or accept new evidence but consider only the record of the trial courts and oral or written arguments (briefs) submitted by attorneys. Federal law provides that every individual has a right to appeal his or her case, so courts of appeals have little discretion in hearing appeals. Appellate judges themselves estimate that more than 80 percent of all appeals are "frivolous"—that is, they are without any real basis at all. These courts require nearly 100 circuit court judges, appointed for life by the president and confirmed by the Senate. Normally, three judges serve together on a panel to hear appeals. More than 90 percent of the cases decided by circuit courts of appeals end at this level. Further appeal to the Supreme Court is not automatic; the Supreme Court itself decides what appeals it will consider. Hence, for most cases, the decision of the circuit court of appeals is final.

THE U.S. SUPREME COURT

The U.S. Supreme Court
Official Web site provides recent decisions, case dockets, oral arguments, public information, etc.
www. supremecourtus.gov

The Supreme Court of the United States is the final interpreter of all matters involving the U.S. Constitution and federal laws and treaties, whether the case began in a federal district court or in a state court. The Supreme Court determines for itself whether to accept an appeal and consider a case. It may do so if a "substantial federal question" is at issue in the case or if "special and important reasons" apply. Any four justices can grant an appeal. However, the Supreme Court denies most cases submitted to it; the Court need not give any reason for denying appeal or certiorari.* Each year about 8,000 appeals, usually submitted as *writs of certiorari* (literally "to make more certain"), are received by the Supreme Court, but the Court accepts less than 150 cases a year.

In the early days of the republic, the size of the U.S. Supreme Court fluctuated, but since 1869 its membership has remained at nine: the chief justice and eight associate justices. The Supreme Court is in session each year from October through June, hearing oral arguments, accepting written briefs, conferring, and rendering opinions.

THE JURISDICTION OF THE FEDERAL COURT SYSTEM

In the U.S. federal system, each state maintains its own court system. The federal courts are not necessarily superior to state courts; both state and federal courts operate independently. But because the U.S. Supreme Court has appellate jurisdiction over state supreme courts as well as over lower federal courts, the Supreme Court oversees the nation's entire judicial system.

State courts have general jurisdiction in all criminal and civil cases. According to Article III of the U.S. Constitution, federal court jurisdiction extends to:

- Cases arising under the Constitution, federal laws, or treaties.
- Cases involving ambassadors, public ministers or counsels, or maritime and admiralty laws.

---

*The Supreme Court technically must hear *writs of appeal*, but only a few matters qualify. Among them are cases involving clear constitutional issues (for example, a finding that a federal law is unconstitutional, that a state law is in conflict with federal law, or that a state law is in violation of the U.S. Constitution). *Writs of certiorari* are granted when four members agree that an issue involves a "substantial federal question."

- Cases in which the U.S. government is a party.
- Cases between two or more states.
- Cases between a state and a citizen of another state.
- Cases between citizens of different states.
- Cases between two or more states.
- Cases between a state or a citizen and a foreign government or citizen of another nation.

Obviously, it is not difficult "to make a federal case out of it," regardless of what "it" might be. The Constitution contains many vaguely worded guarantees—"due process of law," "equal protection of the laws," protection from "cruel and unusual punishment" and "unreasonable searches and seizures," and so forth—which allow nearly every party to any case to claim that a federal question is involved and that a federal court is the proper forum.

APPEALS FROM STATE COURTS

The great bulk of the national caseload begins and ends in state court systems. The federal courts do not intervene once a state court has started hearing a case, except in rare circumstances. And Congress has stipulated that legal disputes between citizens of different states must involve $75,000 or more in order to be heard in federal court. Moreover, parties to cases in state courts must "exhaust their remedies"—that is, appeal their case all the way through the state courts—before the federal courts will hear their appeal. Appeals from state supreme courts go directly to the U.S. Supreme Court and not to federal district or circuit courts. Usually appeals from state supreme courts to the U.S. Supreme Court are made on the grounds that the case raises "a federal question"—that is, a question on the application of the U.S. Constitution or federal law. The U.S. Supreme Court reviews only a small fraction of appeals from state court decisions.

FEDERAL COURT CASELOADS

Of the 10 million civil and criminal cases begun in the nation's courts each year, less than 3 percent (250,000) are filed in federal district courts. State and local courts hear the great bulk of legal cases. The U.S. Constitution "reserves" general police powers to the states so that crimes and civil disputes are generally matters of state and local concern. Murder, robbery, assault, and rape are normally state offenses rather than federal crimes. Federal crimes generally center on offenses (1) against the U.S. government or its property; (2) against U.S. government officials or employees while they are on duty; (3) that involve crossing state lines (such as nationally organized crime, unlawful escape across state lines, taking kidnapping victims across state lines); (4) that interfere with interstate commerce; and (5) that occur on federal territories or on the seas. (However, see Focus: Make It a Federal Crime!)

JUDICIAL POWER: ACTIVISM VERSUS SELF-RESTRAINT

Great legal scholars have argued the merits of activism versus self-restraint in judicial decision making for more than a century.[5] Proponents of judicial *self-restraint* argue that because justices are not popularly elected, the Supreme Court should move cautiously

| FOCUS | "MAKE IT A FEDERAL CRIME!" |

Washington politicians are continually pressured to make "a federal crime" out of virtually every offense in society. Neither Democrats nor Republicans, liberals nor conservatives, are willing to risk their political futures by telling their constituents that a particular crime is a state responsibility, not a subject for their own attention. So Washington lawmakers continue to add offenses to the ever lengthening list of federal crimes.

Traditionally, the federal government's criminal responsibilities were limited to the enforcement of a relatively narrow range of federal laws, including laws dealing with counterfeiting, tax evasion, bank fraud and embezzlement, robbery or theft of federally insured funds, interstate criminal activity, and murder or assault of a federal official. Although some federal criminal laws overlapped state laws, most criminal activity—murder, rape, robbery, assault, burglary, theft, auto theft, gambling, drug offenses, and sex offenses—fell under state jurisdiction. Indeed, the *police power* was believed to be one of the "reserved" powers of the states referred to in the Tenth Amendment.

But over time Congress has made more and more offenses *federal* crimes. Today, federal crimes range from drive-by shootings to obstructing sidewalks in front of abortion clinics. Any violent offense motivated by racial, religious, or ethnic animosity is a "hate crime" subject to federal prosecution. "Racketeering" and "conspiracy" (organizing and communicating with others about the intent to commit a crime) is a federal crime. The greatest impact of federal involvement in law enforcement is found in drug-related crime. Drug offenders may be tried in either federal or state courts or both. Federal drug laws carry heavier penalties than those of most of the states.

Only recently has the U.S. Supreme Court recognized that federalizing crime may impinge on the reserved powers of the states. In 1994, Congress passed a popular Violence Against Women Act that allowed victims of gender-motivated violence, including rape, to sue their attackers for monetary damages in federal court. Congress defended its constitutional authority to involve itself in crimes against women by citing the commerce clause, arguing that crimes against women interfered with interstate commerce, a power given to the federal government in Article I of the Constitution. But in 2000, the Supreme Court said, "The Constitution requires a distinction between what is truly national and what is truly local, and there is no better example of the police power, which the Founders undeniably left reposed in the states and denied the central government than the suppression of violent crime."[a]

———————

[a]*United States v. Morrison* 529 U.S. 598 (2000).

and avoid direct confrontation with legislative and executive authority. Justice Felix Frankfurter wrote, "The only check upon our own exercise of power is our own sense of self-restraint. For the removal of unwise laws from the statute books, appeal lies not to the courts but to the ballot and to the processes of democratic government."[6]

However, Frankfurter was arguing a minority position on the Court. The dominant philosophy of the Supreme Court under Chief Justice Earl Warren (1953–1969) was one of *judicial activism*. The Warren Court believed it should shape constitutional meaning to fit its estimate of the needs of contemporary society. By viewing the Constitution as a deliberately broad and flexible document, one can avoid dozens of new constitutional amendments to accommodate a changing society. The strength of the U.S. Constitution lies in its flexibility—its relevance to contemporary society.[7]

The Supreme Court's posture of judicial activism, combined with its lifetime appointments, greatly strengthens its elitist character. If a nonelective institution such as the federal judiciary assumes a strong, activist role in national policy making, the result is an even more elitist political system. This is true whether the Supreme Court is active on behalf of liberal or conservative policies. Liberals who praise the virtues of judicial activism, who urge the Court to stand against the misguided policies of an elected president and Congress, must recognize the elitist nature of their argument.

RULES OF RESTRAINT

Even an activist Supreme Court adheres to some general rules of judicial self-restraint. These rules include the following:

- The Court will not pass upon the constitutionality of legislation in a nonadversary proceeding but only in an actual case. Thus, the Court will not advise the president or Congress on constitutional questions.
- The Court will not anticipate a question on constitutional law; it does not decide hypothetical cases.
- The Court will not formulate a rule of constitutional law broader than required by the precise facts to which it must be applied.
- The Court will not pass upon a constitutional question if some other ground exists upon which it may dispose of the case.
- When doubt exists about the constitutionality of a law, the Court will try to interpret the meaning of a law so as to give it a constitutional meaning and avoid the necessity of declaring it unconstitutional.
- A complainant must have exhausted all remedies available in lower federal courts or state courts before the Supreme Court accepts review.
- Occasionally the Court defers to Congress and the president and classifies an issue as a political question, and refuses to decide it. The Court has stayed out of foreign and military policy areas.
- If the Court holds a law unconstitutional, it will confine its decision to the particular section of the law that is unconstitutional; the rest of the statute stays intact.[8]

STARE DECISIS

Courts are also limited by the principle of *stare decisis,* which means that the issue has already been decided in earlier cases. Reliance on precedent is a fundamental notion in law. Indeed, the underlying common law of England and the United States is composed simply of past decisions. Students of the law learn through the case-study method: the study of previous decisions. Reliance on precedent gives stability to the law; if every decision were new law, then no one would know what the law is from day to day. Yet judicial activists are frequently willing to discard precedent. Former justice William O. Douglas, who seldom felt restrained by legal precedent, justified disregard of precedent as follows:

> *The decisions of yesterday or of the last century are only the starting points.... A judge looking at a constitutional decision may have compulsions to revere the past history and accept what was once written. But he remembers above all else that it is the Constitution which he swore to support and defend, not the gloss which his predecessors may have put on it. So he comes to formulate his own laws, rejecting some earlier ones as false and embracing others. He cannot do otherwise unless he lets men long dead and unaware of the problems of the age in which he lives do his thinking for him.*[9]

ORIGINAL INTENT

Should the Constitution be interpreted in terms of the intentions of its original writers or according to the morality of society today? Most jurists agree that the Constitution is a living document, that it must be interpreted by each generation in the light of current conditions, and that to do otherwise would soon render the document obsolete. But in interpreting the document, whose values should prevail—the values of the judges or the values of its writers? The doctrine of original intent takes the values of the Founders as expressed in the text of the Constitution and applies them to current conditions. Defenders of original intent argue that the words in the document must be given their historical meaning and that meaning must restrain courts as well as the legislative and executive branches of government. The Supreme Court should not set aside laws made by elected representatives unless they conflict with the original intent of the Founders. A Supreme Court that sets aside laws because they do not accord with today's moral standards is simply substituting its own morality for that of elected bodies. Such decisions lack democratic legitimacy, because there is no reason why judges' moral views should prevail over those of elected representatives. But this original intent doctrine has had little influence among the activists on the Supreme Court.

WISDOM VERSUS CONSTITUTIONALITY

Distinguished jurists have long urged the Supreme Court to exercise self-restraint. A law may be unwise, unjust, unfair, or even stupid and yet still be constitutional. One cannot equate the wisdom of the law with its constitutionality, and the Court should decide only the constitutionality and not the wisdom of a law. Justice Oliver Wendell Holmes once lectured his colleague, 61-year-old Justice Harlan Stone, on this point:

> *Young man, about 75 years ago I learned that I was not God. And so, when the people . . . want to do something I can't find anything in the Constitution expressly forbidding them to do, I say, whether I like it or not, "Goddamn it, let 'em do it."*[10]

However, the actual role of the Supreme Court in the nation's power struggles suggests that the Court indeed equates wisdom with constitutionality. People frequently cite broad phrases in the Fifth and Fourteenth Amendments, establishing constitutional standards of "due process of law" and "equal protection of the laws," when attacking laws they believe are unfair or unjust. Most Americans have come to believe that laws that are simply unwise must also be unconstitutional and that the courts have become the final arbiters of fairness and justice.

| FOCUS | THE SUPREME COURT CHOOSES A PRESIDENT |

The presidential election of 2000 was unique in American history in that the outcome was decided by the Supreme Court of the United States. The Supreme Court's decision in *Bush v. Gore* rested on legal issues, but the 5 to 4 decision of the justices raised the question of the Court's political partisanship.

On the morning after election day, 2000, it became clear that the outcome of the presidential election depended on Florida's twenty-five electoral college votes. Florida law provides for a recount when the margin of victory is less than one-half of 1 percent. The Florida secretary of state, separately elected Republican Katherine Harris, held a machine recount as well as a count of absentee ballots. But she declined to accept any recount returns from counties after November 14, the date set by Florida law as a final date for the submission of election returns to the secretary. She declared George Bush the winner of the state's electoral votes by a margin of 537.

Armies of lawyers descended on Florida's capital city, Tallahassee. Gore's lawyers demanded *manual* recounts of the ballots in the state's three largest, and most Democratic, counties—Miami-Dade, Broward (Fort Lauderdale), and Palm Beach. The Florida Supreme Court (with its seven justices, all appointed by Democratic governors) set aside the state's legal deadline for recounts, and county canvassing boards began the tedious hand count of punch card ballots. The Florida court instructed the canvassers to determine the "intent" of the voter from the condition of each ballot. This gave rise to arguments over "hanging chads," "dimpled chads," and so on (a chad is the small square that is supposed to be punched out of the ballot by the voter).

The Bush legal team appealed directly to the U.S. Supreme Court, arguing, first of all, that the U.S. Constitution gives the power to appoint presidential electors "in such Manner as the *Legislature* thereof may direct" (Article II, Section 1) and that the Florida Supreme Court overreached its authority when it set aside the legislative-enacted deadline for recounts. They also argued that hand counts in counties were late, unreliable, subjective, and open to partisan bias.

Only the U.S. Supreme Court seemed to possess sufficient legitimacy to resolve the first contested presidential election in more than a century. The Supreme Court held that "the use of standardless manual recounts violates the Equal Protection and Due Process Clauses [of the Constitution].... The judgment of the Supreme Court of Florida is reversed." The narrow 5 to 4 decision appeared to follow partisan lines, with Justices O'Connor, Kennedy, Rehnquist, Scalia, and Thomas voting in the majority to allow Florida's secretary of state to certify that state's electoral votes for Bush. Justices Souter, Stevens, Ginsburg, and Breyer dissented, arguing that the U.S. Supreme Court should not interfere with Florida's manual recount.

Al Gore had won the popular vote across the nation by 500,000 votes. Many Democrats charged that the U.S. Supreme Court had acted in a partisan manner and allowed Bush to "steal" the election.

SUPREME COURT POLITICS

Once appointed, the jobs of Supreme Court justices do not depend on public opinion, partisan shifts in Congress or the presidency, or indeed the outcome of democratic politics. Supreme Court justices make decisions based on their own political and judicial philosophies.

Most cases do not present a clear liberal–conservative dimension, and even fewer present a partisan—Democratic versus Republican—dimension. (However, see Focus: The Supreme Court Chooses a President.) Each case presents a separate set of facts, and even justices who share a general philosophy may perceive the central facts of a case differently. So ideological blocs are not always good predictors of voting outcomes on the Supreme Court.

TABLE 13.2 | LIBERAL AND CONSERVATIVE VOTING BLOCS ON THE SUPREME COURT

	The Warren Court	The Burger Court	The Rehnquist Court	The Roberts Court[*]
	1968	1975	2004	2008
Liberal	Earl Warren Hugo Black William O. Douglas Thurgood Marshall William J. Brennan Abe Fortas	William O. Douglas Thurgood Marshall William J. Brennan	John Paul Stevens Ruth Bader Ginsburg Stephen G. Breyer David Souter	John Paul Stevens Ruth Bader Ginsburg Stephen G. Breyer David Souter
Moderate	Potter Stewart Byron White	Potter Stewart Byron White Lewis Powell Harry Blackmun	Anthony Kennedy Sandra Day O'Connor	Anthony Kennedy John Roberts
Conservative	John Marshall Harlan	Warren Burger William Rehnquist	William Rehnquist Antonin Scalia Clarence Thomas	Samual Alito Antonin Scalia Clarence Thomas

[*]All blocs have been designated by the authors. Blocs on the Roberts Court are more speculative inasmuch as the Court has yet to decide many cases.

CHANGING LIBERAL AND CONSERVATIVE BLOCS ON THE SUPREME COURT

Over time, the ideological composition of the Supreme Court has changed (see Table 13.2). The liberal bloc, once headed by Chief Justice Earl Warren, dominated Court decision making from the mid-1950s through the end of the 1960s. The liberal bloc gradually weakened following President Richard Nixon's appointment of Warren Burger as chief justice in 1969, but not all of Nixon's appointees joined the conservative bloc; Justice Harry Blackmun and Justice Lewis Powell frequently joined in voting with

the liberal bloc. Among Nixon's appointees, only William Rehnquist consistently adopted conservative positions. President Gerald Ford's only appointee to the Court, John Paul Stevens, began as a moderate but later joined the liberal bloc. As a result, the Burger Court, although generally not as active as the Warren Court, still did not reverse any earlier liberal decisions.

President Ronald Reagan campaigned on a pledge to restrain the liberal activism of the Court. His first appointee, and the first woman on the Court, Sandra Day O'Connor, turned out to be less conservative than expected, especially on women's issues and abortion rights. When Chief Justice Burger retired in 1986, Reagan seized the opportunity to strengthen the conservative bloc by elevating Justice Rehnquist to Chief Justice and appointing a strong conservative, Antonin Scalia, to the Court. Reagan added Anthony Kennedy to the Court in 1988, but he turned out to be less conservative than Reagan had hoped. If Reagan had succeeded in getting the powerful conservative voice of Robert Bork on the Court, the Court might have reversed some of its earlier liberal decisions. But the Democratic Senate rejected Bork, and David Souter, the man ultimately confirmed, compiled a generally liberal voting record.

George H. W. Bush's appointment of the conservative Clarence Thomas as a replacement for the liberal Thurgood Marshall gave the conservative bloc a strong voice on the Court. But President Bill Clinton's appointees, Ruth Bader Ginsburg and Stephen G. Breyer, predictably reinforced the liberal bloc. On key questions the moderate bloc held the balance of power on the Supreme Court. Sandra Day O'Connor was the leader of the moderates on the Court (see Focus: The Supreme Court and Abortion).

President George W. Bush replaced conservative Chief Justice William Rehnquist with John Roberts, who is expected to be more moderate than his predecessor. And Bush replaced moderate Sandra Day O'Connor with Samuel Alito, who is expected to help hold the conservative bloc together.

DO THE COURTS RULE THE NATION?

George C. Wallace once put the argument bluntly: "Thugs and federal judges have just about taken charge of this country."[11] Others have also worried about the increasing role of the judiciary—the ability of courts to intrude into people's lives in ways unprecedented in history. One need not be a "conservative" in politics to be concerned about the extent to which we now rely on a nonelected judiciary to solve our problems, rather than on democratically elected executives and legislators.

GROWING RELIANCE ON THE COURTS

Law Info
Web site offering legal documents, legal help guides, attorney references, and so forth.
www.lawinfo.com

Harvard Law School professor Archibald Cox, who became famous as the first Watergate prosecutor, warned that "excessive reliance upon courts instead of self-government through democratic processes, may deaden the people's sense of moral and political responsibility for their own future, especially in matters of liberty, and may stunt the growth of political capacity that results from the exercise of the ultimate powers of decision."[12] For good or for ill, Americans have come to rely on courts to solve problems once handled by legislatures, local officials, school boards, teachers, parents, or other social organizations.

FOCUS | THE SUPREME COURT AND ABORTION

It is ironic indeed that a nation that thinks of itself as a democracy must call upon a nonelective, lifetime elite to decide its most contentious issues.

Historically, abortions for any purpose other than saving the life of the mother were criminal offenses under most state laws. A few states permitted abortions in cases of rape or incest or to protect the health of the woman. Then in 1970, New York, Alaska, Hawaii, and Washington enacted laws that in effect permitted abortion at the request of the woman involved and the concurrence of her physician. A growing proabortion coalition formed, including the American Civil Liberties Union, a new National Association for the Repeal of Abortion Laws, Planned Parenthood, and women's organizations, including the National Organization for Women.

At about the same time, the Supreme Court was developing a new constitutional right—the right of privacy—partly in response to a case brought to it by Planned Parenthood in 1965. When Estelle Griswold opened a birth control clinic on behalf of the Planned Parenthood League of Connecticut, the state found her in violation of a Connecticut law prohibiting the use of contraceptives. She challenged the constitutionality of the statute, and in its ruling in *Griswold v. Connecticut*, the Supreme Court struck down the law by a vote of 7 to 2.[a] Voting for the majority were Brennan, Clark, Douglas, Goldberg, Harlan, Warren, and White. Dissenting were Black and Stewart.

The right to privacy is nowhere specifically stated in the Constitution. But Justice Douglas found it in "the penumbras formed by emanations from" the First, Third, Fourth, Ninth, and Fifteenth Amendments. Justices Goldberg, Warren, and Brennan found it in the Ninth Amendment: "The enumeration of the Constitution of certain rights, shall not be contrived to deny or disparage others retained by the people." Justice Harlan found the right in the word *liberty* in the Fourteenth Amendment. The fact that *Griswold* dealt with reproduction gave encouragement to groups advocating abortion rights.

When Norma McCorvey sought an abortion in Texas in 1969, her doctor refused, citing a state law prohibiting abortion except to save a woman's life. McCorvey bore the child and gave it up for adoption but then enlisted the aid of two young attorneys, Linda Coffee and Sarah Weddington, who challenged the Texas law in federal courts on a variety of constitutional grounds, including the right to privacy. *Amicus curiae* briefs were filed by a wide assortment of groups on both sides of the issue. McCorvey became "Jane Roe," and *Roe v. Wade* became one of the most controversial cases in the Court's history.[b]

The Supreme Court ruled in 1973 that the constitutional right to privacy as well as the Fourteenth Amendment's guarantee of "liberty" included a woman's decision to bear or not to bear a child. The Court ruled that the word *person* in the Constitution did *not* include the unborn child; therefore the Fifth and Fourteenth Amendments' guarantee of "life, liberty and property" did not protect the "life" of the fetus. The Court also ruled that a state's power to protect the health and safety of the mother could not justify *any* restriction on abortion in the first three months of pregnancy. Between the third and sixth months of pregnancy, a state could set standards for abortion procedures in order to protect the health of women, but a state could not prohibit abortions. Only in the final three months could a state prohibit or regulate abortion to protect the unborn. Voting with the majority were Blackmun, Brennan, Burger, Douglas, Marshall, Powell, and Stewart. Dissenting were Rehnquist and White.

Roe v. Wade set off a political conflagration. A new movement was mobilized to restrict the scope of the decision and if possible to bring about its overturn. Congress defeated efforts to pass a constitutional amendment restricting abortion or declaring that life begins at conception. However, Congress banned the use of federal funds under Medicaid (medical care for the poor) for abortions except to protect the life of a woman. The Supreme Court upheld the ban, holding that there was no constitutional obligation for governments to pay for abortions.[c]

Initial efforts by some states to restrict abortion ran into Supreme Court opposition.[d] But opponents of abortion won a victory in *Webster v. Reproductive Health Services* in 1989.[e] In this case, the Supreme Court upheld a Missouri law denying public funds for abortions that were not necessary to preserve the life of the woman, and denying the use of public facilities or employees in performing or assisting in abortions. More important, the justices recognized the state's "interest in the protection of human life when viability is possible," and they upheld Missouri's requirement for a test of "viability" after twenty weeks and prohibition on abortions of a viable fetus except to save a woman's life.

Webster gave hope to prolife groups that the Supreme Court might eventually overturn *Roe v. Wade*. Justices Rehnquist and White had dissented in the original *Roe v. Wade* case; they were now joined in upholding restrictions on abortion by three new Reagan appointees, O'Connor, Kennedy, and Scalia. Dissenting were Blackmun, Brennan, Marshall, and Stevens.

However, the current Supreme Court appears to have chosen a policy of affirming a woman's right to abortion while upholding modest restrictions, as evidenced by its ruling in *Planned Parenthood of Pennsylvania v. Casey* in 1992.[f] In this case, the Supreme Court upheld a series of restrictions on abortion enacted by Pennsylvania: that physicians must inform women of risks and alternatives; that women must wait twenty-four hours after requesting an abortion before having one, and that minors must have the consent of parents or a judge. It struck down only the requirement that spouses be notified.

Justice Sandra Day O'Connor took the lead in forming a moderate swing bloc on the Court, consisting of herself, Kennedy, and Souter. (Blackmun and Stevens voted to uphold *Roe v. Wade* with *no* restrictions, making the vote 5 to 4.) O'Connor's majority opinion strongly reaffirmed the fundamental right of abortion, both on the basis of the Fourteenth Amendment and on the principle of *stare decisis*. But the majority also upheld a state's right to protect any fetus that reached the point of "viability." The Court went on to establish a new standard for constitutionally evaluating restrictions: they must not impose an "undue burden" on women seeking abortion or place "substantial obstacles" in her path. All of Pennsylvania's restrictions met this standard and were upheld, except spousal notification.

A number of states have attempted to outlaw an abortion procedure known as "intact dilation and evacuation" or "partial birth" abortion. This procedure, which is used in less than 1 percent of all abortions, involves partial delivery of the fetus feet-first, then vacuuming out the brain and crushing the skull to ease complete removal. Congress also voted to ban this procedure several times, only to have President Clinton veto the bans. In a surprise 5 to 4 decision, with Justice O'Conner supporting the majority, the Supreme Court declared a Nebraska law prohibiting the procedure to be an unconstitutional "undue burden" on a woman's right to an abortion. The Nebraska law failed to make an exception in its prohibition of the procedure "for the preservation of the health of the mother."[g] Congress again voted to ban "partial birth" abortions in 2004, and President George W. Bush signed the ban into law. In 2007, the Supreme Court (by a 5 to 4 decision) found that the federal ban did *not* create an "undue burden" on a woman's right to an abortion and was constitutional.[h]

---

[a]*Griswold v. Connecticut*, 381 U.S. 479 (1965).

[b]*Roe v. Wade*, 400 U.S. 113 (1973).

[c]*Harris v. McRae*, 448 U.S. 297 (1980).

[d]*Planned Parenthood of Missouri v. Danforth*, 418 U.S. 52 (1976); *Belloti v. Baird*, 443 U.S. 662 (1979); *Akron v. Akron Center for Reproductive Health*, 103 S. Ct. 2481 (1983).

[e]*Webster v. Reproductive Health Services*, 492 U.S. 111 (1989).

[f]*Planned Parenthood of Pennsylvania v. Casey*, 505 U.S. 110 (1992).

[g]*Stenberg v. Carhart*, June 28, 2000.

[h]*Gonzales v. Earhart*, April 18, 2007.

COURT CONGESTION

Nearly one million lawyers practice in the United States. Each year the nation's courts try more than 10 million cases, most of them in state and local courts. Over 250,000 cases begin in federal courts each year. Most of these cases will be settled before trial, but about 25,000 (10 percent) go to trial. People appeal more than 50,000 cases to U.S. courts of appeal each year. And the U.S. Supreme Court receives about 8,000 appeals each year, although it accepts and decides on fewer than 200 of them.

The growing number of legal cases not only raises questions about the increasing power of a nonelected, lifetime judicial elite but also overburdens the court system and creates many injustices. As more and more cases get into the judicial system, congestion and costs mount. Cases may be backed up on court dockets for years. As a result, injured parties in civil cases must suffer long delays before receiving compensation. Defendants in criminal cases who are free on bail may deliberately delay the trial, hoping that witnesses will move away or forget important details or that victims will grow frustrated and give up trying to prosecute. Most lawsuits require attorneys on both sides, and attorneys are expensive. The longer a case drags on, the more expensive it is likely to be.

PLEA BARGAINING

Congestion forces prosecuting attorneys in criminal cases to *plea bargain* with defendants—that is, to make special arrangements for criminal defendants to plead guilty in exchange for reduced charges. For example, a prosecutor may reduce the charge of rape to sexual assault, which usually carries a lighter penalty. The prosecutor enters into such a bargain to avoid the delays and costs of a trial; the defendant makes such a bargain to escape serious penalty for the crime. Estimates suggest that 90 percent of all criminal cases are now plea bargained.

JUDICIAL REFORMS

Federal courts are so well insulated from popular pressure and from congressional and presidential pressures that we will probably have to wait for them to "reform" themselves. If federal judges are slow in handling cases, if their decisions are arbitrary, if congestion and confusion reign in their courtrooms, if they bog themselves down in details of managing school districts or prisons or hospitals, if they are lazy or poorly trained in the law, if they are in poor health or senile, no one can do much about it. Only five federal court judges have ever been impeached and convicted by Congress. In 1989, Federal District Court Judge L. C. Hastings became the first sitting judge in more than fifty years to be impeached, tried, and found guilty by the Congress. (Ironically, the politically popular and flamboyant Hastings won election to Congress from a reapportioned majority black South Florida district in 1992 and has won reelection ever since then.) Other judges have resigned under fire: federal judge Otto Kerner (former governor of Illinois) resigned his judicial post only five days before he was scheduled to enter prison for income tax evasion, perjury, bribery, and mail fraud. In short, the U.S. citizenry has little control over the judiciary, despite the control it exercises over all of us.

THE COURTS: AN ELITIST INTERPRETATION

The Supreme Court determines many of the nation's most important policies. Indeed, most political questions sooner or later end up in the courts. Any fair examination of the court system in the United States will reveal the elitist character of judicial decision making.

1. The Supreme Court is the elitist branch of the national government. Nine justices—none of whom is elected and all of whom serve for life—can void the acts of popularly elected presidents, Congresses, governors, legislatures, school boards, and city councils.

2. The principle of judicial review of congressional acts grew out of the Founders' distrust of popularly elected officials subject to influence by popular majorities. Judicial review enables the courts to protect constitutional principles against attacks by elected bodies.

3. The social backgrounds of judges reflect close ties to upper-class segments of society. Presidents may attempt to influence court decisions through their selection of judges, but life terms make judges independent of presidential or congressional influence once they are appointed.

4. Because justices are not popularly elected, some scholars and jurists have urged self-restraint in judicial policy making. They argue that the Supreme Court should decide only the constitutionality of a law, not its wisdom; the Court should not substitute its own judgment for the judgment of elected representatives. But over the years judicial activism has augmented the power of judges. Justices have used broad phrases in the Constitution such as "due process of law" and "equal protection of the law" to strike down laws they believe are unfair or unjust.

5. Even an activist Supreme Court adheres to some rules of restraint. It does not give advisory opinions or decide hypothetical cases or decide on the constitutionality of a law until an actual case directly involving the law comes before it.

6. Americans have come to rely on courts to resolve key conflicts in society. There are more lawyers and more court cases in the United States than any other nation in the world.

SELECTED READINGS

Baum, Lawrence. *The Supreme Court*, 9th ed. Washington, D.C.: C.Q. Press, 2006. A readable introduction to the Supreme Court as a political institution, the book covers the selection of justices, the nature of cases decided, the process of decision making, and the impact of the Supreme Court's decisions.

Carp, Robert A., and Ronald Stidham. *The Federal Courts*, 4th ed. Washington, D.C.: CQ Press, 2001. An overview of the federal judicial system, arguing that federal judges and Supreme Court justices function as part of the political system and engage in policy making that influences all our lives.

Carp, Robert A., Ronald Stidham, and Kenneth L. Manning. *Judicial Process in America*, 7th ed. Washington, D.C., 2007. A comprehensive review of the American judicial system at all levels.

Neubauer, David W., and Stephen S. Weinhold. *Judicial Politics, Law, Courts, and Politics in the United States*. Belmont, Calif.: Wadsworth, 2004. Introduction to the judicial process with controversial cases in each chapter.

Schwartz, Bernard. *A History of the Supreme Court*. New York: Oxford University Press, 1995. A comprehensive one-volume history of the nation's highest court and the influence the Court has had on American politics and society.

U.S. Supreme Court decisions are available at most public and university libraries as well as at law libraries in volumes of *United States Reports*. Court opinions are cited by the names of the parties, for example, *Brown* v. *Board of Education of Topeka, Kansas*, followed by a reference number, such as 347 U.S. 483 (1954). The first number in the citation (347) is the volume number, "U.S." refers to *United States Reports;* the subsequent number is the page on which the decision begins; the year the case was decided is in parentheses.

NOTES

1. Alexis de Tocqueville, *Democracy in America* (New York: Mentor Books, 1956), p. 73.

2. James Madison, Alexander Hamilton, and John Jay, *The Federalist* (New York: Modern Library, 1937), p. 505.

3. Joseph W. Bishop, "The Warren Court Is Not Likely to Be Overruled," *New York Times Magazine* (September 7, 1969), p. 31.

4. John R. Schmidhausery, *The Supreme Court* (New York: Holt, Rinehart & Winston, 1960), p. 59.

5. Frank Jerone, *Law and the Modern Mind* (New York: Coward-McCann, 1930); Benjamin N. Cardozo, *The Nature of the Judicial Process* (New Haven, Conn.: Yale University Press, 1921); Roscoe Pound, *Justice According to Law* (New Haven, Conn.: Yale University Press, 1951).

6. *West Virginia State Board of Education v. Barnette,* 319 U.S. 624 (1943).

7. Archibald Cox, *The Warren Court* (Cambridge, Mass.: Harvard University Press, 1968), p. 2.

8. Henry Abraham, *The Judicial Process* (New York: Oxford University Press, 1968), pp. 310–326.

9. Justice William O. Douglas, "Stare Decisis," *Record* (April 1947).

10. Quoted by Charles P. Curtis, *Lions Under the Throne* (Boston: Houghton Mifflin, 1947), p. 281.

11. *Newsweek* (January 10, 1977), p. 42.

12. Archibald Cox, *The Role of the Supreme Court in American Government* (New York: Oxford University Press, 1976), p. 103.

The importance of denationalizing conflicts can hardly be overestimated, particularly in a large country like the United States where there is great diversity in resources and local problems.

Robert A. Dahl

AMERICAN FEDERALISM: ELITES IN STATES AND COMMUNITIES

Elites are themselves stratified, with national elites supported by subelites in states and communities. Decentralization—decision making by subelites—reduces strain on the national political system and on national elites by keeping many issues out of the national arena. National conflict is reduced by allowing subelites to pursue their own policies within the separate states and communities; they need not battle for a single national policy to be applied uniformly throughout the land. For example, subelites who wish to raise taxes and spend more money for public schools can do so in their own states and communities, and those who wish to reduce taxes and eliminate what some consider to be educational "frills" can also do so within their own states and communities.

Americans have more confidence in state and local government than the federal government (see Table 14.1). Moreover, the masses would prefer that governmental power be concentrated at the state rather than the federal level and they believe that local and state governments do the best job. Yet, as we will see in this chapter, *power in America has shifted over time to Washington and away from states and communities.*

FEDERALISM: THE ORIGINAL DIVISION OF POWER BETWEEN NATION AND STATES

The U.S. Constitution divides power between two separate authorities, the nation and the states, each of which can directly enforce its own laws on individuals through its own courts. There are more than 86,000 separate governments in the United States, of which more than 60,000 have the power to levy their own taxes. The Constitution endows *states* with all governmental powers not vested specifically in the national government or reserved to the people. All other governmental jurisdictions are subdivisions of states. States may create, alter, or abolish these other units of government by amending state laws or constitutions.

TABLE 14.1 | MASS ATTITUDES TOWARD FEDERAL, STATE, AND LOCAL GOVERNMENTS

Confidence

How much confidence do you have in these institutions?

1997			2003		
Your local government					
Great deal	11%	} 31%	Great deal	18%	} 68%
Quite a lot	20		Fair amount	50	
Some	46		Not much	23	
Very little	21		None	8	
Your state government					
Great deal	6%	} 23%	Great deal	12%	} 53%
Quite a lot	17		Fair amount	41	
Some	53		Not much	34	
Very little	23		None	12	
The federal government					
Great deal	4%		Great deal	9%	
Quite a lot	11		Fair amount	40	
Some	47		Not much	32	
Very little	37		None	9	

Power

Where should power be concentrated?

State government	64%
Federal government	26

Best Job

Which level of government does the best job of dealing with the problems it faces?

Federal	14%
State	34
Local	41

Note: All figures are percentages of the U.S. public in national opinion surveys. "No opinion" and "Don't know" are not shown.

Source: Gallup/CNN/*USA Today* polls reported in *Polling Report*. February 10, 1997; and Gallup, September 2003.

"**Look, the American people don't want to be bossed around by federal bureaucrats. They want to be bossed around by state bureaucrats.**"

American federalism differs from a "unitary" political system in that the central government has no constitutional authority to determine, alter, or abolish the power of the states. At the same time, American federalism differs from a confederation of states, in which the national government depends on its states for power. The American system shares authority and power constitutionally and practically.

The U.S. Constitution originally defined federalism in terms of (1) the powers exercised by the national government (delegated powers) and the national supremacy clause; (2) the powers reserved to the states; (3) the powers denied by the Constitution to both the national government and the states; and (4) the constitutional provisions giving the states a role in the composition of the national government.

DELEGATED POWERS

The U.S. Constitution lists eighteen grants of power to Congress, including authority over war and foreign affairs, authority over the economy ("interstate commerce"), control over the money supply, and power to tax and spend "to pay the debts and provide for the common defense and general welfare." Finally, after seventeen specific grants of power comes the power "to make all laws which shall be necessary and proper for carrying into execution the foregoing powers and all other powers vested by this Constitution in the government of the United States or in any department or officer thereof." This statement is generally known as the "necessary and proper" clause.

These delegated powers, when coupled with the assertion of "national supremacy" in Article VI, ensure a powerful national government. The national supremacy clause is specific in asserting the supremacy of federal laws:

The Constitution, and the laws of the United States which shall be made in pursuance thereof; and all treaties made or which shall be made under the authority of the

United States, shall be the supreme law of the land; and the judges in every state shall be bound thereby, anything in the constitution or laws of any state to the contrary notwithstanding.

RESERVED POWERS

Despite these broad grants of power to the national government, the states retained considerable governing power from the beginning of the republic. The Tenth Amendment reassured the states that "the powers not delegated to the United States ... are reserved to the states respectively, or to the people." The states generally retain control over property and contract law, criminal law, marriage and divorce, the provision of education, highways, and social welfare activities. The states control the organization and powers of their own local governments. Finally, the states, like the federal government, retain the power to tax and spend for the general welfare.

POWERS DENIED TO THE STATES

The Constitution denies some powers to both national and state government, namely, the powers to abridge individual rights. The first eight amendments to the U.S. Constitution originally applied only to the national government, but the Fourteenth Amendment, passed by Congress in 1866, provided that the states must also adhere to fundamental guarantees of individual liberty.

The Constitution denies the states some powers in order to safeguard national unity: the powers to coin money, enter into treaties with foreign nations, interfere with the "obligations of contracts," levy taxes on imports and exports, and engage in war, among others.

THE STATES' ROLE IN NATIONAL GOVERNMENT

The states are also basic units in the organizational scheme of the national government. The House of Representatives apportions members to the states by population, and state legislatures draw up their districts. Every state has at least one House representative, regardless of its population. Each state elects two U.S. senators, regardless of its population. The president is chosen by the electoral votes of the states; each state has as many electoral votes as it has senators and House representatives. Finally, three-fourths of the states must ratify amendments to the U.S. Constitution.

POWER FLOWS TO THE NATIONAL ELITE

Over time, governmental power has centralized in Washington. Although the formal constitutional arrangements of federalism remain in place, power has flowed relentlessly toward the national government since the earliest days of the nation.

THE "NECESSARY AND PROPER" CLAUSE

Chief Justice John Marshall added immeasurably to national power in *McCulloch v. Maryland* (1819) when he broadly interpreted the "necessary and proper" clause of Article I, Section 8, of the Constitution. In approving the establishment of a national bank (a power not specifically delegated to the national government in the Constitution), Marshall wrote:

> Let the end be legitimate, let it be within the scope of the Constitution, and all means which are appropriate, which are plainly adopted to that end, which are not prohibited but consistent with the letter and the spirit of the Constitution, are constitutional.

Since then, the "necessary and proper" clause has been called the "implied powers" clause or even the "elastic" clause, suggesting that the national government can do anything not specifically prohibited by the Constitution. Given this tradition, the courts are unlikely to hold an act of Congress unconstitutional solely because no formal constitutional grant of power gives Congress the power to act.

THE CIVIL WAR

The Civil War was the nation's greatest crisis in federalism. Did a state have the right to oppose federal action by force of arms? The issue was decided in the nation's bloodiest war. (Combined casualties in the Civil War, military and civilian, exceeded U.S. casualties in World War II, even though the U.S. population in 1860 was only one-quarter of the population in 1940.) The same issue was at stake when the federal government sent troops to Little Rock, Arkansas, in 1957 and to Oxford, Mississippi, in 1962 to enforce desegregation; however, in those confrontations it was clear which side held the military advantage.

CIVIL RIGHTS

Over the years, the U.S. Supreme Court has built a national system of civil rights based on the Fourteenth Amendment. This amendment rose out of the Civil War: "No *state* shall . . . deprive any person of life, liberty, or property, without due process of law; nor deny to any person within its jurisdiction the equal protection of the laws." In early cases, the Supreme Court held that the general guarantee of "liberty" in the first phrase (the "due process" clause) prevents states from interfering with free speech, the press, religion, and other personal liberties. Later, particularly after *Brown v. Board of Education of Topeka, Kansas* in 1954, the Supreme Court also used the "equal protection" clause to ensure fairness and equality of opportunity throughout the nation.

THE INTERSTATE COMMERCE CLAUSE

The growth of national power under the interstate commerce clause is also an important development in American federalism. The Industrial Revolution created a national economy governable only by a national government. Yet until the 1930s the Supreme Court placed many obstacles in the way of government regulation of the economy. Finally, in *National Labor Relations Board v. Jones & Laughlin Steel Corporation* (1937), the Supreme Court recognized the principle that Congress could regulate production and distribution of goods and services for a national market under the interstate commerce clause. As a result, the national government gained control over wages, prices, production, marketing, labor relations, and all other important aspects of the national economy.

| ## THE SHIFT OF POWER

Over time power in the U.S. federal system has shifted to the national government. The most important developments in this shift in power have been:

- A broad interpretation of the "necessary and proper" clause, obscuring the notion of "delegated powers."
- The victory of the national government in the Civil War, demonstrating that states cannot successfully resist federal power.
- The establishment of a national system of civil rights based on the Fourteenth Amendment,

which brought the federal government into the definition and enforcement of civil rights.

- The growth of federal power under the "interstate commerce" clause as a national industrial economy emerged.
- The growth of federal grants-in-aid to state and local governments as a significant source of revenue for these governments is a major source of federal intervention into state and local affairs.

MONEY AND POWER

Money and power go together. In 1913, when the Sixteenth Amendment gave the national government the power to tax incomes, financial power shifted from the states to Washington. The income tax gave the federal government the authority to raise large sums of money, which it spent for the "general welfare," as well as for defense. Of course, federal land grants to the states began as far back as the famous Northwest Ordinance in 1787, when Congress gave federal land to the states to assist in building public schools. Again, by the Morrill Land Grant Act in 1862, Congress made land grants to the states to promote higher education. But the first major federal *money* grants to the states began shortly after enactment of the federal income tax. Grant programs began in agricultural extension (1914), highways (1916), vocational education (1917), and public health (1918).

Urban Institute
Washington think tank offers viewpoints on federalism and issues confronting state and local governments.
www.urban.org

Gradually the federal government expanded its power in states and communities by use of grants-in-aid. During the Great Depression of the 1930s, the national government used its taxing and spending powers in a number of areas formerly "reserved" to states and communities. Congress began grant-in-aid programs to states and communities for public assistance, unemployment compensation, employment services, child welfare, public housing, and urban renewal.

THE EVOLUTION OF AMERICAN FEDERALISM

American federalism has undergone many changes during the more than 200 years that it has been in existence. And it continues to change over time.

Over time state and local governments throughout the United States became increasingly dependent on federal grant money. From 1960 to 1980 federal grants as a percent of state and local spending rose from about 15 percent to over 27 percent. President Ronald Reagan made significant cutbacks in the flow of federal funds to the states, and by 1990 federal grants constituted only 19 percent of state and local spending (see Figure 14.1). But state-local dependency on federal grants began to creep up again under Presidents Bill Clinton and George W. Bush.

FIGURE 14.1 | STATE AND LOCAL GOVERNMENT DEPENDENCY ON FEDERAL GRANTS

DUAL FEDERALISM

The pattern of federal–state relations during the nation's first hundred years has been described as *dual federalism*. The states and the nation divided most governmental functions. The national government concentrated its attention on the delegated powers—national defense, foreign affairs, tariffs, commerce across state lines, coining money, establishing standard weights and measures, maintaining a post office and building post roads, and admitting new states. State governments decided the important domestic policy issues—slavery (until the Civil War), education, welfare, health, and criminal justice. This separation of policy responsibilities was once compared to a layer cake, with local governments at the base, state governments in the middle, and the national government at the top.

COOPERATIVE FEDERALISM

The Industrial Revolution, bringing the development of a national economy; the income tax, which shifted financial resources to the national government; and the challenges of two world wars and the Great Depression all combined to end the strict distinction between national and state concerns. The new pattern of federal–state relations was labeled *cooperative federalism*. Both the nation and the states exercised responsibilities for welfare, health, highways, education, and criminal justice. This merging of policy responsibilities was compared to a marble cake. "As the colors are mixed in a marble cake, so functions are mixed in the American federal system."[1]

The Great Depression of the 1930s forced states to ask for federal financial assistance in dealing with poverty, unemployment, and old age. Governors welcomed massive federal public-works projects. In addition, the federal government intervened directly in economic affairs, labor relations, business practices, and agriculture. Through the grant-in-aid device, the national government cooperated with the states in public assistance, employment services, child welfare, public housing, urban renewal, highway building, and vocational education.

Yet even during this period when the nation and the states shared responsibility, the national government emphasized cooperation in achieving common national and state goals. Congress generally acknowledged that it had no direct constitutional authority to regulate public health, safety, or welfare. Congress relied primarily on its powers to tax and spend for the general welfare in providing financial assistance to state and local governments to achieve shared goals. Congress did not usually legislate directly on local matters.

CENTRALIZED FEDERALISM

Over the years it became increasingly difficult to maintain the fiction that the national government was merely assisting the states in performing their domestic responsibility. By the time President Lyndon B. Johnson launched the Great Society in 1964, the federal government clearly set forth its own national goals. Virtually all problems confronting American society—from solid-waste disposal and water and air pollution to consumer safety, home insulation, noise abatement, and even metric conversion— were declared to be national problems. Congress legislated directly on any matter it chose. The Supreme Court no longer concerned itself with the reserved powers of the states; the Tenth Amendment lost most of its meaning. The pattern of federal–state relations became centralized.

NEW FEDERALISM

The term *new federalism* has been applied to efforts to return power and responsibility to states and communities. Actually, the term was first used by President Nixon in the early 1970s to describe his general-revenue-sharing proposal: the direct allocation of federal tax revenues to state and local governments to use for general purposes with no strings attached. Later, the term referred to a series of proposals by President Reagan to reduce state and local dependency on federal revenues and return powers to states and communities.

To implement the new federalism, Reagan consolidated many *categorical grants* (by which the federal government specifies individual projects or programs in cities and states) into a few large *block grant* programs (by which the federal government provides funds for use by states and cities for broad purposes, such as law enforcement and community development, with state and local officials deciding on specific projects or programs). These block grants provide greater flexibility in the use of federal funds and allow state and local officials to exercise more power over projects and programs within their jurisdictions. Reagan also ended the federal government's general-revenue-sharing program, which had funneled billions of dollars annually to states and cities. These efforts succeeded for a time in slowing the growth of federal grant money to the states and even in reducing state and local reliance on federal funds.

REPRESENTATIONAL FEDERALISM

Despite the attempts at the new federalism, the flow of power toward national elites continued. In 1985, the U.S. Supreme Court ended all pretense of constitutional protection of state power in its *Garcia* decision.[2] Before this case it was generally believed that the states were constitutionally protected from direct congressional coercion in matters traditionally "reserved" to the states. The Congress could bribe states with grant-in-aid money to enact federal programs—or threaten them with the loss of such aid if they failed to conform to federal rules—but Congress was careful to avoid direct orders to state and local governments. However, in the *Garcia* case, the Supreme Court upheld a federal law requiring state and local governments to obey federal wage and hour rules. The Court dismissed the argument that the nature of American federalism and the reserved powers clause of the Tenth Amendment prevented Congress from legislating directly in state and local affairs. The Court declared that there were no constitutionally protected state powers and that the only protection given the states is in congressional and presidential elections. This weakened view of American federalism—that there is no constitutional protection for state power other than the states' role in electing the members of Congress and the president—has been labeled *representational federalism*.

COERCIVE FEDERALISM

Traditionally, Congress avoided issuing direct orders to state and local governments. Rather, Congress sought to influence them by offering grants of money with federal rules, regulations, and "guidelines" attached. In theory, at least, state and local governments were free to forgo the money and ignore the strings attached to it. But over time, Congress has undertaken to issue direct regulations in areas traditionally reserved for the states.

Federal mandates are direct orders to state and local governments to perform a particular activity or service to comply with federal laws and performance of their functions. Federal mandates occur in a wide variety of areas, for example:

Age Discrimination Act (1986): Outlaws mandatory retirement ages
for public as well as private employees, including police, firefighters, and
state college and university faculty.

Asbestos Hazard Emergency Act (1986): Orders school districts to inspect
for asbestos hazards and remove asbestos from school buildings when necessary.

Safe Drinking Water Act (1986): Establishes national requirements
for municipal water supplies and regulates municipal waste treatment plants.

Clean Air Act (1990): Prohibits municipal incinerators and also
requires additional inspections in certain urban areas.

Americans with Disabilities Act (1990): Requires all state and local
government buildings to promote handicapped access.

Council of State Governments
Official organization of U.S. states, providing information on their governmental structures, officials, and current issues.
www.csg.org

National Voter Registration Act (1993): Requires states to register voters at driver's license, welfare, and unemployment compensation offices.

No Child Left Behind Act (2001): Requires states and their school districts to test public school pupils.

Help America Vote Act (2003): Requires states to modernize registration and voting procedures.

Real ID Act (2005): Sets national standard for drivers' licenses and requires states to link their records to a national database. (Takes effect May 2008.)

Many of these mandates impose heavy costs on state and local governments. When no federal monies are provided to cover these costs, the mandates are said to be *unfunded mandates*. Governors, mayors, and other state and local officials frequently complain about unfunded mandates.

DEVOLUTION: FEDERALISM REVIVED?

In recent years, both Congress and the Supreme Court have shown a renewed interest in federalism. In Congress this interest was reflected in the Welfare Reform Act of 1996, and in the Supreme Court it was reflected in several cases dealing with congressional powers under the interstate commerce clause of the U.S. Constitution.

WELFARE REFORM AND "DEVOLUTION"

In the 1990s, the Washington buzzword was "devolution"—the passing down of responsibilities from the national government to the states. The Welfare Reform Act of 1996 was heralded by Congress as a devolution of responsibility for welfare cash aid to the states. A new Temporary Assistance to Needy Families (TANF) federal *grant* program to the states replaced the 60-year-old Aid to Families with Dependent Children (AFDC) federal *entitlement* program of cash aid to low-income mothers and children. (After twice vetoing the act, President Bill Clinton signed it to improve his reelection chances, despite the opposition of most liberals in Washington.) And indeed, the act does grant greater responsibility to the states regarding cash welfare aid (although food stamps, Medicaid, and other aid remain as federal entitlements). States are granted broad flexibility in determining eligibility benefit levels for persons receiving cash aid. For example, states can deny additional cash payments for children born to women already receiving welfare assistance, and states can deny cash payments to parents younger than age eighteen who do not live with an adult and attend school. But conservatives in Congress added their own "strings" to TANF grants: federally aided cash grants for most recipients were limited to two continuing years and five years over their lifetime. So it appears that national elites—liberals and conservatives, Democrats and Republicans— are all prepared to add strings to federal money to advance their own ideas about welfare.

THE SUPREME COURT'S REASSERTION OF FEDERALISM

The U.S. Supreme Court has rendered several recent decisions that appear to be somewhat more respectful of the powers of the states and somewhat less accepting of their being trampled on by the national government.

In 1995, the Supreme Court held that the politically popular Gun Free School Zone Act exceeded the constitutionally delegated powers of Congress. It was the first High Court opinion in more than sixty years that recognized limits on the national government's power over interstate commerce. The Justice Department had argued that keeping schools gun free would reduce crime and that the reduction in crime would facilitate interstate commerce. The Court rejected this argument, holding that such tenuous reasoning would remove virtually all limits to federal power: "To uphold the Government's contention here, we would have to pile inference upon inference in a manner that would convert congressional authority under the Commerce Clause to a general police power of the sort retained by the states."[3]

In another victory for federalism, the Supreme Court invalidated a provision of a popular law of Congress—the Brady Handgun Violence Protection Act. The Court decided in 1997 that this law's command to local law enforcement officers to conduct background checks on gun purchasers violated "the very principle of separate state sovereignty."[4] Then in 1999 the Supreme Court held that states were shielded in their own courts from lawsuits in which private parties seek to enforce federal mandates. In an opinion that surveyed the history of American federalism, Justice Kennedy wrote: "Congress has vast power but not all power.... When Congress legislates in matters affecting the states it may not treat these sovereign entities as mere prefectures or corporations."[5] And in 2000 the Supreme Court surprised Congress and challenged public opinion by holding that the Violence Against Women Act also invaded the reserved police powers of the states. "The Constitution requires a distinction between what is truly national and what is truly local."[6]

National Conference of State Legislatures This Web site provides information on fifty state legislatures and the issues they confront. *www.ncsl.org*

However, all these recent Supreme Court rulings reaffirming federalism have come in narrow 5 to 4 decisions. The closeness of these votes, together with the fact that these decisions contrast with more than a half century of Court support for national power, provide no guarantee that the Court or the nation will continue to move in the direction of strengthening federalism.

MASS INFLUENCE IN THE STATES

Potentially, the masses can exercise more direct influence in state politics than in national politics. This is true despite the facts that voters' knowledge about state and local politics is less than their knowledge of national politics and voter participation in state and local elections is lower than that in national elections. But unlike national politics, the masses in state and local politics have access to the initiative and referendum—provisions found in the constitutions of eighteen states. They also have access to the recall—provisions found in the constitutions of sixteen states (see Table 14.2).

The U.S. Constitution has no provision for national referenda. Americans cannot vote on federal laws or amendments to the U.S. Constitution. The nation's Founders were profoundly skeptical of "direct democracy"—the people themselves initiating and deciding policy questions by popular vote. The Founders believed that government ultimately rested on the consent of the governed. But their notion of "republicanism" envisioned decision making by representatives of the people, not the people themselves.

TABLE 14.2 | INITIATIVE AND RECALL IN THE STATES

Initiative for Constitutional Amendments (Signatures Required to Get on Ballot)*	Recall (Signatures Required to Force a Recall Election)†
Arizona (15%)	Alaska (25%)
Arkansas (10%)	Arizona (25%)
California (8%)	California (12%)
Colorado (5%)	Colorado (25%)
Florida (8%)	Georgia (15%)
Illinois (8%)	Idaho (20%)
Massachusetts (3%)	Kansas (40%)
Michigan (10%)	Louisiana (33%)
Mississippi (12%)	Michigan (25%)
Missouri (8%)	Montana (10%)
Montana (10%)	Nevada (25%)
Nebraska (10%)	North Dakota (25%)
Nevada (10%)	Oregon (15%)
North Dakota (4% of state population)	Rhode Island (15%)
Ohio (10%)	Washington (25%)
Oklahoma (15%)	Wisconsin (25%)
Oregon (8%)	
South Dakota (10%)	

*Figures expressed as percentage of vote in last governor's election.
†Figures are percentages of voters in last general election of the official sought to be recalled.
Source: Book of the States, 2005–2006.

THE POPULIST MOVEMENT IN THE STATES

At the beginning of the twentieth century a strong populist movement in the midwestern and western states attacked railroads, banks, corporations, and the political institutions that were said to be in their pockets. The people believed that their elected representatives were ignoring the needs of farmers, debtors, and laborers. They wished to bypass governors and legislatures and directly enact popular laws for railroad rate regulation, relief of farm debt, and monetary expansion. The populists were largely responsible for replacing party conventions with the primary elections we use today. They were also successful in bringing about the Seventeenth Amendment to the U.S. Constitution, which requires that U.S. senators be directly elected by the voters rather than chosen by state legislatures. Finally, the populists were responsible for the widespread adoption of three forms of direct democracy: the initiative, the referendum, and the recall.

THE INITIATIVE   The initiative is a device by which a specific number or percentage of voters, through the use of a petition, can have a proposed state constitutional amendment or state law placed on the ballot for adoption or rejection by the voters of a state. This process bypasses the legislature and allows citizens to propose laws and constitutional amendments.

THE REFERENDUM   The referendum is a device by which the electorate must approve either a decision of the legislature or a citizen-proposed initiative before it becomes law. The initiative and the referendum go hand-in-hand to allow citizens to directly alter the laws or constitution of their state.

THE RECALL   Recall elections allow voters to remove elected officials before their term expires. The recall election is initiated by a petition. The number of signatures required is usually expressed as a percentage of the votes cast in the last election for the official being recalled. Recall petitions are rarely successful. But one of the most celebrated successful recalls was the 2003 recall of California governor Gray Davis and his replacement by Arnold Schwarzenegger (see Focus: Arnold: From Bodybuilder to Superstar to Governor).

THE POLITICS OF STATE INITIATIVES

State initiatives have generally reflected mass attitudes rather than elites' preferences. Among the more popular initiatives in recent years are limiting terms for public officials, banning same-sex marriages, limiting taxes of various kinds, making English the official language, allowing gambling, allowing marijuana for medicinal purposes, prohibiting state funds for abortion, and allowing physician-assisted suicide.

Of course, citizen initiatives are often backed by "special interests"—specific businesses or industries, labor unions, government employees, religious organizations, the gambling industry, and so on. In other words, many initiative movements are not really initiated by individual citizens. Often a great deal of money is spent for paid workers to gather the necessary signatures and then later to promote the initiative on television and radio and in newspaper advertisements.

The masses overwhelmingly support the initiative process. Most elites bitterly oppose it. Indeed, nearly two-thirds of Americans say that it is a good idea to let citizens place issues directly on the ballot:

QUESTION: *Many states have laws that allow citizens to place initiatives directly on the ballot by collecting petition signatures. If the initiative is approved by voters on election day, it becomes law. Is this a good idea?*[7]

Yes	64%
No	17
Not sure	19

Yet despite the popularity of the initiative process, legislators in a majority of states have managed to stave off granting initiative rights to their citizens.

| FOCUS | ARNOLD: FROM BODYBUILDER TO SUPERSTAR TO GOVERNOR |

Arnold's message to California Governor Gray Davis: "Hasta la vista, baby!" In 2003, Davis became only the second governor in history to be recalled by the voters. Arnold himself had never held political office. He had risen from an impoverished immigrant who barely spoke English, to champion bodybuilder, to world-famous movie star, to Kennedy family in-law, to governor of America's largest state.

Sixteen states include recall provisions in their constitutions: petitions signed by a specified number of voters (12 percent in California) force incumbent officials to face the voters and risk being ousted before the end of their term. Petition drives for a California governor's recall had failed on thirty-one previous occasions; even Governor Ronald Reagan faced three recall attempts.

So what did Gray Davis do to deserve ouster only one year after his reelection to a second term? Unlike impeachment, a successful recall does not require specific charges of malfeasance or criminal conduct in office. Voters can recall an officeholder for any reason or for no reason. But Davis was particularly inept: he failed to act decisively during California's electricity blackouts of 2000 and 2001, which resulted in higher utility bills; he engaged in reckless spending despite an economic downturn and consequently drowned the state in red ink; and perhaps most enraging to voters, he tripled the car license tax.

Arnold's father had been a local police chief in Austria and a Nazi Party member before World War II. Arnold donated hundreds of thousands of dollars to the Simon Wiesenthal Center, a Jewish human rights organization, and asked the Center to investigate his father's activities. The Center found no evidence that his father had committed any war crimes.

Arnold spent his teenage years developing his body in the hope of one day becoming Mr. Universe. At age twenty he fulfilled his dream and then came to America to pursue his second goal, to become a movie actor. His 1982 *Conan the Barbarian* became a

cult classic; in 1984, he starred in *The Terminator* and later made two sequels.

Arnold revealed an interest in politics by becoming involved with the Special Olympics and serving on President George H. W. Bush's council on physical fitness. In 2002, he sponsored a California initiative to spend more money for before- and afterschool programs. He offered few specifics in his campaign for governor: "I am a man of the people." "We have tough choices ahead." "For the people to win, politics as usual must lose." When the liberal *Los Angeles Times* charged Arnold with "groping" women on movie sets, Arnold's wife, television personality Maria Shriver, came to his defense. His poll numbers actually went up following the charges. Davis lost the recall vote 54 to 46 percent. Arnold won 48 percent of the vote in the 135-candidate race. Later he would try to use the referenda to enact policies that the Democratic-controlled legislature had refused to pass, including a proposal to reduce the influence of public employee unions. Schwarzenegger lost that referenda battle, and his approval ratings dropped.

Yet the "Terminator" proved resilient, winning reelection in 2006 with a comfortable 56 percent of the vote. His victory enhanced his political influence nationwide. (But because Schwarzenegger is not a natural born U.S. citizen, he is barred by the Constitution from becoming president). He abandoned his partisan attacks on the Democratic legislature and transformed himself into a consensus-builder. He negotiated agreements on an increase in the state minimum wage, increases in school spending, and cutting air pollution and saving energy. He threatened to sue the federal government if it did not allow California to raise requirements for fuel economy in new cars. (He customized his 800 horsepower Hummer into an environmentally clean vehicle.) He restructured his image as an independent-minded governor: "I'm for the people."

THE OLD-COMMUNITY ECONOMIC ELITES

Most of the nation's economic resources are controlled by *national* institutions—industrial corporations, banks, utilities, insurance companies, investment firms, and the national government. Most of the forces shaping life in American communities

| FOCUS | CORPORATE ELITE STRUCTURES IN THE STATES |

Cohesive elite structures are more likely to emerge in states in which relatively few major industrial corporations are located. The following table lists the number of corporations in the Fortune 500 in each state. Some states have no large corporation located in them: Alaska, Hawaii, Montana, New Mexico, North Dakota, Vermont, and Wyoming. This indicates that no large national corporation locates its home office there. Nonetheless, these states, because of their mostly rural, nondiversified economies, are likely to have fairly cohesive elite

structures. Likewise, the states with only a few major corporations (Arkansas, for instance, with Wal-Mart and Dillard's retail store headquarters and Tyson's chicken processing) are also likely to have relatively unified elite structures.

In contrast, states with large numbers of corporations engaged in a wide variety of industrial activities are likely to have plural elite structures. California and New York, for example, are too large and diversified and house too many top-ranked corporations to be dominated by a unified elite.

TYPES OF ELITE STRUCTURES (RANKED BY NUMBER OF MAJOR INDUSTRIAL HEADQUARTERS LOCATED IN THE STATE)

Likely Plural Elite Structures

| California | 53 | Texas | 44 | Ohio | 29 | Michigan | 24 |
| New York | 41 | Illinois | 34 | Pennsylvania | 26 | New Jersey | 23 |

Likely Increasingly Diversified Elite Structures

Minnesota	19	Georgia	16	Florida	13	Washington	10
Virginia	18	Massachusetts	14	Missouri	12	Wisconsin	10
Connecticut	17	North Carolina	14				

Likely Dominant Elite among Lesser Elites

| Colorado | 8 | Indiana | 6 | Maryland | 6 | Nebraska | 5 |
| Tennessee | 7 | Kentucky | 6 | Arkansas | 5 | Oklahoma | 4 |

Likely Unified Elite Structures

Arizona	3	Iowa	2	Oregon	1	Montana	0
Nevada	3	Louisiana	2	South Carolina	1	New Mexico	0
Alabama	2	Rhode Island	2	Utah	1	North Dakota	0
Delaware	2	Kansas	1	Alaska	0	Vermont	0
Idaho	2	New Hampshire	1	Hawaii	0	Wyoming	0

Source: Authors' count from data supplied in *Fortune*, April 5, 2004.

arise outside these communities; community leaders cannot make war or peace or cause inflation or recession or determine interest rates or the money supply. But there is one economic resource—land—that is controlled by *community* elites. Land is a valuable resource: capital investment, labor and management, and production must be placed somewhere.

Traditionally, community power structures were composed primarily of landed interests whose goal was to intensify the use of their land and add to its value. These community elites sought to maximize land values, real estate commissions, builders' profits, rent payments, and mortgage interest and to increase revenues to commercial enterprises serving the community. Communities were traditionally dominated by mortgage lending banks, real estate developers, builders, and landowners. They were joined by owners or managers of local utilities, department stores, attorneys and title companies, and others whose wealth is affected by land use. Local bankers who financed the real estate developers and builders were often at the center of the elite structure. Unquestionably, these community elites competed among themselves for wealth, profit, power, and preeminence. But they shared a consensus about intensifying the use of land.

Growth was the shared elite value. The old-community elite was indeed a "growth machine."[8] The old-community elite believed that capital investment in the community would raise land values, expand the labor force, generate demand for housing and commercial services, and enhance the local tax base. Attracting investors required the provision of good transportation facilities—highways, streets, rail access, and water and airport facilities. It required the provision of utilities—water, gas and electrical power, solid-waste disposal, and sewage treatment. It required the provision of good municipal services, especially fire and police protection; the elimination of harassing business regulations and the reduction of taxes on new investments to the lowest feasible levels; the provision of a capable and cooperative labor force educated for the needs of productive capital and motivated to work; and, finally, the provision of sufficient amenities—cultural, recreational, aesthetic—to provide the corporate managers with a desirable lifestyle.

Traditional community elites strove for consensus. They believed that community economic growth—increased capital investment, more jobs, and improved business conditions—benefited the entire community. According to Paul E. Peterson, community residents share a common interest in the economic well-being of the city: "Policies and programs can be said to be in the interest of cities whenever the policies maintain or enhance the economic position, social prestige, or political power of the city as a whole."[9] Economic elites themselves would have agreed with Peterson.

Local government officials were expected to share in the elite consensus. Economic prosperity was necessary to protect the fiscal base of local government. Growth in local budgets and public employment and in governmental services depends on growth in the local economy. Governmental growth expanded the power, prestige, and status of government officials. Moreover, economic growth was usually good politics. Growth-oriented candidates for public office usually had larger campaign treasuries than antigrowth candidates. Finally, according to Peterson, most local politicians had "a sense of community responsibility." They knew that if the economy of the community declines, "local business will suffer, workers will lose employment opportunities, cultural life will decline, and city land values will fall."[10]

<hr>

FOCUS | ## Mayor Rudy Giuliani

In the aftermath of the terrorist attack of September 11, 2001, New York City Mayor Rudy Giuliani led his city—and the nation—through a horrendous period of turmoil. His efforts inspired *Time* magazine to name him Person of the Year. When major crises, from natural disasters to terrorist attacks, strike at the United States, it is state and local elites who bear the initial responsibility for crisis management.

As the grandson of Italian immigrants, Giuliani rose from Catholic high school in Brooklyn, through Manhattan College in the Bronx, to New York University Law School, graduating magna cum laude in 1968. He served in various federal prosecutor positions prior to being appointed U.S. attorney for the Southern District of New York in 1983, where he earned a reputation as a hard-nosed prosecutor of white-collar criminals. He lost a race for mayor of New York City in 1989 but came back to win that post in 1993.

As New York's Mayor, Giuliani quickly established himself as a leader who would govern a city previously declared "ungovernable" by scholars and commentators. He introduced the "broken windows" crime-fighting strategy to the city, then ranked among the most crime-ridden in the nation. He insisted on arrests for petty offenses (such as subway turnstile jumping, graffiti, vandalism, and aggressive panhandling) in order not only to improve the quality of life in the city but also to lead to the capture of suspects wanted for more serious crimes. The strategy was coupled with the use of the latest computer mapping technology to track crime statistics and pinpoint unusual activity in specific neighborhoods. The introduction of these hard-line tactics created more than a little controversy among civil libertarians and many minority group leaders. But over a five-year period the city's overall crime rate fell by an unprecedented 57 percent and murders fell by 65 percent. New York City became the safest big city in the country. Although a Republican in an overwhelmingly Democratic city, Giuliani was reelected in 1997 by a wide margin.

On September 11, 2001, Giuliani raced to the World Trade Center Towers even before the second plane hit. He was nearly trapped inside a makeshift command center when the towers imploded. He then led a platoon of city officials threw ash and smoke to set up a new command center. He took to the airwaves to calm and reassure New Yorkers and made hundreds of rapid-fire decisions about security and rescue operations. His charismatic presence, compassionate words, and reassuring messages won him the acclamation "Mayor of the World."[a]

<hr>

[a]*Time,* January 7, 2002.

<hr>

THE NEW-COMMUNITY POLITICAL ELITES

Today, in many American communities, the old economic elites have been replaced by new political elites. Many of the old economic elites sold their businesses to national corporations and vacated their positions of community leadership. Locally owned stores and factories became manager-directed plants and chain stores. The result was a weakening of community loyalties in the business sector. The new corporate managers could easily decide, in response to national economic conditions, to close the local plant or store with minimal concern for the impact on the community. Local banks were merged into national banking corporations, and local bankers were replaced by banking executives with few community ties. City newspapers that were once independently owned by families who lived in the communities were bought up by giant newspaper and publication chains. Instead of editors and reporters who expected to live the lives of their communities, city newspapers came to be staffed with people who hope to move up in the corporate hierarchy—people who strive primarily to advance their own careers, not the interests of the local community.

The nationalization of the U.S. economy and the resulting demise of locally owned enterprises created a vacuum of leadership in community affairs. Professional politicians moved into this vacuum in city after city, largely replacing the local bankers, real estate developers, chambers of commerce, and old-style newspaper editors who had dominated community politics for generations. The earlier economic elites were only part-time politicians who used local government to promote their economic interests. The new professional political elites work full-time at local politics. They are drawn primarily by personal ambition, not so much for the wealth as for the power and celebrity that accompany running for and winning public office. They are not "screened" by economic elites or political parties; rather, they nominate themselves, raise their own funds, organize their own campaigns, and create their own publicity.

The political elites are independent entrepreneurs. They win office "by selling themselves to the voters, in person, one at a time, day after day. People who do not like to do this, people who do not like to knock on strangers' doors or who find it tedious to repeat the same thirty-second personal introduction thousands of times, are at a severe disadvantage."[11] Thus, over time, these full-time political elites drive out the part-time economic elites.

The new political elites seldom have a large financial stake in the community, aside from their homes. They are *not* corporate leaders or bankers or developers. They may be lawyers, but they are not highly successful lawyers from prestigious law firms; rather, they are "political activists with law degrees."[12] They are not strongly committed to the community's economic growth. They do not necessarily seek community consensus on behalf of prosperity.

On the contrary, it's fashionable among new political elites to complain loudly about the problems created by growth—congestion, pollution, noise, unsightly development, or the replacement of green spaces with concrete slabs. No-growth movements appeal to people who already own their houses and do not intend to sell them, people whose jobs are secure in government bureaucracies or tenured professorships, people who may be displaced from their homes and neighborhoods by new facilities, and people who see no direct benefit to themselves from growth. These no-growth movements (or, to use the current euphemism, "growth-management" movements) are *not* mass movements. They do *not* express the aspirations of workers for jobs or renters for their own homes. Instead, they reflect the upper-middle-class lifestyle preferences of educated, affluent, articulate homeowners. Growth brings ugly factories, cheap commercial outlets, hamburger stands, fried chicken franchises, and "undesirable" residents. Even if new business or industry would help hold down local taxes, these affluent citizens would still oppose it, preferring to retain the appearance or lifestyle of their communities.

New political elites waving the no-growth banner challenge traditional economic elites in many large and growing cities in the West and South. The no-growth leaders may themselves have been beneficiaries of community growth only five or ten years ago, but they quickly perceive their own political interest in slowing or halting additional growth.

Halting or curtailing growth serves the financial interest of homeowners, apartment owners, and owners of already developed commercial property. Curtailing growth serves to freeze out competition from new homes, apartment complexes, and commercial centers. It allows owners of existing homes and properties to raise

| **IN BRIEF** | ## The Shift in Community Power |

Community power has been shifting from traditional economic elites to newer political elites.

Traditional community power structures include mortgage lending banks, real estate developers, builders, and landowners, along with attorneys and title companies and others whose wealth was affected by land use decisions. Growth was the shared elite value. Consensus existed on community economic growth—increased capital investment, more jobs, and improved business conditions, all assumed to benefit the entire community. Governmental elites reflected the consensus of economic elites.

Today, in many American communities, old economic elites are being replaced by new political elites. Traditional local economic elites are being displaced by national managers of plants and chain

stores, weakening the community loyalties of the business sector. Professional political actors are moving into this vacuum, largely replacing the local bankers, real estate developers, chambers of commerce, and old-style newspaper editors who dominated community politics for generations. Aside from the value of their own homes, these new political elites seldom have much financial stake in the community. They are frequently opposed to economic growth and the problems it creates—congestion, pollution, noise, unsightly development, and environmental problems. No-growth movements appeal to people who already own their own houses, whose jobs are secure, and who see no direct benefit to themselves from economic growth.

prices and rents to new residents. It is no surprise that "neighborhood associations" led by upper- and upper-middle-class homeowners are at the forefront of no-growth politics.

Municipal government offers the tools to challenge the old growth elites. Communities may restrict growth through zoning laws, subdivision control restrictions, utility regulations, building permits, and environmental regulations. Opposition to street widening, road building, or tree cutting can slow or halt development. Public utilities needed for development—water lines, sewage disposal facilities, fire houses, and so on—can be postponed indefinitely. High development fees, "impact fees," utility hookup charges, and building permit fees can all be used to discourage growth. Environmental laws and even historic preservation laws can be employed aggressively to halt development.

FEDERALISM: AN ELITIST INTERPRETATION

The existence of political subelites within the larger American political system permits some decentralization of decision making. Decentralization, or decision making by subelites, reduces potential strain on the consensus of national elites. Each subelite group sets its own policies in its own state and community, without battling over a single national policy to be applied uniformly throughout the land. The following propositions summarize our consideration of American federalism and our comparative analysis of elites in states and communities.

1. American federalism divides power constitutionally between national and state governments, each of which can directly enforce its own laws on individuals through its own courts. The Constitution itself cannot be amended without the consent of the national government (two-thirds of both houses of Congress) and the states (three-fourths of the legislatures).

2. Over time, however, power has centralized in Washington owing to (1) a broad interpretation of the "necessary and proper" clause granting the national government the power to do anything not specifically prohibited by the Constitution, (2) the victory of the national government in the Civil War, (3) the establishment of a national system of civil rights, (4) the growth of national power under the interstate commerce clause, and (5) the growth of federal grants-in-aid to state and local governments.

3. The principal instrument of national power in states and communities is the federal "grant-in-aid." Federal grants now provide about 25 percent of all state and local government revenue. Federal rules, regulations, and guidelines accompanying the grants give the federal government great power over the activity of local governments.

4. Despite some efforts to return power to states and communities, power continues to flow toward national elites. The Supreme Court, in its *Garcia* decision, removed all constitutional protections for state power, other than the states' role in electing the members of Congress and the president.

5. Congress turned to the "devolution" of responsibility for cash welfare payments from the federal government to the states in the Welfare Reform Act of 1996. The Supreme Court reversed the direction of its holdings expanding federal power in several recent cases in which it held that Congress had exceeded its "delegated" powers. It remains to be seen whether these trends toward restoring federalism will continue.

6. Traditional community power structures concern themselves with economic growth. These community power structures are dominated by banks, real estate developers, builders, and landowners, all of whom benefit directly from increasing the value of land. These power structures mobilize mass support for local growth policies by promising more jobs.

7. New community political elites have arisen in many cities to replace old community economic elites. As the economy nationalized, locally owned businesses, banks, and newspapers were replaced by national corporations and chains, whose managers have fewer ties to community affairs. Local political elites moved into the vacuum of power. These new elites are self-nominated, full-time professional politicians.

8. The new political elites are not necessarily committed to economic growth. They frequently endorse "growth management" proposals designed to halt or curtail growth. These new elites do *not* reflect mass interests but rather the preferences of upper-middle-class, educated, articulate homeowners for avoiding noise and pollution, ugly factories, cheap commercial outlets, and "undesirable" residents.

SELECTED READINGS

Dahl, Robert A. *Who Governs?* New Haven, Conn.: Yale University Press, 1961. This classic study is perhaps the most important pluralist community power book. Using a decisional approach, Dahl finds that a variety of separate elites make decisions in different issue areas.

Dye, Thomas R., and Susan A. MacManus. *Politics in States and Communities*, 11th ed. Upper Saddle

River, N.J.: Prentice-Hall, 2003. Authoritative text on state and local politics and public policy.

Ehrenhalt, Alan. *The United States of Ambition.* New York: Time Books, 1991. A description of fundamental changes in community, state, and national politics over the last thirty years, illustrated with a series of case studies. Ehrenhalt argues that in communities across the country new professional political elites have grabbed power from the old economic elites. The new political elites nominate themselves and win elections through hard work and self-promotion. They are not committed to community prosperity so much as to their own careers.

Hunter, Floyd. *Community Power Structure.* Chapel Hill: University of North Carolina Press, 1953. Although classical elitism has its origins in European sociological theory, much of the American controversy over elitism has resulted from community power research. This book was one of the first community power studies reporting elitist results.

Nagel, Robert, F. *The Implosion of Federalism.* New York: Oxford University Press, 2001. America's political institutions are collapsing into the center, reducing the opportunities for mass participation.

Notes

1. Morton Grodzins, *The American System* (Chicago: Rand McNally, 1966), p. 265.
2. *Garcia v. San Antonio Metropolitan Authority,* 469 U.S. 528 (1985).
3. *United States v. Lopez,* 514 U.S. 549 (1995).
4. *Printz v. United States,* 521 U.S. 890 (1997).
5. *Alden v. Maine,* 67 U.S.L.W. 1401 (1999).
6. *Brzonkala v. Morrison* (May 15, 2000).
7. *Rasmussen Research,* March 3, 1998.
8. See Harvey Molotch,"The City as Growth Machine," *American Journal of Sociology,* 82 (September 1976): 309–330; and "Capital and Neighborhood in the United States," *Urban Affairs Quarterly,* 14 (March 1979): 289–312.
9. Paul E. Peterson, *City Limits* (Chicago: University of Chicago Press, 1981), p. 20.
10. Peterson, *City Limits,* p. 29.
11. Alan Ehrenhalt, *The United States of Ambition* (New York: Time Books, 1991), p. 15.
12. Ehrenhalt, *Ambition,* p. 16.

The social origins of protest leaders are rather similar to, instead of strikingly different from, the social origins of leaders of established parties with whom they clash.

Anthony Oberschall

CIVIL RIGHTS: ELITE RESPONSE TO PROTEST

People without access to the resources of interest-group politics and people whose values are substantially at odds with the prevailing public policies occasionally enter protest movements. These protest *movements* sometimes lead to the establishment of protest *organizations* designed to represent and shape mass movements. This shaping and organizing is where protest movements and the protest organizations either succeed or fail.

Established elites do not ignore protests. Rather they may (1) make symbolic gestures to pacify the active protesters (co-opting them through programs that bring protest leaders into the "system"), (2) limit protests through repression (increased law enforcement), or (3) do both simultaneously. Often elite response is a combination of accommodation and repression, with heavier doses of accommodation handed out to movements whose goals are within the general framework of elite consensus.

As organizations arise to direct the aspirations of protest movements, the advantages of accommodation increase. Protest leaders find that by moderating their demands, they can gain a portion of their original goals and also achieve for themselves and the organization a stake in the elite system. Thus, protest movements that become protest organizations eventually come to share the elite consensus.

Protest movements tend to be cyclical. Many fail to achieve organizational stability and soon fade from memory. Others successfully travel the road from protest to organization to accommodation, but the price is high. Movement toward political success requires not only accommodation to the acceptable norms of established elites but also organizational leadership by people with negotiating skills and the willingness to sustain activity for long periods of time. Protest leaders, irrespective of the movements they represent, do *not* come from the lower strata of society.

The experience of women and minorities in the United States offers instruction in how white elites have responded to protest movements over the years. Although Hispanics are

TABLE 15.1 | RACIAL AND ETHNIC GROUPS IN AMERICA

	Number	Percentage of Population
White, not Hispanic	197,840,800	67.4
Hispanic Americans	41,322,100	14.1
African Americans	37,502,300	12.3
Asian or Pacific Islander Americans	12,326,200	4.8
Native Americans, Eskimos, Aleuts	2,824,800	1.5
Total Population	293,655,400	100.0*

*The sum of populations is larger than the total because some people belong to more than one racial group.

Source: U.S. Census Bureau. www.census.gov.

now the nation's largest minority (see Table 15.1), we have chosen initially to focus on the long history of African American protest and elite response to it.

THE HISTORY OF BLACK SUBJUGATION

The place of blacks in American society has been a central issue of domestic politics in the United States since the first black slaves stepped onto these shores in 1619. The American nation as a whole, with its democratic tradition, has felt strong conflicting sentiments about slavery, segregation, and discrimination. White America has harbored an ambivalence toward blacks—a recognition of the evils of inequality but a reluctance to take steps to eliminate it. This "American dilemma" reflects the larger issue of the American masses' attitudes toward democracy: commitment to abstract ideals with substantially less commitment to their practice.[1] To a large extent, we can view the struggle of African Americans for full citizenship as a dialogue—sometimes violent, sometimes peaceful—between the demands of black counterelites and the response of dominant white elites.

ABOLITION

In 1865, the Thirteenth Amendment abolished slavery everywhere in the United States. The Fourteenth Amendment, passed in 1867 by a Republican Congress that intended to reconstruct southern society after the Civil War, made "equal protection of the laws" a command for every state to obey. The Fifteenth Amendment, passed in 1869, prohibited federal and state governments from abridging the right to vote "on account of race, color, or previous condition of servitude." In addition, Congress passed a series of civil rights statutes in the 1860s and 1870s guaranteeing newly freed African Americans protection in the exercise of their constitutional rights. The Civil Rights Act of 1875 specifically outlawed segregation by privately owned businesses offering to serve the public. Between 1865 and the early 1880s, the success of the civil rights movement was evident in widespread black voting throughout the South, the presence of many blacks in federal and state offices, and the almost equal treatment afforded blacks in theaters, restaurants, hotels, and public transportation.

THE RISE OF WHITE SUPREMACY

By 1877, support for Reconstruction policies began to crumble. In what was labeled the Compromise of 1877, the national government agreed to end military occupation of the South, give up its efforts to rearrange southern society, and lend tacit approval to white supremacy in that region. In return, the southern states pledged their support to the Union, accepted national supremacy, and agreed to permit the Republican presidential candidate, Rutherford B. Hayes, to assume the presidency, although the Democratic candidate, Samuel Tilden, had received a majority of the popular vote in the disputed election of 1876. The Supreme Court adhered to the terms of this compromise. In the famous Civil Rights Cases of 1883, the Supreme Court declared unconstitutional those federal civil rights laws preventing discrimination by private individuals. By denying Congress the power to protect blacks from discrimination, the Court paved the way for the imposition of segregation as the prevailing social system of the South. In the 1880s and 1890s, white southerners imposed segregation in public accommodations, housing, education, employment, and almost every other sector of private and public life. By 1895, most southern states had passed laws *requiring* racial segregation in education and in public accommodations.

In *Plessy v. Ferguson*, in 1896, the Supreme Court upheld state laws requiring segregation. Although segregation laws involved state action, the Court held that segregating the races did not violate the equal protection clause of the Fourteenth Amendment so long as people in each race received equal treatment. Schools and other public facilities that were "separate but equal" won constitutional approval:

> *The object of the Amendment was undoubtedly to enforce the absolute equality of the two races before the law, but in the nature of things it could not have been intended to abolish distinctions based upon color or to enforce social, as distinguished from political, equality, or a commingling of the two races upon terms unsatisfactory to either. Laws permitting, and even requiring, their separation in places where they are liable to be brought into contact do not necessarily imply the inferiority of either race to the other, and have been generally, if not universally, recognized as within the competency of the state legislatures in the exercise of their police power. The most common instance of this is connected with the establishment of separate schools for white and colored children, which has been held to be a valid exercise of the legislative power.*[2]

The violence that occurred during that period was almost entirely one-sided: whites attacked blacks. The pattern of race relations at the turn of the century was clearly one of violent repression, exclusion of blacks from jobs and labor unions, and rigid segregation. African Americans lost most of what they had gained during Reconstruction.

TWENTIETH-CENTURY ELITE ATTITUDE CHANGE

The first African American organizations emerged in response to the repressive pattern of the late nineteenth century, notably, the National Association for the Advancement of Colored People (NAACP) and the National Urban League in 1909 and 1910, respectively. These organizations sought black equality through court action and other legal means. They were dominated by middle-class blacks and upper-class whites. They accepted the premise that they could effect meaningful change within the American legal system. They were conservative in that their techniques required commitment to the institutional status quo. They disavowed attempts to change or overthrow the basic political and economic structure of the society; they simply sought to integrate blacks into the existing society. In other words, they took literally the ideology and premises of the American democratic system that "all men are created equal."

BROWN V. BOARD OF EDUCATION OF TOPEKA, KANSAS

NAACP Legal Defense Fund
Founded in 1940 by Thurgood Marshall to provide legal assistance to poor African Americans. Originally affiliated with the NAACP, now a separate organization.
www.naacpldf.org

The long labors of the NAACP finally paid off in 1954 in the historic *Brown v. Board of Education of Topeka, Kansas* decision, in which the Court reversed the *Plessy v. Ferguson* doctrine of "separate but equal."

> *Segregation of white and colored children in public schools has a detrimental effect upon the colored children. The impact is greater when it has the sanction of law, for the policy of separating the races is usually interpreted as denoting the inferiority of the Negro group. A form of inferiority affects the motivation of a child to learn. Segregation with the sanction of law, therefore, has a tendency to retard the educational and mental development of Negro children and to deprive them of some of the benefits they would receive in a racially integrated school system.*[3]

Note that this first great step toward racial justice in the twentieth century was taken by the *nonelective* branch of the federal government. Nine men, secure in their positions with lifetime appointments, responded to the legal arguments of highly educated black leaders, one of whom—Thurgood Marshall—would later become a Supreme Court justice himself. The decision was made by a judicial elite, not by the people or their elected representatives.

MASS RESISTANCE TO DESEGREGATION

Although the Supreme Court had spoken forcefully in the *Brown* case in declaring segregation unconstitutional, from a political viewpoint the battle over segregation was just beginning. Segregation would remain a part of American life, regardless of its constitutionality, until effective power was brought to bear to end it. The Supreme Court, by virtue of the American system of federalism and separation of powers, has little formal power at its disposal. Congress, the president, state governors and legislatures, and even mobs of people have more power at their disposal than the federal judiciary. The Supreme Court must rely largely on the other branches of the federal government and on the states to enforce the law of the land.

In 1954, the practice of segregation was widespread and deeply ingrained in American life. Seventeen states *required* the segregation of races in public schools:

Alabama	Mississippi	Texas	Maryland
Arkansas	North Carolina	Virginia	Missouri
Florida	South Carolina	Delaware	Oklahoma
Georgia	Tennessee	Kentucky	West Virginia
Louisiana			

The U.S. Congress required school segregation in Washington, D.C. Four other states (Arizona, Kansas, New Mexico, and Wyoming) authorized segregation at local option. Unless the national political elite directly challenged the political power of the white majority in the South, the pattern of segregation was unlikely to change.

Initially, the Supreme Court placed primary responsibility for enforcing its decision on local officials and school boards, in effect returning power to the white subelites in the South. As a result, the white South developed many schemes to resist integration. Ten years after *Brown*, only about 2 percent of the blacks in the South attended integrated schools; the other 98 percent remained in segregated schools. In short, for a decade the decision meant little to the overwhelming majority of blacks, whose frustrations intensified as they saw the discrepancy between the Supreme Court's intent and the behavior of local officials.

PRESIDENTIAL USE OF FORCE

The historic *Brown* decision might have been rendered meaningless had President Dwight Eisenhower not decided to use military force in 1957 to secure the enforcement of a federal court order to desegregate Little Rock's Central High School. Governor Orval Faubus had posted state units of the Arkansas National Guard at the high school to prevent federal marshals from carrying out federal court orders to admit black students. President Eisenhower officially called the Arkansas National Guard units into federal service, ordered them to leave the high school, and replaced them with units of the U.S. 101st Airborne Division under orders to enforce desegregation. Eisenhower had not publicly spoken on behalf of desegregation, but the direct threat to national power posed by a state governor caused the president to assert the power of the national elite. President John F. Kennedy also used federal troops to enforce desegregation at the University of Mississippi in 1962.

CREATIVE DISORDER

THE MONTGOMERY BUS BOYCOTT

The King Center
Biography of Martin Luther King Jr., together with news and information from the Atlanta King Center.
http://thekingcenter. com

In 1955, an African American woman, Rosa Parks, refused to ride in the back of a bus in Montgomery, Alabama. Her act brought about the Montgomery boycott in which blacks refused to use the public transportation system until they could sit wherever they preferred; this action was the first significant step away from the NAACP's legalism. The Montgomery bus boycott, however, also required mass-oriented leadership. A young African American minister named Martin Luther King Jr. gained instant national prominence through the bus boycott and provided overall leadership in the struggle to eliminate discrimination and segregation from private life. King's father was the pastor of one of the South's largest and most influential congregations, the Ebenezer Baptist Church in Atlanta, Georgia. Martin Luther King Jr. received his doctorate from Boston University and began his ministry in Montgomery, Alabama. The dramatic appeal and the eventual success of the boycott in Montgomery brought King nationwide attention and led to the creation in 1957 of the Southern Christian Leadership Conference (SCLC).

The SCLC emerged in 1957 as the first southern-oriented civil rights group. Although substantially more militant than the older black organizations, it was nevertheless explicitly nonviolent. The purposes of mass demonstrations were to challenge the legality of both legal and de facto segregation and to prick the conscience of white elites.

NONVIOLENT DIRECT ACTION

Under King's leadership, the civil rights movement developed and refined political techniques for minorities in American politics, including nonviolent direct action, a form of protest that involves breaking "unjust" laws in an open, "loving," nonviolent fashion. The general notion of civil disobedience is not new; it has played an important role in American history, from the Boston Tea Party to the abolitionists who illegally hid runaway slaves, to the suffragettes who demonstrated for women's voting rights, to the labor organizers who formed the nation's major industrial unions, to the civil rights workers of the early 1960s, who deliberately violated segregation laws. The purpose of the nonviolent direct action is to call attention, or to "bear witness," to the existence of injustice. In the words of King, civil disobedience "seeks to dramatize the issue so that it can no longer be ignored."[4]

There was to be no violence in true civil disobedience, and only "unjust" laws were broken. Moreover, the law was to be broken "openly, lovingly" and with a willingness to accept the penalty. Punishment was actively sought rather than avoided because it helped to emphasize the injustice of the law. The object was to stir the conscience of an elite and win support for measures that would eliminate the injustices. Willingly accepting punishment for the violation of an unjust law demonstrated the strength of conviction. The dramatization of injustice made news; the public's sympathy was won when injustices were spotlighted; and the willingness of demonstrators to accept punishment was visible evidence of their sincerity. Cruelty or violence directed against the demonstrators by police or others played into the hands of protesters by further emphasizing the injustices they were experiencing.

It is important to note that King's tactics relied primarily on an appeal to the conscience of white elites. The purpose of demonstrations was to call attention to injustice and stimulate established elites to remedy the injustice by lawful means. The purpose of civil disobedience was to dramatize injustice; only *unjust* laws were to be broken "openly and lovingly," and punishment was accepted to demonstrate sincerity. King did *not* urge black masses to remedy injustice themselves by any means necessary, and he did *not* urge the overthrow of established elites.

In 1964, Martin Luther King received the Nobel Peace Prize in recognition of his unique contributions to the development of nonviolent methods of social change.

"I HAVE A DREAM"

The culmination of the nonviolent philosophy was a giant, yet orderly, march on Washington, held on August 28, 1963. More than 200,000 blacks and whites participated in the march, which was endorsed by many labor leaders, religious groups, and political figures. The march ended at the Lincoln Memorial, where King delivered his most eloquent appeal, titled "I Have a Dream":

> *I have a dream. It is a dream deeply rooted in the American dream. I have a dream that one day this nation will rise up and live out the true meaning of its creed: We hold these truths to be self-evident that all men are created equal.*

In response, President Kennedy sent a civil rights bill to Congress, which was passed after his assassination—a bill that became the Civil Rights Act of 1964.

THE CIVIL RIGHTS ACT OF 1964

The Civil Rights Act of 1964 passed both houses of Congress by better than a two-thirds favorable vote; it won the overwhelming support of both Republican and Democratic members of Congress. It was signed into law on July 4, 1964. It ranks with the Emancipation Proclamation, the Fourteenth Amendment, and *Brown v. Board of Education of Topeka, Kansas* as one of the most important steps toward full equality for blacks in America. Among its most important provisions are the following:

U.S. Commission on Civil Rights
National clearing-house on information regarding discrimination because of race, color, religion, sex, age, disability, or national origin. Publishes reports, findings, and recommendations.
www.usccr.gov

Title II: It is unlawful to discriminate or segregate persons on the grounds of race, color, religion, or national origin in any public accommodation, including hotels, motels, restaurants, movies, theaters, sports arenas, entertainment houses, and other places that offer to serve the public. This prohibition extends to all establishments whose operations affect interstate commerce or whose discriminatory practices are supported by state action.

Title VI: Each federal department and agency shall take action to end discrimination in all programs or activities receiving federal financial assistance in any form. This action shall include termination of financial assistance.

Title VII: It shall be unlawful for any employer or labor union to discriminate against any individual in any fashion in employment because of his race, color, religion, sex, or national origin, and that an Equal Employment Opportunity Commission shall be established to enforce this provision by investigation, conference, conciliation, persuasion, and if need be, civil action in federal court.

The Civil Rights Act of 1964 brought about tangible gains for southern blacks. The withdrawal of federal grant-in-aid money as a sanction was a remarkable innovation in federal enforcement of civil rights. When the U.S. Office of Education began to apply pressure in the South, its progress was impressive compared with that of the preceding ten years.

RACIAL INEQUALITY AND AFFIRMATIVE ACTION

The gains of the early civil rights movement were primarily gains in *opportunity* rather than in *results*. Racial politics today centers on the actual inequalities between whites and minorities in incomes, jobs, housing, health, education, and other conditions of life.

TABLE 15.2 | MINORITY LIFE CHANCES

	1970	1985	1995	2005
Median Income of Families				
White	$10,236	$29,152	$36,822	$56,700
Black	6,279	16,786	23,059	35,158
Hispanic	(NA)	19,027	23,535	35,401
Percentage of Persons below Poverty Level				
White	9.7%	11.4%	11.2%	10.8%
Black	31.3	31.3	29.3	24.7
Hispanic	26.9	29.0	30.3	21.9
Unemployment Rate				
White	6.3%	6.2%	4.7%	4.4%
Black	14.3	15.1	10.5	10.0
Hispanic	10.1	10.5	8.9	6.0

Source: *Statistical Abstract of the United States 2007*, p. 449, 459, 396.

CONTINUING INEQUALITIES

The problem of inequality is often posed as differences in the "life chances" of whites and minorities (see Table 15.2). The average income of a black family is only 65 percent of the average white household income. More than 24 percent of black families are below the recognized poverty line, whereas less than 11 percent of whites live in poverty. The black unemployment rate is more than twice as high as the white unemployment rate. The civil rights movement of the 1960s opened up new opportunities for black Americans, but equality of opportunity is not the same as equality of results.

OPPORTUNITY VERSUS RESULTS

Most Americans are concerned more with equality of opportunity than with equality of results. Equality of opportunity refers to the ability to make of oneself what one can, to develop one's talents and abilities, and to be rewarded for work, initiative, and achievement. It means that everyone comes to the same starting line with the same chance of success, that whatever differences develop over time are a result of abilities, talents, initiative, hard work, and perhaps good luck. Equality of results refers to the equal sharing of income, jobs, contracts, and material rewards, regardless of ability, talent, initiative, or work.

What public policies should be pursued to achieve equality? Is it sufficient that government eliminate discrimination, guarantee equality of opportunity to blacks and whites, and apply color-blind standards to both groups? Or should government take action to overcome the results of past unequal treatment of blacks: preferential or compensatory treatment that will favor black applicants for university admission and scholarships, job hiring and promotion, and other opportunities for advancement in life?

Increasingly, the goal of the civil rights movement has shifted from the traditional goal of *equality of opportunity* to one of affirmative action to establish goals and timetables to achieve *equality of results*. Although usually avoiding the term *quota*, affirmative action tests the success of equal employment opportunity by observing whether certain groups achieve admissions, jobs, and promotions in proportion to their numbers in the population, and it allows for preferential or compensatory treatment to overcome the results of past discrimination.

The constitutional question posed by affirmative action programs is whether they discriminate against whites in violation of the equal protection clause of the Fourteenth Amendment. Clearly, this is a question for the Supreme Court to resolve, but unfortunately the Court has failed to develop a clear-cut answer.

THE BAKKE CASE

In an early case, *Regents of the University of California v. Bakke* (1978), the Supreme Court struck down a special admissions program for minorities at a state medical school on the grounds that it excluded a white applicant because of his race and violated his rights under the equal protection clause.[5] Allan Bakke had applied to the University of California Davis Medical School two consecutive years and was rejected; in both years black applicants with significantly lower grade-point averages and medical aptitude test scores were accepted through a special admissions program that reserved sixteen minority places in a class of one hundred. The University of California did not deny that its admissions decisions were based on race. Instead, it argued that the objective of its racial classification was "benign," that is, designed to assist minorities, not to hinder them. The Supreme Court held that this objective was legitimate and that race and ethnic origin may be considered in reviewing applications to a state school without violating the equal protection clause. However, the Court also held that a separate admissions program for minorities with a specified quota of openings that were unavailable to white applicants did violate the equal protection clause. The Court ordered Bakke admitted to medical school and the elimination of the special admissions program. It recommended that California consider developing an admissions program that considered disadvantaged racial or ethnic background as a "plus" in an overall evaluation of an application but did not set numerical quotas or exclude any persons from competing for all positions.

AFFIRMATIVE ACTION AS A REMEDY FOR PAST DISCRIMINATION

The Supreme Court is willing to approve affirmative action programs where there is evidence of past discriminatory actions. In *United States v. Paradise* (1987), the Court upheld a rigid 50 percent black quota system for promotions in the Alabama Department of Safety, which had excluded blacks from the ranks of state troopers before 1972 and had not promoted any blacks higher than corporal before 1984. In a 5 to 4 decision, the majority stressed the long history of discrimination in the agency as a reason for upholding the quota system. Whatever burdens were imposed on innocent parties were outweighed by the need to correct the effects of past discrimination.[6]

SUPREME COURT POLICY

Affirmative action programs are more likely to be found constitutional when:

- They are adopted in response to a past history of discrimination.
- They are narrowly tailored to remedy the effects of previous discrimination.

- They serve a legitimate and important social or educational objective.
- They do not absolutely bar whites or men from competing or participating.

LIMITS ON AFFIRMATIVE ACTION

However, in the absence of past discrimination, the Supreme Court has expressed concern about whites who are directly and adversely affected by government action solely because of their race. In *Firefighters Local Union v. Stotts* (1984), the Court ruled that a city could not lay off white firefighters in favor of black firefighters with less seniority.[7] In *Richmond v. Crosen* (1989), the Court held that a minority set-aside program in Richmond, Virginia, which mandated that 30 percent of all city construction contracts must go to "blacks, Spanish-speaking, Orientals, Indians, Eskimos, or Aleuts," violated the equal protection clause of the Fourteenth Amendment.[8]

It is important to note that the Supreme Court has never adopted the color-blind doctrine, first espoused by Justice Harlan in his dissent from *Plessy v. Ferguson*, that "Our Constitution is colorblind, and neither knows nor tolerates classes among citizens." If the equal protection clause required that the laws of the United States and the states be truly color blind, then no racial guidelines, goals, or quota would be tolerated. Occasionally, this view has been expressed in minority dissents.[9]

The Court has held that racial classifications in law must be subject to "strict scrutiny." This means that race-based actions by government—any disparate treatment of the races by federal, state, or local public agencies—must be found necessary to remedy past proven discrimination or to further clearly identified, compelling, and legitimate government objectives (see Focus: "Diversity" in Higher Education). Moreover, race-based actions must be "narrowly tailored" so as not to adversely affect the rights of individuals. In striking down a federal construction contract "set-aside" program for small businesses owned by racial minorities, the Court expressed skepticism about governmental racial classifications: "There is simply no way of determining what classifications are 'benign' and 'remedial' and what classifications are in fact motivated by illegitimate notions of racial inferiority or simple racial politics."[10]

ELITE VERSUS MASS RESPONSE TO CIVIL RIGHTS

Progress in civil rights policy—from *Brown v. Board of Education of Topeka, Kansas* through the Civil Rights Act of 1964 to affirmative action programs today—has been a response of a national elite to conditions affecting a minority of Americans. Advances in civil rights have *not* come about because of demands by the white majority of citizens. On the contrary, the civil rights policies of the national elite have met with varying degrees of resistance from white masses in states and communities.

"Diversity" in Higher Education

Educational elites—university presidents and administrators, public and private—identify "diversity" as an institutional goal, a term that refers to racial and ethnic representation in the student body and the faculty.

Elites argue that students benefit when they interact with others from different cultural heritages. "Students must be engaged with diverse peers if we expect learning and development to occur," and the existence of a racially and ethnically diverse student body is "a necessary condition" for such engagement. There is some evidence that students admitted under policies designed to increase diversity do well in their postcollege careers.

But despite numerous efforts to develop scientific evidence that racial or ethnic diversity on the campus improves learning, no definitive conclusions have emerged. Educational research on this topic is clouded by political and ideological conflict.

Diversity and Affirmative Action
Even if diversity provides educational benefits, the question arises of how to achieve it. Diversity is closely linked to affirmative action programs on campuses throughout the nation. When affirmative action programs are designed as special efforts to recruit and encourage qualified minority students to attend college, they enjoy widespread public support. But when affirmative action programs include preferences for minority applicants over equally or better qualified nonminorities, public support falters and constitutional questions arise.

Diversity as a Constitutional Question
The U.S. Supreme Court has held that the equal protection clause of the Fourteenth Amendment requires that racial classifications be subject to "strict scrutiny." This means that race-based actions by governments—any disparate treatment of racial or ethnic groups by federal, state, or local public agencies, including colleges and universities—must be found necessary to advance a "compelling government interest" and must be "narrowly tailored" to further that interest.

The U.S. Supreme Court held in 2003 that diversity may be a compelling government interest because it "promotes cross-racial understanding, helps to break down racial stereotypes, and enables [students] to better understand persons of different races."[a] This opinion was written by Justice Sandra Day O'Connor in a case involving the University of Michigan Law School's affirmative action program. In a 5 to 4 decision, O'Connor, writing for the majority, said that the Constitution "does not prohibit the law school's narrowly tailored use of race in admissions decisions to further a compelling interest in obtaining the educational benefits that flow from a diverse student body." However, in a companion case involving the University of Michigan's affirmative action program for undergraduate admissions, the Supreme Court held that the admissions policy was "not narrowly tailored to achieve respondents' asserted interest in diversity" and therefore violated the equal protection clause of the Fourteenth Amendment.[b] The Court again recognized that diversity may be a compelling interest but rejected an affirmative action plan that made race the decisive factor for even minimally qualified minority applicants. Yet the Supreme Court restated its support for limited affirmative action programs that use race as a "plus" factor—the position the Court has held since the *Bakke* case in 1978.

[a]*Gratz v. Bollinger* 539 U.S. 244 (2003).
[b]*Grutter v. Bollinger* 539 U.S. 306 (2003).

Mass Opinion about Discrimination

The attitudes of white masses toward blacks in the United States are ambivalent. Most whites believe that blacks face little discrimination in jobs, housing, or education and that any differences between whites and blacks in society is a result of blacks' lack of education and motivation. In contrast, most blacks believe that differences between blacks and whites in standards of living are "mainly due to discrimination." Whites

"I think I preferred it before he became an equal-opportunity employer."

constitute a large majority of the nation's population. If public policy reflected the views of this majority, there would be little civil rights legislation.

MASS OPINION ABOUT AFFIRMATIVE ACTION

Affirmative action is more popular among elites than masses. Overall, the American public opposes racial preferences in hiring, promotion, and admissions:

Which comes closer to your view about evaluating students for admission to a college or university? Applicants should be admitted solely on the basis of merit, even if that results in few minority students being admitted. Or, an applicant's racial and ethnic background should be considered to help promote diversity on college campuses, even if that means admitting some minority students who otherwise would not be admitted.

	Solely Merit	Race/Ethnicity Considered	Unsure
All	69	27	4
Whites	75	22	3
Blacks	44	49	7
Hispanics	59	36	5

Source: Gallup poll, June 2003.

FOCUS | WOMEN AND MINORITIES ACQUIRING ELITE STATUS

Increasing numbers of women and minorities are moving into elite positions in business, finance, the media, and government. Today most boards of directors of Fortune 500 corporations include at least two or three women and minorities among their fourteen to sixteen directors. A generation ago these directors were usually symbolic gestures, but increasingly women are breaking the "glass ceiling" to head major corporations. Women have recently served as chief executive officer of PepsiCo, Xerox, eBay, Archer Daniels Midland, Kraft Foods, Sara Lee, Avon, and Harpo Inc. (Oprah Winfrey, America's richest self-made woman). Other corporations in which women serve as chief financial officer or vice chair include Citigroup, Procter & Gamble, Johnson & Johnson, Disney ABC, Hewlett-Packard, and Time Inc.

A generation ago, women Cabinet members were appointed largely for symbolic representation, and they were appointed to second-level Cabinet positions. But there is no doubt that Secretary of State Condoleeza Rice exercised real power in the Bush administration, as did Secretary of State Madeline Albright in the Clinton administration.

In the Congress we have noted that women occupied seventy-one seats (16 percent) in the House of Representatives that was elected in 2006, and Nancy Pelosi serves as speaker of the House. In the Senate sixteen women (16 percent) now hold seats, including presidential candidate Hillary Clinton. And in 2006, thirty-nine African Americans were elected

to the House (9 percent), and one, Barack Obama, to the U.S. Senate. Hispanics are the nation's largest minority, 14 percent, but they occupy only twenty-three (6 percent) House seats; currently two Hispanics serve in the U.S. Senate.

Note the dramatic increase in minority representation in the House of Representatives following the 1990 census redistricting (see figure on page 364). This came about, first of all, as a result of Congress' 1982 strengthening of the Voting Rights Act of 1965 by outlawing any electoral arrangement that has the *effect* of weakening minority voting power (replacing an earlier *intent* test with this *effects* test). And in 1986 the Supreme Court interpreted this test to require state legislatures to redistrict their states in a way that maximized minority representation—creating "majority-minority" districts wherever possible.[a] (Later the Court would modify this decision by holding that bizarre-shaped districts based solely or predominantly on race were unconstitutional.[b]) These actions by Congress and the Supreme Court clearly strengthened African American and Hispanic representation in Congress. But the rise of women to power has continued uninterrupted over the past thirty years.

_____

[a]*Thornburg v. Gingles* 478 U.S. 30 (1986).

[b]*Shaw v. Reno* 125 L. Ed. 2d 511 (1993); *Hunt v. Cromartie* 532 U.S. 234 (2001).

According to one scholar:

Americans' response to pollsters' questions leave little doubt that they believe that equality of access and opportunity rather than of condition or result should be the defining principle of our commitment to egalitarianism. ... They disapprove of making race or ethnicity a legitimate or predominant ground for awarding jobs, social benefits, or opportunities.[11]

AFFIRMATIVE ACTION IN MASS REFERENDA

White masses have turned to citizens' initiatives to battle racial preferences. We have already suggested that elites generally consider popular referenda votes to be a threat to democratic values as well as elite governance (see Chapter 5). Such votes are clearly a threat to affirmative action.

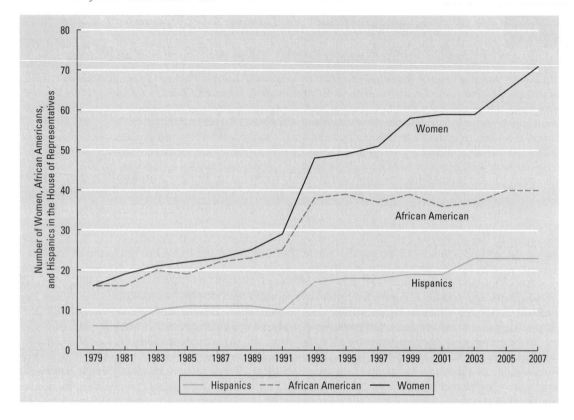

The California Civil Rights Initiative, "Prop 209," was placed on that state's ballot by citizens' initiative in 1996 and was approved by 54 percent of the state's voters. The initiative added the following phrase to the state's constitution:

> *Neither the state of California nor any of its political subdivisions or agents shall use race, sex, color, ethnicity or national origin as a criterion for either discriminating against, or granting preferential treatment to, any individual or group in the operation of the State's system of public employment, public education or public contracting.*

The key words are "or granting preferential treatment to." Opponents challenged the California Civil Rights Initiative in federal courts, arguing that by preventing minorities and women from seeking preferential treatment under law, the initiative violated the equal protection clause of the Fourteenth Amendment. But a circuit court of appeals held, and the U.S. Supreme Court affirmed, that a

> *ban on race or gender preferences, as a matter of law or logic, does not violate the Equal Protection Clause in any conventional sense. … Impediments to preferential treatment do not deny equal protection.*[12]

The success of the California initiative inspired similar mass movements in other states; Washington adopted a similar state constitutional amendment in 1998. Michigan voters approved a state-wide ban on affirmative action programs in public education, employment, and state contracts in 2006. The referendum, "Proposition 2," was opposed by elites in the political, business, and academic worlds, including both Democratic and Republican gubernatorial candidates. Nonetheless, 58 percent of Michigan voters favored banning affirmative action. Proposition 2 gathered the most support from men (60 percent) and whites (59 percent). It gathered less support from women (47 percent) and very little support from blacks (14 percent). The referendum effort was led by Ward Connerly, an African American businessman who had led the California Civil Rights Initiative in 1996, together with Jennifer Gratz, who had been denied admission to the University of Michigan Law School and had been the plaintiff in an unsuccessful Supreme Court challenge to "diversity" as a justification for affirmative action programs.[13] Following voter approval of the referendum banning affirmative action, the president of the University of Michigan announced her intention "not to allow our University" to end its affirmative action efforts.[14]

American Civil Rights Institute
Leading a nation-wide effort to ban racial or gender preferences.
www.acir.org

FEMINISM IN AMERICA

Feminism in America is nearly as old as the nation itself. In 1776, Abigail Adams wrote to her husband, John Adams, at the Second Continental Congress while it was debating whether to declare American independence:

> *I long to hear that you have declared an independency. And in the new code of laws which I suppose it will be necessary for you to make, I desire you would remember the ladies, and be more generous and favorable to them than your ancestors.... If particular care and attention is not paid to the ladies, we are determined to foment a rebellion and will not hold ourselves bound by any laws in which we have no voice or representation.[15]*

The political movement forecast by Abigail Adams did not really emerge until a generation later.

THE FIRST WAVE

The "first wave" of active feminist politics grew out of the pre–Civil War antislavery movement. The first generation of feminists, including Lucretia Mott, Elizabeth Cady Stanton, Lucy Stone, and Susan B. Anthony, learned to organize, hold public meetings, and conduct petition campaigns as abolitionists. After the Civil War, women were successful in changing many state laws that abridged the property rights of married women and treated them as chattel (property) of their husbands. Activists were also successful in winning some protection for women in the workplace, including state laws limiting women's hours of work, working conditions, and physical demands. At that time, these laws were regarded as progressive.

The most successful feminist efforts of the 1800s centered on protections of women in families. The perceived threats to women's well-being were their husbands' drinking, gambling, and consorting with prostitutes. Women led the Anti-Saloon League and succeeded in outlawing gambling and prostitution in every state except Nevada and provided the major source of moral support for the Eighteenth Amendment (prohibition).

In the early twentieth century, the feminist movement concentrated on women's suffrage—the drive to guarantee women the right to vote. The early suffragettes used

League of Women Voters
Oldest women's organization focuses on "making democracy work," with information on voting rights, campaign finance, lobby, ethics, etc.
www.lwv.org

mass demonstrations, parades, picketing, and occasional disruption and civil disobedience tactics similar to those of the civil rights movement of the 1960s. The culmination of their efforts was the 1920 passage of the Nineteenth Amendment to the Constitution: "The right of citizens of the United States to vote shall not be denied or abridged by the United States or by any state on account of sex." The suffrage movement spawned the League of Women Voters.

The goal of this first wave of feminist activity was *equality*. When a delegation of American women was excluded from the World Anti-Slavery Convention in London in 1840, they realized that the cause of emancipation affected them as well as slaves. On July 19, 1848, they met in Seneca Falls, across the New York border in Canada, to draw up "The Seneca Falls Declaration of Sentiments and Resolutions." The Resolution parallels the Declaration of Independence and reads in part:

> We hold these truths to be self-evident: that all men and women are created equal;...

EQUITY FEMINISM

Today, equality remains the goal of what might be labeled *equity feminism*. Equity feminism continues in the classic liberal tradition of seeking equal opportunity for women and men, equal treatment for every individual, equal justice for all. It builds on the earlier feminist efforts to gain for women the rights that men had taken for granted. The principles of equity feminism remain the vision of the vast majority of women in the United States. A majority of women say that there continues to be a need for a strong women's movement in America to guarantee equality. Yet, paradoxically perhaps, a majority of women also decline to call themselves "feminists."[16] This reluctance to identify with the term may derive from views currently expressed by the elites of national women's organizations.

GENDER FEMINISM

NOW
Leading feminist organization, with news, information, and argument on a wide range of issues.
www.now.org

A "second wave" of feminism, which we have labeled *gender feminism*, currently prevails in leadership circles in leading feminist organizations such as the National Organization for Women (NOW). Gender feminism goes beyond a demand for equality and becomes "a call for liberation."[17] Women must not look to men to grant their freedom; rather, they must choose their own freedom. They must liberate themselves from the patriarchal family and the male-dominated society. This requires, first of all, that women become aware of their oppression; "consciousness raising" exposes the oppression of women that is inherent in sex roles, family structure, education, religion, the economy, and many other aspects of society. The next imperative is for women to transform themselves personally and collectively from powerlessness to power and in so doing to reform and restructure society's institutions to reflect feminine values.[18]

VARIATIONS OF GENDER FEMINISM

Gender feminism includes a number of camps with diverse views of both the source of women's oppression and strategies for its elimination. "Radical feminism" perceives male dominance in virtually all of society's institutions and seeks revolutionary restructuring of these institutions. Rape, pornography, sexual harassment, and domestic violence are visible products of a deeper "phallocentric" culture. Men are largely unaware of the devaluation and repression in women's experience—they "just don't get it." "Socialist feminism," following the doctrine of Marx, sees male oppression arising from capitalism, which gives men control of "the means of reproduction" as well as "the means of production." "Liberal feminism" focuses on the early socialization of children into clearly differentiated sex roles and seeks reform measures, including nonsexist education. "Postmodern feminists" perceive sexism in ways of thinking and speaking and seek to reconstruct philosophy, history, and language to liberate them from "masculinist modes and patriarchal ideology" of "dead white European males."

WOMEN AND WORK

Modern feminism has been driven by the changing role of women in America's workforce. In 1960, less than one-third of married women worked. Today most married women work. Indeed, economic pressures on family budgets today have sent more than 70 percent of married women into the workforce, including women with children.

THE DUAL LABOR MARKET

Despite increases in the number and proportion of working women, the nation's occupational fields are still divided between traditionally male and female jobs. Women continue to dominate the traditional "pink-collar" jobs (see Table 15.3). Women have made important inroads in traditionally male white-collar occupations—doctors, lawyers, and architects, for example—although men still remain in the majority in these professions. However, women have only begun to break into the "blue-collar" occupations usually dominated by men. Blue-collar jobs usually pay more than pink-collar jobs.

THE EARNINGS GAP

The existence of this "dual" labor market, with male-dominated blue-collar jobs distinguishable from female-dominated pink-collar jobs, continues to be a major obstacle to economic equality between men and women.

Despite protections under federal laws, women continue to earn substantially less than men do. Today women, on average, earn about 80 percent of what men do (see Table 15.4). This earnings gap is not primarily a product of *direct discrimination;* women in the same job with the same skills, qualifications, experience, and work record are not generally paid less than men. Such direct discrimination has been illegal since the Civil Rights Act of 1964. Rather, the earnings gap is primarily a product of a division in the labor market between traditionally male and female jobs, with lower salaries paid in traditionally female occupations.

TABLE 15.3 | THE DUAL LABOR MARKET

		Percentage Female		
		1960	1983	2005
"White collar"	Women are increasingly entering white-collar occupational fields traditionally dominated by men:			
	Architects	3	13	24
	Computer analysts	11	28	29
	College and university teachers	28	36	46
	Engineers	1	6	12
	Lawyers and judges	4	16	29
	Physicians	10	16	29
"Pink collar"	Women continue to be concentrated in occupational fields traditionally dominated by women:			
	Nurses	97	96	92
	Elementary school teachers	89	83	81
	Secretaries	98	99	97
	Waitress/waiter	91	88	73
"Blue collar"	Women continue to be largely shut out of blue-collar occupational fields traditionally dominated by men:			
	Carpenters	1	1	2
	Mechanics	1	1	2
	Firefighters	0	4	13
	Police officers	1	9	13
	Truck drivers	1	3	5
	Bartenders (the only "blue-collar" job to be largely taken over by women)	21	48	58

Source: *Statistical Abstract of the United States 2006*, pp. 402–403.

GENDER EQUALITY IN CIVIL RIGHTS LAWS

Title VII of the Civil Rights Act of 1964 prevents sexual (as well as racial) discrimination in hiring, pay, and promotions. The Equal Employment Opportunity Commission, the federal agency charged with eliminating discrimination in employment, has established guidelines barring stereotyped classifications of "men's jobs" and "women's jobs." The courts have repeatedly struck down state laws and employer practices that differentiate between men and women in hours, pay, retirement age, and so forth.

The federal Equal Credit Opportunity Act of 1974 prohibits sex discrimination in credit transactions. Federal law prevents banks, credit unions, savings and loan associations, retail stores, and credit card companies from denying credit

TABLE 15.4 | THE EARNINGS GAP

Median Annual Earnings of Women as a Percentage of Median Annual Earnings of Men	
1972	59%
1978	59%
1983	62%
1985	67%
1987	70%
1996	72%
1999	74%
2002	78%
2005	80%

Source: *Statistical Abstract of the United States 2006*, p. 428.

Equal Employment Opportunity Commission
Federal EEOC Web site with information on what constitutes discrimination by age, disability, race, ethnicity, religion, gender; how to file a charge; and guidance for employers.
www.eeoc.gov

because of sex or marital status. However, these businesses may still deny credit for a poor or nonexistent credit rating, and some women who have always maintained accounts in their husband's name may still face credit problems if they apply in their own name.

Title IX of the Education Act Amendment of 1972 deals with sex discrimination in education. This federal law bars discrimination in admissions, housing, rules, financial aid, faculty and staff recruitment and pay, and—most troublesome of all—athletics. The last problem has proven difficult because men's football and basketball programs have traditionally brought in the money to finance all other sports, and men's football and basketball have received the largest share of school athletic budgets.

CULTURAL DIVISIONS OF LABOR

Working women face obstacles not encountered by men. Women who work are still likely to do more housework than men. Most women are still expected to follow their husbands wherever their jobs take them. Working outside the home is a tough decision, and some women who have made this decision later reverse it. Studying a group of women who became adults in the 1970s, sociologist Kathleen Gerson describes two types of women, domestic and nondomestic:

> Those who developed non-domestic orientations sought to restructure the sexual division of labor at home and at work and also to redefine traditional ideologies of child rearing. They met opposition from domestically oriented women who found it in their interest to preserve traditional arrangements and beliefs. The study found emerging divisions among women that promise to add to the social turmoil generated by women's changing position.[19]

Like all other groups that strive to build consensus among disparate elements (such as consumers, businesspeople, and the working class), the size of the potential clientele for women's movements creates both the raw material of political power and the discord that diminishes political power.

FEMINISM AND ELITISM

Center for American Women and Politics
Rutgers University center with information and studies of women in politics.
www.rci.rutgers.edn/ ncoop

It is our argument that feminist ideology and political activists are concentrated among women elites—politically active, often university based, highly educated women. "They hold the keys to many bureaucratic fiefdoms, research centers, women's studies programs, tenure committees, and para-academic organizations."[20] They claim to speak for all women, but not all women, or even all feminists, share the view that women's oppression is a product of a male culture that exalts individualism, competition, and violence. Yet, as elite theory predicts, the more moderate female majority is "not temperamentally suited to activism. . . . They do not network. They do not ally. They do not threaten their opponents with loss of jobs or loss of patronage. They are not especially litigious."[21]

WORKING WOMEN, EDUCATED WOMEN, AND FEMINISM

Employed women and housewives* differ in their attitudes toward feminist issues. Support for feminist ideology is greater among employed women than housewives. Opinion polls report that *unmarried* women with college educations and jobs are most likely to identify themselves as feminists. *Married* women, even those with college educations and jobs, are somewhat less likely to identify themselves as feminists. And relatively few married non–college graduates not in the workforce identify themselves as feminists.

The women's movement suffers from a perception that it is more upper class, more liberal, and indeed more elitist than the mainstream. To combat this elitist image, feminist organizations in recent years have tried to become more "family friendly." Feminist organizations were strong supporters of the Family and Medical Leave Act of 1993. Yet even so, the leading women's lobbying groups in Washington—NOW, the Women's Legal Defense Fund, the American Nurses Association, the National Federation of Business and Professional Women, the American Association of University Women—tend to emphasize the concerns of well-educated, professionally employed women.

THE "GLASS CEILING"

Relatively few women have climbed the ladder to become president or chief executive officer or director of the nation's largest industrial corporations, banks, utilities, newspapers, or television networks. Large numbers of women are entering the legal profession, but as yet few are senior partners in the largest and most prestigious law firms.

---

*The U.S. Census Bureau defines "working [employed] women" as women who are employed outside the home, "housewives" as women who, regardless of marital status, work solely in the home. This text uses the same convention in categorizing women.

IN BRIEF	FEMINISM

Feminists politics today centers on:

- The dual labor market
- The earnings gap
- Cultural divisions between educated professional women, less educated working women, and housewives

- A "glass ceiling" that appears to slow women's advancement to top elite positions
- Sexual harassment

National Association of Scholars
College professors opposed to "political correctness" on campuses.
www.nas.org

The barriers to women's advancement to elite positions are often subtle, giving rise to the term *glass ceiling*. There are many explanations for the glass ceiling, but all are controversial or questionable: Women choose staff assignments rather than fast-track operating-head assignments. Women are cautious and unaggressive in corporate politics. Women have lower expectations about peak earnings and positions, and these expectations become self-fulfilling. Women bear children, and even during relatively short maternity absences they fall behind their male counterparts. Women are less likely to want to change locations than men, and immobile executives are worth less to a corporation than mobile ones. Female executives in sensitive positions come under even more pressure than men in similar posts. Female executives believe that they get much more scrutiny than men and must work harder to succeed. And at all levels, increasing attention has been paid to sexual harassment (see Focus: Elites, Masses, and Sexual Harassment). Finally, it is important to note that affirmative action efforts by governments—notably the Equal Employment Opportunity Commission—are directed primarily at entry-level positions rather than senior management posts.

CIVIL RIGHTS: AN ELITIST INTERPRETATION

Elite theory helps us to understand the development of protest movements and organizations, their accommodation by governing elites, and their eventual moderation and incorporation into the elite structure. Elites modify public policy to defuse protest movements; they grant symbolic victories and elite status to protest leaders in exchange for the moderation of their demands and their support for the system. The masses frequently resist even these accommodationist policies. Progress in civil rights is an elite response to minority appeals, not to mass demands.

1. The first governmental institution to act for equality of opportunity for blacks in the twentieth century was the Supreme Court. The Court, structurally the furthest removed from the influence of the white masses, was the first to apply liberal public-regarding policies to blacks. Elected elites who are more accessible to the white masses were slower to act on black rights than were appointed elites.

2. Elected white elites did not respond to black requests until faced with a prolonged campaign of nonviolent civil disobedience, public demonstrations, and creative disorder and crises. In general, elites have responded by making modest changes in the system to maintain stability. Often these changes are only symbolic.

FOCUS | ELITES, MASSES, AND SEXUAL HARASSMENT

What is "sexual harassment"? Various surveys report that up to one-third of female workers say they have experienced sexual harassment on the job.[a] But it is not always clear exactly what kind of behavior constitutes "sexual harassment."

Elite Definition

The U.S. Supreme Court has provided some guidance in the development of sexual harassment definitions and prohibitions. Title VII of the Civil Rights Act of 1964 makes it "an unlawful employment practice to discriminate against any individual with respect to his [sic] compensation, terms, conditions or privileges of employment because of such individual's race, color, religion, sex, or national origin." In the employment context, the U.S. Supreme Court has approved the following definition of sexual harassment:

> Unwelcome sexual advances, requests for sexual favors, and other verbal or physical conduct of a sexual nature constitute sexual harassment when (1) submission to such conduct is made either explicitly or implicitly a term or condition of an individual's employment; (2) submission to or rejection of such conduct by an individual, is used as the basis for employment decisions affecting such individual; or (3) such conduct has the purpose or effect of unreasonably interfering with an individual's work performance or creating an intimidating, hostile, or offensive working environment.[b]

There are no great difficulties in defining sexual harassment when jobs or promotions are conditioned on the granting of sexual favors. But several problems arise in defining a "hostile working environment." This phrase may include offensive utterances, sexual innuendoes, dirty jokes, the display of pornographic material, and unwanted proposals for dates. First, it would appear to include speech and hence raise First Amendment questions regarding how far speech may be curtailed by law in the workplace. Second, the definition depends more on the subjective feelings of the individual employee about what is "offensive" and "unwanted" than on an objective standard of behavior that is easily understood by all. Justice Sandra Day O'Connor wrestled with the definition of a "hostile work environment" in *Harris v. Forklift Systems* in 1993. She held that a plaintiff need not show that the utterances caused psychological injury but that a "reasonable person," not just the plaintiff, must perceive the work environment to be hostile or abusive. Presumably, a single incident would not constitute harassment; rather, courts should consider "the frequency of the discriminatory conduct," "its severity," and whether it "unreasonably interferes with an employee's work performance."[c]

Mass Definitions

Masses appear to be divided on what they think constitutes sexual harassment. Surveys indicate that women are somewhat more likely to perceive sexual harassment in various behaviors than men (see table). But neither women nor men are likely to perceive it to include repeated requests for a date, the telling of dirty jokes, or comments on attractiveness—even though these behaviors often inspire formal complaints.

3. Elimination of legal discrimination and guaranteed equality of opportunity have largely resulted from the efforts of black middle-class groups who share a dominant elite consensus and who appeal to the conscience of white elites to extend that consensus to include blacks.

4. Elites have not responded to demands that go beyond accepted elite consensus, for example, demands for absolute equality that have replaced demands for equality of opportunity. New mass-oriented black counterelites have emerged to contend with established middle-class black elites. Mass counterelites have less respect for the rules of the game than do either white elites or established middle-class black leaders.

5. Affirmative action—defined as preferential treatment for minorities and women in employment and education—is more likely to be supported by

QUESTION:*"Here is a list of some different situations.*

We're interested in knowing whether you think they are forms of sexual harassment—not just inappropriate or in bad taste, but sexual."

DEFINITELY IS SEXUAL HARASSMENT

	Men	Women
If a male boss makes it clear to a female employee that she must go to bed with him for a promotion	91%	92%
If a male boss asks very direct questions of a female employee about her personal sexual practices and preferences	59%	68%
If a female boss asks very direct questions of a male employee about his personal sexual practices and preferences	47%	57%
If a man once in a while asks a female employee of his to go out on dates, even though she has said no in the past	15%	21%
If a man once in a while tells dirty jokes in the presence of female employees	15%	16%
If a male boss tells a female employee that she looks very attractive today	3%	5%

Source: Roper Organization as reported in *American Enterprise*, September/October 1993, p. 93.

University Policies

Students and professors beware! Most university policies go well beyond both Supreme Court rulings and opinion polls in defining what constitutes sexual harassment, including:

- "Remarks about a person's clothing."
- "Suggestive or insulting sounds."
- "Leering at or ogling of a person's body."
- "Nonsexual slurs about one's gender."
- "Remarks that degrade another person or group on the basis of gender."[d]

The National Association of Scholars worries that overly broad and vague definitions of sexual harassment can undermine academic freedom and inhibit classroom discussions of important yet sensitive topics, including human sexuality, gender differences, sexual roles, and gender politics. Teaching and research on such topics, in their view, must not be constrained by the threat that the views expressed will be labeled "insensitive," "uncomfortable," or "incorrect"; faculty members must feel free to provide their best academic and professional advice to students, collectively and individually, without fear that their comments will be officially labeled "offensive" or "unwelcome"; and students must feel free to express themselves on matters of gender, whether or not their ideas are biased, immature, or crudely expressed.

---

[a]*Washington Post*, National Weekly Edition, March 7, 1993.
[b]*Meritor Savings Bank v. Vinson*, 477 U.S. 57 (1986).
[c]*Harris v. Forklift Systems*, 126 L. Ed. 2d 295 (1993).
[d]Statements in student and faculty handbooks, State University System of Florida.

elites than by the masses. Mass opposition to such preferential treatment is widespread and growing over time.

6. Leaders of the women's movement are professional, educated, upper-middle-class women whose views are not universally shared by the masses of women in the United States. Yet it is difficult to mobilize masses of women on behalf of feminist goals.

7. Differences prevail even among feminist elites regarding both the nature of the obstacles to women's advancement and the remedial strategies to be pursued. Should the women's movement focus primarily on achieving equality, securing special protections, or radically restructuring male-dominated society?

SELECTED READINGS

Barker, Lucius J., and Mack H. Jones. *African Americans and the American Political System*, 4th ed. Upper Saddle River, N.J.: Prentice-Hall, 1999. A comprehensive analysis of African American politics, examining access to the judicial arena, the interest-group process, political parties, Congress, and the White House.

Conway, M. Margaret, Gertrude A. Sternagel, and David W. Ahern. *Women and Political Participation*, 2nd ed. Washington, D.C.: CQ Press, 2004. A review of changes in American political culture brought about by the increasing power of women.

Fox-Genovese, Elizabeth. *Feminism Is Not the Story of My Life*. New York: Doubleday, 1995. A critique of radical feminism for failing to understand the central importance of marriage and motherhood in women's lives, and a discussion of how public policy could ease the clashing demands of work and family on women.

Harrison, Brigid C. *Women in American Politics*. Belmont, Calif.: Wadsworth, 2003. A comprehensive text on the role of women in interest groups, parties, elections, Congress, the executive branch, and the judiciary.

Kirkpatrick, Jeane. *Political Women*. New York: Basic Books, 1978. This early book explores the conditions leading to women's seeking political office, written by the former UN ambassador.

Myrdal, Gunnar. *An American Dilemma*, 2nd ed. Vol. 1: *The Negro in a White Nation*. Vol. 2: *The Negro Social Structure*. New York: McGraw-Hill, 1964. Originally published in 1944, Myrdal's classic study is one of the most comprehensive analyses of the situation of blacks in the United States. It draws broadly from many disciplines.

Sommers, Christina Hoff. *Who Stole Feminism?* New York: Simon & Schuster, 1994. A controversial critique of gender feminism by an equity feminist.

Thernstrom, Stephen, and Abigail Thernstrom. *America in Black and White*. New York: Simon & Schuster, 1997. An information-rich analysis tracing social and economic progress of African Americans and arguing that gains in education and employment were greater *before* the introduction of affirmative action programs.

NOTES

1. Gunnar Myrdal, *An American Dilemma* (New York: McGraw-Hill, 1964), vol. 1, p. xxi.
2. *Plessy v. Ferguson*, 163 U.S. 537 (1896).
3. *Brown v. Board of Education of Topeka, Kansas*, 347 U.S. 483 (1954).
4. Martin Luther King Jr., "Letter from Birmingham City Jail," April 16, 1963.
5. *Regents of the University of California v. Bakke*, 438 U.S. 265 (1978).
6. *United States v. Paradise*, 480 U.S. 149 (1987).
7. *Firefighters Local Union v. Stotts*, 467 U.S. 561 (1984).
8. *Richmond v. Crosen*, 109 S. Ct. 706 (1989).
9. See Justice Antonin Scalia's dissenting opinion in *Johnson v. Transportation Agency of Santa Clara County*, 480 U.S. 616 (1987).
10. *Adarand Construction v. Pena*, 132 L. Ed. 2d 158 (1995).
11. John H. Bunzel, "Affirmative Reactions," *Public Opinion* (February/March 1986), p. 49.
12. *Coalition for Economic Equity v. Pete Wilson*, Ninth Circuit Court of Appeals, April 1997.

13. *Guatz v. Bollinger* 539 U.S. 244 (2003).
14. *Detroit Free Press*, November 9, 2006.
15. Reprinted in Alice Rossi, ed., *The Feminist Papers from Adams to de Beauvoir* (New York: Columbia University Press, 1993).
16. *Time/CNN* poll reported in *Time* (March 9, 1992), p. 54.
17. Marilyn Pearsall, *Women and Values*, 2nd ed. (Belmont, Calif.: Wadsworth, 1993), p. xi.
18. Alison M. Jaggar, *Feminist Politics and Human Nature* (Totowa, N.J.: Rowman & Littlefield, 1988). See also Maggie Homm, ed., *Modern Feminism* (New York: Columbia University Press, 1992).
19. Kathleen Gerson, *Hard Choices* (Berkeley: University of California Press, 1985), pp. 216–217.
20. Christina Hoff Sommers, *Who Stole Feminism?* (New York: Simon & Schuster, 1994), p. 273.
21. Sommers, *Who Stole Feminism?* p. 274.

Governments don't have time to think about the broader longer-range issues. It seemed to make sense to persuade a group of private, qualified citizens to get together to identify the key issues affecting the world and possible solutions.

David Rockefeller, commenting on the creation of the Trilateral Commission

ELITES AND NATIONAL SECURITY

The elite struggle for power is universal. International politics, like all politics, is a struggle for power—a struggle among global elites. The distinguished political scientist Hans Morganthau once observed:

> *Whatever the ultimate aims of international politics, power is always the immediate aim. Statesmen and peoples may ultimately seek freedom, security, prosperity or power itself. They may define their goals in terms of a religious, philosophic, economic, or social ideal. ... But whenever they strive to realize their goal by means of international politics they are striving for power.*[1]

NUCLEAR THREATS TO SECURITY

Nuclear weapons made the world infinitely more dangerous. During the Cold War the nuclear arsenals of the United States and the Soviet Union threatened a human Holocaust. Yet, paradoxically, the very destructiveness of nuclear weapons caused elites on both sides to exercise extreme caution in relations with each other. Scores of wars, large and small, were fought by different nations during the Cold War years (1945–1989), yet U.S. and Soviet troops never engaged in direct combat against each other.

DETERRENCE

To avoid nuclear war, elites in the United States relied primarily on a policy of *deterrence*. Deterrence is based on the idea that *rational* elites in other countries can be dissuaded from launching a nuclear attack by threatening a devastating retaliatory strike. Deterrence seeks to avoid the worst scenario—a surprise first strike against America's nuclear forces. It emphasizes second-strike capability—the ability of American nuclear forces to survive a surprise attack and then inflict unacceptable levels of destruction on the enemy's homeland. Enemy elites are made aware of

America's second-strike capability. Deterrence is really a *psychological* defense against an attack by a *rational* elite that does not wish to risk total destruction of their homeland.

By the early 1970s, a nuclear balance existed between the United States and the Soviet Union. Neither side could consider launching a nuclear attack because of the terrible consequences that the other side could inflict in retaliation. This mutual "balance of terror" maintained the nuclear peace. In effect, the populations of each nation were being held hostage against a nuclear attack. Commentators label this balance of terror as *mutual assured destruction* or MAD.

Arms Control
Texts of all nuclear arms control treaties and agreements.
www.armscontrol.org

NEGOTIATIONS OVER NUCLEAR ARMS

Rational leaders in the United States and the Soviet Union engaged in negotiations over nuclear arms control for many years. (The development of reconnaissance satellites in the 1960s made it possible for each nation to monitor the strategic weapons possessed by the other. Space photography opened the way for both nations to seek stability through arms control.) Following the election of Richard Nixon as president in 1968, the United States, largely guided by former Harvard professor Henry Kissinger (national security adviser to the president and later secretary of state), began negotiations with the Soviet Union over strategic nuclear arms. The first result was the SALT I agreement in 1972, which consisted of a treaty limiting antiballistic missiles (ABMs) and an agreement placing numerical ceilings on offensive missiles. (The ABM Treaty reflected the MAD theory that the populations of each nation should be *un*defended in order to hold them hostage against a first strike attack by either nation.) After seven more years of negotiations, a lengthy and complicated SALT II agreement was reached that set overall limits on "strategic nuclear launch vehicles"—intercontinental ballistic missiles (ICBMs), submarine launched ballistic missiles (SLBMs), and long-range bombers. The SALT II Treaty was never officially ratified by the U.S. Senate; President Jimmy Carter withdrew the treaty from Senate consideration following the Soviet Union's 1979 attack on Afghanistan. But both sides continued to agree to the terms of the Treaty.

When Ronald Reagan came to the White House in 1981 he insisted that any new agreements with the Soviet Union include *reductions* in nuclear weapons, not just limits reflecting existing levels of these weapons. He also insisted on equality and verification—"trust but verify." The result was the Strategic Arms Reduction Talks (START). After years of negotiations, the START I Treaty was signed in 1991 by President George H. W. Bush and Mikhail Gorbachev. It was the first agreement that actually reduced the numbers and types of nuclear warheads and missiles. A far-reaching START II agreement was signed in 1993 by President Bush and the new Russian President Boris Yeltsin. It further reduced total nuclear warheads as well as eliminated multiwarheaded land-based missiles (MIRVs). The capstone of strategic nuclear arms reductions is the Treaty of Moscow signed by President George W. Bush and Russian President Vladimir Putin in 2002. The effects of the Moscow Treaty, together with earlier reductions in nuclear weapons, will be to reduce the nuclear arsenals of the former adversaries by over 80 percent from Cold War levels (see Figure 16.1).

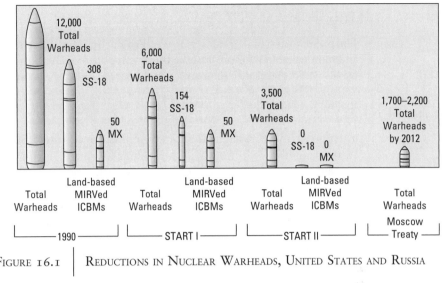

FIGURE 16.1 | REDUCTIONS IN NUCLEAR WARHEADS, UNITED STATES AND RUSSIA

NUCLEAR TERRORISM

The threat of nuclear attack from *rational* elites can be reduced or eliminated through a policy of deterrence. But today nuclear threats are arising from "nondeterrable" sources: nuclear missiles launched by a rogue nation led by an irrational elite, and nuclear weapons brought to the United States by terrorist groups. Over time global nuclear and ballistic missile proliferation steadily increases the likelihood of these types of threats. More national elites have joined the global nuclear club—China, India, Pakistan, Israel (considered rational), as well as North Korea and Iran (considered capable of irrational actions). Nuclear technology is increasingly available to terrorist groups.

Missile Defense
Missile Defense Agency Web site in the Department of Defense.
www.mda.mil

ANTIBALLISTIC MISSILE DEFENSES

As early as 1983 President Ronald Reagan urged that instead of deterring nuclear war through fear of retaliation, the United States should seek a technological defense against nuclear missiles. Reagan's Strategic Defense Initiative (SDI) was initially a research program to explore means of destroying enemy nuclear missiles in space before they could reach their targets. Reagan's SDI was directed against a possible massive attack by the Soviet Union. The media quickly labeled the effort "Star Wars." The end of the Cold War refocused ballistic missile defense (BMD) against more limited yet more likely threats from rogue nations. ABM technology is extremely complex, comparable to "hitting a bullet with a bullet." To date, testing has produced both successes and failures. But the threat from North Korea inspired President George W. Bush to announce a limited deployment of sea- and ground-based missile interceptors in the Pacific area in 2004. He also notified the Russians that the United States was withdrawing from the provisions of the SALT I Anti-Ballistic Missile Treaty of 1972.

NATO AND EUROPEAN SECURITY

The preservation of democracy in Western Europe was the centerpiece of U.S. foreign and military policy for most of the twentieth century. The United States fought in two world wars to preserve democracy in Europe.

ORIGINS OF NATO

NATO
The official North Atlantic Treaty Organization Web site contains basic facts about the alliance, current NATO news and issues, and important NATO policies.
www.nato.int

In response to aggressive Soviet moves in Europe after World War II, the United States, Canada, Belgium, Britain, Denmark, France, Iceland, Italy, Luxembourg, the Netherlands, Norway, and Portugal joined in the North Atlantic Treaty Organization (NATO). Each nation pledged that "an armed attack against one... shall be considered an attack against them all." Greece and Turkey joined in 1952 and West Germany in 1955. To give this pledge credibility, a joint NATO military command was established with a U.S. commanding officer (the first was General of the Army Dwight D. Eisenhower). After the formation of NATO, the Soviets made no further advances in Western Europe. The Soviets themselves, in response to NATO, drew up a comparable treaty among their own Eastern European satellite nations—the Warsaw Pact. It included Poland, Hungary, Czechoslovakia, Romania, Bulgaria, and the German Democratic Republic (the former East Germany).

THE COLLAPSE OF COMMUNISM IN EASTERN EUROPE

The dramatic collapse of the communist governments of Eastern Europe in 1989—Poland, Hungary, Romania, Bulgaria, and East Germany—vastly reduced the threat of a military attack on Western Europe. The dismantling of communist governments came about as a direct result of President Mikhail Gorbachev's decision to renounce the use of Soviet military force to keep them in power. For over forty years, the communist governments of Eastern Europe were supported by Soviet tanks; bloody Soviet military operations put down civilian uprisings in Hungary in 1956 and Czechoslovakia in 1968. The threat of Soviet military intervention crushed the Solidarity movement in Poland in 1981, yet that same movement became the government of Poland in 1989. Any effort today by a Russian leader to reimpose control over Eastern European nations would probably result in widespread bloodshed.

GERMANY UNITED

The collapse of the Berlin Wall in 1989 and the formal unification of Germany in 1990 rearranged the balance of military power in central Europe. Today Germany is the strongest military power in Europe. It remains a member of NATO.

THE COLLAPSE OF THE WARSAW PACT AND THE USSR

The Warsaw Pact collapsed following the ouster of communist governments in the Eastern European nations and was officially dissolved in 1991. Its former members requested the withdrawal of Russian troops from their territory; the Russian government complied, although withdrawals were slowed by economic conditions in that nation.

At the same time strong independence movements emerged in the republics of the USSR. Lithuania, Estonia, and Latvia—Baltic Sea nations that had been forcibly incorporated into the Soviet Union in 1939—led the way to independence in 1991. Soon all fifteen republics declared their independence, and the Union of Soviet Socialist Republics officially ceased to exist after December 31, 1991. Russian President Boris Yeltsin took over the offices of former Soviet Union President Mikhail Gorbachev. The red flag with its banner and sickle atop the Kremlin was replaced by the flag of the Russian Republic.

NATO TODAY

The residual threat to Western Europe posed by Russian forces, even under a hostile regime, is very weak. The Russian military, over 4 million strong as late as 1990, is now down to less than 2 million, a number that is smaller than the forces of the European NATO countries, exclusive of U.S. forces. And even if an anti-Western regime were to emerge in Moscow, considerable time would be required to reconstitute a Russian force capable of threatening Western Europe.

However, the total withdrawal of U.S. military forces from Western Europe would probably mean an end to the NATO alliance. The United States has already reduced its "forward presence" in Europe by over half. Proponents of a continued U.S. military presence in Europe argue that it provides reassurance and stability as democracy emerges in Eastern Europe; they note that both our old allies and new friends in Europe have urged the United States to remain involved in European security. Opponents counter that the Western European nations are now quite capable of shouldering the burden of their own security.

NATO EXPANSION

Despite Russian objections, NATO extended its membership eastward in 1997 by admitting Poland, Hungary, and the Czech Republic. Proponents of NATO expansion argued successfully that a historic opportunity existed to solidify freedom and democracy in Eastern Europe by admitting those nations to NATO. Russia was reassured that it would be "consulted" on NATO policies, but was given no veto powers over these policies or no guarantee that other Eastern European nations might also be admitted to NATO in the future. Indeed, in 2003 NATO admitted seven former Communist countries of Eastern Europe—Estonia, Latvia, and Lithuania, together with Bulgaria, Romania, Slovakia, and Slovenia. NATO now includes a total of twenty-six nations (see Figure 16.2).

NATO AND ETHNIC CONFLICTS

Traditionally, NATO forces were never deployed outside of Western Europe. Yet ethnic wars in the former communist nation of Yugoslavia, and the media coverage of the hardships endured by the people there, inspired NATO to intervene and deploy troops to Bosnia in 1995 to halt conflict raging among Serbs, Croats, and Muslims. The United States provided about one-third of the ground troops deployed in Bosnia as "peacekeepers." Yet some argued that U.S. national security interests were not at

FIGURE 16.2 | NATO TODAY

*NATO members, United States and Canada not shown.

stake in southeastern European ethnic conflicts and therefore American troops should not be exposed to the dangers of intervention.

NATO again acted militarily to halt ethnic conflict in Kosovo in 1999. NATO's objective was to force Serbian troop withdrawal from the largely Muslim province. NATO relied exclusively on bombing from the air to force the Serbian withdrawal. Despite some controversy, even among NATO nations, as well as denunciations from Russia and China, NATO aircraft and missiles hit targets in both Kosovo and Serbia itself. (Even the Chinese embassy in the Serbian capital of Belgrade was bombed, apparently by mistake.) Eventually, Serbian troops were withdrawn from Kosovo; they were replaced by NATO troops (and a small contingent of Russian troops).

NATO in Afghanistan

The United States turned over command of its military forces in Afghanistan to NATO in 2003. NATO created an International Security Assistance Force, officially under U.N. auspices, "to assist the Islamic Republic of Afghanistan in creating a stable and secure environment for the people of Afghanistan." Some thirty-seven nations contribute troops to this force, but the United States contributes the largest number. To date NATO forces have failed to capture Osama bin Laden and to eliminate Taliban forces from Afghan mountainous regions along the Pakistan border.

ELITES DEBATE THE USE OF MILITARY FORCE

All modern presidents have acknowledged that the most agonizing decisions they have made were to send U.S. military forces into combat. These decisions cost lives. The masses are willing to send their sons and daughters into danger—and even to see some of them wounded and killed—but only if a president convinces them that the outcome "is worth dying for." Elites must be able to explain and justify to the masses why lives must be sacrificed.

The Powell Doctrine

Department of Defense (DoD) Official DoD Web site is the starting point for information on all branches of the U.S. military. *www.defenselink.mil*

The U.S. military learned many bitter lessons in its long bloody experience in Vietnam. As a young officer in that war, Colin Powell developed ideas for the use of military force that reflected his experience. He developed a series of criteria for the use of force while he served as Chief of the Combined Chiefs of Staff, National Security Adviser, and later Secretary of State. The Powell Doctrine includes these ideas:

- The United States should commit its military forces only in support of vital national interests.
- If military forces are committed, they must have clearly defined military objectives—the destruction of enemy forces and/or the capture of enemy-held territory.
- Any commitment of U.S. forces must be of such strength as to ensure overwhelming and decisive victory with the fewest possible casualties.
- Before committing U.S. military forces, there must be reasonable assurances that the effort has the support of the American people and the Congress.
- The commitment of U.S. military forces should be a last resort, after political, economic, and diplomatic efforts have failed.

These guidelines for the use of military force are widely supported within the U.S. military itself. Contrary to Hollywood's stereotypes, military leaders are extremely reluctant to go to war when no vital interests of the United States are at stake, where there are no clear-cut military objectives, without the support of the American people or the Congress, or without sufficient force to achieve speedy and decisive victory with minimal casualties. Colin Powell himself was able to implement these guidelines in the first Gulf War in 1991 (see Chapter 3). Military leaders are wary of seeing their troops placed in danger merely to advance diplomatic goals, or to engage in "peacekeeping," or to "stabilize governments" or to "show the flag." They are reluctant to undertake humanitarian missions while being shot at.

War as Politics

Global Security
News and information about weapons, forces, and military conflicts around the world.
www.globalsecurity. org

In contrast to military leaders, political elites often reflect the view that "war is a continuation of politics by other means"—a view commonly attributed to nineteenth-century German theorist of war Karl von Clausewitz. Military force may be used to protect interests that are important to the United States but not necessarily vital. Otherwise American elites would be rendered largely impotent in world affairs. Diplomatic efforts to achieve satisfactory results often depend on the express or implied threat of military force. Political elites have demonstrated a willingness to use military force for a variety of missions in addition to the conduct of conventional war:

- Demonstrating U.S. resolve in crisis situations.
- Demonstrating U.S. support for democratic governments.
- Protecting U.S. citizens living abroad.
- Peacemaking among warring factions or nations.
- Peacekeeping where hostile factions or nations have accepted a peace agreement.
- Providing humanitarian aid often under warlike conditions.
- Assisting in the war against drug trafficking.

In pursuit of such objectives, recent U.S. presidents have sent troops to Lebanon in 1982 to stabilize the government (Reagan), to Grenada in 1983 to rescue American medical students and restore democratic government (Reagan), to Panama in 1989 to oust drug-trafficking General Manuel Antonio Noriega from power and to protect U.S. citizens (Bush), to Somalia in 1992–1993 to provide emergency humanitarian aid (Bush and Clinton), to Haiti in 1994 (Clinton) to restore constitutional government and again to Haiti in 2004 (Bush), and to Bosnia and Kosovo (Clinton) for peace-keeping among warring ethnic factions.

The War on Terrorism

Terrorism Research Center
Web site dedicated to "informing the public of phenomena of terrorism and information warfare." It contains news, analytical essays on terrorist issues, and many links to other terrorism materials and research sources.
www.terrorism.com

The war on terrorism* creates several new conditions for the use of military force. These include:

- Direct attacks against terrorist forces to capture or kill them. These operations are usually carried out by highly trained Special Operations Forces.
- Attacks on nations that harbor terrorists, allow terrorist to maintain bases, or supply and equip terrorist organizations. In 2001 the United States relied principally on Special Forces working in conjunction with tribal forces in Afghanistan to attack Al Queda terrorists and topple the Taliban regime that harbored and supported Al Queda.

---

*Title 22 of the *U.S. Code*, Section 2656 (d): "The term 'terrorism' means premeditated, politically motivated violence perpetrated against noncombatant targets by subnational groups or clandestine agents, usually intended to influence an audience."

| IN BRIEF | **ELITES DIFFER OVER THE USE OF FORCE** |

- Political elites argue that U.S. military forces may be used to protect interests that are important to the nation but not necessarily vital, including peacemaking, peacekeeping, the support of democratic governments, and humanitarian aid.
- Military elites argue that U.S. military forces should be used only to protect vital national interests, that they be given clear military objectives, that they employ overwhelming strength,

that they have the support of Congress and the American people, and that they should be used only as a last resort.

- The war on terror has placed additional responsibilities on the U.S. military, including direct attacks on terrorists, attacks on nations that harbor terrorists, and preemptive strikes on regimes that threaten to use weapons of mass distraction.

- Preemptive attacks on regimes that threaten to use weapons of mass destruction—chemical, biological, or nuclear weapons—against the United States or its allies, or to supply terrorist organizations with these weapons. Preemptive military action represents a reversal of traditional U.S. policy. Historically the United States acted militarily only in response to a direct attack on its own forces or those of its allies. But the terrorist attack on the World Trade Center in New York and the Pentagon in Washington on September 11, 2001, initiated the current war on terrorism. The Bush administration argues that the war in Iraq is a part of the war on terrorism. The argument for preemptive military action was summarized by President Bush's Secretary of State, Condeleeza Rice: "We cannot wait until the smoking gun becomes a mushroom cloud."

FOCUS | ELITE FOREIGN POLICY MAKING: THE COUNCIL ON FOREIGN RELATIONS

The influence of the Council on Foreign Relations (CFR) throughout government is so pervasive that it is difficult to distinguish the CFR from government programs. "The Council on Foreign Relations, while not financed by government, works so closely with it that it is difficult to distinguish council actions stimulated by government from autonomous actions."[a] Of course, the CFR denies that it exercises any control over U.S. foreign policy. Indeed, its by-laws declare that "the Council shall not take any position on questions of foreign policy and no person is authorized to speak or purport to speak for the Council on such matters."[b] But policy initiation and consensus building do not require the CFR to officially adopt policy positions.

The history of CFR policy accomplishments is dazzling. It developed the Kellogg Peace Pact in the 1920s, stiffened U.S. opposition to Japanese Pacific expansion in the 1930s, designed major portions of the United Nations' charter, and devised the "containment" policy to halt Soviet expansion in Europe after World War II. It also laid the groundwork for the NATO agreement and devised the Marshall Plan for European recovery. In the Kennedy and Johnson administrations, the Council took the lead in formulating U.S. policy in Southeast Asia—including both the initial decision to intervene militarily in Vietnam and the later decision to withdraw. Secretary of State Henry Kissinger avoided directly attributing U.S. policy to the CFR peace plan, but the plan itself eventually became the basis of the January 1973 Paris Peace Agreement.

Following Vietnam, the CFR, under David Rockefeller's tenure as chairman, developed an international campaign on behalf of "human rights" with money from the Ford, Lilly, Mellon, and Rockefeller Foundations. The campaign became the centerpiece of the Carter administration's foreign policy.

The Council takes pride in the success of the Cold War containment policy, which was first outlined by CFR member George Kennan in his 1947 "X" article in CFR's leading publication, *Foreign Affairs*. But it recognizes that the end of the Cold War necessitates another restructuring of fundamental policy goals. Above all, the Council seeks to keep the United States actively involved in international politics, that is, to avoid isolationism, trade barriers, and "xenophobia." Its members actively support U.S. aid to Russia and other former Soviet republics; the North American Free Trade Agreement, the World Trade Organization, and other efforts to stimulate global trade; an active U.S. role in peace efforts in the Middle East, Bosnia, and other republics of the former Yugoslavia; and the development of a strategy for dealing with the Islamic world.

The CFR strongly supports multinationalism in U.S. foreign policy. It disdains American "unilateralism"—foreign and military policy initiatives that do not have widespread support among Western European nations or the United Nations generally. The CFR backed Secretary of State Colin Powell in his unsuccessful effort to convince the U.N. Security Council to back the U.S. invasion of Iraq. Disappointed at the U.N.'s refusal to enforce more than a dozen of its resolutions, all of which were ignored by Saddam Hussein, the CFR supported the initial invasion of Iraq. But as the U.S. occupation of Iraq grew more costly and with no end in sight, the CFR began to search for an "exit strategy." The CFR rejected Bush's goal of establishing a democracy in Iraq as unrealistic and urged the president to place greater emphasis on regional diplomacy in the Middle East, including a revival of the Israeli-Palestinian peace process, as a way of bringing stability to Iraq. When President George W. Bush insisted on a "stay the course" policy, the CFR turned to the creation of the Iraq Study Group. (The Iraq Study Group was composed largely of CFR members.) The CFR strongly supports the recommendations of the Iraq Study Group.[c] Yet the Council continues to warn that the United States must not "retreat into our own borders or into any kind of isolationism."[d]

---

[a]Lester Milbraith, "Interest Groups in Foreign Policy," in *Domestic Sources of Foreign Policy*, James Rosenau, ed. (New York: Free Press, 1967), p. 247.

[b]Council on Foreign Relations, *Annual Report* (1992), p. 174.

[c]*The Iraq Study Group Report* (New York: Random House Vintage Books, 2006).

[d]www.cfr.org/publications/Iraq

Afghanistan: "Operation Enduring Freedom"

The military phase of the war on terrorism began October 7, 2001, when U.S. Air Force and Navy aircraft began attacks on known Al Queda bases in Afghanistan. Simultaneously, U.S. Special Forces began to organize and lead anti-Taliban fighters, including several tribal groups calling themselves the Northern Alliance, in a campaign against the ruling Taliban. Coming so soon after the 9/11 attack on the United States, the U.S. military effort in Afghanistan enjoyed widespread international support. A coalition of nations participated in "Operation Enduring Freedom"; some, including Britain and Canada contributed combat troops, while others including Pakistan, Saudi Arabia, and Uzbekistan allowed U.S. forces to base operations in their territory. Kabul, the capital of Afghanistan, was occupied by anti-Taliban forces on November 13, 2001. By April, 2002, Al Queda and Taliban forces had been either destroyed or scattered into small groups in the mountainous areas of Afghanistan and neighboring Pakistan. However, the leader of Al Queda, Osama bin Laden, escaped capture. A new government was installed in Kabul, but various tribal chiefs throughout Afghanistan continue to exercise independent power. And the Taliban remained a strong force in the mountainous regions of Southern Afghanistan. In 2004 the United States officially turned over command of allied military forces in Afghanistan to NATO.

THE WAR IN IRAQ

Elites lose the support of the masses when they fail to produce victories in war. And the masses lose confidence in elite governance when the elites themselves cannot agree on a course of action.

"Operation Iraqi Freedom"

At the end of the Gulf War in 1991, the Iraqi regime of Saddam Hussein agreed to destroy all its chemical and biological weapons and to end its efforts to acquire nuclear weapons. United Nations inspectors were to verify Iraqi compliance with these conditions. But Saddam's regime refused to cooperate. In 1998 he ordered the inspectors out of the country. Over a twelve-year period Iraq violated at least a dozen U.N. resolutions. Following a U.S. military buildup in the region in late 2002, Saddam allowed U.N. inspectors to return but continued to obstruct their work. On March 19, 2003, after giving Saddam a forty-eight hour warning to leave Iraq, the United States and Great Britain launched air strikes designed to eliminate Saddam and his top command.

At different times President Bush stated the purposes of "Operation Iraqi Freedom" as (1) the elimination of Iraq's weapons of mass destruction, (2) a "regime change" for Iraq to end the threat that Saddam posed for his neighbors and to free the Iraqi people from his oppressive rule, and (3) to ensure that Saddam would not harbor or assist terrorist organizations. But President Bush and Secretary of State Colin Powell failed to secure U.N. Security Council approval for military action. Among the permanent members of the Security Counsel, only the British, with the strong support of Prime Minister Tony Blair, were prepared to offer significant military support for the war against Saddam. Mass opinion in America supported military action, but opinion in Europe opposed it. France and Germany led the diplomatic opposition, Turkey refused to let U.S. troops use its territory to attack Iraq, and the United States was obliged to rely primarily on Kuwait, Qatar, and the other smaller Gulf states for regional support.

The U.S. military wanted to wage war in the fashion of the successful Gulf War—a period of heavy air bombardment to "prepare the battlefield," followed by a massive ground attack using overwhelming military force. But Secretary of Defense Donald Rumsfeld wanted a "leaner" fighting force in Iraq. He deployed fewer than half of the air, ground, and naval forces that had been used in the Gulf War. And he began the air and ground attacks simultaneously.

American and British soldiers and Marines took just twenty-one days to sweep the 350 miles from the Kuwait border to downtown Baghdad. The British 3rd Armored Division, with Australian support, captured the port city of Basra; the U.S. 3rd Infantry Division moved up the west side of the Euphrates River; and the U.S. 1st Marine Division moved up the east side. Special Operations Forces, together with elements of the 101st Airborne Division, joined Kurdish forces in northern Iraq. Special Operations Forces also acted quickly to secure Iraq's oil fields and prevent their destruction. At first progress was hindered by the requirement that soldiers wear heavy chemical protection gear and carry decontamination equipment. But neither chemical nor biological weapons were used against U.S. forces. The advance on Baghdad was speeded up and the city was captured with precious few casualties.

THE OCCUPATION OF IRAQ

The American occupation of Iraq started out poorly and proceeded over time to become worse. Planning for post-war Iraq appeared nonexistent. The U.S. administrator for Iraq, Paul Bremmer, began by dismissing the entire Iraqi Army, sending thousands of well-armed unemployed young men into the streets. The United States promised to restore infrastructure—water, electricity, roads, etc.—yet Bremmer pursued a policy of dismissing virtually all Iraqi managers and technicians on the grounds that they had been Bathists (Saddam's ruling party members). Later, the United States would be obliged to begin recruiting and training an Iraqi Army and police force and bringing in U.S. contract workers, managers, and technicians. Bremmer was fired after one year.

Soon, Iraqi street mobs that had earlier torn down Saddam's statue began demonstrations against the American presence. An insurgent movement seemed to surprise Secretary of Defense Donald Rumsfeld. He steadfastly refused to send additional U.S. troops to Iraq to handle the insurgency and insisted that a new Iraqi government could eventually recruit and train enough troops to contain the insurgency. No weapons of mass destruction were found despite an intensive search. Saddam himself was captured and turned over to the Iraqis who conducted a bizarre show trial that allowed Saddam to rally his followers. Three years after his capture he was convicted of mass murder and executed by hanging. Bush's critics at home and abroad increasingly complained of the president's "unilateralism"—his willingness to go to war without the support of the United Nations, and they charged that he misled Congress, the U.N., and the American people about the existence of weapons of mass destruction.

IRAQI GOVERNANCE

The population of Iraq is composed of three major factions: the Kurds, who occupy most of Northeastern Iraq; the Shiites, who occupy most of Southern Iraq; and the

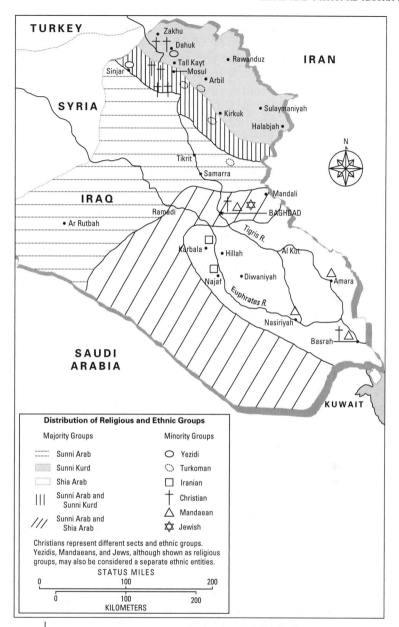

FIGURE 16.3 | DISTRIBUTION OF RELIGIOUS GROUPS IN IRAQ

Source: *Iraq Study Group Report.*

Sunnis, who occupy Central Iraq. Baghdad itself is divided between Sunni and Shiite neighborhoods (see Figure 16.3). The Sunnis have long dominated Iraq. Saddam's family was Sunni. Yet the Shiites are the largest faction, with more than half of the total population of Iraq. Over the years, the Kurds have fought for a separate Kurdistan, an outcome strongly opposed by neighboring Turkey.

Iraq held its first nationwide election in fifty years in 2003, despite violence and threats of violence. Nearly 60 percent of the population participated, many proudly displaying their blue-inked thumbs to signal that they had voted. The result was a new constitution that was approved in a second vote that year. However, a substantial number of Sunnis boycotted the elections, fearing a loss of their power and the ascendancy of the Shiites. The United States officially turned over sovereignty to a new Iraqi government in 2004.

THE INSURGENCY

Attacks on U.S. forces and the Iraqi Army and police grew in intensity and deadliness month after month. Most attacks against Americans came from disaffected Sunni Arabs, including former elements of the Saddam regime. Al Queda was responsible for a portion of the violence, including the more spectacular suicide attacks, truck bombs, and attacks on religious and political targets. The insurgency raised the flag of "Jihad" and brought in thousands of Islamic radical foreign fighters. The Shiites organized their own militia, the strongest being the Mahdi Army, with as many as 60,000 fighters led by Moqtada al-Sadr. Large areas of Iraq came under the control of one or another of these insurgent groups.

American military forces suffered a gruesome toll in lives and limbs. By 2006 over 3,000 American troops had been killed and 20,000 wounded, many from "improvised explosive devices." U.S. Army and Marine forces approached the "breaking point." Nearly every Army and Marine combat unit, and several National Guard and Reserve units, were rotated into Iraq more than once. Rotations were typically one year for Army units and seven months for Marine units. The strain on U.S. forces worldwide became clearly evident, with both personnel and equipment wearing down.

"STAY THE COURSE"

U.S. policy in Iraq focused primarily on security. The key phrase was "clear, hold, and build." U.S. military forces were to clear neighborhoods and cities, towns and regions, of insurgents; then hold the cleared areas with U.S.-trained and -equipped Iraqi Army and police forces; and then to begin to rebuild infrastructure. U.S. forces were able to "clear" many areas, but there were too few troops to "hold" these areas. Iraqi forces were unable or unwilling to halt insurgents from reoccupying these areas after the U.S. troops left. Very little "building" took place. The Bush administration declined to increase U.S. troop strength (despite early recommendations that 500,000 troops would be required to effectively occupy Iraq). Despite U.S. training and equipment and the presence of U.S. advisers in Iraqi units, Iraqi security forces made only "fitful progress toward becoming a reliable fighting force loyal to the national government."[2]

Many members of the Iraqi security forces remained loyal to their sectarian—Shiite or Sunni—goals, rather than the agenda of the national government. Many of these units simply refuse to carry out assigned missions.

Nevertheless, President Bush continued to argue that the war in Iraq was central to the worldwide war against terrorism. He argued that an abrupt withdrawal ("cut and run") would encourage radical Islamic terrorists around the world.

Failure is not an option. Iraq would become a safe haven from which terrorists could plan attacks against American interests abroad, and our allies. Middle East reformers would never again fully trust American assurances of support for democracy in human rights in the region. Iraq is the central front in the global war on terror.[3]

CIVIL WAR

Iraq gradually disintegrated into a bloody civil war, with Sunni and Shiite forces committing atrocities against each other. By 2006 most of the violence in Iraq was occurring among various factions; thousands of Iraqi were victims of sectarian killings. The Shiites, the majority of Iraq's population, gained power for the first time in more than a thousand years. Above all, the Shiites are interested in preserving that power. The Sunnis fear displacement and the loss of their traditional position of power in Iraq. The Kurds seek at a minimum quasi-independence and control over the oil resources in their region. The Shiites also seek control over oil resources in southern Iraq. But the areas with the largest Sunni population lack oil resources, so the Sunni fight to maintain control of all of Iraq. Corruption is rampant throughout Iraq, the judiciary is weak, oil production is down, and the government is unable to produce an acceptable plan of national reconciliation.

THE IRAQ STUDY GROUP

Elites frequently create special commissions to deal with particularly vexing national problems. From the Warren Commission report on the assassination of President John F. Kennedy in 1963 to the present, this device has been employed to find consensus among elites and to reassure the masses that the elites are governing wisely.

A bipartisan Iraq Study Group (ISG) was created in 2006 to review the situation in Iraq and propose a new strategy for the way forward. The ISG was co-chaired by former Secretary of State James A. Baker III and former House Foreign Relations Committee Chairman Lee H. Hamilton. The ISG Report did not criticize Bush's original decision to invade Iraq, but taken as a whole the report was a clear rebuke of Bush's policies in Iraq and a rejection of the president's "we are winning" description of the war. "The situation in Iraq is grave and deteriorating. There is no path to guaranteed success, but the prospects can be improved."[4] The report made seventy-nine specific recommendations, including:

- A new diplomatic offensive in the region, including contacts with Syria and Iran, to convince other nations that chaos in Iraq would destabilize the entire region.
- Accelerated efforts by the Iraqi government to achieve national reconciliation, including an agreement between Kurds, Shiites, and Sunnis to end sectarian violence and come to an agreement over the distribution of oil revenues.
- Continued training and support of Iraqi security forces and continued economic support *only* if the Iraqi government made progress toward

FOCUS │ MASS OPPOSITION TO THE WAR IN IRAQ

Americans demand quick victory in war. With the exception of World War II, American public support for wars, notably Korea (1950–1953) and Vietnam (1965–1973), declined steadily as casualties rose and no end appeared in sight. The initial "rally 'round the flag" support for military action begins to wane after the first year of combat. Quick victories with few casualties, as in the Gulf War (1991), inspire support for the president and his decision to go to war. Prolonged stalemates with mounting casualties gradually erode public support for war.

Shortly after the war in Iraq began, most Americans thought Iraq was worth going to war over. Indeed, this opinion climbed to 76 percent immediately following the capture of Baghdad. But as American casualties mounted and no end to the fighting appeared in sight, mass opinion in support of the war declined rapidly. By late 2004 a majority of Americans believed that Iraq was not worth going to war over (see figure).

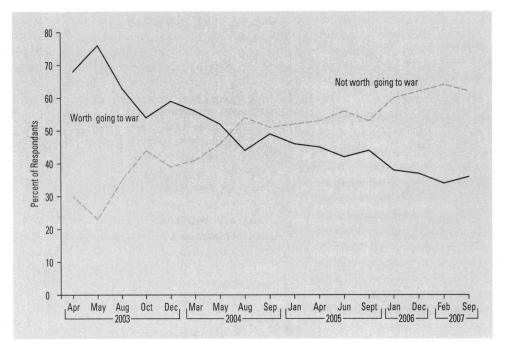

Source: Data derived from Gallup polls.

national reconciliation. Reconciliation should include a reintegration of Bathists into the government and far-reaching amnesty for insurgents and sectarian militias.

- Changing the primary mission of U.S. troops to advice and support of Iraqi military and police forces, and increasing the number of U.S. military advisers embedded with Iraqi forces.

- The withdrawal of all U.S. combat troops by early 2008. The U.S. would maintain a military presence in Kuwait, Bahrain, and Qatar, and continue to fight Al Queda and other terrorist organizations in the region.

The "Surge"

President Bush ignored the recommendations of the Iraqi Study Group and opted instead for a "surge" in U.S. troops in Iraq. The surge added about 30,000 troops bringing the U.S. total to over 168,000 troops. Democrats in the Congress, many of whom were elected in November 2006, on the pledge to end the war, failed to cut off funds for operations in Iraq. U.S. policy became that of "buying time," first for the training of Iraqi security forces, and secondly, for allowing Sunni, Shiite, and Kurdish factions to reach national reconciliation.

The Drawdown

In September 2007, five years into the U.S. occupation of Iraq, the commander of U.S. forces, General David Petraeus, reported only "uneven" improvements in security, continuing concerns about sectarian violence, stresses on U.S. troops from prolonged tours of duty, and a failure of Iraq's political leadership to reach any significant agreements among the warring factions. President Bush pledged a modest drawdown in U.S. troops in Iraq, but gave no indication of any foreseeable U.S. military withdrawal from the war-torn country.

DEFENSE POLICY MAKING

In theory, the formulation of defense policy begins with an assessment of the range of threats to the nation and its interests. Once major threats have been identified, the next step is to develop strategies designed to counter them. Once strategies have been devised, defense policy making must determine the appropriate forces (military units, personnel, weapons, training, readiness, and so on) required to implement them. Finally budgets must be calculated to finance the required force levels.

National Security Council
NSC membership, functions, press releases, and information on national security issues. *www. whitehouse.gov/nsc*

But in fact differences among elites arise at each step in this policy-making process—differing assessments of the nature of the threats facing the nation, the right strategies to confront these threats, the force levels necessary to implement strategies, and the funds required to provide these forces. Indeed, elites often reverse the process, deciding first on the amount of money that is to be allocated to defense, then structuring strategies and forces to stay within budget limits, and then estimating threats based on the forces available to meet them. Of course, this reversal of rational policy making places the nation in peril.

The National Security Council

The president, as Commander-in-Chief, relies principally upon the National Security Council (NSC) to develop and coordinate security policy. The NSC is chaired by the president and includes the vice president, secretary of state, and secretary of defense. A National Security Adviser heads the staff of the NSC. The Chairman of the Joint Chiefs of Staff and the Director of Central Intelligence (DCI) advises the NFC. The DCI is responsible for assembling and analyzing intelligence on national security threats developed within the intelligence community (see "Intelligence and the Presidency" in Chapter 10). The NSC advises the president on threats and overall strategies and forces required to meet these threats.

DEFENSE PLANNING

Planning in the Department of Defense (DoD) is a continuous process, supervised by the Joint Chiefs of Staff (JCS). The JCS is composed of the Chief of the JCS, a Vice Chief, the Chief of Staff of the Army, the Chief of Naval Operations, the Chief of Staff of the Air Force, and the Commandant of the Marine Corps. In addition to serving on the JCS, these military officers head their respective branches of the armed services. An important policy document produced by the JCS is the *Quadrennial Defense Review*.

ASSESSMENT OF CURRENT THREATS

American Security Council
Organization providing summary information on national security threats.
www.ascusa.org

Currently, the Department of Defense views the global war on terror as the most serious threat to the nation's security. According to the 2006 *Quadrennial Defense Review*, "The enemies in this war are not traditional conventional military forces but rather dispersed, global terrorist networks that exploit Islam to advance radical political plans. These enemies have the avowed aim of acquiring and using nuclear and biological weapons to murder hundreds of thousands of Americans and others around the world."

REORGANIZING THE NATION'S DEFENSES

Under the supervision of Secretary of Defense Donald Rumsfeld, the U.S. military was reconfigured to emphasize *joint* (Army, Navy, Air Force, and Marine) operations and to "become more agile and capable of rapid action in exploiting information advantages to increase operational effectiveness." The chain of command extends from the president to the secretary of defense, to the chief of the JCS, to the various regional commands. Each command encompasses all military forces in their region. (Central Command—CENCOM—is responsible for all military activity in the Middle East.) The basic unit of operations for the Army was changed from the division (with 12,000 to 16,000 men) to the brigade (with 3,000 to 4,000 men).

CURRENT FORCE LEVELS

The end of the Cold War rationalized deep cuts in military forces and defense budgets in the 1990s. The Army was reduced to ten active combat divisions and the Air Force to twelve fighter wings. The Navy now possesses twelve carrier strike forces (a carrier strike force typically includes one aircraft carrier with seventy-five to eighty-five aircraft, plus defending cruisers, destroyers, frigates, attack submarines, and support ships). The Marine Corps retained all three of its Marine Expeditionary Forces (each MEF includes one Marine division, one Marine air wing, and supporting services). (See Table 16.1.) National Guard and Reserve forces have been assigned a larger and more active role. There are about an additional 1.2 million persons in the guard and reserve forces. Military deployments in Iraq and Afghanistan have required about one-third of these forces to be called to active duty.

CURRENT MISSIONS

The war on terrorism has brought a new emphasis on nonconventional forces and tactics (to meet what DoD refers to as "asymmetrical threats"). Special Operations Forces played

TABLE 16.1 | U.S. COMBAT FORCES

End of Cold War	1990	2000	2007
Active duty personnel (in millions)	2.1	1.4	1.4
Army divisions (brigades)	18	10	37
Navy carrier battle groups	15	12	12
Marine expeditionary forces	3	3	3
Air Force fighter wings	24	12	10

Source: Office of the Secretary of Defense.

a central role in defeating the Taliban regime in Afghanistan. Special Operations Forces on the ground, together with manned and unmanned surveillance aircraft, provided the targeting intelligence for U.S. air attacks from carriers in the Arabian Sea and even longer-range bombers based in the continental United States. These attacks allowed Afghan forces opposed to the regime to capture the capital, Kabul, two months after the initiation of Operation Enduring Freedom. Army, Navy, and Air Force Special Operations Forces are currently being expanded and strengthened. They are being trained to adapt quickly to changing circumstances, to communicate intelligence to conventional forces, and to engage in both open and covert military operations.

U.S. military forces are currently deployed in more than 120 countries around the world. The largest deployments are in Iraq, South Korea, and Afghanistan, but U.S. forces are also deployed in Qatar, Bahrain, Saudi Arabia, Kuwait, Bosnia, Kosovo, the Philippines, Japan, Cuba, Columbia, Honduras, as well as the NATO countries. Traditionally U.S. military forces were trained for combat not "peacekeeping" or "nation-building." But currently the U.S. military is tailoring more of its training, doctrine, and equipment to these missions. This means increasing the numbers of military police, civil affairs units, local force trainers, and humanitarian relief supply units.

STRETCHED TOO THIN?

Over the past decade U.S. military forces have been assigned increasing numbers of war-fighting, peacekeeping, nation-building, and humanitarian missions. Yet force levels have remained minimal. But experience has taught the U.S. military that casualties can be kept low only when an overwhelming military force is employed quickly and decisively. Lives are lost when minimal forces are sent into combat, when they have inadequate air combat support, or when they are extended over too wide an area. Current numbers of Army and Air Force combat units and the limited transport and support services available to the military are inadequate to deal with more than a single major regional conflict. Potential regional foes—for example Iran and North Korea—possess modern heavy armor and artillery forces. The United States does not have the military capability to confront two of these regional enemies simultaneously. Moreover, commitments of U.S. troops to peacekeeping and humanitarian missions divert resources, training, and morale away from war-fighting. Morale is also affected when U.S. military forces are deployed abroad for long periods of time.

HOMELAND SECURITY

The terrorist attack of September 11, 2001 (9/11) resulted in 3,000 civilian deaths at the World Trade Center in New York and the Pentagon in Washington. "9/11" awakened America to the threat of terrorism—deliberate attacks on civilian targets by enemies who are willing to sacrifice themselves and their people to their cause.

MASS RESPONSE TO THE WAR ON TERRORISM

On the evening of September 11, President George W. Bush spoke to the American people from the Oval Office in a nationally televised address:

> The pictures of airplanes flying into buildings, fires burning, huge structures collapsing, have filled us with disbelief, terrible sadness, and a quiet, unyielding anger. These mass murders were intended to frighten our nation into chaos and retreat. But they failed, our country is strong. . . .These deliberate and deadly attacks were more than acts of terror. They were acts of war.[5]

The president outlined a broad "response to terrorism" to be fought both at home and abroad through diplomatic, military, financial, homeland security, and humanitarian means.

America's initial response to the terrorist attack of 9/11 was precisely the opposite of the intention of the terrorists. National pride and confidence in national leadership soared in the aftermath of the attack. American flags flew throughout the country. Trust in government rose to levels not seen since the 1960s. Presidential approval ratings reached dramatic highs. Support for military action was overwhelming. (See Table 16.2.) But over time this "rally 'round the flag" effect diminished. Trust in government and support for the president returned to their pre-9/11 levels. Indeed, as the war in Iraq became a bloody stalemate, Americans came to believe that "it was not worth going to war in Iraq." Presidential approval ratings sunk to new lows.

ELITE RESPONSE TO TERRORISM

Elites typically respond to perceived threats to national security with repressive measures: from Lincoln's suspension of the *writ of habeas corpus* during the Civil War; through the Sedition Act of 1918 during World War I that outlawed "disloyal" speech; through the Smith Act of 1940 that made it unlawful to "advocate, abet, advise, or teach" the desirability of overthrowing the government; through the internment of thousands of Japanese Americans living on the West Coast during World War II; through laws placing additional prohibitions on communists during the Cold War; to the current restrictions enacted immediately following 9/11 to pursue the war on terrorism.

THE AVIATION AND TRANSPORTATION SECURITY ACT OF 2001

Congress created a new Transportation Security Agency, later placed in the new Department of Homeland Security, which, among other things, federalized airport passenger screening, required the screening of baggage, authorized federal marshals

TABLE 16.2 | MASS RESPONSE TO THE WAR ON TERRORISM

Do you approve or disapprove of the way George W. Bush is handling the job of president?

	Approve	Disapprove
May 2001	55	40
September 2001	89	9
January 2003	59	38
April 2004	53	44
May 2004	46	48
September 2005	39	58
November 2005	37	60
February 2006	38	60
June 2006	36	57
November 2006	33	62
May 2007	34	63
September 2007	33	62

Do you approve or disapprove of the way George W. Bush is handling the campaign against terrorism?

	Approve	Disapprove
December 2001	90	6
April 2002	80	17
January 2003	66	31
April 2004	52	45
May 2004	41	58
May 2006	47	45
December 2006	42	55
May 2007	47	50
September 2007	45	52

Source: Various *Gallup* polls.

on domestic and international flights, and tightened airport security throughout the United States.

THE PATRIOT ACT

An even more sweeping enactment followed: the Patriot Act of 2001, officially the Uniting and Strengthening America Act by Providing Appropriate Tools Required to Intercept and Obstruct Terrorism. The act was passed nearly unanimously in the

Senate (98 to 1) and overwhelmingly in the House (337 to 66), with the support of both Democrats and Republicans.

Among the key provisions of the Patriot Act are:

- *Roving Wiretaps.* Allows wiretaps of any telephones that suspects might use instead of requiring separate warrants for each line.
- *Internet Tracking.* Allows law enforcement authorities to track Internet communications, that is, to "surf the Web" without obtaining warrants.
- *Business Records.* Allows investigators to obtain information from credit cards, bank records, consumer purchases, libraries, schools and colleges, etc.
- *Foreign Intelligence Surveillance Court.* A special Foreign Intelligence Surveillance Court may issue search warrants on an investigator's assertion that the information sought is relevant to a terrorist investigation. No showing of "probable cause" is required. The warrant is not made public, in order to avoid "tipping off" the subject.
- *Property Seizure.* Authorizes the seizure of the property of suspected terrorists. Persons whose property is seized bear the burden of proof that the property was not used for terrorist purposes in order to secure the return of their property.
- *Detention.* Allows the detention of suspected terrorists for lengthy periods without judicial recourse.
- *Aliens Reporting and Detention.* Authorizes the Immigration and Naturalization Service to require reporting by aliens of selected nations and indefinite detention of illegal aliens suspected of terrorist connections.
- *Prohibits Harboring of Terrorists.* Creates a new federal crime: knowingly harboring persons who have committed, or are about to commit, a terrorist act.

The Patriot Act was extended in 2005 with relatively few technical changes.

ENEMY COMBATANTS

The U.S. military detains hundreds of "enemy combatants" abroad and at Guantanamo Bay, Cuba. These include persons captured in the fighting in Afghanistan and Iraq, as well as some terrorists captured in other nations. Traditionally, prisoners of war are not entitled to rights under the U.S. Constitution. But they are to be afforded humane treatment under the international Geneva Convention. They may be detained for the duration of a war. The category of "enemy combatant" appears to be analogous to prisoner of war. However, the war on terrorism does not appear to have a specific duration.

But in 2004 the U.S. Supreme Court held the enemy combatants captured on the battlefield and "imprisoned in territory over which the United States exercises an exclusive jurisdiction and control" are entitled to constitutional rights, including habeas corpus—the right to bring their case to U.S. courts.[6] President Bush established special military commissions to try detainees. But the Supreme Court struck down these commissions because Congress had not established them by law, and they did not operate under the rules of the Uniform Code of Military Justice which Congress had enacted years ago. The Court said that the president's powers as commander-in-chief did not grant him the power to hold and try detainees without congressional legislation.[7] Bush then promptly asked Congress for the power to establish special military tribunals with special rules to try detainees, and Congress immediately did so.

THE DEPARTMENT OF HOMELAND SECURITY

Department of Homeland Security
Official Web site for information on travel, transportation, homeland protection, and threat status.
www.dhs.gov

Elites often create new bureaucratic organizations to symbolize their commitment to protect the masses. In October 2001, less than one month after the 9/11 attack, President Bush issued an executive order establishing an Office of Homeland Security that was expected to "coordinate" the counterterrorist activities of over forty separate bureaucracies. Then later in 2002, in response to growing criticism that he had not done enough to reassure the masses of the federal government's commitment to protect them from terrorism, President Bush proposed, and Congress established, a new Department of Homeland Security.

The stated mission of the new department is to prevent terrorist attacks within the United States, to reduce America's vulnerability to terrorism, and to minimize damage and recover from attacks that do occur. The new department includes the U.S. Customs Service (formerly part of the Department of the Treasury); the Immigration and Naturalization Service (INS) renamed Immigration and Customs Enforcement (ICE), and the Border Patrol (formerly part of the Department of Justice); the Transportation Security Administration (formerly part of the Department of Transportation); the United States Coast Guard (formerly part of the Department of Transportation); the Secret Service (formerly part of the Department of the Treasury); and FEMA, the Federal Emergency Management Agency (formerly an independent agency). Perhaps the most publicized activity of the Department of Homeland Security is its "Security Advisory System," a scale of five conditions indicating increasing risk of terrorist attack (see Figure 16.4). But the conditions, indicated by colors, have had little effect on the general public.

Central Intelligence Agency
CIA official Web site, with history, news, and links to its *World Fact Book*, with information on every nation.
www.cia.gov

INTEGRATING FOREIGN AND DOMESTIC INTELLIGENCE

Perhaps the greatest obstacle to the government's effectiveness in fighting terrorism is the failure to integrate foreign intelligence with domestic antiterrorist intelligence. The Federal Bureau of Investigation (FBI) has the principal responsibility for counterterrorism *within* the United States. The Central Intelligence Agency (CIA) is responsible for gathering and analyzing intelligence on terrorist activity *outside* of the United States. Indeed, prior to the passage of the Patriot Act, the CIA was prohibited by law from gathering intelligence on individuals or groups within the United States or even sharing information with the FBI about American citizens that the CIA gathered abroad. Indeed, *The 9/11 Commission Report* concluded that a contributing cause to the 9/11 attack was the failure of agencies to communicate among themselves.[8] The Commission recommended that the "wall" between domestic and foreign intelligence be removed, that a National Counterintelligence Center be established under the Director of Central Intelligence (see Chapter 10), and that efforts be undertaken to discourage a "culture" in which various agencies believe they "own" information. But the CIA and the FBI continue largely along separate paths.

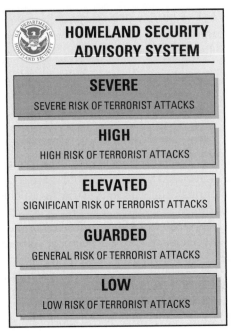

FIGURE 16.4 | THE HOMELAND SECURITY ADVISORY SYSTEM

Source: Department of Homeland Security.

NATIONAL SECURITY: AN ELITIST INTERPRETATION

American elites, like elites of every nation, seek power in the international arena. National security is a primary responsibility of any government. National security is a product of economic, diplomatic, and, most of all, military power.

1. During the long cold war, deterrence strategy prevented nuclear war by making the consequences of a nuclear attack unacceptable to rational elites in both the United States and the former Soviet Union. Neither side could consider launching a strike because of the terrible consequences if the other side in the conflict retaliated. This mutual balance of terror was referred to as "mutual assured destruction" or "MAD."
2. Negotiations between American and Russian elites resulted in a series of agreements—SALT I, SALT II, START I, START II, and the Treaty of Moscow—that eventually reduced nuclear weapons to a small fraction of Cold War levels.
3. Current nuclear weapons strategies focus on nondeterrable threats— weapons launched from terrorist nations or terrorist groups that are not deterred by the threat of a retaliatory strike on their own people. Antiballistic missiles were first proposed by President Ronald Reagan and later deployed by President George W. Bush. Despite technological challenges, antiballistic missile defenses represent the only safeguard against missile attack by a rogue nation.

4. The collapse of Communist governments in Eastern Europe, the unification of Germany, and dissolution of the Soviet Union greatly diminished the threat to European security. Today NATO is confronted with the question of the admission of Eastern European nations and the question of whether it is wise to deploy its troops on missions outside of Western Europe.

5. Elites appear divided over policy guidelines regarding when to use military force. Most military leaders argue that troops should be used only to protect vital national interests, where there are clearly defined military objectives, and with the support of Congress and the American people. Furthermore, military force should be used to achieve speedy and decisive victory with minimum casualties, and only as a last resort.

6. In contrast, political and diplomatic leaders argue that troops may be used in support of important political objectives and humanitarian goals. These may include support for democratic governments, peacemaking among warring factions or nations, peacekeeping where hostile parties have agreed to settlement, and the provision of humanitarian aid.

7. The initial decision to go to war in Iraq was widely supported by both elites and masses. But the prolonged occupation of Iraq gradually eroded mass support. Elites divided over the future course of action in Iraq, with the president arguing the importance of remaining there, and other elites, including the prestigious Iraq Study Group, arguing for an exit strategy.

8. The American people responded to the 9/11 attack with strong support for the nation's leadership as well as security measures designed to reduce the threat of terrorism.

9. Historically, elites have responded to national security threats with repressive measures. The Patriot Act was supported in Congress by large majorities of both parties. It gave federal law enforcement authorities sweeping new powers of searches, seizures, surveillance, and detention of suspects in fighting the war on terrorism.

10. The war on terrorism has placed greater restrictions on the liberties of Americans. As in the past, Americans have supported restrictions on their liberties when confronted with perceived serious threats to their security.

SELECTED READINGS

Clausewitz, Carl von. *On War*. Edited and translated by Michael Howard and Peter Paret. Princeton, N.J.: Princeton University Press, 1984. The classic theory of war and military operations, emphasizing their political character; first published in 1832.

Combs, Cynthia C. *Terrorism in the 21st Century*, 4th ed. Upper Saddle River, N.J.: Prentice-Hall, 2006. History of terrorism, terrorist operations, and responses to terrorism, written for those not familiar with the topic.

Hastedt, Glenn P. *American Foreign Policy: Past, Present, Future*, 6th ed. Upper Saddle River, N.J.: Prentice-Hall, 2006. A foreign policy text that deals with national security issues within the broader context of foreign policy.

International Institute for Strategic Studies. *The Military Balance*. London: International Institute for Strategic Studies, published annually. Careful description of the military forces of more than 160 countries; this book is considered the most authoritative public information available.

Kegley, Charles W. *The New Global Terrorism.*
Upper Saddle River, N.J.: Prentice-Hall, 2003.
Describing post-9/11 terrorism, its multiple roots,
and leading ideas for winning the "war on global
terrorism."

Magstadt, Thomas M. *An Empire If You Can Keep It:
Power and Principle in American Foreign Policy.*
Washington, D.C.: CQ Press, 2004.

Comprehensive text on American foreign policy,
describing its history, the Cold War, the Gulf War,
September 11, and the war on terrorism.

Snow, Donald M. *When America Fights: The Uses of
U.S. Military Force.* Washington, D.C.: CQ Press,
2000. Questions U.S. military involvement in
"peacekeeping" operations. Discusses the use of
force in relation to U.S. national interests.

Notes

1. Hans Morganthau, *Politics Among Nations,*
   5th ed. (New York: Alfred A. Knopf, 1973), p. 27.
2. *Iraq Study Group Report.* Authorized edition.
   (New York: Vintage Books, 2006), p. 37
3. President George W. Bush, *National Strategy for
   Victory in Iraq,* November 1, 2005.
   www.whitehouse.gov.
4. *Iraq Study Group Report.* Authorized edition.
   (New York: Vintage Books, 2006), p. ix.
5. *Presidential Address to the Nation,* September 11,
   2001.
6. *Rasul v. Bush* 524 U.S. 466 (2004).
7. *Hamden v. Rumsfeld,* June 29, 2006.
8. *The 9/11 Commission Report* (New York: W. W.
   Norton, 2003).

The kind of elitists I admire are those who ruthlessly seek out and encourage intelligence and who believe that competition—and, inevitably, some measure of failure—will do more for character than coddling ever can. My kind of elitist does not grade on a curve and is willing to flunk the whole class.

William A. Henry III

What Can Students Do?

Regardless of what students are told by high school graduation speakers about their ability to reshape the world, elites—not students—govern the nation. It will be a long while before anyone in college today occupies a position of power allowing him or her to shape American society. In the meantime, what can students really do to help preserve democratic values?

1. *Avoid being exploited or used by demagogues of the left or right.* It is wise to lower your expectations about short-term possibilities for change. Excessive idealism, coupled with impatience to change society now, leads only to bitterness and disillusionment. In the long run, these feelings may reduce rather than increase your political effectiveness. Excessive idealism can also expose you to the demagogic appeals of those politicians who exploit others' idealism for their own advantage. Understanding your personal limits in shaping the world and resolving society's problems is important. It is time to reexamine adolescent optimism about "changing the world."

2. *Develop your powers to think critically.* You will benefit from reexamining the "truths" taught in the public schools—looking beyond the slogans of democracy (and of Marxism) to the realities of power in contemporary society. Just as this book has tried to reexamine traditional teachings about American government, concerned students should also critically reexamine the economic system, the social system, the communications system, and even the accepted "truths" of the physical and biological sciences. Developing your independent powers of social and political analysis can help you resist the flood tide of popular rhetoric, the symbolic posturing of politicians, and the pseudoscience of the bureaucratic social engineers. You can learn to be wary of the politician or bureaucrat who promises to solve society's problems with a stroke of the pen: to end racism, eliminate poverty, cure the sick, prevent crime, clean

"Résumés over there."

the air and water, provide new energy, all without imposing any new taxes or further restricting individual freedom. You will learn that society's problems have no simple solutions.

3. *Master the technological revolution rather than letting it master you.* For example, you should endeavor to learn about one or more aspects of technology in the pursuit of your education. If computers are going to direct your life, why not learn some computer technology yourself? The same applies to social institutions. If laws regulate your life, why not master some aspects of the law yourself, even as an undergraduate? If you are going to be the object of the administrative, managerial, and budgetary practices of large bureaucracies, why not learn something about these subjects, for self-defense if nothing else? If you are not majoring in any of the physical or biological sciences, why not explore some of these courses—perhaps on a pass-fail basis if your school permits it? The more you know about today's technology, the less impressed you will be when someone tells you that certain policies are "technological requirements."

4. *Become familiar with the meaning of individual freedom and dignity throughout the ages.* Read about and understand the human quest for freedom in many times and cultures—from St. Thomas More to Aleksandr Solzhenitsyn, from Antigone to Galileo. You should also learn to view American democracy from a world perspective, comparing the personal freedoms we enjoy with those existing in other nations. It is one thing to struggle against mindless corporate and governmental bureaucracies in this country but quite another to conclude that the United States is "not worth saving"—especially when

viewing the personal liberties of Americans in the context of the personal restrictions in many other nations.

5. *Maintain a healthy distrust of government and assume responsibility for your own life.* Personal freedom is most endangered when we place too much trust in government, see great idealism in its actions, and have unquestioning faith in our public leaders. Democratic values—individual dignity, freedom of speech and the press, rights of dissent, personal liberty—are safer when we are suspicious of government and its power and worry about its size and complexity. Perhaps the most important danger to a free people is that they "politicize" all the problems confronting them as individuals, blame government and "society" for the problems that beset them, and therefore excuse themselves from personal efforts to confront these problems. If we look to government to resolve all our problems, our social dependency will increase, and we will assume less responsibility for our lives. The traditional democratic value is to encourage individuals to shape their own destinies.

We the People of the United States, in Order to form a more perfect Union, establish Justice, insure domestic Tranquility, provide for the common defense, promote the general Welfare, and secure the Blessings of Liberty to ourselves and our Posterity, do ordain and establish this Constitution for the United States of America.

Preamble to the Constitution of the United States of America

THE CONSTITUTION OF THE UNITED STATES OF AMERICA

ARTICLE I

Section 1 All legislative Powers herein granted shall be vested in a Congress of the United States, which shall consist of a Senate and House of Representatives.

Section 2 The House of Representatives shall be composed of Members chosen every second Year by the People of the several States, and the Electors in each State shall have the Qualifications requisite for Electors of the most numerous Branch of the State Legislature.

No Person shall be a Representative who shall not have attained to the age of twenty five Years, and been seven Years a Citizen of the United States, and who shall not, when elected, be an Inhabitant of that State in which he shall be chosen.

Representatives and direct Taxes shall be apportioned among the several States which may be included within this Union, according to their respective Numbers, *which shall be determined by adding to the whole Number of free Persons, including those bound to Service for a Term of Years, and excluding Indians not taxed, three fifths of all other persons.*[†]

The actual Enumeration shall be made within three Years after the first Meeting of the Congress of the United States, and within every subsequent Term of ten Years, in such Manner as they shall by Law direct. The Number of Representatives shall not exceed one for every thirty Thousand, but each State shall have at Least one Representative, and until such enumeration shall be made, the State of New Hampshire shall be entitled to chuse three, Massachusetts eight, Rhode-Island and Providence Plantations one, Connecticut five, New York six, New Jersey

---

[†]Superseded by the Fourteenth Amendment. Throughout, italics indicate passages altered by subsequent amendments.

four, Pennsylvania eight, Delaware one, Maryland six, Virginia ten, North Carolina five, South Carolina five, and Georgia three.

When vacancies happen in the Representation from any State, the Executive Authority thereof shall issue Writs of Election to fill such Vacancies.

The House of Representatives shall chuse their Speaker and other Officers; and shall have the sole Power of Impeachment.

Section 3 The Senate of the United States shall be composed of two Senators from each State, *chosen by the Legislature thereof,*[*] for six Years; and each Senator shall have one Vote.

Immediately after they shall be assembled in Consequence of the first Election, they shall be divided as equally as may be into three Classes. The Seats of the Senators of the first Class shall be vacated at the Expiration of the second Year, of the second Class at the Expiration of the fourth Year, and of the third Class at the Expiration of the sixth Year, so that one third may be chosen every second Year; *and if Vacancies happen by Resignation, or otherwise, during the Recess of the Legislature of any State, the Executive thereof may make temporary Appointments until the next Meeting of the Legislature, which shall then fill such Vacancies.*[**] No Person shall be a Senator who shall not have attained to the Age of thirty Years, and been nine Years a Citizen of the United States, and who shall not, when elected, be an Inhabitant of the State for which he shall be chosen.

The Vice President of the United States shall be President of the Senate, but shall have no Vote, unless they be equally divided.

The Senate shall chuse their other Officers, and also a President pro tempore, in the Absence of the Vice President, or when he shall exercise the Office of President of the United States.

The Senate shall have the sole Power to try all Impeachments. When sitting for that Purpose, they shall be on Oath or Affirmation. When the President of the United States is tried, the Chief Justice shall preside: And no Person shall be convicted without the Concurrence of two thirds of the Members present.

Judgment in Cases of Impeachment shall not extend further than to removal from Office, and disqualification to hold and enjoy any Office of Honor, Trust or Profit under the United States: but the party convicted shall nevertheless be liable and subject to Indictment, Trial, Judgment and Punishment, according to Law.

Section 4 The Times, Places and Manner of holding Elections for Senators and Representatives, shall be prescribed in each State by the Legislature thereof; but the Congress may at any time by Law make or alter such Regulations, except as to the Places of chusing Senators.

The congress shall assemble at least once in every Year, and such Meeting shall be on the first Monday in December, unless they shall by Law appoint a different Day.[†]

---

[*]See the Seventeenth Amendment.

[**]See the Seventeenth Amendment.

[†]See the Twentieth Amendment.

Section 5 Each House shall be the Judge of the Elections, Returns and Qualifications of its own Members, and a Majority of each shall constitute a Quorum to do Business; but a smaller Number may adjourn from day to day, and may be authorized to compel the Attendance of absent Members, in such Manner, and under such Penalties as each House may provide.

Each House may determine the Rules of its Proceedings, punish its Members for disorderly Behaviour, and, with the Concurrence of two thirds, expel a Member.

Each House shall keep a Journal of its Proceedings, and from time to time publish the same, excepting such Parts as may in their Judgment require Secrecy; and the Yeas and Nays of the Members of either House on any question shall, at the Desire of one fifth of those Present, be entered on the Journal.

Neither House, during the Session of Congress, shall, without the Consent of the other, adjourn for more than three days, nor to any other Place than that in which the two Houses shall be sitting.

Section 6 The Senators and Representatives shall receive a Compensation for their Services, to be ascertained by law, and paid out of the Treasury of the United States. They shall in all Cases, except Treason, Felony and Breach of the Peace, be privileged from Arrest during their Attendance at the Session of their respective Houses, and in going to and returning from the same; and for any Speech or Debate in either House, they shall not be questioned in any other Place.

No Senator or Representative shall, during the Time for which he was elected, be appointed to any civil Office under the Authority of the United States, which shall have been created, or the Emoluments whereof shall have been encreased during such time; and no Person holding any Office under the United States, shall be a Member of either House during his Continuance in Office.

Section 7 All Bills for raising Revenue shall originate in the House of Representatives; but the Senate may propose or concur with Amendments as on other Bills.

Every Bill which shall have passed the House of Representatives and the Senate, shall, before it become a Law, be presented to the President of the United States; If he approves he shall sign it, but if not he shall return it, with his Objections to that House in which it shall have originated, who shall enter the Objections at large on their Journal, and proceed to reconsider it.

If after such Reconsideration two thirds of that House shall agree to pass the Bill, it shall be sent, together with the Objections, to the other House, by which it shall likewise be reconsidered, and if approved by two thirds of that House, it shall become a Law. But in all such Cases the Votes of both Houses shall be determined by Yeas and Nays, and the Names of the Persons voting for and against the Bill shall be entered on the Journal of each House respectively. If any Bill shall not be returned by the President within ten Days (Sundays excepted) after it shall have been presented to him, the Same shall be a Law, in like Manner as if he had signed it, unless the Congress by their Adjournment prevent its Return, in which Case it shall not be a Law.

Every Order, Resolution, or Vote to which the concurrence of the Senate and House of Representatives may be necessary (except on a question of Adjournment) shall be presented to the President of the United States; and before the Same shall take Effect, shall be approved by him, or being disapproved by him, shall be repassed by two thirds of the Senate and House of Representatives, according to the Rules and Limitations prescribed in the Case of a Bill.

Section 8 The Congress shall have Power To lay and collect Taxes, Duties, Imposts and Excises, to pay the Debts and provide for the common Defense and general Welfare of the United States; but all Duties, Imposts and Excises shall be uniform throughout the United States; To borrow Money on the credit of the United States; To regulate Commerce with foreign Nations, and among the several States, and with the Indian Tribes; To establish a uniform Rule of Naturalization, and uniform Laws on the subject of Bankruptcies throughout the United States; To coin Money, regulate the Value thereof, and of foreign Coin, and fix the Standard of Weights and Measures; To provide for the Punishment of counterfeiting the Securities and current Coin of the United States; To establish Post Offices and post Roads; To promote the Progress of Science and useful Arts, by securing for limited times to Authors and Inventors the exclusive Right to their respective Writings and Discoveries; To constitute Tribunals inferior to the Supreme Court; To define and punish Piracies and Felonies committed on the high Seas, and Offences against the Law of Nations; To declare War, grant Letters of Marque and Reprisal, and make Rules concerning Captures on Land and Water; To raise and support Armies, but no Appropriation of Money to that Use shall be for a longer Term than two Years; To provide and maintain a Navy; To make Rules for the Government and Regulation of the land and naval Forces; To provide for calling forth the Militia to execute the Laws of the Union, suppress Insurrections and repel Invasions; To provide for organizing, arming, and disciplining the Militia, and for governing such Part of them as may be employed in the Service of the United States, reserving to the States respectively, the Appointment of the Officers, and the Authority of training the Militia according to the discipline prescribed by Congress; To exercise exclusive Legislation in all Cases whatsoever, over such District (not exceeding ten Miles square) as may, by Cession of particular States, and the Acceptance of Congress, become the Seat of the Government of the United States, and to exercise like Authority over all Places purchased by the Consent of the Legislature of the State in which the Same shall be, for the Erection of Forts, Magazines, Arsenals, dock-Yards, and other needful Buildings;—And To make all Laws which shall be necessary and proper for carrying into Execution the foregoing Powers, and all other Powers vested by this Constitution in the Government of the United States, or in any Department or Officer thereof.

Section 9 The Migration or Importation of such Persons as any of the States now existing shall think proper to admit, shall not be prohibited by the Congress prior to the Year one thousand eight hundred and eight, but a Tax or duty may be imposed on such Importation, not exceeding ten dollars for each Person.

The Privilege of the Writ of Habeas Corpus shall not be suspended, unless when in Cases of Rebellion or Invasion the public Safety may require it.

No Bill of Attainder or ex post facto Law shall be passed.

No Capitation, or other direct, Tax shall be laid, unless in Proportion to the Census or Enumeration herein before directed to be taken.

No Tax or Duty shall be laid on Articles exported from any State.

No Preference shall be given by any Regulation of Commerce or Revenue to the Ports of one State over those of another: nor shall Vessels bound to, or from, one State be obliged to enter, clear, or pay Duties in another.

No Money shall be drawn from the Treasury, but in Consequence of Appropriations made by Law; and a regular Statement and Account of the Receipts and Expenditures of all public Money shall be published from time to time.

No Title of Nobility shall be granted by the United States: And no Person holding any Office or Profit or Trust under them, shall, without the Consent of the Congress, accept of any present, Emolument, Office, or Title, of any kind whatever, from any King, Prince, or foreign State.

Section 10 No State shall enter into any Treaty, Alliance, or Confederation; grant Letters of Marque and Reprisal; coin Money; emit Bills of Credit; make any Thing but gold and silver Coin a Tender in Payment of Debts; pass any Bill of Attainder, ex post facto Law, or Law impairing the Obligation of Contracts, or grant any Title of Nobility.

No State shall, without the Consent of the Congress, lay any Imposts or Duties on Imports or Exports, except what may be absolutely necessary for executing its inspection Laws: and the net Produce of all Duties and Imposts, laid by any State on Imports or Exports, shall be for the Use of the Treasury of the United States; and all such Laws shall be subject to the Revision and Control of the Congress.

No State shall, without the Consent of Congress, lay any Duty of Tonnage, keep Troops, or Ships of War in time of Peace, enter into any Agreement or Compact with another State, or with a foreign Power, or engage in War, unless actually invaded, or in such imminent Danger as will not admit of delay.

ARTICLE II

Section 1 The executive Power shall be vested in a President of the United States of America. He shall hold Office during the Term of four Years, and, together with the Vice President, chosen for the same Term, be elected, as follows: Each State shall appoint, in such Manner as the Legislature thereof may direct, a Number of Electors, equal to the whole Number of Senators and Representatives to which the State may be entitled in the Congress: but no Senator or Representative, or Person holding an Office of Trust or Profit under the United States, shall be appointed an Elector.

The Electors shall meet in their respective States, and vote by Ballot for two Persons, of whom one at least shall not be an Inhabitant of the same State with themselves. And they shall make a List of all the Persons voted for, and of the Number of Votes for each; which List they shall sign and certify, and transmit sealed to the Seat of the Government of the United States, directed to the President of the Senate. The President of the Senate shall, in the Presence of the Senate and House of Representatives, open all the Certificates, and the Votes shall then be counted. The Person having the greatest Number of Votes shall be the President, if such Number be a Majority of the whole Number of Electors appointed; and if there be more than one who have such Majority, and have an equal Number of Votes, then the House of Representatives shall immediately chuse by Ballot one of them for President, and if no Person have a Majority, then from the five highest on the List the said House shall in like Manner chuse the President. But in chusing the President, Votes shall be taken by States, the Representation from each State having one Vote: A quorum for this Purpose shall consist of a Member or Members from two thirds of the States, and a Majority of all the States shall be necessary to a Choice. In every Case, after the Choice of the President, the Person having the greatest Number of Votes of the Electors shall be the Vice President. But if there should remain two or more who have equal Votes, the Senate shall chuse from them by Ballot the Vice President.*

The Congress may determine the Time of chusing the Electors, and the Day on which they shall give their Votes; which Day shall be the same throughout the United States.

No Person except a natural born Citizen, or a Citizen of the United States, at the time of the Adoption of this Constitution, shall be eligible to the Office of President; neither shall any Person be eligible to that Office who shall not have attained to the Age of thirty five Years, and been fourteen Years a Resident within the United States.

In Case of the Removal of the President from Office, or of his Death, Resignation, or Inability to discharge the Powers and Duties of the said Office, the Same shall devolve on the Vice President, and the Congress may by Law provide for the Case of Removal, Death, Resignation or Inability, both of the President and Vice President, declaring what Officer shall then act as President, and such Officer shall act accordingly, until the Disability be removed, or a President shall be elected.**

The President shall, at stated Times, receive for his Services, a Compensation which shall neither be encreased nor diminished during the Period for which he shall have been elected, and he shall not receive within the Period any other Emolument from the United States, or any of them.

Before he enter on the Execution of his Office, he shall take the following Oath or Affirmation:—"I do solemnly swear (or affirm) that I will faithfully execute the Office of President of the United States, and will to the best of my Ability, preserve, protect and defend the Constitution of the United States."

Section 2 The President shall be the Commander in Chief of the Army and Navy of the United States, and of the Militia of the several States, when called into the actual Service of the United States; he may require the Opinion, in writing, of the principal Officer in each of the executive Departments, upon any Subject relating to the Duties of their respective Offices, and he shall have Power to grant Reprieves and Pardons for Offences against the United States, except in Cases of Impeachment.

He shall have Power, by and with the Advice and Consent of the Senate, to make Treaties, provided two thirds of the Senators present concur; and he shall nominate, and by and with the Advice and consent of the Senate, shall appoint

*Superseded by the Twelfth Amendment.

**See the Twenty-fifth Amendment.

Ambassadors, other public Ministers and Consuls, Judges of the Supreme Court, and all other Officers of the United States, whose Appointments are not herein otherwise provided for, and which shall be established by Law: but the Congress may by Law vest the Appointment of such inferior officers, as they think proper, in the President alone, in the Courts of Law, or in the Heads of Departments.

The President shall have Power to fill up all Vacancies that may happen during the Recess of the Senate, by granting Commissions which shall expire at the End of their next Session.

Section 3 He shall from time to time give to the Congress Information of the State of the Union, and recommend to their Consideration such Measures as he shall judge necessary and expedient; he may, on extraordinary Occasions, convene both Houses, or either of them, and in Case of Disagreement between them, with Respect to the Time of Adjournment, he may adjourn them to such Time as he shall think proper; he shall receive Ambassadors and other public Ministers; he shall take Care that the Laws be faithfully executed, and shall Commission all the Officers of the United States.

Section 4 The President, Vice President, and all civil Officers of the United States, shall be removed from Office on Impeachment for, and Conviction of, Treason, Bribery, or other high Crimes and Misdemeanors.

ARTICLE III

Section 1 The judicial Power of the United States, shall be vested in one supreme Court and in such inferior Courts as the Congress may from time to time ordain and establish. The Judges, both of the supreme and inferior Courts, shall hold their Offices during good Behaviour, and shall, at stated times, receive for their Services, a Compensation, which shall not be diminished during their Continuance in Office.

Section 2 The judicial Power shall extend to all Cases, in Law and Equity, arising under this Constitution, the Laws of the United States, and Treaties made, or which shall be made, under their Authority;—to all Cases affecting Ambassadors, other public Ministers and Consuls;—to all Cases of admiralty and maritime Jurisdiction;—to Controversies to which the United States shall be a Party;—to Controversies between two or more States;—*between a State and Citizens of another State;**—between Citizens of different States;—between Citizens of the same State claiming Lands under Grants of different States, and *between a State or the Citizens thereof, and foreign States, Citizens, or Subjects.*†

In all Cases affecting Ambassadors, other public Ministers and Consuls, and those in which a State shall be Party, the supreme Court shall have original Jurisdiction. In all the other Cases before mentioned, the supreme Court shall have appellate Jurisdiction, both as to Law and Fact, with such Exceptions, and under such Regulations as the Congress shall make.

---

*See the Eleventh Amendment.
†See the Eleventh Amendment.

The Trial of all Crimes, except in Cases of Impeachment, shall be by Jury; and such Trial shall be held in the State where the said Crimes shall have been committed; but when not committed within any State, the Trial shall be at such Place or Places as the Congress may by Law have directed.

Section 3 Treason against the United States, shall consist only in levying War against them, or in adhering to their Enemies, giving them Aid and Comfort. No Person shall be convicted of Treason unless on the Testimony of two Witnesses to the same overt Act, or on Confession in open Court.

The Congress shall have Power to declare the Punishment of Treason, but no Attainder of Treason shall work Corruption of Blood, or Forfeiture except during the Life of the Person attained.

ARTICLE IV

Section 1 Full Faith and Credit shall be given in each State to the public Acts, Records, and judicial Proceedings of every other State. And the Congress may by general Laws prescribe the Manner in which such Acts, Records, and Proceedings shall be proved, and the Effect thereof.

Section 2 The Citizens of each State shall be entitled to all Privileges and Immunities of Citizens in the several States.

A Person charged in any State with Treason, Felony, or other Crime, who shall flee from Justice, and be found in another State, shall on Demand of the executive Authority of the State from which he fled, be delivered up, to be removed to the State having Jurisdiction of the Crime.

*No Person held to Service of Labour in one State, under the Laws thereof, escaping into another, shall, in Consequence of any Law or Regulation therein, be discharged from such Service or Labour, but shall be delivered up on Claim of the Party to whom such Service of Labour may be due.**

Section 3 New States may be admitted by the Congress into this Union; but no new State shall be formed or erected within the Jurisdiction of any other State; nor any State be formed by the Junction of two or more States, or Parts of States, without the Consent of the Legislatures of the States concerned as well as of the Congress.

The Congress shall have Power to dispose of and make all needful Rules and Regulations respecting the Territory or other Property belonging to the United States; and nothing in this Constitution shall be so construed as to Prejudice any claims of the United States, or of any particular State.

Section 4 The United States shall guarantee to every State in this Union a Republican Form of Government, and shall protect each of them against Invasion; and on Application of the Legislature, or of the Executive (when the Legislature cannot be convened) against domestic Violence.

---

*See the Thirteenth Amendment.

ARTICLE V

The Congress, whenever two thirds of both Houses shall deem it necessary, shall propose Amendments to this Constitution, or, on the Application of the Legislatures of two thirds of the several States, shall call a Convention for proposing Amendments, which, in either Case, shall be valid to all Intents and Purposes, as Part of this Constitution, when ratified by the Legislatures of three fourths of the several States, or by Conventions in three fourths thereof, as the one or the other Mode of Ratification may be proposed by the Congress; Provided that no Amendment which may be made prior to the Year One thousand eight hundred and eight shall in any Manner affect the first and fourth clauses in the Ninth Section of the first Article; and that no State, without its Consent, shall be deprived of its equal Suffrage in the Senate.

ARTICLE VI

All debts contracted and Engagements entered into, before the Adoption of this Constitution, shall be as valid against the United States under this Constitution, as under the Confederation.

This Constitution, and the Laws of the United States which shall be made in Pursuance thereof; and all Treaties made, or which shall be made, under the Authority of the United States, shall be the supreme Law of the Land; and the Judges in every State shall be bound thereby, any Thing in the Constitution or Laws of any State to the Contrary notwithstanding.

The Senators and Representatives before mentioned, and the Members of the several State Legislatures, and all executive and judicial Officers, both of the United States and of the several States, shall be bound by Oath or Affirmation, to support this Constitution; but no religious Test shall ever be required as a Qualification to any Office or public Trust under the United States.

ARTICLE VII

The Ratification of the Conventions of nine States, shall be sufficient for the Establishment of this Constitution between the States so ratifying the Same.

Done in Contention by the Unanimous Consent of the States present the Seventeenth Day of September in the Year of our Lord one thousand seven hundred and eighty seven and of the Independence of the United States of America the Twelfth. In witness whereof We have hereunto subscribed our Names.

Articles in Addition to, and Amendment of, the Constitution of the United States of America, Proposed by Congress, and Ratified by the Several States, Pursuant to the Fifth Article of the Original Constitution.

AMENDMENT I

(Ratification of the first ten amendments was completed December 15, 1791.)

Congress shall make no law respecting an establishment of religion, or prohibiting the free exercise thereof; or abridging the freedom of speech, or of the press; or the right of the people peaceably to assemble, and to petition the Government for a redress of grievances.

AMENDMENT II

A well regulated Militia, being necessary to the security of a free State, the right of the people to keep and bear Arms, shall not be infringed.

AMENDMENT III

No Soldier shall, in time of peace be quartered in any house, without the consent of the Owner, nor in time of war, but in a manner to be prescribed by law.

AMENDMENT IV

The right of the people to be secure in their persons, houses, papers, and effects, against unreasonable searches and seizures, shall not be violated, and no Warrants shall issue, but upon probable cause, supported by Oath or affirmation, and particularly describing the place to be searched, and the persons or things to be seized.

AMENDMENT V

No person shall be held to answer for a capital, or otherwise infamous crime, unless on a presentment or indictment of a Grand Jury, except in cases arising in the land or naval forces, or in the Militia, when in actual service in time of War or public danger; nor shall any person be subject for the same offence to be twice put in jeopardy of life or limb; nor shall be compelled in any criminal case to be a witness against himself, nor be deprived of life, liberty, or property, without due process of law; nor shall private property be taken for public use, without just compensation.

AMENDMENT VI

In all criminal prosecutions, the accused shall enjoy the right to a speedy and public trial, by an impartial jury of the State and district wherein the crime shall have been committed, which district shall have been previously ascertained by law, and to be informed of the nature and cause of the accusation; to be confronted with the witnesses against him; to have compulsory process for obtaining witnesses in his favor, and to have the Assistance of Counsel for his defense.

AMENDMENT VII

In Suits at common law, where the value in controversy shall exceed twenty dollars, the right of trial by jury shall be preserved, and no fact tried by a jury, shall be otherwise reexamined in any Court of the United States, than according to the rules of the common law.

AMENDMENT VIII

Excessive bail shall not be required, nor excessive fines imposed, nor cruel and unusual punishments inflicted.

AMENDMENT IX

The enumeration in the Constitution, of certain rights, shall not be construed to deny or disparage others retained by the people.

AMENDMENT X

The powers not delegated to the United States by the Constitution, nor prohibited by it to the States, are reserved to the States respectively, or to the people.

AMENDMENT XI (1795)

The Judicial power of the United States shall not be construed to extend to any suit in law or equity, commenced or prosecuted against one of the United States by Citizens of another State, or by Citizens or Subjects of any Foreign State.

AMENDMENT XII (1804)

The Electors shall meet in their respective states and vote by ballot for President and Vice President, one of whom, at least, shall not be an inhabitant of the same state with themselves; they shall name in their ballots the person voted for as President, and in distinct ballots the person voted for as Vice President, and they shall make distinct lists of all persons voted for as President, and of all persons voted for as Vice President, and of the number of votes for each, which lists they shall sign and certify, and transmit sealed to the seat of the government of the United States, directed to the President of the Senate;—The President of the Senate shall, in the presence of the Senate and House of Representatives, open all the certificates and the votes shall then be counted;—the person having the greatest number of votes for President, shall be the President, if such number be a majority of the whole number of Electors appointed; and if no person have such majority, then from the persons having the highest numbers not exceeding three on the list of those voted for as President, the House of Representatives shall choose immediately, by ballot, the President. But in choosing the President, the votes shall be taken by states, the representation from each state having one vote; a quorum for this purpose shall consist of a member or members from two-thirds of the states, and a majority of all the states shall be necessary to a choice. And if the House of Representatives shall not choose a President whenever the right of choice shall devolve upon them, *before the fourth day of March next following,** then the Vice President shall act as President, as in the case of the death or other constitutional disability of the President.— The person having the greatest number of votes as Vice President shall be the Vice President, if such number be a majority of the whole number of Electors appointed, and if no person have a majority, then from the two highest numbers on the list, the Senate shall choose the Vice President; a quorum for the purpose shall consist of two-thirds of the whole number of Senators, and a majority of the whole number shall be necessary to a choice.

---

*Altered by the Twentieth Amendment.

But no person constitutionally ineligible to the office of President shall be eligible to that of Vice President of the United States.

AMENDMENT XIII (1865)

Section 1 Neither slavery nor involuntary servitude, except as a punishment for crime whereof the party shall have been duly convicted, shall exist within the United States, or any place subject to their jurisdiction.

Section 2 Congress shall have the power to enforce this article by appropriate legislation.

AMENDMENT XIV (1868)

Section 1 All persons born or naturalized in the United States, and subject to the jurisdiction thereof, are citizens of the United States and the State wherein they reside. No State shall make or enforce any law which shall abridge the privileges or immunities of citizens of the United States; nor shall any State deprive any person of life, liberty, or property, without due process of law; nor deny to any person within its jurisdiction the equal protection of the laws.

Section 2 Representatives shall be apportioned among the several States according to their respective numbers, counting the whole number of persons in each State, excluding Indians not taxed. But when the right to vote at any election for the choice of electors for President and Vice President of the United States, Representatives in Congress, the Executive and Judicial officers of a State, or the members of the Legislature thereof, is denied to any of the male inhabitants of such State, being twenty-one years of age, and citizens of the United States, or in any way abridged, except for participation in rebellion, or other crime, the basis of representation therein shall be reduced in the proportion which the number of such male citizens shall bear to the whole number of male citizens twenty-one years of age in such State.

Section 3 No person shall be a Senator or Representative in Congress, or elector of President and Vice President, or hold any office, civil or military, under the United States, or under any State, who, having previously taken an oath, as a member of Congress, or as an officer of the United States, or as a member of any State legislature, or as an executive or judicial officer of any State, to support the Constitution of the United States, shall have engaged in insurrection or rebellion against the same, or given aid or comfort to the enemies thereof. But Congress may by a vote of two-thirds of each House, remove such disability.

Section 4 The validity of the public debt of the United States, authorized by law, including debts incurred for payment of pensions and bounties for services in suppressing insurrection or rebellion, shall not be questioned.

But neither the United States nor any State shall assume or pay any debt or obligation incurred in aid of insurrection or rebellion against the United States, or any claim for the loss or emancipation of any slave; but all debts, obligations, and claims shall be held illegal and void.

Section 5 The Congress shall have power to enforce, by appropriate legislation, the provisions of this article.

AMENDMENT XV (1870)

Section 1 The right of citizens of the United States to vote shall not be denied or abridged by the United States or by any State on account of race, color, or previous condition of servitude.

Section 2 The Congress shall have power to enforce this article by appropriate legislation.

AMENDMENT XVI (1913)

The Congress shall have power to lay and collect taxes on incomes, from whatever source derived, without apportionment among the several States, and without regard to any census or enumeration.

AMENDMENT XVII (1913)

The Senate of the United States shall be composed of two Senators from each State, elected by the people thereof, for six years; and each Senator shall have one vote. The electors in each State shall have the qualifications requisite for electors of the most numerous branch of the State legislature.

When vacancies happen in the representation of any State in the Senate, the executive authority of such State shall issue writs of election to fill such vacancies: *Provided,* That the legislature of any State may empower the executive thereof to make temporary appointments until the people fill the vacancies by election as the legislature may direct.

This amendment shall not be so construed as to affect the election or term of any Senator chosen before it becomes valid as part of the Constitution.

AMENDMENT XVIII (1919)

Section 1 After one year from the ratification of this article the manufacture, sale, or transportation of intoxicating liquors within, the importation thereof into, or the exportation thereof from the United States and all territory subject to the jurisdiction thereof for beverage purposes is hereby prohibited.

Section 2 The Congress and the several States shall have concurrent power to enforce this article by appropriate legislation.

Section 3 This article shall be inoperative unless it shall have been ratified as an amendment to the Constitution by the legislatures of the several States, as provided in the Constitution, within seven years from the date of submission hereof to the States by the Congress.*

AMENDMENT XIX (1920)

The right of citizens of the United States to vote shall not be denied or abridged by the United States or by any State on account of sex.

Congress shall have power to enforce this article by appropriate legislation.

AMENDMENT XX (1933)

Section 1 The terms of the President and Vice President shall end at noon on the 20th day of January, and the terms of Senators and Representatives at noon on the 3rd day of January, of the years in which such terms would have ended if this article had not been ratified; and the terms of their successors shall then begin.

Section 2 The Congress shall assemble at least once in every year, and such meeting shall begin at noon on the 3rd day of January, unless they shall by law appoint a different day.

Section 3 If, at the time fixed for the beginning of the term of the President, the President elect shall have died, the Vice President elect shall become President. If a President shall not have been chosen before the time fixed for the beginning of his term, or if the President elect shall have failed to qualify, then the Vice President elect shall act as President until a President shall have qualified; and the Congress may by law provide for the case wherein neither a President elect nor a Vice President elect shall have qualified, declaring who shall then act as President, or the manner in which one who is to act shall be selected, and such person shall act accordingly until a President or Vice President shall have qualified.

Section 4 The Congress may by law provide for the case of the death of any of the persons from whom the House of Representatives may choose a President whenever the right of choice shall have devolved upon them, and for the case of the death of any of the persons from whom the Senate may choose a Vice President whenever the right of choice shall have devolved upon them.

Section 5 Sections 1 and 2 shall take effect on the 15th day of October following ratification of this article.

Section 6 This article shall be inoperative unless it shall have been ratified as an amendment to the Constitution by the legislatures of three-fourths of the several States within seven years from the date of its submission.

---

*Repealed by the Twenty-first Amendment.

AMENDMENT XXI (1933)

Section 1 The eighteenth article of amendment to the Constitution of the United States is hereby repealed.

Section 2 The transportation or importation into any State, Territory, or possession of the United States for delivery or use therein of intoxicating liquors, in violation of the laws thereof, is hereby prohibited.

Section 3 This article shall be inoperative unless it shall have been ratified as an amendment to the Constitution by conventions in the several States, as provided in the Constitution, within seven years from the date of submission thereof to the States by the Congress.

AMENDMENT XXII (1951)

Section 1 No person shall be elected to the office of the President more than twice, and no person who has held the office of President, or acted as President for more than two years of a term to which some other person was elected President shall be elected to the office of President more than once. But this Article shall not apply to any person holding the office of President when this Article was proposed by the Congress, and shall not prevent any person who may be holding the office of President, or acting as President, during the term within which this Article becomes operative from holding the office of President or acting as President during the remainder of such term.

Section 3 This article shall be inoperative unless it shall have been ratified as an amendment to the Constitution by the legislatures of three-fourths of the several States within seven years from the date of its submission to the States by the Congress.

AMENDMENT XXIII (1961)

Section 1 The District constituting the seat of Government of the United States shall appoint in such manner as the Congress may direct: A number of electors of President and Vice President equal to the whole number of Senators and Representatives in Congress to which the District would be entitled if it were a State, but in no event more than the least populous State; they shall be in addition to those appointed by the States, but they shall be considered, for the purposes of the election of President and Vice President, to be electors appointed by a State; and they shall meet in the District and perform such duties as provided by the twelfth article of amendment.

Section 2 The Congress shall have power to enforce this article by appropriate legislation.

AMENDMENT XXIV (1964)

Section 1 The right of citizens of the United States to vote in any primary or other election for President or Vice President, for electors for President or Vice President, or for Senator or Representative in Congress, shall not be denied or abridged by the United States or any state by reason of failure to pay any poll tax or other tax.

Section 2 The Congress shall have the power to enforce this article by appropriate legislation.

AMENDMENT XXV (1967)

Section 1 In case of the removal of the President from office or of his death or resignation, the Vice President shall become President.

Section 2 Whenever there is a vacancy in the office of the Vice President, the President shall nominate a Vice President who shall take office upon confirmation by a majority vote of both Houses of Congress.

Section 3 Whenever the President transmits to the President pro tempore of the Senate and the Speaker of the House of Representatives his written declaration that he is unable to discharge the powers and duties of his office, and until he transmits to them a written declaration to the contrary, such powers and duties shall be discharged by the Vice President as Acting President.

Section 4 Whenever the Vice President and a majority of either the principal officers of the executive departments or of such other body as Congress may by law provide, transmit to the President pro tempore of the Senate and the Speaker of the House of Representatives their written declaration that the President is unable to discharge the powers and duties of his office, the Vice President shall immediately assume the powers and duties of the office as Acting President.

Thereafter, when the President transmits to the President pro tempore of the Senate and the Speaker of the House of Representatives his written declaration that no inability exists, he shall resume the powers and duties of his office unless the Vice President and a majority of either the principal officers of the executive departments or of such other body as Congress may by law provide, transmit within four days to the President pro tempore of the Senate and the Speaker of the House of Representatives their written declaration that the President is unable to discharge the powers and duties of his office. Thereupon Congress shall decide the issue, assembling within forty-eight hours for that purpose if not in session. If the Congress, within twenty-one days after the receipt of the latter written declaration, or, if Congress is not in session, within twenty-one days after Congress is required to assemble, determines by two-thirds vote of both Houses that the President is unable to discharge the powers and duties of his office, the Vice President shall continue to discharge the same as Acting President; otherwise, the President shall resume the powers and duties of his office.

AMENDMENT XXVI (1971)

Section 1 The right of citizens of the United States, who are eighteen years of age or older, to vote shall not be denied or abridged by the United States or any state on account of age.

Section 2 The Congress shall have the power to enforce this article by appropriate legislation.

AMENDMENT XXVII (1992)

No law, varying the compensation for the service of the Senators and Representatives, shall take effect, until an election of Representatives shall have intervened.*

---

* The Twenty-seventh Amendment (1992), proposed in 1789 by James Madison, became law more than two centuries later when ratified by the Michigan legislature on May 7, 1992.

INDEX